The Edmonton Oilers

Also by K. Michael Gaschnitz

Professional Sports Statistics: A North American Team-by-Team, and Major Non-Team Events, Year-by-Year Reference, 1876 through 1996 (McFarland, 1997)

The Edmonton Oilers

K. MICHAEL GASCHNITZ

McFarland & Company, Inc., Publishers
Jefferson, North Carolina, and London

This work is not associated with the Edmonton Oilers or the National Hockey League. The names Edmonton Oilers, National Hockey League, NHL, and the names of other NHL teams are the property of the respective teams and leagues.

Library of Congress Cataloguing-in-Publication Data

Gaschnitz, K. Michael.
The Edmonton Oilers / K. Michael Gaschnitz.
p. cm.
Includes bibliographical references and index.
ISBN 0-7864-1252-6 (softcover : 50# alkaline paper) ♾
1. Edmonton Oilers (Hockey team)—History.
2. Edmonton Oilers (Hockey team)—Statistics. I. Title.
GV848.E36 G37 2003
796.962'64'09712334—dc21 2002006973

British Library cataloguing data are available

Manufactured in the United States of America

McFarland & Company, Inc., Publishers
Box 611, Jefferson, North Carolina 28640
www.mcfarlandpub.com

Thank you, Laureen Tarr, for your help and suggestions

Contents

Preface

The current 2002-03 season marks the 24th anniversary of the Edmonton Oilers as a member of the National Hockey League. Founded in 1972 during the heyday of professional sports expansion, the Oilers played their first seven seasons in the World Hockey Association (WHA). The WHA was one of many rebel leagues founded in the 1970s to provide competition against the more established leagues.

In 1979 Edmonton was one of four former WHA clubs to be accepted into the NHL. Through the dedicated efforts of the owners, the management and the fans, Edmonton is the only team that still exists in its original location. The Oilers are to the NHL what the Green Bay Packers are to the National Football League—a successful small market team.

Though the definition of a sports dynasty is something not carved in stone, it is probably safe to say that the Oilers may be the last hockey team ever to be considered a dynasty. Even Detroit, which has had great success recently, cannot yet be considered a team which defines and dominates an era, such as the Canadiens of the 1970s, Islanders of the early 1980s or the Oilers of the mid to late 1980s. With salaries continuing to escalate and players constantly in search of greener pastures it has become much harder to keep a championship team together. One only has to look at baseball's Florida Marlins, who won the World Series in 1997 and were virtually dismantled the following year.

The team was led in its glory years by superstar Wayne Gretzky, who was elected to the Hall of Fame in 1999. The Oilers of that era also included potential Hall of Fame players such as Mark Messier, Paul Coffey, Jari Kurri, Glenn Anderson, and Grant Fuhr. With stars such as these it is little wonder that Edmonton won five Stanley Cups in seven seasons.

Though knowledgeable Oiler fans may vilify longtime owner Peter Pocklington for not holding onto this large core of star players, especially Gretzky, in hindsight it must be realized that paying the salaries of such players for much longer than he did would have quickly bankrupted the team. Even Pocklington's willingness to lose money in order to keep the team in Edmonton would have quickly waned in the face of such huge salary increases. Whatever else Oiler fans may have thought of him, it was he who was responsible for keeping the team in the city for 21 years.

In May of 1998 the team was taken over by the Edmonton Investors Group, a corporation put together by a number of the city's well-known entrepreneurs. This group would grow to over thirty by the end of the year. With the influx of new capital the team should be able to stay in Edmonton indefinitely.

The following pages contain more information than a fan of the Edmonton Oilers would probably ever want to know. Included is a brief summary of each season. This summary encompasses individual regular season and post-season statistics for every player as well as team statistics for each season. Following the seasonal summaries is an alphabetical list of every player to don an Oiler uniform and his statistics for each year.The reader will also find a summary of all five Stanley Cup winning games, team records, award winners, individual milestones, transactions, the WHA, the Sky Reach Center, and much more in Part Three.

Part One

Season Summaries and Statistics

1979-80

The Edmonton Oilers were granted a National Hockey League franchise on June 22, 1979. The Oilers, Hartford Whalers, Quebec Nordiques and Winnipeg Jets were the four teams that joined the NHL from the defunct World Hockey Association in time to open the 1979-80 season. Despite some recent financial woes, the Oilers are the only club still operating in their original location. This is a tribute to the people who put together and run the team; to the city of Edmonton; and, most of all, to the fans.

Edmonton's rabid hockey fans eagerly anticipated the arrival of a major league team when in the summer of 1972 "Wild" Bill Hunter, a flamboyant local entrepreneur, was granted a franchise in the fledgling World Hockey Association (see "The WHA" in Part Three).

Following five years of rivalry and financial bloodletting the WHA approached the NHL about the possibility of a merger. However the NHL governors rejected the merger bid. John Ziegler, president of the National Hockey League, stated that "after very careful and due consideration, the proposed plan of expansion was put to the governors and it failed to receive the requisite majority for approval, and thus any possible expansion for the 1977-78 season has gone by the board at this point."

Team owner Peter Pocklington, undeterred by this setback, remained intent on bringing the city of Edmonton a National Hockey League franchise. He began assembling the personnel to realize this goal.

The first piece of the puzzle was put in place with the hiring of Larry Gordon in June of 1978. Gordon would be the team's first general manager, and along with Glen Sather was one of two vice presidents who worked closely with Pocklington in the operation of the team.

The second and arguably most influential part of the puzzle was already at work in the organization. High Prairie, Alberta–born Glen Sather came to the Oilers after playing the 1975-76 season with the Minnesota North Stars of the NHL "Slats" played 81 games, scoring 19 goals and adding 34 assists in the 1976-77 season with the WHA Oilers. Late in the season he became the playing coach, replacing Bep Guidolin behind the Oilers' bench for the final 18 games of the season, recording nine wins, seven losses and two ties.

Sather guided the team to a first place finish the following year, the first and only time the Oilers finished atop the WHA standings, and he remained behind the bench when the team joined the National Hockey League in 1979. Sather was also named as a vice-president of the new NHL franchise, and along with Larry Gordon would help put the new team together.

On November 3, 1978, the Oilers added the final ingredient which virtually guaranteed their acceptance into the National Hockey League. In July of that year former Oiler owner Nelson Skalbania signed teenage phenomenon Wayne Gretzky to a personal services contract. "The Great One," fresh from a 182 point season with the Sault Ste. Marie Greyhounds of the OHL, inked a \$1.75 million contract with Skalbania's Indianapolis Racers. After signing Gretzky, Skalbania began experiencing financial problems and sold Gretzky, Eddie Mio and Peter Driscoll to former partner Peter Pocklington for \$850,000 in cash. Gretzky ended up playing only eight games for the Racers, scoring three goals and adding three assists.

Gretzky almost ended up as a member of the Winnipeg Jets as Skalbania wanted to play backgammon for his contract with Jets co-owner Michael Gobuty. The stakes would have been Gretzky's contract against one-third ownership of the Jets. Gobuty declined the offer. But no matter on which team he played, Gretzky's presence in the league virtually guaranteed that a number of WHA teams would be included in the NHL in the near future.

The 1979-80 team had a number of players left over from the previous WHA season including Brett Callighen, Ron Chipperfield, Peter Driscoll, Dave Dryden, Bill "Cowboy" Flett, Al Hamilton, Dave Hunter, Blair MacDonald, Ed Mio, Dave Semenko, Risto Siltanen, and Stan Weir as well as Gretzky. They would all return to the team for the Oilers' first NHL season.

On August 9, 1979, at the NHL entry draft, which took place at the Queen Elizabeth Hotel in Toronto, the team added three more players who would go on to form the nucleus of future Stanley Cup winning teams. Drafted 21st overall from the Quebec Remparts of the Quebec Major Junior Hockey League was defenseman Kevin Lowe. Lowe would go on to become the longest serving Oiler, appearing in more games and playing more seasons than any other player.

The Oilers did not have a second round draft choice, as they had traded it to Minnesota to reacquire the rights to Dave Semenko but in the third round they chose future superstar Mark Messier. "The Moose" had played in the WHA during the ill-fated league's final season, scoring one goal and adding ten assists while playing 52 games for Indianapolis and Cincinnati. Messier was only 17 years of age though and was still eligible for the NHL draft.

Also drafted in the third round, and 69th overall was fleet-footed and talented Glenn Anderson, who would also go on to become a future star. Anderson had scored 26 goals and 29 assists in 40 games for the University of Denver in the 1978-79 season. "Mork," as he was known, did not appear in any games for the Oilers in the year following his selection, opting instead to play for the Canadian National team, for whom he scored 42 points in 49 games.

On October 10, 1979, the Oilers played their first regular season game in the NHL, with veteran Ron Chipperfield as team captain. Playing in venerable Chicago Stadium the Oilers faced off against the Blackhawks and future Hall of Fame goaltender Tony Esposito. Oilers goaltender Dave Dryden faced 27 shots and the Oilers gave the 'Hawks all they could handle before losing 4–2. Kevin Lowe scored the first goal in the Oilers' NHL history at 9:49 of the first period.

After this first mini road-trip the Oilers came home to play their first games in Northlands Coliseum. Their first home game took place on October 13, 1979, against the Detroit Red Wings. The Oilers tied the Wings 3–3 as Ed Mio and Rogie Vachon faced each other in goal. The team's first win came on October 19, 1979, versus the Quebec Nordiques. Edmonton scored six goals on goaltender Michel Dion, and defeated Quebec by a score of 6–3. This was the first of 28 wins which the Oilers would register in their first season.

The Oilers were 17–25–10 (.423) at the All-Star break. By season's end the team's high powered offense, with their run and gun style of attack, had scored the most goals in their division. However this freewheeling style often left the team's goaltenders defenseless, and the shell-shocked netminders allowed the most goals in the division and the second most in the entire league.

Veteran Al Hamilton missed 33 games with a separated shoulder, while hard-nosed winger Brett Callighen sat out the final 18 regular season games due to an eye injury. He would however return in time for the playoffs.

Wayne Gretzky finished the season tied with Marcel Dionne for the lead in league scoring with 137 points. Dionne, however, was awarded the Art Ross Trophy on the basis of having scored more goals than Gretzky.

The Oilers met the Philadelphia Flyers in the first round of the playoffs. Edmonton lost the first two games, both in Philadelphia, a 4–3 overtime thriller April 8, and a 5–1 lopsided loss the following night. On April 11, Flyer goaltender Phil Myre faced off against Oiler Ron Low in the first NHL playoff game ever played in Edmonton. Tied after regulation, Ken Linseman finally ended the Oilers' playoff dreams at 3:56 of the second overtime period.

1979-80 Regular Season Scoring

#		*Ht.*	*Wt.*	*Age*	*GP*	*G*	*A*	*Pts.*	*Shots*	*%*	*GW*	*GT*	*PP*	*SH*	*P/M*	*PIM*
99	Gretzky	71	165	18	79	51	86	137	284	18.0	6	4	13	1	15	21
14	MacDonald (A)	70	180	26	80	46	48	94	266	17.3	6	1	13	2	1	6
21	Weir	73	170	27	79	33	33	66	129	25.6	2	2	3	2	2	40
18	Callighen	71	175	26	59	23	35	58	159	14.5	0	2	8	0	-1	72
20	Lumley	72	185	25	80	20	38	58	145	13.8	6	0	1	0	15	138
12	Hunter	71	195	21	80	12	31	43	109	11.0	3	0	1	2	7	103
5	Hicks	72	185	24	78	9	31	40	122	7.4	1	0	5	2	18	52
7	Chipperfield (C)	71	180	25	67	18	19	37	129	14.0	1	1	2	1	-15	24
8	Siltanen	68	185	21	64	6	29	35	116	5.2	0	0	1	0	-9	26
11	Messier	73	190	18	75	12	21	33	113	10.6	1	1	1	1	-10	120
26	Price	74	200	24	75	11	21	32	95	11.6	0	1	2	0	4	134
4	Lowe	74	197	20	64	2	19	21	86	2.3	0	0	2	0	1	70
17	Connor	74	200	25	38	7	13	20	44	15.9	0	0	0	0	2	136
19	Ashby	73	185	24	18	10	9	19	31	32.3	1	0	3	0	1	0
3	Hamilton	74	210	33	31	4	15	19	34	11.8	0	0	1	0	-2	20
16	Schmautz	69	172	34	29	8	8	16	46	17.4	0	0	2	0	-4	20
2	Fogolin (A)	72	200	24	80	5	10	15	90	5.6	0	0	0	0	-8	104
27	Semenko	75	215	22	67	6	7	13	43	14.0	1	0	1	0	-13	135
6	Campbell	69	190	26	72	2	11	13	80	2.5	0	0	0	0	-18	196

#		*Ht.*	*Wt.*	*Age*	*GP*	*G*	*A*	*Pts.*	*Shots*	*%*	*GW*	*GT*	*PP*	*SH*	*P/M*	*PIM*
47	Murdoch	71	180	23	10	5	2	7	35	14.3	0	0	1	0	0	4
19	Flett	73	205	36	20	5	2	7	26	19.2	0	0	1	0	-17	2
24	Driscoll	72	190	25	39	1	5	6	23	4.3	0	1	0	0	-11	54
16	Newman	73	195	27	10	3	1	4	16	18.8	0	0	0	0	-1	0
9	Makkonen	72	190	24	9	2	2	4	11	18.2	0	0	0	0	-2	0
35	Corsi	70	180	25	26	0	3	3	0	0.0	0	0	0	0	0	6
30	Low	73	205	29	11	0	1	1	0	0.0	0	0	0	0	0	0
31	Mio	70	180	25	34	0	1	1	0	0.0	0	0	0	0	0	4
1	Cutts	75	190	26	6	0	0	0	0	0.0	0	0	0	0	0	6
33	Bednarski	70	195	27	1	0	0	0	2	0.0	0	0	0	0	0	0
22	Carter	73	205	21	2	0	0	0	0	0.0	0	0	0	0	0	0
33	Baltimore	74	200	27	2	0	0	0	2	0.0	0	0	0	0	4	4
23	Forbes	74	200	22	2	0	0	0	3	0.0	0	0	0	0	-4	0
25	Toal	72	178	20	3	0	0	0	1	0.0	0	0	0	0	0	0
9	Harrison	71	185	32	3	0	0	0	3	0.0	0	0	0	0	-1	0
10	Areshenkoff	72	175	22	4	0	0	0	3	0.0	0	0	0	0	-4	0
15	Tidey	72	182	24	5	0	0	0	4	0.0	0	0	0	0	-3	8
22	Popiel	68	170	36	10	0	0	0	12	0.0	0	0	0	0	-5	0
15	Bianchin	70	180	26	11	0	0	0	7	0.0	0	0	0	0	-4	7
33	Dupuis	71	167	27	1	0	0	0	0	0.0	0	0	0	0	0	0
28	Dryden	73	186	38	14	0	0	0	0	0.0	0	0	0	0	0	0
	Bench														16	
		72	188	26	80	301	501	802	2269	13.3	28	13	61	11	-8	1528

1979-80 Goaltender Records

	GP	*Min.*	*GA*	*W*	*L*	*T*	*Ave.*	*SA*	*Pct.*	*SO*	*EN*
Ron Low	11	650	37	8	2	1	3.42	804	0.891	0	0
Don Cutts	6	269	16	1	2	1	3.57	142	0.887	0	1
Jim Corsi	26	1366	83	8	14	3	3.65	644	0.871	0	3
Bob Dupuis	1	60	4	0	1	0	4.00	35	0.886	0	1
Ed Mio	34	1711	120	9	13	5	4.21	915	0.869	1	2
Dave Dryden	14	744	53	2	7	3	4.27	350	0.849	0	2
	80	4800	322	28	39	13	4.03	2890	0.892	1	9

Coach: Glen Sather 28-39-13

1979-80 Scoring vs. Opposition

	Atl.	*Bost.*	*Buff.*	*Chi.*	*Col.*	*Det.*	*Hart.*	*L.A.*	*Minn.*	*Mont.*
Ashby	1–0–1	0–0–0	0–0–0	0–0–0	0–0–0	0–1–1	0–0–0	0–0–0	0–0–0	1–1–2
Callighen	0–0–0	1–0–1	2–2–4	0–2–2	1–4–5	1–3–4	0–1–1	2–4–6	1–3–4	0–1–1
Campbell	0–0–0	0–0–0	0–2–2	0–1–1	0–3–3	1–0–1	0–0–0	0–0–0	0–1–1	0–0–0
Chipperfield	0–1–1	0–2–2	0–1–1	1–0–1	1–0–1	0–0–0	0–1–1	2–1–3	2–0–2	0–1–1
Connor	0–0–0	1–0–1	0–1–1	0–1–1	0–0–0	0–0–0	0–0–0	1–2–3	0–2–2	0–1–1
Corsi	0–0–0	0–0–0	0–0–0	0–0–0	0–0–0	0–0–0	0–0–0	0–0–0	0–0–0	0–1–1
Driscoll	0–1–1	0–0–0	0–0–0	0–0–0	0–0–0	0–0–0	0–0–0	0–0–0	0–0–0	0–0–0
Flett	1–0–1	0–0–0	0–0–0	0–0–0	0–0–0	0–0–0	0–0–0	0–0–0	0–0–0	0–0–0
Fogolin	1–1–2	1–0–1	0–0–0	1–2–3	1–1–2	0–1–1	0–0–0	0–0–0	0–0–0	0–0–0
Gretzky	3–3–6	0–2–2	1–6–7	0–5–5	2–4–6	4–5–9	1–2–3	6–6–12	2–2–4	3–3–6
Hamilton	0–1–1	0–0–0	0–0–0	0–1–1	0–0–0	0–0–0	0–0–0	0–0–0	0–1–1	0–1–1
Hicks	1–1–2	0–1–1	2–2–4	0–2–2	0–1–1	1–1–2	0–1–1	0–3–3	0–1–1	0–0–0
Hunter	0–2–2	0–1–1	2–5–7	2–3–5	1–2–3	0–2–2	1–2–3	0–1–1	0–3–3	0–3–3
Lowe	0–0–0	0–0–0	0–2–2	1–1–2	0–4–4	0–0–0	0–0–0	0–3–3	0–1–1	0–2–2
Lumley	1–1–2	0–1–1	2–3–5	2–4–6	1–3–4	3–0–3	1–1–2	0–2–2	0–2–2	4–1–5
MacDonald	1–4–5	1–0–1	2–3–5	1–0–1	3–1–4	4–5–9	1–0–1	2–5–7	2–0–2	2–3–5
Makkonen	1–0–1	0–0–0	0–0–0	0–0–0	0–0–0	0–0–0	0–0–0	0–0–0	0–0–0	1–1–2
Messier	3–0–3	0–1–1	0–1–1	2–3–5	1–1–2	1–1–2	0–0–0	0–0–0	2–0–2	1–0–1
Mio	0–0–0	0–0–0	0–0–0	0–0–0	0–0–0	0–1–1	0–0–0	0–0–0	0–0–0	0–0–0
Murdoch	0–0–0	0–0–0	0–0–0	1–0–1	1–0–1	2–1–3	0–0–0	0–0–0	0–0–0	1–0–1
Newman	0–0–0	1–1–2	0–0–0	0–0–0	0–0–0	0–0–0	0–0–0	0–0–0	0–0–0	0–0–0
Price	1–3–4	1–0–0	0–1–1	2–1–3	0–0–0	0–0–0	2–2–4	1–2–3	0–0–0	0–1–1
Schmautz	0–1–1	0–0–0	1–0–1	0–0–0	0–2–2	0–0–0	1–0–1	2–0–2	0–0–0	1–0–1
Semenko	1–0–1	0–0–0	0–0–0	2–0–2	0–1–1	0–1–1	0–0–0	0–0–0	0–0–0	0–0–0

	Atl.	*Bost.*	*Buff.*	*Chi.*	*Col.*	*Det.*	*Hart.*	*L.A.*	*Minn.*	*Mont.*
Siltanen	0–1–1	0–1–1	1–1–2	1–1–2	0–1–1	0–1–1	0–0–0	1–3–4	0–3–3	0–0–0
Weir	0–2–2	0–0–0	6–4–10	2–1–3	3–0–3	0–4–4	1–3–4	2–2–4	3–0–3	1–2–3

	NYI.	*NYR.*	*Phil.*	*Pitt.*	*Que.*	*St.L.*	*Tor.*	*Van.*	*Wash.*	*Winn.*
Ashby	2–1–3	1–1–2	0–0–0	2–2–4	0–0–0	0–0–0	3–3–6	0–0–0	0–0–0	0–0–0
Callighen	1–2–3	1–0–1	2–1–3	1–2–3	2–1–3	3–2–5	2–1–3	0–3–3	1–2–3	2–2–4
Campbell	0–1–1	0–0–0	0–0–0	1–0–1	0–0–0	1–0–1	0–0–0	0–1–1	0–1–1	0–1–1
Chipperfield	2–1–3	1–0–1	0–1–1	1–2–3	1–0–1	1–2–3	2–1–3	0–2–2	2–2–4	2–1–3
Connor	0–0–0	1–0–1	0–2–2	1–0–1	0–0–0	1–1–2	1–1–2	0–0–0	1–1–2	0–0–0
Corsi	0–0–0	0–0–0	0–0–0	0–0–0	0–0–0	0–1–1	0–0–0	0–0–0	0–0–0	0–0–0
Driscoll	1–1–2	0–0–0	0–0–0	0–0–0	0–0–0	0–0–0	0–2–2	0–0–0	0–1–1	0–0–0
Flett	1–2–3	0–0–0	0–0–0	0–0–0	0–0–0	0–1–1	0–0–0	0–0–0	3–0–3	0–0–0
Fogolin	0–0–0	0–0–0	0–0–0	0–1–1	0–0–0	0–1–1	0–1–1	0–0–0	1–1–2	0–1–1
Gretzky	5–5–10	0–2–2	1–5–6	7–5–12	3–4–7	2–4–6	4–10–14	2–1–3	2–9–11	4–2–6
Hamilton	0–1–1	1–2–3	0–0–0	1–1–2	1–1–2	0–0–0	0–0–0	1–2–3	0–1–1	0–0–0
Hicks	0–4–4	0–0–0	1–1–2	0–3–3	1–3–4	1–1–2	0–3–3	0–0–0	0–3–3	0–2–2
Hunter	0–1–1	0–1–1	0–0–0	1–0–1	2–2–4	0–0–0	0–0–0	1–1–2	0–1–1	1–4–5
Lowe	0–1–1	0–0–0	0–0–0	0–3–3	0–0–0	0–0–0	1–0–1	0–0–0	0–1–1	0–0–0
Lumley	0–3–3	1–1–2	0–2–2	1–1–2	1–0–1	0–1–1	1–3–4	1–2–3	0–2–2	3–4–7
MacDonald	4–3–7	1–1–2	2–2–4	4–4–8	4–1–5	0–2–2	4–5–9	0–2–2	4–5–9	2–1–3
Makkonen	0–0–0	0–0–0	0–0–0	0–0–0	0–0–0	0–0–0	0–0–0	0–0–0	0–0–0	0–1–1
Messier	0–1–1	0–2–2	1–0–1	0–0–0	1–1–2	1–1–2	0–2–2	0–1–1	0–2–2	0–3–3
Mio	0–0–0	0–0–0	0–0–0	0–0–0	0–0–0	0–0–0	0–0–0	0–0–0	0–0–0	0–1–1
Murdoch	0–0–0	0–0–0	0–0–0	0–1–1	0–0–0	0–0–0	0–0–0	0–0–0	0–0–0	0–0–0
Newman	1–0–1	0–0–0	0–0–0	0–0–0	0–0–0	0–0–0	1–0–1	0–0–0	0–0–0	0–0–0
Price	0–3–3	1–1–2	1–1–2	1–3–4	0–0–0	0–0–0	0–0–0	0–2–2	1–2–3	0–0–0
Schmautz	0–0–0	0–1–1	0–0–0	0–1–1	0–0–0	0–0–0	0–0–0	1–0–1	2–2–4	0–0–0
Semenko	0–0–0	0–1–1	0–0–0	1–1–2	0–0–0	0–0–0	0–0–0	1–0–1	1–2–3	1–0–1
Siltanen	0–2–2	0–1–1	0–1–1	0–1–1	0–1–1	1–3–4	0–5–5	2–0–2	0–0–0	0–3–3
Weir	1–1–2	1–0–1	2–0–2	0–2–2	1–3–4	0–0–0	3–0–3	1–2–3	4–1–5	2–4–6

1979–80–Goaltender Record vs. Opposition

	GP	*Min.*	*GA*	*EN*	*SO*	*Ave.*	*W–L–T*	*Opposition*
Jim Corsi	2	95	9	0	0	5.68	0–2–0	Boston
	1	60	5	0	0	5.00	1–0–0	Buffalo
	3	127	9	0	0	4.25	1–2–0	Colorado
	1	60	3	0	0	3.00	0–0–1	Hartford
	3	159	7	0	0	2.64	1–1–1	Los Angeles
	1	32	0	0	0	0.00	1–0–0	Minnesota
	2	120	9	0	0	4.50	0–2–0	Montreal
	1	36	3	0	0	5.00	0–1–0	N.Y. Islanders
	1	60	4	0	0	4.00	0–1–0	N.Y. Rangers
	1	60	5	0	0	5.00	0–1–0	Philadelphia
	1	20	1	0	0	3.00	0–0–0	Pittsburgh
	2	120	5	0	0	2.50	0–2–0	Quebec
	2	120	11	0	0	5.50	0–1–1	St. Louis
	1	57	0	0	0	0.00	1–0–0	Toronto
	2	120	8	0	0	4.00	1–1–0	Vancouver
	1	60	2	0	0	2.00	1–0–0	Washington
	1	60	2	0	0	2.00	1–0–0	Winnipeg
Don Cutts	1	60	4	0	0	4.00	0–1–0	Atlanta
	1	21	0	0	0	0.00	0–0–0	Los Angeles
	1	28	3	0	0	6.43	0–0–0	Minnesota
	1	40	4	0	0	6.00	0–1–0	Pittsburgh
	1	60	3	0	0	3.00	1–1–0	St. Louis
	1	60	2	0	0	2.00	0–0–1	Winnipeg
Dave Dryden	1	60	7	0	0	7.00	0–1–0	Atlanta
	1	60	4	0	0	4.00	0–1–0	Boston
	1	31	4	0	0	7.74	0–1–0	Buffalo
	2	120	6	0	0	3.00	1–1–0	Chicago
	1	60	4	0	0	4.00	0–1–0	Hartford
	1	5	2	0	0	24.00	0–1–0	N. Y. Rangers

	GP	Min.	GA	EN	SO	Ave.	W–L–T	Opposition
	2	120	7	0	0	3.50	0–1–1	Philadelphia
	2	71	8	0	0	6.76	0–1–1	Toronto
	1	60	4	0	0	4.00	0–0–1	Vancouver
	1	60	3	0	0	3.00	1–0–0	Washington
	1	60	8	0	0	8.00	0–1–0	Winnipeg
Bob Dupuis	1	60	5	0	0	5.00	0–1–0	Philadelphia
Ron Low	1	60	4	0	0	4.00	1–0–0	Atlanta
	1	60	4	0	0	4.00	1–0–0	Chicago
	1	60	2	0	0	2.00	1–0–0	Colorado
	1	60	2	0	0	2.00	1–0–0	Detroit
	1	60	1	0	0	1.00	0–0–1	Minnesota
	1	60	7	0	0	7.00	0–1–0	Montreal
	1	60	2	0	0	2.00	1–0–0	N.Y. Rangers
	1	60	2	0	0	2.00	1–0–0	Pittsburgh
	1	60	3	0	0	3.00	1–0–0	Quebec
	1	60	5	0	0	5.00	1–0–0	Toronto
	1	50	5	0	0	6.00	0–1–1	Vancouver
Ed Mio	1	60	5	0	0	5.00	0–0–1	Atlanta
	2	85	4	0	0	2.82	0–1–0	Boston
	3	149	13	0	0	5.23	0–1–1	Buffalo
	1	60	2	0	0	2.00	1–0–0	Chicago
	2	53	2	0	0	2.26	0–0–0	Colorado
	3	180	14	0	0	4.67	0–2–1	Detroit
	2	120	6	0	1	3.00	1–1–0	Hartford
	1	60	9	0	0	9.00	0–1–0	Los Angeles
	2	120	11	0	0	5.50	0–1–1	Minnesota
	1	60	3	0	0	3.00	1–0–0	Montreal
	4	204	14	0	0	4.18	2–0–1	N.Y. Islanders
	2	115	14	0	0	7.30	0–1–0	N.Y. Rangers
	2	120	5	0	0	2.50	2–0–0	Pittsburgh
	1	60	3	0	0	3.00	1–0–0	Quebec
	1	60	2	0	0	2.00	0–1–0	St. Louis
	2	52	5	0	0	5.77	0–0–0	Toronto
	1	10	0	0	0	0.00	0–0–0	Vancouver
	2	120	8	0	0	4.00	1–1–0	Washington
	1	60	4	0	0	4.00	0–1–0	Winnipeg

1979-80 Schedule Results

Date	Team	Score		Team	Score
Oct. 10	Edmonton	2	at	Chicago	4
Oct. 13	Detroit	3	at	Edmonton	3
Oct. 14	Vancouver	4	at	Edmonton	4
Oct. 19	Quebec	3	at	Edmonton	6
Oct. 21	Minnesota	5	at	Edmonton	5
Oct. 23	Edmonton	3	at	Islanders	3
Oct. 24	Edmonton	2	at	Rangers	10
Oct. 26	Edmonton	3	at	Atlanta	7
Oct. 28	Washington	6	at	Edmonton	4
Oct. 30	Edmonton	1	at	St. Louis	2
Nov. 2	Islanders	5	at	Edmonton	7
Nov. 4	Boston	2	at	Edmonton	1
Nov. 7	Edmonton	3	at	Detroit	5
Nov. 8	Edmonton	2	at	Boston	4
Nov. 11	Toronto	6	at	Edmonton	3
Nov. 13	Edmonton	5	at	Washington	3
Nov. 15	Edmonton	3	at	Philadelphia	5
Nov. 17	Edmonton	0	at	Hartford	4
Nov. 18	Edmonton	7	at	Buffalo	9
Nov. 21	Edmonton	4	at	Toronto	4
Nov. 24	Philadelphia	2	at	Edmonton	2
Nov. 28	Chicago	2	at	Edmonton	4
Nov. 30	Islanders	3	at	Edmonton	5
Dec. 5	Edmonton	1	at	Minnesota	6
Dec. 7	Edmonton	3	at	Winnipeg	8
Dec. 9	Hartford	0	at	Edmonton	3
Dec. 12	Atlanta	5	at	Edmonton	5
Dec. 14	Montreal	3	at	Edmonton	5
Dec. 16	Winnipeg	4	at	Edmonton	3
Dec. 19	Detroit	6	at	Edmonton	4
Dec. 21	Edmonton	4	at	Colorado	5
Dec. 22	Edmonton	3	at	Los Angeles	9
Dec. 26	Colorado	3	at	Edmonton	4
Dec. 28	Edmonton	5	at	Vancouver	3
Dec. 30	Quebec	2	at	Edmonton	1
Jan. 2	Hartford	3	at	Edmonton	3
Jan. 5	Los Angeles	3	at	Edmonton	3
Jan. 7	Edmonton	3	at	Montreal	4
Jan. 9	Edmonton	2	at	Quebec	3
Jan. 11	Rangers	6	at	Edmonton	2
Jan. 13	Buffalo	5	at	Edmonton	6
Jan. 16	Edmonton	5	at	Washington	2
Jan. 17	Edmonton	1	at	Boston	7
Jan. 19	Edmonton	5	at	Pittsburgh	2
Jan. 20	Edmonton	4	at	Buffalo	4
Jan. 23	Pittsburgh	3	at	Edmonton	4
Jan. 26	Toronto	3	at	Edmonton	8
Jan. 27	Philadelphia	5	at	Edmonton	3

Date	Visitor			Home	
Jan. 29	Edmonton	2	at	St. Louis	3
Jan. 30	Edmonton	8	at	Los Angeles	1
Feb. 1	Winnipeg	2	at	Edmonton	9
Feb. 3	Los Angeles	3	at	Edmonton	5
Feb. 6	St. Louis	6	at	Edmonton	3
Feb. 8	Atlanta	4	at	Edmonton	2
Feb. 10	Edmonton	2	at	Winnipeg	2
Feb. 13	Edmonton	5	at	Minnesota	3
Feb. 15	Washington	2	at	Edmonton	8
Feb. 17	St. Louis	5	at	Edmonton	5
Feb. 19	Edmonton	2	at	Hartford	6
Feb. 20	Edmonton	1	at	Rangers	4
Feb. 22	Edmonton	1	at	Colorado	3
Feb. 24	Boston	4	at	Edmonton	2
Feb. 27	Edmonton	5	at	Chicago	2
Feb. 29	Buffalo	4	at	Edmonton	2
Mar. 1	Vancouver	5	at	Edmonton	2
Mar. 4	Edmonton	4	at	Islanders	6
Mar. 6	Edmonton	4	at	Montreal	5
Mar. 8	Edmonton	4	at	Pittsburgh	5
Mar. 9	Edmonton	3	at	Philadelphia	5
Mar. 12	Edmonton	6	at	Quebec	3
Mar. 14	Chicago	4	at	Edmonton	6
Mar. 15	Montreal	7	at	Edmonton	3
Mar. 19	Rangers	2	at	Edmonton	4
Mar. 21	Pittsburgh	2	at	Edmonton	9
Mar. 25	Edmonton	5	at	Atlanta	4
Mar. 26	Edmonton	5	at	Detroit	2
Mar. 29	Edmonton	8	at	Toronto	5
April 1	Edmonton	0	at	Vancouver	5
April 2	Minnesota	1	at	Edmonton	1
April 4	Colorado	2	at	Edmonton	6

Opponent	*Home W–L–T*	*Road W–L–T*
Atlanta	0–1–1	1–1–0
Boston	0–2–0	0–2–0
Buffalo	1–1–0	0–1–1
Chicago	2–0–0	1–1–0
Colorado	2–0–0	0–2–0
Detroit	0–1–1	1–1–0
Hartford	1–0–1	0–2–0
Los Angeles	1–0–1	1–1–0
Minnesota	0–0–2	1–1–0
Montreal	1–1–0	0–2–0
Islanders	2–0–0	0–1–1
Rangers	1–1–0	0–2–0
Philadelphia	0–1–1	0–2–0
Pittsburgh	2–0–0	1–1–0
Quebec	1–1–0	1–1–0
St. Louis	0–1–1	0–2–0
Toronto	1–1–0	1–0–1
Vancouver	0–1–1	1–1–0
Washington	1–1–0	2–0–0
Winnipeg	1–1–0	0–1–1

Opponent	*Overall W–L–T*	*GF–GA*
Atlanta	1–2–1	15–20
Boston	0–4–0	6–17
Buffalo	1–2–1	19–22
Chicago	3–1–0	17–12
Colorado	2–2–0	15–13
Detroit	1–2–1	12–16
Hartford	1–2–1	8–13
Los Angeles	2–1–1	19–18
Minnesota	1–1–2	12–15
Montreal	1–3–0	15–19
Islanders	2–1–1	19–17
Rangers	1–3–0	9–22
Philadelphia	0–3–1	11–17
Pittsburgh	3–1–0	22–12
Quebec	2–2–0	15–11
St. Louis	0–3–1	11–16
Toronto	2–1–1	23–18
Vancouver	1–2–1	11–17
Washington	3–1–0	22–13
Winnipeg	1–2–1	17–16

1979-80 Playoff Scoring

#		*GP*	*G*	*A*	*Pts.*	*GW*	*OT*	*PP*	*SH*	*PIM*
99	Wayne Gretzky	3	2	1	3	0	0	0	0	0
11	Mark Messier	3	1	2	3	0	0	0	1	2
14	Blair MacDonald	3	0	3	3	0	0	0	0	0
47	Don Murdoch	3	2	0	2	0	0	0	0	0
18	Brett Callighen	3	0	2	2	0	0	0	0	0
20	Dave Lumley	3	1	0	1	0	0	1	0	12
4	Kevin Lowe	3	0	1	1	0	0	0	0	0
3	Al Hamilton	1	0	0	0	0	0	0	0	0
8	Risto Siltanen	2	0	0	0	0	0	0	0	2
19	Don Ashby	3	0	0	0	0	0	0	0	0
30	Ron Low	3	0	0	0	0	0	0	0	0
24	Peter Driscoll	3	0	0	0	0	0	0	0	0
2	Lee Fogolin	3	0	0	0	0	0	0	0	4
5	Doug Hicks	3	0	0	0	0	0	0	0	2
6	Colin Campbell	3	0	0	0	0	0	0	0	11
26	Pat Price	3	0	0	0	0	0	0	0	11
12	Dave Hunter	3	0	0	0	0	0	0	0	7
21	Stan Weir	3	0	0	0	0	0	0	0	2
27	Dave Semenko	3	0	0	0	0	0	0	0	2
		3	6	9	15	0	0	1	0	55

1979-80 Playoff Goaltending

	GP	Min.	GA	W	L	Ave.	SA	Pct.	SO	EN
Ron Low	3	212	12	0	3	3.40	127	.906	0	0

Date			Result			Winning Goaltender	Winning Goal
April 8, 1980	Edmonton	3	at	Philadelphia	4	Pete Peeters	Bobby Clarke[1]
April 9, 1980	Edmonton	1	at	Philadelphia	5	Pete Peeters	Bobby Clarke
April 11, 1980	Philadelphia	3	at	Edmonton	2	Phil Myre	Ken Linseman[2]

[1]-8:06 of overtime
[2]-23:56 of overtime

Table 1. Oilers Yearly Record

Season	*GP*	*W*	*L*	*T*	*OL*	*GF*	*GA*	*Pts*	*Pct.*	*Finish*
2000-01	82	39	28	12	3	243	222	93	.549	2nd Northwest
1999-00	82	32	34	16	8	230	211	88	.488	2nd Northwest
1998-99	82	33	37	12	NA	230	226	78	.476	2nd Northwest
1997-98	82	35	37	10	NA	215	223	80	.488	3rd Pacific
1996-97	82	36	37	9	NA	252	247	81	.494	3rd Pacific
1995-96	82	30	44	8	NA	240	304	68	.415	5th Pacific
1994-95	48	17	27	4	NA	136	183	38	.396	5th Pacific
1993-94	84	25	45	14	NA	261	305	64	.381	6th Pacific
1992-93	84	26	50	8	NA	242	337	60	.357	5th Smythe
1991-92	80	36	34	10	NA	295	297	82	.513	3rd Smythe
1990-91	80	37	37	6	NA	272	272	80	.500	3rd Smythe
1989-90	80	38	28	14	NA	315	283	90	.563	2nd Smythe
1988-89	80	38	34	8	NA	325	306	84	.525	3rd Smythe
1987-88	80	44	25	11	NA	363	288	99	.619	2nd Smythe
1986-87	80	50	24	6	NA	372	284	106	.663	lst Smythe
1985-86	80	56	17	7	NA	426	310	119	.744	1st Smythe
1984-85	80	49	20	11	NA	401	298	109	.681	1st Smythe
1983-84	80	57	18	5	NA	446	314	119	.744	1st Smythe
1982-83	80	47	21	12	NA	424	315	106	.663	1st Smythe
1981-82	80	48	17	15	NA	417	295	111	.694	1st Smythe
1980-81	80	29	35	16	NA	328	327	74	.463	4th Smythe
1979-80	80	28	39	13	NA	301	322	69	.431	4th Smythe
TOTAL	1748	830	688	227	11	6734	6169	1898	.543	

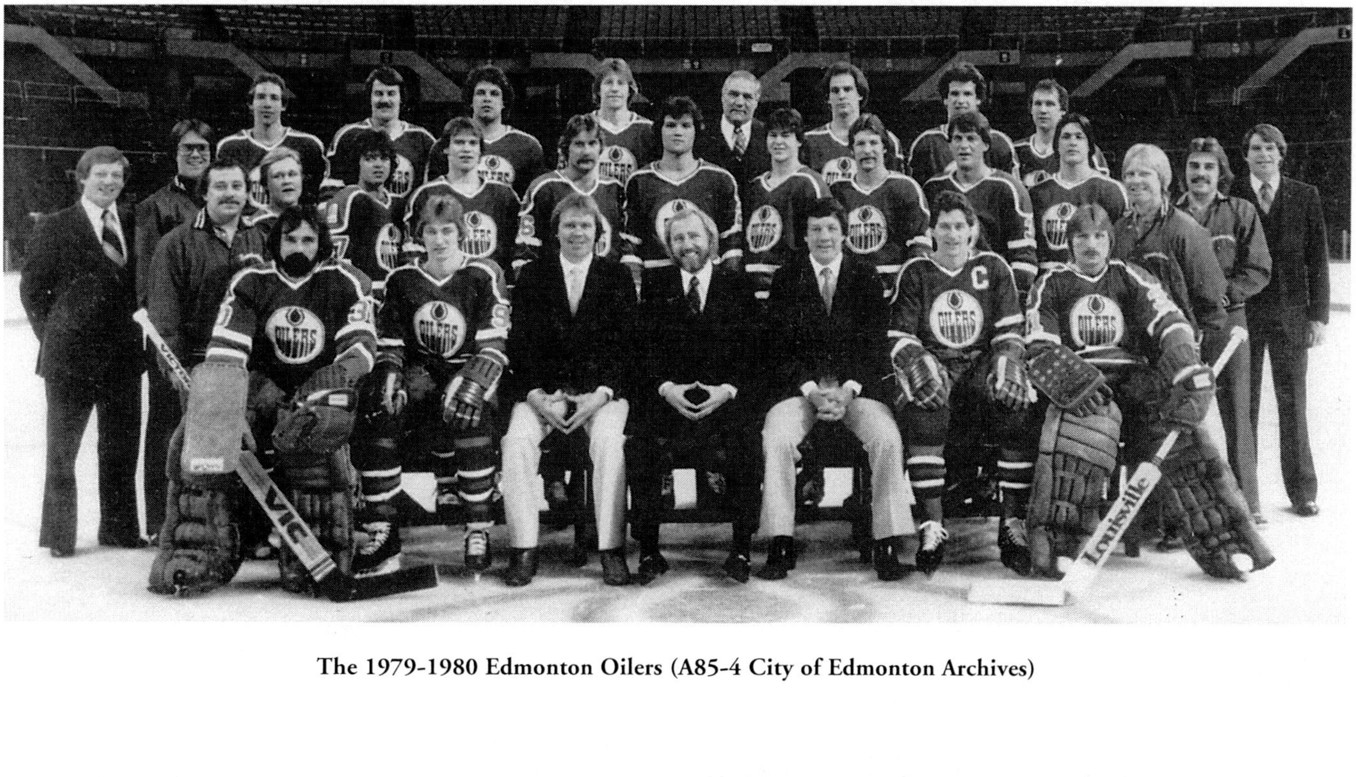

The 1979-1980 Edmonton Oilers (A85-4 City of Edmonton Archives)

1980-81

Glen Sather replaced Larry Gordon as the Oilers' general manager in June of 1980. Gordon had taken over as owner, president and G.M. of the Wichita Wind of the Central Hockey League. He would later come to an agreement with Peter Pocklington to run the team as the Oiler's minor league affiliate.

At this year's entry draft, Sather drafted three players who would become instrumental in helping the Oilers win future Stanley Cups. In the first round, sixth overall, Sather picked Paul Coffey the talented defenseman from the Kitchener Rangers of the Ontario Hockey League. Coffey had scored 71 points in 52 games for the Rangers and was named to the league's second All-Star Team.

Drafted 69th overall from Jokerit of the Finnish Ice Hockey League was winger Jari Kurri. During the 1979-80 season Kurri had scored 39 points in 33 games for the Helsinki based team and would shortly begin his NHL career. He would go on to become the highest scoring European player in league history. Kurri and Glenn Anderson, the 69th overall draft choice from 1979, would both join the team this year and became major contributors to all five of the Oiler Cup victories.

Drafted in the seventh round from Billings of the Western Hockey League, Andy Moog became the first goaltender ever chosen by the Oilers in the entry draft. Moog would be influential in helping the Oilers win three Stanley Cups.

Over the summer Sather named Bryan Watson as head coach but had some difficulty finding an assistant coach. Passed over for the head coaching position with the Oilers, Dave Dryden had quit the team over the summer to accept the head coaching and managing duties with the Peterborough Petes of the OHA. Ralph Backstrom was also expected to sign with the Oilers but opted instead to take the assistant coaching position with the Los Angeles Kings. Sather finally settled on veteran coach Billy Harris, who had both WHA and international experience. Blair MacDonald was named as captain and was in turn replaced by Lee Fogolin after MacDonald was traded to Vancouver. Wayne Gretzky wore the captain's "C" for one game before Fogolin took over the duties on a full time basis.

The team made a fine off-season acquisition with the signing of free agent Matti Hagman. Hagman, a part-time firefighter in his native Finland, had been out of the NHL for two seasons but would score 112 points in 147 games for the team over the next two years.

The Oilers opened their second season on October 10, with a 7–4 loss to Quebec. The team's first victory would come on the road this season, when they defeated the New York Rangers by a score of 4–2. It was the club's fifth game of the season.

Glen Sather replaced his close friend "Bugsy" Watson as coach after the team managed only four wins and 13 points in their first 18 games. Due to a rash of injuries incurred throughout the year the team won a total of only 29 games, finishing the year with 74 points, good enough for fourth place in the Smythe Division.

Wayne Gretzky's regular winger Brett Callighen played the first six games but then sat out the next 25 due to complications from the eye injury he had sustained the previous year. Defenseman Doug Hicks broke his wrist on October 26 in a game against Los Angeles and sat out 21 games. On November 29, Dave Lumley sprained his shoulder in a game against Boston and was out of the lineup for 14 games. Rookie Glenn Anderson also missed five weeks due to a knee injury while captain Blair MacDonald missed seven games due to a cracked finger. The goaltending corps was also hard hit, as last year's savior Ron Low missed five weeks with a broken thumb. Ed Mio also suffered a broken thumb and missed the final ten games of the season.

The Oilers were 17–28–9–(.398) at the All-Star break. The team finished the season sixth in goals scored with 328 but their porous defense was still allowing too many goals, finishing 15th in the league in goals against. The team ended the season with only one loss in their final 12 games.

Wayne Gretzky led the league in scoring, outdistancing last year's rival Marcel Dionne by 19 points.

Glen Sather played rookie goaltender Andy Moog in the first round of the playoffs against the highly favored Montreal Canadiens. The "Habs" had finished 29 points ahead of Edmonton in the regular season but with Moog in goal the Oilers shut the door on the Montreal team, allowing only six goals in the three games while scoring 15 of their own. The Oilers then faced the defending Stanley Cup champion New York Islanders. They extended the series to six games before finally bowing out 5–2 to the Islanders in an April 24 game in Edmonton.

1980-81 Regular Season Scoring

#		*Ht.*	*Wt.*	*Age*	*GP*	*G*	*A*	*Pts.*	*Shots*	*S%*	*GW*	*GT*	*PP*	*SH*	*P/M*	*PIM*
99	Gretzky	71	165	19	80	55	109	164	261	21.1	3	2	15	4	41	28
17	Kurri	73	185	20	75	32	43	75	202	15.8	1	2	9	0	26	40
11	Messier	72	190	19	72	23	40	63	179	12.8	1	1	4	0	-12	102

#		*Ht.*	*Wt.*	*Age*	*GP*	*G*	*A*	*Pts.*	*Shots*	*S%*	*GW*	*GT*	*PP*	*SH*	*P/M*	*PIM*
18	Callighen	71	182	27	55	25	35	60	127	19.7	1	1	6	0	13	32
8	Siltanen	67	158	22	79	17	36	53	209	8.1	3	2	7	1	5	54
10	Hagman	73	184	25	75	20	33	53	96	20.8	0	0	2	0	4	16
9	Anderson	71	175	20	58	30	23	53	160	18.8	5	2	10	3	4	24
14	MacDonald (C)	70	180	27	51	19	24	43	134	14.2	1	0	5	0	-8	27
4	Lowe	74	197	21	79	10	24	34	115	8.7	2	0	4	0	-10	94
21	Weir	73	170	28	70	12	20	32	84	14.3	2	1	1	0	-7	40
7	Coffey	73	185	19	74	9	23	32	113	8.0	0	0	2	0	4	130
26	Price	74	200	25	59	8	24	32	90	8.9	0	1	0	0	-7	193
2	Fogolin (C)	72	204	25	80	13	17	30	89	14.6	1	1	0	4	2	139
12	Hunter	71	195	22	78	12	16	28	104	11.5	3	3	0	0	-12	98
5	Hicks	72	185	25	59	5	16	21	109	4.6	0	0	1	1	21	76
27	Semenko	75	200	23	58	11	8	19	42	26.2	2	0	4	0	-4	80
47	Murdoch	71	180	24	40	10	9	19	102	9.8	2	0	4	0	-16	18
20	Lumley	72	185	26	53	7	9	16	54	13.0	1	0	0	0	-15	74
15	Brackenbury	70	197	28	58	2	7	9	20	10.0	0	0	0	0	-3	153
22	Huddy	72	200	21	12	2	5	7	23	8.7	0	0	1	0	1	6
19	Ashby	73	185	25	6	2	3	5	13	15.4	1	0	1	0	-1	2
24	Driscoll	72	190	26	21	2	3	5	17	11.8	0	0	1	0	1	43
31	Mio	70	180	26	43	0	5	5	0	0.0	0	0	0	0	0	6
30	Low	73	205	30	24	0	3	3	0	0.0	0	0	0	0	0	0
6	J. Hughes	71	200	26	18	0	3	3	9	0.0	0	0	0	0	-6	30
33	Edwards	69	165	33	15	0	2	2	0	0.0	0	0	0	0	0	0
23	Roulston	73	184	23	11	1	1	2	9	11.1	0	0	0	0	-3	2
6	Lariviere	72	190	26	13	0	2	2	8	0.0	0	0	0	0	9	6
35	Moog	68	165	20	7	0	1	1	0	0.0	0	0	0	0	0	0
28	Sommer	72	180	23	3	1	0	1	1	100.0	0	0	0	0	0	7
23	Bladon	73	195	28	1	0	0	0	0	0.0	0	0	0	0	-1	0
1	LoPresti	73	195	26	2	0	0	0	0	0.0	0	0	0	0	0	0
16	P. Hughes	73	180	25	2	0	0	0	3	0.0	0	0	0	0	-3	0
77	Unger	72	185	33	13	0	0	0	13	0.0	0	0	0	0	-9	6
	Bench															18
		72	186	25	80	328	544	872	2386	13.7	29	16	77	13	9	1544

1980-81 Goaltender Records

	GP	*Min.*	*GA*	*W*	*L*	*T*	*Ave.*	*SA*	*Pct.*	*SO*	*EN*
Gary Edwards	17	729	44	5	3	4	3.62	326	0.865	0	0
Andy Moog	7	313	20	3	3	0	3.83	206	0.903	0	0
Ed Mio	43	2393	155	16	15	9	3.89	1115	0.861	0	4
Ron Low	24	1260	93	5	13	3	4.43	661	0.859	0	2
Pete LoPresti	2	105	8	0	1	0	4.57	46	0.826	0	1
	80	4800	327	29	35	16	4.09	2354	0.861	0	7

Coach: Bryan Watson 4-9-5
Coach: Glen Sather 25-26-11

1980-81 Scoring vs. Opposition

	Bost.	*Buff.*	*Calg.*	*Chi.*	*Col.*	*Det.*	*Hart.*	*L.A.*	*Minn.*	*Mont.*
Ashby	–––	–––	–––	0–2–2	–––	–––	–––	–––	–––	–––
Anderson	2–0–2	1–0–1	0–0–0	1–0–1	2–1–3	1–0–1	3–0–3	1–2–3	2–0–2	2–2–4
Bladon	–––	–––	–––	–––	0–0–0	–––	–––	–––	–––	–––
Brackenbury	0–0–0	0–1–1	0–0–0	0–0–0	0–0–0	0–1–1	0–0–0	0–0–0	0–0–0	0–0–0
Callighen	2–1–3	2–1–3	1–3–4	1–1–2	0–2–2	1–4–5	1–1–2	0–0–0	3–0–3	0–2–2
Coffey	0–1–1	0–2–2	3–0–3	1–2–3	1–0–1	0–1–1	0–3–3	0–1–1	0–0–0	0–1–1
Driscoll	0–0–0	0–1–1	0–0–0	–––	0–0–0	0–0–0	0–1–1	0–0–0	–––	0–0–0
Fogolin	0–0–0	0–1–1	1–2–3	0–1–1	1–1–2	2–0–2	0–0–0	1–0–1	0–0–0	0–2–2
Gretzky	1–3–4	0–2–2	3–5–8	4–8–12	0–6–6	1–7–8	2–8–10	5–4–9	1–5–6	1–6–7
Hagman	0–2–2	1–2–3	0–1–1	0–2–2	0–0–0	1–0–1	3–2–5	2–3–5	0–2–2	3–1–4
Hicks	1–0–1	0–0–0	0–4–4	1–1–2	0–1–1	1–0–1	0–0–0	0–2–2	0–1–1	0–0–0
Huddy	0–0–0	0–0–0	–––	1–1–2	0–0–0	–––	0–1–1	–––	–––	–––
Hughes, J.	–––	0–0–0	0–0–0	0–0–0	–––	0–0–0	0–0–0	–––	0–0–0	0–0–0
Hughes, P.	0–0–0	–––	–––	–––	–––	–––	–––	–––	–––	–––

	Bost.	*Buff.*	*Calg.*	*Chi.*	*Col.*	*Det.*	*Hart.*	*L.A.*	*Minn.*	*Mont.*
Hunter	2–1–3	1–2–3	0–0–0	0–0–0	0–0–0	0–3–3	1–0–1	1–0–1	1–1–2	1–0–1
Kurri	1–2–3	1–1–2	1–3–4	4–2–6	2–0–2	1–1–2	2–2–4	2–3–5	2–2–4	3–2–5
Lariviere	0–0–0	———	0–0–0	———	0–0–0	0–0–0	0–0–0	0–0–0	0–0–0	———
Lowe	0–2–2	1–0–1	1–0–1	1–2–3	0–2–2	0–1–1	1–3–4	1–0–1	0–1–1	0–1–1
Lumley	0–0–0	0–0–0	0–0–0	1–3–4	0–0–0	1–0–1	0–0–0	0–0–0	0–0–0	0–0–0
MacDonald	0–1–1	2–1–3	1–2–3	1–2–3	2–0–2	0–0–0	1–1–2	0–0–0	0–1–1	1–3–4
Messier	1–2–3	0–1–1	0–3–3	1–1–2	0–0–0	2–2–4	4–4–8	1–3–4	0–1–1	1–3–4
Murdoch	1–0–1	0–1–1	1–0–1	1–1–2	1–0–1	1–1–2	1–2–3	1–1–2	———	0–0–0
Price	0–4–4	2–1–3	0–1–1	0–3–3	1–0–1	0–2–2	0–1–1	1–0–1	0–0–0	1–1–2
Roulston	———	———	———	———	———	1–0–1	———	0–0–0	———	0–0–0
Semenko	0–0–0	0–0–0	3–0–3	1–0–1	0–0–0	0–0–0	1–2–3	0–1–1	0–0–0	0–0–0
Siltanen	1–1–2	1–2–3	0–2–2	0–3–3	0–0–0	3–3–6	3–2–5	0–2–2	0–2–2	0–0–0
Sommer	———	———	———	0–0–0	———	———	———	———	———	1–0–1
Unger	0–0–0	———	0–0–0	———	0–0–0	0–0–0	0–0–0	0–0–0	0–0–0	———
Weir	1–3–4	1–2–3	0–0–0	3–1–4	0–0–0	0–1–1	0–1–1	0–0–0	0–0–0	0–0–0

	NYI.	*NYR.*	*Phil.*	*Pitt.*	*Que.*	*St.L.*	*Tor.*	*Van.*	*Wash.*	*Winn.*
Ashby	———	———	0–0–0	———	———	0–0–0	0–1–1	0–1–1	———	1–0–1
Anderson	1–3–4	1–2–3	1–2–3	3–6–9	0–1–1	2–1–3	4–0–4	4–0–4	0–1–1	3–2–5
Bladon	———	———	———	———	———	———	———	———	———	———
Brackenbury	0–0–0	0–0–0	0–1–1	0–1–1	1–0–1	1–1–2	0–0–0	0–0–0	0–1–1	0–0–0
Callighen	0–1–1	1–0–1	0–3–3	2–0–2	1–4–5	2–1–3	1–4–5	4–1–5	1–2–3	2–4–6
Coffey	0–0–0	0–2–2	0–0–0	1–3–4	0–0–0	1–2–3	0–1–1	0–1–1	0–1–1	1–1–2
Driscoll	———	0–1–1	0–0–0	———	0–0–0	0–0–0	1–0–1	1–0–1	1–0–1	0–0–0
Fogolin	0–1–1	0–2–2	2–0–2	0–1–1	1–1–2	1–0–1	1–0–1	1–0–1	1–2–3	1–2–3
Gretzky	4–3–7	3–5–8	6–2–8	2–7–9	4–6–10	6–7–13	4–5–9	2–7–9	2–4–6	4–9–13
Hagman	1–2–3	1–2–3	0–1–1	2–4–6	1–2–3	1–1–2	2–2–4	2–2–4	1–1–2	1–2–3
Hicks	0–0–0	0–1–1	0–1–1	1–0–1	0–0–0	0–3–3	0–0–0	0–0–0	1–1–2	0–0–0
Huddy	0–1–1	0–1–1	———	———	0–0–0	———	1–0–1	1–0–1	———	———
Hughes, J.	0–1–1	0–0–0	0–0–0	0–0–0	———	0–0–0	0–1–1	0–1–1	0–0–0	0–0–0
Hughes, P.	0–0–0	———	———	———	———	———	———	———	———	———
Hunter	0–0–0	0–2–2	0–0–0	1–0–1	1–0–1	0–2–2	0–1–1	0–1–1	1–3–4	2–1–3
Kurri	3–3–6	0–0–0	0–1–1	2–1–3	3–5–8	———	2–3–5	1–5–6	0–2–2	0–4–4
Lariviere	0–0–0	———	———	0–1–1	———	———	0–0–0	0–0–0	———	0–1–1
Lowe	0–1–1	0–0–0	1–0–1	0–0–0	0–1–1	1–4–5	0–3–3	0–3–3	1–0–1	2–2–4
Lumley	0–0–0	2–1–3	0–1–1	1–1–2	0–0–0	0–1–1	1–0–1	1–0–1	0–0–0	0–2–2
MacDonald	1–2–3	1–1–2	1–0–1	0–0–0	1–2–3	1–2–3	1–2–3	1–2–3	1–0–1	3–2–5
Messier	2–3–5	2–2–4	2–2–4	4–6–10	0–0–0	1–2–3	0–0–0	0–0–0	0–0–0	1–3–4
Murdoch	0–0–0	0–0–0	0–1–1	0–0–0	0–1–1	0–1–1	1–0–1	1–0–1	1–0–1	0–0–0
Price	0–1–1	0–1–1	0–2–2	———	2–0–2	0–0–0	0–1–1	0–1–1	0–3–3	1–2–3
Roulston	0–0–0	0–1–1	0–0–0	———	0–0–0	———	———	———	0–0–0	0–0–0
Semenko	1–0–1	3–1–4	0–1–1	0–0–0	0–1–1	1–1–2	0–0–0	0–0–0	0–0–0	0–0–0
Siltanen	1–0–1	0–0–0	0–1–1	1–3–4	2–1–3	1–4–5	0–1–1	0–1–1	0–4–4	4–1–5
Sommer	———	———	———	———	———	———	———	———	0–0–0	———
Unger	0–0–0	———	———	0–0–0	———	———	0–0–0	0–0–0	———	0–0–0
Weir	1–0–1	0–0–0	0–1–1	0–3–3	0–2–2	1–3–4	0–0–0	0–0–0	3–1–4	0–1–1

1980-81 Goaltender Records vs. Opposition

	GP	*Min.*	*GA*	*EN*	*SO*	*Ave.*	*W–L–T*	*Opposition*
Gary Edwards	1	20	4	0	0	12.00	0–1–1	Boston
	1	60	2	0	0	2.00	0–0–1	Buffalo
	1	24	4	0	0	10.00	0–0–0	Calgary
	1	60	4	0	0	4.00	0–0–1	Colorado
	1	60	2	0	0	2.00	1–0–0	Detroit
	1	60	2	0	0	2.00	1–0–0	Hartford
	2	120	11	0	0	5.50	1–0–1	Los Angeles
	2	120	4	0	0	2.00	1–0–1	Minnesota
	1	60	5	0	0	5.00	0–1–0	N.Y. Islanders
	1	60	3	0	0	3.00	1–0–0	Philadelphia
	1	24	1	0	0	2.50	0–0–0	Pittsburgh
	1	1	0	0	0	0.00	0–0–0	Vancouver
	1	60	2	0	0	2.00	1–0–0	Winnipeg

	GP	Min.	GA	EN	SO	Ave.	W–L–T	Opposition
Pete LoPresti	1	60	6	1	0	6.00	0–0–1	Quebec
	1	45	2	0	0	2.67	0–0–0	Washington
Ron Low	1	60	6	0	0	6.00	0–1–0	Boston
	2	120	5	0	0	2.50	1–1–0	Buffalo
	1	60	3	0	0	3.00	1–0–0	Calgary
	1	60	3	0	0	3.00	1–0–0	Chicago
	1	60	4	0	0	4.00	0–1–0	Colorado
	1	9	3	0	0	20.00	0–0–0	Hartford
	1	60	4	0	0	4.00	0–0–1	Los Angeles
	2	83	9	0	0	6.51	0–2–0	Minnesota
	1	59	3	1	0	3.05	0–1–0	Montreal
	2	120	8	0	0	4.00	0–1–1	N.Y. Islanders
	2	120	7	0	0	3.50	1–1–0	N.Y. Rangers
	1	60	8	0	0	8.00	0–1–0	Philadelphia
	1	8	4	0	0	30.00	0–0–0	Quebec
	1	60	6	0	0	6.00	0–1–0	St. Louis
	2	120	8	0	0	4.00	0–1–1	Toronto
	1	60	4	0	0	4.00	0–1–0	Vancouver
	2	80	6	1	0	4.50	0–1–0	Washington
	1	60	2	0	0	2.00	1–0–0	Winnipeg
Ed Mio	1	40	1	0	0	1.50	0–0–0	Boston
	1	60	5	0	0	5.00	0–0–1	Buffalo
	3	156	14	0	0	5.38	0–2–1	Calgary
	3	180	12	0	0	4.00	2–1–0	Chicago
	2	120	6	0	0	3.00	0–2–0	Colorado
	3	180	9	1	0	3.00	1–1–1	Detroit
	3	171	13	0	0	4.56	1–1–1	Hartford
	1	58	6	0	0	6.21	0–1–0	Los Angeles
	1	37	1	0	0	1.62	0–0–0	Minnesota
	3	148	8	0	0	3.24	2–1–0	Montreal
	1	60	8	0	0	8.00	0–0–1	N.Y. Islanders
	2	119	11	1	0	5.55	0–1–1	N.Y. Rangers
	1	60	2	0	0	2.00	1–0–0	Philadelphia
	3	156	15	0	0	5.77	1–1–1	Pittsburgh
	3	172	8	1	0	2.79	1–2–0	Quebec
	3	180	12	0	0	4.00	1–1–1	St. Louis
	2	120	5	0	0	2.50	2–0–0	Toronto
	2	120	6	1	0	3.00	1–1–0	Vancouver
	3	115	8	0	0	4.17	1–1–1	Washington
	2	120	5	0	0	2.50	2–0–0	Winnipeg
Andy Moog	2	120	12	0	0	6.00	1–1–0	Boston
	1	2	1	0	0	30.00	0–0–0	Los Angeles
	1	32	1	0	0	1.88	0–0–0	Montreal
	1	60	2	0	0	2.00	0–1–0	Philadelphia
	1	60	2	0	0	2.00	1–0–0	Pittsburgh
	1	59	2	0	0	2.03	1–0–0	Vancouver

1980-81 Schedule Results

Date	Team	Score		Team	Score
Oct. 10	Quebec	7	at	Edmonton	4
Oct. 12	Colorado	3	at	Edmonton	2
Oct. 15	Edmonton	0	at	Buffalo	2
Oct. 18	Edmonton	5	at	Islanders	5
Oct. 19	Edmonton	4	at	Rangers	2
Oct. 22	Calgary	3	at	Edmonton	5
Oct. 24	Minnesota	4	at	Edmonton	2
Oct. 26	Los Angeles	4	at	Edmonton	4
Oct. 29	Toronto	4	at	Edmonton	4
Nov. 1	Washington	2	at	Edmonton	2
Nov. 3	Pittsburgh	4	at	Edmonton	4
Nov. 5	Edmonton	3	at	Vancouver	4
Nov. 7	Edmonton	4	at	Winnipeg	2
Nov. 9	St. Louis	6	at	Edmonton	4
Nov. 13	Edmonton	1	at	Philadelphia	8
Nov. 15	Edmonton	2	at	Toronto	4
Nov. 16	Edmonton	5	at	Chicago	4
Nov. 19	Vancouver	6	at	Edmonton	4
Nov. 23	Buffalo	3	at	Edmonton	6
Nov. 25	Edmonton	3	at	Colorado	4
Nov. 26	Chicago	3	at	Edmonton	10
Nov. 28	Edmonton	4	at	Hartford	6
Nov. 29	Edmonton	3	at	Boston	6
Dec. 5	Rangers	5	at	Edmonton	1
Dec. 7	Hartford	4	at	Edmonton	6
Dec. 10	Islanders	3	at	Edmonton	2
Dec. 13	Edmonton	1	at	Montreal	4
Dec. 14	Edmonton	5	at	Quebec	6
Dec. 16	Edmonton	3	at	Detroit	4
Dec. 17	Edmonton	2	at	Washington	5

Dec. 20	Montreal	3	at	Edmonton	4
Dec. 23	Edmonton	4	at	Los Angeles	7
Dec. 27	Detroit	4	at	Edmonton	4
Dec. 28	Philadelphia	2	at	Edmonton	1
Dec. 30	Edmonton	3	at	Calgary	5
Jan. 2	Boston	5	at	Edmonton	7
Jan. 3	Toronto	1	at	Edmonton	4
Jan. 7	Washington	3	at	Edmonton	6
Jan. 9	Hartford	6	at	Edmonton	6
Jan. 11	Edmonton	6	at	Quebec	3
Jan. 12	Edmonton	0	at	Montreal	5
Jan. 14	Edmonton	7	at	Toronto	4
Jan. 16	Edmonton	5	at	Buffalo	5
Jan. 17	Edmonton	6	at	St.Louis	7
Jan. 21	Vancouver	1	at	Edmonton	5
Jan. 23	Rangers	7	at	Edmonton	4
Jan. 24	Edmonton	1	at	Minnesota	6
Jan. 28	Montreal	1	at	Edmonton	9
Jan. 30	Chicago	2	at	Edmonton	4
Feb. 1	Edmonton	4	at	Washington	7
Feb. 3	Edmonton	3	at	St. Louis	3
Feb. 4	Edmonton	3	at	Chicago	6
Feb. 6	Winnipeg	4	at	Edmonton	10
Feb. 8	Calgary	10	at	Edmonton	4
Feb. 13	Quebec	4	at	Edmonton	2
Feb. 15	Buffalo	2	at	Edmonton	2
Feb. 18	St. Louis	2	at	Edmonton	9
Feb. 20	Boston	5	at	Edmonton	1
Feb. 21	Edmonton	5	at	Winnipeg	1
Feb. 24	Edmonton	2	at	Los Angeles	5
Feb. 25	Philadelphia	2	at	Edmonton	6
Feb. 27	Detroit	2	at	Edmonton	5
Feb. 28	Edmonton	1	at	Colorado	3
Mar. 3	Edmonton	8	at	Islanders	8
Mar. 4	Edmonton	5	at	Rangers	5
Mar. 7	Edmonton	5	at	Philadelphia	3
Mar. 8	Edmonton	4	at	Pittsburgh	6
Mar. 12	Islanders	5	at	Edmonton	0
Mar. 15	Edmonton	3	at	Calgary	3
Mar. 16	Pittsburgh	6	at	Edmonton	7
Mar. 18	Edmonton	5	at	Minnesota	3
Mar. 20	Minnesota	1	at	Edmonton	1
Mar. 21	Los Angeles	6	at	Edmonton	6
Mar. 23	Edmonton	2	at	Boston	7
Mar. 25	Edmonton	7	at	Hartford	2
Mar. 28	Edmonton	4	at	Detroit	2
Mar. 29	Edmonton	5	at	Pittsburgh	2
April 1	Colorado	4	at	Edmonton	4
April 3	Edmonton	7	at	Vancouver	2
April 4	Winnipeg	2	at	Edmonton	7

Opponent	*Home W–L–T*	*Road W–L–T*
Boston	1–1–0	0–2–0
Buffalo	1–0–1	0–1–1
Calgary	1–1–0	0–1–1
Chicago	2–0–0	1–1–0
Colorado	0–1–1	0–2–0
Detroit	1–0–1	1–1–0
Hartford	1–0–1	1–1–0
Los Angeles	0–0–2	0–2–0
Minnesota	0–1–1	1–1–0
Montreal	2–0–0	0–2–0
Islanders	0–2–0	0–0–2
Rangers	0–2–0	1–0–1
Philadelphia	1–1–0	1–1–0
Pittsburgh	1–0–1	1–1–0
Quebec	0–2–0	1–1–0
St. Louis	1–1–0	0–1–1
Toronto	1–1–0	0–1–1
Vancouver	1–1–0	1–1–0
Washington	1–1–0	0–2–0
Winnipeg	2–0–0	2–0–0

Opponent	*Overall W–L–T*	*GF–GA*
Boston	1–3–0	13–23
Buffalo	1–1–2	13–12
Calgary	1–2–1	15–21
Chicago	3–1–0	22–15
Colorado	0–3–1	10–14
Detroit	2–1–1	16–12
Hartford	2–1–1	23–18
Los Angeles	0–2–2	16–22
Minnesota	1–2–1	9–14
Montreal	2–2–0	14–13
Islanders	0–2–2	15–21
Rangers	1–2–1	14–19
Philadelphia	2–2–0	13–15
Pittsburgh	2–1–1	20–18
Quebec	1–3–0	17–20
St. Louis	1–2–1	22–18
Toronto	1–2–1	17–13
Vancouver	2–2–0	19–13
Washington	1–3–0	14–17
Winnipeg	4–0–0	26–9

1980-81 Playoff Scoring

#		*GP*	*G*	*A*	*Pts.*	*GW*	*OT*	*PP*	*SH*	*PIM*
99	Wayne Gretzky	9	7	14	21	1	0	2	1	4
9	Glenn Anderson	9	5	7	12	0	0	3	0	12
17	Jari Kurri	9	5	7	12	0	0	0	0	4
18	Brett Callighen	9	4	4	8	1	0	1	0	6
7	Paul Coffey	9	4	3	7	0	0	1	0	22
11	Mark Messier	9	2	5	7	0	0	0	0	13
10	Matti Hagman	9	4	1	5	2	0	0	0	6
6	Garry Lariviere	9	0	3	3	0	0	0	0	8
8	Risto Siltanen	9	2	0	2	1	0	2	0	8
5	Doug Hicks	9	1	1	2	0	0	0	0	4

#		GP	G	A	Pts.	GW	OT	PP	SH	PIM
4	Kevin Lowe	9	0	2	2	0	0	0	0	11
20	Dave Lumley	7	1	0	1	0	0	0	0	4
33	Gary Edwards	1	0	0	0	0	0	0	0	0
15	Curt Brackenbury	2	0	0	0	0	0	0	0	0
16	Pat Hughes	5	0	5	5	0	0	0	0	16
21	Stan Weir	5	0	0	0	0	0	0	0	2
77	Garry Unger	8	0	0	0	0	0	0	0	2
2	Lee Fogolin	9	0	0	0	0	0	0	0	12
35	Andy Moog	9	0	0	0	0	0	0	0	0
12	Dave Hunter	9	0	0	0	0	0	0	0	28
27	Dave Semenko	8	0	0	0	0	0	0	0	5
	Bench									2
		9	35	52	87	5	0	9	1	169

1980-81 Playoff Goaltending

	GP	Min.	GA	W	L	Ave.	SA	Pct.	SO	EN
Andy Moog	9	526	32	5	4	3.65	271	.886	0	1
Gary Edwards	1	20	2	0	0	6.00	6	.667	0	0
	9	546	35	5	4	3.85	277	.877	0	1

Date			Result			Winning Goaltender	Winning Goal
April 8, 1981	Edmonton	6	at	Montreal	3	Andy Moog	Brett Callighen
April 9, 1981	Edmonton	3	at	Montreal	1	Andy Moog	Risto Siltanen
April 11, 1981	Montreal	2	at	Edmonton	6	Andy Moog	Wayne Gretzky
April 16, 1981	Edmonton	2	at	N.Y. Islanders	8	Billy Smith	John Tonelli
April 17, 1981	Edmonton	3	at	N.Y. Islanders	6	Billy Smith	Denis Potvin
April 19, 1981	N.Y. Islanders	2	at	Edmonton	5	Andy Moog	Matti Hagman
April 20, 1981	N.Y. Islanders	5	at	Edmonton	4	Roland Melanson	Ken Morrow[1]
April 22, 1981	Edmonton	4	at	N.Y. Islanders	3	Andy Moog	Matti Hagman
April 24, 1981	N.Y. Islanders	5	at	Edmonton	2	Billy Smith	Bob Nystrom

[1]-5:41 of overtime

The Skyreach Center before renovations? No. This is the Oilers' first home, the Edmonton Gardens. This game, circa 1922, features the Edmonton Eskimos of the old Western Canada (professional) Hockey League. Note the goal judge standing behind the net. (EA349-2 City of Edmonton Archives.)

Table 2. Oilers Yearly Home Record

Season	*GP*	*W*	*L*	*T*	*OL*	*GF*	*GA*	*Pts*	*Pct.*	*Rank*
2000-01	41	24	10	7	2	125	91	55	.671	T7
1999-00	41	18	14	9	3	118	94	48	.549	T13
1998-99	41	17	19	5	NA	113	112	39	.476	T19
1997-98	41	20	16	5	NA	103	103	45	.549	11th
1996-97	41	21	16	4	NA	124	117	46	.561	12th
1995-96	41	15	21	5	NA	118	143	35	.427	23rd
1994-95	24	11	12	1	NA	69	84	23	.479	T19
1993-94	42	17	22	3	NA	147	147	37	.440	21st
1992-93	42	16	21	5	NA	132	151	37	.440	20th
1991-92	40	22	13	5	NA	151	121	49	.613	T11
1990-91	40	22	15	3	NA	134	119	47	.588	T11
1989-90	40	23	11	6	NA	165	130	52	.650	5th
1988-89	40	21	16	3	NA	172	150	45	.563	10th
1987-88	40	28	8	4	NA	197	126	60	.750	1st
1986-87	40	29	6	5	NA	199	124	63	.788	1st
1985-86	40	32	6	2	NA	228	141	66	.825	2nd
1984-85	40	26	7	7	NA	207	136	59	.738	2nd
1983-84	40	31	5	4	NA	241	135	66	.825	1st
1982-83	40	25	9	6	NA	212	148	56	.700	7th
1981-82	40	31	5	4	NA	244	138	66	.825	2nd
1980-81	40	17	13	10	NA	178	151	44	.550	T14
1979-80	40	17	14	9	NA	165	145	43	.538	T14
TOTALS	874	483	279	112	5	3542	2806	1081	.617	

1981-82

The Oilers began the 1981-82 season with Glen Sather behind the bench as coach. He was joined by last year's assistant Billy Harris and newcomer Ted Green.

Sather again had good success in this year's draft, which was held June 10 in the Montreal Forum. In the first round, the Oilers chose goaltender Grant Fuhr from the Victoria Cougars of the Western Hockey League. Fuhr, the eighth overall choice, became the highest drafted goaltender since John Davidson, who was drafted fifth overall in 1973. Fuhr had led the Cougars to the championship of the WHL in 1981 with a league leading 2.78 goals against average, earning himself a first team All-Star berth in the process. Fuhr would play on all five of the Oilers' Stanley Cup teams.

The other solid prospect drafted this year was Steve Smith. The hulking 6'4", 190 pound native of Scotland was chosen 111th over-all from the London Knights of the Ontario Hockey League. Smith would be an integral part of the Oilers' blue line corps in three Stanley Cup victories.

The team finally won a season opening game, defeating the Colorado Rockies by a score of 7–4. The Oilers split the first six games of the season, winning three and losing three. They then caught fire, winning 32 and tying 10 of their next 52 games, for a .690 average by the All-Star break.

The team was no doubt inspired by the stellar goaltending of rookie sensation Grant Fuhr. Beginning on October 21 with a 5–2 win over the Hartford Whalers and ending on January 13 with a 6–6 tie against Washington, Fuhr would post a 23-game undefeated streak. The streak included 15 wins and 8 ties. This remains as the longest undefeated streak by a goaltender in his first NHL season. Fuhr would team up with last year's playoff hero Andy Moog to give the Oilers the best young netminding duo in the league.

Wayne Gretzky led the league in scoring with an unheard of 212 points. This was 65 points better than runner-up Mike Bossy of the New York Islanders. Gretzky scored an amazing 92 goals and added 120 assists.

On December 30, having already scored 45 goals in 38 games, Gretzky went on a scoring spree in game number 39 against goaltender Pete Peeters and the Philadelphia Flyers. Having scored four goals by the early minutes of the third period, the Oiler star needed only one more goal for number 50. With his characteristic sense of the dramatic Gretzky scored his 50th into an empty net with three seconds left in the game as the Oilers defeated the Flyers 7–5. The 50 goals in 39 games wiped out the mark set by Rocket Richard and Mike Bossy, who each scored 50 goals in 50 games.

Sophomore defenseman Paul Coffey added 89 points to the Oilers offense and was named to the league's 2nd All-Star team.

Most of the star players were injury free throughout the year, but Risto Siltanen missed 17 games over the length of the season with a nagging groin injury and Dave Hunter missed the same number of games due to a knee injury he received in a December 5 game against Vancouver. Hard luck Brett Callighen also missed six weeks with a cracked clavicle and Pat Hughes missed two weeks with strained knee ligaments.

The team finished atop the Smythe Division, 37 points ahead of their previous year's pace and 34 points in front of second place Vancouver. Only the reigning Stanley Cup champion New York Islanders ended the season with more points than the Oilers, registering 118 points.

The Oilers increased their goal scoring output by over one goal per game, becoming the first team in league history to score over 400 goals. Team defense also improved dramatically. Only six other teams allowed fewer goals against than the Oilers, who had managed to knock 30 goals off of last year's total. The team looked set to make a serious run for the Stanley Cup.

Edmonton's defense faltered however in the postseason series against Los Angeles, allowing 27 goals, and the team bowed out of the playoffs in five games.

1981-82 Regular Season Scoring

#		*Ht.*	*Wt.*	*Age*	*GP*	*G*	*A*	*Pts*	*Shots*	*S%*	*GW*	*GT*	*PP*	*SH*	*P/M*	*PIM*
99	Gretzky	71	170	20	80	92	120	212	369	24.9	12	4	18	6	81	26
9	Anderson	71	175	21	80	38	67	105	252	15.1	8	2	9	0	46	71
7	Coffey	73	185	20	80	29	60	89	234	12.4	1	0	13	0	35	106
11	Messier	73	190	20	78	50	38	88	235	21.3	3	2	10	0	21	119
17	Kurri	73	185	21	71	32	54	86	211	15.2	5	1	6	1	38	32
20	Lumley	72	185	27	66	32	42	74	148	21.6	6	3	4	1	12	96
8	Siltanen	68	185	23	63	15	48	63	143	10.5	1	0	6	0	13	26
10	Hagman	73	184	26	72	21	38	59	94	22.3	2	0	5	0	15	18
16	Hughes	73	180	26	68	24	22	46	167	14.4	0	1	4	2	21	99
4	Lowe	74	197	22	80	9	31	40	110	8.2	2	0	1	1	46	63
12	Hunter	71	195	23	63	16	22	38	124	12.9	3	1	0	0	33	63
2	Fogolin (C)	72	200	26	80	4	25	29	98	4.1	0	0	0	0	40	154
18	Callighen	71	175	28	46	8	19	27	87	9.2	1	0	3	0	16	28
27	Semenko	75	215	24	59	12	12	24	54	22.2	1	0	4	0	7	194
5	Hicks	72	185	26	49	3	20	23	44	6.8	0	0	1	0	6	55
6	Lariviere	72	190	27	62	1	21	22	46	2.2	0	0	0	0	27	41
77	Unger	72	185	34	46	7	13	20	62	11.3	2	0	0	0	8	69
21	Weir	73	170	29	51	3	13	16	29	10.3	1	0	1	0	0	13
22	Huddy	71	203	22	41	4	11	15	84	4.8	0	1	0	0	17	46
24	Roulston	73	184	24	35	11	3	14	54	20.4	0	0	0	1	-6	22
26	Forbes	74	200	24	16	1	7	8	14	7.1	0	0	0	0	14	26
1	Fuhr	70	181	19	48	0	6	6	0	0.0	0	0	0	0	0	6
14	Boschman	72	185	21	11	2	3	5	4	50.0	0	0	0	0	2	37
19	Berry	69	165	21	15	2	3	5	9	22.2	0	0	0	0	-6	9
23	Habscheid	72	179	18	7	1	3	4	7	14.3	0	0	1	0	5	2
28	Nethery	73	185	24	3	0	2	2	1	0.0	0	0	0	0	1	2
15	Brackenbury	70	197	29	14	0	2	2	2	0.0	0	0	0	0	2	12
35	Moog	68	165	21	8	0	1	1	0	0.0	0	0	0	0	0	2
28	Strueby	73	186	18	3	0	0	0	1	0.0	0	0	0	0	0	0
14	Podubny	73	203	21	4	0	0	0	2	0.0	0	0	0	0	-1	0
25	Jackson	75	210	25	8	0	0	0	4	0.0	0	0	0	0	0	18
30	Low	73	205	31	29	0	0	0	0	0.0	0	0	0	0	0	2
	Bench															20
		72	187	24	80	417	706	1123	2689	15.5	48	15	86	12	103	1477

1981-82 Goaltender Records

	GP	*Min.*	*GA*	*W*	*L*	*T*	*Ave.*	*SA*	*Pct.*	*SO*	*EN*
Grant Fuhr	48	2845	157	28	5	14	3.31	1545	0.898	0	2
Ron Low	29	1556	100	17	7	1	3.86	790	0.873	0	2
Andy Moog	8	399	32	3	5	0	4.81	197	0.838	0	2
	80	4800	295	48	17	15	3.69	2532	0.883	0	6

Coach: Glen Sather 48-17-15

1981-82 Scoring vs. Opposition

	Bos.	*Buff.*	*Calg.*	*Chi.*	*Col.*	*Det.*	*Hart.*	*L.A.*	*Minn.*	*Mont.*
Anderson	3–2–5	1–2–3	2–6–9	1–1–2	3–6–9	4–5–9	1–3–4	3–11–14	1–2–3	3–0–3
Berry	0–0–0	———	0–2–2	———	1–0–1	———	———	1–0–1	0–0–0	———
Boschman	———	0–0–0	1–1–2	———	0–0–0	———	———	0–0–0	———	———
Brackenbury	———	———	0–0–0	0–0–0	0–0–0	0–0–0	0–0–0	0–0–0	———	0–1–1
Callighen	0–0–0	0–0–0	1–3–4	1–0–1	2–1–3	0–0–0	0–1–1	———	0–1–1	0–0–0
Coffey	0–2–2	0–0–0	4–4–8	2–3–5	3–4–7	2–2–4	1–0–1	3–6–9	0–2–2	1–2–3
Fogolin	0–0–0	0–0–0	1–2–3	0–1–1	0–3–3	0–0–0	0–1–1	———	0–1–1	0–2–2
Forbes	0–0–0	———	0–0–0	0–1–1	0–0–0	0–0–0	———	0–1–1	0–0–0	0–0–0
Gretzky	1–4–5	4–2–6	9–11–20	4–7–11	5–11–16	2–7–9	5–3–8	13–9–22	5–7–12	1–6–7
Habscheid	———	———	———	0–0–0	———	———	———	0–1–1	———	0–0–0
Hagman	2–1–3	0–0–0	3–5–8	1–0–1	0–2–2	1–4–5	2–3–5	1–4–5	0–3–3	0–0–0
Hicks	———	0–0–0	0–1–1	1–2–3	0–3–3	0–0–0	1–0–1	1–3–4	0–1–1	0–0–0
Huddy	0–0–0	2–0–2	0–3–3	0–0–0	1–0–1	0–0–0	0–1–1	0–2–2	0–0–0	0–0–0
Hughes, P.	0–0–0	1–2–3	4–2–6	1–1–2	2–5–7	2–1–3	0–1–1	3–1–4	1–0–1	1–0–1
Hunter	0–0–0	1–1–2	2–1–3	0–2–2	1–1–2	0–4–4	1–0–1	2–8–10	0–0–0	1–2–3
Jackson	0–0–0	———	———	———	———	0–0–0	0–0–0	———	0–0–0	———
Kurri	1–0–1	1–3–4	1–9–10	0–1–1	5–6–11	2–1–3	1–5–6	———	3–2–5	0–1–1
Lariviere	0–0–0	0–0–0	0–3–3	0–0–0	0–1–1	0–2–2	0–1–1	0–2–2	0–1–1	0–1–1
Lowe	0–0–0	0–0–0	1–5–6	1–0–1	2–7–9	1–2–3	0–1–1	0–3–3	1–1–2	0–0–0
Lumley	1–0–1	0–1–1	1–2–3	1–1–2	3–4–7	1–1–2	1–0–1	4–5–9	3–5–8	1–1–2
Messier	0–4–4	0–1–1	6–5–11	1–0–1	5–4–9	3–0–3	1–3–4	10–4–14	4–0–4	1–0–1
Nethery	———	———	———	———	———	———	———	0–2–2	———	———
Podubny	0–0–0	———	———	———	0–0–0	———	———	———	———	———
Roulston	0–0–0	0–0–0	0–0–0	0–0–0	2–0–2	0–0–0	1–0–1	0–0–0	0–0–0	0–0–0
Semenko	0–0–0	0–0–0	3–0–3	1–2–3	2–2–4	0–0–0	0–0–0	1–2–3	0–0–0	———
Siltanen	0–0–0	1–3–4	1–4–5	1–2–3	0–5–5	0–4–4	0–5–5	4–5–9	0–3–3	0–0–0
Strueby	———	———	———	0–0–0	———	0–0–0	———	0–0–0	———	———
Unger	0–0–0	0–0–0	0–4–4	0–0–0	4–0–4	0–2–2	1–0–1	0–1–1	0–1–1	0–0–0
Weir	0–0–0	———	1–0–1	0–1–1	0–3–3	1–0–1	0–0–0	0–4–4	0–2–2	0–0–0

	NYI.	*NYR.*	*Phil.*	*Pitt.*	*Que.*	*St.L.*	*Tor.*	*Van.*	*Wash.*	*Winn.*
Anderson	0–2–2	1–1–2	1–6–7	4–1–5	3–2–5	2–3–5	1–3–4	2–8–10	1–0–1	1–3–4
Berry	———	———	0–0–0	———	———	———	0–0–0	0–2–2	———	———
Boschman	———	———	———	0–2–2	———	———	———	1–0–1	———	0–0–0
Brackenbury	0–0–0	———	0–0–0	0–0–0	0–0–0	0–0–0	0–0–0	———	0–1–1	———
Callighen	0–1–1	0–0–0	0–0–0	0–1–1	1–2–3	0–0–0	1–0–1	1–1–2	———	0–1–1
Coffey	2–0–2	3–4–7	1–6–7	1–5–6	0–4–4	0–4–4	0–1–1	2–3–5	2–3–5	2–5–7
Fogolin	0–2–2	1–0–1	0–0–0	1–1–2	0–2–2	0–1–1	0–0–0	0–1–1	0–1–1	0–0–0
Forbes	0–0–0	———	———	———	0–1–1	0–0–0	———	1–2–3	———	0–1–1
Gretzky	2–7–9	4–5–9	9–3–12	5–4–9	4–5–9	6–4–10	3–2–5	4–14–18	4–5–9	2–4–6
Habscheid	———	———	———	———	———	———	———	0–2–2	———	1–0–1
Hagman	0–1–1	0–2–2	0–2–2	2–3–5	3–2–5	1–1–2	0–2–2	3–1–4	1–2–3	1–1–2
Hicks	0–1–1	0–1–1	0–0–0	0–0–0	0–3–3	0–1–1	0–1–1	0–2–2	0–1–1	0–1–1
Huddy	———	0–0–0	0–0–0	0–1–1	0–0–0	1–3–4	0–1–1	0–0–0	0–0–0	0–0–0
Hughes, P.	2–0–2	0–2–2	0–0–0	1–2–3	2–0–2	0–1–1	1–3–4	2–1–3	0–0–0	1–0–1
Hunter	0–1–1	2–2–4	0–0–0	2–0–2	0–0–0	1–0–1	1–1–2	0–1–1	1–0–1	1–1–2
Jackson	0–0–0	0–0–0	———	———	———	0–0–0	———	0–0–0	———	———
Kurri	0–1–1	0–3–3	1–1–2	1–3–4	2–2–4	3–2–5	1–1–2	3–4–7	3–3–6	1–1–2
Lariviere	0–0–0	0–0–0	0–0–0	1–2–3	0–2–2	0–1–1	0–1–1	0–1–1	0–2–2	0–0–0
Lowe	0–0–0	0–2–2	0–1–1	1–3–4	0–1–1	1–0–1	0–0–0	1–5–6	0–0–0	0–0–0
Lumley	1–1–2	1–2–3	1–2–3	1–0–1	3–1–4	1–4–5	0–1–1	6–6–12	1–4–5	1–2–3
Messier	2–1–3	1–1–2	3–1–4	1–4–5	3–3–6	0–4–4	2–1–3	4–0–4	2–1–3	1–1–2
Nethery	———	———	0–0–0	———	———	———	———	0–0–0	———	———
Podubny	———	———	———	———	———	———	———	0–0–0	———	———
Roulston	———	3–0–3	0–1–1	0–0–0	0–0–0	2–1–3	2–1–3	1–0–1	0–0–0	0–0–0
Semenko	1–0–1	0–0–0	0–1–1	0–1–1	0–0–0	0–0–0	0–0–0	3–3–6	0–0–0	1–1–2
Siltanen	1–2–3	1–3–4	0–1–1	1–1–2	2–6–8	0–0–0	0–2–2	2–1–3	0–0–0	1–1–2
Strueby	———	———	———	———	———	———	———	———	———	———
Unger	1–1–2	0–0–0	0–0–0	0–1–1	0–1–1	1–0–1	0–1–1	0–1–1	0–0–0	0–0–0
Weir	0–0–0	1–0–1	0–1–1	0–1–1	0–0–0	0–0–0	0–0–0	0–0–0	0–1–1	0–0–0

1981-82 Goaltender Records vs. Opposition

	GP	*Min.*	*GA*	*EN*	*SO*	*Ave.*	*W–L–T*	*Opposition*
Grant Fuhr	2	120	6	0	0	3.00	0–0–2	Boston
	2	120	4	0	0	2.00	2–0–0	Buffalo
	4	216	10	0	0	2.78	2–0–1	Calgary
	1	60	1	0	0	1.00	1–0–0	Chicago
	3	180	11	1	0	3.67	2–1–0	Colorado
	1	60	4	0	0	4.00	0–0–1	Detroit
	2	120	6	0	0	3.00	1–0–1	Hartford
	7	417	23	0	0	3.31	4–1–2	Los Angeles
	2	113	5	0	0	2.65	1–0–1	Minnesota
	3	180	12	0	0	4.00	0–1–2	Montreal
	2	120	8	0	0	4.00	1–0–1	N.Y. Islanders
	3	180	10	0	0	3.33	3–0–0	N.Y. Rangers
	2	120	9	0	0	4.50	2–0–0	Philadelphia
	1	60	3	0	0	3.00	1–0–0	Pittsburgh
	1	60	6	0	0	6.00	1–0–0	St. Louis
	2	120	11	0	0	5.50	1–1–0	Toronto
	5	300	13	0	0	2.60	4–0–1	Vancouver
	2	120	7	0	0	3.50	1–0–1	Washington
	3	180	6	1	0	2.00	2–1–0	Winnipeg
Ron Low	1	59	4	1	0	4.07	0–1–0	Boston
	1	59	3	0	0	3.05	0–1–0	Buffalo
	4	185	13	0	0	4.22	2–1–0	Calgary
	1	60	3	0	0	3.00	0–0–1	Chicago
	3	180	11	0	0	3.67	2–0–1	Colorado
	2	120	7	0	0	3.50	2–0–0	Detroit
	1	60	4	0	0	4.00	1–0–0	Hartford
	2	62	2	0	0	1.94	1–0–0	Los Angeles
	2	48	7	0	0	8.75	0–0–0	Minnesota
	1	60	8	0	0	8.00	0–1–0	Philadelphia
	2	120	5	0	0	2.50	2–0–0	Pittsburgh
	3	180	17	0	0	5.66	1–2–0	Quebec
	2	120	5	0	0	2.50	2–0–0	St. Louis
	1	60	1	0	0	1.00	1–0–0	Toronto
	2	119	6	0	0	3.03	1–1–0	Vancouver
	1	60	3	0	0	3.00	1–0–0	Washington
Andy Moog	2	79	7	1	0	5.32	1–1–0	Calgary
	1	59	6	1	0	6.10	0–1–0	Chicago
	2	119	0	0	0	0.00	1–0–0	Minnesota
	1	60	4	0	0	4.00	0–1–0	N.Y. Islanders
	1	60	6	0	0	6.00	0–1–0	Vancouver

1981-82 Schedule Results

Oct. 7	Colorado	4	at	Edmonton	7	Nov. 15	Edmonton	5	at	Rangers	3
Oct. 9	Edmonton	2	at	Vancouver	6	Nov. 17	Edmonton	5	at	St. Louis	1
Oct. 10	Edmonton	7	at	Los Angeles	4	Nov. 19	Edmonton	2	at	Minnesota	2
Oct. 14	Winnipeg	4	at	Edmonton	2	Nov. 21	Vancouver	3	at	Edmonton	8
Oct. 16	Calgary	4	at	Edmonton	8	Nov. 23	Detroit	4	at	Edmonton	8
Oct. 18	Edmonton	5	at	Chicago	7	Nov. 25	Los Angeles	4	at	Edmonton	11
Oct. 20	Edmonton	5	at	Calgary	4	Nov. 27	Chicago	1	at	Edmonton	8
Oct. 21	Hartford	2	at	Edmonton	5	Nov. 29	Edmonton	10	at	Winnipeg	2
Oct. 23	Pittsburgh	3	at	Edmonton	8	Dec. 1	Edmonton	3	at	Montreal	3
Oct. 24	Edmonton	3	at	Colorado	1	Dec. 2	Edmonton	8	at	Quebec	9
Oct. 27	Edmonton	3	at	Islanders	4	Dec. 4	Vancouver	3	at	Edmonton	7
Oct. 28	Edmonton	5	at	Rangers	3	Dec. 5	Edmonton	3	at	Vancouver	3
Oct. 31	Quebec	4	at	Edmonton	11	Dec. 9	Edmonton	5	at	Los Angeles	5
Nov. 4	Toronto	4	at	Edmonton	6	Dec. 13	Islanders	3	at	Edmonton	4
Nov. 7	Colorado	5	at	Edmonton	4	Dec. 16	Edmonton	7	at	Colorado	4
Nov. 11	Edmonton	4	at	Hartford	4	Dec. 17	Edmonton	5	at	Calgary	4
Nov. 12	Edmonton	2	at	Boston	5	Dec. 19	Minnesota	6	at	Edmonton	9
Nov. 14	Edmonton	5	at	Islanders	5	Dec. 20	Calgary	7	at	Edmonton	5

Dec. 23	Vancouver	1	at	Edmonton	6
Dec. 27	Los Angeles	3	at	Edmonton	10
Dec. 30	Philadelphia	5	at	Edmonton	7
Dec. 31	Edmonton	1	at	Vancouver	3
Jan. 2	Boston	4	at	Edmonton	4
Jan. 6	Colorado	3	at	Edmonton	5
Jan. 9	Calgary	2	at	Edmonton	7
Jan. 10	Edmonton	1	at	Calgary	5
Jan. 13	Edmonton	6	at	Washington	6
Jan. 14	Edmonton	2	at	Philadelphia	8
Jan. 16	Edmonton	1	at	Toronto	7
Jan. 17	Edmonton	4	at	Detroit	4
Jan. 20	St. Louis	6	at	Edmonton	8
Jan. 22	Edmonton	4	at	Vancouver	3
Jan. 24	Colorado	4	at	Edmonton	7
Jan. 26	Edmonton	6	at	St. Louis	4
Jan. 27	Edmonton	3	at	Chicago	3
Jan. 29	Buffalo	1	at	Edmonton	3
Jan. 31	Philadelphia	4	at	Edmonton	7
Feb. 3	Montreal	6	at	Edmonton	3
Feb. 6	Toronto	1	at	Edmonton	5
Feb. 7	Rangers	4	at	Edmonton	8
Feb. 12	Washington	3	at	Edmonton	5
Feb. 14	Boston	2	at	Edmonton	2
Feb. 17	Minnesota	4	at	Edmonton	7
Feb. 19	Hartford	4	at	Edmonton	7
Feb. 21	Edmonton	7	at	Detroit	3
Feb. 24	Edmonton	6	at	Buffalo	3
Feb. 27	Edmonton	4	at	Pittsburgh	1
Feb. 28	Edmonton	4	at	Washington	1
Mar. 2	Edmonton	3	at	Montreal	3
Mar. 3	Edmonton	4	at	Quebec	6
Mar. 6	Edmonton	2	at	Colorado	5
Mar. 10	Edmonton	2	at	Los Angeles	3
Mar. 12	Buffalo	3	at	Edmonton	2
Mar. 13	Vancouver	3	at	Edmonton	5
Mar. 15	Los Angeles	3	at	Edmonton	3
Mar. 17	Pittsburgh	4	at	Edmonton	10
Mar. 19	Calgary	3	at	Edmonton	3
Mar. 25	Edmonton	7	at	Calgary	2
Mar. 26	Edmonton	6	at	Colorado	6
Mar. 28	Edmonton	6	at	Los Angeles	2
Mar. 31	Los Angeles	3	at	Edmonton	7
April 4	Winnipeg	1	at	Edmonton	2

Opponent	*Home W–L–T*	*Road W–L–T*
Boston	0–0–2	0–1–0
Buffalo	1–1–0	1–0–0
Calgary	2–1–1	3–1–0
Chicago	1–0–0	0–1–1
Colorado	3–1–0	2–1–1
Detroit	1–0–0	1–0–1
Hartford	2–0–0	0–0–1
Los Angeles	3–0–1	2–1–1
Minnesota	2–0–0	0–0–1
Montreal	0–1–0	0–0–2
Islanders	1–0–0	0–1–1
Rangers	1–0–0	2–0–0
Philadelphia	2–0–0	0–1–0
Pittsburgh	2–0–0	1–0–0
Quebec	1–0–0	0–2–0
St. Louis	1–0–0	2–0–0
Toronto	2–0–0	0–1–0
Vancouver	4–0–0	1–2–1
Washington	1–0–0	1–0–1
Winnipeg	1–1–0	1–0–0

Opponent	*Overall W–L–T*	*GF–GA*
Boston	0–1–2	8–11
Buffalo	2–0–1	11–7
Calgary	5–2–1	41–31
Chicago	1–1–1	16–11
Colorado	5–2–1	41–32
Detroit	2–0–1	19–10
Hartford	2–0–1	16–10
Los Angeles	5–1–2	51–27
Minnesota	2–0–1	18–11
Montreal	0–1–2	9–12
Islanders	1–1–1	12–12
Rangers	3–0–0	18–10
Philadelphia	2–1–0	16–17
Pittsburgh	3–0–0	22–8
Quebec	1–2–0	23–19
St. Louis	3–0–0	19–11
Toronto	2–1–0	12–12
Vancouver	5–2–1	36–25
Washington	2–0–1	15–10
Winnipeg	2–1–0	14–7

1981-82 Playoff Scoring

#		*GP*	*G*	*A*	*Pts*	*OT*	*PP*	*SH*	*P/M*	*PIM*
99	Wayne Gretzky	5	5	7	12	1	1	1	1	8
9	Glenn Anderson	5	2	5	7	1	0	0	0	8
17	Jari Kurri	5	2	5	7	0	0	0	0	10
8	Risto Siltanen	5	3	2	5	0	0	1	0	10
20	Dave Lumley	5	2	1	3	0	0	0	0	21
16	Pat Hughes	5	2	1	3	0	0	0	0	6
22	Charlie Huddy	5	1	2	3	0	0	0	1	14
11	Mark Messier	5	1	2	3	0	0	0	0	8
4	Kevin Lowe	5	0	3	3	0	0	0	0	0
2	Lee Fogolin	5	1	1	2	0	0	0	0	14
7	Paul Coffey	5	1	1	2	0	0	1	0	6
21	Randy Gregg	4	0	2	2	0	0	0	0	12
10	Matti Hagman	3	1	0	1	0	0	0	0	0

#		GP	G	A	Pts	OT	PP	SH	P/M	PIM
77	Garry Unger	4	1	0	1	0	0	0	0	23
24	Tom Roulston	5	1	0	1	0	0	0	0	2
14	Laurie Boschman	3	0	1	1	0	0	0	0	4
6	Garry Lariviere	4	0	1	1	0	0	0	0	0
12	Dave Hunter	5	0	1	1	0	0	0	0	26
1	Grant Fuhr	5	0	1	1	0	0	0	0	0
18	Brett Callighen	2	0	0	0	0	0	0	0	2
27	Dave Semenko	4	0	0	0	0	0	0	0	2
		5	23	36	59	2	1	3	2	176

1981-82 Playoff Goaltending

	GP	Min.	GA	W	L	Ave.	SA	Pct.	SO	EN
Grant Fuhr	5	309	26	2	3	5.05	177	.859	0	1

Date			Result			Winning Goaltender	Winning Goal
April 7, 1982	Los Angeles	10	at	Edmonton	8	Mario Lessard	Charlie Simmer
April 8, 1982	Los Angeles	2	at	Edmonton	3	Grant Fuhr	Wayne Gretzky[1]
April 10, 1982	Edmonton	5	at	Los Angeles	6	Mario Lessard	Daryl Evans[2]
April 12, 1982	Edmonton	3	at	Los Angeles	2	Grant Fuhr	Glenn Anderson
April 13, 1982	Los Angeles	7	at	Edmonton	4	Mario Lessard	Bernie Nicholls

[1]6:20 of overtime
[2]2:35 of overtime

Table 3. Oilers Yearly Road Record

Season	GP	W	L	T	OL	GF	GA	Pts	Pct.	Rank
2000-01	41	16	19	5	1	119	130	38	.451	T19
1999-00	41	14	20	7	5	112	117	40	.427	T11
1998-99	41	16	18	7	NA	117	114	39	.476	T8
1997-98	41	15	21	5	NA	112	120	35	.427	T17
1996-97	41	15	21	5	NA	128	130	35	.427	15th
1995-96	41	15	23	3	NA	122	161	33	.402	17th
1994-95	24	6	15	3	NA	67	99	15	.313	T21
1993-94	42	8	23	11	NA	114	158	27	.321	23rd
1992-93	42	10	29	3	NA	110	186	23	.274	22nd
1991-92	40	14	21	5	NA	144	176	33	.413	T11
1990-91	40	15	22	3	NA	138	153	33	.413	T12
1989-90	40	15	17	8	NA	150	153	38	.475	T4
1988-89	40	17	18	5	NA	153	156	39	.488	T4
1987-88	40	16	17	7	NA	166	162	39	.488	T4
1986-87	40	21	18	1	NA	173	160	43	.538	T1
1985-86	40	24	11	5	NA	198	169	53	.663	1st
1984-85	40	23	13	4	NA	194	162	50	.625	1st
1983-84	40	26	13	1	NA	205	179	53	.663	1st
1982-83	40	22	12	6	NA	212	167	50	.625	1st
1981-82	40	17	12	11	NA	173	157	45	.563	2nd
1980-81	40	12	22	6	NA	150	176	30	.375	T14
1979-80	40	11	25	4	NA	136	177	26	.325	T15
TOTALS	874	348	410	115	6	3193	3362	817	.464	

Former team owner Peter Pocklington. (EA340-1847 City of Edmonton Archives).

1982-83

The 1982-83 season again saw Glen Sather behind the bench as coach. Ted Green and John Muckler who had replaced the departed Billy Harris, were named assistant coaches.

The only player drafted this year to have much of an influence on the team's future was 30-year-old former Czech star Jaroslav Pouzar, who was chosen 83rd overall. The virtually indestructible Czech would play 186 regular season games in the span of four seasons for the Oilers and help them win two Stanley Cups.

Even though they came up empty at the draft table the Oilers did make a major free agent signing at the beginning

Longtime Oiler President and General Manager, Glen Sather. (A96-182 City of Edmonton Archives.)

of the season. Randy Gregg, a medical student, had played the previous season with the Kokudo Bunnies of the Japanese league, and had signed with the team in October. The former University of Alberta player was highly sought after by the Rangers, Calgary and the Oilers, but would finally settle on playing in his hometown. Gregg would be a key member of all five Stanley Cup–winning teams. The Oilers also picked up veteran Ken Linseman from Hartford. Linseman would play on a line with Messier and Anderson.

The "Rat," as Linseman was sometimes known, would miss eight games due to two separate four game suspensions, the first for a gouging incident in a fight during an exhibition game against Toronto and the second for being involved in a fight with a Los Angeles player under the stands in a game on February 3. Center Laurie Boschman would also receive a three game suspension for being the first one off the bench during an altercation.

The team remained relatively healthy throughout the course of the season. Glenn Anderson missed seven games due to an ankle injury, while Lee Fogolin missed eight with the flu. Mark Messier also missed two games with a chipped bone in his wrist.

Following the playoff disappointment of 1982, the Oilers started the 1983 season slowly, playing only .500 hockey for the first 24 games. The team then caught fire, winning 21, losing 7 and tying 4, posting a winning percentage of .625 at the All-Star break. From November 24—when the team was 9–9–6 until the end of the season the Oilers registered an impressive 38 wins, 12 losses and 6 ties. Edmonton again finished atop the Smythe Division, 28 points ahead of Calgary and only 4 points behind Boston to tie Philadelphia for second place overall in the entire league.

The Oilers again led the league in scoring, finishing with 424 goals. This was 74 goals more than runner-up Montreal. The team's defense though lost a little ground, allowing 20 more goals than they had the previous year, finishing 11th in goals against.

Four Oilers players finished in the top ten in scoring, as Gretzky, Messier, Anderson and Kurri all finished with over 100 points. Paul Coffey finished with 96 points and tied for 13th in scoring.

The team reached the Stanley Cup finals for the first time in their history, losing only one game on the way. Edmonton scored an astounding 74 goals in the 12 games while allowing only 33 and were a good bet to knock off the aging Stanley Cup champion New York Islanders in the final round. The Oilers however ran into the hot goaltending of Billy Smith in the Islanders' net and lost the series in four straight games.

1982-83 Regular Season Scoring

#		Ht.	Wt.	Age	GP	G	A	Pts	Shots	S%	GW	GT	PP	SH	P/M	PIM
99	Gretzky	72	170	21	80	71	125	196	348	20.4	9	1	18	6	60	59
11	Messier	72	207	21	77	48	58	106	237	20.3	2	5	12	1	19	72
9	Anderson	71	180	22	72	48	56	104	243	19.8	10	3	11	0	41	70
17	Kurri	72	185	22	80	45	59	104	218	20.6	3	1	10	1	47	22
7	Coffey	72	203	21	80	29	67	96	259	11.2	2	0	9	1	52	87
13	Linseman	71	175	24	72	33	42	75	141	23.4	3	0	10	4	16	181
22	Huddy	72	199	23	76	20	37	57	151	13.2	2	0	7	0	62	58
16	Hughes	71	190	27	80	25	20	45	144	17.4	7	1	2	5	0	85
24	Roulston	73	196	25	67	19	21	40	107	17.8	2	0	2	0	29	24
4	Lowe	73	191	23	80	6	34	40	92	6.5	0	0	1	0	39	43
20	Lumley	71	182	28	72	13	24	37	96	13.5	1	0	2	0	19	158
10	Pouzar	71	202	30	74	15	18	33	86	17.4	2	0	2	0	17	57
12	Hunter	71	199	24	80	13	18	31	113	11.5	0	0	0	1	12	120

#		*Ht.*	*Wt.*	*Age*	*GP*	*G*	*A*	*Pts*	*Shots*	*S%*	*GW*	*GT*	*PP*	*SH*	*P/M*	*PIM*
21	Gregg	76	216	26	80	6	22	28	94	6.4	2	0	0	2	15	54
27	Semenko	75	215	25	75	12	15	27	69	17.4	1	0	0	0	19	141
14	Boschman	72	183	22	62	8	12	20	59	13.6	0	1	0	0	3	183
2	Fogolin (C)	72	203	27	72	0	18	18	66	0.0	0	0	0	0	24	92
23	Habscheid	72	179	19	32	3	10	13	19	15.8	0	0	0	0	14	14
19	Lindstrom	72	180	31	10	6	5	11	21	28.6	0	0	0	0	5	2
29	Jackson	75	210	26	71	2	8	10	72	2.8	1	0	0	1	12	136
35	Moog	69	170	22	50	0	4	4	0	0.0	0	0	0	0	0	16
28	Blum	75	203	23	5	0	3	3	0	0.0	0	0	0	0	2	24
77	Unger	72	184	35	16	2	0	2	14	14.3	0	0	0	0	1	8
6	Lariviere	72	194	28	17	0	2	2	15	0.0	0	0	0	0	13	14
33	Middlebrook	67	160	27	1	0	0	0	0	0.0	0	0	0	0	0	0
25	Strueby	73	186	19	1	0	0	0	0	0.0	0	0	0	0	-2	0
30	Low	73	210	32	3	0	0	0	0	0.0	0	0	0	0	0	0
26	Nachbaur	74	200	23	4	0	0	0	0	0.0	0	0	0	0	-1	17
31	Fuhr	70	201	20	32	0	0	0	0	0.0	0	0	0	0	0	6
	Bench															28
		72	192	25	80	424	678	1102	2664	15.9	47	12	86	22	112	1771

1982-83 Goaltender Record

	GP	*Min.*	*GA*	*W*	*L*	*T*	*Ave*	*SA*	*Pct.*	*SO*	*EN*
Middlebrook	1	60	3	1	0	0	3.00	33	0.909	0	0
Andy Moog	50	2833	167	33	8	7	3.54	1531	0.891	1	1
Grant Fuhr	32	1803	129	13	12	5	4.29	974	0.867	0	4
Ron Low	3	104	10	0	1	0	5.78	55	0.815	0	1
	80	4800	315	47	21	12	3.94	2593	0.881	1	6

Coach: Glen Sather 47-21-12

1982-83 Scoring vs. Opposition

	Bost.	*Buff.*	*Calg.*	*Chi.*	*Det.*	*Hart.*	*L.A.*	*Minn.*	*Mont.*	*N.J.*
Anderson	1–2–3	1–2–3	5–7–12	3–2–5	2–2–4	1–3–4	9–7–16	4–2–6	1–2–3	3–2–5
Blum	———	———	0–3–3	———	———	0–0–0	———	———	———	———
Boschman	0–1–1	0–0–0	1–1–2	0–0–0	0–0–0	1–0–1	1–4–5	0–2–2	1–1–2	0–0–0
Coffey	0–1–1	1–3–4	2–3–5	4–4–8	2–2–4	3–1–4	1–8–9	4–3–7	1–1–2	2–4–6
Fogolin	0–1–1	0–0–0	0–2–2	0–0–0	0–2–2	0–2–2	0–2–2	0–0–0	0–0–0	0–0–0
Gregg	0–0–0	0–1–1	0–2–2	0–0–0	0–4–4	0–1–1	2–0–2	1–1–2	0–0–0	0–0–0
Gretzky	1–3–4	2–5–7	5–9–14	2–5–7	1–10–11	4–4–8	7–12–19	3–9–12	3–4–7	3–4–7
Habscheid	———	0–0–0	0–1–1	0–1–1	0–0–0	0–1–1	1–1–2	1–1–2	0–0–0	0–1–1
Huddy	1–0–1	0–1–1	1–4–5	2–1–3	2–2–4	0–3–3	1–7–8	1–2–3	1–1–2	1–2–3
Hughes	3–0–3	1–0–1	1–2–3	2–2–4	2–0–2	1–2–3	2–3–5	0–1–1	0–0–0	0–1–1
Hunter	1–0–1	1–1–2	3–2–5	1–2–3	0–1–1	1–0–1	3–0–3	0–0–0	0–0–0	1–1–2
Jackson	0–0–0	0–0–0	1–1–2	0–2–2	0–0–0	0–2–2	0–1–1	1–0–1	0–0–0	0–0–0
Kurri	2–1–3	3–1–4	4–5–9	3–2–5	3–3–6	1–3–4	1–8–9	0–2–2	2–0–2	3–2–5
Lariviere	0–0–0	0–0–0	0–0–0	0–0–0	0–0–0	———	0–0–0	———	0–0–0	———
Lindstrom	———	1–2–3	0–0–0	———	1–0–1	———	2–0–2	———	———	———
Linseman	1–2–3	1–1–2	4–2–6	2–4–6	1–1–2	0–2–2	2–3–5	3–3–6	0–2–2	2–3–5
Lowe	0–1–1	0–4–4	0–3–3	0–0–0	0–3–3	0–0–0	0–2–2	0–1–1	0–0–0	0–1–1
Lumley	0–1–1	1–0–1	0–3–3	0–1–1	0–1–1	0–1–1	3–2–5	0–2–2	0–2–2	0–3–3
Messier	0–0–0	1–1–2	5–7–12	1–6–7	4–0–4	1–1–2	5–7–12	2–5–7	4–4–8	2–3–5
Nachbaur	———	———	0–0–0	———	———	0–0–0	———	———	———	———
Pouzar	0–1–1	1–1–2	1–2–3	0–0–0	1–0–1	0–2–2	3–2–5	0–0–0	0–0–0	0–0–0
Roulston	1–2–3	1–2–3	2–1–3	0–0–0	0–2–2	3–0–3	0–1–1	0–0–0	0–1–1	2–0–2
Semenko	0–0–0	0–0–0	2–1–3	0–0–0	0–0–0	0–1–1	3–1–4	2–0–2	1–0–1	0–0–0
Strueby	———	———	———	———	———	———	———	———	———	———
Unger	———	0–0–0	0–0–0	———	0–0–0	1–0–1	———	———	———	0–0–0

	NYI.	*NYR.*	*Phil.*	*Pitt.*	*Que.*	*St.L.*	*Tor.*	*Van.*	*Wash.*	*Winn.*
Anderson	1–0–1	1–0–1	1–0–1	5–2–7	1–2–3	3–3–6	0–1–1	3–5–8	1–3–4	2–9–11
Blum	0–0–0	———	———	———	———	———	———	0–0–0	———	———
Boschman	0–0–0	0–0–0	0–0–0	1–0–1	1–0–1	0–0–0	1–0–1	1–0–1	0–0–0	0–3–3

	NYI.	*NYR.*	*Phil.*	*Pitt.*	*Que.*	*St.L.*	*Tor.*	*Van.*	*Wash.*	*Winn.*
Coffey	0–1–1	2–2–4	0–3–3	0–1–1	1–5–6	0–4–4	1–3–4	1–8–9	0–4–4	4–5–9
Fogolin	0–0–0	0–1–1	0–1–1	0–1–1	0–0–0	0–0–0	0–1–1	0–3–3	0–1–1	0–1–1
Gregg	0–0–0	1–0–1	0–0–0	0–1–1	0–0–0	0–5–5	0–0–0	0–2–2	0–2–2	2–3–5
Gretzky	1–3–4	3–3–6	1–4–5	4–4–8	4–9–13	3–2–5	5–6–11	9–11–20	4–3–7	6–14–20
Habscheid	0–0–0	0–0–0	———	0–0–0	———	0–2–2	———	0–0–0	1–2–3	0–0–0
Huddy	1–0–1	1–3–4	0–1–1	0–1–1	1–1–2	1–0–1	0–2–2	1–3–4	1–0–1	4–3–7
Hughes	0–1–1	2–1–3	2–0–2	1–1–2	0–1–1	2–0–2	1–1–2	2–2–4	0–0–0	3–2–5
Hunter	0–0–0	0–1–1	0–0–0	0–2–2	0–0–0	0–3–3	0–1–1	1–2–3	0–0–0	1–2–3
Jackson	0–0–0	0–0–0	0–0–0	0–0–0	0–0–0	0–0–0	0–1–1	0–0–0	0–0–0	0–1–1
Kurri	1–2–3	0–2–2	2–0–2	1–3–4	3–4–7	1–2–3	4–2–6	6–6–12	0–3–3	5–8–13
Lariviere	———	———	———	0–0–0	———	0–1–1	———	0–1–1	0–0–0	0–0–0
Lindstrom	———	0–0–0	———	———	———	———	0–0–0	0–2–2	———	2–1–3
Linseman	1–1–2	0–2–2	1–0–1	3–3–6	1–2–3	1–2–3	0–0–0	4–4–8	2–1–3	4–3–7
Lowe	0–1–1	0–2–2	1–0–1	1–6–7	0–2–2	0–1–1	0–1–1	0–1–1	1–1–2	3–4–7
Lumley	0–2–2	2–1–3	0–0–0	1–1–2	1–1–2	0–0–0	0–1–1	2–0–2	1–1–2	2–0–2
Messier	1–2–3	0–1–1	0–1–1	1–5–6	3–0–3	1–1–2	1–2–3	9–7–16	2–1–3	5–5–10
Nachbaur	———	———	———	———	———	———	0–0–0	0–0–0	———	———
Pouzar	0–0–0	1–1–2	1–1–2	0–2–2	1–0–1	1–0–1	2–1–3	2–2–4	1–2–3	0–1–1
Roulston	2–0–2	2–1–3	0–1–1	3–0–3	1–1–2	1–1–2	0–1–1	0–2–2	0–2–2	1–3–4
Semenko	0–2–2	0–2–2	0–0–0	0–1–1	1–0–1	0–1–1	1–2–3	1–1–2	0–0–0	1–3–4
Strueby	———	———	———	———	———	0–0–0	———	———	———	———
Unger	0–0–0	0–0–0	0–0–0	0–0–0	0–0–0	1–0–1	———	0–0–0	0–0–0	0–0–0

1982-83 Goaltender Records vs. Opposition

	GP	*Min.*	*GA*	*EN*	*SO*	*Ave.*	*W–L–T*	*Opposition*
Grant Fuhr	1	60	5	0	0	5.00	0–1–0	Boston
	1	40	2	0	0	3.00	0–1–0	Buffalo
	5	300	26	0	0	5.20	2–1–2	Calgary
	1	60	7	1	0	7.00	0–1–0	Chicago
	1	60	4	0	0	4.00	0–1–0	Detroit
	2	120	6	0	0	3.00	2–0–0	Hartford
	2	120	7	0	0	3.50	1–1–0	Minnesota
	1	60	2	0	0	2.00	1–0–0	Montreal
	1	60	1	0	0	1.00	1–0–0	New Jersey
	2	120	9	1	0	4.50	0–2–0	N.Y. Islanders
	1	60	2	0	0	2.00	1–0–0	N.Y. Rangers
	1	60	7	0	0	7.00	0–1–0	Philadelphia
	1	20	4	0	0	12.00	0–0–0	Pittsburgh
	2	100	12	0	0	7.20	0–1–1	Quebec
	2	120	7	0	0	3.50	1–0–1	St. Louis
	2	120	4	0	0	2.00	2–0–0	Toronto
	2	120	8	0	0	4.00	1–1–0	Vancouver
	1	60	3	0	0	3.00	0–0–1	Washington
	3	143	13	2	0	5.45	1–1–0	Winnipeg
Ron Low	1	47	5	0	0	6.38	0–0–0	Boston
	1	20	1	1	0	3.00	0–0–0	Los Angeles
	1	38	4	0	0	6.32	0–1–0	Winnipeg
L. Middlebrook	1	60	3	0	0	3.00	1–0–0	New Jersey
Andy Moog	2	73	6	0	0	4.93	1–1–0	Boston
	3	140	10	0	0	4.29	2–0–0	Buffalo
	3	180	11	0	0	3.67	2–1–0	Calgary
	2	120	8	0	0	4.00	1–0–1	Chicago
	2	120	12	0	0	6.00	2–0–0	Detroit
	1	60	4	0	0	4.00	0–0–1	Hartford
	8	460	28	0	0	3.65	5–1–2	Los Angeles
	1	60	4	0	0	4.00	1–0–0	Minnesota
	2	120	7	0	0	3.50	1–1–0	Montreal
	1	60	4	0	0	4.00	1–0–0	New Jersey
	1	60	4	0	0	4.00	0–1–0	N.Y. Islanders
	2	120	2	0	0	1.00	2–0–0	N.Y. Rangers
	2	120	6	1	0	3.00	1–1–0	Philadelphia
	3	140	10	0	0	4.29	2–1–0	Pittsburgh
	2	80	5	0	0	3.75	1–0–0	Quebec

GP	*Min.*	*GA*	*EN*	*SO*	*Ave.*	*W–L–T*	*Opposition*
1	60	5	0	0	5.00	1–0–0	St. Louis
1	60	6	0	0	6.00	0–0–1	Toronto
6	380	17	0	0	2.68	4–1–1	Vancouver
2	120	6	0	0	3.00	2–0–0	Washington
5	300	12	0	1	2.40	5–0–0	Winnipeg

1982-83 Schedule Results

Oct. 5	Calgary	5	at	Edmonton	7
Oct. 8	Islanders	6	at	Edmonton	6
Oct. 9	Edmonton	6	at	Vancouver	3
Oct. 12	Edmonton	4	at	Calgary	9
Oct. 14	Edmonton	4	at	Hartford	4
Oct. 16	Edmonton	6	at	Boston	6
Oct. 17	Edmonton	4	at	Buffalo	6
Oct. 20	Hartford	2	at	Edmonton	4
Oct. 21	Boston	5	at	Edmonton	3
Oct. 24	Edmonton	5	at	Winnipeg	9
Oct. 27	Chicago	4	at	Edmonton	4
Oct. 29	Los Angeles	3	at	Edmonton	6
Oct. 31	Vancouver	3	at	Edmonton	2
Nov. 3	Winnipeg	2	at	Edmonton	7
Nov. 5	Rangers	1	at	Edmonton	5
Nov. 8	Edmonton	5	at	Quebec	5
Nov. 10	Edmonton	4	at	Pittsburgh	5
Nov. 11	Edmonton	5	at	New Jersey	1
Nov. 13	Edmonton	4	at	Philadelphia	3
Nov. 14	Edmonton	7	at	Rangers	2
Nov. 16	Edmonton	2	at	Islanders	4
Nov. 20	Vancouver	3	at	Edmonton	3
Nov. 21	Quebec	9	at	Edmonton	7
Nov. 24	Washington	3	at	Edmonton	3
Nov. 26	Edmonton	6	at	Winnipeg	5
Nov. 28	Edmonton	7	at	Detroit	5
Dec. 1	Philadelphia	4	at	Edmonton	2
Dec. 4	Calgary	5	at	Edmonton	7
Dec. 5	Los Angeles	3	at	Edmonton	7
Dec. 7	St. Louis	2	at	Edmonton	3
Dec. 9	Edmonton	3	at	Los Angeles	3
Dec. 11	Edmonton	4	at	Minnesota	5
Dec. 17	New Jersey	4	at	Edmonton	10
Dec. 19	Montreal	2	at	Edmonton	5
Dec. 22	Minnesota	2	at	Edmonton	8
Dec. 23	Edmonton	6	at	Los Angeles	2
Dec. 26	Edmonton	4	at	Calgary	4
Dec. 29	Chicago	8	at	Edmonton	6
Dec. 31	Edmonton	8	at	Vancouver	1
Jan. 1	Winnipeg	3	at	Edmonton	5
Jan. 4	Edmonton	6	at	Calgary	3
Jan. 5	Edmonton	8	at	Winnipeg	3
Jan. 7	Pittsburgh	2	at	Edmonton	7
Jan. 9	Detroit	4	at	Edmonton	3
Jan. 11	Edmonton	7	at	St. Louis	5
Jan. 12	Edmonton	10	at	Chicago	4
Jan. 15	Edmonton	10	at	Minnesota	4
Jan. 18	Edmonton	3	at	Los Angeles	3
Jan. 19	Vancouver	4	at	Edmonton	9
Jan. 22	Edmonton	3	at	Vancouver	4
Jan. 23	Los Angeles	6	at	Edmonton	8
Jan. 26	Toronto	6	at	Edmonton	6
Jan. 29	Calgary	4	at	Edmonton	5
Jan. 30	Islanders	4	at	Edmonton	2
Feb. 3	Los Angeles	7	at	Edmonton	4
Feb. 4	Montreal	3	at	Edmonton	7
Feb. 11	Quebec	3	at	Edmonton	7
Feb. 14	Edmonton	2	at	Montreal	4
Feb. 17	Edmonton	3	at	Philadelphia	7
Feb. 19	Edmonton	10	at	Pittsburgh	7
Feb. 20	Edmonton	5	at	Buffalo	4
Feb. 22	Edmonton	1	at	Calgary	4
Feb. 23	Washington	3	at	Edmonton	6
Feb. 25	St. Louis	5	at	Edmonton	5
Feb. 27	Winnipeg	0	at	Edmonton	3
Mar. 1	Edmonton	4	at	New Jersey	3
Mar. 2	Edmonton	5	at	Washington	3
Mar. 5	Edmonton	6	at	Toronto	3
Mar. 6	Edmonton	2	at	Boston	5
Mar. 8	Edmonton	9	at	Hartford	4
Mar. 11	Rangers	1	at	Edmonton	3
Mar. 13	Buffalo	2	at	Edmonton	6
Mar. 16	Vancouver	3	at	Edmonton	4
Mar. 19	Detroit	7	at	Edmonton	9
Mar. 21	Edmonton	4	at	Toronto	1
Mar. 23	Edmonton	4	at	Winnipeg	7
Mar. 26	Edmonton	9	at	Los Angeles	3
Mar. 29	Edmonton	7	at	Vancouver	4
April 1	Winnipeg	2	at	Edmonton	7
April 3	Calgary	3	at	Edmonton	3

Opponent	*Home W–L–T*	*Road W–L–T*
Boston	0–1–0	0–1–1
Buffalo	1–0–0	1–1–0
Calgary	3–0–1	1–2–1
Chicago	0–1–1	1–0–0
Detroit	1–1–0	1–0–0
Hartford	1–0–0	1–0–1
Los Angeles	3–1–0	2–0–2
Minnesota	1–0–0	1–1–0
Montreal	2–0–0	0–1–0
New Jersey	1–0–0	2–0–0
Islanders	0–2–0	0–1–0
Rangers	2–0–0	1–0–0
Philadelphia	0–1–0	1–1–0
Pittsburgh	1–0–0	1–1–0
Quebec	1–1–0	0–0–1
St. Louis	1–0–1	1–0–0
Toronto	0–0–1	2–0–0
Vancouver	2–1–1	3–1–0
Washington	1–0–1	1–0–0
Winnipeg	4–0–0	2–2–0

Opponent	Overall W–L–T	GF–GA	Opponent	Overall W–L–T	GF–GA
Boston	0–2–1	11–16	Islanders	0–3–0	8–14
Buffalo	2–1–0	15–12	Rangers	3–0–0	15–4
Calgary	4–2–2	37–37	Philadelphia	1–2–0	9–14
Chicago	1–1–1	20–16	Pittsburgh	2–1–0	21–14
Detroit	2–1–0	19–16	Quebec	1–1–1	19–17
Hartford	2–0–1	17–10	St. Louis	2–0–1	15–12
Los Angeles	5–1–2	46–30	Toronto	2–0–1	16–10
Minnesota	2–1–0	22–11	Vancouver	5–2–1	42–25
Montreal	2–1–0	14–9	Washington	2–0–1	14–9
New Jersey	3–0–0	19–8	Winnipeg	6–2–0	45–31

1982-83 Playoff Scoring

#		GP	G	A	Pts	Shots	S%	GW	OT	PP	SH	P/M	PIM
99	Wayne Gretzky	16	12	26	38	76	15.8	3	0	2	3	19	4
17	Jari Kurri	16	8	15	23	31	25.8	0	0	2	2	15	8
11	Mark Messier	15	15	6	21	50	30.0	2	0	4	2	10	14
9	Glenn Anderson	16	10	10	20	49	20.4	2	0	1	0	4	32
7	Paul Coffey	16	7	7	14	42	16.7	0	0	2	2	15	14
13	Ken Linseman	16	6	8	14	31	19.4	1	0	1	0	7	22
19	Willy Lindstrom	16	2	11	13	31	6.5	0	0	1	0	12	4
12	Dave Hunter	16	4	7	11	16	25.0	0	0	0	0	8	60
4	Kevin Lowe	16	1	8	9	19	5.3	0	0	0	0	8	10
16	Pat Hughes	16	2	5	7	31	6.5	1	0	0	0	10	14
22	Charlie Huddy	15	1	6	7	47	2.1	0	0	0	0	12	10
29	Don Jackson	16	3	3	6	16	18.8	0	0	0	0	9	30
21	Randy Gregg	16	2	4	6	16	12.5	1	0	0	1	13	13
14	Ray Cote	14	3	2	5	17	17.6	0	0	0	0	6	4
2	Lee Fogolin	16	0	5	5	15	0.0	0	0	0	0	8	36
24	Tom Roulston	16	1	2	3	13	7.7	0	0	0	0	-1	0
10	Jaroslav Pouzar	1	2	0	2	2	100.0	1	0	1	0	1	0
27	Dave Semenko	15	1	1	2	13	7.7	0	0	0	0	-1	69
6	Garry Lariviere	1	0	1	1	0	0.0	0	0	0	0	2	0
35	Andy Moog	16	0	1	1	0	0.0	0	0	0	0	0	2
31	Grant Fuhr	1	0	0	0	0	0.0	0	0	0	0	0	0
77	Garry Unger	1	0	0	0	0	0.0	0	0	0	0	0	0
26	Don Nachbaur	2	0	0	0	0	0.0	0	0	0	0	-1	7
20	Dave Lumley	16	0	0	0	4	0.0	0	0	0	0	-1	19
		16	80	128	208	519	15.4	11	0	14	10	20	372

1982-83 Playoff Goaltending

	GP	Min.	GA	W	L	Ave	SA	Pct.	SO	EN
Grant Fuhr	1	11	0	0	0	0.00	4	1.000	0	0
Andy Moog	16	949	48	11	5	3.00	463	0.896	0	2
	16	960	50	11	5	3.13	467	0.893	0	2

Date			Result			Winning Goaltender	Winning Goal
April 6, 1983	Winnipeg	3	at	Edmonton	6	Andy Moog	Wayne Gretzky
April 7, 1983	Winnipeg	4	at	Edmonton	3	Andy Moog	Mark Messier
April 9, 1983	Edmonton	4	at	Winnipeg	3	Andy Moog	Ken Linseman
April 14, 1983	Calgary	3	at	Edmonton	6	Andy Moog	Pat Hughes
April 15, 1983	Calgary	1	at	Edmonton	5	Andy Moog	Randy Gregg
April 17, 1983	Edmonton	10	at	Calgary	2	Andy Moog	Wayne Gretzky
April 18, 1983	Edmonton	5	at	Calgary	6	Don Edwards	Greg Meredith
April 20, 1983	Calgary	1	at	Edmonton	9	Andy Moog	Mark Messier
April 24, 1983	Chicago	4	at	Edmonton	8	Andy Moog	Wayne Gretzky
April 26, 1983	Chicago	2	at	Edmonton	8	Andy Moog	Glenn Anderson
May 1, 1983	Edmonton	3	at	Chicago	2	Andy Moog	Glenn Anderson
May 3, 1983	Edmonton	6	at	Chicago	3	Andy Moog	Jaroslav Pouzar
May 10, 1983	N.Y. Islanders	2	at	Edmonton	0	Billy Smith	Duane Sutter

Date			*Result*			*Winning Goaltender*	*Winning Goal*
May 12, 1983	N.Y. Islanders	6	at	Edmonton	3	Billy Smith	Bob Bourne
May 14, 1983	Edmonton	1	at	N.Y. Islanders	5	Billy Smith	Bob Bourne
May 17, 1983	Edmonton	2	at	N.Y. Islanders	4	Billy Smith	Mike Bossy

Table 4. Oilers All Time Regular Season Overtime Record

Season		*Overall*				*Home*				*Away*		
	GP	*W*	*L*	*T*	*GP*	*W*	*L*	*T*	*GP*	*W*	*L*	*T*
2000-01	*20*	*5*	*3*	*12*	*12*	*3*	*2*	*7*	*8*	*2*	*1*	*5*
1999-00	*28*	*4*	*8*	*16*	*13*	*1*	*3*	*9*	*15*	*3*	*5*	*7*
1998-99	*19*	*3*	*4*	*12*	*8*	*0*	*3*	*5*	*11*	*3*	*1*	*7*
1997-98	*15*	*3*	*2*	*10*	*6*	*0*	*1*	*5*	*9*	*3*	*1*	*5*
1996-97	*16*	*1*	*6*	*9*	*8*	*1*	*3*	*4*	*8*	*0*	*3*	*5*
1995-96	*14*	*4*	*2*	*8*	*8*	*2*	*1*	*5*	*6*	*2*	*1*	*3*
1994-95	*7*	*1*	*2*	*4*	*2*	*1*	*0*	*1*	*5*	*0*	*2*	*3*
1993-94	*21*	*1*	*6*	*14*	*7*	*0*	*4*	*3*	*14*	*1*	*2*	*11*
1992-93	*17*	*5*	*4*	*8*	*9*	*2*	*2*	*5*	*8*	*3*	*2*	*3*
1991-92	*12*	*0*	*2*	*10*	*5*	*0*	*0*	*5*	*7*	*0*	*2*	*5*
1990-91	*15*	*4*	*5*	*6*	*7*	*2*	*2*	*3*	*8*	*2*	*3*	*3*
1989-90	*20*	*5*	*1*	*14*	*10*	*3*	*1*	*6*	*10*	*2*	*0*	*8*
1988-89	*15*	*4*	*3*	*8*	*5*	*1*	*1*	*3*	*10*	*3*	*2*	*5*
1987-88	*16*	*3*	*2*	*11*	*5*	*0*	*1*	*4*	*11*	*3*	*1*	*7*
1986-87	*14*	*5*	*3*	*6*	*8*	*2*	*1*	*5*	*6*	*3*	*2*	*1*
1985-86	*14*	*5*	*2*	*7*	*6*	*3*	*1*	*2*	*8*	*2*	*1*	*5*
1984-85	*12*	*0*	*1*	*11*	*7*	*0*	*0*	*7*	*5*	*0*	*1*	*4*
1983-84	*9*	*4*	*0*	*5*	*5*	*1*	*0*	*4*	*4*	*3*	*0*	*1*
TOTAL	*284*	*57*	*56*	*171*	*131*	*22*	*26*	*83*	*153*	*35*	*30*	*88*

1983-84

The Oilers picked up a couple of fine prospects at this year's entry draft. General manager Glen Sather chose 6 foot 4 inch, 215 pound defenseman Jeff Beukeboom from Sault Ste. Marie of the OHA where he had recorded 25 assists and 143 penalty minutes for the Greyhounds. Beukeboom would win three Stanley Cups as a member of the Oilers and one with the New York Rangers.

Chosen 82nd overall was Finnish Junior player Esa Tikkanen. Tikkanen would be a part of four Oiler Stanley Cup teams. "The Grate One" gained a reputation as one of the finest defensive forwards of the era and perfectly complemented the team's attack oriented style of play.

Sather also made a couple of key transactions to fine-tune the team in their quest for the Stanley Cup. Signed to a free agent contract at the start of the season was defensive center Pat Conacher who played in 45 regular season contests. Conacher appeared in only three playoff games, but teamed with Pat Hughes and fellow newcomer Kevin McClelland he was instrumental in shutting down the Islanders' top scoring line in the final series.

In December the team obtained rugged center Kevin McClelland from the Penguins for little used forward Tom Roulston. McClelland would have a fine regular season and also contributed 10 points in 18 postseason games. McClelland played seven years for the Oilers and in four of these seasons he helped the team win the Stanley Cup.

The trio of Anderson, Messier and Linseman was rated as the fastest line in the league by *Hockey News*. The players were rated one, two and five respectively in individual speed by the weekly publication.

For the first time in five years the team's coaching staff returned intact from the previous year. Part way through the season Lee Fogolin voluntarily gave up his captaincy to Wayne Gretzky.

The Oilers engineered their best start ever this season. They won the first seven games, lost two of the next three, won the next eight, lost a 5–3 game to Chicago and then won four straight. The team was 38–9–5 (.779) at the All-Star break. In late January, around the same time that Wayne Gretzky was sitting out six games with a shoulder injury, Mark Messier was suspended six games for slashing Thomas Gradin of Vancouver. The team lost five of the six games in which Gretzky did not dress. Jari Kurri also missed several games in January with a groin pull.

Edmonton finished 37 points ahead of the Flames atop the Smythe Division and 15 points ahead of the Bruins and Islanders, who tied for second overall in the league standings. The offense was in high gear during the regular

Mark Messier won the Conn Smythe Trophy in 1984. (662A13A File 15 City of Edmonton Archives.)

season with 86 more goals than runner-up Quebec. The team finished second in goals against in the wide open Campbell Conference, but were tied for tenth overall in the entire league.

Wayne Gretzky again led the league in scoring, outdistancing teammate Paul Coffey by 79 points. The Oilers finished with three players in the top ten in scoring and had four players with over 100 points. Glenn Anderson just missed out with 99 points.

Of Gretzky's 205 points, 153 of them came in an amazing 51–game scoring streak in which he scored 61 goals and 92 assists. The streak began on October 5, 1983, the first game of the season, and continued until January 27, 1984.

The team destroyed Winnipeg in the first round of the playoffs, winning three straight games and outscoring the Jets 18–7. They then ran into a roadblock in the guise of the Calgary Flames. Edmonton won three of the first four games before Calgary won the next two to force a game seven in Edmonton which the Oilers won 7–4. After the Calgary series the rest of the playoffs were rather anticlimactic. The Oilers defeated Minnesota four straight games in the semifinal series, and knocked off the defending champion New York Islanders four games to one to win their first Stanley Cup.

1983-84 Regular Season Scoring

#		*Ht.*	*Wt.*	*Age*	*GP*	*G*	*A*	*Pts.*	*Shots*	*SH%*	*GW*	*GT*	*PP*	*SH*	*P/M*	*PIM*
99	Gretzky (C)	72	170	22	74	87	118	205	324	26.9	11	0	20	12	76	39
7	Coffey	72	200	22	80	40	86	126	258	15.5	4	1	14	1	52	104
17	Kurri	72	185	23	64	52	61	113	194	26.8	4	1	10	5	38	14
11	Messier	72	205	22	73	37	64	101	219	16.9	7	0	7	4	40	165
9	Anderson	71	180	23	80	54	45	99	277	19.5	11	1	11	4	41	65
13	Linseman	70	175	25	72	18	49	67	105	17.1	2	0	5	1	30	119
16	Hughes	71	190	28	77	27	28	55	164	16.5	3	0	2	3	18	61
12	Hunter	71	200	25	80	22	26	48	117	18.8	3	0	1	1	25	90
4	Lowe	73	185	24	80	4	42	46	81	4.9	1	0	1	0	37	59
22	Huddy	72	197	24	75	8	34	42	161	5.0	0	0	3	0	50	43
21	Gregg	76	210	27	80	13	27	40	91	14.3	2	0	2	1	40	56
19	Lindstrom	73	172	32	73	22	16	38	116	19.0	3	1	2	0	17	38
10	Pouzar	71	200	31	67	13	19	32	87	14.9	0	0	2	0	17	44
24	McClelland	72	180	21	52	8	20	28	65	12.3	2	0	0	2	9	127
20	Lumley	71	180	29	56	6	15	21	44	13.6	0	1	0	0	14	68
2	Fogolin (C)	72	200	28	80	5	16	21	73	6.8	0	0	0	0	33	125
29	Jackson	75	210	27	60	8	12	20	57	14.0	2	0	0	1	28	120
27	Semenko	75	210	26	52	6	11	17	39	15.4	2	0	0	0	9	118
31	Fuhr	70	185	21	45	0	14	14	0	0.0	0	0	0	0	0	6
24	Roulston	73	192	26	24	5	7	12	38	13.2	0	0	1	0	0	16
15	Conacher	68	185	24	45	2	8	10	18	11.1	0	0	0	0	-2	31
9	Chartraw	74	210	29	24	2	6	8	23	8.7	0	0	0	0	5	21
18	Berry	69	170	23	13	2	3	5	18	11.1	0	0	0	1	6	10
25	Summanen	71	185	21	2	1	4	5	3	33.3	0	0	0	0	4	2
5	Playfair	75	200	19	2	1	1	2	2	50.0	0	0	0	0	4	2
26	Gorence	72	190	26	12	1	1	2	7	14.3	0	0	0	0	0	0
8	Sherven	72	185	20	2	1	0	1	5	20.0	0	0	0	0	1	0
23	Habscheid	72	180	20	9	1	0	1	6	16.7	0	0	0	0	-3	6
26	Strueby	73	186	20	1	0	1	1	1	0.0	0	0	0	0	2	2

#		*Ht.*	*Wt.*	*Age*	*GP*	*G*	*A*	*Pts.*	*Shots*	*SH%*	*GW*	*GT*	*PP*	*SH*	*P/M*	*PIM*
28	Blum	75	200	24	4	0	1	1	3	0.0	0	0	0	0	0	2
35	Moog	69	170	23	38	0	1	1	0	0.0	0	0	0	0	0	4
8	Jalonen	75	190	23	3	0	0	0	0	0.0	0	0	0	0	-2	0
6	Clark	73	180	19	1	0	0	0	0	0.0	0	0	0	0	0	0
8	S. Graves	70	175	19	2	0	0	0	2	0.0	0	0	0	0	0	0
25	Kerr	70	180	26	3	0	0	0	3	0.0	0	0	0	0	-3	0
14	Cote	71	170	22	13	0	0	0	12	0.0	0	0	0	0	-5	2
	Bench															18
		72	188	24	80	446	736	1182	2613	17.1	57	5	81	36	128	1577

1983-84 Goaltender Records

	GP	*Min.*	*GA*	*W*	*L*	*T*	*Ave.*	*SA*	*Pct.*	*SO*	*EN*
Andy Moog	38	2212	139	27	8	1	3.77	1179	0.882	1	2
Grant Fuhr	45	2625	171	30	10	4	3.91	1463	0.883	1	2
	80	4837	314	57	18	5	3.89	2642	0.881	2	4

Coach: Glen Sather 57-18-5

1983-84 Scoring vs. Opposition

	Bost.	*Buff.*	*Calg.*	*Chi.*	*Det.*	*Hart.*	*L.A.*	*Minn.*	*Mont.*	*N.J.*
Anderson	2–0–2	1–3–4	5–5–10	1–0–1	0–4–4	4–1–5	9–1–10	2–3–5	3–1–4	0–2–2
Berry	———	0–0–0	0–0–0	0–0–0	0–0–0	———	1–0–1	0–0–0	———	0–1–1
Blum	———	———	———	———	———	———	0–0–0	0–0–0	———	———
Chartraw	0–0–0	0–0–0	0–2–2	0–0–0	———	0–0–0	0–1–1	———	0–0–0	———
Clark	———	———	———	———	———	0–0–0	———	———	———	———
Coffey	1–3–4	0–2–2	3–10–13	1–2–3	3–1–4	0–5–5	5–12–17	2–1–3	0–4–4	2–2–4
Conacher	0–0–0	0–0–0	0–0–0	1–0–1	0–0–0	0–0–0	0–2–2	0–0–0	0–0–0	0–0–0
Cote	———	0–0–0	0–0–0	0–0–0	———	———	0–0–0	———	———	0–0–0
Fogolin	0–0–0	0–0–0	1–0–1	1–1–2	1–0–1	0–1–1	1–2–3	0–0–0	0–1–1	0–1–1
Gorence	———	0–0–0	———	0–1–1	0–0–0	———	1–0–1	———	———	———
Graves	———	———	———	———	0–0–0	0–0–0	———	———	———	———
Gregg	1–2–3	2–0–2	2–6–8	0–1–1	1–2–3	0–0–0	1–2–3	1–0–1	0–0–0	0–0–0
Gretzky	0–2–2	0–4–4	7–11–18	1–4–5	7–6–13	3–1–4	4–15–19	6–6–12	2–3–5	4–8–12
Habscheid	———	———	0–0–0	———	0–0–0	———	———	0–0–0	———	———
Huddy	0–0–0	0–0–0	2–4–6	0–3–3	1–0–1	0–1–1	2–3–5	0–4–4	0–0–0	1–1–2
Hughes	1–0–1	2–1–3	9–1–10	0–1–1	1–0–1	0–1–1	4–3–7	0–1–1	0–0–0	0–1–1
Hunter	1–1–2	1–1–2	2–4–6	2–0–2	1–3–4	1–0–1	1–1–2	0–0–0	0–0–0	0–1–1
Jackson	0–1–1	0–0–0	1–0–1	0–0–0	0–0–0	0–0–0	1–2–3	0–2–2	0–0–0	0–0–0
Kerr	0–0–0	———	———	———	———	0–0–0	———	———	———	———
Kurri	0–0–0	2–1–3	7–9–16	4–1–5	1–3–4	1–0–1	2–3–5	5–2–7	2–2–4	6–1–7
Lindstrom	0–0–0	0–0–0	0–1–1	2–0–2	1–1–2	0–0–0	2–3–5	1–0–1	0–0–0	6–1–7
Linseman	1–2–3	0–0–0	5–8–13	0–3–3	1–1–2	0–1–1	3–8–11	0–0–0	1–1–2	0–1–1
Lowe	0–0–0	0–1–1	0–7–7	0–3–3	1–1–2	0–1–1	0–5–5	0–3–3	0–1–1	0–4–4
Lumley	0–0–0	1–2–3	1–1–2	0–0–0	0–1–1	0–0–0	1–1–2	1–1–2	0–1–1	0–0–0
McClelland	0–1–1	0–1–1	2–6–8	1–0–1	0–0–0	0–1–1	1–1–2	0–1–1	0–0–0	0–1–1
Messier	1–1–2	2–3–5	4–4–8	1–4–5	3–3–6	0–4–4	2–2–4	0–8–8	2–2–4	1–1–2
Playfair	———	———	———	———	———	———	———	0–0–0	———	1–1–2
Pouzar	0–0–0	1–1–2	2–1–3	0–1–1	0–1–1	1–0–1	1–2–3	0–0–0	1–0–1	0–2–2
Roulston	———	0–1–1	———	0–0–0	0–0–0	———	0–0–0	0–0–0	0–0–0	0–2–2
Semenko	0–0–0	0–0–0	0–2–2	0–0–0	0–1–1	0–0–0	0–1–1	0–0–0	0–0–0	———
Sherven	———	———	0–0–0	———	———	———	1–0–1	———	———	———
Strueby	———	———	———	———	———	———	———	———	———	0–1–1
Summanen	———	———	0–2–2	———	———	———	1–2–3	———	———	———

	NYI.	*NYR.*	*Phil.*	*Pitt.*	*Que.*	*St.L.*	*Tor.*	*Van.*	*Wash.*	*Winn.*
Anderson	0–1–1	2–4–6	2–0–2	2–3–5	1–1–2	1–1–2	2–2–4	9–7–16	2–1–3	6–5–11
Berry	———	———	———	———	0–0–0	———	———	0–1–1	0–1–1	1–0–1
Blum	———	———	———	———	———	0–0–0	———	———	———	0–1–1
Chartraw	1–0–1	0–0–0	0–0–0	0–0–0	0–0–0	0–0–0	0–2–2	1–0–1	0–0–0	0–0–0
Coffey	2–1–3	0–3–3	2–2–4	4–3–7	2–8–10	0–3–3	0–3–3	4–9–13	2–4–6	7–8–15
Conacher	0–0–0	0–3–3	0–0–0	0–0–0	0–1–1	0–0–0	0–0–0	———	1–1–2	0–1–1

	NYI.	*NYR.*	*Phil.*	*Pitt.*	*Que.*	*St.L.*	*Tor.*	*Van.*	*Wash.*	*Winn.*
Cote	0–0–0	———	0–0–0	———	———	———	———	0–0–0	———	———
Fogolin	1–0–1	0–0–0	0–0–0	0–1–1	0–0–0	0–0–0	0–2–2	0–2–2	0–0–0	0–4–4
Gorence	0–0–0	———	0–0–0	———	———	———	———	0–0–0	———	———
Gregg	0–0–0	0–1–1	1–1–2	1–1–2	0–1–1	0–1–1	0–1–1	0–4–4	1–0–1	2–3–5
Gretzky	1–2–3	5–2–7	1–3–4	6–5–11	3–7–10	5–6–11	4–1–5	9–15–24	3–6–9	16–11–27
Habscheid	———	———	———	———	———	———	0–0–0	0–0–0	0–0–0	1–0–1
Huddy	1–0–1	0–2–2	1–0–1	0–3–3	0–4–4	0–0–0	0–3–3	0–2–2	0–0–0	0–3–3
Hughes	1–2–3	2–0–2	1–0–1	1–3–4	0–3–3	0–1–1	0–0–0	3–5–8	2–1–3	0–4–4
Hunter	1–2–3	1–1–2	0–0–0	0–1–1	1–0–1	0–1–1	1–1–2	1–4–5	1–3–4	7–2–9
Jackson	0–0–0	0–1–1	0–0–0	1–1–2	0–0–0	2–0–2	0–1–1	1–4–5	2–0–2	0–1–1
Jalonen	———	———	———	———	———	———	———	———	———	0–0–0
Kerr	———	———	———	———	———	———	———	———	0–0–0	———
Kurri	0–1–1	1–3–4	0–3–3	2–4–6	4–2–6	1–2–3	1–2–3	7–5–12	2–3–5	4–14–18
Lindstrom	1–2–3	0–1–1	0–0–0	1–1–2	3–1–4	0–0–0	2–0–2	2–3–5	1–1–2	0–1–1
Linseman	0–0–0	1–2–3	0–2–2	0–2–2	0–2–2	0–3–3	1–2–3	4–5–9	0–2–2	1–4–5
Lowe	1–0–1	0–1–1	0–1–1	0–3–3	0–1–1	0–0–0	1–1–2	0–3–3	0–1–1	1–5–6
Lumley	0–0–0	0–0–0	0–0–0	1–0–1	1–1–2	0–0–0	0–3–3	0–3–3	0–0–0	0–1–1
McClelland	0–1–1	1–0–1	0–1–1	1–2–3	0–0–0	0–0–0	0–0–0	0–2–2	0–0–0	2–2–4
Messier	0–2–2	2–2–4	0–2–2	2–3–5	3–2–5	2–3–5	3–2–5	4–6–10	1–3–4	4–6–10
Pouzar	0–0–0	1–0–1	1–0–1	1–0–1	1–1–2	2–0–2	0–0–0	1–4–5	0–2–2	0–3–3
Roulston	———	0–0–0	———	0–0–0	0–1–1	0–0–0	1–0–1	2–1–3	2–0–2	0–2–2
Semenko	0–0–0	0–0–0	0–0–0	0–1–1	2–2–4	0–0–0	0–2–2	3–1–4	0–0–0	1–1–2

1983-84 Goaltender Records vs. Opposition

	GP	*Min.*	*GA*	*EN*	*SO*	*Ave.*	*W–L–T*	*Opposition*
Grant Fuhr	2	120	2	0	1	1.00	2–0–0	Boston
	2	120	6	0	0	3.00	1–1–0	Buffalo
	5	300	16	0	0	3.20	5–0–0	Calgary
	2	119	8	1	0	4.03	1–1–0	Chicago
	1	60	3	0	0	3.00	1–0–0	Detroit
	1	31	7	0	0	13.55	0–1–0	Hartford
	3	180	9	0	0	3.00	3–0–0	Los Angeles
	3	189	13	0	0	4.13	2–0–1	Minnesota
	3	180	5	0	0	1.66	2–1–0	Montreal
	2	125	7	0	0	3.36	1–0–1	New Jersey
	2	120	11	1	0	5.50	0–2–0	N.Y. Islanders
	2	121	7	0	0	3.47	1–1–0	N.Y. Rangers
	2	125	7	0	0	3.36	0–1–1	Philadelphia
	1	60	4	0	0	4.00	1–0–0	Quebec
	2	120	12	0	0	6.00	1–1–0	St. Louis
	1	60	4	0	0	4.00	1–0–0	Toronto
	4	212	20	0	0	5.66	2–0–1	Vancouver
	3	180	16	0	0	5.33	2–1–0	Washington
	4	197	14	0	0	4.26	4–0–0	Winnipeg
Andy Moog	1	60	4	0	0	4.00	0–1–0	Boston
	1	60	0	0	1	0.00	1–0–0	Buffalo
	3	185	12	0	0	3.89	2–0–1	Calgary
	1	60	3	0	0	3.00	1–0–0	Chicago
	2	120	6	0	0	3.00	2–0–0	Detroit
	3	129	10	0	0	4.65	2–0–0	Hartford
	5	300	20	0	0	4.00	3–1–0	Los Angeles
	1	60	4	0	0	4.00	1–0–0	New Jersey
	1	60	4	1	0	4.00	0–1–0	N.Y. Islanders
	1	60	4	0	0	4.00	1–0–0	N.Y. Rangers
	1	60	4	1	0	4.00	0–1–0	Philadelphia
	3	180	8	0	0	2.67	3–0–0	Pittsburgh
	2	125	6	0	0	2.88	2–0–0	Quebec
	1	60	8	0	0	8.00	0–1–0	St. Louis
	2	120	11	0	0	5.50	1–1–0	Toronto
	5	268	12	0	0	2.69	4–1–0	Vancouver
	5	285	22	0	0	4.63	4–0–0	Winnipeg

1983-84 Schedule Results

Date	Visitor			Home	
Oct. 5	Toronto	4	at	Edmonton	5
Oct. 7	Edmonton	8	at	Winnipeg	6
Oct. 9	Minnesota	4	at	Edmonton	3 OT
Oct. 12	Detroit	3	at	Edmonton	8
Oct. 15	Edmonton	4	at	Calgary	3
Oct. 16	Calgary	1	at	Edmonton	5
Oct. 18	Edmonton	10	at	Vancouver	7
Oct. 20	Edmonton	2	at	Los Angeles	7
Oct. 22	Vancouver	5	at	Edmonton	5 OT
Oct. 26	Edmonton	3	at	Toronto	8
Oct. 29	Edmonton	2	at	Montreal	1
Oct. 30	Edmonton	5	at	Rangers	4 OT
Nov. 2	Washington	3	at	Edmonton	11
Nov. 5	Pittsburgh	3	at	Edmonton	7
Nov. 6	Edmonton	8	at	Winnipeg	5
Nov. 8	Edmonton	7	at	Quebec	4
Nov. 9	Edmonton	7	at	Washington	4
Nov. 12	Edmonton	7	at	Detroit	3
Nov. 13	Edmonton	3	at	Chicago	5
Nov. 18	Buffalo	0	at	Edmonton	7
Nov. 19	New Jersey	4	at	Edmonton	13
Nov. 21	Winnipeg	6	at	Edmonton	7
Nov. 23	Edmonton	7	at	Los Angeles	3
Nov. 25	Edmonton	2	at	Minnesota	2 OT
Nov. 26	Edmonton	6	at	St. Louis	8
Nov. 30	Philadelphia	3	at	Edmonton	3 OT
Dec. 3	Los Angeles	3	at	Edmonton	7
Dec. 4	Islanders	4	at	Edmonton	2
Dec. 7	Vancouver	4	at	Edmonton	5
Dec. 10	Edmonton	2	at	Vancouver	3
Dec. 13	Edmonton	5	at	Islanders	8
Dec. 14	Edmonton	9	at	Rangers	4
Dec. 17	Quebec	1	at	Edmonton	8
Dec. 18	Edmonton	7	at	Winnipeg	5
Dec. 21	Winnipeg	4	at	Edmonton	7
Dec. 23	Calgary	5	at	Edmonton	5 OT
Dec. 26	Edmonton	6	at	Calgary	3
Dec. 28	Edmonton	4	at	Vancouver	2
Dec. 30	Boston	0	at	Edmonton	2
Jan. 3	Edmonton	9	at	Calgary	6
Jan. 4	Minnesota	8	at	Edmonton	12
Jan. 7	Hartford	3	at	Edmonton	5
Jan. 9	Edmonton	7	at	Detroit	3
Jan. 11	Edmonton	5	at	Chicago	3
Jan. 13	Edmonton	1	at	Buffalo	3
Jan. 15	Edmonton	5	at	New Jersey	4
Jan. 18	Vancouver	5	at	Edmonton	7
Jan. 20	Los Angeles	5	at	Edmonton	7
Jan. 21	Edmonton	6	at	Los Angeles	3
Jan. 25	Edmonton	6	at	Vancouver	4
Jan. 27	New Jersey	3	at	Edmonton	3 OT
Jan. 28	Los Angeles	4	at	Edmonton	2
Feb. 3	Calgary	5	at	Edmonton	10
Feb. 5	Edmonton	2	at	Washington	9
Feb. 7	Edmonton	3	at	Islanders	5
Feb. 9	Edmonton	3	at	Philadelphia	4
Feb. 11	Edmonton	1	at	Boston	4
Feb. 12	Edmonton	0	at	Hartford	11
Feb. 15	Winnipeg	4	at	Edmonton	7
Feb. 17	Boston	2	at	Edmonton	5
Feb. 19	Pittsburgh	3	at	Edmonton	7
Feb. 21	Edmonton	6	at	St. Louis	5
Feb. 22	Edmonton	9	at	Pittsburgh	2
Feb. 24	Calgary	3	at	Edmonton	5
Feb. 25	Toronto	3	at	Edmonton	8
Feb. 27	Edmonton	6	at	Winnipeg	5 OT
Feb. 29	Philadelphia	5	at	Edmonton	3
Mar. 4	Montreal	1	at	Edmonton	6
Mar. 7	Chicago	4	at	Edmonton	7
Mar. 10	Rangers	3	at	Edmonton	2
Mar. 11	Vancouver	2	at	Edmonton	12
Mar. 13	Edmonton	6	at	Quebec	5 OT
Mar. 15	Edmonton	2	at	Montreal	3
Mar. 17	Los Angeles	1	at	Edmonton	9
Mar. 18	Buffalo	3	at	Edmonton	4
Mar. 21	Hartford	3	at	Edmonton	5
Mar. 24	St. Louis	7	at	Edmonton	1
Mar. 25	Winnipeg	2	at	Edmonton	3
Mar. 27	Edmonton	9	at	Calgary	2
Mar. 31	Edmonton	4	at	Los Angeles	3

Opponent	*Home W–L–T*	*Road W–L–T*
Boston	2–0–0	0–1–0
Buffalo	2–0–0	0–1–0
Calgary	3–0–1	4–0–0
Chicago	1–0–0	1–1–0
Detroit	1–0–0	2–0–0
Hartford	2–0–0	0–1–0
Los Angeles	3–1–0	3–1–0
Minnesota	2–0–0	0–0–1
Montreal	1–0–0	1–1–0
New Jersey	1–0–1	1–0–0
Islanders	0–1–0	0–2–0
Rangers	0–1–0	2–0–0
Philadelphia	0–1–1	0–1–0
Pittsburgh	2–0–0	1–0–0
Quebec	1–0–0	2–0–0
St. Louis	0–1–0	1–1–0
Toronto	2–0–0	0–1–0
Vancouver	3–0–1	3–1–0
Washington	1–0–0	1–1–0
Winnipeg	4–0–0	4–0–0

Opponent	*Overall W–L–T*	*GF–GA*
Boston	2–1–0	10–6
Buffalo	2–1–0	12–6
Calgary	7–0–1	53–28
Chicago	2–1–0	15–12
Detroit	3–0–0	22–9
Hartford	2–1–0	10–17
Los Angeles	6–2–0	44–27
Minnesota	2–0–1	18–12
Montreal	2–1–0	11–5
New Jersey	2–0–1	21–11
Islanders	0–3–0	12–17
Rangers	2–1–0	16–11
Philadelphia	0–2–1	9–12
Pittsburgh	3–0–0	23–8
Quebec	3–0–0	21–10
St. Louis	1–2–0	13–20
Toronto	2–1–0	16–15
Vancouver	6–1–1	51–31
Washington	2–1–0	20–16
Winnipeg	8–0–0	53–37

1983-84 Playoff Scoring

#		GP	G	A	Pts.	Shots	SH%	GW	OT	PP	SH	P/M	PIM
99	Wayne Gretzky	19	13	22	35	86	15.1	3	0	2	0	18	12
17	Jari Kurri	19	14	14	28	60	23.3	0	0	4	0	9	13
11	Mark Messier	19	8	18	26	63	12.7	2	0	1	1	9	19
7	Paul Coffey	19	8	14	22	66	12.1	1	0	2	0	21	21
9	Glenn Anderson	19	6	11	17	68	8.8	1	0	1	0	6	33
13	Ken Linseman	19	10	4	14	44	22.7	4	0	3	1	5	65
16	Pat Hughes	19	2	11	13	44	4.5	0	0	0	0	14	12
12	Dave Hunter	17	5	5	10	25	20.0	0	0	1	1	10	14
19	Willy Lindstrom	19	5	5	10	30	16.7	0	0	3	0	7	10
27	Dave Semenko	19	5	5	10	25	20.0	1	0	0	0	11	44
24	Kevin McClelland	18	4	6	10	32	12.5	1	0	0	0	13	42
21	Randy Gregg	19	3	7	10	32	9.4	1	1	0	0	16	21
4	Kevin Lowe	19	3	7	10	19	15.8	0	0	0	0	13	16
22	Charlie Huddy	12	1	9	10	35	2.9	0	0	0	0	18	8
20	Dave Lumley	19	2	5	7	21	9.5	0	0	0	0	6	44
25	Raimo Summanen	5	1	4	5	11	9.1	0	0	0	0	2	0
2	Lee Fogolin	19	1	4	5	22	4.5	0	0	0	0	10	23
10	Jaroslav Pouzar	14	1	2	3	14	7.1	1	0	0	0	0	12
29	Don Jackson	19	1	2	3	16	6.3	0	0	0	0	9	32
31	Grant Fuhr	16	0	3	3	0	0.0	0	0	0	0	0	4
15	Pat Conacher	3	1	0	1	3	33.3	0	0	0	0	1	2
28	Larry Melnyk	6	0	1	1	1	0.0	0	0	0	0	1	0
9	Rick Chartraw	1	0	0	0	0	0.0	0	0	0	0	-1	2
35	Andy Moog	7	0	0	0	0	0.0	0	0	0	0	0	2
		19	94	159	253	717	13.1	15	1	17	3	24	451

1983-84 Playoff Goaltending

	GP	Min.	GA	W	L	Ave.	SA	Pct.	SO	EN
Grant Fuhr	16	883	44	11	4	2.99	491	0.910	1	0
Andy Moog	7	263	12	4	0	2.74	110	0.891	0	0
	19	1146	56	15	4	2.93	601	0.907	1	0

Date			*Result*			*Winning Goaltender*	*Winning Goal*
April 4, 1984	Winnipeg	2	at	Edmonton	9	Grant Fuhr	Paul Coffey
April 5, 1984	Winnipeg	4	at	Edmonton	5	Grant Fuhr	Randy Gregg[1]
April 7, 1984	Edmonton	4	at	Winnipeg	1	Grant Fuhr	Dave Semenko
April 12, 1984	Calgary	2	at	Edmonton	5	Grant Fuhr	Wayne Gretzky
April 13, 1984	Calgary	6	at	Edmonton	5	Don Edwards	Carey Wilson[2]
April 15, 1984	Edmonton	3	at	Calgary	2	Grant Fuhr	Jaroslav Pouzar
April 16, 1984	Edmonton	5	at	Calgary	3	Grant Fuhr	Mark Messier
April 18, 1984	Calgary	5	at	Edmonton	4	Rejean Lemelin	Mike Eaves
April 20, 1984	Edmonton	4	at	Calgary	5	Rejean Lemelin	Lanny McDonald[3]
April 22, 1984	Calgary	4	at	Edmonton	7	Grant Fuhr	Ken Linseman
April 24, 1984	Minnesota	1	at	Edmonton	7	Grant Fuhr	Wayne Gretzky
April 26, 1984	Minnesota	3	at	Edmonton	4	Andy Moog	Wayne Gretzky
April 28, 1984	Edmonton	8	at	Minnesota	5	Andy Moog	Ken Linseman
May 1, 1984	Edmonton	3	at	Minnesota	1	Grant Fuhr	Ken Linseman
May 10, 1984	Edmonton	1	at	N.Y. Islanders	0	Grant Fuhr	Kevin McClelland
May 12, 1984	Edmonton	1	at	N.Y. Islanders	6	Billy Smith	Greg Gilbert
May 15, 1984	N.Y. Islanders	2	at	Edmonton	7	Grant Fuhr	Glenn Anderson
May 17, 1984	N.Y. Islanders	2	at	Edmonton	7	Andy Moog	Mark Messier
May 19, 1984	N.Y. Islanders	2	at	Edmonton	5	Andy Moog	Ken Linseman

[1] 00:21 of overtime
[2] 3:42 of overtime
[3] 1:04 of overtime

1983-84 Stanley Cup Winning Game

May 19, 1984: Northlands Coliseum, Edmonton

Attendance: 17,498

Oilers

Starting Lineup: **35**-Andy Moog (Goal), **2**-Lee Fogolin (Defense), **4**-Kevin Lowe (Defense), **9**-Glenn Anderson (Left Wing), **11**-Mark Messier (Center), **19**-Willy Lindstrom (Right Wing).

Remaining Players: 7-Paul Coffey, **15**-Pat Conacher, **21**-Randy Gregg, **99**-Wayne Gretzky, **22**-Charlie Huddy, **16**-Pat Hughes, **29**-Don Jackson, **17**-Jari Kurri, **13**-Ken Linseman, **20**-Dave Lumley, **24**-Kevin McClelland, **10**-Jaroslav Pouzar, **27**-Dave Semenko, **30**-Mike Zanier (backup goaltender).

Average: Age-25.3 years, Height-71.9 inches, Weight-189.7 pounds, Years Experience-3.17 years

Islanders

Starting Lineup: **31**-Billy Smith (Goal), **5**-Denis Potvin (Defense), **3**-Tomas Jonsson (Defense), **9**-Clark Gillies (Left Wing), **19**-Bryan Trottier (Center), **8**-Pat Flatley (Right Wing).

Remaining Players: **22**-Mike Bossy, **4**-Paul Boutilier, **17**-Greg Gilbert, **91**-Butch Goring, **28**-Anders Kallur, **16**-Pat LaFontaine, **26**-Dave Langevin, **6**-Ken Morrow, **23**-Bob Nystrom, **7**-Stefan Persson, **21**-Brent Sutter, **12**-Duane Sutter, **27**-John Tonelli, **1**-Roland Melanson (backup goaltender, replaced Smith at the start of the second period).

Average: Age-26.2 years, Height-72.2 inches, Weight-192.4 pounds, Years Experience-5.3 years.

Officials

Referee: Bryan Lewis, Linesmen: John D'Amico and Ray Scapinello

Game Summary

1st Period

Goals: Edmonton-Gretzky (Kurri) 12:08
Edmonton-Gretzky (Kurri) 17:26

Penalties: Edmonton (too many men-served by Willy Lindstrom)-00:47, New York (Pat Flatley-elbowing)-4:09, New York (Stefan Persson-high sticking)-6:48, New York (Duane Sutter-roughing)-18:47

2nd Period

Goals: Edmonton-Linseman (Gretzky, Huddy) PP 00:38
Edmonton-Kurri (Coffey, Anderson) PP 4:59

Penalties: New York (Duane Sutter-hooking)-4:19, Edmonton (Semenko-high sticking)-10:22

3rd Period

Goals: New York-LaFontaine (Gillies, Flatley) 00:13
New York-LaFontaine (Gillies) 00:35
Edmonton-Lumley 19:47

Penalties: New York (Flatley-interference)-16:45

Shots on Goal: Edmonton 9-5-6-20
New York 8-6-11-25

Table 5. Oilers Team Averages

	1980	*1981*	*1982*	*1983*	*1984*	*1985*	*1986*	*1987*	*1988*	*1989*	*1990*
Experience	*1.3*	*2.0*	*3.4*	*2.3*	*3.2*	*3.6*	*4.3*	*4.4*	*4.4*	*4.6*	*4.7*
Age	*24.6*	*24.4*	*25.2*	*24.5*	*25.8*	*25.9*	*25.9*	*26.1*	*24.2*	*26.1*	*27.1*
Height	*71.9*	*71.9*	*72.0*	*72.4*	*72.3*	*72.4*	*72.2*	*72.3*	*72.2*	*73.0*	*73.2*
Weight	*189.5*	*186.1*	*185.1*	*190.0*	*188.8*	*190.0*	*189.8*	*192.7*	*196.3*	*198.6*	*193.3*

	1991	*1992*	*1993*	*1994*	*1995*	*1996*	*1997*	*1998*	*1999*	*2000*	*2001*
Experience	*5.1*	*4.3*	*4.7*	*3.1*	*3.3*	*3.0*	*3.9*	*3.8*	*4.3*	*3.5*	*3.4*
Age	*26.8*	*26.1*	*26.6*	*24.7*	*25.3*	*24.8*	*26.1*	*26.4*	*26.2*	*25.3*	*25.3*
Height	*73.3*	*73.1*	*73.2*	*73.0*	*73.0*	*72.8*	*72.9*	*73.0*	*73.2*	*73.5*	*73.1*
Weight	*196.3*	*192.1*	*196.2*	*196.7*	*199.8*	*197.2*	*201.5*	*201.3*	*204.9*	*205.4*	*202.4*

*includes only the top 20 players in games played each season including both goaltenders (Height in inches)

1984-85

Glen Sather made few changes during the summer. The ones he did make however were key to the Oilers' defense of the Cup.

Picked up from the Boston Bruins on June 21, in a trade for Ken Linseman, was Mike Krushelnyski. Krushelnyski, playing for most of the season on a line with Wayne Gretzky and Jari Kurri, scored a career high 88 points.

Also picked up by Sather was center Bill Carroll, who had signed a free agent contract at the beginning of the season. Carroll had played on three Cup winning teams with the Islanders and would help the Oilers win their second Cup this year. Midway through the season Mark Napier was obtained from Minnesota and played in parts of three seasons with the Oilers. Playing on a line with Messier and Anderson he would also be instrumental in helping the team defend the Cup.

The 1984-85 season saw the team get off to a record start. Of their first 15 games the Oilers won 12 and tied 3 to set a new league standard for the longest undefeated streak from the start of a season. This eclipsed a 40-year-old record set by Montreal, who had won 11 and tied 3 in the 1943-44 season. The Oilers had a record of 40–10–6 (.768) at the All-Star break.

The team finished atop the much improved Smythe

Division again this season, with 109 points, four points behind the Flyers in the overall league standings. For the fourth consecutive season Edmonton scored more than 400 goals; they remain the only team in league history to reach the 400 goal plateau. The Oilers showed a marked improvement defensively finishing eighth in goals allowed.

Injuries did not play a major part in the team's fortunes this year as most of the star players except for Mark Messier remained injury free during the season. Messier missed 15 games in November and December due to stretched ligaments in his left knee and also received a 10 game suspension for injuring Calgary's Jamie Macoun in a fight December 26. Star winger Jari Kurri also missed three games in January with a bruised tailbone and four games in late March due to a broken bone in his hand. The goaltending corps however did have a few injury problems as Grant Fuhr was out almost a month with a partial separation of the shoulder and Andy Moog sat out the last month of the season with a knee injury.

Wayne Gretzky won his fifth consecutive scoring title, registering 208 points, 73 points ahead of teammate Jari Kurri, Paul Coffey with 121 points was the third member of the Oilers to finish in the top ten in scoring. All three players would make this year's first All-Star Team.

The Oilers won only four of their final ten regular season games, and it looked as if their plans for of a second Stanley Cup title had derailed. The team though got the tonic it needed when they met the Los Angeles Kings in the first round of the playoffs. The Kings had finished 27 points below Edmonton in the Smythe Division and were no match for the powerful Oilers. Winning the series against Los Angeles in three straight games, they then met Winnipeg in the Division finals, defeating the Jets in four straight games. After sweeping the first two series the Oilers met Chicago in the conference finals.

1985 Stanley Cup Parade (EA340-1755 City of Edmonton Archives.)

Edmonton won the first two games against the Black Hawks, outscoring them 18–5, but then the team's nine game postseason winning streak came to an end, as Chicago won the next two games at home. Back in the friendly confines of Northlands Coliseum the Oilers again dominated Chicago, outscoring them 18–7 in the final two games.

The Oilers then met league champion Philadelphia in the championship series. After being defeated 4–1 in Philadelphia in the opening game the Oilers won the final four games to capture their second Stanley Cup.

1984-85 Regular Season Scoring

#		Ht.	Wt.	Age	GP	G	A	Pts.	Shots	SH%	GW	GT	PP	SH	P/M	PIM
99	Gretzky (C)	72	170	23	80	73	135	208	358	20.4	7	2	8	11	98	52
17	Kurri	72	188	24	73	71	64	135	261	27.2	13	3	14	3	77	30
7	Coffey	72	203	23	80	37	84	121	284	13.0	6	0	12	2	55	97
26	Krushelnyski	74	200	24	80	43	45	88	187	23.0	4	1	13	0	56	60
9	Anderson	71	180	24	80	42	39	81	258	16.3	6	0	12	1	24	69
11	Messier	72	207	23	55	23	31	54	136	16.9	1	0	4	5	9	57
22	Huddy	72	200	25	80	7	44	51	146	4.8	1	1	3	0	50	46
12	Hunter	71	200	26	80	17	19	36	119	14.3	1	0	1	1	0	122
18	Napier	70	185	27	33	9	26	35	50	18.0	0	1	3	0	12	19
19	Lindstrom	73	185	33	80	12	20	32	98	12.2	1	0	1	0	5	18
16	Hughes	71	190	29	73	12	13	25	98	12.2	0	0	1	1	-7	85
4	Lowe	73	191	25	80	4	21	25	83	4.8	1	0	1	0	11	104
24	McClelland	72	190	22	62	8	15	23	96	8.3	3	0	0	0	-11	205
21	Gregg	76	212	28	57	3	20	23	58	5.2	0	0	0	0	28	32
29	Jackson	75	210	28	78	3	17	20	47	6.4	0	0	0	0	28	141
27	Semenko	75	210	27	69	6	12	18	50	12.0	1	0	0	0	5	172
2	Fogolin	72	203	29	79	4	13	17	63	6.3	1	0	0	1	17	126
20	Carroll	70	190	25	65	8	9	17	44	18.2	1	0	0	0	0	22
8	Sherven	72	185	21	37	9	7	16	49	18.4	1	0	1	0	-2	10
10	Pouzar	71	202	32	33	4	8	12	36	11.1	1	0	0	0	3	28
28	Melnyk	72	180	24	28	0	11	11	8	0.0	0	0	0	0	12	25

#		*Ht.*	*Wt.*	*Age*	*GP*	*G*	*A*	*Pts.*	*Shots*	*SH%*	*GW*	*GT*	*PP*	*SH*	*P/M*	*PIM*
23	Habscheid	72	180	21	26	5	3	8	30	16.7	0	0	2	0	-2	4
8	Lumley	71	180	30	12	1	3	4	10	10.0	0	0	0	0	-1	13
25	Summanen	71	185	22	9	0	4	4	5	0.0	0	0	0	0	-1	0
31	Fuhr	70	185	22	46	0	3	3	0	0.0	0	0	0	0	0	6
18	Martin	71	195	29	4	0	2	2	6	0.0	0	0	0	0	3	0
33	Baron	71	180	25	1	0	0	0	0	0.0	0	0	0	0	0	0
32	Reaugh	76	190	19	1	0	0	0	0	0.0	0	0	0	0	0	0
14	Cote	71	165	23	2	0	0	0	1	0.0	0	0	0	0	0	2
5	S. Smith	74	200	21	2	0	0	0	3	0.0	0	0	0	0	-2	2
30	Zanier	71	183	22	3	0	0	0	0	0.0	0	0	0	0	0	0
35	Moog	69	170	24	39	0	0	0	0	0.0	0	0	0	0	0	8
	Bench															12
		72	190	25	80	401	668	1069	2584	15.5	49	8	76	25	105	1567

1984-85 Goaltender Records

	GP	*Min.*	*GA*	*W*	*L*	*T*	*Ave.*	*SA*	*Pct.*	*SO*	*EN*
Andy Moog	39	2019	111	22	9	3	3.30	1050	0.894	1.5	1
Marco Baron	1	33	2	0	1	0	3.64	9	0.778	0	0
Grant Fuhr	46	2559	165	26	8	7	3.87	1426	0.884	1.5	1
Mike Zanier	3	185	12	1	1	1	3.89	100	0.880	0	0
Daryl Reaugh	1	60	5	0	1	0	5.00	35	0.853	0	1
	80	4856	298	49	20	11	3.68	2620	0.886	3	3

Coach: Glen Sather 49-20-11

1984-85 Scoring vs. Opposition

	Bost.	*Buff.*	*Calg.*	*Chi.*	*Det.*	*Hart.*	*L.A.*	*Minn.*	*Mont.*	*N.J.*
Anderson	2–0–2	3–0–3	2–2–4	6–0–6	1–2–3	0–2–2	2–5–7	3–0–3	1–0–1	1–1–2
Carroll	1–1–2	0–0–0	0–0–0	0–0–0	0–0–0	0–0–0	0–3–3	1–1–2	0–1–1	0–0–0
Coffey	1–2–3	0–6–6	7–11–18	4–4–8	0–4–4	2–6–8	5–6–11	2–3–5	0–1–1	0–1–1
Cote	———	0–0–0	———	———	———	———	———	———	———	———
Fogolin	0–1–1	0–1–1	0–1–1	0–1–1	0–0–0	0–0–0	0–3–3	1–0–1	0–2–2	0–0–0
Gregg	0–2–2	0–0–0	0–2–2	0–2–2	0–0–0	1–1–2	0–0–0	0–1–1	0–0–0	0–0–0
Gretzky	2–4–6	3–4–7	7–14–21	1–7–8	4–9–13	2–6–8	7–16–23	4–4–8	2–2–4	1–6–7
Habscheid	0–0–0	———	0–0–0	———	———	0–0–0	———	0–0–0	———	0–1–1
Huddy	0–1–1	1–2–3	0–3–3	2–0–2	1–2–3	0–2–2	1–4–5	0–2–2	0–0–0	0–1–1
Hughes	0–1–1	0–1–1	1–3–4	0–0–0	0–0–0	1–0–1	2–3–5	0–0–0	0–0–0	0–0–0
Hunter	1–1–2	0–1–1	2–0–2	0–2–2	1–0–1	1–2–3	3–0–3	0–1–1	0–2–2	0–0–0
Jackson	0–1–1	0–1–1	0–0–0	0–1–1	0–2–2	0–2–2	2–2–4	0–0–0	1–1–2	0–0–0
Krushelnyski	1–1–2	1–1–2	4–6–10	1–0–1	4–1–5	4–0–4	4–6–10	1–2–3	1–1–2	3–1–4
Kurri	4–2–6	2–3–5	8–7–15	1–0–1	5–5–10	3–1–4	6–12–18	2–1–3	1–1–2	4–2–6
Lindstrom	0–0–0	0–0–0	1–0–1	0–2–2	0–1–1	0–1–1	3–0–3	2–2–4	0–0–0	0–0–0
Lowe	1–0–1	0–0–0	1–1–2	0–4–4	0–1–1	0–1–1	1–0–1	0–0–0	0–0–0	0–0–0
Lumley	———	0–0–0	———	0–1–1	0–2–2	———	1–0–1	0–0–0	———	———
Martin	———	———	———	———	———	———	———	———	———	0–0–0
McClelland	1–1–2	0–0–0	2–2–4	1–0–1	0–0–0	0–1–1	0–1–1	0–1–1	1–1–2	0–0–0
Melnyk	———	0–0–0	0–2–2	0–1–1	0–0–0	0–1–1	0–2–2	0–0–0	0–0–0	0–0–0
Messier	0–0–0	4–1–5	3–3–6	0–3–3	1–3–4	0–1–1	2–3–5	1–0–1	0–0–0	0–0–0
Napier	0–1–1	0–3–3	1–3–4	0–3–3	1–1–2	2–1–3	1–4–5	0–1–	0–0–0	0–1–1
Pouzar	0–1–1	0–0–0	0–0–0	0–0–0	———	1–2–3	1–0–1	———	0–1–1	0–0–0
Semenko	0–0–0	1–0–1	0–0–0	0–0–0	1–0–1	0–0–0	0–1–1	0–3–3	1–0–1	0–0–0
Sherven	0–0–0	———	0–1–1	1–0–1	0–0–0	0–0–0	———	1–1–2	0–1–1	0–0–0
Smith	———	———	———	———	0–0–0	———	———	———	———	———
Summanen	———	———	0–1–1	———	———	0–0–0	0–0–0	———	———	———

	NYI.	*NYR.*	*Phil.*	*Pitt.*	*Que.*	*St.L.*	*Tor.*	*Van.*	*Wash.*	*Winn.*
Anderson	0–3–3	1–2–3	2–1–3	2–2–4	0–1–1	2–2–4	3–1–4	5–7–12	1–3–4	5–5–10
Carroll	1–0–1	1–0–1	0–0–0	0–1–1	2–0–2	0–1–1	0–1–1	1–0–1	0–0–0	1–0–1
Coffey	2–3–5	1–3–4	4–1–5	0–3–3	2–3–5	2–3–5	0–3–3	3–13–16	0–2–2	2–6–8
Cote	———	———	———	0–0–0	———	———	———	———	———	———
Fogolin	0–0–0	0–0–0	0–0–0	0–0–0	1–0–1	0–0–0	0–0–0	1–1–2	0–1–1	1–2–3

	NYI.	*NYR.*	*Phil.*	*Pitt.*	*Que.*	*St.L.*	*Tor.*	*Van.*	*Wash.*	*Winn.*
Gregg	0–0–0	0–1–1	0–0–0	0–0–0	0–2–2	0–0–0	0–2–2	1–3–4	0–1–1	1–3–4
Gretzky	3–6–9	3–2–5	2–4–6	4–4–8	3–6–9	7–5–12	6–5–11	4–11–15	2–7–9	6–13–19
Habscheid	0–0–0	0–1–1	———	0–0–0	———	0–0–0	0–0–0	2–13	———	3–0–3
Huddy	0–2–2	0–4–4	0–3–3	0–2–2	0–3–3	2–2–4	0–1–1	0–4–4	0–0–0	0–6–6
Hughes	1–0–1	0–1–1	0–0–0	0–1–1	1–0–1	1–0–1	1–0–1	2–1–3	1–0–1	1–2–3
Hunter	1–0–1	2–0–2	0–0–0	0–1–1	1–4–5	1–1–2	1–1–2	1–2–3	0–0–0	2–1–3
Jackson	0–0–0	0–1–1	0–0–0	0–0–0	0–3–3	0–0–0	0–0–0	0–2–2	0–0–0	0–0–0
Krushelnyski	2–3–5	4–2–6	0–2–2	2–1–3	1–2–3	2–3–5	3–3–6	2–4–6	2–0–2	1–6–7
Kurri	4–4–8	2–2–4	2–2–4	1–3–4	3–2–5	1–6–7	3–4–7	6–3–9	4–1–5	9–3–12
Lindstrom	0–0–0	0–1–1	0–1–1	1–0–1	0–0–0	0–3–3	0–0–0	3–4–7	1–2–3	1–3–4
Lowe	0–1–1	0–1–1	0–1–1	0–0–0	0–1–1	0–0–0	0–2–2	1–2–3	0–2–2	0–4–4
Lumley	———	0–0–0	0–0–0	———	———	———	0–0–0	———	———	0–0–0
Martin	———	———	———	0–0–0	0–2–2	———	———	———	———	———
McClelland	0–0–0	0–0–0	0–0–0	1–0–1	0–1–1	0–1–1	0–1–1	1–1–2	0–1–1	1–3–4
Melnyk	0–0–0	0–2–2	———	0–0–0	0–0–0	0–1–1	0–0–0	0–1–1	0–0–0	0–1–1
Messier	2–0–2	1–0–1	1–1–2	0–0–0	0–0–0	1–3–4	0–4–4	5–2–7	0–1–1	2–6–8
Napier	0–1–1	0–2–2	0–1–1	1–0–1	1–1–2	———	1–2–3	0–1–1	1–0–1	0–0–0
Pouzar	0–0–0	0–0–0	0–1–1	0–0–0	0–0–0	0–1–1	———	0–0–0	0–1–1	2–1–3
Semenko	0–0–0	0–1–1	0–1–1	0–0–0	1–2–3	1–0–1	0–1–1	0–2–2	0–1–1	1–0–1
Sherven	0–0–0	———	0–0–0	0–0–0	3–0–3	0–0–0	1–0–1	0–2–2	2–1–3	1–1–2
Smith	———	———	———	———	———	———	———	0–0–0	———	———
Summanen	0–0–0	0–1–1	———	0–1–1	———	———	———	0–1–1	———	———

1984-85 Goaltender Records vs. Opposition

	GP	*Min.*	*GA*	*EN*	*SO*	*Ave.*	*W-L-T*	*Opposition*
Marco Baron	1	33	2	0	0	3.64	0–1–0	Los Angeles
Grant Fuhr	2	80	5	0	0	3.00	1–0–0	Boston
	3	185	12	0	0	3.89	2–0–1	Buffalo
	5	285	18	0	0	3.79	3–0–1	Calgary
	3	180	9	0	0	3.00	3–0–0	Chicago
	1	60	6	0	0	6.00	1–0–0	Detroit
	2	100	8	0	0	4.80	1–1–0	Hartford
	6	352	24	0	0	4.09	3–2–1	Los Angeles
	2	120	8	0	0	4.00	2–0–0	Minnesota
	2	120	5	1	0	2.50	1–1–0	Montreal
	1	26	3	0	0	6.92	0–1–0	New Jersey
	3	185	12	0	0	3.89	2–0–1	N.Y. Islanders
	1	20	6	0	0	18.00	0–0–0	N.Y. Rangers
	2	125	6	0	0	2.88	1–0–1	Pittsburgh
	2	100	2	0	0	1.20	1–0–0	Quebec
	1	60	6	0	0	6.00	1–0–0	St. Louis
	2	84	4	0	0	2.86	0–0–1	Toronto
	5	310	18	0	1	3.48	2–2–1	Vancouver
	1	60	5	0	0	5.00	1–0–0	Washington
	2	111	8	0	0	4.32	1–1–0	Winnipeg
Andy Moog	2	100	5	0	0	3.00	1–1–0	Boston
	3	140	8	0	0	3.43	2–1–0	Calgary
	2	120	8	0	0	4.00	2–0–0	Detroit
	2	80	5	0	0	3.75	1–0–0	Hartford
	3	100	9	0	0	5.40	1–0–0	Los Angeles
	1	60	3	0	0	3.00	1–0–0	Minnesota
	1	60	4	0	0	4.00	0–1–0	Montreal
	3	154	6	0	0	2.34	2–0–0	New Jersey
	2	100	3	0	0	1.80	1–1–0	N.Y. Rangers
	3	180	16	1	0	5.33	0–3–0	Philadelphia
	1	60	4	0	0	4.00	0–1–0	Pittsburgh
	2	80	3	0	0	2.25	2–0–0	Quebec
	2	120	3	0	0	1.50	2–0–0	St. Louis
	2	101	4	0	0	2.38	2–0–0	Toronto
	2	125	4	0	1	1.92	1–0–1	Vancouver
	2	130	6	0	0	2.77	0–0–2	Washington
	6	309	20	0	0	3.88	4–1–0	Winnipeg
Daryl Reaugh	1	60	5	0	0	5.00	0–1–0	Winnipeg

	GP	Min.	GA	EN	SO	Ave.	W–L–T	Opposition
Mike Zanier	1	60	3	0	0	3.00	1–0–0	Calgary
	1	65	3	0	0	2.77	0–0–1	N.Y. Rangers
	1	60	6	0	0	6.00	0–1–0	Vancouver

1984-85 Schedule Results

Date	Visitor			Home	
Oct. 11	Edmonton	2	at	Los Angeles	2 OT
Oct. 12	St. Louis	1	at	Edmonton	5
Oct. 14	Quebec	2	at	Edmonton	9
Oct. 16	Boston	2	at	Edmonton	7
Oct. 18	Edmonton	7	at	Minnesota	5
Oct. 19	Edmonton	7	at	Winnipeg	4
Oct. 21	Calgary	4	at	Edmonton	6
Oct. 24	Washington	3	at	Edmonton	3 OT
Oct. 26	Los Angeles	2	at	Edmonton	8
Oct. 30	Vancouver	0	at	Edmonton	7
Nov. 2	Chicago	2	at	Edmonton	4
Nov. 4	Edmonton	2	at	Winnipeg	1
Nov. 6	Edmonton	3	at	Pittsburgh	3 OT
Nov. 8	Edmonton	3	at	New Jersey	2
Nov. 9	Edmonton	8	at	Washington	5
Nov. 11	Edmonton	5	at	Philadelphia	7
Nov. 14	Montreal	4	at	Edmonton	2
Nov. 15	Edmonton	2	at	Calgary	6
Nov. 17	Vancouver	0	at	Edmonton	7
Nov. 21	Winnipeg	5	at	Edmonton	7
Nov. 24	St. Louis	6	at	Edmonton	7
Nov. 27	Edmonton	7	at	Toronto	1
Nov. 29	Edmonton	4	at	Boston	2
Nov. 30	Edmonton	4	at	Hartford	2
Dec. 5	Islanders	4	at	Edmonton	6
Dec. 7	Minnesota	3	at	Edmonton	6
Dec. 8	Edmonton	2	at	Vancouver	3 OT
Dec. 13	Edmonton	2	at	Los Angeles	7
Dec. 15	Edmonton	8	at	St. Louis	2
Dec. 17	Edmonton	2	at	New Jersey	5
Dec. 19	Los Angeles	3	at	Edmonton	7
Dec. 21	Vancouver	3	at	Edmonton	1
Dec. 22	Calgary	1	at	Edmonton	7
Dec. 26	Edmonton	5	at	Calgary	6
Dec. 29	Detroit	3	at	Edmonton	6
Dec. 30	Edmonton	7	at	Vancouver	7OT
Jan. 2	Philadelphia	5	at	Edmonton	2
Jan. 4	Winnipeg	4	at	Edmonton	7
Jan. 6	Edmonton	7	at	Winnipeg	2
Jan. 8	Edmonton	4	at	Quebec	0
Jan. 10	Edmonton	5	at	Montreal	2
Jan. 12	Edmonton	3	at	Pittsburgh	4
Jan. 13	Edmonton	5	at	Buffalo	4
Jan. 16	Islanders	3	at	Edmonton	3 OT
Jan. 18	Edmonton	4	at	Vancouver	4 OT
Jan. 19	Vancouver	5	at	Edmonton	7
Jan. 21	Los Angeles	7	at	Edmonton	8
Jan. 25	New Jersey	2	at	Edmonton	4
Jan. 26	Pittsburgh	3	at	Edmonton	6
Jan. 28	Calgary	3	at	Edmonton	4
Jan. 29	Edmonton	4	at	Calgary	2
Feb. 2	Rangers	1	at	Edmonton	5
Feb. 3	Hartford	3	at	Edmonton	6
Feb. 6	Edmonton	2	at	Winnipeg	6
Feb. 8	Edmonton	5	at	Minnesota	3
Feb. 9	Edmonton	6	at	Detroit	5
Feb. 15	Edmonton	7	at	Rangers	8
Feb. 16	Edmonton	4	at	Philadelphia	5
Feb. 18	Edmonton	6	at	Buffalo	4
Feb. 19	Edmonton	9	at	Toronto	4
Feb. 22	Quebec	3	at	Edmonton	6
Feb. 23	Washington	3	at	Edmonton	3 OT
Feb. 27	Montreal	4	at	Edmonton	1
Mar. 1	Los Angeles	5	at	Edmonton	4
Mar. 3	Winnipeg	6	at	Edmonton	3
Mar. 5	Edmonton	5	at	Calgary	3
Mar. 9	Rangers	3	at	Edmonton	3 OT
Mar. 10	Edmonton	3	at	Vancouver	6
Mar. 13	Detroit	6	at	Edmonton	7
Mar. 15	Buffalo	4	at	Edmonton	4 OT
Mar. 17	Edmonton	4	at	Los Angeles	5
Mar. 20	Chicago	4	at	Edmonton	6
Mar. 22	Toronto	3	at	Edmonton	3 OT
Mar. 26	Edmonton	7	at	Islanders	5
Mar. 28	Edmonton	3	at	Boston	6
Mar. 29	Edmonton	7	at	Hartford	8
Mar. 31	Edmonton	7	at	Chicago	3
April 2	Edmonton	6	at	Los Angeles	4
April 5	Calgary	5	at	Edmonton	5 OT
April 6	Winnipeg	6	at	Edmonton	5

Opponent	*Home W–L–T*	*Road W–L–T*
Boston	1–0–0	1–1–0
Buffalo	0–0–1	2–0–0
Calgary	3–0–1	3–1–0
Chicago	2–0–0	1–0–0
Detroit	2–0–0	1–0–0
Hartford	1–0–0	1–1–0
Los Angeles	3–1–0	1–2–1
Minnesota	1–0–0	2–0–0
Montreal	0–2–0	1–0–0
New Jersey	1–0–0	1–1–0
Islanders	1–0–1	1–0–0
Rangers	1–0–1	0–1–0
Philadelphia	0–1–0	0–2–0
Pittsburgh	1–0–0	0–1–1
Quebec	2–0–0	1–0–0
St. Louis	2–0–0	1–0–0
Toronto	0–0–1	2–0–0
Vancouver	3–1–0	0–2–2
Washington	0–0–2	1–0–0
Winnipeg	2–2–0	3–1–0

Opponent	*Overall W–L–T*	*GF–GA*
Boston	2–1–0	14–10
Buffalo	2–0–1	15–12
Calgary	6–1–1	39–29
Chicago	3–0–0	17–9
Detroit	3–0–0	19–14
Hartford	2–1–0	17–13
Los Angeles	4–3–1	41–35

Opponent	*Overall W–L–T*	*GF–GA*
Minnesota	3–0–0	18–11
Montreal	1–2–0	8–10
New Jersey	2–1–0	9–9
Islanders	2–0–1	16–12
Rangers	1–1–1	15–12
Philadelphia	0–3–0	11–17
Pittsburgh	1–1–1	12–10
Quebec	3–0–0	19–5
St. Louis	3–0–0	20–9
Toronto	2–0–1	19–8
Vancouver	3–3–2	38–28
Washington	1–0–2	14–11
Winnipeg	5–3–0	40–34

1984-85 Playoff Scoring

#		*GP*	*G*	*A*	*Pts.*	*Shots*	*SH%*	*GW*	*OT*	*PP*	*SH*	*P/M*	*PIM*
99	Wayne Gretzky	18	17	30	47	67	25.4	3	0	4	2	28	4
7	Paul Coffey	18	12	25	37	66	18.2	4	0	3	1	26	44
17	Jari Kurri	18	19	12	31	89	21.3	2	0	1	2	24	6
9	Glenn Anderson	18	10	16	26	47	21.3	1	1	2	0	11	38
11	Mark Messier	18	12	13	25	56	21.4	1	0	1	1	13	12
22	Charlie Huddy	18	3	17	20	50	6.0	0	0	1	0	20	17
26	Mike Krushelnyski	18	5	8	13	37	13.5	2	0	2	0	9	22
18	Mark Napier	18	5	5	10	20	25.0	0	0	1	0	8	7
12	Dave Hunter	18	2	5	7	31	6.5	0	0	0	0	5	33
19	Willy Lindstrom	18	5	1	6	20	25.0	1	0	0	0	4	8
21	Randy Gregg	17	0	6	6	17	0.0	0	0	0	0	19	12
4	Kevin Lowe	16	0	5	5	20	0.0	0	0	0	0	5	8
2	Lee Fogolin	18	3	1	4	10	30.0	1	1	0	0	8	16
28	Larry Melnyk	12	1	3	4	15	6.7	0	0	0	0	10	26
24	Kevin McClelland	18	1	3	4	22	4.5	0	0	0	0	4	75
10	Jaroslav Pouzar	9	2	1	3	12	16.7	0	0	0	0	2	2
31	Grant Fuhr	18	0	3	3	0	0.0	0	0	0	0	0	2
16	Pat Hughes	10	1	1	2	3	33.3	0	0	0	0	1	4
35	Andy Moog	2	0	0	0	0	0.0	0	0	0	0	0	0
14	Esa Tikkanen	3	0	0	0	3	0.0	0	0	0	0	-1	2
8	Dave Lumley	8	0	0	0	2	0.0	0	0	0	0	-5	29
20	Bill Carroll	9	0	0	0	4	0.0	0	0	0	0	3	4
29	Don Jackson	9	0	0	0	6	0.0	0	0	0	0	4	64
27	Dave Semenko	14	0	0	0	5	0.0	0	0	0	0	2	39
		18	98	155	253	602	16.3	15	2	15	6	30	474

1984-85 Playoff Goaltending

	GP	*Min.*	*GA*	*W*	*L*	*Ave.*	*SA*	*Pct.*	*SO*	*EN*
Andy Moog	2	20	0	0	0	0.00	3	1.000	0	0
Grant Fuhr	18	1064	55	15	3	3.10	522	0.894	0	2
	18	1084	57	15	3	3.17	525	0.891	0	2

Date			*Result*			*Winning Goaltender*	*Winning Goal*
April 10, 1985	Los Angeles	2	at	Edmonton	3	Grant Fuhr	Lee Fogolin[1]
April 11, 1985	Los Angeles	2	at	Edmonton	4	Grant Fuhr	Mike Krushelnyski
April 13, 1985	Edmonton	4	at	Los Angeles	3	Grant Fuhr	Glenn Anderson[2]
April 18, 1985	Winnipeg	2	at	Edmonton	4	Grant Fuhr	Paul Coffey
April 20, 1985	Winnipeg	2	at	Edmonton	5	Grant Fuhr	Paul Coffey
April 23, 1985	Edmonton	5	at	Winnipeg	4	Grant Fuhr	Wayne Gretzky
April 25, 1985	Edmonton	8	at	Winnipeg	3	Grant Fuhr	Jari Kurri
May 4, 1985	Chicago	2	at	Edmonton	11	Grant Fuhr	Paul Coffey
May 7, 1985	Chicago	3	at	Edmonton	7	Grant Fuhr	Jari Kurri
May 9, 1985	Edmonton	2	at	Chicago	5	Murray Bannerman	Darryl Sutter
May 12, 1985	Edmonton	6	at	Chicago	8	Murray Bannerman	Steve Larmer
May 14, 1985	Chicago	5	at	Edmonton	10	Grant Fuhr	Wayne Gretzky
May 16, 1985	Edmonton	8	at	Chicago	2	Grant Fuhr	Mark Messier
May 21, 1985	Edmonton	1	at	Philadelphia	4	Pelle Lindbergh	Ron Sutter
May 23, 1985	Edmonton	3	at	Philadelphia	1	Grant Fuhr	Willy Lindstrom
May 25, 1985	Philadelphia	3	at	Edmonton	4	Grant Fuhr	Mike Krushelnyski
May 28, 1985	Philadelphia	3	at	Edmonton	5	Grant Fuhr	Wayne Gretzky
May 30, 1985	Philadelphia	3	at	Edmonton	8	Grant Fuhr	Paul Coffey

[1]3:01 of overtime
[2]00:46 of overtime

1984-85 Stanley Cup Winning Game

May 30, 1985: Northlands Coliseum, Edmonton Attendance: 17,498

Oilers

Starting Lineup: **31**-Grant Fuhr (Goal), **4**-Kevin Lowe (Defense), **2**-Lee Fogolin (Defense), **9**-Glenn Anderson (Left Wing), **11**-Mark Messier (Center), **18**-Mark Napier (Right Wing).

Remaining Players: **20**-Billy Carroll, **7**-Paul Coffey, **21**-Randy Gregg, **99**-Wayne Gretzky, **22**-Charlie Huddy, **16**-Pat Hughes, **12**-Dave Hunter, **29**-Don Jackson, **26**-Mike Krushelnyski, **17**-Jari Kurri, **19**-Willy Lindstrom, **24**-Kevin McClelland, **27**-Dave Semenko, **35**-Andy Moog (backup goaltender).

Average: Age-25.6 years, Height-72.3 inches, Weight-194.7 pounds, Years Experience-3.57 years

Flyers

Starting Lineup: **35**-Bob Froese (Goal), **8**-Brad Marsh (Defense), **3**-Doug Crossman (Defense), **6**-Joe Paterson (Left Wing), **25**-Peter Zezel (Center), **32**-Murray Craven (Right Wing).

Remaining Players: **42**-Todd Bergen, **21**-Dave Brown, **9**-Miroslav Dvorak, **27**-Thomas Eriksson, **17**-Ed Hospodar, **2**-Mark Howe, **20**-Dave Poulin, **26**-Brian Propp, **23**-Ilka Sinisalo, **24**-Derek Smith, **15**-Rich Sutter, **14**-Ron Sutter, **22**-Rick Tocchet, **33**-Darren Jensen (backup goaltender).

Average: Age-24.8 years, Height-72.5 inches, Weight-189.5 pounds, Years Experience-2.15 years

Officials

Referee: Bryan Lewis, Linesmen: Leon Stickle, Ron Finn

Game Summary

1st Period

Goals: Edmonton-Kurri (Gretzky, Huddy) 4:54
Edmonton-Lindstrom (Messier) 5:31
Philadelphia-Rich Sutter (Smith) 7:23
Edmonton-Coffey (Gretzky) 15:31
Edmonton-Coffey (Huddy, Kurri) PP 17:57

Penalties: Edmonton (Don Jackson-slashing)-1:03, Philadelphia (Dave Brown-slashing)-1:03, Philadelphia-(Hospodar-holding)-8:45, Edmonton (Jackson-roughing)-15:40, Philadelphia (Doug Crossman -hooking)-16:47

2nd Period

Goals: Edmonton-Messier (unassisted) 9:18
Edmonton-Krushelnyski (Gretzky, Kurri) 10:20
Edmonton-Gretzky (Kurri, Coffey) 16:49

Penalties: Philadelphia (Rick Tocchet-slashing)-3:43, Philadelphia (Rick Tocchet-holding)-6:44, Edmonton (Mark Messier-hooking)-7:05, Edmonton (Kevin McClelland-roughing)-12:23, Philadelphia (Rich Sutter-cross-checking)-12:23 Edmonton (Glenn Anderson-roughing) 15:36, Philadelphia (Paterson-roughing)-15:36, Philadelphia (Dave Brown-roughing) 19:55, Edmonton (Kevin McClelland-roughing)-19:55

3rd period

Goals: Philadelphia-Propp (Howe, Poulin) 1:59 PP
Edmonton-Messier (unassisted) 3:39
Philadelphia-Rich Sutter (Smith) 7:05

Penalties: Edmonton (Messier-hooking)-00:38, Edmonton (Coffey-roughing)-1:55, Philadelphia (Zezel-roughing)-1:55, Edmonton (Jackson-tripping)-3:57, Edmonton (Lowe-highsticking)-8:23, Philadelphia (Craven-hooking)-12:28, Philadelphia (Froese-slashing, served by Rich Sutter) 12:38, Philadelphia (Brown-5 minutes for fighting, 10 minute misconduct) 15:22, Philadelphia (Brad Marsh-5 minutes for fighting, 10 minute misconduct, game misconduct) 15:22, Edmonton (Don Jackson-4 minutes for roughing, 10 minute misconduct) 15:22, Edmonton McClelland (5 minutes for fighting, 10 minute misconduct, game misconduct) 15:22

Shots on Goal: Edmonton 12-17-12-41
Philadelphia 7-8-7-22

Note: At 12:51 of the third period Grant Fuhr stopped Dave Poulin on a penalty shot.

Table 6. Oilers All Time Regular Season Penalty Killing Record

Year	*Dis*	*PPGA*	*Road* *%*	*SHGF*	*Dis*	*PPGA*	*Home* *%*	*SHGF*	*Dis*	*PPGA*	*Overall* *%*	*SHGF*	*Rank*
2001	*204*	*38*	*81.4*	*7*	*169*	*23*	*86.4*	*6*	*373*	*61*	*83.6*	*13*	*16th*
2000	*188*	*25*	*86.7*	*3*	*179*	*29*	*83.8*	*6*	*367*	*54*	*85.3*	*9*	*T10*
1999	*204*	*32*	*84.3*	*1*	*170*	*35*	*79.4*	*7*	*374*	*67*	*82.1*	*8*	*21st*
1998	*203*	*28*	*86.2*	*2*	*203*	*38*	*81.3*	*8*	*406*	*66*	*83.7*	*10*	*22nd*
1997	*173*	*31*	*82.1*	*6*	*165*	*28*	*83.0*	*3*	*338*	*59*	*82.5*	*9*	*18th*
1996	*213*	*46*	*78.4*	*7*	*204*	*34*	*83.3*	*3*	*417*	*80*	*80.8*	*10*	*18th*
1995	*115*	*27*	*76.5*	*3*	*118*	*25*	*78.8*	*5*	*233*	*52*	*77.7*	*8*	*25th*
1994	*211*	*42*	*80.1*	*0*	*190*	*36*	*81.1*	*2*	*401*	*78*	*80.5*	*2*	*T20*
1993	*243*	*56*	*77.0*	*10*	*221*	*50*	*77.4*	*7*	*464*	*106*	*77.2*	*17*	*21st*
1992	*236*	*57*	*75.8*	*6*	*187*	*36*	*80.7*	*6*	*423*	*93*	*78.0*	*12*	*21st*
1991	*195*	*41*	*79.0*	*8*	*193*	*39*	*79.8*	*5*	*388*	*80*	*79.4*	*13*	*15th*
1990	*220*	*45*	*79.5*	*9*	*197*	*37*	*81.2*	*13*	*417*	*82*	*80.3*	*22*	*T10*
1989	*242*	*48*	*80.2*	*14*	*210*	*30*	*85.7*	*13*	*452*	*78*	*82.7*	*27*	*2nd*
1988	*232*	*49*	*78.9*	*10*	*215*	*37*	*82.8*	*10*	*447*	*86*	*80.8*	*20*	*7th*
1987	*210*	*38*	*81.9*	*14*	*162*	*36*	*77.8*	*14*	*372*	*74*	*80.1*	*28*	*9th*
1986	*209*	*47*	*77.5*	*10*	*200*	*30*	*85.0*	*17*	*409*	*77*	*81.2*	*27*	*2nd*
1985	*179*	*44*	*75.4*	*6*	*174*	*32*	*81.6*	*19*	*353*	*76*	*78.5*	*25*	*5th*
1984	*200*	*41*	*79.5*	*20*	*186*	*36*	*80.6*	*16*	*386*	*77*	*80.1*	*36*	*9th*
1983	*214*	*54*	*74.8*	*18*	*182*	*35*	*80.8*	*4*	*396*	*89*	*77.5*	*22*	*10th*
1982									*371*	*67*	*81.9*	*12*	*T1*
1981	*180**	*44*	*75.6*	*7*	*170**	*41*	*75.9*	*6*	*348*	*85*	*75.6*	*13*	*T14*
1980									*315*	*74*	*76.5*	*11*	*14th*

*Estimate

1985-86

After finishing last season in second place, General Manager Glen Sather again chose late in the entry draft, held June 15 at the Toronto Convention Center. He had little luck until the ninth round, when he chose an 18-year-old left winger from the Moose Jaw Warriors of the Western Hockey League. While not blessed with the offensive talent of other Oiler stars, Kelly Buchberger would go on to play 12 seasons with the team, eventually becoming captain and helping them win two Stanley Cups.

Assistant coach Ted Green took a one year sabbatical to pursue business opportunities, and former Philadelphia Flyers head coach Bob McCammon joined the team to assist Sather and John Muckler behind the bench.

Glen Sather, seldom one to stand pat, made two significant additions to the team in the off-season. Signed to a free agent contract from the Boston Bruins was defensive center Craig MacTavish. MacTavish played on three Cup winners as an Oiler, chipping in more than his share of points even though he was often assigned to check the opponents' top lines.

Also obtained this year, in a trade with Pittsburgh, was Marty McSorley. McSorley was a versatile player who could play either on the wing or on defense and was a menacing presence on the ice. McSorley was part of two Cup winning teams and while thought of mainly as an enforcer, he would, in 1991 as a member of the Los Angeles Kings, be a co-winner (with Theo Fleury) of the league's plus/minus award.

The team got off to a good start this year winning their first five games and eight of their first ten. The team was 36–11–6 (.736) at the All-Star break and ended the season with 119 points. This equaled a team high. The Calgary Flames finished 30 points behind the Oilers in the Smythe Division. Edmonton again scored over 400 goals while allowing 310, which was only 13th best in the league.

Although a number of players sat out various amounts of time with injuries, the team's depth of talent meant that overall performance did not suffer. Mark Messier was out of the lineup for 17 games with a hairline fracture of his left foot, while Glenn Anderson sat out an eight game suspension. Mike Krushelnyski missed 17 games with a sprained knee suffered in a game against Chicago in early December, and after returning to the lineup for 13 games, missed nine more when the injury flared up again. Esa Tikkanen also missed 16 games from the middle of December to the middle of January with a broken bone in his right foot, while Don Jackson missed ten games with a cracked cheekbone suffered in a game against Detroit on February 11th. Goaltender Grant Fuhr again suffered a shoulder injury, missing ten games.

For the sixth consecutive year Wayne Gretzky won the Art Ross Trophy, tallying 215 points. His 163 assists alone would have allowed him to win the scoring title. Finishing third and fourth in scoring were Paul Coffey with 138 points and Jari Kurri with 131. Glenn Anderson also scored over 100 points.

Losing only five of their final 25 games the Oilers were poised to win their third consecutive Stanley Cup. The Oilers walked all over the Vancouver Canucks in the first round series. The Canucks, in losing all three games, were outscored 17–5 by Edmonton. In the next series versus Calgary the Oilers were continually playing catch-up hockey with the Flames. The Flames won games one, three, and five while Edmonton won games two, four and six. The teams met in the deciding game on April 30 in Edmonton.

With the score tied 2–2 early in the third period, rookie defenseman Steve Smith picked up the puck behind the Oiler net and attempted to clear it out of the zone. Unfortunately the puck hit the pads of goaltender Grant Fuhr and ricocheted into his own goal. While Smith will always carry the stigma of scoring on his own team, goaltender Grant Fuhr must also accept some of the blame. With no Calgary Flame in the Edmonton zone, Fuhr had taken his eyes off of the play and was looking up ice, paying no attention at all to the Oiler defenseman.

The Oilers could not score the equalizer and their quest for a third straight Cup had ended.

1985-86 Regular Season Scoring

#		*Ht.*	*Wt.*	*Age*	*GP*	*G*	*A*	*Pts.*	*Shots*	*SH%*	*GW*	*GT*	*PP*	*SH*	*P/M*	*PIM*
99	Gretzky (C)	72	170	24	80	52	163	215	350	14.9	6	1	11	3	71	46
7	Coffey	72	203	24	79	48	90	138	307	15.6	3	1	9	9	61	120
17	Kurri	72	188	25	78	68	63	131	236	28.8	9	1	16	6	45	22
9	Anderson	71	180	25	72	54	48	102	243	22.2	9	0	18	2	38	90
11	Messier (A)	72	207	24	63	35	49	84	201	17.4	7	0	10	5	36	68
18	Napier	70	185	28	80	24	32	56	117	20.5	4	1	3	1	13	14
14	MacTavish	72	185	27	74	23	24	47	121	19.0	5	0	4	1	17	70
22	Huddy	72	200	26	76	6	35	41	151	4.0	0	0	1	0	30	55
26	Krushelnyski	74	200	25	54	16	24	40	98	16.3	1	1	3	0	11	22
25	Summanen	71	185	23	73	19	18	37	83	22.9	4	0	1	0	7	16

#		Ht.	Wt.	Age	GP	G	A	Pts.	Shots	SH%	GW	GT	PP	SH	P/M	PIM
12	Hunter	71	200	27	62	15	22	37	110	13.6	1	0	0	0	37	77
24	McClelland	72	190	23	79	11	25	36	104	10.6	1	0	0	0	9	266
21	Gregg	76	212	29	64	2	26	28	55	3.6	0	0	0	0	30	47
2	Fogolin (A)	72	203	30	80	4	22	26	71	5.6	0	0	0	0	48	129
5	S. Smith	75	208	22	55	4	20	24	74	5.4	1	0	1	0	30	166
33	McSorley	73	190	22	59	11	12	23	72	15.3	2	0	0	0	9	265
20	Lumley	71	180	31	46	11	9	20	33	33.3	1	0	1	0	13	35
27	Semenko	75	210	28	69	6	12	18	51	11.8	0	0	0	0	0	141
4	Lowe	73	191	26	74	2	16	18	57	3.5	0	0	0	0	24	90
10	Tikkanen	71	185	20	35	7	6	13	44	15.9	2	0	0	0	5	28
29	Jackson	75	210	29	45	2	8	10	34	5.9	0	0	0	0	2	93
28	Melnyk	72	180	25	6	2	3	5	4	50.0	0	0	0	0	8	11
13	Jalo	71	185	23	3	0	3	3	3	0.0	0	0	0	0	2	0
8	Sherven	72	185	22	5	1	1	2	6	16.7	0	0	0	0	0	4
31	Fuhr	70	185	23	40	0	2	2	0	0.0	0	0	0	0	0	0
35	Moog	69	170	25	47	0	2	2	0	0.0	0	0	0	0	0	8
20	Carroll	70	190	26	5	0	2	2	0	0.0	0	0	0	0	2	0
19	Rogers	69	170	31	8	1	0	1	6	16.7	0	0	0	0	-2	0
28	Solheim	75	210	24	6	1	0	1	8	12.5	0	0	0	0	-2	5
15	Brubaker	74	210	27	4	1	0	1	4	25.0	0	0	0	0	1	12
34	Hopkins	73	210	26	1	0	0	0	0	0.0	0	0	0	0	0	0
15	Moller	72	190	23	1	0	0	0	2	0.0	0	0	0	0	0	0
16	Odelein	72	195	19	4	0	0	0	2	0.0	0	0	0	0	1	0
	Bench															28
		72	193	25	80	426	737	1163	2647	16.1	56	5	78	27	115	1928

1985-86 Goaltender Records

	GP	Min.	GA	W	L	T	Ave.	SA	Pct.	SO	EN
Andy Moog	47	2664	164	27	9	7	3.69	1480	0.889	1	2
Grant Fuhr	40	2184	143	29	8	0	3.93	1296	0.890	0	1
	80	4848	310	56	17	7	3.84	2776	0.888	1	3

Coach: Glen Sather 56-17-7

1985-86 Scoring vs. Opposition

	Bost.	Buff.	Calg.	Chi.	Det.	Hart.	L.A.	Minn.	Mont.	N.J.
Anderson	2–3–5	0–1–1	10–3–13	5–4–9	5–2–7	0–2–2	9–5–14	2–5–7	1–1–2	1–0–1
Brubaker	———	———	———	———	———	———	0–0–0	———	———	———
Carroll	———	———	———	0–1–1	———	———	0–0–0	———	———	———
Coffey	1–4–5	2–2–4	4–6–10	0–2–2	3–9–12	2–4–6	9–11–20	0–3–3	2–2–4	2–2–4
Fogolin	0–0–0	0–0–0	0–2–2	1–1–2	0–1–1	0–2–2	0–5–5	0–0–0	0–2–2	0–2–2
Gregg	0–1–1	0–0–0	0–2–2	0–3–3	0–1–1	0–0–0	1–5–6	0–0–0	0–0–0	0–0–0
Gretzky	2–5–7	1–4–5	4–20–24	0–8–8	1–8–9	3–6–9	6–21–27	1–5–6	3–5–8	1–7–8
Huddy	0–1–1	0–0–0	1–7–8	0–0–0	0–1–1	1–3–4	0–1–1	1–0–1	0–1–1	1–1–2
Hunter	0–0–0	0–0–0	0–3–3	0–1–1	0–0–0	1–0–1	1–2–3	0–0–0	0–1–1	0–1–1
Jackson	0–0–0	0–0–0	0–3–3	0–2–2	0–0–0	0–1–1	0–0–0	0–0–0	0–0–0	0–0–0
Jalo	———	———	———	———	0–2–2	———	———	———	———	———
Krushelnyski	0–0–0	1–0–1	0–1–1	1–0–1	1–1–2	0–1–1	1–5–6	1–0–1	1–1–2	2–1–3
Kurri	1–1–2	2–2–4	5–7–12	4–0–4	3–2–5	2–2–4	10–8–18	4–0–4	2–2–4	2–4–6
Lowe	0–2–2	1–0–1	0–0–0	0–1–1	0–0–0	0–0–0	0–3–3	0–1–1	0–0–0	0–0–0
Lumley	2–1–3	0–0–0	0–0–0	1–0–1	———	2–0–2	1–1–2	———	1–0–1	0–0–0
MacTavish	1–1–2	0–1–1	5–2–7	0–1–1	0–0–0	0–0–0	3–1–4	0–2–2	1–3–4	1–1–2
McClelland	0–0–0	0–1–1	2–1–3	1–4–5	1–2–3	0–2–2	0–1–1	0–1–1	0–0–0	0–2–2
McSorley	0–0–0	0–0–0	2–1–3	4–1–5	0–1–1	1–0–1	1–1–2	0–0–0	0–0–0	1–0–1
Melnyk	———	———	———	———	———	———	0–1–1	———	———	———
Messier	2–3–5	1–3–4	4–4–8	1–2–3	3–6–9	2–1–3	3–8–11	1–1–2	1–1–2	2–0–2
Napier	0–1–1	0–1–1	1–2–3	1–3–4	2–1–3	0–0–0	4–6–10	3–2–5	1–3–4	1–0–1
Odelein	0–0–0	0–0–0	———	———	———	———	———	———	———	———
Rogers	———	———	0–0–0	———	———	0–0–0	1–0–1	———	———	0–0–0
Semenko	1–0–1	0–0–0	0–0–0	1–0–1	0–1–1	1–0–1	0–2–2	0–0–0	0–1–1	0–0–0
Sherven	———	———	0–0–0	———	———	0–1–1	———	———	———	———
Smith	0–0–0	1–2–3	0–3–3	0–0–0	0–0–0	0–0–0	0–2–2	0–2–2	1–0–1	1–0–1

	Bost.	*Buff.*	*Calg.*	*Chi.*	*Det.*	*Hart.*	*L.A.*	*Minn.*	*Mont.*	*N.J.*
Solheim	0–0–0	0–0–0	———	———	———	———	———	———	———	———
Summanen	1–0–1	0–0–0	2–6–8	0–2–2	1–1–2	1–1–2	3–1–4	0–0–0	0–1–1	1–1–2
Tikkanen	0–0–0	———	0–0–0	0–0–0	2–0–2	0–0–0	0–1–1	0–0–0	0–0–0	0–1–1

	NYI.	*NYR.*	*Phil.*	*Pitt.*	*Que.*	*St.L.*	*Tor.*	*Van.*	*Wash.*	*Winn.*
Anderson	2–2–4	0–1–1	0–2–2	1–3–4	2–3–5	2–0–2	4–3–7	1–4–5	1–0–1	6–4–10
Brubaker	———	———	———	———	———	———	———	0–0–0	1–0–1	———
Carroll	———	———	———	———	———	———	———	0–0–0	0–1–1	0–0–0
Coffey	3–1–4	1–2–3	1–1–2	2–2–4	4–2–6	1–4–5	3–9–12	6–9–15	1–1–2	1–14–15
Fogolin	1–0–1	0–0–0	0–0–0	0–1–1	0–2–2	0–2–2	0–0–0	1–1–2	0–0–0	1–1–2
Gregg	0–1–1	0–0–0	0–0–0	0–3–3	0–0–0	0–0–0	0–5–5	0–1–1	0–2–2	1–2–3
Gretzky	1–4–5	0–5–5	3–2–5	2–6–8	1–11–12	0–7–7	8–3–11	5–16–21	1–3–4	9–17–26
Hopkins	———	———	———	———	0–0–0	———	———	———	———	———
Huddy	0–1–1	0–0–0	0–1–1	0–1–1	0–1–1	0–1–1	0–1–1	2–6–8	0–0–0	0–8–8
Hunter	0–1–1	2–0–2	1–1–2	0–2–2	1–1–2	0–0–0	0–2–2	5–4–9	1–1–2	3–2–5
Jackson	1–0–1	0–1–1	0–0–0	1–1–2	0–0–0	0–0–0	0–0–0	0–0–0	0–0–0	0–0–0
Jalo	———	———	———	———	———	———	———	———	———	0–1–1
Krushelnyski	3–2–5	0–0–0	0–0–0	2–0–2	0–0–0	0–0–0	0–1–1	2–3–5	0–0–0	1–8–9
Kurri	2–2–4	1–2–3	2–3–5	3–1–4	2–3–5	4–1–5	2–7–9	7–7–14	2–1–3	8–8–16
Lowe	0–2–2	0–1–1	0–1–1	0–0–0	1–0–1	0–1–1	0–0–0	0–3–3	0–0–0	0–1–1
Lumley	0–0–0	0–0–0	0–0–0	1–1–2	0–0–0	0–1–1	0–1–1	3–2–5	0–1–1	0–1–1
MacTavish	1–1–2	0–0–0	0–1–1	3–1–4	1–0–1	0–0–0	1–2–3	2–4–6	0–0–0	4–3–7
McClelland	0–2–2	0–1–1	0–0–0	0–1–1	0–0–0	2–0–2	1–1–2	3–2–5	0–1–1	1–3–4
McSorley	0–0–0	0–0–0	0–0–0	1–0–1	0–0–0	0–1–1	0–1–1	1–5–6	0–0–0	0–1–1
Melnyk	———	———	1–0–1	———	———	———	1–0–1	0–2–2	0–0–0	———
Messier	0–2–2	2–1–3	1–1–2	1–1–2	0–1–1	2–3–5	0–4–4	4–4–8	0–1–1	5–2–7
Moller	0–0–0	———	———	———	———	———	———	———	———	———
Napier	0–3–3	2–0–2	0–0–0	0–2–2	1–1–2	1–0–1	2–0–2	2–5–7	0–0–0	3–2–5
Odelein	———	———	———	———	0–0–0	———	0–0–0	———	———	———
Rogers	———	———	0–0–0	———	———	———	———	0–0–0	———	0–0–0
Semenko	0–0–0	0–0–0	0–0–0	0–0–0	2–3–5	1–1–2	0–2–2	0–2–2	0–0–0	0–0–0
Sherven	———	———	0–0–0	———	———	———	0–0–0	———	———	1–0–1
Smith	0–1–1	0–0–0	0–0–0	0–2–2	0–0–0	0–0–0	1–1–2	0–4–4	0–0–0	0–3–3
Solheim	———	———	———	———	1–0–1	———	0–0–0	———	0–0–0	———
Summanen	0–1–1	1–1–2	0–0–0	0–0–0	0–0–0	0–1–1	2–0–2	4–0–4	1–1–2	2–1–3
Tikkanen	0–1–1	0–0–0	0–0–0	0–1–1	0–0–0	1–1–2	———	3–1–4	———	1–0–1

1985-86 Goaltender Records vs. Opposition

	GP	*Min.*	*GA*	*EN*	*SO*	*Ave.*	*W–L–T*	*Opposition*
Grant Fuhr	1	60	3	0	0	3.00	1–0–0	Boston
	1	60	3	1	0	3.00	0–1–0	Buffalo
	4	240	13	0	0	3.25	4–0–0	Calgary
	2	88	7	0	0	4.77	2–0–0	Chicago
	1	60	2	0	0	2.00	1–0–0	Detroit
	1	60	5	0	0	5.00	1–0–0	Hartford
	4	240	15	0	0	3.75	4–0–0	Los Angeles
	1	24	3	0	0	7.50	0–0–0	Minnesota
	1	60	2	0	0	2.00	1–0–0	Montreal
	2	121	10	0	0	4.96	2–0–0	New Jersey
	1	60	4	0	0	4.00	1–0–0	N.Y. Islanders
	2	120	9	0	0	4.50	0–2–0	N.Y. Rangers
	1	61	1	0	0	0.98	1–0–0	Philadelphia
	2	120	7	0	0	3.50	1–1–0	Quebec
	1	60	7	0	0	7.00	0–1–0	St. Louis
	3	132	12	0	0	5.45	2–1–0	Toronto
	3	180	9	0	0	3.00	3–0–0	Vancouver
	1	60	5	0	0	5.00	0–1–0	Washington
	8	378	26	1	0	4.13	5–1–0	Winnipeg
Andy Moog	2	122	8	0	0	3.93	1–1–0	Boston
	2	120	7	0	0	3.50	1–1–0	Buffalo
	4	245	20	0	0	4.90	2–1–1	Calgary
	2	92	8	0	0	5.22	1–0–0	Chicago

GP	*Min.*	*GA*	*EN*	*SO*	*Ave.*	*W–L–T*	*Opposition*
2	120	5	0	0	2.50	2–0–0	Detroit
2	120	4	0	0	2.00	2–0–0	Hartford
4	250	16	0	0	3.84	2–0–2	Los Angeles
3	158	9	0	0	3.42	2–1–0	Minnesota
2	121	7	0	0	3.47	2–0–0	Montreal
1	60	2	0	0	2.00	1–0–0	New Jersey
2	130	8	0	0	3.69	0–0–2	N.Y. Islanders
1	62	2	0	0	1.94	1–0–0	N.Y. Rangers
2	120	8	0	0	4.00	1–1–0	Philadelphia
3	180	13	0	0	4.33	2–1–0	Pittsburgh
1	60	4	0	0	4.00	1–0–0	Quebec
2	125	8	0	0	3.84	1–0–1	St. Louis
2	48	5	0	0	6.25	0–0–0	Toronto
5	305	14	0	1	2.75	4–0–1	Vancouver
2	124	9	1	0	4.35	0–2–0	Washington
3	102	7	0	0	4.12	1–1–0	Winnipeg

1985-86 Schedule Results

Date	Visitor			Home	
Oct. 10	Winnipeg	3	at	Edmonton	4
Oct. 13	St. Louis	3	at	Edmonton	6
Oct. 16	Islanders	4	at	Edmonton	6
Oct. 18	Boston	2	at	Edmonton	3
Oct. 20	Edmonton	8	at	Los Angeles	5
Oct. 23	Edmonton	3	at	Winnipeg	9
Oct. 25	Calgary	3	at	Edmonton	5
Oct. 28	Edmonton	6	at	Calgary	4
Oct. 30	Winnipeg	3	at	Edmonton	7
Nov. 1	Buffalo	2	at	Edmonton	0
Nov. 3	Toronto	1	at	Edmonton	7
Nov. 5	Edmonton	6	at	Vancouver	4
Nov. 6	Edmonton	4	at	Los Angeles	4 OT
Nov. 8	Vancouver	0	at	Edmonton	13
Nov. 12	Edmonton	2	at	Washington	5
Nov. 14	Edmonton	3	at	Philadelphia	5
Nov. 16	Edmonton	4	at	Islanders	4 OT
Nov. 17	Edmonton	3	at	Rangers	2 OT
Nov. 19	Edmonton	5	at	Quebec	4
Nov. 20	Edmonton	5	at	Montreal	4 OT
Nov. 23	New Jersey	2	at	Edmonton	3
Nov. 27	Vancouver	5	at	Edmonton	5 OT
Nov. 30	Hartford	5	at	Edmonton	8
Dec. 1	Calgary	3	at	Edmonton	5
Dec. 3	Edmonton	8	at	Los Angeles	4
Dec. 5	Los Angeles	6	at	Edmonton	6 OT
Dec. 7	Minnesota	4	at	Edmonton	8
Dec. 8	Chicago	3	at	Edmonton	4
Dec. 10	Edmonton	3	at	St. Louis	7
Dec. 11	Edmonton	12	at	Chicago	9
Dec. 13	Edmonton	6	at	Winnipeg	3
Dec. 15	Vancouver	3	at	Edmonton	5
Dec. 18	Washington	5	at	Edmonton	2
Dec. 20	Los Angeles	4	at	Edmonton	9
Dec. 22	Winnipeg	7	at	Edmonton	5
Dec. 29	Edmonton	5	at	Vancouver	3
Dec. 31	Philadelphia	3	at	Edmonton	4
Jan. 2	Edmonton	4	at	Calgary	3
Jan. 4	Hartford	3	at	Edmonton	4
Jan. 5	Calgary	3	at	Edmonton	6
Jan. 8	Edmonton	9	at	Toronto	11
Jan. 10	Edmonton	3	at	Quebec	5
Jan. 11	Edmonton	6	at	Montreal	3
Jan. 13	Edmonton	5	at	Boston	3
Jan. 15	Edmonton	4	at	Hartford	1
Jan. 18	Rangers	5	at	Edmonton	4
Jan. 22	Pittsburgh	7	at	Edmonton	4
Jan. 24	New Jersey	6	at	Edmonton	7 OT
Jan. 25	Los Angeles	2	at	Edmonton	5
Jan. 27	Edmonton	4	at	Chicago	3
Jan. 29	Edmonton	5	at	St. Louis	5 OT
Jan. 31	Calgary	4	at	Edmonton	7
Feb. 1	Edmonton	4	at	Calgary	4 OT
Feb. 6	Edmonton	6	at	New Jersey	5
Feb. 8	Edmonton	4	at	Washington	5
Feb. 9	Edmonton	2	at	Buffalo	4
Feb. 11	Edmonton	3	at	Detroit	2
Feb. 14	Quebec	2	at	Edmonton	8
Feb. 16	Buffalo	5	at	Edmonton	7
Feb. 19	Toronto	5	at	Edmonton	9
Feb. 22	Boston	6	at	Edmonton	5 OT
Feb. 24	Montreal	2	at	Edmonton	3
Feb. 26	Edmonton	8	at	Winnipeg	2
Mar. 2	Philadelphia	1	at	Edmonton	2 OT
Mar. 4	Edmonton	6	at	Vancouver	2
Mar. 5	Los Angeles	3	at	Edmonton	6
Mar. 7	Pittsburgh	3	at	Edmonton	5
Mar. 9	Edmonton	7	at	Los Angeles	3
Mar. 11	Edmonton	0	at	Minnesota	4
Mar. 12	Edmonton	8	at	Winnipeg	5
Mar. 14	Detroit	3	at	Edmonton	12
Mar. 18	Winnipeg	2	at	Edmonton	6
Mar. 21	Minnesota	4	at	Edmonton	5 OT
Mar. 25	Edmonton	7	at	Detroit	2
Mar. 26	Edmonton	8	at	Pittsburgh	3
Mar. 28	Edmonton	2	at	Rangers	4
Mar. 29	Edmonton	4	at	Islanders	4 OT
April 2	Vancouver	4	at	Edmonton	8
April 4	Edmonton	3	at	Calgary	9
April 6	Edmonton	3	at	Vancouver	2

Opponent	*Home W-L-T*	*Road W-L-T*
Boston	1–1–0	1–0–0
Buffalo	1–1–0	0–1–0
Calgary	4–0–0	2–1–1
Chicago	1–0–0	2–0–0

Opponent	Home W–L–T	Road W–L–T
Detroit	1–0–0	2–0–0
Hartford	2–0–0	1–0–0
Los Angeles	3–0–1	3–0–1
Minnesota	2–0–0	0–1–0
Montreal	1–0–0	2–0–0
New Jersey	2–0–0	1–0–0
Islanders	1–0–0	0–0–2
Rangers	0–1–0	1–1–0

Opponent	Home W–L–T	Road W–L–T
Philadelphia	2–0–0	0–1–0
Pittsburgh	1–1–0	1–0–0
Quebec	1–0–0	1–1–0
St. Louis	1–0–0	0–1–1
Toronto	2–0–0	0–1–0
Vancouver	3–0–1	4–0–0
Washington	0–1–0	0–2–0
Winnipeg	3–1–0	3–1–0

Opponent	Overall W–L–T	GF–GA
Boston	2–1–0	13–11
Buffalo	1–2–0	9–11
Calgary	6–1–1	40–33
Chicago	3–0–0	20–15
Detroit	3–0–0	22–7
Hartford	3–0–0	16–9
Los Angeles	6–0–2	53–31
Minnesota	2–1–0	13–12
Montreal	3–0–0	14–9
New Jersey	3–0–0	16–12

Opponent	Overall W–L–T	GF–GA
Islanders	1–0–2	4–12
Rangers	1–2–0	9–11
Philadelphia	2–1–0	9–9
Pittsburgh	2–1–0	17–13
Quebec	2–1–0	16–11
St. Louis	1–1–1	14–15
Toronto	2–1–0	25–17
Vancouver	7–0–1	51–23
Washington	0–3–0	8–15
Winnipeg	6–2–0	47–34

1985-86 Playoff Scoring

#		GP	G	A	Pts.	Shots	SH%	GW	OT	PP	SH	P/M	PIM
99	Wayne Gretzky	10	8	11	19	42	19.0	2	0	4	1	0	2
17	Jari Kurri	10	2	10	12	25	8.0	0	0	0	1	1	4
9	Glenn Anderson	10	8	3	11	38	21.1	2	1	1	0	2	14
11	Mark Messier	10	4	6	10	23	17.4	0	0	0	2	1	18
7	Paul Coffey	10	1	9	10	33	3.0	0	0	1	0	0	30
26	Mike Krushelnyski	10	4	5	9	15	26.7	2	0	1	0	3	16
14	Craig MacTavish	10	4	4	8	17	23.5	0	0	1	0	6	11
10	Esa Tikkanen	8	3	2	5	19	15.8	0	0	0	0	1	7
12	Dave Hunter	10	2	3	5	18	11.1	0	0	0	0	7	23
18	Mark Napier	10	1	4	5	14	7.1	0	0	0	0	6	0
4	Kevin Lowe	10	1	3	4	16	6.3	0	0	0	0	6	15
25	Raimo Summanen	5	1	1	2	6	16.7	0	0	0	0	2	0
20	Dave Lumley	3	0	2	2	1	0.0	0	0	0	0	0	2
22	Charlie Huddy	7	0	2	2	5	0.0	0	0	0	0	3	0
2	Lee Fogolin	8	0	2	2	7	0.0	0	0	0	0	3	10
33	Marty McSorley	8	0	2	2	4	0.0	0	0	0	0	3	50
21	Randy Gregg	10	1	0	1	6	16.7	0	0	0	0	3	12
24	Kevin McClelland	10	1	0	1	7	14.3	0	0	0	0	-1	32
5	Steve Smith	6	0	1	1	5	0.0	0	0	0	0	4	14
31	Grant Fuhr	9	0	1	1	0	0.0	0	0	0	0	0	0
6	Jeff Beukeboom	1	0	0	0	1	0.0	0	0	0	0	1	4
35	Andy Moog	1	0	0	0	0	0.0	0	0	0	0	0	0
27	Dave Semenko	6	0	0	0	1	0.0	0	0	0	0	0	32
29	Don Jackson	8	0	0	0	7	0.0	0	0	0	0	3	21
		10	41	71	112	310	13.2	6	1	8	4	5	317

1985-86 Playoff Goaltending

	GP	Min.	GA	W	L	Ave.	SA	Pct.	SO	EN
Andy Moog	1	60	1	1	0	1.00	27	0.963	0	0
Grant Fuhr	9	541	28	5	4	3.11	273	0.897	0	1
	10	601	30	6	4	3.00	300	0.900	0	1

Date	Result					Winning Goaltender	Winning Goal
April 9, 1986	Vancouver	3	at	Edmonton	7	Grant Fuhr	Mike Krushelnyski
April 10, 1986	Vancouver	1	at	Edmonton	5	Andy Moog	Wayne Gretzky
April 12, 1986	Edmonton	5	at	Vancouver	1	Grant Fuhr	Mike Krushelnyski
April 18, 1986	Calgary	4	at	Edmonton	1	Mike Vernon	Gary Suter
April 20, 1986	Calgary	5	at	Edmonton	6	Grant Fuhr	Glenn Anderson[1]

Date			***Result***			***Winning Goaltender***	***Winning Goal***
April 22, 1986	Edmonton	2	at	Calgary	3	Mike Vernon	Joel Otto
April 24, 1986	Edmonton	7	at	Calgary	4	Grant Fuhr	Wayne Gretzky
April 26, 1986	Calgary	4	at	Edmonton	1	Mike Vernon	Lanny McDonald
April 28, 1986	Edmonton	5	at	Calgary	2	Grant Fuhr	Glenn Anderson
April 30, 1986	Calgary	3	at	Edmonton	2	Mike Vernon	Perry Berezan

[1]-at 1:04 of overtime

Table 7. Oilers All Time Regular Season Power Play Record

			Road				***Home***				***Overall***		
Year	***Adv***	***PPGF***	***%***	***SHGA***	***Adv***	***PPGF***	***%***	***SHGA***	***Adv***	***PPGF***	***%***	***SHGA***	***Rank***
2001	*199*	*31*	*15.6*	*2*	*199*	*28*	*14.1*	*1*	*398*	*59*	*14.8*	*3*	*21st*
2000	*172*	*27*	*15.7*	*1*	*167*	*26*	*15.6*	*3*	*339*	*53*	*15.6*	*4*	*T17*
1999	*231*	*32*	*13.9*	*5*	*207*	*31*	*15.0*	*5*	*438*	*63*	*14.4*	*10*	*T17*
1998	*238*	*44*	*18.5*	*5*	*245*	*33*	*13.5*	*6*	*483*	*77*	*15.9*	*11*	*12th*
1997	*199*	*36*	*18.1*	*8*	*207*	*37*	*17.9*	*5*	*406*	*73*	*18.0*	*13*	*6th*
1996	*223*	*38*	*17.0*	*7*	*229*	*34*	*14.8*	*5*	*452*	*72*	*15.9*	*12*	*T20*
1995	*121*	*20*	*16.5*	*5*	*138*	*22*	*15.9*	*3*	*259*	*42*	*16.2*	*8*	*18th*
1994	*188*	*34*	*18.1*	*1*	*214*	*40*	*18.7*	*8*	*402*	*74*	*18.4*	*9*	*T15*
1993	*200*	*29*	*14.5*	*4*	*216*	*37*	*17.1*	*6*	*416*	*66*	*15.9*	*10*	*23rd*
1992	*179*	*30*	*16.8*	*11*	*187*	*38*	*20.3*	*4*	*366*	*68*	*18.6*	*15*	*14th*
1991	*165*	*30*	*18.2*	*2*	*196*	*33*	*16.8*	*2*	*361*	*63*	*17.5*	*4*	*17th*
1990	*194*	*39*	*20.1*	*4*	*213*	*45*	*21.1*	*2*	*407*	*84*	*20.6*	*6*	*12th*
1989	*202*	*39*	*19.3*	*7*	*217*	*44*	*20.3*	*10*	*419*	*83*	*19.8*	*17*	*T16*
1988	*199*	*38*	*19.1*	*5*	*203*	*50*	*24.6*	*6*	*402*	*88*	*21.9*	*11*	*7th*
1987	*155*	*38*	*24.5*	*5*	*163*	*32*	*19.6*	*5*	*318*	*70*	*22.0*	*8*	*7th*
1986	*134*	*35*	*26.1*	*7*	*161*	*43*	*26.7*	*8*	*295*	*78*	*26.4*	*15*	*1st*
1985	*128*	*28*	*21.9*	*2*	*165*	*46*	*27.9*	*3*	*293*	*74*	*25.3*	*5*	*2nd*
1984	*156*	*40*	*25.6*	*7*	*162*	*41*	*25.3*	*5*	*318*	*81*	*25.5*	*12*	*2nd*
1983	*154*	*45*	*29.2*	*0*	*140*	*41*	*29.3*	*6*	*294*	*86*	*29.3*	*6*	*1st*
1982									*341*	*86*	*25.2*	*8*	*4th*
1981	*164**	*37*	*22.6*	*2*	*186**	*40*	*21.5*	*5*	*347*	*77*	*22.2*	*7*	*T12*
1980									*282*	*61*	*21.6*	*4*	*12th*

*Estimate

1986-87

Ted Green rejoined the team's coaching staff after a one year absence. Bob McCammon was named as director of player development and John Muckler returned as co-coach.

The only player of note to come out of this year's draft was Tony Hand. Hand, a 5'10" native of Edinburgh, Scotland, was drafted from the Murrayfield Racers of the British Ice Hockey Association and remains as the only Scottish born and trained player ever taken in the NHL's entry draft.

Sather again made a couple of off season moves to bolster his team in an attempt to regain the Cup. Toronto's 1st choice in the 1980 draft, defenseman Craig Muni, was signed as a free agent in August. Muni, who would often be paired with Kevin Lowe, was a solid defenseman who could dish out devastating open ice hits and would help the team win three Cups.

The other major acquisition was Finnish defenseman Reijo Ruotsalainen, obtained from the Rangers just prior to the start of the season. At 5'8" and 170 pounds Ruotsalainen was rather small for a defenseman but he possessed a devastating shot and could move the puck out of his own end almost as well as Paul Coffey. Ruotsalainen played only 16 games in the regular season, scoring 13 points before returning to his native Finland. He rejoined the team in time for the playoffs, playing in 21 games and registering seven points. Following the playoff he again returned to Finland where he played two years before returning to the Oilers in 1990. He played only ten regular season games but again shone in the playoffs, appearing in 22 games, and scoring 13 points to win his second Stanley Cup.

Sather would make one more move in March in a bid to increase the team's chances to regain the championship. Acquired from Minnesota for future considerations was Kent Nilsson. Known as "Magic," Nilsson scored 17 points in 17 regular season games, but teamed with Anderson and Messier, he scored 21 points in 19 playoff games. This nominal second line would take much of the pressure off of the Gretzky line.

Defenseman Paul Coffey missed 21 games throughout the season with back spasms, while Steve Smith missed a number of games with a hip flexor and Charlie Huddy also missed some games with a bruised knee. The team was 37-15-5-.693 at the All-Star break.

For the sixth year in a row the Oilers finished on top of the Smythe Division and led the NHL in overall points in a much tighter league. For the first time in five years the team scored fewer than 400 goals, but they still led the league in scoring. They were able to cut down on their goals against by 26, finishing 10th in defense.

Wayne Gretzky again led the league in scoring, with 183 points, outdistancing teammate Jari Kurri who was second with 108. Mark Messier would finish fourth with 107 points.

The Oilers met the Los Angeles Kings in the first round of the playoffs. The Kings, who had finished 36 points behind Edmonton in the regular season, were no match for the hungry Oilers. Edmonton won the series four games to one and won game two in Edmonton by a score of 13–3. After defeating the Kings they met the Jets in the division finals, sweeping that series in four straight games. After getting by Detroit in the conference finals in five games the Oilers came up against the Flyers in the championship series.

Even without leading scorer Tim Kerr, the Flyers gave the Oilers all they could handle. After falling behind in the series three games to one the Flyers came back to win the next two to tie the series. With game number seven taking place in Edmonton, the home team was not to be denied and the Oilers would win their third Cup in four years.

Grant Fuhr (left) and Andy Moog with the Stanley Cup. (A96-15 City of Edmonton Archives.)

1986-87 Regular Season Scoring

#		*Ht.*	*Wt.*	*Age*	*GP*	*G*	*A*	*Pts.*	*Shots*	*SH%*	*GW*	*GT*	*PP*	*SH*	*P/M*	*PIM*
99	Gretzky (C)	72	170	25	79	62	121	183	288	21.5	4	0	13	7	70	28
17	Kurri	72	190	26	79	54	54	108	211	25.6	10	0	12	5	35	41
11	Messier (A)	73	205	25	77	37	70	107	208	17.8	5	0	7	4	21	73
10	Tikkanen	71	185	21	76	34	44	78	126	27.0	6	1	7	0	44	120
9	Anderson	71	185	26	80	35	38	73	188	18.6	5	0	7	1	27	65
7	Coffey	72	200	25	59	17	50	67	165	10.3	3	0	10	2	12	49
26	Krushelnyski	74	200	26	80	16	35	51	89	18.0	2	0	4	1	26	67
14	MacTavish	72	190	28	79	20	19	39	140	14.3	2	0	1	4	9	55
4	Lowe (A)	74	195	27	77	8	29	37	99	8.1	1	0	2	2	41	94
28	Muni	74	200	24	79	7	22	29	69	10.1	2	0	0	0	45	85
24	McClelland	74	200	24	72	12	13	25	76	15.8	1	0	0	0	-4	238
21	Gregg	76	215	30	52	8	16	24	59	13.6	2	0	0	0	36	42
5	S. Smith	76	210	23	62	7	15	22	71	9.9	1	0	2	0	11	165
65	Napier	70	185	29	62	8	13	21	88	9.1	0	0	0	1	3	2

#		*Ht.*	*Wt.*	*Age*	*GP*	*G*	*A*	*Pts.*	*Shots*	*SH%*	*GW*	*GT*	*PP*	*SH*	*P/M*	*PIM*
22	Huddy	72	200	27	58	4	15	19	75	5.3	0	0	0	0	27	35
15	Nilsson	73	195	29	17	5	12	17	25	20.0	0	0	1	0	10	4
25	Summanen	71	185	24	48	10	7	17	55	18.2	0	0	0	0	-1	15
12	Hunter	71	200	28	77	6	9	15	84	7.1	1	0	0	1	1	79
29	Ruotsalainen	68	170	26	16	5	8	13	52	9.6	1	0	3	0	8	6
6	Beukeboom	76	210	21	44	3	8	11	24	12.5	1	0	1	0	7	124
33	McSorley	73	210	23	41	2	4	6	32	6.3	0	0	0	0	-4	159
20	Pouzar	71	202	34	12	2	3	5	11	18.2	1	0	0	0	3	6
8	Kulak	70	180	23	23	3	1	4	30	10.0	1	0	0	0	3	41
18	Gare	69	175	32	18	1	3	4	22	4.5	0	0	0	0	2	6
2	Fogolin	72	200	31	35	1	3	4	37	2.7	0	0	0	0	-2	17
23	Lemay	71	185	24	10	1	2	3	7	14.3	0	0	0	0	2	36
25	Moller	72	190	24	6	2	1	3	10	20.0	0	0	0	0	2	0
15	S. Graves	70	180	22	12	2	0	2	12	16.7	1	0	0	0	-2	0
31	Fuhr	70	185	24	44	0	2	2	0	0.0	0	0	0	0	0	6
35	Moog	69	170	26	46	0	2	2	0	0.0	0	0	0	0	0	8
19	Lacombe	71	205	22	1	0	0	0	0	0.0	0	0	0	0	-1	2
20	Lumley	72	185	32	1	0	0	0	0	0.0	0	0	0	0	0	0
8	Van Dorp	76	225	25	3	0	0	0	3	0.0	0	0	0	0	-1	25
27	Semenko	75	215	29	5	0	0	0	1	0.0	0	0	0	0	0	0
	Bench															26
		72	194	26	80	372	619	991	2357	15.8	50	1	70	28	92	1719

1986-87 Goaltender Records

	GP	*Min.*	*GA*	*W*	*L*	*T*	*Ave.*	*SA*	*Pct.*	*SO*	*EN*
Grant Fuhr	44	2388	137	22	13	3	3.44	1149	0.881	0	1
Andy Moog	46	2461	144	28	11	3	3.51	1218	0.882	0	2
	80	4849	284	50	24	6	3.51	2367	0.880	0	3

Coach: Glen Sather 50-24-6

1986-87 Scoring vs. Opposition

	Bost.	*Buff.*	*Calg.*	*Chi.*	*Det.*	*Hart.*	*L.A.*	*Minn.*	*Mont.*	*N.J.*
Anderson	1–1–2	2–1–3	3–2–5	2–1–3	1–3–4	1–0–1	3–5–8	1–0–1	1–1–2	1–1–2
Beukeboom	———	0–0–0	1–0–1	0–1–1	0–1–1	0–0–0	1–0–1	0–2–2	0–0–0	0–0–0
Coffey	0–1–1	0–1–1	2–10–12	0–0–0	0–3–3	2–1–3	2–3–5	———	1–4–5	2–4–6
Fogolin	0–1–1	———	1–0–1	0–0–0	0–0–0	0–0–0	0–0–0	0–0–0	0–1–1	———
Gare	0–0–0	———	0–0–0	0–0–0	0–0–0	0–1–1	0–0–0	0–0–0	0–1–1	———
Graves	———	———	———	0–0–0	———	———	0–0–0	0–0–0	———	———
Gregg	0–0–0	0–1–1	2–0–2	0–0–0	1–0–1	0–1–1	1–1–2	1–1–2	0–1–1	1–0–1
Gretzky	4–1–5	2–3–5	5–8–13	2–7–9	2–9–11	1–4–5	4–17–21	3–4–7	2–4–6	0–6–6
Huddy	0–0–0	1–0–1	1–1–2	0–0–0	———	0–0–0	0–2–2	1–0–1	0–0–0	0–0–0
Hunter	1–0–1	1–0–1	0–1–1	1–3–4	0–0–0	0–0–0	2–0–2	0–0–0	0–0–0	0–1–1
Krushelnyski	0–3–3	0–3–3	3–1–4	0–4–4	0–1–1	0–2–2	2–4–6	0–0–0	1–1–2	1–1–2
Kulak	———	1–0–1	0–0–0	———	0–0–0	———	1–0–1	———	———	0–0–0
Kurri	0–1–1	2–2–4	2–1–3	2–0–2	5–2–7	1–0–1	7–10–17	1–4–5	3–1–4	4–2–6
Lacombe	———	———	———	———	———	———	———	———	———	0–0–0
Lemay	———	0–1–1	1–1–2	———	———	0–0–0	———	———	———	0–0–0
Lowe	0–0–0	0–1–1	0–4–4	0–1–1	2–0–2	0–0–0	1–3–4	0–2–2	0–1–1	0–0–0
Lumley	———	———	———	———	———	———	0–0–0	———	———	———
MacTavish	2–1–3	1–0–1	0–1–1	0–2–2	0–0–0	2–1–3	5–3–8	2–0–2	1–1–2	0–1–1
McClelland	0–0–0	0–2–2	1–1–2	2–0–2	0–0–0	0–0–0	2–2–4	0–0–0	0–0–0	0–0–0
McSorley	0–0–0	———	0–0–0	1–1–2	0–0–0	———	1–1–2	———	0–0–0	———
Messier	0–4–4	1–1–2	1–8–9	4–2–6	1–4–5	2–2–4	2–9–11	0–2–2	3–3–6	0–4–4
Moller	0–0–0	0–0–0	———	———	———	0–0–0	0–0–0	———	———	1–1–2
Muni	0–1–1	0–0–0	1–2–3	0–0–0	0–0–0	1–0–1	2–3–5	0–0–0	1–2–3	2–0–2
Napier	1–1–2	0–0–0	0–0–0	0–2–2	0–0–0	0–0–0	1–2–3	0–0–0	0–0–0	———
Nilsson	0–1–1	0–0–0	1–0–1	———	0–0–0	1–3–4	2–2–4	———	0–1–1	1–2–3
Pouzar	0–0–0	0–0–0	0–1–1	———	0–0–0	0–0–0	0–0–0	———	1–0–1	0–2–2
Ruotsalainen	0–0–0	1–1–2	0–0–0	———	0–1–1	0–1–1	2–1–3	———	0–1–1	2–3–5
Semenko	———	———	0–0–0	———	———	———	0–0–0	———	———	———
Smith	1–0–1	0–0–0	0–0–0	2–0–2	1–0–1	0–0–0	0–2–2	0–0–0	0–0–0	0–0–0

	Bost.	*Buff.*	*Calg.*	*Chi.*	*Det.*	*Hart.*	*L.A.*	*Minn.*	*Mont.*	*N.J.*
Summanen	0–0–0	0–1–1	0–1–1	0–0–0	0–0–0	0–0–0	3–0–3	0–0–0	0–1–1	0–0–0
Tikkanen	0–0–0	1–2–3	4–1–5	2–3–5	2–2–4	0–2–2	4–3–7	2–2–4	0–0–0	1–3–4
Van Dorp	———	———	0–0–0	———	———	———	———	———	———	0–0–0

	NYI.	*NYR.*	*Phil.*	*Pitt.*	*Que.*	*St.L.*	*Tor.*	*Van.*	*Wash.*	*Winn.*
Anderson	2–3–5	3–1–4	0–1–1	3–2–5	2–0–2	0–1–1	1–2–3	3–6–9	2–2–4	3–5–8
Beukeboom	0–0–0	0–1–1	0–0–0	0–0–0	0–0–0	0–2–2	0–0–0	1–0–1	0–0–0	0–1–1
Coffey	1–1–2	1–4–5	0–2–2	1–0–1	0–2–2	0–0–0	1–1–2	2–6–8	2–3–5	0–4–4
Fogolin	0–0–0	0–0–0	0–0–0	———	0–0–0	0–0–0	———	0–1–1	0–0–0	0–0–0
Gare	0–0–0	———	———	———	0–0–0	0–0–0	0–0–0	1–1–2	0–0–0	———
Graves	0–0–0	———	0–0–0	1–0–1	0–0–0	———	———	0–0–0	———	1–0–1
Gregg	0–2–2	0–0–0	0–1–1	0–2–2	1–0–1	0–0–0	1–1–2	0–4–4	0–0–0	0–1–1
Gretzky	1–5–6	4–4–8	3–1–4	1–7–8	5–7–12	2–3–5	2–7–9	10–15–25	1–1–2	8–8–16
Huddy	0–1–1	0–1–1	0–1–1	0–0–0	0–0–0	0–2–2	0–0–0	0–4–4	0–1–1	1–2–3
Hunter	0–0–0	0–3–3	0–0–0	0–0–0	0–0–0	0–0–0	0–0–0	0–1–1	1–0–1	0–0–0
Krushelnyski	1–1–2	2–3–5	0–1–1	0–2–2	1–1–2	0–0–0	1–1–2	1–3–4	1–0–1	2–3–5
Kulak	———	1–1–2	0–0–0	0–0–0	0–0–0	0–0–0	0–0–0	0–0–0	———	0–0–0
Kurri	1–3–4	1–4–5	3–2–5	2–0–2	0–4–4	3–2–5	4–4–8	10–8–18	0–1–1	3–3–6
Lemay	———	———	———	———	———	———	———	———	———	0–0–0
Lowe	0–2–2	0–2–2	0–0–0	0–1–1	0–1–1	3–1–4	0–1–1	0–5–5	0–1–1	2–3–5
MacTavish	1–0–1	0–0–0	1–1–2	0–1–1	0–0–0	2–1–3	0–1–1	1–1–2	1–2–3	1–2–3
McClelland	0–0–0	2–1–3	0–0–0	0–0–0	1–0–1	1–2–3	1–1–2	0–1–1	1–0–1	2–2–4
McSorley	0–0–0	0–0–0	0–1–1	0–0–0	0–0–0	0–0–0	0–0–0	0–1–1	0–0–0	0–0–0
Messier	4–1–5	3–5–8	2–0–2	1–2–3	0–3–3	2–1–3	1–1–2	5–8–13	0–4–4	5–6–11
Moller	———	———	———	———	———	———	1–0–1	———	———	———
Muni	0–1–1	0–1–1	0–0–0	0–0–0	0–1–1	0–2–2	0–3–3	0–5–5	0–0–0	0–1–1
Napier	0–1–1	1–0–1	0–0–0	0–1–1	1–0–1	1–3–4	0–0–0	2–0–2	0–2–2	1–1–2
Nilsson	———	———	———	———	———	———	0–1–1	0–1–1	———	0–1–1
Pouzar	———	———	———	———	———	———	———	1–0–1	0–0–0	———
Ruotsalainen	———	———	———	———	———	———	0–0–0	———	———	0–0–0
Semenko	———	0–0–0	———	———	———	———	———	0–0–0	———	———
Smith	0–0–0	0–2–2	0–0–0	0–1–1	0–1–1	0–1–1	1–3–4	1–1–2	0–0–0	1–4–5
Summanen	0–0–0	1–1–2	0–0–0	0–0–0	0–1–1	0–0–0	1–0–1	2–1–3	1–0–1	2–1–3
Tikkanen	2–1–3	1–3–4	0–3–3	1–0–1	4–3–7	1–4–5	3–2–5	4–5–9	1–1–2	1–4–5

1986-87 Goaltender Records vs. Opposition

	GP	*Min.*	*GA*	*EN*	*SO*	*Ave.*	*W–L–T*	*Opposition*
Grant Fuhr	2	121	8	0	0	3.97	0–2–0	Boston
	1	60	2	0	0	2.00	1–0–0	Buffalo
	5	305	25	0	0	4.92	0–4–1	Calgary
	2	124	7	0	0	3.39	1–1–0	Chicago
	2	119	6	0	0	3.03	2–0–0	Detroit
	1	60	3	0	0	3.00	1–0–0	Hartford
	4	270	15	0	0	3.33	3–0–1	Los Angeles
	2	79	2	0	0	1.52	2–0–0	Minnesota
	1	60	3	0	0	3.00	1–0–0	Montreal
	1	60	4	0	0	4.00	0–1–0	New Jersey
	2	127	5	0	0	2.36	1–0–1	N.Y. Islanders
	2	121	10	0	0	3.48	2–0–0	N.Y. Rangers
	3	120	6	0	0	3.00	0–1–0	Philadelphia
	1	60	3	0	0	3.00	1–0–0	Quebec
	2	120	4	0	0	2.00	2–0–0	St. Louis
	3	123	7	0	0	3.41	1–1–0	Toronto
	2	120	4	0	0	2.00	2–0–0	Vancouver
	1	60	5	0	0	5.00	0–1–0	Washington
	5	280	18	1	0	3.86	2–2–0	Winnipeg
Andy Moog	1	60	2	0	0	2.00	1–0–0	Boston
	2	122	9	0	0	4.43	1–1–0	Buffalo
	3	179	14	0	0	4.69	1–2–0	Calgary
	1	60	5	1	0	5.00	0–1–0	Chicago
	2	61	3	0	0	2.95	1–0–0	Detroit
	2	120	6	1	0	3.00	1–1–0	Hartford
	5	220	20	0	0	5.45	1–2–1	Los Angeles

GP	Min.	GA	EN	SO	Ave.	W–L–T	Opposition
2	108	7	0	0	3.89	0–0–1	Minnesota
2	125	7	0	0	3.36	2–0–0	Montreal
2	120	10	0	0	5.00	2–0–0	New Jersey
1	60	1	0	0	1.00	1–0–0	N.Y. Islanders
1	60	4	0	0	4.00	1–0–0	N.Y. Rangers
2	60	5	0	0	5.00	1–1–0	Philadelphia
3	180	9	0	0	3.00	2–1–0	Pittsburgh
2	120	3	0	0	1.50	2–0–0	Quebec
1	60	1	0	0	1.00	1–0–0	St. Louis
2	57	3	0	0	3.16	1–0–0	Toronto
6	365	19	0	0	3.12	5–0–1	Vancouver
2	120	8	0	0	4.00	1–1–0	Washington
4	202	8	0	0	2.38	3–1–0	Winnipeg

1986-87 Schedule Results

Date	Visitor			Home	
Oct. 9	Edmonton	1	at	Philadelphia	2
Oct. 11	Edmonton	5	at	Montreal	4 OT
Oct. 12	Edmonton	3	at	Winnipeg	5
Oct. 15	Quebec	2	at	Edmonton	5
Oct. 17	Detroit	3	at	Edmonton	4
Oct. 19	Edmonton	6	at	Los Angeles	7
Oct. 21	Chicago	1	at	Edmonton	9
Oct. 22	Edmonton	3	at	Calgary	6
Oct. 24	Boston	2	at	Edmonton	6
Oct. 26	Vancouver	2	at	Edmonton	3
Oct. 29	Washington	3	at	Edmonton	6
Oct. 31	Edmonton	6	at	Vancouver	2
Nov. 2	Los Angeles	5	at	Edmonton	5 OT
Nov. 5	Calgary	3	at	Edmonton	1
Nov. 7	Edmonton	4	at	Calgary	6
Nov. 8	Montreal	3	at	Edmonton	4
Nov. 11	Edmonton	3	at	Islanders	2 OT
Nov. 13	Edmonton	3	at	Boston	4 OT
Nov. 15	Edmonton	2	at	Hartford	6
Nov. 16	Edmonton	8	at	Rangers	6
Nov. 19	Rangers	4	at	Edmonton	5 OT
Nov. 22	Vancouver	2	at	Edmonton	5
Nov. 24	Edmonton	5	at	Calgary	6
Nov. 26	Winnipeg	3	at	Edmonton	4
Nov. 28	Chicago	6	at	Edmonton	5 OT
Dec. 3	Islanders	1	at	Edmonton	7
Dec. 5	Edmonton	4	at	Pittsburgh	2
Dec. 7	Edmonton	2	at	Philadelphia	5
Dec. 9	Edmonton	3	at	Minnesota	2
Dec. 10	Edmonton	7	at	Winnipeg	4
Dec. 12	Winnipeg	1	at	Edmonton	6
Dec. 14	Edmonton	4	at	Los Angeles	2
Dec. 17	Quebec	3	at	Edmonton	5
Dec. 19	Vancouver	2	at	Edmonton	4
Dec. 20	Los Angeles	8	at	Edmonton	8 OT
Dec. 23	Winnipeg	2	at	Edmonton	1
Dec. 28	Philadelphia	4	at	Edmonton	6
Dec. 30	Edmonton	7	at	Vancouver	3
Jan. 3	Edmonton	8	at	Los Angeles	1
Jan. 7	Los Angeles	6	at	Edmonton	1
Jan. 9	St. Louis	1	at	Edmonton	5
Jan. 11	Calgary	3	at	Edmonton	5
Jan. 13	Edmonton	5	at	Detroit	3
Jan. 15	Edmonton	4	at	Quebec	1
Jan. 17	Edmonton	7	at	Toronto	4
Jan. 18	Edmonton	5	at	Buffalo	6 OT
Jan. 21	Edmonton	5	at	Winnipeg	3
Jan. 23	Rangers	4	at	Edmonton	7
Jan. 24	Pittsburgh	2	at	Edmonton	4
Jan. 27	Edmonton	4	at	Vancouver	4 OT
Jan. 28	Vancouver	3	at	Edmonton	7
Jan. 30	Minnesota	2	at	Edmonton	2 OT
Feb. 1	Edmonton	4	at	Chicago	6
Feb. 3	Edmonton	4	at	St. Louis	2
Feb. 4	Edmonton	6	at	Minnesota	5 OT
Feb. 6	Islanders	3	at	Edmonton	3 OT
Feb. 8	St. Louis	2	at	Edmonton	6
Feb. 15	Washington	5	at	Edmonton	3
Feb. 18	Toronto	2	at	Edmonton	9
Feb. 22	Edmonton	2	at	Winnipeg	5
Feb. 24	Edmonton	2	at	Pittsburgh	5
Feb. 25	Edmonton	2	at	New Jersey	4
Feb. 27	Edmonton	2	at	Washington	5
Mar. 4	Edmonton	8	at	Vancouver	5
Mar. 6	Los Angeles	3	at	Edmonton	9
Mar. 7	Montreal	3	at	Edmonton	5
Mar. 11	Detroit	3	at	Edmonton	6
Mar. 14	Buffalo	3	at	Edmonton	5
Mar. 15	Hartford	1	at	Edmonton	4
Mar. 17	New Jersey	4	at	Edmonton	7
Mar. 19	Edmonton	4	at	Calgary	5
Mar. 20	Calgary	6	at	Edmonton	3
Mar. 23	Edmonton	7	at	New Jersey	6
Mar. 25	Edmonton	5	at	Hartford	3
Mar. 26	Edmonton	1	at	Boston	4
Mar. 28	Edmonton	2	at	Toronto	4
Mar. 29	Edmonton	3	at	Buffalo	2
Mar. 31	Winnipeg	4	at	Edmonton	5 OT
April 2	Calgary	4	at	Edmonton	4 OT
April 4	Edmonton	7	at	Los Angeles	3

Opponent	Home W–L–T	Road W–L–T
Boston	1–0–0	0–2–0
Buffalo	1–0–0	1–1–0
Calgary	1–2–1	0–4–0
Chicago	1–1–0	0–1–0
Detroit	2–0–0	1–0–0
Hartford	1–0–0	1–1–0
Los Angeles	1–1–2	3–1–0
Minnesota	0–0–1	2–0–0
Montreal	2–0–0	1–0–0
New Jersey	1–0–0	1–1–0

Opponent	*Home W–L–T*	*Road W–L–T*
Islanders	1–0–1	1–0–0
Rangers	2–0–0	1–0–0
Philadelphia	1–0–0	0–2–0
Pittsburgh	1–0–0	1–1–0
Quebec	2–0–0	1–0–0
St. Louis	2–0–0	1–0–0
Toronto	1–0–0	1–1–0
Vancouver	4–0–0	3–0–1
Washington	1–1–0	0–1–0
Winnipeg	3–1–0	2–2–0

Opponent	*Overall W–L–T*	*GF–GA*
Boston	1–2–0	10–10
Buffalo	2–1–0	13–11
Calgary	1–6–1	29–39
Chicago	1–2–0	18–13
Detroit	3–0–0	15–9
Hartford	2–1–0	11–10
Los Angeles	4–2–2	48–35
Minnesota	2–0–1	11–9
Montreal	3–0–0	14–10
New Jersey	2–1–0	16–14
Islanders	2–0–1	13–6
Rangers	3–0–0	20–14
Philadelphia	1–2–0	9–11
Pittsburgh	2–1–0	10–9
Quebec	3–0–0	14–6
St. Louis	3–0–0	15–5
Toronto	2–1–0	18–10
Vancouver	7–0–1	44–23
Washington	1–2–0	11–13
Winnipeg	5–3–0	33–27

1986-87 Playoff Scoring

#		*GP*	*G*	*A*	*Pts*	*Shots*	*SH%*	*GW*	*OT*	*PP*	*SH*	*P/M*	*PIM*
99	Wayne Gretzky	21	5	29	34	55	9.1	0	0	2	0	10	6
11	Mark Messier	21	12	16	28	62	19.4	1	0	1	2	13	16
9	Glenn Anderson	21	14	13	27	62	22.6	2	1	4	0	13	59
17	Jari Kurri	21	15	10	25	52	28.8	5	1	4	1	11	20
15	Kent Nilsson	21	6	13	19	46	13.0	0	0	2	0	11	6
7	Paul Coffey	17	3	8	11	45	6.7	1	0	1	0	7	30
14	Craig MacTavish	21	1	9	10	35	2.9	0	0	0	0	1	16
10	Esa Tikkanen	21	7	2	9	39	17.9	1	0	1	0	1	20
21	Randy Gregg	18	3	6	9	29	10.3	1	0	1	0	8	17
22	Charlie Huddy	21	1	7	8	34	2.9	0	0	0	0	12	21
33	Marty McSorley	21	4	3	7	21	19.0	1	0	0	0	8	65
26	Mike Krushelnyski	21	3	4	7	29	10.3	1	0	0	0	4	18
29	Reijo Ruotsalainen	21	2	5	7	46	4.3	1	0	1	0	8	10
12	Dave Hunter	21	3	3	6	27	11.1	0	0	0	0	4	20
4	Kevin Lowe	21	2	4	6	21	9.5	1	0	0	2	8	22
24	Kevin McClelland	21	2	3	5	24	8.3	0	0	0	0	-6	43
5	Steve Smith	15	1	3	4	17	5.9	0	0	0	0	9	45
23	Moe Lemay	9	2	1	3	7	28.6	1	0	0	0	1	11
20	Jaroslav Pouzar	5	1	1	2	9	11.1	0	0	0	0	4	2
28	Craig Muni	14	0	2	2	11	0.0	0	0	0	0	2	17
31	Frant Fuhr	19	0	1	1	0	0.0	0	0	0	0	0	0
16	Kelly Buchberger	3	0	0	0	1	0.0	0	0	0	0	0	5
35	Andy Moog	2	0	0	0	0	0.0	0	0	0	0	0	0
8	Wayne Van Dorp	3	0	0	0	1	0.0	0	0	0	0	0	2
		21	87	144	231	673	12.9	16	2	17	5	14	471

1986-87 Playoff Goaltending

	GP	*Min.*	*GA*	*W*	*L*	*Ave.*	*SA*	*Pct.*	*SO*	*EN*
Grant Fuhr	19	1148	47	14	5	2.46	511	0.908	0	2
Andy Moog	2	120	8	2	0	4.00	37	0.784	0	0
	21	1268	57	16	5	2.71	548	0.896	0	2

Date			*Result*			*Winning Goaltender*	*Winning Goal*
April 8, 1987	Los Angeles	5	at	Edmonton	2	Roland Melanson	Dave Williams
April 9, 1987	Los Angeles	3	at	Edmonton	13	Andy Moog	Randy Gregg
April 11, 1987	Edmonton	6	at	Los Angeles	5	Andy Moog	Jari Kurri
April 12, 1987	Edmonton	6	at	Los Angeles	3	Grant Fuhr	Esa Tikkanen
April 14, 1987	Los Angeles	4	at	Edmonton	5	Grant Fuhr	Glenn Anderson
April 21, 1987	Winnipeg	2	at	Edmonton	3	Grant Fuhr	Glenn Anderson[1]
April 23, 1987	Winnipeg	3	at	Edmonton	5	Grant Fuhr	Moe Lemay
April 25, 1987	Edmonton	5	at	Winnipeg	2	Grant Fuhr	Jari Kurri

Date		*Result*				*Winning Goaltender*	*Winning Goal*
April 27, 1987	Edmonton	4	at	Winnipeg	2	Grant Fuhr	Reijo Ruotsalainen
May 5, 1987	Detroit	3	at	Edmonton	1	Greg Stefan	Joey Kocur
May 7, 1987	Detroit	1	at	Edmonton	4	Grant Fuhr	Jari Kurri
May 9, 1987	Edmonton	2	at	Detroit	1	Grant Fuhr	Marty McSorley
May 11, 1987	Edmonton	3	at	Detroit	2	Grant Fuhr	Mike Krushelnyski
May 13, 1987	Detroit	3	at	Edmonton	6	Grant Fuhr	Mark Messier
May 17, 1987	Philadelphia	2	at	Edmonton	4	Grant Fuhr	Paul Coffey
May 20, 1987	Philadelphia	2	at	Edmonton	3	Grant Fuhr	Jari Kurri[2]
May 22, 1987	Edmonton	5	at	Philadelphia	5	Ron Hextall	Brad McCrimmon
May 24, 1987	Edmonton	4	at	Philadelphia	1	Grant Fuhr	Kevin Lowe
May 26, 1987	Philadelphia	4	at	Edmonton	3	Ron Hextall	Rick Tocchet
May 28, 1987	Edmonton	2	at	Philadelphia	3	Ron Hextall	J.J. Daigneault
May 31, 1987	Philadelphia	1	at	Edmonton	3	Grant Fuhr	Jari Kurri

[1]00:36 of overtime
[2]6:50 of overtime

1986-87 Stanley Cup Winning Game

May 31, 1987: Northlands Coliseum, Edmonton

Attendance: 17, 502

Oilers

Starting Lineup: **31**-Grant Fuhr (Goal), **4**-Kevin Lowe (Defense), **28**-Craig Muni (Defense), **9**-Glenn Anderson (Left Wing), **11**-Mark Messier (Center), **15**-Kent Nilsson (Right Wing).

Remaining Players: 7-Paul Coffey, **21**-Randy Gregg, **99**-Wayne Gretzky, **22**-Charlie Huddy, **12**-Dave Hunter, **26**-Mike Krushelnyski, **17**-Jari Kurri, **14**-Craig MacTavish, **24**-Kevin McClelland (dressed but did not play due to illness), **33**-Marty McSorley, **29**-Reijo Ruotsalainen, **5**-Steve Smith, **10**-Esa Tikkanen, **35**-Andy Moog (backup goaltender).

Average: Age-25.6 years, Height-72.5 inches, Weight-195.0 pounds, Years Experience-5.3 years.

Flyers

Starting Lineup: **27**-Ron Hextall (Goal), **8**-Brad Marsh (Defense), **28**-Kjell Samuelsson (Defense), **26**-Brian Propp (Left Wing), **20**-Dave Poulin (Center), **22**-Rick Tocchet (Right Wing).

Remaining Players: **21**-Dave Brown, **18**-Lindsay Carson, **32**-Murray Craven, **3**-Doug Crossman, **15**-J.J. Daigneault, **9**-Pelle Eklund, **2**-Mark Howe, **10**-Brad McCrimmon, **19**-Scott Mellanby, **23**-Ilka Sinisalo, **24**-Derek Smith, **14**-Ron Sutter, **25**-Peter Zezel, **33**-Glenn Resch (backup goaltender).

Average: Age-25.7 years, Height-72.6 inches, Weight-191.3 pounds, Years Experience-3.8 years

Officials

Referee: Andy Van Hellemond, Linesmen: John D'Amico and Ron Finn

Game Summary

1st Period

Goals: Philadelphia-Craven (Eklund, Crossman) 1:41 PP
Edmonton-Messier (Anderson, Nilsson) 7:45

Penalties: Edmonton (Mark Messier-cross-checking) 00:34, Edmonton (Coffey-holding) 1:13, Philadelphia (Poulin-hooking) 4:22

2nd period

Goals: Edmonton-Kurri (Gretzky) 14:59

Penalties: Philadelphia-(Sinisalo-hooking) 3:39, Philadelphia (Marsh-holding)-12:15, Edmonton (Steve Smith-roughing)-15:27, Philadelphia (Scott Mellanby-roughing)-15:27, Edmonton (Mark Messier-charging)-16:02

3rd period

Goals: Edmonton-Anderson (Huddy)17:36

Penalties: Philadelphia (Tocchet-roughing)-4:31, Philadelphia (Hextall-roughing, served by Eklund)-4:31, Edmonton (MacTavish-roughing)-4:31, Edmonton (McSorley-roughing)-4:31, Edmonton (Tikkanen-roughing)-14:16, Philadelphia (Crossman-holding)-14:16

Shots on Goal:	Edmonton	18-13-12-43
	Philadelphia	12-6-2-20

1987-88

Unlike most other seasons, Glen Sather made no off-season moves to improve the club, but major changes were in the offing. Defenseman Paul Coffey, no longer able to get along with Sather, had asked to be traded, and on November 24 he got his wish. Coffey was traded to Pittsburgh with veteran Dave Hunter and minor leaguer Wayne Van Dorp for Craig Simpson, Moe Mantha, Dave Hannan and Chris Joseph. While missing the two veterans in the dressing room, on the ice the effect of the trade was negligible. Craig Simpson provided 43 goals in 59 games, while Hannan was a Dave Hunter–type player with good defensive skills. Mantha and Joseph played well on defense when called upon.

Also joining the team this year was defensive forward Normand Lacombe. Lacombe played in only one game after being obtained near the end of the 1987 season from Buffalo, for veteran Lee Fogolin, but appeared in 53 regular season games this season.

The Oilers were without one other star this season. Goaltender Andy Moog, not happy with his backup role to Grant Fuhr, had also asked to be traded. Moog ended up playing nearly all of the season with the Canadian National Team while his spot on the Oiler roster was taken by Daryl Reaugh. With the absence of Moog, Fuhr played in a record 75 games. In March Sather traded Moog to Boston for Geoff Courtnall and Bill Ranford. Ranford more than made up for the loss of Moog and would be a star in the Oiler net for years to come.

General Manager Glen Sather came up with a fine prospect at this year's entry draft. Geoff Smith, a 6'3" defenseman from the St. Albert Saints of the AJHL, would be named to the NHL'S All Rookie Team, recording 15 points in 74 games. The Oilers won six of their first eight games and were 30–18–7 (.609) at the All-Star break.

This was a season of change for the team. For the first time since the 1980-81 season Edmonton did not finish at the top of the Smythe Division nor lead the league in scoring. The Calgary Flames managed to post four more wins and six more points to finish at the top of the division for the first time in their history. The Flames also managed to score more goals than the Oilers in the regular season. The Oilers finished second to the Flames, Calgary scoring 397 goals and the Oilers 363.

Also for the first time since the team entered the league, Wayne Gretzky did not lead the league in scoring. Gretzky finished 19 points behind Mario Lemieux in the scoring race, due in part to having missed 13 games in the middle of the season with a sprained right knee. Gretzky and Messier were the only Edmonton players to finish in the top ten in scoring and the only two Oilers to score over 100 points.

Kevin Lowe missed ten games with a fractured bone in his left wrist while Jeff Beukeboom missed four games with a lacerated right hand. Although Grant Fuhr played 31 more games in goal than in the previous season he managed to record an almost identical goals against average as in 1987 and the team finished 8th in defense.

With the absence of Coffey and Moog, the Oilers did not look to be favored to repeat as Cup champions. In the first round series against Winnipeg, who had finished 22 points back of Edmonton, the Oilers knocked off the Jets in five games. The Oilers then met perennial rival Calgary in the division final series and had little trouble with the Flames, defeating them in four games.

The Oilers then went on to the conference final series, meeting the much improved Detroit Red Wings who had finished only six points behind the Oilers in the overall standings. The Oilers easily defeated the Wings four games to one.

After breezing through the first three rounds the Oilers advanced to the Stanley Cup final series for the fifth time in six years. Edmonton won the first three games, outscoring Boston 12–6 and it appeared that the team might win the Stanley Cup on the road for the first time.

On May 24, the teams met in game four in the Boston Garden. Just as Edmonton had scored their third goal to tie the game with 3:23 left in the second period the lights went out in the arena. With little chance of the power coming back on league president John Ziegler canceled the game. According to league bylaws a canceled game would be replayed at the end of a series if necessary. The Oilers made it unnecessary however as they won the May 26 game in Edmonton to wrap up Stanley Cup number four.

1987-88 Regular Season Scoring

#		*Ht.*	*Wt.*	*Age*	*GP*	*G*	*A*	*Pts.*	*Shots*	*S%*	*GW*	*GT*	*PP*	*SH*	*P/M*	*PIM*
99	Gretzky (C)	72	170	26	64	40	109	149	211	19.0	3	0	9	5	39	24
11	Messier (A)	73	205	26	77	37	74	111	182	20.3	7	2	12	3	21	103
17	Kurri	72	190	27	80	43	53	96	207	20.8	5	1	10	3	25	30
9	Anderson	71	185	27	80	38	50	88	255	14.9	3	0	16	1	5	58
10	Tikkanen	71	185	22	80	23	51	74	142	16.2	2	0	6	1	21	153
18	Simpson	74	185	20	59	43	21	64	118	36.4	5	0	18	0	15	43
5	S. Smith	76	210	24	79	12	43	55	116	10.3	1	0	5	0	40	286
26	Krushelnyski	74	200	27	76	20	27	47	124	16.1	0	0	4	0	26	64
22	Huddy	72	200	28	77	13	28	41	163	8.0	2	1	2	0	23	71
14	MacTavish	72	190	29	80	15	17	32	90	16.7	5	0	0	3	-3	47
33	McSorley	73	210	24	60	9	17	26	66	13.6	1	0	0	0	23	223
6	Beukeboom	76	210	22	73	5	20	25	76	6.6	1	0	1	0	27	201
4	Lowe (A)	74	195	28	70	9	15	24	82	11.0	2	0	2	1	18	89
12	Hannan	70	175	26	51	9	11	20	62	14.5	2	1	0	2	12	43
28	Muni	74	200	25	72	4	15	19	56	7.1	0	0	0	1	32	77
19	Lacombe	71	205	23	53	8	9	17	44	18.2	2	0	1	0	-3	36
24	McClelland	74	200	25	74	10	6	16	61	16.4	0	0	0	0	1	281
23	Acton	68	170	29	26	3	6	9	26	11.5	1	0	1	0	-10	21
15	Courtnall	72	165	25	12	4	4	8	32	12.5	1	0	0	0	1	15
31	Fuhr	70	185	25	75	0	8	8	0	0.0	0	0	0	0	0	16
15	S. Graves	70	175	23	21	3	4	7	21	14.3	0	0	0	0	13	10
12	Hunter	71	200	29	21	3	3	6	18	16.7	0	0	0	0	1	6
20	Mantha	74	195	26	25	0	6	6	50	0.0	0	0	0	0	7	26

#		*Ht.*	*Wt.*	*Age*	*GP*	*G*	*A*	*Pts.*	*Shots*	*S%*	*GW*	*GT*	*PP*	*SH*	*P/M*	*PIM*
20	Dykstra	74	210	25	15	2	3	5	15	13.3	0	0	0	0	1	39
37	McMurchy	69	165	24	9	4	1	5	11	36.4	1	0	0	0	2	8
8	Miner	70	180	22	14	2	3	5	16	12.5	0	0	0	0	-4	16
27	Shudra	73	180	20	10	0	5	5	8	0.0	0	0	0	0	5	6
2	Joseph	73	195	18	7	0	4	4	1	0.0	0	0	0	0	-3	6
32	Wiemer	76	200	26	12	1	2	3	24	4.2	0	0	0	0	7	15
21	Gregg	76	215	31	15	1	2	3	20	5.0	0	0	0	0	4	8
30	Ranford	70	170	21	6	0	2	2	0	0.0	0	0	0	0	0	0
36	Odelein	72	195	21	12	0	2	2	17	0.0	0	0	0	0	-2	33
2	Ennis	72	205	20	5	1	0	1	9	11.1	0	0	1	0	0	10
16	Buchberger	74	190	21	19	1	0	1	10	10.0	0	1	0	0	-1	81
18	Lamb	69	180	23	2	0	0	0	0	0.0	0	0	0	0	0	0
20	Metcalfe	72	195	20	2	0	0	0	0	0.0	0	0	0	0	-1	0
30	Skorodenski	73	180	27	3	0	0	0	0	0.0	0	0	0	0	0	0
34	Donnelly	71	185	25	4	0	0	0	3	0.0	0	0	0	0	0	4
23	Lemay	71	185	25	4	0	0	0	5	0.0	0	0	0	0	-1	2
29	Reaugh	76	190	22	6	0	0	0	0	0.0	0	0	0	0	0	0
	Bench															22
		72	191	24	80	363	621	984	2341	15.5	44	6	88	20	73	2173

1987-88 Goaltender Record

	GP	*Min.*	*GA*	*W*	*L*	*T*	*Ave.*	*SA*	*Pct.*	*SO*	*EN*
Ranford	6	325	16	3	0	2	2.95	159	0.889	0	0
Fuhr	75	4304	246	40	24	9	3.43	2066	0.881	4	5
Reaugh	6	176	14	1	1	0	4.78	114	0.870	0	0
Skorodenski	3	61	7	0	0	0	6.86	25	0.720	0	0
	80	4866	288	44	25	11	3.55	2364	0.878	4	5

Coach: Glen Sather 44-25-11

1987-88 Scoring vs. Opposition

	Bost.	*Buff.*	*Calg.*	*Chi.*	*Det.*	*Hart.*	*L.A.*	*Minn.*	*Mont.*	*N.J.*
Acton	0–2–2	———	0–0–0	1–0–1	0–0–0	1–0–1	0–0–0	0–0–0	0–0–0	0–0–0
Anderson	3–2–5	1–2–3	9–5–14	0–0–0	0–2–2	1–2–3	5–5–10	1–2–3	0–0–0	2–4–6
Beukeboom	0–1–1	0–3–3	1–2–3	1–1–2	0–0–0	1–0–1	0–2–2	0–2–2	1–0–1	1–0–1
Buchberger	0–0–0	0–0–0	0–0–0	———	0–0–0	———	———	0–0–0	0–0–0	———
Courtnall	———	3–0–3	———	———	0–0–0	———	1–0–1	0–2–2	0–0–0	———
Donnelly	———	———	———	———	———	———	———	———	0–0–0	———
Dykstra	0–0–0	———	0–0–0	0–0–0	1–0–1	———	0–0–0	———	———	———
Ennis	———	———	0–0–0	———	0–0–0	———	0–0–0	———	0–0–0	———
Graves	———	1–0–1	0–1–1	1–0–1	0–0–0	———	0–0–0	———	———	———
Gregg	———	0–0–0	0–0–0	———	0–0–0	———	0–0–0	0–0–0	0–0–0	———
Gretzky	1–4–5	2–5–7	4–11–15	2–3–5	0–5–5	1–2–3	6–12–18	7–6–13	0–1–1	2–8–10
Hannan	0–0–0	0–0–0	0–0–0	0–0–0	0–0–0	0–2–2	0–3–3	0–0–0	1–0–1	2–0–2
Huddy	1–0–1	0–2–2	1–5–6	1–2–3	0–0–0	0–1–1	2–3–5	0–0–0	1–1–2	1–1–2
Hunter	0–0–0	0–0–0	0–0–0	0–0–0	0–0–0	———	1–0–1	———	0–0–0	0–0–0
Joseph	———	0–0–0	0–0–0	0–0–0	0–0–0	———	———	———	———	0–2–2
Krushelnyski	0–0–0	1–4–5	3–1–4	0–1–1	1–0–1	1–2–3	1–1–2	1–0–1	0–2–2	0–3–3
Kurri	1–2–3	0–1–1	2–5–7	0–1–1	1–2–3	1–2–3	5–6–11	4–6–10	0–1–1	2–6–8
Lacombe	1–0–1	0–0–0	0–0–0	1–0–1	0–1–1	0–0–0	1–2–3	0–0–0	1–0–1	0–0–0
Lamb	0–0–0	———	0–0–0	———	———	———	———	———	———	———
Lemay	0–0–0	———	———	———	———	0–0–0	———	———	———	———
Lowe	0–2–2	0–0–0	0–2–2	0–1–1	0–0–0	1–3–4	1–2–3	0–0–0	0–0–0	0–0–0
MacTavish	0–1–1	1–0–1	3–2–5	0–1–1	1–0–1	1–1–2	1–2–3	1–1–2	0–0–0	0–0–0
Mantha	0–0–0	0–0–0	0–0–0	0–0–0	0–1–1	0–1–1	0–0–0	0–0–0	0–0–0	0–1–1
McClelland	0–0–0	2–1–3	1–1–2	0–0–0	0–0–0	0–0–0	2–1–3	0–1–1	0–0–0	0–0–0
McMurchy	———	0–0–0	0–0–0	———	———	———	0–0–0	———	———	1–0–1
McSorley	0–0–0	0–0–0	0–1–1	1–0–1	0–0–0	1–1–2	1–3–4	0–0–0	0–0–0	0–2–2
Messier	1–2–3	3–4–7	2–8–10	1–5–6	2–2–4	1–0–1	5–7–12	1–3–4	0–0–0	3–5–8
Metcalfe	0–0–0	———	———	———	———	0–0–0	———	———	———	———
Miner	0–0–0	———	1–0–1	———	———	———	0–1–1	0–0–0	0–0–0	0–0–0
Muni	0–0–0	0–0–0	0–2–2	0–0–0	0–0–0	0–0–0	0–0–0	0–1–1	0–0–0	1–3–4

	Bost.	*Buff.*	*Calg.*	*Chi.*	*Det.*	*Hart.*	*L.A.*	*Minn.*	*Mont.*	*N.J.*
Odelein	———	0–1–1	0–0–0	0–0–0	———	0–0–0	0–0–0	0–0–0	———	0–0–0
Shudra	———	0–3–3	0–0–0	0–0–0	———	———	0–0–0	———	———	0–0–0
Simpson	0–0–0	2–1–3	2–1–3	2–2–4	5–1–6	2–1–3	5–2–7	1–1–2	0–1–1	0–0–0
Smith	2–0–2	0–1–1	2–3–5	0–0–0	0–2–2	1–2–3	1–3–4	1–4–5	0–3–3	1–0–1
Tikkanen	0–0–0	0–1–1	2–4–6	1–2–3	0–2–2	0–0–0	1–9–10	4–3–7	2–1–3	4–0–4
Wiemer	———	0–1–1	0–0–0	0–0–0	———	———	1–0–1	———	0–0–0	0–0–0

	NYI.	*NYR.*	*Phil.*	*Pitt.*	*Que.*	*St.L.*	*Tor.*	*Van.*	*Wash.*	*Winn.*
Acton	0–0–0	0–0–0	0–0–0	0–2–2	———	0–0–0	0–0–0	0–1–1	———	1–1–2
Anderson	1–2–3	2–1–3	4–0–4	1–1–2	0–0–0	1–3–4	1–4–5	3–10–13	0–1–1	3–4–7
Beukeboom	0–0–0	0–0–0	0–0–0	0–1–1	0–1–1	0–1–1	0–1–1	0–2–2	0–1–1	0–2–2
Buchberger	0–0–0	———	0–0–0	0–0–0	1–0–1	———	———	———	0–0–0	0–0–0
Courtnall	0–1–1	0–0–0	———	———	———	0–0–0	0–1–1	0–0–0	———	0–0–0
Donnelly	———	———	———	———	0–0–0	———	———	0–0–0	———	———
Dykstra	0–0–0	0–0–0	———	0–0–0	———	0–0–0	1–2–3	0–1–1	———	0–0–0
Ennis	———	———	———	———	0–0–0	———	———	———	———	———
Graves	1–0–1	0–1–1	0–0–0	0–0–0	0–1–1	———	0–0–0	0–0–0	0–1–1	0–0–0
Gregg	0–0–0	0–0–0	0–1–1	———	———	1–0–1	0–0–0	0–1–1	———	0–0–0
Gretzky	1–2–3	3–4–7	1–8–9	0–2–2	0–2–2	0–7–7	3–5–8	5–13–18	0–0–0	2–9–11
Hannan	0–1–1	0–0–0	1–0–1	3–2–5	0–0–0	0–0–0	0–1–1	1–2–3	0–0–0	1–0–1
Huddy	0–1–1	1–1–2	0–1–1	1–1–2	0–0–0	2–1–3	0–1–1	1–3–4	1–0–1	0–4–4
Hunter	———	0–0–0	———	1–0–1	0–0–0	0–0–0	———	1–3–4	———	0–0–0
Joseph	———	———	———	———	———	———	———	———	0–1–1	0–1–1
Krushelnyski	2–0–2	0–0–0	1–1–2	2–3–5	1–2–3	0–0–0	1–0–1	3–5–8	0–1–1	2–1–3
Kurri	2–1–3	1–3–4	1–2–3	2–2–4	1–2–3	4–1–5	3–1–4	7–4–11	1–0–1	5–5–10
Lacombe	0–1–1	1–0–1	0–0–0	0–1–1	0–0–0	1–0–1	———	1–1–2	0–0–0	1–3–4
Lemay	———	———	———	———	———	———	———	———	0–0–0	0–0–0
Lowe	0–0–0	0–0–0	1–0–1	1–2–3	1–0–1	0–1–1	0–0–0	1–2–3	1–0–1	2–0–2
MacTavish	0–1–1	0–1–1	0–0–0	0–1–1	0–0–0	0–2–2	0–0–0	3–2–5	0–1–1	4–1–5
Mantha	0–0–0	———	0–0–0	———	———	———	0–0–0	0–1–1	0–0–0	0–2–2
McClelland	0–1–1	2–0–2	0–0–0	0–0–0	1–0–1	0–0–0	0–1–1	2–0–2	0–0–0	0–0–0
McMurchy	———	3–1–4	———	0–0–0	———	0–0–0	———	———	———	0–0–0
McSorley	0–1–1	0–0–0	1–1–2	1–1–2	0–0–0	0–2–2	0–1–1	4–0–4	0–0–0	0–4–4
Messier	0–0–0	1–5–6	1–0–1	1–6–7	1–2–3	2–4–6	2–4–6	6–8–14	1–1–2	3–8–11
Miner	0–0–0	———	———	———	0–0–0	1–0–1	0–0–0	0–2–2	———	———
Muni	0–0–0	0–0–0	0–0–0	0–1–1	0–0–0	0–0–0	2–0–2	0–6–6	0–0–0	1–2–3
Odelein	0–0–0	———	0–0–0	0–0–0	0–1–1	———	———	———	———	0–0–0
Shudra	———	0–0–0	———	0–1–1	0–1–1	0–0–0	———	———	———	0–0–0
Simpson	4–0–4	0–0–0	2–3–5	2–2–4	1–0–1	3–1–4	1–1–2	6–1–7	1–1–2	4–2–6
Smith	0–3–3	0–4–4	0–3–3	1–2–3	1–1–2	2–3–5	0–1–1	0–5–5	0–0–0	0–3–3
Tikkanen	0–2–2	1–6–7	1–3–4	1–2–3	0–0–0	0–4–4	1–3–4	2–5–7	0–1–1	3–3–6
Wiemer	———	0–0–0	———	0–0–0	0–0–0	0–1–1	———	———	———	0–0–0

1987-88 Goaltender Records vs. Opposition

	GP	*Min.*	*GA*	*EN*	*SO*	*Ave.*	*W–L–T*	*Opposition*
Grant Fuhr	3	177	12	0	0	4.07	1–1–1	Boston
	3	180	6	0	1	2.00	3–0–0	Buffalo
	8	483	32	1	0	3.98	3–4–1	Calgary
	3	179	12	2	0	4.02	1–2–0	Chicago
	3	140	12	1	0	5.14	1–2–0	Detroit
	2	120	3	0	0	1.50	2–0–0	Hartford
	8	453	29	0	0	3.84	4–2–2	Los Angeles
	3	145	7	0	0	2.90	2–0–0	Minnesota
	3	180	13	0	0	4.33	0–3–0	Montreal
	3	180	19	0	0	6.33	1–2–0	New Jersey
	3	179	9	0	0	3.02	1–2–0	N.Y. Islanders
	3	105	9	0	0	5.14	1–1–0	N.Y. Rangers
	3	165	5	0	1	1.82	2–1–0	Philadelphia
	3	180	8	0	0	2.67	3–0–0	Pittsburgh
	3	185	10	0	0	3.24	1–1–1	Quebec
	2	121	9	0	0	4.46	2–0–0	St. Louis
	2	125	6	0	0	2.88	1–0–1	Toronto
	7	382	18	0	0	2.83	7–0–0	Vancouver

	GP	Min.	GA	EN	SO	Ave.	W-L-T	Opposition
	3	179	7	1	0	2.35	1-2-0	Washington
	7	442	20	0	2	2.71	3-1-3	Winnipeg
Bill Ranford	1	40	5	0	0	7.50	0-0-1	Minnesota
	1	40	1	0	0	1.50	0-0-0	N.Y. Rangers
	1	60	2	0	0	2.00	1-0-0	St. Louis
	1	60	4	0	0	4.00	1-0-0	Toronto
	1	65	3	0	0	2.77	0-0-1	Vancouver
	1	60	1	0	0	1.00	1-0-0	Winnipeg
Daryl Reaugh	1	40	2	0	0	3.00	0-0-0	Detroit
	1	59	4	0	0	4.07	0-1-0	Hartford
	1	7	0	0	0	0.00	0-0-0	Los Angeles
	1	35	4	0	0	6.86	1-0-0	N.Y. Rangers
	1	14	2	0	0	8.57	0-0-0	Philadelphia
	1	20	2	0	0	6.00	0-0-0	Vancouver
W. Skorodenski	1	8	0	0	0	0.00	0-0-0	Boston
	1	30	3	0	0	6.00	0-0-0	Los Angeles
	1	23	4	0	0	10.43	0-0-0	Vancouver

1987-88 Schedule Results

Date	Visitor	Score		Home	Score
Oct. 9	Detroit	4	at	Edmonton	1
Oct. 11	Edmonton	9	at	Los Angeles	2
Oct. 14	Calgary	5	at	Edmonton	4
Oct. 16	Edmonton	5	at	Calgary	2
Oct. 17	Boston	3	at	Edmonton	4
Oct. 21	Los Angeles	2	at	Edmonton	6
Oct. 23	Edmonton	5	at	Vancouver	4 OT
Oct. 24	Vancouver	5	at	Edmonton	9
Oct. 27	Edmonton	0	at	Quebec	5
Oct. 28	Edmonton	1	at	Montreal	3
Oct. 31	Edmonton	5	at	New Jersey	6
Nov. 1	Edmonton	7	at	Rangers	6
Nov. 4	Rangers	2	at	Edmonton	7
Nov. 5	Edmonton	4	at	Calgary	4 OT
Nov. 7	Buffalo	0	at	Edmonton	5
Nov. 10	Edmonton	4	at	Los Angeles	4 OT
Nov. 14	Edmonton	6	at	St. Louis	5 OT
Nov. 15	Edmonton	4	at	Chicago	5
Nov. 18	Quebec	1	at	Edmonton	4
Nov. 20	Pittsburgh	1	at	Edmonton	4
Nov. 22	Edmonton	3	at	Winnipeg	4 OT
Nov. 25	New Jersey	8	at	Edmonton	7 OT
Nov. 27	Chicago	3	at	Edmonton	4
Nov. 29	Edmonton	5	at	Buffalo	2
Dec. 1	Edmonton	2	at	Washington	4
Dec. 2	Edmonton	4	at	Detroit	7
Dec. 5	Toronto	2	at	Edmonton	5
Dec. 6	Minnesota	4	at	Edmonton	10
Dec. 9	Winnipeg	0	at	Edmonton	2
Dec. 11	Vancouver	1	at	Edmonton	2
Dec. 12	Edmonton	6	at	Vancouver	3
Dec. 16	Edmonton	5	at	Los Angeles	7
Dec. 18	Winnipeg	5	at	Edmonton	5 OT
Dec. 19	Hartford	4	at	Edmonton	3
Dec. 22	Los Angeles	2	at	Edmonton	5
Dec. 26	Edmonton	5	at	Calgary	4
Dec. 28	Vancouver	3	at	Edmonton	7
Dec. 30	Philadelphia	0	at	Edmonton	6
Jan. 2	Edmonton	0	at	Washington	2
Jan. 4	Edmonton	2	at	Boston	2 OT
Jan. 6	Edmonton	5	at	Hartford	1
Jan. 8	Edmonton	4	at	Winnipeg	4 OT
Jan. 9	Islanders	1	at	Edmonton	5
Jan. 11	Washington	2	at	Edmonton	3
Jan. 13	Calgary	3	at	Edmonton	5
Jan. 15	Winnipeg	4	at	Edmonton	4 OT
Jan. 18	Edmonton	4	at	Montreal	6
Jan. 19	Edmonton	4	at	Quebec	4 OT
Jan. 21	Edmonton	1	at	Philadelphia	3
Jan. 23	Edmonton	2	at	Islanders	3
Jan. 25	Edmonton	6	at	Pittsburgh	4
Jan. 29	Calgary	5	at	Edmonton	4
Jan. 30	Hartford	2	at	Edmonton	5
Feb. 3	New Jersey	5	at	Edmonton	8
Feb. 6	Edmonton	2	at	Los Angeles	7
Feb. 11	Edmonton	7	at	Vancouver	2
Feb. 12	Boston	7	at	Edmonton	4
Feb. 14	Vancouver	6	at	Edmonton	7
Feb. 17	Toronto	4	at	Edmonton	4 OT
Feb. 19	Pittsburgh	3	at	Edmonton	7
Feb. 21	Edmonton	4	at	Winnipeg	3 OT
Feb. 23	Edmonton	6	at	St. Louis	4
Feb. 24	Edmonton	4	at	Chicago	6
Feb. 28	Calgary	3	at	Edmonton	2
Mar. 1	Los Angeles	3	at	Edmonton	5
Mar. 4	Philadelphia	4	at	Edmonton	7
Mar. 5	Edmonton	4	at	Calgary	7
Mar. 7	Edmonton	6	at	Winnipeg	0
Mar. 9	Montreal	4	at	Edmonton	1
Mar. 12	Edmonton	3	at	Vancouver	3 OT
Mar. 15	Buffalo	4	at	Edmonton	6
Mar. 18	Winnipeg	1	at	Edmonton	4
Mar. 20	Edmonton	5	at	Minnesota	5 OT
Mar. 22	Edmonton	6	at	Detroit	4
Mar. 24	Edmonton	1	at	Rangers	6
Mar. 26	Edmonton	4	at	Islanders	5
Mar. 28	Edmonton	6	at	Toronto	4
Mar. 30	Minnesota	3	at	Edmonton	6
April 1	St. Louis	2	at	Edmonton	5
April 3	Los Angeles	5	at	Edmonton	5 OT

Opponent	*Home W–L–T*	*Road W–L–T*
Boston	1–1–0	0–0–1
Buffalo	2–0–0	1–0–0
Calgary	1–3–0	2–1–1
Chicago	1–0–0	0–2–0
Detroit	0–1–0	1–1–0
Hartford	1–1–0	1–0–0
Los Angeles	3–0–1	1–2–1
Minnesota	2–0–0	0–0–1
Montreal	0–1–0	0–2–0
New Jersey	1–1–0	0–1–0
Islanders	1–0–0	0–2–0
Rangers	1–0–0	1–1–0
Philadelphia	2–0–0	0–1–0
Pittsburgh	2–0–0	1–0–0
Quebec	1–0–0	0–1–1
St. Louis	1–0–0	2–0–0
Toronto	1–0–1	1–0–0
Vancouver	4–0–0	3–0–1
Washington	1–0–0	0–2–0
Winnipeg	2–0–2	2–1–1

Opponent	*Overall W–L–T*	*GF–GA*
Boston	1–1–1	10–12
Buffalo	3–0–0	16–6
Calgary	3–4–1	33–33
Chicago	1–2–0	12–14
Detroit	1–2–0	11–15
Hartford	2–1–0	13–7
Los Angeles	4–2–2	41–32
Minnesota	2–0–1	21–12
Montreal	0–3–0	6–13
New Jersey	1–2–0	20–19
Islanders	1–2–0	11–9
Rangers	2–1–0	15–14
Philadelphia	2–1–0	14–7
Pittsburgh	3–0–0	17–8
Quebec	1–1–1	8–10
St. Louis	3–0–0	17–11
Toronto	2–0–1	15–10
Vancouver	7–0–1	46–27
Washington	1–2–0	5–8
Winnipeg	4–1–3	32–21

1987-88 Playoff Scoring

#		*GP*	*G*	*A*	*Pts*	*Shots*	*S%*	*GW*	*OT*	*PP*	*SH*	*P/M*	*PIM*
99	Wayne Gretzky	19	12	31	43	62	19.4	3	1	5	1	9	16
11	Mark Messier	19	11	23	34	42	26.2	0	0	7	1	9	29
17	Jari Kurri	19	14	17	31	57	24.6	3	1	5	0	15	12
10	Esa Tikkanen	19	10	17	27	42	23.8	1	0	5	0	2	72
9	Glenn Anderson	19	9	16	25	43	20.9	1	0	4	0	5	49
18	Craig Simpson	19	13	6	19	33	39.4	3	0	3	0	4	26
5	Steve Smith	19	1	11	12	26	3.8	0	0	1	0	16	55
26	Mike Krushelnyski	19	4	6	10	18	22.2	0	0	0	0	4	12
22	Charlie Huddy	13	4	5	9	33	12.1	0	0	2	0	2	10
21	Randy Gregg	19	1	8	9	22	4.5	1	0	0	0	17	24
24	Kevin McClelland	19	2	3	5	13	15.4	0	0	0	0	-1	68
28	Craig Muni	19	0	4	4	11	0.0	0	0	0	0	7	31
19	Normand Lacombe	19	3	0	3	17	17.6	1	0	0	0	0	28
33	Marty McSorley	16	0	3	3	15	0.0	0	0	0	0	2	67
15	Geoff Courtnall	19	0	3	3	33	0.0	0	0	0	0	2	23
23	Keith Acton	7	2	0	2	10	20.0	2	0	0	0	4	16
12	Dave Hannan	12	1	1	2	11	9.1	1	0	0	0	-3	8
4	Kevin Lowe	19	0	2	2	9	0.0	0	0	0	0	2	26
31	Grant Fuhr	19	0	1	1	0	0.0	0	0	0	0	0	6
14	Craig MacTavish	19	0	1	1	12	0.0	0	0	0	0	0	31
32	Jim Wiemer	2	0	0	0	3	0.0	0	0	0	0	-2	2
6	Jeff Beukeboom	7	0	0	0	2	0.0	0	0	0	0	-1	16
		19	87	158	245	514	16.9	16	2	32	2	19	627

1987-88 Playoff Goaltending

	GP	*Min.*	*GA*	*W*	*L*	*Ave.*	*SA*	*Pct.*	*SO*	*EN*
Grant Fuhr	19	1136	55	16	2	2.90	471	0.883	0	1
	19	1136	56	16	2	2.95	472	0.881	0	1

Date			*Result*			*Winning Goaltender*	*Winning Goal*
April 6, 1988	Winnipeg	4	at	Edmonton	7	Grant Fuhr	Craig Simpson
April 7, 1988	Winnipeg	2	at	Edmonton	3	Grant Fuhr	Craig Simpson
April 9, 1988	Edmonton	4	at	Winnipeg	6	Daniel Berthiaume	Randy Gilhen
April 10, 1988	Edmonton	5	at	Winnipeg	3	Grant Fuhr	Normand Lacombe
April 12, 1988	Winnipeg	2	at	Edmonton	6	Grant Fuhr	Jari Kurri
April 19, 1988	Edmonton	3	at	Calgary	1	Grant Fuhr	Jari Kurri
April 21, 1988	Edmonton	5	at	Calgary	4	Grant Fuhr	Wayne Gretzky[1]
April 23, 1988	Calgary	2	at	Edmonton	4	Grant Fuhr	Glenn Anderson

Date			*Result*			*Winning Goaltender*	*Winning Goal*
April 25, 1988	Calgary	4	at	Edmonton	6	Grant Fuhr	Dave Hannan
May 3, 1988	Detroit	1	at	Edmonton	4	Grant Fuhr	Randy Gregg
May 5, 1988	Detroit	3	at	Edmonton	5	Grant Fuhr	Craig Simpson
May 7, 1988	Edmonton	2	at	Detroit	5	Glen Hanlon	Bob Probert
May 9, 1988	Edmonton	4	at	Detroit	3	Grant Fuhr	Jari Kurri[2]
May 11, 1988	Detroit	4	at	Edmonton	8	Grant Fuhr	Keith Acton
May 18, 1988	Boston	1	at	Edmonton	2	Grant Fuhr	Keith Acton
May 20, 1988	Boston	2	at	Edmonton	4	Grant Fuhr	Wayne Gretzky
May 22, 1988	Edmonton	6	at	Boston	3	Grant Fuhr	Esa Tikkanen
May 24, 1988	Edmonton	3	at	Boston	3	**Game canceled due to power failure.**	
May 26, 1988	Boston	3	at	Edmonton	6	Grant Fuhr	Wayne Gretzky

[1]7:54 of overtime
[2]11:02 of overtime

1987-88 Stanley Cup Winning Game

May 26, 1988: Northlands Coliseum, Edmonton

Attendance: 17,500

Oilers

Starting Lineup: **31**-Grant Fuhr (Goal), **28**-Craig Muni (Defense) **4**-Kevin Lowe (Defense), **18**-Craig Simpson (Left Wing), **11**-Mark Messier (Center), **9**-Glenn Anderson (Right Wing).

Remaining Players: **23**-Keith Acton, **15**-Geoff Courtnall, **21**-Randy Gregg, **99**-Wayne Gretzky, **22**-Charlie Huddy, **26**-Mike Krushelnyski, **17**-Jari Kurri, **19**-Normand Lacombe, **14**-Craig MacTavish, **24**-Kevin McClelland, **33**-Marty McSorley, **5**-Steve Smith, **10**-Esa Tikkanen, **30**-Bill Ranford (backup goaltender).

Average: Age-25.8 years, Height-72.6 inches, Weight-192.9 pounds, Years Experience-4.35 years

Bruins

Starting Lineup: **35**-Andy Moog (Goal), **6**-Gord Kluzak (Defense), **77**-Ray Bourque (Defense), **12**-Randy Burridge (Left Wing),**11**-Steve Kasper (Center), **39**-Greg Johnston (Right Wing).

Remaining Players: **18**-Keith Crowder, **40**-Greg Hawgood, **23**-Craig Janney, **27**-Bob Joyce, **36**-Moe Lemay, **28**-Reed Larson, **13**-Ken Linseman, **16**-Rick Middleton, **8**-Cam Neely, **10**-Bill O'Dwyer, **42**-Bob Sweeney, **22**-Michael Thelven, **26**-Glen Wesley, **1**-Rejean Lemelin (backup goaltender).

Average: Age-24.6 years, Height-71.6 inches, Weight-188.7 pounds, Years Experience-4.63 years

Officials

Referee: Andy Van Hellemond, Linesmen: Ron Finn and Ray Scapinello

Game Summary

1st Period

Goals: Boston-Kasper (Burridge, Bourque) 00:43
Edmonton-Lacombe (Muni, Lowe) 6:07
Boston-Linseman (Bourque) 9:44 PP
Edmonton-Tikkanen (Kurri, Gretzky) 15:03PP

Penalties: Boston (Ray Bourque-high sticking)-3:55, Edmonton (Esa Tikkanen-hooking)-8:30, Edmonton (Messier-slashing)-9:16, Boston (Crowder-hooking)-13:29

2nd Period

Goals: Edmonton-Krushelnyski (McClelland, Lowe) 6:38
Edmonton-Gretzky (Tikkanen, S. Smith) 9:44 PP
Edmonton-Simpson (Gretzky, Gregg) 19:58

Penalties: Edmonton (Simpson-unsportsmanlike conduct)-00:52, Boston (Larson-tripping)-3:31, Boston-(Moe Lemay-roughing)-7:08, Edmonton (Normand Lacombe-roughing)-7:08, Boston (Michael Thelven-holding)-8:00, Boston (too many men, served by Bob Joyce)-10:42, Edmonton (Anderson-hooking)-11:55

3rd Period

Goals: Edmonton-Tikkanen (Kurri, Gregg) 1:21
Boston-Kasper (Johnston, Wesley) 6:35

Penalties: Edmonton (Krushelnyski-holding)-12:09, Edmonton (Tikkanen-double minor for high sticking, Tikkanen's second penalty served by Simpson)-14:38, Boston (Ken Linseman-high sticking)-14:38, Edmonton (Krushelnyski-hooking)-18:48

Shots on Goal: Edmonton 8-10-8-26
Boston 8-6-5-19

Table 8. Oilers All Time Regular Season Overtime Record vs. Opponents

Team	*Overall*				*Home*				*Away*			
	GP	*W*	*L*	*T*	*GP*	*W*	*L*	*T*	*GP*	*W*	*L*	*T*
Anaheim	*7*	*2*	*3*	*2*	*1*	*0*	*1*	*0*	*6*	*2*	*2*	*2*
Atl. Thrashers	*0*	*0*	*0*	*0*	*0*	*0*	*0*	*0*	*0*	*0*	*0*	*0*
Boston	*8*	*1*	*4*	*3*	*2*	*0*	*1*	*1*	*6*	*1*	*3*	*2*
Buffalo	*12*	*4*	*2*	*6*	*3*	*2*	*0*	*1*	*9*	*2*	*2*	*5*
Calgary	*18*	*2*	*4*	*12*	*9*	*1*	*1*	*7*	*9*	*1*	*3*	*5*
Carolina	*3*	*0*	*0*	*3*	*2*	*0*	*0*	*2*	*1*	*0*	*0*	*1*
Chicago	*17*	*5*	*3*	*9*	*9*	*2*	*3*	*4*	*8*	*3*	*0*	*5*
Colorado	*7*	*1*	*2*	*4*	*4*	*0*	*1*	*3*	*3*	*1*	*1*	*1*
Dallas	*6*	*1*	*2*	*3*	*5*	*1*	*2*	*2*	*1*	*0*	*0*	*1*
Detroit	*7*	*0*	*1*	*6*	*4*	*0*	*0*	*4*	*3*	*0*	*1*	*2*
Florida	*3*	*0*	*0*	*3*	*1*	*0*	*0*	*1*	*2*	*0*	*0*	*2*
Hartford	*5*	*1*	*0*	*4*	*2*	*1*	*0*	*1*	*3*	*0*	*0*	*3*

Alberta Premier Peter Lougheed (left) and Edmonton Mayor Laurence Decore with the Stanley Cup in 1988. (EA340-1387 City of Edmonton Archives.)

Team		*Overall*				*Home*				*Away*		
	GP	*W*	*L*	*T*	*GP*	*W*	*L*	*T*	*GP*	*W*	*L*	*T*
Los Angeles	30	3	5	22	16	2	4	10	14	1	1	12
Montreal	7	4	1	2	1	1	0	0	6	3	1	2
Nashville	2	0	2	1	1	0	1	0	1	0	0	1
New Jersey	11	3	2	6	8	1	2	5	3	2	0	1
N.Y. Islanders	11	1	0	10	5	0	0	5	6	1	0	5
N.Y. Rangers	14	4	2	8	5	1	1	3	9	3	1	5
North Stars	11	4	0	7	5	2	0	3	6	2	0	4
Ottawa	4	0	1	3	2	0	0	2	2	0	1	1
Philadelphia	8	1	1	6	5	1	0	4	3	0	1	2
Phoenix	5	1	2	2	3	1	0	2	2	0	2	0
Pittsburgh	5	1	1	3	1	1	0	0	4	0	1	3
Quebec	4	2	1	1	1	0	1	0	3	2	0	1
St. Louis	11	2	4	5	3	1	1	1	8	1	4	3
San Jose	11	1	1	9	6	0	0	6	5	1	1	3
Tampa Bay	5	3	0	2	1	1	0	0	4	2	0	2
Toronto	6	0	1	5	5	0	1	4	1	0	0	1
Vancouver	25	4	8	13	10	1	4	5	15	3	4	8
Washington	6	2	1	3	4	1	1	2	2	1	0	1
Wild	2	1	0	1	1	0	0	1	1	1	0	0
Winnipeg	13	2	4	7	6	1	1	4	7	1	3	3

1988-89

A new era was about to begin in the home of the Stanley Cup champions. With the team having won four Stanley Cups in five years, the veterans on the team were commanding higher salaries. In an effort to reduce the payroll, General Manager Glen Sather traded superstar Wayne Gretzky to the Los Angeles Kings. Gretzky had led the league in scoring from 1979 through 1987 and although he had not won the scoring championship last year he was still the dominant player in the league. Also included in the deal were defenseman and enforcer Marty McSorley and forward Mike Krushelnyski. Obtained from the Kings were young star Jimmy Carson, untested Martin Gelinas and three of the Kings' future first round draft choices. The Oilers also received a reported $15 million in cash. Mark Messier took over Gretzky's responsibilities as team captain.

At the June 11 entry draft, held at the Montreal Forum, the Oilers used their first choice to select gigantic 18-year-old defenseman Francois Leroux from the St. Jean Castors of the QMJHL. At 6'5" and 220 pounds Leroux had scored 11 points in 58 games for the Castors during the 1988 season however he would play in only 11 games for the Oilers over parts of five seasons.

The team was 27–23–6 (.536) at the All-Star break and for the first time the All-Star game was held in Edmonton. With all the new faces on the team the Oilers experienced their worst season since 1980-81. The team finished in third place in the Smythe Division, 33 points behind the division leading Calgary Flames and seven points behind second place Los Angeles. Edmonton finished 4th in team offense and 11th in defense.

Jari Kurri led the team in scoring with 102 points, and Jimmy Carson, while not making the fans forget about Gretzky, had a fine season and managed to record 100 points. They were the only two Oilers to finish in the top ten in the scoring race.

Grant Fuhr again played the lion's share of games in net and although he played in 16 fewer games than in 1988, he allowed almost a half a goal per game more. This reflected the teams' overall defensive shortcomings rather than any erosion of Fuhr's skills.

Defending Cup champion Edmonton went on to meet the second place Los Angeles Kings in the first round of the playoffs. Although the Oilers started strongly, winning three of the first four games, the Kings rebounded from this setback, winning the next three games in succession and taking the series in seven games.

1988-89 Regular Season Scoring

#		Ht.	Wt.	Age	GP	G	A	Pts.	Shots	S%	GW	GT	PP	SH	P/M	PIM
17	Kurri	73	195	28	76	44	58	102	214	20.6	8	1	10	5	19	69
12	Carson	72	185	20	80	49	51	100	240	20.4	5	1	19	0	3	36
11	Messier (C)	73	210	27	72	33	61	94	164	20.1	4	1	6	6	-5	130
10	Tikkanen	73	200	23	67	31	47	78	151	20.5	4	0	6	8	10	92
18	Simpson	74	192	21	66	35	41	76	121	28.9	4	0	17	0	-3	80
9	Anderson (A)	73	190	28	79	16	48	64	212	7.5	3	0	7	0	-16	93
14	MacTavish	73	195	30	80	21	31	52	120	17.5	2	2	2	4	10	55
22	Huddy	72	210	29	76	11	33	44	178	6.2	0	0	5	2	0	52
19	Lacombe	72	205	24	64	17	11	28	71	23.9	1	0	2	0	2	57
23	Acton	68	170	30	46	11	15	26	74	14.9	1	0	0	1	9	47
4	Lowe (A)	74	195	29	76	7	18	25	85	8.2	1	0	0	0	26	98
5	S. Smith	76	215	25	35	3	19	22	47	6.4	0	0	0	0	5	97
24	McClelland	74	205	26	79	6	14	20	43	14.0	0	0	0	0	-10	161
28	Muni	75	200	26	69	5	13	18	40	12.5	1	0	0	0	43	71
21	Gregg	76	215	32	57	3	15	18	42	7.1	1	0	1	0	-9	28
16	Buchberger	74	190	22	66	5	9	14	57	8.8	1	0	1	0	-14	234
26	Redmond	71	195	23	21	3	10	13	29	10.3	0	0	3	0	-10	12
23	Jonsson	70	185	28	20	1	10	11	46	2.2	0	0	1	0	-12	22
15	Frycer	72	200	29	14	5	5	10	33	15.2	0	0	2	0	2	18
7	Lamb	69	180	24	20	2	8	10	20	10.0	0	0	1	0	4	14
2	Joseph	74	210	19	44	4	5	9	36	11.1	0	0	0	0	-9	54
25	Adams	74	200	28	49	4	5	9	49	8.2	1	0	0	0	1	72
27	Larson	72	195	32	10	2	7	9	19	10.5	0	0	0	1	1	15
27	Hunter	71	195	30	32	3	5	8	44	6.8	0	0	0	0	-5	22
37	Halward	73	200	33	24	0	7	7	8	0.0	0	0	0	0	-3	25
6	Beukeboom	76	215	23	36	0	5	5	26	0.0	0	0	0	0	2	94
20	Gelinas	71	195	18	6	1	2	3	14	7.1	0	0	0	0	-1	0
32	D. Brown	77	205	26	22	0	2	2	14	0.0	0	0	0	0	-4	56
8	D. Smith	71	186	25	19	1	1	2	15	6.7	0	0	0	0	-1	9
8	LeBlanc	73	195	24	2	1	0	1	5	20.0	0	0	0	0	0	0
32	May	73	200	23	3	1	0	1	3	33.3	1	0	0	0	0	7

#		Ht.	Wt.	Age	GP	G	A	Pts.	Shots	S%	GW	GT	PP	SH	P/M	PIM
34	Ware	77	205	21	2	0	1	1	0	0.0	0	0	0	0	1	11
26	Hammond	73	190	25	5	0	1	1	1	0.0	0	0	0	0	-2	8
31	Fuhr	70	189	26	59	0	1	1	0	0.0	0	0	0	0	0	6
32	Fotiu	74	210	36	1	0	0	0	0	0.0	0	0	0	0	1	0
35	Leroux	77	217	18	2	0	0	0	0	0.0	0	0	0	0	1	0
36	Odelein	72	205	22	2	0	0	0	0	0.0	0	0	0	0	-1	2
33	Issel	76	196	21	4	0	0	0	1	0.0	0	0	0	0	-1	0
34	Cochrane	74	205	30	12	0	0	0	3	0.0	0	0	0	0	-2	52
30	Ranford	70	170	22	29	0	0	0	0	0.0	0	0	0	0	0	2
	Bench															20
		73	198	26	80	325	559	884	2225	14.6	38	5	83	27	14	1921

1988-89 Goaltender Record

	GP	Min.	GA	W	L	T	Ave.	SA	Pct.	SO	EN
Bill Ranford	29	1509	88	15	8	2	3.50	718	0.877	1	1
Grant Fuhr	59	3341	213	23	26	6	3.83	1714	0.875	1	4
	80	4860	306	38	34	8	3.78	2432	0.874	2	5

Coach: Glen Sather 38-34-8

1988-89 Scoring vs. Opposition

	Bost.	Buff.	Calg.	Chi.	Det.	Hart.	L.A.	Minn.	Mont.	N.J.
Acton	———	3–3–6	1–1–2	1–0–1	0–0–0	0–0–0	0–0–0	0–0–0	0–0–0	0–1–1
Adams	0–1–1	0–1–1	0–0–0	0–0–0	0–0–0	0–0–0	1–0–1	0–0–0	0–0–0	0–0–0
Anderson	0–1–1	0–2–2	1–2–3	0–2–2	0–4–4	0–2–2	3–6–9	0–1–1	2–1–3	1–0–1
Brown	0–0–0	———	0–0–0	———	0–0–0	0–0–0	0–0–0	———	0–0–0	———
Buchberger	0–1–1	0–0–0	1–0–1	0–1–1	0–1–1	0–0–0	0–1–1	0–0–0	0–0–0	0–1–1
Beukeboom	0–0–0	0–1–1	0–1–1	0–1–1	0–0–0	0–0–0	0–0–0	0–0–0	0–0–0	0–0–0
Carson	0–1–1	4–3–7	5–5–10	0–1–1	4–1–5	1–5–6	4–6–10	3–3–6	2–1–3	1–2–3
Cochrane	0–0–0	0–0–0	0–0–0	———	———	———	———	———	———	0–0–0
Fotiu	———	———	0–0–0	———	———	———	———	———	———	———
Frycer	———	———	0–1–1	1–0–1	1–1–2	———	1–2–3	———	———	0–0–0
Gelinas	———	———	———	———	———	———	0–0–0	1–0–1	———	———
Gregg	1–0–1	0–1–1	0–4–4	0–0–0	0–0–0	1–0–1	0–0–0	0–1–1	0–1–1	0–1–1
Halward	0–0–0	———	0–1–1	0–2–2	0–1–1	0–1–1	0–0–0	———	0–0–0	0–0–0
Hammond	———	———	———	———	———	———	0–0–0	0–0–0	———	———
Huddy	0–0–0	0–0–0	1–1–2	0–1–1	1–3–4	1–1–2	2–4–6	2–1–3	0–1–1	0–1–1
Hunter	0–0–0	———	0–0–0	0–1–1	1–2–3	0–1–1	1–0–1	———	0–0–0	0–0–0
Issel	———	———	0–0–0	———	———	———	———	0–0–0	0–0–0	———
Jonsson	0–1–1	———	0–0–0	———	0–0–0	0–1–1	1–2–3	———	0–1–1	———
Joseph	0–0–0	0–0–0	0–0–0	0–0–0	0–1–1	0–0–0	1–0–1	0–0–0	1–0–1	0–0–0
Kurri	0–1–1	1–5–6	2–5–7	0–0–0	1–4–5	0–2–2	6–4–10	0–1–1	1–1–2	0–1–1
Lacombe	0–0–0	0–0–0	4–2–6	0–0–0	1–0–1	2–0–2	1–1–2	1–0–1	0–0–0	0–0–0
Lamb	1–0–1	———	0–1–1	———	———	0–1–1	0–1–1	———	0–0–0	———
Larson	———	1–0–1	0–0–0	———	———	———	1–0–1	0–0–0	———	———
Lowe	0–0–0	0–1–1	1–1–2	0–1–1	1–1–2	0–0–0	0–3–3	0–0–0	0–1–1	0–0–0
MacTavish	0–1–1	1–1–2	4–1–5	2–0–2	1–3–4	1–1–2	1–6–7	1–1–2	0–2–2	0–0–0
May	———	———	1–0–1	———	———	———	———	0–0–0	0–0–0	———
McClelland	2–0–2	0–1–1	1–3–4	0–0–0	0–1–1	0–1–1	0–0–0	0–1–1	0–0–0	1–0–1
Messier	0–3–3	1–4–5	2–3–5	1–1–2	1–5–6	4–2–6	5–9–14	0–2–2	1–3–4	0–0–0
Muni	0–0–0	0–1–1	0–1–1	0–1–1	1–0–1	1–0–1	0–0–0	0–0–0	1–0–1	0–0–0
Odelein	———	———	0–0–0	———	———	———	———	———	———	———
Redmond	0–0–0	———	1–1–2	0–0–0	1–0–1	———	0–2–2	———	———	0–0–0
Simpson	2–0–2	1–2–3	2–5–7	1–0–1	2–1–3	0–3–3	5–5–10	0–0–0	1–0–1	1–0–1
Smith, D.	0–0–0	0–0–0	0–0–0	———	———	0–0–0	0–0–0	———	0–1–1	0–0–0
Smith, S.	0–0–0	1–3–4	0–1–1	0–0–0	0–0–0	1–1–2	1–3–4	0–1–1	0–2–2	0–2–2
Tikkanen	1–1–2	4–3–7	0–5–5	1–0–1	0–1–1	2–3–5	2–4–6	1–0–1	1–2–3	1–0–1
Ware	———	———	———	———	———	———	0–0–0	———	———	———

	NYI.	NYR.	Phil.	Pitt.	Que.	St.L.	Tor.	Van.	Wash.	Winn.
Acton	———	0–0–0	0–0–0	1–0–1	2–1–3	0–1–1	1–1–2	1–2–3	0–1–1	1–4–5
Adams	0–0–0	0–0–0	0–0–0	0–1–1	1–0–1	0–0–0	1–1–2	0–1–1	0–0–0	1–0–1

	NYI.	*NYR.*	*Phil.*	*Pitt.*	*Que.*	*St.L.*	*Tor.*	*Van.*	*Wash.*	*Winn.*
Anderson	0–1–1	0–5–5	0–1–1	1–2–3	0–2–2	3–3–6	4–2–6	0–3–3	1–2–3	0–6–6
Brown	0–0–0	0–0–0	0–0–0	0–0–0	———	0–2–2	———	0–0–0	0–0–0	0–0–0
Buchberger	1–0–1	0–0–0	0–0–0	0–0–0	1–3–4	0–0–0	2–0–2	0–0–0	0–0–0	0–1–1
Beukeboom	0–0–0	0–0–0	———	0–0–0	0–0–0	0–1–1	0–0–0	0–1–1	0–0–0	0–0–0
Carson	2–1–3	3–2–5	1–2–3	1–2–3	3–2–5	3–2–5	4–5–9	4–2–6	1–3–4	3–2–5
Cochrane	———	———	———	0–0–0	0–0–0	———	0–0–0	0–0–0	———	0–0–0
Frycer	———	0–0–0	———	———	1–0–1	———	———	1–0–1	———	0–1–1
Gelinas	0–2–2	———	———	———	———	———	———	0–0–0	———	0–0–0
Gregg	0–1–1	0–0–0	0–0–0	1–2–3	0–0–0	0–1–1	0–0–0	0–0–0	0–0–0	0–3–3
Halward	0–0–0	0–0–0	0–0–0	0–1–1	———	———	———	0–0–0	0–0–0	0–1–1
Hammond	———	———	———	———	———	———	———	0–1–1	———	0–0–0
Huddy	0–1–1	1–3–4	1–2–3	0–2–2	0–0–0	0–0–0	0–3–3	0–1–1	0–2–2	2–7–9
Hunter	0–0–0	0–0–0	0–0–0	0–0–0	———	0–0–0	———	0–0–0	0–0–0	1–1–2
Issel	0–0–0	———	———	———	———	———	———	———	———	———
Jonsson	0–0–0	———	0–2–2	0–0–0	———	0–0–0	———	0–1–1	0–0–0	0–2–2
Joseph	0–0–0	0–1–1	0–0–0	0–0–0	0–0–0	0–0–0	0–1–1	1–1–2	0–0–0	1–1–2
Kurri	0–4–4	1–2–3	2–1–3	3–2–5	7–1–8	1–3–4	4–9–13	7–4–11	1–1–2	7–7–14
Lacombe	3–0–3	2–0–2	0–2–2	1–0–1	0–3–3	0–0–0	0–1–1	1–1–2	0–0–0	1–1–2
Lamb	0–2–2	———	0–0–0	0–0–0	———	0–0–0	———	0–1–1	0–0–0	1–2–3
Larson	———	———	———	———	———	———	0–5–5	———	———	0–2–2
LeBlanc	———	———	———	———	———	———	———	0–0–0	———	1–0–1
Leroux	———	0–0–0	———	0–0–0	———	———	———	———	———	———
Lowe	0–2–2	1–2–3	0–0–0	1–0–1	1–2–3	0–0–0	0–1–1	0–0–0	0–0–0	2–3–5
MacTavish	1–1–2	0–2–2	1–0–1	0–3–3	1–4–5	0–1–1	0–0–0	2–2–4	1–0–1	4–2–6
McClelland	0–0–0	0–0–0	0–1–1	0–0–0	0–1–1	0–0–0	0–1–1	2–1–3	0–0–0	0–3–3
Messier	1–0–1	2–1–3	1–0–1	1–2–3	2–4–6	3–3–6	0–2–2	2–6–8	1–0–1	5–11–16
Muni	0–1–1	0–0–0	0–0–0	0–1–1	0–1–1	1–0–1	0–2–2	0–1–1	0–1–1	1–3–4
Odelein	———	———	———	———	———	———	———	0–0–0	———	———
Redmond	0–1–1	0–0–0	0–1–1	0–2–2	0–2–2	———	———	0–0–0	1–0–1	0–1–1
Simpson	2–3–5	3–3–6	2–1–3	1–3–4	0–1–1	3–2–5	2–3–5	2–5–7	0–2–2	5–2–7
Smith, D.	1–0–1	———	———	0–0–0	0–0–0	0–0–0	0–0–0	———	———	0–0–0
Smith, S.	0–0–0	0–2–2	———	0–0–0	0–1–1	0–2–2	0–1–1	0–0–0	0–0–0	0–0–0
Tikkanen	0–1–1	2–1–3	0–1–1	4–3–7	0–2–2	0–6–6	5–5–10	0–2–2	3–0–3	4–7–11
Ware	———	———	———	———	———	———	———	0–1–1	———	———

1988-89 Goaltender Records vs. Opposition

	GP	*Min.*	*GA*	*EN*	*SO*	*Ave.*	*W–L–T*	*Opposition*
Grant Fuhr	2	119	7	2	0	3.53	0–2–0	Boston
	3	187	12	0	0	3.85	2–0–1	Buffalo
	6	307	25	1	0	4.89	1–3–1	Calgary
	3	165	12	0	0	4.36	0–2–1	Chicago
	3	115	7	1	0	3.65	1–2–0	Detroit
	2	120	6	0	0	3.00	2–0–0	Hartford
	7	418	31	0	0	4.45	4–3–0	Los Angeles
	2	128	5	0	0	2.34	1–0–1	Minnesota
	3	160	9	0	1	3.38	1–1–0	Montreal
	3	185	7	0	0	2.27	1–2–0	New Jersey
	1	60	2	0	0	2.00	1–0–0	N.Y. Islanders
	1	59	3	0	0	3.05	0–1–0	N.Y. Rangers
	2	125	5	0	0	2.40	1–0–1	Philadelphia
	2	80	5	0	0	3.75	1–0–0	Pittsburgh
	2	120	5	0	0	2.50	2–0–0	St. Louis
	1	60	2	0	0	2.00	1–0–0	Toronto
	6	360	25	0	0	4.17	1–5–0	Vancouver
	3	185	16	0	0	5.19	1–2–0	Washington
	7	390	29	0	0	4.46	2–3–1	Winnipeg
Bill Ranford	1	62	4	0	0	3.87	0–1–0	Boston
	4	178	9	0	1	3.03	1–2–0	Calgary
	1	20	1	0	0	3.00	0–0–0	Chicago
	2	64	10	0	0	9.38	0–0–0	Detroit
	1	58	6	1	0	6.21	0–1–0	Hartford
	1	62	5	0	0	4.84	0–1–0	Los Angeles
	1	65	3	0	0	2.77	0–0–1	Minnesota

GP	Min.	GA	EN	SO	Ave.	W–L–T	Opposition
1	20	2	0	0	6.00	0–1–0	Montreal
2	120	6	0	0	3.00	1–1–0	N.Y. Islanders
2	120	7	0	0	3.50	2–0–0	N.Y. Rangers
1	65	1	0	0	0.92	0–0–1	Philadelphia
2	100	7	0	0	4.20	1–1–0	Pittsburgh
3	180	9	0	0	3.00	3–0–0	Quebec
1	60	4	0	0	4.00	1–0–0	St. Louis
2	120	3	0	0	1.50	2–0–0	Toronto
2	120	5	0	0	2.50	2–0–0	Vancouver
2	95	6	0	0	3.79	2–0–0	Winnipeg

1988-89 Schedule Results

Date	Visitor	Score		Home	Score
Oct. 7	Islanders	1	at	Edmonton	5
Oct. 9	Winnipeg	4	at	Edmonton	5
Oct. 12	Vancouver	6	at	Edmonton	2
Oct. 14	Edmonton	1	at	Calgary	6
Oct. 16	Edmonton	3	at	Winnipeg	3 OT
Oct. 17	Minnesota	3	at	Edmonton	3 OT
Oct. 19	Los Angeles	6	at	Edmonton	8
Oct. 23	Edmonton	5	at	Vancouver	6
Oct. 25	Edmonton	5	at	Los Angeles	4
Oct. 29	Washington	3	at	Edmonton	4 OT
Oct. 30	Chicago	5	at	Edmonton	2
Nov. 2	St. Louis	4	at	Edmonton	5
Nov. 4	Buffalo	3	at	Edmonton	7
Nov. 6	Edmonton	2	at	Detroit	5
Nov. 8	Edmonton	7	at	Pittsburgh	3
Nov. 9	Edmonton	3	at	New Jersey	2 OT
Nov. 12	Edmonton	6	at	Toronto	2
Nov. 13	Edmonton	5	at	Buffalo	4 OT
Nov. 16	Winnipeg	2	at	Edmonton	1 OT
Nov. 19	Toronto	1	at	Edmonton	9
Nov. 20	Edmonton	4	at	Winnipeg	7
Nov. 23	Edmonton	3	at	Minnesota	3 OT
Nov. 24	Edmonton	4	at	St. Louis	2
Nov. 26	Edmonton	5	at	Montreal	7
Nov. 28	Edmonton	7	at	Quebec	4
Nov. 30	Vancouver	2	at	Edmonton	4
Dec. 2	Calgary	7	at	Edmonton	4
Dec. 4	Rangers	6	at	Edmonton	10
Dec. 7	Quebec	3	at	Edmonton	8
Dec. 8	Edmonton	3	at	Calgary	5
Dec. 10	Winnipeg	7	at	Edmonton	6
Dec. 14	Edmonton	8	at	Toronto	2
Dec. 15	Edmonton	3	at	Boston	4 OT
Dec. 17	Edmonton	4	at	Hartford	2
Dec. 19	Edmonton	5	at	Buffalo	5 OT
Dec. 21	Vancouver	2	at	Edmonton	1
Dec. 23	Calgary	1	at	Edmonton	4
Dec. 31	Montreal	4	at	Edmonton	2
Jan. 2	Edmonton	3	at	Minnesota	2 OT
Jan. 4	Quebec	2	at	Edmonton	4
Jan. 7	Edmonton	2	at	Calgary	7
Jan. 8	Calgary	0	at	Edmonton	6
Jan. 10	Edmonton	4	at	Los Angeles	5 OT
Jan. 13	Edmonton	3	at	Washington	5
Jan. 15	Edmonton	0	at	New Jersey	1
Jan. 16	Edmonton	2	at	Chicago	2 OT
Jan. 18	Edmonton	9	at	Winnipeg	4
Jan. 20	Philadelphia	1	at	Edmonton	1 OT
Jan. 21	Pittsburgh	7	at	Edmonton	4
Jan. 23	Rangers	3	at	Edmonton	2
Jan. 25	Chicago	6	at	Edmonton	3
Jan. 28	Edmonton	7	at	Los Angeles	6
Jan. 31	Edmonton	2	at	Vancouver	6
Feb. 1	Vancouver	3	at	Edmonton	4
Feb. 3	Detroit	5	at	Edmonton	8
Feb. 5	New Jersey	4	at	Edmonton	2
Feb. 9	Edmonton	3	at	Philadelphia	1
Feb. 11	Edmonton	2	at	Boston	5
Feb. 12	Edmonton	3	at	Rangers	1
Feb. 14	Edmonton	3	at	Islanders	5
Feb. 17	Washington	8	at	Edmonton	2
Feb. 19	Boston	4	at	Edmonton	2
Feb. 21	Hartford	4	at	Edmonton	7
Feb. 24	Los Angeles	1	at	Edmonton	4
Feb. 25	St. Louis	3	at	Edmonton	5
Mar. 1	Montreal	0	at	Edmonton	3
Mar. 3	Edmonton	7	at	Winnipeg	4
Mar. 5	Edmonton	4	at	Pittsburgh	2
Mar. 6	Edmonton	4	at	Philadelphia	4 OT
Mar. 8	Edmonton	3	at	Hartford	7
Mar. 11	Calgary	5	at	Edmonton	5 OT
Mar. 12	Los Angeles	6	at	Edmonton	3
Mar. 15	Detroit	8	at	Edmonton	6
Mar. 16	Edmonton	0	at	Vancouver	3
Mar. 19	Islanders	2	at	Edmonton	3
Mar. 21	Los Angeles	4	at	Edmonton	3
Mar. 23	Winnipeg	4	at	Edmonton	5
Mar. 25	Edmonton	2	at	Los Angeles	4
Mar. 29	Edmonton	5	at	Vancouver	2
April 2	Edmonton	2	at	Calgary	4

Opponent	Home W–L–T	Road W–L–T
Boston	0–1–0	0–2–0
Buffalo	1–0–0	1–0–1
Calgary	2–1–1	0–4–0
Chicago	0–2–0	0–0–1
Detroit	1–1–0	0–1–0
Hartford	1–0–0	1–1–0
Los Angeles	2–2–0	2–2–0
Minnesota	1–0–0	1–0–1
Montreal	2–2–0	0–1–0
New Jersey	0–1–0	1–1–0
Islanders	2–0–0	0–1–0
Rangers	1–1–0	1–0–0
Philadelphia	0–0–1	1–0–1
Pittsburgh	0–1–0	2–0–0
Quebec	2–0–0	1–0–0
St. Louis	2–0–0	1–0–0

Opponent	Home W-L-T	Road W-L-T
Toronto	1-0-0	2-0-0
Vancouver	2-2-0	1-3-0
Washington	1-1-0	0-1-0
Winnipeg	2-2-0	2-1-1

Opponent	Overall W-L-T	GF-GA
Boston	0-3-0	7-13
Buffalo	2-0-1	17-12
Calgary	2-5-1	27-35
Chicago	0-2-1	7-13
Detroit	1-2-0	16-18
Hartford	2-1-0	14-13
Los Angeles	4-4-0	36-36
Minnesota	1-0-2	9-8
Montreal	1-2-0	10-11
New Jersey	2-1-0	5-7
Islanders	2-1-0	11-8
Rangers	2-1-0	15-10
Philadelphia	1-0-2	8-6
Pittsburgh	2-1-0	15-12
Quebec	3-0-0	19-9
St. Louis	3-0-0	14-9
Toronto	3-0-0	23-5
Vancouver	3-5-0	23-30
Washington	1-2-0	9-16
Winnipeg	4-3-1	40-35

1988-89 Playoff Scoring

#		GP	G	A	Pts	Shots	S%	GW	OT	PP	SH	P/M	PIM
11	Mark Messier	7	1	11	12	23	4.3	0	0	0	0	-1	8
17	Jari Kurri	7	3	5	8	17	17.6	0	0	0	1	-2	6
5	Steve Smith	7	2	2	4	6	33.3	1	0	0	0	3	20
10	Esa Tikkanen	7	1	3	4	17	5.9	0	0	0	0	-1	12
12	Jimmy Carson	7	2	1	3	15	13.3	1	0	1	0	0	6
19	Normand Lacombe	7	2	1	3	10	20.0	0	0	0	0	3	21
9	Glenn Anderson	7	1	2	3	16	6.3	0	0	1	0	-1	8
4	Kevin Lowe	7	1	2	3	11	9.1	0	0	0	0	-1	4
28	Craig Muni	7	0	3	3	4	0.0	0	0	0	0	-1	8
23	Tomas Jonsson	4	2	0	2	6	33.3	0	0	2	0	1	6
22	Charlie Huddy	7	2	0	2	17	11.8	0	0	1	0	-2	4
18	Craig Simpson	7	2	0	2	10	20.0	1	0	1	0	-3	10
7	Mark Lamb	6	0	2	2	8	0.0	0	0	0	0	1	8
24	Kevin McClelland	7	0	2	2	7	0.0	0	0	0	0	3	16
21	Randy Gregg	7	1	0	1	8	12.5	0	0	0	0	4	4
14	Craig MacTavish	7	0	1	1	10	0.0	0	0	0	0	1	8
6	Jeff Beukeboom	1	0	0	0	0	0.0	0	0	0	0	0	2
8	John LeBlanc	1	0	0	0	2	0.0	0	0	0	0	0	0
37	Doug Halward	2	0	0	0	0	0.0	0	0	0	0	-2	0
27	Dave Hunter	6	0	0	0	5	0.0	0	0	0	0	-2	0
32	Dave Brown	7	0	0	0	5	0.0	0	0	0	0	-2	6
31	Grant Fuhr	7	0	0	0	0	0.0	0	0	0	0	0	0
		7	20	35	55	197	10.2	3	0	6	1	-10	157

1988-89 Playoff Goaltending

	GP	Min.	GA	W	L	Ave.	SA	Pct	SO	EN
Grant Fuhr	7	417	24	3	4	3.43	227	0.894	1	1
	7	420	25	3	4	3.57	227	0.890	1	1

Date	Result					Winning Goaltender	Winning Goal
April 5, 1989	Edmonton	4	at	Los Angeles	3	Grant Fuhr	Craig Simpson
April 6, 1989	Edmonton	2	at	Los Angeles	5	Kelly Hrudey	Chris Kontos
April 8, 1989	Los Angeles	0	at	Edmonton	4	Grant Fuhr	Jimmy Carson
April 9, 1989	Los Angeles	3	at	Edmonton	4	Grant Fuhr	Steve Smith
April 11, 1989	Edmonton	2	at	Los Angeles	4	Kelly Hrudey	Luc Robitaille
April 13, 1989	Los Angeles	4	at	Edmonton	1	Kelly Hrudey	Jim Wiemer
April 15, 1989	Edmonton	3	at	Los Angeles	6	Kelly Hrudey	Bernie Nicholls

All-Star Game Summary

February 7, 1989 at Northlands Coliseum — Campbell Conference 9 — Wales Conference 5

Players on the Ice

Campbell Conference: **Grant Fuhr** (G), Mike Vernon (G), Dave Ellett (D), Dave Manson (D), **Kevin Lowe** (D), Gary Suter (D), Paul Reinhart (D), Steve Duchesne (LW), Joe Mullen

(RW), Bernie Nicholls (C), Gary Leeman (D), **Mark Messier** (LW), **Jimmy Carson** (C), Brett Hull (RW), **Jari Kurri** (RW), Steve Yzerman (C), Dino Ciccarelli (RW), Luc Robitaille (LW), Joe Nieuwendyk (C), Wayne Gretzky (C), **Glen Sather** (coach)

Wales Conference: Rejean Lemelin (G), Sean Burke (G), Kevin Stevens (D), Paul Coffey (D), Larry Robinson (D), Glen Wesley (D), Phil Housley (D), Ray Bourque (D), Cam Neely (RW), Kevin Dineen (RW), John MacLean (RW), Bobby Smith (C), Pat LaFontaine (C), Mike Ridley (C), Brian Mullen (LW), Rick Tocchet (RW), Mike McPhee (LW), Rob Brown (C), Mario Lemieux (C), Walt Poddubny (C), Mats Naslund (LW, chosen but did not play due to injury), Terry O'Reilly (coach)

1st period
1. Kurri (Gretzky, Robitaille) 1:07, **2.** Gretzky (Duchesne) 4:33, **3.** Neely (Lemieux, Stevens) 9:47 PP, **4.** Poddubny (Ridley, Robinson) 10:38
Penalty: Messier 9:35

2nd period
5. Wesley (LaFontaine, B. Mullen) 3:16, **6.** J. Mullen (Messier, Nieuwendyk) 7:57, **7.** Yzerman (Duchesne, Ciccarelli) 17:21, **8.** Leeman (Carson) 17:35
Penalty: Bourque (13:44

3rd period
9. Poddubny (Tocchet, Robinson) 4:40, **10.** J. Mullen (Manson) 6:53, **11.** Ridley (Bourque, Tocchet) 9:35, **12.** Robitaille (Kurri, Gretzky) 12:18, **13.** Carson (Leeman, Hull) 14:35 **14.** Messier (Nieuwendyk, J. Mullen) 17:14
Penalties: none

Goaltenders:	Campbell Conference	Fuhr	30 minutes	3 goals against
		Vernon	30 minutes	2 goals against
	Wales Conference	Lemelin	30 minutes	3 goals against
		Burke	30 minutes	6 goals against

Shots on Goal By:	Campbell Conference	13-10-14-37
	Wales Conference	14-9-15-38

Attendance: 17,503

Names in boldface indicate players from the Oilers.

1989-90

For the first time since joining the NHL the Oilers did not have Glen Sather behind the bench as coach. Wishing to concentrate more on his managerial duties, Sather appointed longtime assistant John Muckler as the new head coach. Replacing Muckler as co-coach was former Oiler goaltender Ron Low.

At the June 17 entry draft held at the Metropolitan Sports Center in Bloomington, Sather drafted a number of players who would end up playing a few games for the Oilers. These players would include Josef Beranek, Peter White and Anatoli Semenov.

Early in the season and with the Oilers playing less than stellar hockey, Glen Sather made a blockbuster deal in an attempt to shake up the team. From the Red Wings, Edmonton obtained forward Adam Graves, defenseman Jeff Sharples, talented but erratic Czech winger Petr Klima and former first over-all draft choice Joe Murphy. In exchange the Oilers gave up last year's 100 point man Jimmy Carson, rugged forward Kevin McClelland and a draft choice.

The deal seemed to spark the Oilers. Before the trade the team had won four, lost five and tied four others but following the trade they won 34, lost 23 and tied 10 and were 24–15–9 (.594) at the All-Star break.

Thanks to a mid-season stretch in which they lost only 3 of 20 games played, the Oilers ended the season with 90 points and finished second to Calgary in the Smythe Division. Although the team scored 10 fewer goals this year than last year they more than made up for it in defense as they trimmed 23 goals from their total of last year.

Captain Mark Messier had a career high 129 points to finish second in the scoring race behind former longtime teammate Wayne Gretzky who finished the season with 142 points. Bill Ranford took over much of the goaltending duties from Grant Fuhr, and the 3.19 average he recorded was the lowest of any of the Oilers' number one goaltenders since the team joined the league.

Although the Oilers were without stars such as Gretzky, Coffey, Moog and Fuhr, they still had a core of veterans who had been through the playoff wars many times over. Even so Edmonton was not expected to advance far into the playoffs.

The first round of the playoffs found the Oilers squared off with the Winnipeg Jets. The teams split the first two games which were played in Edmonton, and then the Jets won both games in Winnipeg. It looked as if the Edmonton's Stanley Cup hopes might be in jeopardy. However once the Oilers returned to the friendly confines of Northlands Coliseum they got their second wind and defeated the Jets 4–3 and then won the remaining two games, winning the series four games to three.

Edmonton then met Los Angeles in the division final series. The Kings had defeated division leading Calgary four games to two in the other divisional series. Behind the enthusiastic play of the Oilers "Kid Line" of Joe Murphy,

From left to right: Jari Kurri, Barry Fraser, Esa Tikkanen. (A96-182 City of Edmonton Archives.)

Adam Graves and Martin Gelinas the Oilers easily swept the Kings in four games.

Norris Division champion Chicago then met the Oilers in the conference finals. This series was very similar to the Winnipeg series against the Oilers. The teams split the first two games in Edmonton and then Chicago won game three. As in the Winnipeg series though, the Oilers rebounded to win the final three games and advanced to the Stanley Cup finals for the sixth time in eight years.

Edmonton did not look to be favored to win the Cup against the league leading Boston Bruins. But with the "Kid Line" again leading the way and Bill Ranford at the top of his game the Oilers defeated the Bruins in five games. Ranford allowed only eight goals in the five games and was named the winner of the Conn Smythe Trophy as the most valuable player in the playoffs. Mark Messier capped off a spectacular regular season by scoring 31 points in 22 playoff games. Craig Simpson also had 31 points, 16 of them goals. The Oilers had won their fifth Stanley Cup in seven years.

1989-90 Regular Season Scoring

#		*Ht.*	*Wt.*	*Age*	*GP*	*G*	*A*	*Pts*	*Shots*	*S%*	*GW*	*GT*	*PP*	*SH*	*P/M*	*PIM*
11	Messier (C)	73	210	28	79	45	84	129	211	21.3	3	2	13	6	19	79
17	Kurri (A)	73	195	29	78	33	60	93	201	16.4	2	1	10	2	18	48
9	Anderson	73	190	29	73	34	38	72	204	16.7	7	1	17	1	-1	107
10	Tikkanen	73	200	24	79	30	33	63	199	15.1	6	0	6	4	17	161
18	Simpson	74	195	22	80	29	32	61	129	22.5	2	1	7	0	-2	180
85	Klima	72	190	25	63	25	28	53	149	16.8	3	0	7	0	-1	66
14	MacTavish	73	195	31	80	21	22	43	109	19.3	5	0	1	6	13	89
5	S. Smith	76	215	26	75	7	34	41	125	5.6	1	0	3	0	6	171
4	Lowe (A)	74	195	30	78	7	26	33	74	9.5	0	0	2	1	18	140
7	Lamb	69	180	25	58	12	16	28	81	14.8	2	0	2	0	10	42
8	Murphy	73	190	22	62	7	18	25	101	6.9	0	0	2	0	1	56
20	Gelinas	71	195	19	46	17	8	25	71	23.9	2	2	5	0	0	30
21	Gregg	76	215	33	48	4	20	24	41	9.8	0	0	0	0	24	42

#		*Ht.*	*Wt.*	*Age*	*GP*	*G*	*A*	*Pts*	*Shots*	*S%*	*GW*	*GT*	*PP*	*SH*	*P/M*	*PIM*
22	Huddy	72	210	30	70	1	23	24	119	0.8	1	0	1	0	-13	56
12	A. Graves	71	200	21	63	9	12	21	84	10.7	1	0	1	0	5	123
29	Ruzicka	73	175	26	25	11	6	17	52	21.2	1	0	4	0	-21	10
28	Muni	75	200	27	71	5	12	17	42	11.9	0	0	0	2	22	81
25	G. Smith	75	190	20	74	4	11	15	66	6.1	0	0	1	0	13	52
6	Beukeboom	76	215	24	46	1	12	13	36	2.8	0	0	0	0	5	86
26	Ruotsalainen	68	170	29	10	1	7	8	28	3.6	0	0	0	0	-1	6
16	Buchberger	74	205	23	55	2	6	8	35	5.7	2	0	0	0	-8	168
19	Lacombe	72	200	25	15	5	2	7	15	33.3	0	0	0	0	4	21
26	Eriksson	76	224	24	20	3	3	6	23	13.0	0	0	1	0	-1	24
32	D. Brown	77	205	27	60	0	6	6	32	0.0	0	0	0	0	-3	145
12	Carson	73	200	21	4	1	2	3	11	9.1	0	0	1	0	-2	0
24	McClelland	74	205	27	10	1	1	2	7	14.3	0	0	0	0	-1	13
2	Joseph	74	210	20	4	0	2	2	5	0.0	0	0	0	0	-2	2
30	Ranford	70	170	23	56	0	2	2	0	0.0	0	0	0	0	0	18
35	Greenlay	75	200	21	2	0	1	1	0	0.0	0	0	0	0	0	0
35	Leroux	77	220	19	3	0	1	1	0	0.0	0	0	0	0	-2	0
15	Sim	74	180	19	3	0	1	1	0	0.0	0	0	0	0	0	2
36	Bell	73	190	24	1	0	0	0	1	0.0	0	0	0	0	0	0
35	Exelby	69	170	24	1	0	0	0	0	0.0	0	0	0	0	0	0
23	Lehmann	73	185	25	1	0	0	0	0	0.0	0	0	0	0	1	0
36	Maciver	71	180	25	1	0	0	0	0	0.0	0	0	0	0	-1	0
34	Ware	77	208	22	3	0	0	0	1	0.0	0	0	0	0	-1	4
33	Reddick	68	170	25	11	0	0	0	0	0.0	0	0	0	0	0	0
31	Fuhr	70	186	27	21	0	0	0	0	0.0	0	0	0	0	0	2
	Bench															22
		73	196	25	80	315	529	844	2252	14.0	38	7	84	22	30	2046

1989-90 Goaltender Records

	GP	*Min.*	*GA*	*W*	*L*	*T*	*Ave.*	*SA*	*Pct.*	*SO*	*EN*
Eldon Reddick	11	604	31	5	4	2	3.08	283	0.890	0	2
Bill Ranford	56	3107	165	24	16	9	3.19	1463	0.887	1	5
Grant Fuhr	21	1081	70	9	7	3	3.88	532	0.868	1	0
Randy Exelby	1	60	5	0	1	0	5.00	30	0.833	0	1
Mike Greenlay	2	20	4	0	0	0	12.00	17	0.765	0	0
	80	4882	283	38	28	14	3.48	2325	0.878	2	8

Coach: John Muckler 38-28-14

1989-90 Scoring vs. Opposition

	Bost.	*Buff.*	*Calg.*	*Chi.*	*Det.*	*Hart.*	*L.A.*	*Minn.*	*Mont.*	*N.J.*
Anderson	0–1–1	1–3–4	2–5–7	0–0–0	1–1–2	0–0–0	2–3–5	3–3–6	2–1–3	0–2–2
Beukeboom	0–0–0	0–1–1	0–0–0	0–0–0	0–1–1	1–0–1	0–1–1	0–0–0	0–0–0	0–1–1
Brown	0–1–1	0–0–0	0–1–1	0–1–1	0–0–0	0–1–1	0–0–0	0–0–0	0–0–0	0–0–0
Buchberger	0–0–0	0–0–0	1–0–1	0–2–2	0–0–0	0–0–0	0–0–0	0–0–0	0–0–0	0–0–0
Carson	0–0–0	———	———	———	———	———	0–2–2	———	———	———
Eriksson	1–0–1	0–1–1	0–0–0	0–0–0	———	———	0–0–0	———	0–1–1	0–0–0
Gelinas	2–0–2	———	5–0–5	0–0–0	———	0–1–1	0–0–0	0–1–1	1–0–1	0–0–0
Graves	0–0–0	0–0–0	1–1–2	3–0–3	0–1–1	0–1–1	0–0–0	0–1–1	0–0–0	0–0–0
Gregg	———	0–0–0	0–0–0	0–2–2	0–2–2	0–1–1	1–2–3	1–2–3	0–3–3	0–0–0
Huddy	0–0–0	1–1–2	0–2–2	0–1–1	0–1–1	0–0–0	0–2–2	0–1–1	0–1–1	0–0–0
Joseph	0–1–1	———	———	———	———	———	0–1–1	———	———	———
Klima	0–1–1	0–2–2	2–3–5	0–1–1	1–3–4	0–1–1	5–3–8	0–0–0	0–0–0	1–0–1
Kurri	0–2–2	2–5–7	2–4–6	1–1–2	1–3–4	1–2–3	4–9–13	1–3–4	3–4–7	3–1–4
Lacombe	———	———	———	1–0–1	0–0–0	———	1–0–1	0–0–0	0–0–0	———
Lamb	0–1–1	0–0–0	0–0–0	0–0–0	1–0–1	0–1–1	2–3–5	0–0–0	3–1–4	0–1–1
Leroux	0–0–0	———	———	———	———	———	0–0–0	———	———	———
Lowe	0–1–1	1–1–2	1–0–1	0–1–1	0–1–1	0–0–0	1–4–5	1–1–2	0–1–1	0–2–2
MacTavish	0–0–0	1–2–3	2–2–4	1–1–2	2–2–4	1–1–2	2–1–3	3–1–4	0–2–2	1–0–1
McClelland	0–0–0	———	———	———	———	———	1–0–1	———	0–0–0	0–0–0
Messier	1–2–3	2–5–7	1–9–10	1–5–6	2–2–4	2–3–5	4–8–12	1–5–6	2–2–4	2–2–4
Muni	0–0–0	0–0–0	0–0–0	0–0–0	0–0–0	0–0–0	3–3–6	1–0–1	0–1–1	0–0–0

	Bost.	Buff.	Calg.	Chi.	Det.	Hart.	L.A.	Minn.	Mont.	N.J.
Murphy	0–0–0	0–2–2	0–2–2	2–0–2	2–0–2	0–1–1	0–0–0	0–1–1	0–1–1	0–0–0
Ruotsalainen	———	———	0–0–0	———	———	0–0–0	———	———	0–1–1	0–0–0
Ruzicka	———	———	0–1–1	———	1–0–1	1–0–1	2–1–3	0–0–0	———	1–0–1
Sim	0–0–0	———	———	———	———	———	———	———	———	———
Simpson	0–0–0	3–1–4	1–2–3	2–1–3	3–0–3	1–2–3	5–3–8	1–1–2	2–1–3	0–1–1
Smith, G.	0–0–0	0–0–0	0–0–0	0–1–1	0–0–0	0–0–0	0–1–1	0–2–2	0–0–0	0–0–0
Smith, S.	0–0–0	2–0–2	1–4–5	1–2–3	1–1–2	0–0–0	0–7–7	0–1–1	0–0–0	0–2–2
Tikkanen	1–0–1	2–5–7	2–1–3	0–1–1	0–3–3	2–0–2	3–2–5	2–0–2	0–3–3	1–3–4
Ware	0–0–0	———	———	———	———	———	0–0–0	———	———	———

	NYI.	NYR.	Phil.	Pitt.	Que.	St.L.	Tor.	Van.	Wash.	Winn.
Anderson	0–1–1	0–1–1	0–1–1	1–0–1	4–2–6	2–0–2	3–2–5	4–4–8	1–1–2	8–7–15
Bell	———	———	———	0–0–0	———	———	———	———	———	———
Beukeboom	0–0–0	0–0–0	0–0–0	0–1–1	0–1–1	0–1–1	0–0–0	0–1–1	0–1–1	0–3–3
Brown	0–0–0	0–0–0	0–1–1	0–0–0	0–1–1	0–0–0	0–0–0	0–0–0	0–0–0	0–0–0
Buchberger	0–0–0	0–0–0	0–1–1	0–0–0	0–0–0	0–0–0	0–0–0	1–1–2	0–0–0	0–2–2
Carson	———	———	———	———	———	———	———	1–0–1	———	———
Eriksson	0–0–0	1–0–1	0–0–0	0–0–0	0–0–0	———	———	1–0–1	0–1–1	0–0–0
Gelinas	2–2–4	1–0–1	0–0–0	0–1–1	1–2–3	1–0–1	0–0–0	3–0–3	0–0–0	1–1–2
Graves	1–1–2	0–0–0	1–0–1	0–1–1	1–0–1	0–2–2	0–0–0	0–3–3	1–0–1	1–1–2
Gregg	0–0–0	0–0–0	0–1–1	0–0–0	0–0–0	1–2–3	0–0–0	0–0–0	0–3–3	1–2–3
Huddy	0–4–4	0–0–0	0–0–0	0–0–0	0–3–3	0–3–3	0–0–0	0–3–3	0–1–1	0–0–0
Joseph	0–0–0	0–0–0	———	———	———	———	———	———	———	———
Klima	1–2–3	1–3–4	0–0–0	1–0–1	2–0–2	1–1–2	2–2–4	2–3–5	1–3–4	5–0–5
Kurri	2–2–4	2–2–4	0–1–1	0–2–2	1–1–2	1–6–7	2–0–2	1–7–8	2–1–3	4–4–8
Lacombe	3–1–4	0–0–0	———	———	0–0–0	———	0–0–0	0–1–1	———	———
Lamb	2–2–4	0–0–0	0–1–1	2–0–2	1–1–2	0–0–0	0–3–3	0–1–1	0–0–0	1–1–2
Lehmann	———	———	———	———	———	———	———	———	———	0–0–0
Leroux	———	———	———	———	———	———	———	0–1–1	———	———
Lowe	0–2–2	0–0–0	0–0–0	0–1–1	0–1–1	0–1–1	1–0–1	0–2–2	1–2–3	1–5–6
Maciver	———	———	———	———	0–0–0	———	———	———	———	———
MacTavish	0–0–0	0–0–0	1–2–3	1–1–2	2–1–3	0–0–0	0–2–2	2–1–3	2–0–2	0–3–3
McClelland	0–0–0	0–0–0	———	———	0–1–1	———	———	0–0–0	———	0–0–0
Messier	0–2–2	2–3–5	4–0–4	0–3–3	1–3–4	3–4–7	1–5–6	7–9–16	0–5–5	9–7–16
Muni	0–0–0	0–1–1	0–1–1	0–0–0	1–0–1	0–0–0	0–1–1	0–2–2	0–0–0	0–3–3
Murphy	1–1–2	0–0–0	0–1–1	0–0–0	0–1–1	1–1–2	0–1–1	1–2–3	0–2–2	0–2–2
Ruotsalainen	1–0–1	———	———	———	0–1–1	0–3–3	0–0–0	0–0–0	———	0–2–2
Ruzicka	0–0–0	0–0–0	0–0–0	1–1–2	———	2–1–3	0–0–0	2–1–3	1–1–2	0–0–0
Sim	———	———	———	———	———	———	———	———	———	0–1–1
Simpson	1–0–1	0–1–1	1–1–2	1–0–1	0–3–3	2–2–4	1–0–1	2–6–8	1–1–2	2–6–8
Smith, G.	0–3–3	0–0–0	0–1–1	1–1–2	1–0–1	0–0–0	0–0–0	0–0–0	0–0–0	2–2–4
Smith, S.	0–0–0	0–1–1	0–1–1	0–1–1	0–3–3	0–1–1	0–0–0	1–6–7	1–0–1	0–4–4
Tikkanen	1–2–3	1–0–1	1–0–1	0–0–0	0–0–0	3–2–5	2–1–3	4–2–6	2–2–4	3–6–9
Ware	———	———	———	———	———	———	———	0–0–0	———	———

1989-90 Goaltender Records vs. Opposition

	GP	Min.	GA	EN	SO	Ave.	W–L–T	Opposition
Randy Exelby	1	60	5	1	0	5.00	0–1–0	Pittsburgh
Grant Fuhr	1	60	6	0	0	6.00	0–1–0	Boston
	2	120	6	0	1	3.00	1–1–0	Buffalo
	4	205	14	0	0	4.10	1–2–1	Calgary
	1	60	4	0	0	4.00	1–0–0	Chicago
	1	60	2	0	0	2.00	1–0–0	Detroit
	2	122	10	0	0	4.92	2–0–0	Los Angeles
	1	59	5	0	1	5.08	0–1–0	Montreal
	1	20	0	0	0	0.00	0–0–1	New Jersey
	1	60	2	0	0	2.00	1–0–0	N.Y. Islanders
	2	62	4	0	0	3.87	1–0–0	Philadelphia
	2	120	6	0	0	3.00	1–1–0	Pittsburgh
	1	65	3	0	0	2.77	0–0–1	St. Louis
	1	24	2	0	0	5.00	0–0–0	Vancouver
	1	43	6	0	0	8.37	0–1–0	Winnipeg

	GP	*Min.*	*GA*	*EN*	*SO*	*Ave.*	*W–L–T*	*Opposition*
Mike Greenlay	1	20	4	0	0	12.00	0–0–0	Calgary
	1	1	0	0	0	0.00	0–0–0	Los Angeles
Bill Ranford	2	125	6	0	0	2.88	0–1–1	Boston
	4	232	8	0	1	2.07	2–1–0	Calgary
	2	118	9	0	0	4.58	0–2–0	Chicago
	2	119	11	2	0	5.55	0–2–0	Detroit
	3	189	11	0	0	3.49	0–1–2	Hartford
	6	373	24	1	0	3.86	2–2–2	Los Angeles
	2	120	1	0	1	0.50	2–0–0	Minnesota
	2	125	5	0	0	2.40	1–0–1	Montreal
	3	107	11	0	0	6.17	0–1–0	New Jersey
	2	130	8	0	0	3.69	0–0–2	N.Y. Islanders
	2	123	7	0	0	3.41	0–1–1	N.Y. Rangers
	2	117	4	1	0	2.05	1–1–0	Philadelphia
	3	180	5	0	0	1.67	3–0–0	Quebec
	2	75	7	0	0	5.60	1–0–0	St. Louis
	2	119	6	0	0	3.03	1–1–0	Toronto
	6	335	12	1	0	2.15	5–1–0	Vancouver
	3	136	9	0	0	3.97	2–0–0	Washington
	8	392	21	0	0	3.21	4–2–0	Winnipeg
Eldon Reddick	1	60	3	0	0	3.00	1–0–0	Buffalo
	1	40	6	0	0	9.00	0–1–0	Calgary
	1	60	2	0	0	2.00	1–0–0	Minnesota
	1	62	1	0	0	0.97	0–0–1	New Jersey
	1	60	3	2	0	3.00	0–1–0	N.Y. Rangers
	1	45	3	0	0	4.00	1–0–0	St. Louis
	1	60	6	0	0	6.00	0–1–0	Toronto
	2	125	4	0	0	1.92	1–0–1	Vancouver
	1	46	2	0	0	2.61	0–1–0	Washington
	1	45	1	0	0	1.33	1–0–0	Winnipeg

1989-90 Schedule Results

Oct. 5	Edmonton	4	at	Vancouver	1
Oct. 7	Edmonton	6	at	Los Angeles	5
Oct. 11	Vancouver	5	at	Edmonton	2
Oct. 13	Boston	3	at	Edmonton	3 OT
Oct. 15	Los Angeles	5	at	Edmonton	4 OT
Oct. 18	Winnipeg	2	at	Edmonton	7
Oct. 19	Boston	3	at	Edmonton	0
Oct. 22	Edmonton	4	at	Winnipeg	5
Oct. 24	Edmonton	3	at	Islanders	3 OT
Oct. 25	Edmonton	3	at	Rangers	3 OT
Oct. 28	Edmonton	6	at	Quebec	3
Oct. 29	Edmonton	4	at	Montreal	5
Nov. 1	New Jersey	6	at	Edmonton	6 OT
Nov. 3	Calgary	2	at	Edmonton	5
Nov. 4	Pittsburgh	3	at	Edmonton	1
Nov. 6	Edmonton	1	at	Calgary	5
Nov. 9	Edmonton	2	at	Boston	6
Nov. 11	Edmonton	5	at	Washington	3
Nov. 12	Edmonton	5	at	Buffalo	6
Nov. 15	Los Angeles	2	at	Edmonton	2 OT
Nov. 17	Buffalo	0	at	Edmonton	3
Nov. 19	Chicago	4	at	Edmonton	5 OT
Nov. 21	Vancouver	3	at	Edmonton	4
Nov. 24	Edmonton	1	at	Philadelphia	5
Nov. 25	Edmonton	7	at	Islanders	2
Nov. 27	Edmonton	2	at	Edmonton	6
Nov. 30	Edmonton	7	at	Los Angeles	6
Dec. 2	Minnesota	1	at	Edmonton	6
Dec. 3	Toronto	3	at	Edmonton	5
Dec. 8	Los Angeles	4	at	Edmonton	5 OT
Dec. 11	Calgary	3	at	Edmonton	3 OT
Dec. 13	Quebec	1	at	Edmonton	5
Dec. 16	Edmonton	3	at	St. Louis	3 OT
Dec. 17	Edmonton	5	at	Chicago	6
Dec. 19	Edmonton	5	at	Minnesota	0
Dec. 21	Winnipeg	2	at	Edmonton	3
Dec. 23	Calgary	1	at	Edmonton	2
Dec. 27	Philadelphia	1	at	Edmonton	2
Dec. 29	Montreal	2	at	Edmonton	6
Dec. 31	Edmonton	2	at	Winnipeg	3
Jan. 2	Edmonton	6	at	St. Louis	4
Jan. 3	Edmonton	2	at	Chicago	3
Jan. 6	Hartford	4	at	Edmonton	4 OT
Jan. 7	Calgary	3	at	Edmonton	1
Jan. 9	Edmonton	3	at	Calgary	2 OT
Jan. 11	Edmonton	3	at	Los Angeles	3 OT
Jan. 16	Detroit	6	at	Edmonton	4
Jan. 17	Winnipeg	3	at	Edmonton	6
Jan. 23	Rangers	4	at	Edmonton	3
Jan. 25	Los Angeles	6	at	Edmonton	7
Jan. 27	Vancouver	2	at	Edmonton	6
Jan. 30	Edmonton	4	at	Hartford	4 OT
Jan. 31	Edmonton	5	at	Detroit	7
Feb. 2	Edmonton	3	at	Pittsburgh	6
Feb. 4	Edmonton	5	at	Washington	4 OT
Feb. 6	Edmonton	2	at	New Jersey	2 OT
Feb. 7	Edmonton	2	at	Rangers	5
Feb. 11	Winnipeg	4	at	Edmonton	7
Feb. 14	Washington	4	at	Edmonton	3
Feb. 16	Edmonton	2	at	Vancouver	2 OT
Feb. 18	Minnesota	2	at	Edmonton	3
Feb. 20	Edmonton	4	at	Vancouver	2

Feb. 21	Buffalo	3	at	Edmonton	7
Feb. 23	Toronto	6	at	Edmonton	5
Feb. 25	Edmonton	4	at	Calgary	10
Feb. 28	Edmonton	2	at	Los Angeles	4
Mar. 3	Philadelphia	3	at	Edmonton	5
Mar. 4	Vancouver	3	at	Edmonton	6
Mar. 6	Pittsburgh	3	at	Edmonton	4 OT
Mar. 9	Edmonton	5	at	Winnipeg	7
Mar. 10	Edmonton	2	at	Toronto	3
Mar. 13	Edmonton	4	at	Quebec	1
Mar. 14	Edmonton	3	at	Montreal	3 OT
Mar. 17	New Jersey	4	at	Edmonton	1
Mar. 18	Hartford	3	at	Edmonton	1
Mar. 21	St. Louis	6	at	Edmonton	8
Mar. 24	Islanders	5	at	Edmonton	5 OT
Mar. 27	Edmonton	4	at	Vancouver	1
Mar. 30	Edmonton	2	at	Calgary	6
April 1	Edmonton	4	at	Winnipeg	2

Opponent	Home W–L–T	Road W–L–T
Boston	0–1–1	0–1–0
Buffalo	2–0–0	0–1–0
Calgary	2–1–1	1–3–0
Chicago	1–0–0	0–2–0
Detroit	0–1–0	1–1–0
Hartford	0–1–1	0–0–1
Los Angeles	2–1–1	2–1–1
Minnesota	2–0–0	1–0–0
Montreal	1–0–0	0–1–1
New Jersey	0–1–1	0–0–1
Islanders	0–1–1	1–0–1
Rangers	0–1–0	0–1–1
Philadelphia	2–0–0	0–1–0
Pittsburgh	1–1–0	0–1–0
Quebec	1–0–0	2–0–0
St. Louis	1–0–0	1–1–0
Toronto	1–1–0	0–1–0
Vancouver	3–1–0	3–0–1
Washington	0–1–0	2–0–0
Winnipeg	4–0–0	1–3–0

Opponent	Overall W–L–T	GF–GA
Boston	0–2–1	5–12
Buffalo	2–1–0	15–9
Calgary	3–4–1	21–32
Chicago	1–2–0	12–13
Detroit	1–2–0	15–15
Hartford	0–1–2	9–11
Los Angeles	4–2–2	36–35
Minnesota	3–0–0	14–3
Montreal	1–1–1	13–10
New Jersey	0–1–2	9–12
Islanders	1–0–2	15–10
Rangers	0–2–1	8–12
Philadelphia	2–1–0	8–9
Pittsburgh	1–2–0	8–12
Quebec	3–0–0	15–5
St. Louis	2–0–1	17–13
Toronto	1–2–0	12–12
Vancouver	6–1–1	32–19
Washington	2–1–0	13–11
Winnipeg	5–3–0	38–28

1989-90 Playoff Scoring

#		GP	G	A	Pts	Shots	S%	GW	OT	PP	SH	P/M	PIM
18	Craig Simpson	22	16	15	31	42	38.1	3	0	6	0	11	8
11	Mark Messier	22	9	22	31	47	19.1	1	0	1	1	5	20
17	Jari Kurri	22	10	15	25	58	17.2	3	0	6	0	13	18
10	Esa Tikkanen	22	13	11	24	54	24.1	0	0	2	2	12	26
9	Glenn Anderson	22	10	12	22	46	21.7	2	0	2	0	12	20
7	Mark Lamb	22	6	11	17	34	17.6	2	1	1	0	12	2
5	Steve Smith	22	5	10	15	35	14.3	1	0	0	1	15	37
8	Joe Murphy	22	6	8	14	29	20.7	2	1	0	0	1	16
26	Reijo Ruotsalainen	22	2	11	13	55	3.6	0	0	1	0	13	12
12	Adam Graves	22	5	6	11	46	10.9	1	0	0	0	1	17
21	Randy Gregg	20	2	6	8	17	11.8	0	0	1	0	1	16
14	Craig MacTavish	22	2	6	8	21	9.5	0	0	0	0	6	29
22	Charlie Huddy	22	0	6	6	35	0.0	0	0	0	0	11	10
85	Petr Klima	21	5	0	5	25	20.0	1	1	1	0	-2	8
20	Martin Gelinas	20	2	3	5	24	8.3	0	0	0	0	0	6
16	Kelly Buchberger	19	0	5	5	15	0.0	0	0	0	0	2	13
28	Craig Muni	22	0	3	3	13	0.0	0	0	0	0	7	16
4	Kevin Lowe	20	0	2	2	11	0.0	0	0	0	0	3	10
30	Bill Ranford	22	0	2	2	0	0.0	0	0	0	0	0	4
33	Eldon Reddick	1	0	0	0	0	0.0	0	0	0	0	0	0
6	Jeff Beukeboom	2	0	0	0	0	0.0	0	0	0	0	2	0
19	Anatoli Semenov	2	0	0	0	0	0.0	0	0	0	0	-1	0
32	Dave Brown	3	0	0	0	2	0.0	0	0	0	0	0	0
25	Geoff Smith	3	0	0	0	1	0.0	0	0	0	0	0	0
		22	93	154	247	610	15.2	16	3	21	4	26	288

1989-90 Playoff Goaltending

	GP	Min.	GA	W	L	Ave.	SA	Pct.	SO	EN
Eldon Reddick	1	2	0	0	0	0.00	1	1.000	0	0
Bill Ranford	22	1401	59	16	6	2.68	672	0.912	1	1
	22	1405	60	16	6	2.73	673	0.911	1	1

Date	Result						Winning Goaltender	Winning Goal
April 4, 1990	Winnipeg	7	at	Edmonton	5		Bob Essensa	Brent Ashton
April 6, 1990	Winnipeg	2	at	Edmonton	3		Bill Ranford	Mark Lamb[1]
April 8, 1990	Edmonton	1	at	Winnipeg	2		Bob Essensa	Dale Hawerchuk
April 10, 1990	Edmonton	3	at	Winnipeg	4		Bob Essensa	Dave Ellett[2]
April 12, 1990	Winnipeg	3	at	Edmonton	4		Bill Ranford	Mark Messier
April 14, 1990	Edmonton	4	at	Winnipeg	3		Bill Ranford	Jari Kurri
April 16, 1990	Winnipeg	1	at	Edmonton	4		Bill Ranford	Mark Lamb
April 18, 1990	Los Angeles	0	at	Edmonton	7		Bill Ranford	Glenn Anderson
April 20, 1990	Los Angeles	1	at	Edmonton	6		Bill Ranford	Craig Simpson
April 22, 1990	Edmonton	5	at	Los Angeles	4		Bill Ranford	Adam Graves
April 24, 1990	Edmonton	6	at	Los Angeles	5		Bill Ranford	Joe Murphy[3]
May 2, 1990	Chicago	2	at	Edmonton	5		Bill Ranford	Steve Smith
May 4, 1990	Chicago	4	at	Edmonton	3		Greg Millen	Doug Wilson
May 6, 1990	Edmonton	1	at	Chicago	5		Greg Millen	Steve Larmer
May 8, 1990	Edmonton	4	at	Chicago	2		Bill Ranford	Craig Simpson
May 10, 1990	Chicago	3	at	Edmonton	4		Bill Ranford	Jari Kurri
May 12, 1990	Edmonton	8	at	Chicago	4		Bill Ranford	Joe Murphy
May 15, 1990	Edmonton	3	at	Boston	2		Bill Ranford	Petr Klima[4]
May 18, 1990	Edmonton	7	at	Boston	2		Bill Ranford	Jari Kurri
May 20, 1990	Boston	2	at	Edmonton	1		Andy Moog	Greg Johnston
May 22, 1990	Boston	1	at	Edmonton	5		Bill Ranford	Glenn Anderson
May 24, 1990	Edmonton	4	at	Boston	1		Bill Ranford	Craig Simpson

[1]4:21 of overtime [2]21:08 of overtime
[3]4:42 of overtime [4]55:13 of overtime

1989-90 Stanley Cup Winning Game

May 24, 1990: Boston Gardens, Boston

Attendance: 14,448

Oilers

Starting Lineup: **30**-Bill Ranford (Goal), **21**-Randy Gregg (Defense) **22**-Charlie Huddy (Defense), **18**-Craig Simpson (Left Wing), **11**-Mark Messier (Center), **9**-Glenn Anderson (Right Wing).

Remaining Players: **16**-Kelly Buchberger, **20**-Martin Gelinas, **12**-Adam Graves, **85**-Petr Klima, **17**-Jari Kurri, **7**-Mark Lamb, **4**-Kevin Lowe, **14**-Craig MacTavish, **28**-Craig Muni, **8**-Joe Murphy, **26**-Reijo Ruotsalainen, **5**-Steve Smith, **10**-Esa Tikkanen, **33**-Eldon Reddick (backup goaltender).

Average: Age-26.1 years, Height-72.6 inches, Weight-195.8 pounds, Years Experience-4.68 years

Bruins

Starting Lineup: **35**-Andy Moog (Goal), **26**-Glen Wesley (Defense), **77**-Ray Bourque (Defense), **31**-John Carter (Left Wing), **11**-Bob Carpenter (Center), **27**-Dave Christian (Right Wing).

Remaining Players: **12**-Randy Burridge, **42**-John Byce, **34**-Lyndon Byers, **28**-Garry Galley, **18**-Bob Gould, **38**-Greg Hawgood, **23**-Craig Janney, **39**-Greg Johnston, **8**-Cam Neely, **41**-Allen Pedersen, **36**-Brian Propp, **20**-Bob Sweeney, **32**-Don Sweeney, **1**-Rejean Lemelin (backup goaltender).

Average: Age-26.4 years, Height-71.8 inches, Weight-189.2 pounds, Years Experience-4 years

Officials

Referee: Andy Van Hellemond, Linesmen: Swede Knox and Ray Scapinello

Game Summary

1st Period

Goals: none

Penalties: Boston (Bourque-cross-checking)-2:56, Edmonton (Tikkanen-holding)-4:32, Boston (Galley-holding)-4:45

2nd Period

Goals: Edmonton-Anderson (unassisted) 1:17
Edmonton-Simpson (Anderson) 9:31

3rd Period

Goals: Edmonton-Smith (Messier, Simpson) 6:09
Edmonton-Murphy (Gelinas, Lamb) 14:53
Boston-Byers (Sweeney, Bourque) 16:30

Penalties: Edmonton (Huddy-hooking)-7:09, Boston (Bourque-holding)-11:46

Shots on Goal: Edmonton 10-5-7-22
Boston 10-10-10-30

1990-91

John Muckler returned behind the bench for his second season as head coach of the Oilers and was rejoined by Ted Green and Ron Low as associate coaches. It was not a banner year for the Oilers at the league's annual entry draft.

No player from this year's draft has ever appeared in a National Hockey League game with the Oilers or any other NHL team.

After having won the Stanley Cup last year General Manager Glen Sather did not make any major off-season trades and the Oilers iced basically the same lineup as last year, with the notable exceptions of Jari Kurri and Randy Gregg. Kurri played much of the year in the Italian League, while at the age of 34 Randy Gregg decided to retire from the game.

The team got off to their worst start ever, registering only six points in their first 15 games. Included in these 15 games was a nine game losing streak. This was somewhat offset in mid-season when the team won 11 of 15 games. At the All-Star break the Oilers were 22–20–3 (.522).

The team's poor performance was in large part due to the rash of injuries which they endured throughout most of the season. Ken Linseman missed 24 games, nine of them due to an eye injury. Also missing for extended periods because of injury were solid first year player Anatoli Semenov, team captain Mark Messier and goal scoring leader Petr Klima. Only Joe Murphy and Craig MacTavish managed to play in all 80 games.

The team was very inconsistent towards the end of the season and finished 22 points behind division leading Los Angeles. The Oilers' 80-point regular season total was their worst since 1981 but it was still enough to allow them to finish third in the Smythe Division.

The Oilers' once explosive offense sputtered this year and the team finished eleventh in offense and twelfth in goals against. Esa Tikkanen led the team in scoring with a measly 69 points. This was 33 points less than Jari Kurri's total of last season. Bill Ranford was now the Oilers' undisputed number one goaltender, playing in 60 games.

For the twelfth consecutive season the Oilers advanced to the postseason. Meeting the Calgary Flames in the division semifinal series, the two teams split the first six games with the series then moving to Calgary for game seven. In a game which could have gone either way, Esa Tikkanen scored at 6:58 of overtime to put the Oilers into the division finals against Los Angeles.

The Kings won the first game on an overtime goal by Luc Robitaille, but then the veteran Oilers won the next three games, with games two and three going into overtime. Counting the final two games in the Calgary series, the Oilers had played five overtime games in a row. The Kings then came back to win game five, before the Oilers won game six, again in overtime.

After defeating Calgary and Los Angeles the Oilers looked like they should have an easy time reaching the finals. They only had to get by the lowly Minnesota North Stars in the conference final series. In what must rank as one of the great upsets in Stanley Cup history, Minnesota, who had finished with 22 fewer victories than division leading Chicago in the regular season, knocked off the Black Hawks in six games. Then in the Norris Division Finals Minnesota met second place St. Louis, who had finished 37 points ahead of the North Stars. Minnesota defeated the Blues in a six game series.

The Oilers could have hardly wished for a more suitable opponent in the conference finals. The North Stars had just been through two tough series against teams that had finished well ahead of them in the standings, and the veteran Oilers looked like they should have little trouble with them. The Oilers though had little left for the Minnesota series and lost to the North Stars in five games.

1990-91 Regular Season Scoring

#		Ht.	Wt.	Age	GP	G	A	Pts	Shots	S%	GW	GT	PP	SH	P/M	PIM
10	Tikkanen	73	200	25	79	27	42	69	235	11.5	6	0	3	2	22	85
85	Klima	72	190	26	70	40	28	68	204	19.6	5	0	7	1	24	113
11	Messier (C)	73	210	29	53	12	52	64	109	11.0	2	0	3	1	15	34
8	Murphy	73	190	23	80	27	35	62	141	19.1	4	1	4	1	2	35
18	Simpson	74	195	23	75	30	27	57	143	21.0	5	0	15	0	-8	66
9	Anderson	73	190	30	74	24	31	55	193	12.4	4	0	8	0	-7	59
5	S. Smith	76	215	27	77	13	41	54	114	11.4	2	0	4	0	14	193
20	Gelinas	71	195	20	73	20	20	40	124	16.1	2	1	4	0	-7	34
13	Linseman	71	180	32	56	7	29	36	49	14.3	0	0	2	1	15	94
14	MacTavish	73	195	32	80	17	15	32	113	15.0	1	0	2	6	-1	76
19	Semenov	74	190	28	57	15	16	31	101	14.9	1	0	3	1	17	26
22	Huddy	72	210	31	53	5	22	27	90	5.6	0	0	2	0	4	32
12	A. Graves	71	185	22	76	7	18	25	126	5.6	1	0	2	0	-21	127
2	Joseph	74	210	21	49	5	17	22	74	6.8	0	0	2	0	3	59
4	Lowe(A)	74	195	31	73	3	13	16	51	5.9	0	0	0	0	-9	113
25	G. Smith	75	200	21	59	1	12	13	66	1.5	0	0	0	0	13	55
7	Lamb	69	180	26	37	4	8	12	41	9.8	1	0	1	0	-2	25
6	Beukeboom	76	215	25	67	3	7	10	48	6.3	0	0	0	0	6	150
28	Muni	75	200	28	76	1	9	10	47	2.1	0	0	0	0	10	77

#		Ht.	Wt.	Age	GP	G	A	Pts	Shots	S%	GW	GT	PP	SH	P/M	PIM
32	D. Brown	77	205	28	58	3	4	7	32	9.4	0	0	0	0	-7	160
36	Maciver	71	180	26	21	2	5	7	25	8.0	0	0	1	0	1	14
16	Buchberger	74	210	24	64	3	1	4	54	5.6	2	0	0	0	-6	160
30	Ranford	70	170	24	60	0	4	4	0	0.0	0	0	0	0	0	6
35	Leroux	78	221	20	1	0	2	2	1	0.0	0	0	0	0	1	0
24	Aitken	75	200	23	3	0	1	1	0	0.0	0	0	0	0	-1	0
26	Middendorf	76	210	23	3	1	0	1	1	100.0	0	0	0	0	0	2
29	Vyazmikin	73	190	24	4	1	0	1	5	20.0	1	0	0	0	0	0
26	Haas	74	196	22	5	1	0	1	4	25.0	0	0	0	0	-2	0
23	Hawgood	68	175	22	6	0	1	1	9	0.0	0	0	0	0	-2	6
1	Takko	74	185	27	11	0	1	1	0	0.0	0	0	0	0	0	0
33	Reddick	68	170	26	2	0	0	0	0	0.0	0	0	0	0	0	0
15	Srsen	71	180	24	2	0	0	0	2	0.0	0	0	0	0	0	0
26	Van Allen	73	200	23	2	0	0	0	0	0.0	0	0	0	0	0	0
15	Currie	74	195	22	5	0	0	0	5	0.0	0	0	0	0	0	0
31	Fuhr	70	186	28	13	0	0	0	0	0.0	0	0	0	0	0	0
	Bench															22
		73	195	25	80	272	461	733	2207	12.3	37	2	63	13	17	1823

1990-91 Goaltender Records

	GP	Min.	GA	W	L	T	Ave.	SA	Pct.	SO	EN
Grant Fuhr	13	778	39	6	4	3	3.01	380	0.897	1	0
Bill Ranford	60	3415	182	27	27	3	3.20	1705	0.893	0	5
Kari Takko	11	529	37	4	4	0	4.20	279	0.867	0	0
Eldon Reddick	2	120	9	0	2	0	4.50	59	0.847	0	0
	80	4850	272	37	37	6	3.37	2428	0.888	1	5

Coach: John Muckler 37-37-6

1990-91 Scoring vs. Opposition

	Bost.	Buff.	Calg.	Chi.	Det.	Hart.	L.A.	Minn.	Mont.	N.J.
Aitken	———	———	———	———	———	———	———	0–0–0	0–0–0	———
Anderson	1–2–3	1–0–1	4–1–5	1–2–3	1–1–2	0–1–1	1–2–3	0–0–0	0–1–1	1–1–2
Beukeboom	0–0–0	0–0–0	0–1–1	0–0–0	0–0–0	0–0–0	1–2–3	0–0–0	0–0–0	0–0–0
Brown	0–0–0	0–0–0	2–0–2	0–0–0	0–0–0	0–0–0	0–0–0	0–0–0	0–0–0	0–0–0
Buchberger	0–0–0	0–0–0	0–0–0	0–0–0	0–0–0	0–0–0	0–0–0	0–0–0	0–0–0	0–0–0
Currie	———	———	———	———	0–0–0	———	———	0–0–0	0–0–0	———
Gelinas	0–1–1	2–0–2	0–4–4	0–0–0	1–1–2	0–1–1	0–1–1	1–0–1	1–0–1	1–1–2
Graves	0–0–0	0–0–0	0–3–3	0–0–0	2–0–2	0–0–0	0–1–1	0–1–1	0–0–0	0–2–2
Haas	———	———	———	1–0–1	———	———	0–0–0	0–0–0	———	———
Hawgood	———	———	0–0–0	———	———	———	———	———	———	0–1–1
Huddy	1–0–1	0–0–0	1–2–3	1–2–3	———	0–0–0	0–2–2	———	0–0–0	0–0–0
Joseph	0–1–1	0–0–0	2–4–6	1–0–1	0–0–0	0–0–0	0–0–0	0–0–0	0–0–0	0–0–0
Klima	5–2–7	2–1–3	4–5–9	2–0–2	1–0–1	1–3–4	1–4–5	1–1–2	1–0–1	1–0–1
Lamb	2–1–3	0–0–0	0–0–0	0–0–0	0–0–0	0–0–0	1–1–2	0–0–0	0–0–0	———
Linseman	1–4–5	0–1–1	1–1–2	0–0–0	0–1–1	1–2–3	1–2–3	0–0–0	0–0–0	0–0–0
Lowe	0–3–3	0–0–0	0–2–2	0–0–0	0–1–1	1–0–1	0–4–4	0–0–0	0–0–0	0–0–0
Maciver	———	———	0–1–1	———	0–0–0	———	1–0–1	0–0–0	0–1–1	0–0–0
MacTavish	0–1–1	0–0–0	4–0–4	0–2–2	2–1–3	1–0–1	2–1–3	0–0–0	0–1–1	2–0–2
Messier	0–1–1	0–3–3	1–4–5	0–2–2	———	0–1–1	2–4–6	———	0–1–1	0–5–5
Middendorf	———	0–0–0	———	0–0–0	———	———	———	———	———	———
Muni	0–0–0	0–1–1	0–0–0	0–0–0	0–1–1	0–1–1	0–0–0	0–0–0	0–0–0	0–0–0
Murphy	1–2–3	0–1–1	5–1–6	0–1–1	0–3–3	1–3–4	3–1–4	0–2–2	0–2–2	2–1–3
Semenov	0–1–1	0–0–0	0–3–3	———	2–0–2	0–1–1	6–1–7	0–0–0	1–0–1	0–0–0
Simpson	3–1–4	2–4–6	1–4–5	2–0–2	0–1–1	1–0–1	3–2–5	0–0–0	1–0–1	1–1–2
Smith, G.	0–1–1	0–1–1	0–0–0	0–1–1	1–2–3	0–0–0	0–2–2	0–0–0	0–0–0	0–1–1
Smith, S.	1–2–3	2–1–3	1–2–3	0–1–1	0–2–2	0–0–0	1–3–4	0–0–0	0–0–0	2–4–6
Srsen	———	———	———	———	———	———	———	———	———	0–0–0
Tikkanen	0–4–4	0–2–2	1–2–3	0–1–1	1–5–6	3–0–3	1–8–9	1–1–2	1–2–3	1–1–1
Van Allen	———	———	———	———	0–0–0	———	———	———	———	0–0–0
Vyazmikin	———	———	0–0–0	———	———	———	1–0–1	———	———	———

	NYI.	*NYR.*	*Phil.*	*Pitt.*	*Que.*	*St.L.*	*Tor.*	*Van.*	*Wash.*	*Winn.*
Aitken	———	———	———	———	———	———	———	———	0–1–1	———
Anderson	1–3–4	2–0–2	1–2–3	3–2–5	2–3–5	1–0–1	0–2–2	3–4–7	0–1–1	1–3–4
Beukeboom	0–0–0	0–0–0	0–0–0	0–0–0	1–1–2	0–0–0	1–0–1	0–1–1	0–0–0	0–2–2
Brown	0–0–0	0–0–0	0–2–2	0–0–0	1–0–1	0–0–0	0–0–0	0–0–0	0–2–2	0–0–0
Buchberger	0–0–0	0–0–0	1–0–1	0–0–0	0–0–0	0–0–0	0–0–0	1–1–2	0–0–0	1–0–1
Currie	———	———	———	———	0–0–0	———	———	———	———	———
Gelinas	1–0–1	0–2–2	1–0–1	2–0–2	1–2–3	1–0–1	0–0–0	4–4–8	0–1–1	4–2–6
Graves	0–0–0	0–1–1	0–0–0	0–2–2	3–1–4	0–0–0	0–2–2	2–3–5	0–0–0	0–2–2
Haas	———	———	———	———	———	0–0–0	———	———	———	0–0–0
Hawgood	———	———	———	———	———	0–0–0	———	———	0–0–0	0–0–0
Huddy	0–3–3	0–1–1	0–1–1	0–2–2	0–2–2	0–1–1	1–1–2	1–4–5	0–1–1	0–0–0
Joseph	0–3–3	0–0–0	0–0–0	1–1–2	0–1–1	0–0–0	0–0–0	1–5–6	0–1–1	0–1–1
Klima	1–1–2	1–0–1	3–2–5	3–1–4	0–1–1	1–0–1	1–1–2	4–4–8	1–0–1	6–2–8
Lamb	0–1–1	0–0–0	0–0–0	0–0–0	1–0–1	0–0–0	———	0–1–1	0–0–0	0–4–4
Leroux	———	———	———	———	———	———	———	———	———	0–2–2
Linseman	1–1–2	0–2–2	1–2–3	0–4–4	0–0–0	0–0–0	0–1–1	0–4–4	0–2–2	1–2–3
Lowe	0–0–0	0–0–0	0–0–0	0–0–0	0–1–1	0–1–1	0–0–0	1–0–1	1–1–2	0–0–0
Maciver	0–0–0	———	0–0–0	———	0–2–2	———	———	———	0–0–0	1–1–2
MacTavish	0–1–1	0–2–2	1–2–3	0–0–0	0–0–0	0–1–1	0–1–1	2–2–4	3–0–3	0–0–0
Messier	1–2–3	0–3–3	1–4–5	1–4–5	2–3–5	0–1–1	0–2–2	4–10–14	0–0–0	0–2–2
Middendorf	1–0–1	———	———	———	———	———	———	———	———	———
Muni	0–1–1	0–1–1	0–1–1	0–1–1	1–0–1	0–0–0	0–0–0	0–1–1	0–1–1	0–0–0
Murphy	1–1–2	3–1–4	1–3–4	2–2–4	0–3–3	1–2–3	2–0–2	4–3–7	0–0–0	1–3–4
Semenov	0–0–0	0–0–0	2–1–3	2–2–4	1–0–1	1–1–2	0–1–1	0–4–4	0–1–1	0–0–0
Simpson	2–1–3	1–2–3	0–0–0	1–0–1	1–3–4	0–1–1	3–1–4	5–5–10	0–0–0	3–1–4
Smith, G.	0–1–1	0–0–0	0–1–1	0–1–1	0–0–0	0–0–0	0–0–0	0–0–0	0–0–0	0–1–1
Smith, S.	1–0–1	1–0–1	0–6–6	0–2–2	1–2–3	0–1–1	0–1–1	2–10–12	0–0–0	1–4–5
Srsen	———	———	———	———	———	———	———	———	———	0–0–0
Tikkanen	1–1–2	1–1–2	4–2–6	0–1–1	1–2–3	0–0–0	1–0–1	7–4–11	1–0–1	2–5–7
Vyazmikin	———	———	———	———	———	———	———	0–0–0	———	———

1990–91 Goaltender Records vs. Opposition

	GP	*Min.*	*GA*	*EN*	*SO*	*Ave.*	*W–L–T*	*Opposition*
Grant Fuhr	2	125	8	0	0	3.84	0–1–1	Calgary
	1	65	5	0	0	4.62	0–0–1	Detroit
	1	64	4	0	0	3.75	0–1–0	Los Angeles
	1	45	1	0	0	1.33	0–0–1	Minnesota
	2	120	5	0	0	2.50	1–1–0	Montreal
	1	60	0	0	1	0.00	1–0–0	New Jersey
	1	60	1	0	0	1.00	1–0–0	N.Y. Islanders
	1	60	4	0	0	4.00	1–0–0	Philadelphia
	3	180	11	0	0	3.67	2–1–0	Winnipeg
Bill Ranford	3	183	10	1	0	3.28	1–2–0	Boston
	3	181	7	0	0	2.32	2–1–0	Buffalo
	6	360	17	0	0	2.83	3–3–0	Calgary
	3	182	11	0	0	3.63	1–2–0	Chicago
	2	120	6	1	0	3.00	1–1–0	Detroit
	1	60	3	0	0	3.00	1–0–0	Hartford
	6	344	24	1	0	4.19	1–4–1	Los Angeles
	3	140	10	0	0	4.29	0–2–0	Minnesota
	1	59	2	1	0	2.03	0–1–0	Montreal
	2	93	6	0	0	3.87	1–1–0	New Jersey
	2	120	2	0	0	1.00	2–0–0	N.Y. Islanders
	2	125	5	0	0	2.40	1–0–1	N.Y. Rangers
	2	120	6	0	0	3.00	2–0–0	Philadelphia
	3	140	12	0	0	5.14	2–1–0	Pittsburgh
	2	125	9	0	0	4.32	2–0–0	Quebec
	2	120	7	0	0	3.50	0–2–0	St. Louis
	3	137	6	0	0	2.63	1–1–0	Toronto
	7	382	22	0	0	3.46	5–1–0	Vancouver
	2	119	6	0	0	3.03	0–2–0	Washington
	5	300	11	1	0	2.20	1–3–1	Winnipeg
Eldon Reddick	1	60	5	0	0	5.00	0–1–0	Hartford

Eldon Reddick	1	60	4	0	0	4.00	0–1–0	St. Louis
Kari Takko	1	60	2	0	0	2.00	1–0–0	Hartford
	2	80	6	0	0	4.50	1–0–0	Los Angeles
	1	28	3	0	0	6.43	0–0–0	New Jersey
	1	59	4	0	0	4.07	0–1–0	N.Y. Rangers
	1	40	2	0	0	3.00	0–0–0	Pittsburgh
	1	60	2	0	0	2.00	1–0–0	Quebec
	1	42	0	0	0	0.00	1–0–0	Toronto
	2	99	12	0	0	7.27	0–2–0	Vancouver
	1	60	6	0	0	6.00	0–1–0	Washington

1990-91 Schedule Results

Oct. 6	Winnipeg	3	at	Edmonton	3 OT
Oct. 7	Toronto	2	at	Edmonton	3
Oct. 11	Edmonton	5	at	Los Angeles	5 OT
Oct. 14	Edmonton	4	at	Vancouver	5 OT
Oct. 16	St. Louis	5	at	Edmonton	2
Oct. 19	Boston	1	at	Edmonton	8
Oct. 21	Calgary	2	at	Edmonton	1
Oct. 24	Edmonton	1	at	Winnipeg	3
Oct. 25	Edmonton	2	at	Calgary	4
Oct. 28	Washington	1	at	Edmonton	0
Oct. 31	Winnipeg	1	at	Edmonton	0 OT
Nov. 3	New Jersey	5	at	Edmonton	2
Nov. 6	Edmonton	1	at	St. Louis	2
Nov. 8	Edmonton	3	at	Chicago	5
Nov. 10	Edmonton	4	at	Los Angeles	7
Nov. 14	Vancouver	3	at	Edmonton	5
Nov. 16	Buffalo	2	at	Edmonton	4
Nov. 18	Islanders	1	at	Edmonton	3
Nov. 20	Chicago	3	at	Edmonton	1
Nov. 23	Edmonton	2	at	Buffalo	3 OT
Nov. 24	Edmonton	4	at	Toronto	1
Nov. 27	Edmonton	7	at	Pittsburgh	3
Nov. 29	Edmonton	2	at	Boston	4
Dec. 1	Edmonton	4	at	Hartford	2
Dec. 2	Edmonton	6	at	Philadelphia	3
Dec. 5	Quebec	2	at	Edmonton	3
Dec. 7	Rangers	3	at	Edmonton	4
Dec. 9	Calgary	3	at	Edmonton	2
Dec. 12	Vancouver	4	at	Edmonton	5
Dec. 15	Edmonton	3	at	Los Angeles	8
Dec. 18	Los Angeles	3	at	Edmonton	4
Dec. 20	Edmonton	4	at	Vancouver	7
Dec. 22	Edmonton	6	at	Calgary	2
Dec. 23	Vancouver	3	at	Edmonton	4
Dec. 27	Calgary	1	at	Edmonton	4
Dec. 28	Edmonton	5	at	Vancouver	2
Dec. 30	Hartford	3	at	Edmonton	4
Jan. 2	Montreal	3	at	Edmonton	0
Jan. 4	Detroit	2	at	Edmonton	3
Jan. 8	Edmonton	1	at	Pittsburgh	6
Jan. 9	Edmonton	3	at	Detroit	5
Jan. 12	Edmonton	5	at	New Jersey	4 OT
Jan. 13	Edmonton	5	at	Philadelphia	3
Jan. 15	Edmonton	2	at	Rangers	2 OT
Jan. 17	Edmonton	6	at	Islanders	1
Jan. 22	Los Angeles	2	at	Edmonton	4
Jan. 23	Edmonton	5	at	Vancouver	6
Jan. 25	Rangers	4	at	Edmonton	3
Jan. 27	Edmonton	3	at	Winnipeg	2
Jan. 30	Vancouver	4	at	Edmonton	9
Feb. 1	Chicago	3	at	Edmonton	4 OT
Feb. 3	Edmonton	3	at	Buffalo	2
Feb. 5	Edmonton	5	at	Boston	6 OT
Feb. 6	Edmonton	1	at	Hartford	5
Feb. 8	Edmonton	3	at	Washington	6
Feb. 11	Pittsburgh	5	at	Edmonton	7
Feb. 12	St. Louis	4	at	Edmonton	2
Feb. 14	Los Angeles	4	at	Edmonton	2
Feb. 16	Edmonton	2	at	Toronto	3
Feb. 18	Edmonton	4	at	New Jersey	0
Feb. 20	Edmonton	1	at	Minnesota	5
Feb. 22	Detroit	5	at	Edmonton	5 OT
Feb. 24	Quebec	3	at	Edmonton	6
Feb. 27	Edmonton	2	at	Calgary	4
Mar. 1	Minnesota	1	at	Edmonton	1 OT
Mar. 2	Montreal	3	at	Edmonton	1
Mar. 5	Edmonton	5	at	Winnipeg	4
Mar. 6	Edmonton	1	at	Minnesota	5
Mar. 8	Philadelphia	4	at	Edmonton	5
Mar. 10	Washington	5	at	Edmonton	3
Mar. 13	Islanders	1	at	Edmonton	2
Mar. 15	Edmonton	3	at	Winnipeg	4
Mar. 17	Edmonton	4	at	Montreal	2
Mar. 19	Edmonton	7	at	Quebec	6 OT
Mar. 23	Winnipeg	3	at	Edmonton	0
Mar. 24	Los Angeles	4	at	Edmonton	3 OT
Mar. 26	Edmonton	0	at	Los Angeles	2
Mar. 28	Edmonton	4	at	Calgary	4 OT
Mar. 29	Calgary	5	at	Edmonton	6 OT
Mar. 31	Winnipeg	3	at	Edmonton	6

Opponent	*Home W–L–T*	*Road W–L–T*
Boston	1–0–0	0–2–0
Buffalo	1–0–0	1–1–0
Calgary	2–2–0	1–2–1
Chicago	1–1–0	0–1–0
Detroit	1–0–1	0–1–0
Hartford	1–0–0	1–1–0
Los Angeles	2–2–0	0–3–1
Minnesota	0–0–1	0–2–0
Montreal	0–2–0	1–0–0
New Jersey	0–1–0	2–0–0
Islanders	2–0–0	1–0–0
Rangers	1–1–0	0–0–1
Philadelphia	1–0–0	2–0–0
Pittsburgh	1–0–0	1–1–0
Quebec	2–0–0	1–0–0
St. Louis	0–2–0	0–1–0
Toronto	1–0–0	1–1–0
Vancouver	4–0–0	1–3–0
Washington	0–2–0	0–1–0
Winnipeg	1–2–1	2–2–0

Opponent	Overall W–L–T	GF-GA	Opponent	Overall W–L–T	GF-GA
Boston	1–2–0	15–11	Islanders	3–0–0	11–3
Buffalo	2–1–0	9–7	Rangers	1–1–1	9–9
Calgary	3–4–1	27–25	Philadelphia	3–0–0	16–10
Chicago	1–2–0	8–11	Pittsburgh	2–1–0	15–14
Detroit	1–1–1	11–12	Quebec	3–0–0	16–11
Hartford	2–1–0	9–10	St. Louis	0–3–0	5–11
Los Angeles	2–5–1	25–35	Toronto	2–1–0	9–6
Minnesota	0–2–1	3–11	Vancouver	5–3–0	41–34
Montreal	1–2–0	5–8	Washington	0–3–0	6–12
New Jersey	2–1–0	11–9	Winnipeg	3–4–1	21–23

1990–91 Playoff Scoring

#		GP	G	A	Pts	Shots	S%	GW	OT	PP	SH	P/M	PIM
10	Esa Tikkanen	18	12	8	20	76	15.8	3	2	3	0	3	24
18	Craig Simpson	18	5	11	16	21	23.8	0	0	1	0	1	12
11	Mark Messier	18	4	11	15	41	9.8	0	0	1	0	2	16
85	Petr Klima	18	7	6	13	51	13.7	3	1	1	0	–1	16
9	Glenn Anderson	18	6	7	13	43	14.0	0	0	3	0	–2	41
19	Anatoli Semenov	12	5	5	10	28	17.9	0	0	0	0	7	6
22	Charlie Huddy	18	3	7	10	35	8.6	0	0	1	0	9	10
20	Martin Gelinas	18	3	6	9	29	10.3	1	0	0	0	4	25
8	Joe Murphy	15	2	5	7	22	9.1	1	0	1	0	3	14
14	Craig MacTavish	18	3	3	6	24	12.5	1	1	0	0	–3	20
12	Adam Graves	18	2	4	6	48	4.2	0	0	0	0	7	22
7	Mark Lamb	15	0	5	5	14	0.0	0	0	0	0	–4	20
6	Jeff Beukeboom	18	1	3	4	15	6.7	0	0	0	0	–5	28
36	Norm Maciver	18	0	4	4	18	0.0	0	0	0	0	10	8
16	Kelly Buchberger	12	2	1	3	12	16.7	0	0	0	0	–3	25
5	Steve Smith	18	1	2	3	30	3.3	0	0	1	0	–8	45
28	Craig Muni	18	0	3	3	10	0.0	0	0	0	0	5	20
4	Kevin Lowe	14	1	1	2	5	20.0	0	0	0	0	–1	14
31	Grant Fuhr	17	0	2	2	0	0.0	0	0	0	0	0	2
13	Ken Linseman	2	0	1	1	1	0.0	0	0	0	0	1	0
32	Dave Brown	16	0	1	1	11	0.0	0	0	0	0	–2	30
30	Bill Ranford	3	0	0	0	0	0.0	0	0	0	0	0	0
25	Geoff Smith	4	0	0	0	5	0.0	0	0	0	0	5	0
		18	57	96	153	539	10.6	9	4	12	0	28	398

1990-91 Playoff Goaltending

	GP	Min.	GA	W	L	Ave.	SA	Pct.	SO	EN
Bill Ranford	3	135	8	1	2	2.66	78	0.897	0	0
Grant Fuhr	17	1019	51	8	7	3.00	488	0.895	0	1
	18	4850	60	9	9	3.33	567	0.894	0	1

Date	Result					Winning Goaltender	Winning Goal
April 4, 1991	Edmonton	3	at	Calgary	1	Grant Fuhr	Peter Klima
April 6, 1991	Edmonton	1	at	Calgary	3	Mike Vernon	Doug Gilmour
April 8, 1991	Calgary	3	at	Edmonton	4	Grant Fuhr	Joe Murphy
April 10, 1991	Calgary	2	at	Edmonton	5	Grant Fuhr	Esa Tikkanen
April 12, 1991	Edmonton	3	at	Calgary	5	Mike Vernon	Ric Natress
April 14, 1991	Calgary	2	at	Edmonton	1	Mike Vernon	Theo Fleury[1]
April 16, 1991	Edmonton	5	at	Calgary	4	Grant Fuhr	Esa Tikkanen[2]
April 18, 1991	Edmonton	3	at	Los Angeles	4	Kelly Hrudey	Luc Robitaille[3]
April 20, 1991	Edmonton	4	at	Los Angeles	3	Grant Fuhr	Peter Klima[4]
April 22, 1991	Los Angeles	3	at	Edmonton	4	Grant Fuhr	Esa Tikkanen[5]
April 24, 1991	Los Angeles	2	at	Edmonton	4	Grant Fuhr	Martin Gelinas
April 26, 1991	Edmonton	2	at	Los Angeles	5	Kelly Hrudey	Luc Robitaille
April 28, 1991	Los Angeles	3	at	Edmonton	4	Bill Ranford	Craig MacTavish[6]
May 2, 1991	Minnesota	3	at	Edmonton	1	Jon Casey	Dave Gagner
May 4, 1991	Minnesota	2	at	Edmonton	7	Grant Fuhr	Petr Klima

Date			*Result*			*Winning Goaltender*	*Winning Goal*
May 6, 1991	Edmonton	3	at	Minnesota	7	Jon Casey	Bobby Smith
May 8, 1991	Edmonton	1	at	Minnesota	5	Jon Casey	Mike Modano
May 10, 1991	Minnesota	3	at	Edmonton	2	Jon Casey	Bobby Smith

[1]4:40 of overtime [2]6:58 of overtime [3]2:13 of overtime
[4]24:48 of overtime [5]20:48 of overtime [6]16:57 of overtime

Table 9. All Time Regular Season Overtime Scorers

Date	*Scorer*	*Home/Road*	*Opposition*	*Time*	*Goaltender*
October 9, 1983	*Jari Kurri*	*Home*	*Minnesota*	*3:50*	*Gilles Meloche*
October 30, 1983	*Pat Hughes*	*Road*	*Rangers*	*1:18*	*Steve Weeks*
February 27, 1984	*Dave Hunter*	*Road*	*Winnipeg*	*2:10*	*Marc Behrend*
March 13, 1984	*Paul Coffey*	*Road*	*Quebec*	*4:35*	*Daniel Bouchard*
November 17, 1985	*Mark Napier*	*Road*	*Rangers*	*2:06*	*John Vanbiesbrouck*
November 20, 1985	*Mark Messier*	*Road*	*Montreal*	*0:42*	*Steve Penney*
January 24, 1986	*Wayne Gretzky*	*Home*	*New Jersey*	*1:29*	*Craig Billington*
March 2, 1986	*Jari Kurri*	*Home*	*Philadelphia*	*1:29*	*Darren Jensen*
March 21, 1986	*Jari Kurri*	*Home*	*Minnesota*	*1:36*	*Don Beaupre*
October 11, 1986	*Jari Kurri*	*Road*	*Montreal*	*4:49*	*Patrick Roy*
November 11, 1986	*Glenn Anderson*	*Road*	*Islanders*	*2:19*	*Kelly Hrudey*
November 19, 1986	*Glenn Anderson*	*Home*	*Rangers*	*1:05*	*John Vanbiesbrouck*
February 4, 1987	*Randy Gregg*	*Road*	*Minnesota*	*2:12*	*Don Beaupre*
March 31, 1987	*Steve Smith*	*Home*	*Winnipeg*	*1:29*	*Eldon Reddick*
October 23, 1987	*Charlie Huddy*	*Road*	*Vancouver*	*2:51*	*Kirk McLean*
November 14, 1987	*Jari Kurri*	*Road*	*St. Louis*	*1:27*	*Rick Wamsley*
February 21, 1988	*Kevin Lowe*	*Road*	*Winnipeg*	*3:15*	*Daniel Berthiaume*
October 29, 1988	*Jari Kurri*	*Home*	*Washington*	*4:44*	*Clint Malarchuk*
November 9, 1988	*Glenn Anderson*	*Road*	*New Jersey*	*4:46*	*Sean Burke*
November 13, 1988	*Esa Tikkanen*	*Road*	*Buffalo*	*3:25*	*Daren Puppa*
January 2, 1989	*Esa Tikkanen*	*Road*	*Minnesota*	*3:10*	*Jon Casey*
November 19, 1989	*Mark Messier*	*Home*	*Chicago*	*0:08*	*Alain Chevrier*
December 8, 1989	*Mark Lamb*	*Home*	*Los Angeles*	*2:03*	*Kelly Hrudey*
January 9, 1990	*Martin Gelinas*	*Road*	*Calgary*	*2:11*	*Mike Vernon*
February 4, 1990	*Jari Kurri*	*Road*	*Washington*	*3:13*	*Bob Mason*
March 6, 1990	*Craig MacTavish*	*Home*	*Pittsburgh*	*1:17*	*Frank Pietrangelo*
January 12, 1991	*Steve Smith*	*Road*	*New Jersey*	*0:56*	*Chris Terreri*
February 1, 1991	*Petr Klima*	*Home*	*Chicago*	*2:24*	*Ed Belfour*
March 19, 1991	*Mark Messier*	*Road*	*Quebec*	*4:34*	*Ron Tugnutt*
October 15, 1992	*Craig Simpson*	*Road*	*Chicago*	*2:06*	*Jim Waite*
November 28, 1992	*Craig Simpson*	*Home*	*Tampa Bay*	*3:45*	*Wendell Young*
January 17, 1993	*Zdeno Ciger*	*Home*	*Buffalo*	*0:25*	*Tom Draper*
January 31, 1993	*Kelly Buchberger*	*Road*	*Buffalo*	*0:46*	*Tom Draper*
March 17, 1993	*Craig MacTavish*	*Road*	*Rangers*	*0:32*	*John Vanbiesbrouck*
March 31, 1994	*Jason Arnott*	*Road*	*Anaheim*	*1:44*	*Guy Hebert*
April 27, 1995	*Zdeno Ciger*	*Home*	*St. Louis*	*3:19*	*Jon Casey*
November 10, 1995	*Jason Arnott*	*Road*	*Tampa Bay*	*2:41*	*Derek Wilkinson*
December 29, 1995	*Miroslav Satan*	*Home*	*Los Angeles*	*3:44*	*Kelly Hrudey*
January 13, 1996	*Doug Weight*	*Home*	*Buffalo*	*4:49*	*Dominik Hasek*
February 27, 1996	*Mariusz Czerkawski*	*Road*	*Boston*	*4:40*	*Bill Ranford*
January 12, 1997	*Mats Lindgren*	*Home*	*Hartford*	*2:27*	*Sean Burke*
October 19, 1997	*Todd Marchant*	*Road*	*Los Angeles*	*3:05*	*Stephane Fiset*
March 2, 1998	*Scott Fraser*	*Road*	*Colorado*	*0:11*	*Patrick Roy*
March 9, 1998	*Dean McAmmond*	*Road*	*Chicago*	*4:17*	*Jeff Hackett*
November 8, 1998	*Josef Beranek*	*Road*	*Chicago*	*0:34*	*Mark Fitzpatrick*
November 20, 1998	*Andrei Kovalenko*	*Road*	*Anaheim*	*0:39*	*Guy Hebert*
April 12, 1999	*Tom Poti*	*Road*	*San Jose*	*3:55*	*Steve Shields*
January 25, 2000	*Ethan Moreau*	*Road*	*Vancouver*	*4:00*	*Garth Snow*
February 8, 2000	*Jason Smith*	*Road*	*Montreal*	*3:04*	*Jeff Hackett*
April 1, 2000	*Tom Poti*	*Home*	*Phoenix*	*3:07*	*Sean Burke*
April 7, 2000	*Rem Murray*	*Road*	*Vancouver*	*4:01*	*E.N.G.*
November 12, 2000	*Doug Weight*	*Road*	*Minnesota*	*1:24*	*Manny Fernandez*
December 20, 2000	*Anson Carter*	*Home*	*Vancouver*	*2:41*	*Bob Essensa*
December 30, 2000	*Doug Weight*	*Home*	*Montreal*	*1:49*	*Jose Theodore*
February 25, 2001	*Todd Marchant*	*Home*	*Dallas*	*0:31*	*Ed Belfour*

Date	*Scorer*	*Home/Road*	*Opposition*	*Time*	*Goaltender*
March 13, 2001	*Eric Brewer*	*Road*	*Tampa Bay*	*1:17*	*Kevin Weekes*

Most Goals Scored—7 (Jari Kurri), Most Goals Allowed—3 (John Vanbiesbrouck, Kelly Hrudey, Sean Burke), Team Allowing the Most Goals—5 (Chicago), 21 Home Wins, 35 Road Wins, Average Time—2 minutes 27 seconds.

1991-92

With the departure of John Muckler to Buffalo, where he would become head coach of the Sabres, Sather named longtime assistant coach Ted Green as the new head coach. Sather also hired Kevin Primeau to fill the now vacant assistant coaching position. Primeau had been a former Oiler and University of Alberta Golden Bear player and assistant coach and had also been around the international hockey scene in various capacities.

At this year's draft, held in Buffalo, Glen Sather drafted three players who would see some action with the team in the future. Tyler Wright, Martin Rucinsky and David Oliver would play a combined total of 184 games for the Oilers in upcoming seasons, Oliver playing in 141 of them.

In September Sather initiated a number of trades which would leave the Oilers virtually unrecognizable as the team which had won the Stanley Cup two years ago. "Slats" would deal many of the superstars who had helped the team win the championship five times in seven years.

The first to leave was star goaltender Grant Fuhr who was reportedly having trouble with substance abuse. Included in the trade was high scoring winger Glenn Anderson whose scoring production had slipped in recent years, and Craig Berube. In exchange Edmonton got: goaltender Peter Ing; rugged forward Scott Thornton, former Toronto first round draft choice; defenseman Luke Richardson; and Vincent Damphousse, who would lead the team in scoring in his first year in Edmonton.

In October the Oilers traded team leader Mark Messier to the New York Rangers in exchange for tough guy Louie DeBrusk, utility forward Steven Rice and former seventy-goal scorer Bernie Nicholls. Nicholls would not report to the team until December 6.

Gone too were the "Oilers Twin Towers" on defense. In October Steve Smith was traded to Chicago for defenseman Dave Manson, and in November, in an exchange of defensemen, Jeff Beukeboom was traded to the Rangers for David Shaw. Also gone were forward Adam Graves, who was lost to free agency, and defenseman Charlie Huddy, who had been taken in the expansion draft in May by Minnesota.

Already gone from the club was Finnish star Jari Kurri, who had played the previous season in Italy. In May Sather had worked out a deal with Los Angeles in which Kurri could join former line mate Wayne Gretzky on the Kings. Included in the trade was Dave Brown and Corey Foster. In turn the Oilers received Craig Fisher, Scott Mellanby and Craig Berube.

Injuries hampered many of the players this year. Bernie Nicholls missed a couple of games with a pulled abdominal muscle and Petr Klima missed nine games with an assortment of bumps and bruises, including six due to a groin injury. Finnish winger Esa Tikkanen missed 37 games with a fractured left shoulder. Defenseman Geoff Smith also suffered a shoulder injury and missed the final 11 games of the playoffs while newcomer David Maley missed 12 games with a knee injury. Bad knees also plagued Craig Muni who missed the final eight games of the regular season and the first 12 games of the playoffs with a rupture of the ligament in his right knee. Muni had earlier missed 17 games with a pinched nerve in his shoulder.

The team got off to a slow start but gathered momentum towards the middle of the season. The Oilers were 17–23–7 (.436) at the All-Star break, but won 11 of 15 games from January to March. With the change of personnel the Oilers improved their record slightly over the previous year's total. They finished third in the Smythe Division, 14 points behind division leading Vancouver. The team's offense, led by Vincent Damphousse with 89 points, improved this year to sixth overall, scoring 295 goals. The team's defense however appeared confused at times, finishing sixteenth in goals allowed. Bill Ranford appeared in 67 games in net.

In the first round of the playoffs Edmonton met Los Angeles and defeated former teammates Gretzky, Kurri, Huddy, and McSorley in six games. In the division final series the Oilers met the much improved Vancouver Canucks and defeated them in six games.

The team then advanced to the conference final series against Chicago, but the first two series had taken their toll on the Oilers and they bowed out to Chicago in four straight games. This would prove to be their final playoff appearance for four years.

1991-92 Regular Season Scoring

#		Ht.	Wt.	Age	GP	G	A	Pts	Shots	S%	GW	GT	PP	SH	P/M	PIM
21	Damphousse	73	190	24	80	38	51	89	247	15.4	8	1	12	1	10	53
8	Murphy	73	190	24	80	35	47	82	193	18.1	2	2	10	2	17	52
18	Simpson	74	195	24	79	24	37	61	128	18.8	2	0	6	0	8	80
27	Mellanby	73	205	25	80	23	27	50	159	14.5	5	0	7	0	5	197
9	Nicholls	72	185	30	49	20	29	49	115	17.4	2	0	7	0	5	60
24	Manson	74	202	24	79	15	32	47	206	7.3	2	0	7	0	9	220
16	Buchberger	74	210	25	79	20	24	44	90	22.2	3	1	0	4	9	157
19	Semenov	74	190	29	59	20	22	42	105	19.0	3	0	3	0	12	16
36	Maciver	71	180	27	57	6	34	40	69	8.7	3	0	2	0	20	38
85	Klima	72	190	27	57	21	13	34	107	19.6	0	0	5	0	-18	52
14	MacTavish (A)	73	195	33	80	12	18	30	86	14.0	1	0	0	2	-1	98
20	Gelinas	71	195	21	68	11	18	29	94	11.7	0	0	1	0	14	62
10	Tikkanen	73	200	26	40	12	16	28	117	10.3	1	0	6	2	-8	44
42	Beranek	74	185	22	58	12	16	28	79	15.2	1	0	0	0	-2	18
7	Lamb	69	180	27	59	6	22	28	61	9.8	1	0	2	0	4	46
22	Richardson	76	210	22	75	2	19	21	85	2.4	0	0	0	0	-9	118
25	G. Smith	75	200	22	74	2	16	18	61	3.3	0	0	0	0	-5	43
34	Hawgood	70	190	23	20	2	11	13	24	8.3	0	0	0	0	19	22
12	Maley	74	195	28	23	3	6	9	31	9.7	1	0	0	0	8	46
4	Lowe (C)	74	195	32	55	2	8	10	33	6.1	0	0	0	0	-4	107
6	Glynn	76	215	24	25	2	6	8	29	6.9	0	0	0	1	11	6
28	Muni	75	200	29	54	2	5	7	38	5.3	0	0	0	0	11	34
6	Beukeboom	76	215	26	18	0	5	5	7	0.0	0	0	0	0	4	78
12	Mallette	72	215	21	15	1	3	4	9	11.1	0	0	0	0	-1	36
29	DeBrusk	73	225	20	25	2	1	3	7	28.6	1	0	0	0	4	124
1	Ing	74	170	22	12	0	3	3	0	0.0	0	0	0	0	0	0
30	Ranford	70	170	25	67	0	3	3	0	0.0	0	0	0	0	0	4
26	Shaw	74	204	27	12	1	1	2	15	6.7	0	0	0	0	-8	8
23	Currie	74	195	23	7	1	0	1	3	33.3	0	0	0	0	-1	0
17	Thornton	74	200	20	15	0	1	1	11	0.0	0	0	0	0	-6	43
23	Rucinsky	73	185	20	2	0	0	0	1	0.0	0	0	0	0	-3	0
15	Rice	72	215	20	3	0	0	0	2	0.0	0	0	0	0	-2	2
35	Leroux	78	221	21	4	0	0	0	0	0.0	0	0	0	0	-1	7
2	Joseph	74	210	22	7	0	0	0	5	0.0	0	0	0	0	-1	8
33	Foster	69	175	26	10	0	0	0	0	0.0	0	0	0	0	0	2
32	Tugnutt	71	155	24	3	0	0	0	0	0.0	0	0	0	0	0	2
	Bench															24
		73	196	25	80	295	494	789	2217	13.3	36	4	68	12	100	1907

1991-92 Goaltender Records

	GP	Min.	GA	W	L	T	Ave.	SA	Pct.	SO	EN
Norm Foster	10	439	20	5	3	0	2.71	183	0.891	0	0
Bill Ranford	67	3822	228	27	26	10	3.58	1971	0.884	1	5
Peter Ing	12	463	33	3	4	0	4.27	252	0.869	0	1
Ron Tugnutt	3	124	10	1	1	0	4.83	73	0.863	0	0
	80	4858	297	36	34	10	3.67	2479	0.880	1	6

Coach: Ted Green 36-34-10

1991-92 Scoring vs. Opposition

	Bost.	Buff.	Calg.	Chi.	Det.	Hart.	L.A.	Minn.	Mont.	N.J.
Beranek	1–1–2	0–2–2	0–2–2	0–0–0	0–0–0	0–1–1	1–1–2	2–0–2	0–0–0	0–0–0
Beukeboom	———	———	0–0–0	0–0–0	0–0–0	———	0–1–1	———	———	0–0–0
Buchberger	0–1–1	0–1–1	0–1–1	0–1–1	3–1–2	1–1–2	1–1–2	0–0–0	0–0–0	1–1–2
Currie	0–0–0	———	1–0–1	———	———	———	0–0–0	0–0–0	———	0–0–0
Damphousse	2–0–2	2–4–6	3–4–7	2–1–3	1–0–1	2–0–2	3–5–8	4–3–7	2–0–2	0–1–1
DeBrusk	———	0–0–0	0–0–0	0–0–0	0–0–0	1–0–1	0–0–0	0–0–0	———	0–0–0
Gelinas	0–1–1	0–0–0	0–1–1	1–1–2	0–0–0	1–0–1	3–0–3	0–0–0	0–0–0	0–1–1
Glynn	0–1–1	0–0–0	0–0–0	0–0–0	———	0–0–0	0–1–1	0–0–0	0–0–0	0–0–0

	Bost.	***Buff.***	***Calg.***	***Chi.***	***Det.***	***Hart.***	***L.A.***	***Minn.***	***Mont.***	***N.J.***
Hawgood	0–1–1	0–0–0	0–1–1	0–0–0	———	0–0–0	1–2–3	0–1–1	———	1–0–1
Joseph	———	———	———	———	———	0–0–0	———	0–0–0	———	———
Klima	2–1–3	2–2–4	1–2–3	0–0–0	1–0–1	0–0–0	0–2–2	0–0–0	0–1–1	0–0–0
Lamb	0–0–0	0–1–1	1–3–4	1–0–1	0–0–0	0–1–1	0–1–1	0–1–1	0–0–0	0–0–0
Leroux	0–0–0	———	0–0–0	———	———	———	———	———	———	———
Lowe	0–0–0	0–0–0	1–0–1	0–0–0	1–0–1	———	0–0–0	0–0–0	0–0–0	0–0–0
Maciver	0–1–1	0–2–2	0–1–1	0–2–2	0–1–1	0–3–3	0–4–4	0–1–1	1–1–2	0–2–2
MacTavish	1–0–1	0–1–1	0–0–0	0–0–0	0–0–0	1–1–2	0–2–2	2–0–2	0–0–0	1–1–2
Maley	0–0–0	0–0–0	———	0–0–0	———	1–0–1	0–0–0	0–2–2	0–0–0	———
Mallette	0–0–0	0–0–0	0–0–0	———	———	———	0–0–0	———	0–0–0	———
Manson	0–3–3	0–1–1	2–2–4	1–0–1	1–0–1	2–0–2	1–2–3	1–4–5	0–2–2	0–1–1
Mellanby	1–0–1	1–0–1	4–2–6	1–1–2	0–1–1	0–1–1	1–0–1	1–2–3	0–0–0	0–1–1
Muni	0–0–0	0–0–0	0–0–0	1–0–1	0–0–0	0–0–0	0–1–1	0–0–0	0–0–0	0–0–0
Murphy	1–2–3	0–2–2	1–4–5	2–2–4	0–0–0	1–2–3	7–3–10	5–3–8	0–0–0	0–2–2
Nicholls	0–2–2	3–0–3	3–2–5	0–1–1	0–1–1	0–2–2	1–3–4	0–2–2	0–1–1	2–0–2
Rice	———	———	———	———	———	———	———	———	0–0–0	———
Richardson	0–1–1	1–2–3	0–0–0	0–1–1	0–2–2	0–1–1	0–2–2	0–0–0	0–0–0	0–1–1
Rucinsky	———	0–0–0	———	———	———	———	———	0–0–0	———	———
Semenov	2–0–2	1–1–2	1–4–5	0–2–2	0–1–1	0–2–2	2–0–2	1–1–2	0–0–0	1–0–1
Shaw	0–0–0	———	0–0–0	———	0–0–0	———	0–0–0	———	0–0–0	———
Simpson	0–3–3	1–1–2	1–3–4	3–1–4	1–1–2	0–0–0	1–2–3	1–3–4	0–0–0	1–2–3
Smith	0–0–0	0–0–0	1–1–2	0–1–1	0–0–0	0–2–2	0–0–0	0–1–1	0–0–0	0–0–0
Thornton	———	———	0–0–0	0–0–0	0–0–0	———	0–0–0	———	———	0–0–0
Tikkanen	———	0–0–0	1–2–3	1–1–2	1–0–1	———	0–1–1	———	0–0–0	1–0–1

	NYI.	***NYR.***	***Phil.***	***Pitt.***	***Que.***	***S. J.***	***St.L.***	***Tor.***	***Van.***	***Wash.***	***Winn.***
Beranek	1–2–3	0–1–1	0–0–0	1–1–2	0–0–0	1–1–2	1–0–1	1–0–1	2–4–6	1–0–1	0–0–0
Beukeboom	0–1–1	0–1–1	———	———	———	0–0–0	0–0–0	———	0–2–2	0–0–0	———
Buchberger	2–0–2	1–0–1	0–2–2	2–1–3	2–2–	1–2–3	1–0–1	2–0–2	2–5–7	2–0–2	1–4–5
Currie	———	———	———	0–0–0	———	———	———	———	———	0–0–0	———
Damphousse	2–0–2	1–0–1	2–2–4	1–2–3	1–4–5	2–9–11	0–1–1	1–4–5	1–7–8	0–2–2	6–2–8
DeBrusk	0–0–0	0–0–0	0–0–0	———	———	———	0–0–0	———	1–1–2	0–0–0	0–0–0
Gelinas	0–4–4	0–1–1	0–1–1	1–2–3	1–0–1	1–1–2	0–1–1	0–0–0	3–3–6	0–0–0	0–1–1
Glynn	1–1–2	0–0–0	0–0–0	———	0–0–0	0–1–1	0–1–1	0–0–0	0–0–0	———	1–1–2
Hawgood	———	0–0–0	0–0–0	0–1–1	———	0–1–1	———	0–1–1	———	0–0–0	0–3–3
Joseph	0–0–0	———	0–0–0	———	0–0–0	———	———	0–0–0	———	———	———
Klima	1–2–3	0–0–0	0–0–0	1–0–1	0–0–0	4–0–4	0–0–0	1–0–1	5–2–7	———	3–1–4
Lamb	0–1–1	0–0–0	0–0–0	0–0–0	0–3–3	1–2–3	0–1–1	1–0–1	1–2–3	0–2–2	1–4–5
Leroux	———	———	———	———	———	———	———	———	———	0–0–0	———
Lowe	0–0–0	0–0–0	0–0–0	0–1–1	0–1–1	0–0–0	0–0–0	0–0–0	0–3–3	0–0–0	0–2–2
Maciver	0–0–0	———	1–1–2	0–0–0	1–2–3	1–3–4	0–0–0	0–2–2	0–1–1	0–1–1	2–6–8
MacTavish	0–2–2	0–1–1	2–0–2	2–1–3	0–3–3	1–2–3	0–0–0	0–1–1	1–2–3	0–0–0	1–1–2
Maley	0–0–0	1–0–1	0–1–1	———	1–1–2	0–0–0	———	0–1–1	0–0–0	———	0–1–1
Mallette	———	———	0–0–0	0–1–1	0–1–1	0–0–0	———	0–1–1	1–0–1	———	0–0–0
Manson	0–0–0	0–0–0	0–2–2	0–1–1	2–0–2	2–2–4	0–1–1	0–1–1	2–4–6	0–4–4	1–2–3
Mellanby	2–4–6	0–0–0	0–1–1	1–2–3	1–1–2	2–2–4	0–1–1	2–2–4	5–3–8	0–0–0	1–3–4
Muni	0–0–0	0–0–0	0–0–0	0–0–0	0–0–0	0–2–2	0–0–0	0–1–1	1–1–2	0–0–0	0–0–0
Murphy	1–0–1	1–2–3	1–2–3	1–3–4	2–2–4	3–5–8	3–2–5	2–2–4	1–7–8	2–0–2	1–2–3
Nicholls	0–2–2	0–0–0	1–0–1	1–0–1	0–0–0	4–6–10	0–1–1	1–2–3	2–3–5	1–0–1	1–1–2
Rice	———	———	———	———	———	0–0–0	———	———	———	———	0–0–0
Richardson	0–1–1	0–1–1	0–1–1	0–0–0	0–1–1	1–1–2	0–0–0	0–1–1	0–2–2	0–0–0	0–1–1
Semenov	0–0–0	0–1–1	2–0–2	0–2–2	0–1–1	3–3–6	1–0–1	2–1–3	2–3–5	0–0–0	2–0–2
Shaw	———	———	0–0–0	1–1–2	0–0–0	———	———	———	———	———	0–0–0
Simpson	1–1–2	1–0–1	1–2–3	2–1–3	2–3–5	2–3–5	1–0–1	1–2–3	2–3–5	0–2–2	4–1–5
Smith	0–0–0	0–0–0	0–0–0	0–0–0	0–2–2	0–2–2	0–2–2	0–2–2	1–2–3	0–0–0	0–1–1
Thornton	0–0–0	———	———	0–0–0	———	0–0–0	0–1–1	———	0–0–0	———	———
Tikkanen	2–2–4	0–1–1	0–0–0	0–1–1	1–0–1	0–2–2	2–0–2	0–1–1	2–2–4	1–0–1	0–3–3

1991–92 Goaltender Records vs. Opposition

	GP	***Min.***	***GA***	***EN***	***SO***	***Ave.***	***W–L–T***	***Opposition***
Norm Foster	1	18	1	0	0	3.33	0–0–0	Buffalo
	2	90	3	0	0	2.00	1–1–0	Calgary
	1	38	3	0	0	4.74	0–1–0	Chicago

	GP	Min.	GA	EN	SO	Ave.	W–L–T	Opposition
	1	60	1	0	0	1.00	1–0–0	Hartford
	1	26	4	0	0	9.23	0–0–0	Minnesota
	1	60	1	0	0	1.00	1–0–0	Montreal
	1	60	2	0	0	2.00	1–0–0	N.Y. Islanders
	1	60	2	0	0	2.00	1–0–0	Quebec
	1	28	3	0	0	6.43	0–1–0	Winnipeg
Peter Ing	1	40	6	0	0	9.00	0–1–0	Boston
	1	14	1	0	0	4.29	0–0–0	Calgary
	1	59	3	1	0	3.05	0–1–0	Chicago
	1	20	3	0	0	9.00	0–0–0	Los Angeles
	1	34	0	0	0	0.00	1–0–0	Minnesota
	1	60	3	0	0	3.00	1–0–0	N.Y. Islanders
	2	50	5	0	0	6.00	0–1–0	San Jose
	1	65	3	0	0	2.77	0–1–0	St. Louis
	1	60	5	1	0	5.00	1–0–0	Toronto
	1	30	2	0	0	4.00	0–0–0	Vancouver
	1	32	2	0	0	3.75	0–0–0	Winnipeg
Bill Ranford	2	138	8	0	0	3.48	1–1–0	Boston
	3	167	13	0	0	4.67	1–1–1	Buffalo
	6	321	22	1	0	4.11	2–2–1	Calgary
	2	82	3	0	0	2.20	1–1–0	Chicago
	3	185	12	0	0	3.89	0–2–1	Detroit
	2	120	2	0	0	1.00	2–0–0	Hartford
	7	415	28	0	0	4.05	1–3–3	Los Angeles
	2	120	7	0	0	3.50	2–0–0	Minnesota
	2	119	4	0	0	2.01	0–2–0	Montreal
	2	120	3	1	0	1.50	0–1–1	New Jersey
	1	60	2	0	0	2.00	1–0–0	N.Y. Islanders
	2	119	6	0	0	3.03	1–1–0	N.Y. Rangers
	3	179	11	2	0	3.69	1–2–0	Philadelphia
	3	182	14	0	0	4.62	1–2–0	Pittsburgh
	1	60	2	0	0	2.00	1–0–0	Quebec
	7	375	23	0	0	3.68	3–2–1	San Jose
	2	125	5	0	0	2.40	1–0–1	St. Louis
	2	120	11	1	0	5.50	0–2–0	Toronto
	7	390	24	0	1	3.69	5–2–0	Vancouver
	1	59	6	0	0	6.10	0–1–0	Washington
	6	365	22	0	0	3.62	3–2–1	Winnipeg
Ron Tugnutt	2	64	4	0	0	3.75	1–0–0	New Jersey
	1	60	6	0	0	6.00	0–1–0	Washington

1991-92 Schedule Results

Date	Visitor	Score		Home	Score
Oct. 4	Edmonton	2	at	Calgary	9
Oct. 6	Los Angeles	2	at	Edmonton	2 OT
Oct. 8	Edmonton	3	at	Los Angeles	6
Oct. 10	Edmonton	2	at	St. Louis	3 OT
Oct. 12	Calgary	1	at	Edmonton	3
Oct. 15	Edmonton	1	at	Detroit	3
Oct. 17	Edmonton	2	at	Chicago	4
Oct. 19	Edmonton	4	at	Islanders	2
Oct. 20	Edmonton	4	at	Rangers	3
Oct. 23	Washington	6	at	Edmonton	5
Oct. 26	Vancouver	4	at	Edmonton	5
Oct. 27	Edmonton	6	at	Vancouver	3
Oct. 30	St. Louis	2	at	Edmonton	2 OT
Nov. 1	New Jersey	3	at	Edmonton	1
Nov. 3	Edmonton	2	at	Vancouver	7
Nov. 6	Islanders	3	at	Edmonton	5
Nov. 8	Edmonton	2	at	San Jose	6
Nov. 9	Edmonton	4	at	Los Angeles	4 OT
Nov. 13	Edmonton	4	at	Pittsburgh	5 OT
Nov. 14	Edmonton	1	at	Philadelphia	3
Nov. 16	Edmonton	6	at	Quebec	2
Nov. 18	Edmonton	0	at	Montreal	1
Nov. 23	Winnipeg	4	at	Edmonton	0
Nov. 27	Chicago	2	at	Edmonton	6
Nov. 29	San Jose	4	at	Edmonton	4 OT
Dec. 1	Vancouver	0	at	Edmonton	7
Dec. 3	Pittsburgh	3	at	Edmonton	5
Dec. 6	Edmonton	4	at	Winnipeg	4 OT
Dec. 8	San Jose	1	at	Edmonton	3
Dec. 10	Edmonton	7	at	Vancouver	4
Dec. 12	Edmonton	3	at	San Jose	6
Dec. 14	Winnipeg	5	at	Edmonton	7
Dec. 15	Detroit	4	at	Edmonton	1
Dec. 18	Edmonton	7	at	Toronto	5
Dec. 20	Edmonton	4	at	Buffalo	4 OT
Dec. 21	Edmonton	3	at	Boston	6
Dec. 23	Calgary	3	at	Edmonton	5
Dec. 28	Los Angeles	9	at	Edmonton	4
Dec. 29	Montreal	3	at	Edmonton	1
Jan. 2	Edmonton	3	at	Los Angeles	5
Jan. 4	Edmonton	3	at	Calgary	2
Jan. 5	Calgary	3	at	Edmonton	2

Date	Visitor			Home	
Jan. 8	Edmonton	2	at	Winnipeg	5
Jan. 10	Edmonton	2	at	Buffalo	8
Jan. 11	Edmonton	5	at	Detroit	5 OT
Jan. 13	Edmonton	7	at	Minnesota	4
Jan. 15	Vancouver	5	at	Edmonton	3
Jan. 21	San Jose	2	at	Edmonton	9
Jan. 23	Rangers	3	at	Edmonton	1
Jan. 25	Edmonton	2	at	San Jose	5
Jan. 28	Edmonton	5	at	Vancouver	3
Jan. 29	Chicago	4	at	Edmonton	3
Jan. 31	Hartford	1	at	Edmonton	4
Feb. 2	Quebec	2	at	Edmonton	8
Feb. 5	Montreal	1	at	Edmonton	2
Feb. 7	Islanders	2	at	Edmonton	4
Feb. 11	Edmonton	5	at	Minnesota	4
Feb. 13	Edmonton	3	at	Hartford	1
Feb. 15	Edmonton	5	at	Philadelphia	8
Feb. 16	Edmonton	5	at	Toronto	7
Feb. 19	Los Angeles	3	at	Edmonton	4
Feb. 21	Boston	5	at	Edmonton	3
Feb. 23	Buffalo	2	at	Edmonton	5
Feb. 26	Winnipeg	1	at	Edmonton	6
Feb. 28	Philadelphia	2	at	Edmonton	4
Mar. 1	Edmonton	4	at	Winnipeg	2
Mar. 4	Toronto	5	at	Edmonton	2
Mar. 6	St. Louis	3	at	Edmonton	5
Mar. 11	New Jersey	2	at	Edmonton	2 OT
Mar. 14	Hartford	1	at	Edmonton	3
Mar. 17	Edmonton	5	at	Pittsburgh	6
Mar. 19	Edmonton	5	at	New Jersey	3
Mar. 21	Edmonton	4	at	Boston	3
Mar. 22	Edmonton	2	at	Washington	6
Mar. 24	Edmonton	4	at	Calgary	4 OT
Mar. 27	Minnesota	3	at	Edmonton	5
Mar. 29	Los Angeles	2	at	Edmonton	2 OT
Mar. 31	Edmonton	2	at	Calgary	5
April 12	San Jose	4	at	Edmonton	6
April 14	Winnipeg	6	at	Edmonton	2

Opponent	*Home W–L–T*	*Road W–L–T*
Boston	0–1–0	1–1–0
Buffalo	1–0–0	0–1–1
Calgary	2–1–0	1–2–1
Chicago	1–1–0	0–1–0
Detroit	0–1–0	0–1–1
Hartford	2–0–0	1–0–0
Los Angeles	1–1–2	0–2–1
Minnesota	1–0–0	2–0–0
Montreal	1–1–0	0–1–0
New Jersey	0–1–1	1–0–0
Islanders	2–0–0	1–0–0
Rangers	0–1–0	1–0–0
Philadelphia	1–0–0	0–2–0
Pittsburgh	1–0–0	0–2–0
Quebec	1–0–0	1–0–0
San Jose	3–0–1	0–3–0
St. Louis	1–0–1	0–1–0
Toronto	0–1–0	1–1–0
Vancouver	2–1–0	3–1–0
Washington	0–1–0	0–1–0
Winnipeg	2–2–0	1–1–1

Opponent	*Overall W–L–T*	*GF–GA*
Boston	1–2–0	10–14
Buffalo	1–1–1	11–14
Calgary	3–3–1	21–27
Chicago	1–2–0	11–10
Detroit	0–2–1	7–12
Hartford	3–0–0	10–3
Los Angeles	1–3–3	22–31
Minnesota	3–0–0	17–11
Montreal	1–2–0	3–5
New Jersey	1–1–1	8–8
Islanders	3–0–0	13–7
Rangers	1–1–0	5–6
Philadelphia	1–2–0	10–13
Pittsburgh	1–2–0	14–14
Quebec	2–0–0	14–4
San Jose	3–3–1	29–28
St. Louis	1–1–1	9–8
Toronto	1–2–0	14–17
Vancouver	5–2–0	35–26
Washington	0–2–0	7–12
Winnipeg	3–3–1	25–27

1991-92 Playoff Scoring

#		GP	G	A	Pts	Shots	S%	GW	OT	PP	SH	P/M	PIM
8	Joe Murphy	16	8	16	24	32	25.0	2	1	4	0	2	12
9	Bernie Nicholls	16	8	11	19	32	25.0	1	0	4	0	2	25
21	Vincent Damphousse	16	6	8	14	45	13.3	0	0	1	0	5	8
24	Dave Manson	16	3	9	12	47	6.4	0	0	1	0	-2	44
10	Esa Tikkanen	16	5	3	8	37	13.5	1	0	1	0	-1	8
6	Brian Glynn	16	4	1	5	13	30.8	1	0	1	0	1	12
85	Petr Klima	15	1	4	5	22	4.5	0	0	0	0	-1	8
16	Kelly Buchberger	16	1	4	5	12	8.3	0	0	0	0	2	32
22	Luke Richardson	16	0	5	5	11	0.0	0	0	0	0	-2	45
2	Chris Joseph	5	1	3	4	6	16.7	0	0	0	0	2	2
20	Martin Gelinas	15	1	3	4	15	6.7	0	0	0	0	-3	10
14	Craig MacTavish	16	3	0	3	27	11.1	1	0	0	1	4	28
42	Josef Beranek	12	2	1	3	17	11.8	1	0	1	0	-6	0
27	Scott Mellanby	16	2	1	3	26	7.7	1	0	1	0	-3	29
36	Norm Maciver	13	1	2	3	17	5.9	0	0	0	0	3	10

#		*GP*	*G*	*A*	*Pts*	*Shots*	*S%*	*GW*	*OT*	*PP*	*SH*	*P/M*	*PIM*
4	Kevin Lowe	11	0	3	3	7	0.0	0	0	0	0	-2	16
34	Greg Hawgood	13	0	3	3	19	0.0	0	0	0	0	-4	23
19	Anatoli Semenov	8	1	1	2	12	8.3	0	0	0	0	3	6
12	David Maley	10	1	1	2	6	16.7	0	0	0	0	-4	4
7	Mark Lamb	16	1	1	2	13	7.7	0	0	0	0	-5	10
25	Geoff Smith	5	0	1	1	5	0.0	0	0	0	0	2	6
18	Craig Simpson	1	0	0	0	1	0.0	0	0	0	0	0	0
17	Scott Thornton	1	0	0	0	1	0.0	0	0	0	0	-1	0
32	Ron Tugnutt	2	0	0	0	0	0.0	0	0	0	0	0	0
28	Craig Muni	3	0	0	0	3	0.0	0	0	0	0	-4	2
30	Bill Ranford	16	0	0	0	0	0.0	0	0	0	0	0	0
		16	49	81	130	426	11.5	8	1	14	1	-2	340

1991-92 Playoff Goaltending

	GP	*Min.*	*GA*	*W*	*L*	*Ave.*	*SA*	*Pct.*	*SO*	*EN*
Ron Tugnutt	2	60	3	0	0	3.00	34	0.912	0	0
Bill Ranford	16	909	51	8	8	3.19	484	0.895	2	0
	16	971	54	8	8	3.38	518	0.896	2	0

Date			*Result*			*Winning Goaltender*	*Winning Goal*
April 18, 1992	Edmonton	3	at	Los Angeles	1	Bill Ranford	Brian Glynn
April 20, 1992	Edmonton	5	at	Los Angeles	8	Kelly Hrudey	Charlie Huddy
April 22, 1992	Los Angeles	3	at	Edmonton	4	Bill Ranford	Bernie Nicholls
April 24, 1992	Los Angeles	4	at	Edmonton	3	Kelly Hrudey	Luc Robitaille
April 26, 1992	Edmonton	5	at	Los Angeles	2	Bill Ranford	Esa Tikkanen
April 28, 1992	Los Angeles	0	at	Edmonton	3	Bill Ranford	Josef Beranek
May 3, 1992	Edmonton	4	at	Vancouver	3	Bill Ranford	Joe Murphy
May 5, 1992	Edmonton	0	at	Vancouver	4	Kirk McLean	Geoff Courtnall
May 6, 1992	Vancouver	2	at	Edmonton	5	Bill Ranford	Joe Murphy
May 8, 1992	Vancouver	2	at	Edmonton	3	Bill Ranford	Scott Mellanby
May 10, 1992	Edmonton	3	at	Vancouver	4	Kirk McLean	Cliff Ronning
May 12, 1992	Vancouver	0	at	Edmonton	3	Bill Ranford	Craig MacTavish
May 16, 1992	Edmonton	2	at	Chicago	8	Ed Belfour	Mike Peluso
May 18, 1992	Edmonton	2	at	Chicago	4	Ed Belfour	Michel Goulet
May 20, 1992	Chicago	4	at	Edmonton	3	Ed Belfour	Jeremy Roenick[1]
May 22, 1992	Chicago	5	at	Edmonton	1	Ed Belfour	Jeremy Roenick

[1]2:45 of overtime

Table 10. Team Milestone Goals

Goal	*Scorer*	*Assist*	*Assist*	*Date*	*Opposition*	*Per.*	*Time*	*Goaltender*	
				Regular Season					
1000	*Messier*	*Anderson*		*03/13/82*	*Vancouver*	*3*	*6:55*	*Heinz*	*PP*
2000	*Gretzky*	*Anderson*		*11/11/84*	*Philadelphia*	*2*	*8:43*	*Lindbergh*	*ES*
3000	*Tikkanen*	*Kurri*	*Gretzky*	*02/04/87*	*Minnesota*	*3*	*14:11*	*Beaupre*	*PP*
4000	*Ruzicka*	*Gregg*	*Messier*	*01/25/90*	*Los Angeles*	*3*	*4:19*	*Hrudey*	*PP*
5000	*Ciger*	*Arnott*		*12/05/93*	*Dallas*	*2*	*7:05*	*Wakaluk*	*ES*
6000	*McAmmond*	*Hamrlik*	*Weight*	*03/30/98*	*Calgary*	*1*	*2:59*	*Tabaracci*	*PP*
				Regular Season and Playoffs					
1000	*Kurri*	*Gretzky*	*Siltanen*	*02/19/82*	*Hartford*	*2*	*1:42*	*Millen*	*PP*
2000	*McClelland*	*Coffey*		*03/07/84*	*Chicago*	*2*	*15:12*	*Bannerman*	*ES*
3000	*Gretzky*	*Fogolin*		*03/05/86*	*Los Angeles*	*3*	*8:19*	*Melanson*	*ES*
4000	*Kurri*	*Tikkanen*		*05/09/88*	*Detroit*	*OT*	*11:02*	*Hanlon*	*ES*
5000	*Lamb*	*Anderson*	*MacIver*	*02/24/91*	*Quebec*	*3*	*12:22*	*Tugnutt*	*PP*
6000	*Marchant*	*Stapleton*	*Corson*	*02/22/95*	*Dallas*	*3*	*18:51*	*Moog*	*ES*
7000	*Beranek*	*Falloon*	*Poti*	*02/03/99*	*Ottawa*	*2*	*12:16*	*Tugnutt*	*ES*
				Regular Season at Home					
1000	*Lindstrom*	*Linseman*		*03/07/84*	*Chicago*	*1*	*18:01*	*Bannerman*	*ES*
2000	*Lacombe*	*Tikkanen*	*Hunter*	*02/21/89*	*Hartford*	*1*	*15:26*	*Liut*	*ES*
3000	*Weight*	*Czerkawski*	*Smyth*	*12/06/96*	*Ottawa*	*3*	*15:03*	*Tugnutt*	*ES*

Goal	*Scorer*	*Assist*	*Assist*	*Date*	*Opposition*	*Per.*	*Time*	*Goaltender*	
				Regular Season on the Road					
1000	*Krushelnyski*	*Jackson*		*02/09/85*	*Detroit*	*2*	*19:28*	*Micalef*	*ES*
2000	*Gelinas*	*Joseph*	*Muni*	*01/23/91*	*Vancouver*	*3*	*10:16*	*Gamble*	*PP*
3000	*Beranek*	*Robertsson*	*Grier*	*12/11/99*	*New Jersey*	*1*	*14:24*	*Brodeur*	*ES*
				Regular Season and Playoffs at Home					
1000	*Coffey*	*Gretzky*	*Messier*	*01/04/84*	*Minnesota*	*2*	*7:31*	*Meloche*	*PP*
2000	*Hunter*	*Lacombe*	*Muni*	*11/20/87*	*Pittsburgh*	*2*	*16:41*	*Meloche*	*ES*
3000	*Simpson*	*Tikkanen*	*Corson*	*12/18/92*	*Los Angeles*	*2*	*8:30*	*Hrudey*	*PP*
4000	*Cleary*	*Zholtok*	*Weight*	*02/25/01*	*Dallas*	*2*	*14:03*	*Belfour*	*ES*
				Regular Season and Playoffs on the Road					
1000	*Gretzky*	*Kurri*	*Coffey*	*11/11/84*	*Philadelphia*	*2*	*0:57*	*Lindbergh*	*PP*
2000	*Kurri*	*Lamb*	*G. Smith*	*10/24/89*	*Islanders*	*3*	*7:39*	*Healy*	*ES*
3000	*Lindgren*	*Smyth*		*01/08/97*	*Chicago*	*3*	*17:45*	*Hackett*	*ES*

1992-93

As the team's stockpile of stars had become depleted over time Glen Sather was able to complete only one major off-season deal this year. In August he traded last year's leading scorer Vincent Damphousse and a draft choice to Montreal for Shayne Corson, Brent Gilchrist and Vladimir Vujtek.

Sather had little luck at this year's entry draft. Although five of the players drafted would eventually appear in an Oilers uniform only hard hitting forward Kirk Maltby would go on to have a substantial NHL career, eventually playing on two Stanley Cup–winning teams as a member of the Detroit Red Wing. Ted Green, Ron Low and Kevin Primeau all returned to work behind the bench as coaches.

The club got off to a poor start, winning one and tying one of their first ten games, and then won five and tied two of their next seven. With his team sporting an 11–15–4 record, Sather traded original Oiler Kevin Lowe to the Rangers for Roman Oksiuta and a draft choice. This shocking trade did little to shake up the team and in January Sather traded malcontent Bernie Nicholls to New Jersey for Zdeno Ciger and Kevin Todd. Craig MacTavish was named as team captain replacing Kevin Lowe.

On February 24th, Sather made one more major deal, this time obtaining Igor Kravchuk and Dean McAmmond for Joe Murphy. The former first overall draft choice had not appeared in an Oiler uniform since the May 22 playoff game against Chicago.

In March Sather also got rid of one of the last links to the Stanley Cup era, trading Finnish forward Esa Tikkanen to the New York Rangers for Doug Weight. It was a great trade for the Oilers as Weight became the undisputed team leader. He would lead the Oilers in scoring every season from 1994 to 2001 except for the 1999 campaign in which he was severely hampered by injuries.

Unfortunately no amount of wheeling and dealing helped. Edmonton was 19–28–8 (.418) at the All-Star break and won only five of their final 25 games. The team finished the season with 60 points, 41 points behind division leading Vancouver. For the first time since the club joined the NHL they did not qualify for the postseason playoffs. The Oilers would finish 22nd in offense this year and 20th in defense in a totally forgettable season.

Petr Klima led the team in scoring with a minuscule 48 points. To put this in perspective Wayne Gretzky in 1983-84 scored his 48th point in only his 17th game on his way to a 205 point season. Klima's points this season added to those of Esa Tikkanen who led the team in scoring in 1991 and those of Vincent Damphousse who led the team last season would total only 206. Gretzky would score more than 206 points in a *single* season three times in his career with the Oilers.

1992-93 Regular Season Scoring

#		*Ht.*	*Wt.*	*Age*	*GP*	*G*	*A*	*Pts*	*Shots*	*S%*	*GW*	*GT*	*PP*	*SH*	*P/M*	*PIM*
85	Klima	72	190	28	68	32	16	48	175	18.3	2	0	13	0	-15	100
9	Corson	72	205	26	80	16	31	47	164	9.8	1	0	9	2	-19	209
18	Simpson	74	195	25	60	24	22	46	91	26.4	3	0	12	0	-14	36
24	Manson	74	202	25	83	15	30	45	244	6.1	1	1	9	1	-28	210
9	Nicholls	72	185	31	46	8	32	40	86	9.3	1	0	4	0	-16	40
10	Tikkanen	73	200	27	66	14	19	33	162	8.6	3	0	2	4	-11	76
27	Mellanby	73	205	26	69	15	17	32	114	13.2	3	1	6	0	-4	147
16	Buchberger	74	210	26	83	12	18	30	92	13.0	3	0	1	2	-27	133

14	MacTavish	73	195	34	82	10	20	30	101	9.9	3	0	0	3	-16	110
8	Ciger	73	190	23	37	9	15	24	67	13.4	1	0	0	0	-5	6
7	Gelinas	71	195	22	65	11	12	23	93	11.8	1	0	0	0	3	30
41	Gilchrist	71	185	25	60	10	10	20	94	10.6	0	0	2	0	-10	47
26	Podein	74	200	24	40	13	6	19	64	20.3	1	0	2	1	-2	25
34	Hawgood	70	190	24	29	5	13	18	47	10.6	0	0	2	0	-1	35
25	Smith	75	200	23	78	4	14	18	67	6.0	0	0	0	1	-11	30
6	Glynn	76	215	25	64	4	12	16	80	5.0	0	0	2	0	-13	60
15	Todd	70	175	24	25	4	9	13	39	10.3	1	0	0	0	-5	10
22	Richardson	76	210	23	82	3	10	13	78	3.8	0	0	0	2	-18	142
21	Kravchuk	73	200	26	17	4	8	12	42	9.5	0	0	1	0	-8	2
2	Joseph	74	210	23	33	2	10	12	49	4.1	0	0	1	0	-9	48
23	Vujtek	72	190	20	30	1	10	11	49	2.0	0	0	0	0	-1	8
28	Muni	75	200	30	72	0	11	11	51	0.0	0	0	0	0	-15	67
34	Elik	74	190	26	14	1	9	10	28	3.6	0	0	0	0	1	8
29	DeBrusk	73	225	21	51	8	2	10	33	24.2	1	0	0	0	-16	205
36	Werenka	74	204	23	27	5	4	9	38	13.2	1	0	0	1	1	24
42/39	Weight	71	185	21	13	2	6	8	35	5.7	0	0	0	0	-2	10
19	Benning	72	195	26	18	1	7	8	28	3.6	0	0	0	0	-1	59
42	Beranek	74	185	23	26	2	6	8	44	4.5	0	0	0	0	-7	28
12	Rice	72	215	21	28	2	5	7	29	6.9	0	0	0	0	-4	28
20	Van Allen	73	200	25	21	1	4	5	19	5.3	0	0	0	0	-2	6
41	McDougall	72	185	26	4	2	1	3	8	25.0	0	0	0	0	2	4
30	Ranford	70	170	26	67	0	3	3	0	0.0	0	0	0	0	0	10
19	Wright	71	175	19	7	1	1	2	7	14.3	0	0	0	0	-4	19
12	Maley	74	195	29	13	1	1	2	9	11.1	0	0	0	0	-3	29
20	Hudson	73	185	25	5	0	1	1	2	0.0	0	0	0	0	-1	2
17	Thornton	74	200	21	9	0	1	1	7	0.0	0	0	0	0	-4	0
35	Leroux	78	221	22	1	0	0	0	0	0.0	0	0	0	0	0	4
26	Currie	74	195	24	5	0	0	0	11	0.0	0	0	0	0	-4	4
1	Tugnutt	71	155	25	26	0	0	0	0	0.0	0	0	0	0	0	2
	Bench															14
		73	196	25	84	242	396	638	2347	10.3	26	2	66	17	-55	2027

1992-93 Goaltender Records

	GP	*Min.*	*GA*	*W*	*L*	*T*	*Ave.*	*SA*	*Pct.*	*SO*	*EN*
Bill Ranford	67	3753	240	17	38	6	3.84	2065	0.884	1	2
Ron Tugnutt	26	1338	93	9	12	2	4.17	767	0.879	0	2
	84	5099	337	26	50	8	3.97	2836	0.881	1	4

Coach: Ted Green 26-50-8

1992-93 Scoring vs. Opposition

	Bost.	*Buff.*	*Calg.*	*Chi.*	*Det.*	*Hart.*	*L.A.*	*Minn.*
Benning	–––	–––	–––	–––	0–0–0	–––	0–0–0	0–1–1
Beranek	0–0–0	–––	0–0–0	0–1–1	0–0–0	–––	0–0–0	0–0–0
Buchberger	2–0–2	4–1–5	1–0–1	0–0–0	0–0–0	0–2–2	1–1–2	0–2–2
Ciger	0–2–2	1–1–2	1–0–1	0–1–1	3–1–4	0–0–0	1–4–5	0–0–0
Corson	1–1–2	1–1–2	1–1–2	2–0–2	0–3–3	0–0–0	3–2–5	3–3–6
Currie	–––	–––	–––	0–0–0	–––	–––	–––	–––
DeBrusk	0–0–0	–––	2–0–2	2–0–2	0–0–0	–––	0–0–0	1–0–1
Elik	–––	–––	–––	0–2–2	0–0–0	–––	0–0–0	0–0–0
Gelinas	0–0–0	0–2–2	0–1–1	2–0–2	0–0–0	0–0–0	0–1–1	3–0–3
Gilchrist	0–0–0	0–0–0	0–1–1	2–0–2	1–0–1	0–0–0	2–1–3	0–0–0
Glynn	0–1–1	0–0–0	0–1–1	0–1–1	0–0–0	0–1–1	1–0–1	0–0–0
Hawgood	1–1–2	–––	1–3–4	0–1–1	0–1–1	–––	1–1–2	0–2–2
Hudson	–––	–––	0–0–0	–––	–––	–––	0–0–0	–––
Joseph	0–0–0	0–1–1	1–1–2	0–0–0	0–1–1	–––	0–2–2	0–1–1
Klima	1–0–1	0–0–0	2–3–5	0–0–0	0–0–0	1–0–1	2–2–4	0–0–0
Kravchuk	–––	–––	–––	0–3–3	1–1–2	–––	0–1–1	1–0–1
Leroux	–––	–––	–––	–––	–––	–––	–––	–––
MacTavish	0–1–1	0–3–3	0–2–2	1–1–2	0–1–1	2–1–3	0–1–1	1–2–3
Maley	–––	–––	0–0–0	0–0–0	1–0–1	–––	–––	0–1–1

	Bost.	*Buff.*	*Calg.*	*Chi.*	*Det.*	*Hart.*	*L.A.*	*Minn.*
Manson	0–1–1	0–1–1	0–4–4	0–2–2	0–0–0	0–0–0	2–5–7	2–3–5
McDougall	———	———	———	———	———	———	———	———
Mellanby	0–0–0	0–1–1	1–1–2	0–2–2	0–0–0	0–1–1	0–2–2	0–3–3
Muni	0–0–0	0–0–0	0–0–0	0–0–0	0–0–0	0–1–1	0–1–1	0–0–0
Nicholls	0–1–1	———	1–3–4	0–4–4	0–0–0	———	0–3–3	0–1–1
Podein	1–0–1	0–0–0	0–0–0	1–0–1	0–2–2	1–0–1	0–0–0	0–0–0
Rice	———	———	1–0–1	0–0–0	0–0–0	0–0–0	0–0–0	———
Richardson	0–0–0	0–0–0	0–2–2	0–2–2	0–0–0	0–0–0	1–0–1	0–1–1
Simpson	1–3–4	0–2–2	2–1–3	1–0–1	1–0–1	0–1–1	5–1–6	1–1–2
Smith	0–0–0	2–0–2	0–2–2	0–1–1	0–0–0	0–0–0	0–2–2	0–0–0
Thornton	0–0–0	0–0–0	———	———	———	0–0–0	0–0–0	———
Tikkanen	0–0–0	0–1–1	1–0–1	1–1–2	0–0–0	0–2–2	0–3–3	1–0–1
Todd	0–0–0	0–0–0	———	0–0–0	0–1–1	1–1–2	0–0–0	———
Van Allen	———	———	0–3–3	0–0–0	———	———	0–0–0	1–0–1
Vujtek	———	———	0–0–0	0–0–0	———	———	0–0–0	1–2–3
Weight	———	———	0–0–0	———	———	———	1–0–1	0–1–1
Werenka	0–1–1	0–1–1	———	0–0–0	0–0–0	1–1–2	0–0–0	———
Wright	0–0–0	———	———	0–0–0	0–1–1	———	———	———

	Mont.	*N.J.*	*NYI.*	*NYR.*	*Ott.*	*Phil.*	*Pitt.*	*Que.*
Benning	———	0–1–1	0–0–0	———	———	———	0–1–1	0–1–1
Beranek	———	———	1–0–1	———	0–0–0	0–0–0	———	———
Buchberger	0–2–2	0–3–3	0–0–0	0–0–0	0–1–1	1–0–1	0–0–0	0–1–1
Ciger	0–0–0	0–0–0	1–0–1	0–0–0	0–1–1	———	1–1–2	0–1–1
Corson	0–0–0	0–1–1	0–0–0	1–0–1	0–1–1	0–0–0	0–1–1	0–1–1
Currie	———	———	———	———	———	0–0–0	———	———
DeBrusk	0–0–0	0–0–0	0–0–0	0–0–0	———	0–0–0	0–0–0	0–0–0
Elik	———	1–1–2	———	0–2–2	———	———	0–1–1	———
Gelinas	0–0–0	0–1–1	0–1–1	0–0–0	0–1–1	0–0–0	1–0–1	0–0–0
Gilchrist	1–1–2	———	0–1–1	0–0–0	0–0–0	0–0–0	0–0–0	0–0–0
Glynn	1–0–1	0–1–1	1–0–1	0–0–0	0–1–1	0–0–0	0–0–0	0–0–0
Hawgood	1–0–1	———	0–0–0	———	0–1–1	0–0–0	———	———
Hudson	———	———	———	———	———	———	———	———
Joseph	0–0–0	———	———	———	0–0–0	0–1–1	———	———
Klima	2–0–2	1–0–1	2–2–4	1–0–1	0–2–2	1–0–1	2–1–3	2–1–3
Kravchuk	———	0–0–0	———	0–0–0	———	———	0–0–0	———
Leroux	———	———	———	———	———	———	———	———
MacTavish	1–1–2	0–0–0	0–0–0	1–0–1	0–1–1	0–0–0	1–0–1	0–1–1
Maley	———	———	———	———	0–0–0	———	———	———
Manson	0–0–0	0–1–1	0–2–2	1–0–1	0–1–1	0–0–0	0–1–1	0–0–0
McDougall	———	1–0–1	———	0–1–1	———	———	1–0–1	———
Mellanby	0–0–0	———	1–0–1	———	2–0–2	0–0–0	0–2–2	0–0–0
Muni	0–1–1	0–0–0	0–1–1	0–0–0	0–0–0	0–0–0	0–0–0	0–0–0
Nicholls	0–3–3	———	1–2–3	———	1–0–1	0–1–1	———	———
Podein	0–0–0	1–0–1	1–0–1	0–0–0	1–0–1	0–0–0	1–3–4	0–0–0
Rice	0–0–0	0–1–1	0–0–0	0–1–1	———	0–0–0	0–1–1	0–0–0
Richardson	0–0–0	1–0–1	0–0–0	0–0–0	1–0–1	0–0–0	0–1–1	0–0–0
Simpson	0–0–0	———	0–2–2	———	1–0–1	0–0–0	2–0–2	0–0–0
Smith	0–0–0	0–0–0	0–0–0	0–0–0	1–0–1	0–0–0	0–1–1	0–0–0
Thornton	———	———	0–0–0	———	0–0–0	0–0–0	———	———
Tikkanen	0–1–1	1–0–1	0–2–2	0–0–0	0–1–1	0–0–0	1–2–3	3–0–3
Todd	0–1–1	1–1–2	0–1–1	0–0–0	0–0–0	———	0–1–1	0–0–0
Van Allen	———	———	0–0–0	0–0–0	———	0–0–0	———	———
Vujtek	0–0–0	0–0–0	0–0–0	———	0–1–1	———	———	———
Weight	———	0–0–0	———	0–0–0	———	———	0–1–1	———
Werenka	0–0–0	0–0–0	0–0–0	0–0–0	0–0–0	0–0–0	1–0–1	0–0–0
Wright	———	———	———	———	———	———	———	———

	S. J.	*St.L.*	*Tampa*	*Tor.*	*Van.*	*Wash.*	*Win.*
Benning	1–1–2	———	———	0–2–2	0–0–0	———	0–0–0
Beranek	0–0–0	0–1–1	0–1–1	0–0–0	0–2–2	1–1–2	0–0–0
Buchberger	1–1–2	1–0–1	0–1–1	0–1–1	1–0–1	0–0–0	0–2–2
Ciger	1–1–2	———	———	0–0–0	0–0–0	———	0–2–2
Corson	1–1–2	0–1–1	0–3–3	01–1–	2–3–5	1–1–2	0–6–6

	S. J.	*St.L.*	*Tampa*	*Tor.*	*Van.*	*Wash.*	*Win.*
Currie	———	0–0–0	0–0–0	———	———	———	0–0–0
DeBrusk	1–0–1	0–0–0	0–1–1	1–0–1	0–0–0	0–0–0	1–1–2
Elik	0–1–1	———	———	0–1–1	———	———	0–1–1
Gelinas	2–2–4	0–0–0	0–0–0	0–0–0	0–2–2	0–0–0	3–1–4
Gilchrist	0–2–2	0–2–2	0–0–0	0–0–0	2–1–3	———	2–1–3
Glynn	0–1–1	0–1–1	0–0–0	0–1–1	0–2–2	1–0–1	0–1–1
Hawgood	0–0–0	1–0–1	0–0–0	———	0–1–1	0–1–1	0–1–1
Hudson	———	———	———	———	0–1–1	———	0–0–0
Joseph	0–1–1	0–0–0	0–1–1	———	0–0–0	———	1–1–2
Klima	4–1–5	0–0–0	1–0–1	2–0–2	3–3–6	0–0–0	5–1–6
Kravchuk	0–1–1	———	———	0–0–0	———	———	2–2–4
Leroux	———	———	———	0–0–0	———	———	———
MacTavish	1–2–3	0–0–0	0–2–2	0–0–0	1–1–2	0–0–0	1–0–1
Maley	———	0–0–0	0–0–0	———	0–0–0	0–0–0	0–0–0
Manson	2–2–4	1–1–2	1–0–1	1–2–3	1–0–1	1–0–1	3–4–7
McDougall	———	———	———	0–0–0	———	———	———
Mellanby	4–1–5	1–0–1	1–1–2	0–0–0	4–0–4	0–2–2	1–1–2
Muni	0–2–2	0–1–1	0–1–1	0–0–0	0–2–2	0–1–1	0–0–0
Nicholls	0–4–4	0–2–2	0–1–1	1–1–2	1–2–3	0–1–1	3–3–6
Podein	2–1–3	———	———	1–0–1	0–0–0	1–0–1	2–0–2
Rice	0–1–1	0–0–0	1–0–1	0–0–0	———	———	0–1–1
Richardson	0–1–1	0–0–0	0–0–0	0–0–0	0–1–1	0–0–0	0–2–2
Simpson	2–1–3	1–1–2	3–2–5	0–1–1	1–3–4	1–0–1	2–3–5
Smith	0–4–4	0–0–0	0–0–0	0–0–0	1–2–3	0–0–0	0–2–2
Thornton	———	———	———	———	———	0–1–1	0–0–0
Tikkanen	1–2–3	1–0–1	1–1–2	0–0–0	1–0–1	1–1–2	1–2–3
Todd	2–1–3	———	———	———	———	———	0–2–2
Van Allen	0–1–1	0–0–0	0–0–0	———	0–0–0	0–0–0	0–0–0
Vujtek	0–1–1	0–0–0	0–0–0	0–1–1	0–1–1	0–1–1	0–3–3
Weight	0–1–1	———	———	1–0–1	0–1–1	———	0–2–2
Werenka	1–0–1	———	———	0–0–0	———	0–1–1	2–0–2
Wright	———	———	0–0–0	0–0–0	1–0–1	———	0–0–0

1992–93 Goaltender Records vs. Opposition

	GP	*Min.*	*GA*	*EN*	*SO*	*Ave.*	*W–L–T*	*Opposition*
Bill Ranford	1	60	6	0	0	6.00	0–1–0	Boston
	6	365	28	0	0	4.60	1–5–0	Calgary
	4	250	19	0	0	4.56	1–2–1	Chicago
	4	245	8	0	0	1.96	3–0–1	Dallas
	2	119	10	0	0	5.04	0–2–0	Detroit
	2	120	8	0	0	4.00	1–1–0	Hartford
	6	364	26	0	0	4.29	1–4–1	Los Angeles
	2	119	10	0	0	5.04	0–2–0	Montreal
	2	120	9	0	0	4.50	1–1–0	New Jersey
	2	92	6	0	0	3.91	0–0–1	N.Y. Islanders
	2	119	4	0	0	2.02	1–1–0	N.Y. Rangers
	2	40	0	0	0	0.00	0–0–0	Ottawa
	1	65	2	0	0	1.85	0–0–1	Philadelphia
	1	60	4	0	0	4.00	1–0–0	Pittsburgh
	2	118	7	0	0	3.56	0–2–0	Quebec
	5	257	7	1	1	1.63	3–1–0	San Jose
	3	185	15	0	0	4.86	0–2–1	St. Louis
	3	179	9	1	0	3.02	1–2–0	Tampa Bay
	2	80	4	0	0	3.00	0–1–0	Toronto
	5	218	18	0	0	4.95	1–3–0	Vancouver
	2	119	6	0	0	3.03	1–1–0	Washington
	8	459	34	0	0	4.44	1–7–0	Winnipeg
Ron Tugnutt	1	60	3	0	0	3.00	1–0–0	Boston
	2	121	6	0	0	2.98	2–0–0	Buffalo
	1	60	4	0	0	4.00	0–1–0	Calgary
	1	65	2	0	0	1.85	0–0–1	Detroit
	1	60	6	0	0	6.00	0–1–0	Los Angeles
	2	93	10	0	0	6.45	0–2–0	N.Y. Islanders

GP	*Min.*	*GA*	*EN*	*SO*	*Ave.*	*W-L-T*	*Opposition*
2	80	5	0	0	3.75	1–1–0	Ottawa
1	60	4	0	0	4.00	0–1–0	Philadelphia
2	120	6	1	0	3.00	1–1–0	Pittsburgh
1	4	2	0	0	30.00	0–0–0	Quebec
3	157	9	1	0	3.44	2–1–0	San Jose
1	64	3	0	0	2.81	1–0–0	Tampa Bay
2	105	9	0	0	5.14	0–1–1	Toronto
4	203	14	0	0	4.14	1–2–0	Vancouver
2	80	10	0	0	7.50	0–1–0	Winnipeg

Overall Record vs. Opponents

Opponent	*Home*	*Road*	*Overall*	*GF–GA*	*Opponent*
Boston	0–1–0	1–0–0	1–1–0	7–9	Boston
Buffalo	1–0–0	1–0–0	2–0–0	8–6	Buffalo
Calgary	1–3–0	0–3–0	1–6–0	15–32	Calgary
Chicago	0–2–0	1–0–1	1–2–1	12–19	Chicago
Detroit	0–1–1	0–1–0	0–2–1	7–12	Detroit
Hartford	1–0–0	0–1–0	1–1–0	6–8	Hartford
Los Angeles	0–3–1	1–2–0	1–5–1	20–32	Los Angeles
Minnesota	2–0–0	1–0–1	3–0–1	15–8	Minnesota
Montreal	0–1–0	0–1–0	0–2–0	6–10	Montreal
New Jersey	1–0–0	0–1–0	1–1–0	7–9	New Jersey
Islanders	0–0–1	0–2–0	0–2–1	8–16	Islanders
Rangers	0–1–0	1–0–0	1–1–0	4–4	Rangers
Ottawa	1–0–0	0–1–0	1–1–0	7–5	Ottawa
Philadelphia	0–0–1	0–1–0	0–1–1	2–6	Philadelphia
Pittsburgh	1–1–0	1–0–0	2–1–0	11–11	Pittsburgh
Quebec	0–1–0	0–1–0	0–2–0	5–9	Quebec
San Jose	3–0–0	2–2–0	5–2–0	26–18	San Jose
St. Louis	0–1–0	0–1–1	0–2–1	6–15	St. Louis
Tampa Bay	2–0–0	0–2–0	2–2–0	8–13	Tampa Bay
Toronto	0–1–1	0–1–0	0–2–1	7–13	Toronto
Vancouver	2–1–0	0–4–0	2–5–0	19–32	Vancouver
Washington	1–0–0	0–1–0	1–1–0	7–6	Washington
Winnipeg	0–4–0	1–4–0	1–8–0	29–44	Winnipeg

1992-93 Schedule Results

Date	Visitor			Home	
Oct. 6	Vancouver	5	at	Edmonton	4
Oct. 8	Edmonton	2	at	Calgary	7
Oct. 10	Edmonton	2	at	Vancouver	5
Oct. 11	Toronto	3	at	Edmonton	3 OT
Oct. 14	Edmonton	3	at	Winnipeg	7
Oct. 15	Edmonton	4	at	Chicago	3 OT
Oct. 17	Edmonton	2	at	Detroit	4
Oct. 20	Edmonton	1	at	Tampa Bay	6
Oct. 23	Boston	6	at	Edmonton	3
Oct. 25	Calgary	4	at	Edmonton	0
Oct. 28	Minnesota	2	at	Edmonton	5
Oct. 31	Washington	2	at	Edmonton	4
Nov. 3	Ottawa	2	at	Edmonton	5
Nov. 6	Edmonton	6	at	Winnipeg	1
Nov. 7	Edmonton	2	at	Minnesota	2 OT
Nov. 10	Edmonton	4	at	St. Louis	4 OT
Nov. 12	Edmonton	4	at	San Jose	3
Nov. 14	Edmonton	2	at	Los Angeles	6
Nov. 18	Vancouver	2	at	Edmonton	4
Nov. 21	Edmonton	0	at	Vancouver	9
Nov. 22	Islanders	5	at	Edmonton	5 OT
Nov. 25	Los Angeles	3	at	Edmonton	1
Nov. 27	Chicago	8	at	Edmonton	1
Nov. 28	Tampa Bay	3	at	Edmonton	4 OT
Dec. 1	Edmonton	3	at	San Jose	1
Dec. 3	Edmonton	1	at	Vancouver	4
Dec. 5	St. Louis	5	at	Edmonton	1
Dec. 7	Edmonton	3	at	Calgary	6
Dec. 8	Calgary	1	at	Edmonton	3
Dec. 10	Edmonton	3	at	Minnesota	2
Dec. 12	Edmonton	1	at	Tampa Bay	3
Dec. 13	Edmonton	1	at	Islanders	4
Dec. 16	Vancouver	2	at	Edmonton	4
Dec. 18	Los Angeles	5	at	Edmonton	5 OT
Dec. 21	Edmonton	2	at	Calgary	3 OT
Dec. 23	San Jose	2	at	Edmonton	4
Dec. 27	Calgary	7	at	Edmonton	3
Dec. 29	Montreal	6	at	Edmonton	3
Dec. 31	Edmonton	2	at	Winnipeg	3
Jan. 2	Tampa Bay	1	at	Edmonton	2
Jan. 3	Philadelphia	2	at	Edmonton	2 OT
Jan. 5	Edmonton	1	at	St. Louis	6
Jan. 7	Edmonton	3	at	Chicago	3 OT
Jan. 9	Edmonton	3	at	Washington	4
Jan. 10	Edmonton	0	at	Philadelphia	4
Jan. 13	Winnipeg	4	at	Edmonton	1
Jan. 15	Hartford	1	at	Edmonton	3
Jan. 17	Buffalo	2	at	Edmonton	3 OT
Jan. 19	Los Angeles	5	at	Edmonton	4
Jan. 22	Pittsburgh	1	at	Edmonton	2

Jan. 23	Edmonton	5	at	Winnipeg	8	Mar. 7	Edmonton	3	at	San Jose	6
Jan. 27	Detroit	2	at	Edmonton	2 OT	Mar. 10	Detroit	6	at	Edmonton	3
Jan. 31	Edmonton	5	at	Buffalo	4 OT	Mar. 12	New Jersey	4	at	Edmonton	6
Feb. 2	Edmonton	4	at	Boston	3	Mar. 14	Chicago	5	at	Edmonton	4 OT
Feb. 3	Edmonton	2	at	Ottawa	3	Mar. 17	Edmonton	4	at	Rangers	3 OT
Feb. 9	Edmonton	6	at	Los Angeles	3	Mar. 18	Edmonton	1	at	New Jersey	5
Feb. 12	San Jose	0	at	Edmonton	6	Mar. 20	Edmonton	2	at	Toronto	4
Feb. 14	Quebec	3	at	Edmonton	2 OT	Mar. 21	Pittsburgh	6	at	Edmonton	4
Feb. 16	Edmonton	2	at	Islanders	7	Mar. 26	Los Angeles	4	at	Edmonton	1
Feb. 18	Edmonton	5	at	Pittsburgh	4	Mar. 27	Toronto	6	at	Edmonton	2
Feb. 20	Edmonton	3	at	Hartford	7	Mar. 31	Minnesota	2	at	Edmonton	5
Feb. 21	Edmonton	3	at	Montreal	4	April 3	Winnipeg	6	at	Edmonton	4
Feb. 23	Edmonton	3	at	Quebec	6	April 6	Edmonton	2	at	San Jose	5
Feb. 27	Rangers	1	at	Edmonton	0	April 7	Edmonton	4	at	Vancouver	5 OT
Feb. 28	San Jose	1	at	Edmonton	4	April 11	Winnipeg	7	at	Edmonton	5
Mar. 4	Winnipeg	5	at	Edmonton	3	April 13	Calgary	4	at	Edmonton	2
Mar. 6	Edmonton	1	at	Los Angeles	6	April 15	Edmonton	0	at	Winnipeg	3

Table 11. Team Win-Loss Milestones

Milestone	*Date*	*Home/Road*	*Opposition*	*Score*	*Game #*	*%*
		Regular Season Only				
100th win	*March 13, 1982*	*Home*	*Vancouver*	*5-3*	*232*	*.431*
200th win	*March 4, 1984*	*Home*	*Montreal*	*6-1*	*388*	*.515*
300th win	*February 24, 1986*	*Home*	*Montreal*	*3-2*	*542*	*.554*
400th win	*March 1, 1988*	*Home*	*Los Angeles*	*5-3*	*705*	*.567*
500th win	*December 27, 1990*	*Home*	*Calgary*	*4-1*	*915*	*.546*
600th win	*February 27, 1994*	*Home*	*Tampa Bay*	*3-2*	*1189*	*.505*
700th win	*December 5, 1997*	*Home*	*Detroit*	*3-1*	*1450*	*.483*
800th win	*November 5, 2000*	*Road*	*Columbus*	*4-2*	*1682*	*.476*
100th loss	*November 21, 1982*	*Home*	*Quebec*	*7-9*	*263*	*.380*
200th loss	*December 1, 1987*	*Road*	*Washington*	*2-4*	*665*	*.301*
300th loss	*January 25, 1991*	*Home*	*Rangers*	*3-4*	*928*	*.323*
400th loss	*October 11, 1993*	*Road*	*Vancouver*	*1-4*	*1127*	*.355*
500th loss	*February 16, 1996*	*Road*	*Dallas*	*1-6*	*1311*	*.381*
600th loss	*December 6, 1998*	*Home*	*Dallas*	*2-6*	*1527*	*.393*
100th tie	*December 19, 1988*	*Road*	*Buffalo*	*5-5*	*755*	
200th tie	*October 1, 1999*	*Home*	*Rangers*	*1-1*	*1585*	
		Regular Season and Playoffs				
100th win	*February 19, 1982*	*Home*	*Hartford*	*7-4*	*234*	*.427*
200th win	*January 4, 1984*	*Home*	*Minnesota*	*12-8*	*394*	*.508*
300th win	*May 7, 1985*	*Home*	*Chicago*	*7-3*	*541*	*.555*
400th win	*January 21, 1987*	*Road*	*Winnipeg*	*5-3*	*687*	*.582*
500th win	*November 2, 1988*	*Home*	*St. Louis*	*5-4*	*833*	*.600*
600th win	*December 7, 1990*	*Home*	*Rangers*	*4-3*	*1055*	*.569*
700th win	*February 12, 1993*	*Home*	*San Jose*	*6-0*	*1279*	*.547*
800th win	*March 4, 1997*	*Home*	*Los Angeles*	*4-1*	*1586*	*.504*
900th win	*December 21, 1999*	*Home*	*Washington*	*6-2*	*1830*	*.492*
100th loss	*April 10, 1982*	*Road*	*Los Angeles*	*5-6*	*254*	*.394*
200th loss	*November 13, 1986*	*Road*	*Boston*	*3-4*	*658*	*.304*
300th loss	*January 3, 1990*	*Road*	*Chicago*	*2-3*	*968*	*.310*
400th loss	*March 31, 1992*	*Road*	*Calgary*	*2-5*	*1203*	*.333*
500th loss	*March 9, 1994*	*Home*	*Florida*	*3-5*	*1375*	*.364*
600th loss	*February 17, 1997*	*Road*	*Anaheim*	*1-5*	*1579*	*.380*
700th loss	*April 21, 1999*	*Road*	*Dallas*	*1-2*	*1792*	*.391*

1993-94

Ted Green began his third season behind the bench as head coach of the Oilers. Ron Low and Kevin Primeau remained in their posts as associate coaches.

At the June 26 entry draft held in Quebec City the Oilers came up with their best draft choice in years. Drafted seventh overall from the Oshawa Generals was 6'3", 195 pound power forward Jason Arnott. Arnott would have a fine season. He set a team record for rookies, scoring 33

The Oilers practice at West Edmonton Mall.

goals. He also added 35 assists to become only the second Oiler named to the league's Rookie All-Star Team.

Also making the Rookie All-Star Team this year was Russian defenseman Boris Mironov. The Oilers had acquired Mironov in a trade with the Winnipeg Jets. Also picked up in the trade was untested Swedish center Mats Lindgren and a couple of draft choices. In return the Oilers gave up defenseman Dave Manson and a draft choice.

Sather was busy much of the season making trades, although none of the players with the exception of Todd Marchant would have much of a long term effect on the fortunes of the team. Picked up in trades were Bob Beers, Fredrick Olausson, Mike Stapleton, and Brent Grieve. Shayne Corson was named as captain after Craig MacTavish was traded to the Rangers.

The team got off to a terrible start this year with a 4–18–3 record in their first 25 games. Included in this streak was a team record 11 consecutive defeats. The Oilers were 13–28–7 (.344) at the All-Star break.

Following the team's 18th loss in 24 games Glen Sather replaced Green as coach. The Oilers' fortunes improved considerably following Sather's return to the coaching ranks. With Green behind the bench, the team had a record of .188 and with Sather coaching they were .458.

The Oilers finished in last place in the Pacific Division, 33 points behind division leading Calgary. They finished 18th overall in offense and 22nd in defense. Doug Weight, who was picked up from the Rangers late in the 1993 season led the team in scoring with 74 points.

1993-94 Regular Season Scoring

#		*Ht.*	*Wt.*	*Age*	*GP*	*G*	*A*	*Pts*	*Shots*	*S%*	*GW*	*GT*	*PP*	*SH*	*P/M*	*PIM*
39	Weight	71	191	22	84	24	50	74	188	12.8	1	0	4	1	-22	47
7	Arnott	75	195	19	78	33	35	68	194	17.0	4	1	10	0	1	104
8	Ciger	73	190	24	84	22	35	57	158	13.9	1	2	8	0	-11	8
9	Corson	72	200	27	64	25	29	54	171	14.6	3	1	11	0	-8	118
21	Kravchuk	73	200	27	81	12	38	50	197	6.1	2	0	5	0	-12	16
2	Beers	74	200	26	66	10	27	37	152	6.6	0	1	5	0	-11	74
33	Pearson	73	205	24	72	19	18	37	160	11.9	7	0	3	0	-4	165
15	Olausson	74	195	27	55	9	19	28	85	10.6	1	0	6	0	-4	20
12	Rice	72	215	22	63	17	15	32	129	13.2	1	1	6	0	-10	36
10	Byakin	69	185	30	44	8	20	28	51	15.7	3	0	6	0	-3	30
37	McAmmond	71	185	20	45	6	21	27	52	11.5	0	0	2	0	12	16
14	MacTavish	73	195	35	66	16	10	26	97	16.5	1	0	0	0	-20	80
25	Stapleton	70	183	27	23	5	9	14	43	11.6	0	1	1	0	-1	28

#		*Ht.*	*Wt.*	*Age*	*GP*	*G*	*A*	*Pts*	*Shots*	*S%*	*GW*	*GT*	*PP*	*SH*	*P/M*	*PIM*
16	Buchberger	74	210	27	84	3	18	21	93	3.2	0	0	0	0	-20	199
18	Maltby	72	180	21	68	11	8	19	89	12.4	1	0	0	1	-2	74
23	Vujtek	73	190	21	40	4	15	19	66	6.1	0	0	1	0	-7	14
34	Grieve	73	202	24	24	13	5	18	53	24.5	0	1	4	0	4	14
24	Manson	74	202	26	57	3	13	16	144	2.1	0	0	0	0	-4	140
17	Thornton	74	200	22	61	4	7	11	65	6.2	0	0	0	0	-15	104
29	DeBrusk	74	215	22	48	4	6	10	27	14.8	0	0	0	0	-9	185
35	Bennett	76	206	22	48	3	6	9	57	5.3	0	0	1	0	-8	49
27	White	71	200	24	26	3	5	8	17	17.6	0	0	0	0	1	2
26	Podein	74	200	25	28	3	5	8	26	11.5	0	0	0	0	3	8
22	Richardson	76	210	24	69	2	6	8	92	2.2	0	0	0	0	-13	131
5	Werenka	74	205	24	15	0	4	4	11	0.0	0	0	0	0	-1	14
28	Oksiuta	75	220	23	10	1	2	3	18	5.6	0	0	0	0	-1	4
25	G. Smith	75	200	24	21	0	3	3	23	0.0	0	0	0	0	-10	12
20	Mironov	75	196	21	14	0	2	2	23	0.0	0	0	0	0	-4	14
2	Joseph	74	210	24	10	1	1	2	25	4.0	0	0	1	0	-8	28
6	Herbers	76	225	26	22	0	2	2	16	0.0	0	0	0	0	-6	32
30	Ranford	70	185	27	71	0	2	2	0	0.0	0	0	0	0	0	2
36	Marchant	70	170	20	3	0	1	1	5	0.0	0	0	0	0	-1	2
32	Mark	76	218	29	12	0	1	1	8	0.0	0	0	0	0	-2	43
20	Cierny	74	180	19	1	0	0	0	0	0.0	0	0	0	0	-1	0
1	Cowley	72	185	29	1	0	0	0	0	0.0	0	0	0	0	0	0
20	Chychrun	76	215	27	2	0	0	0	2	0.0	0	0	0	0	1	0
34	Martini	76	220	24	2	0	0	0	0	0.0	0	0	0	0	-1	0
20	Zavisha	74	205	21	2	0	0	0	1	0.0	0	0	0	0	-2	0
27	Elik	74	190	27	4	0	0	0	5	0.0	0	0	0	0	0	6
34	Kerch	70	187	26	5	0	0	0	4	0.0	0	0	0	0	-8	2
19	Wright	71	175	20	5	0	0	0	2	0.0	0	0	0	0	-3	4
20	Laforge	74	210	25	5	0	0	0	0	0.0	0	0	0	0	-2	21
31	Brathwaite	67	170	21	19	0	0	0	0	0.0	0	0	0	0	0	0
	Bench															12
	73	198	24	84	261	438	699	2549	10.2	25	8	74	2	-40	1858	

1993-94 Goaltender Records

	GP	*Min.*	*GA*	*W*	*L*	*T*	*Ave.*	*SA*	*Pct.*	*SO*	*EN*
Wayne Cowley	1	57	3	0	1	0	3.16	35	0.914	0	0
Bill Ranford	71	4070	236	22	34	11	3.48	2325	0.898	1	8
Fred Brathwaite	19	982	58	3	10	3	3.54	523	0.889	0	0
	84	5121	305	25	45	14	3.57	2891	0.895	1	8

Coach: Ted Green 3-18-3
Coach: Glen Sather 22-27-11

1993-94 Scoring vs. Opposition

	Ana.	*Bost.*	*Buff.*	*Calg.*	*Chi.*	*Dall.*	*Det.*	*Flor.*
Arnott	2–1–3	0–1–1	2–0–2	2–4–6	0–3–3	1–3–4	0–0–0	1–1–2
Beers	0–0–0	———	0–1–1	2–1–3	1–1–2	0–2–2	1–0–1	0–0–0
Bennett	0–0–0	0–0–0	0–0–0	0–0–0	0–0–0	2–1–3	0–0–0	0–0–0
Buchberger	1–0–1	0–1–1	0–1–1	0–0–0	0–0–0	0–4–4	0–1–1	0–0–0
Byakin	1–1–2	0–0–0	0–0–0	0–1–1	0–0–0	———	1–2–3	1–0–1
Chychrun	———	———	———	———	———	0–0–0	———	———
Cierny	———	———	———	———	———	———	———	———
Ciger	1–1–2	0–0–0	0–0–0	0–3–3	1–1–2	3–1–4	0–1–1	0–4–4
Corson	1–1–2	1–0–1	0–0–0	2–1–3	0–1–1	1–2–3	0–0–0	———
DeBrusk	0–0–0	———	0–0–0	0–1–1	0–1–1	2–0–2	0–0–0	———
Elik	0–0–0	0–0–0	———	0–0–0	———	———	———	———
Grieve	0–0–0	———	———	———	———	———	1–2–3	2–0–2
Herbers	0–0–0	0–0–0	0–0–0	0–0–0	0–0–0	———	0–0–0	———
Joseph	0–0–0	0–0–0	0–1–1	1–0–1	———	———	———	———
Kerch	———	0–0–0	0–0–0	0–0–0	———	———	———	———
Kravchuk	1–1–2	0–2–2	0–0–0	1–2–3	1–0–1	0–2–2	1–1–2	0–2–2
Laforge	———	0–0–0	———	———	0–0–0	———	0–0–0	———

	Ana.	*Bost.*	*Buff.*	*Calg.*	*Chi.*	*Dall.*	*Det.*	*Flor.*
MacTavish	1–0–1	0–0–0	1–0–1	0–0–0	0–0–0	1–2–3	1–1–2	0–0–0
Maltby	0–2–2	0–0–0	0–0–0	1–0–1	0–0–0	0–0–0	2–1–3	1–1–2
Manson	0–2–2	———	0–0–0	1–0–1	0–1–1	0–1–1	0–0–0	0–1–1
Marchant	———	———	———	———	———	———	———	———
Mark	0–0–0	———	———	0–0–0	0–0–0	———	0–0–0	———
Martini	———	———	———	———	———	———	———	———
McAmmond	1–2–3	0–0–0	———	0–1–1	0–1–1	———	1–2–3	0–1–1
Mironov	0–0–0	———	———	———	———	———	0–0–0	0–0–0
Oksiuta	———	———	0–0–0	0–1–1	0–0–0	———	———	———
Olausson	1–0–1	———	0–1–1	0–1–1	0–0–0	0–0–0	1–1–2	0–0–0
Pearson	0–1–1	1–0–1	0–1–1	2–2–4	0–0–0	1–1–2	1–1–2	1–0–1
Podein	0–0–0	———	0–0–0	0–1–1	1–0–1	———	0–0–0	0–0–0
Rice	1–0–1	0–0–0	1–0–1	2–0–2	0–1–1	0–2–2	2–1–3	———
Richardson	0–1–1	0–0–0	0–0–0	0–0–0	0–0–0	0–0–0	0–2–2	0–1–1
Smith	0–1–1	0–0–0	0–1–1	0–0–0	0–0–0	0–0–0	———	———
Stapleton	0–0–0	———	———	———	———	———	1–0–1	0–1–1
Thornton	0–0–0	———	0–0–0	0–1–1	1–0–1	0–0–0	0–0–0	0–0–0
Vujtek	1–1–2	0–0–0	0–0–0	0–1–1	0–0–0	0–0–0	0–1–1	———
Weight	1–3–4	0–0–0	0–2–2	2–5–7	1–1–2	1–2–3	0–2–2	1–0–1
Werenka	———	0–0–0	———	0–1–1	———	0–0–0	———	0–0–0
White	0–0–0	———	———	0–1–1	———	1–0–1	0–0–0	———
Wright	———	———	———	0–0–0	0–0–0	0–0–0	———	———
Zavisha	———	———	———	———	———	———	0–0–0	———

	Hart.	*L.A.*	*Mont.*	*N.J.*	*NYI.*	*NYR.*	*Ott.*	*Phil.*
Arnott	3–0–3	1–2–3	0–1–1	0–1–1	0–1–1	2–1–3	0–0–0	2–0–2
Beers	0–1–1	0–3–3	1–1–2	0–2–2	0–0–0	1–1–2	0–1–1	0–0–0
Bennett	0–0–0	0–0–0	0–0–0	0–0–0	0–0–0	0–0–0	0–2–2	0–0–0
Buchberger	0–0–0	0–1–1	———	0–1–1	0–1–1	0–0–0	0–0–0	0–1–1
Byakin	0–1–1	0–0–0	1–2–3	1–0–1	0–0–0	0–1–1	0–1–1	1–0–1
Chychrun	———	———	———	———	———	———	———	———
Cierny	———	———	———	———	———	———	0–0–0	———
Ciger	2–0–2	2–3–5	1–1–2	0–0–0	0–3–3	0–0–0	0–0–0	0–0–0
Corson	0–4–4	2–1–3	0–2–2	2–0–2	2–0–2	0–0–0	2–1–3	1–2–3
DeBrusk	0–0–0	1–1–2	0–0–0	0–1–1	0–0–0	0–0–0	0–0–0	0–0–0
Elik	———	———	———	———	———	———	———	———
Grieve	0–1–1	4–0–4	———	———	———	0–0–0	———	———
Herbers	0–0–0	———	0–0–0	———	0–0–0	———	0–1–1	———
Joseph	———	0–0–0	———	———	0–0–0	———	0–0–0	———
Kerch	———	———	———	———	———	———	0–0–0	———
Kravchuk	0–1–1	2–1–3	0–2–2	0–0–0	1–0–1	0–0–0	1–1–2	0–2–2
Laforge	———	———	———	———	———	———	———	———
MacTavish	0–0–0	2–1–3	0–0–0	1–0–1	0–1–1	0–0–0	1–0–1	0–0–0
Maltby	0–0–0	1–1–2	0–1–1	1–0–1	1–0–1	0–0–0	0–0–0	0–0–0
Manson	0–1–1	0–3–3	1–0–1	0–0–0	0–0–0	0–0–0	0–0–0	0–0–0
Marchant	———	0–1–1	———	———	———	0–0–0	———	———
Mark	———	0–0–0	———	———	———	———	———	———
Martini	———	———	———	———	———	———	———	———
McAmmond	0–0–0	1–4–5	0–0–0	———	0–1–1	1–2–3	0–0–0	0–0–0
Mironov	———	0–0–0	———	———	———	0–2–2	———	———
Oksiuta	———	———	———	———	0–1–1	———	———	———
Olausson	0–0–0	2–4–6	0–1–1	0–1–1	0–0–0	0–0–0	0–1–1	0–1–1
Pearson	0–0–0	2–1–3	0–0–0	0–1–1	1–2–3	0–0–0	2–1–3	0–1–1
Podein	0–0–0	0–0–0	———	———	———	———	0–1–1	———
Rice	0–1–1	1–2–3	0–1–1	0–0–0	1–2–3	0–0–0	0–0–0	1–0–1
Richardson	0–0–0	0–0–0	0–0–0	0–0–0	0–0–0	0–0–0	0–1–1	0–0–0
Smith	———	0–0–0	0–0–0	———	0–0–0	———	0–0–0	0–0–0
Stapleton	———	2–1–3	———	———	———	0–0–0	———	———
Thornton	0–0–0	2–2–4	0–0–0	0–1–1	0–0–0	0–0–0	0–0–0	0–0–0
Vujtek	0–1–1	0–1–1	3–0–3	———	0–2–2	———	0–0–0	———
Weight	1–0–1	1–6–7	0–0–0	0–1–1	3–1–4	0–0–0	2–4–6	0–2–2
Werenka	———	0–0–0	0–1–1	———	———	———	———	———
White	0–0–0	0–1–1	0–0–0	0–1–1	0–0–0	0–0–0	———	0–0–0
Wright	———	———	———	0–0–0	———	———	———	———

	Pitt.	*Que.*	*S.J.*	*St.L.*	*Tampa*	*Tor.*	*Van.*	*Wash.*	*Winn.*
Arnott	0–3–3	1–0–1	3–2–5	1–1–2	1–0–1	3–2–5	4–3–7	0–1–1	4–4–8
Beers	0–0–0	0–1–1	0–4–4	1–0–1	0–0–0	0–2–2	1–3–4	0–2–2	2–1–3
Bennett	0–0–0	0–1–1	———	1–0–1	0–1–1	0–1–1	0–0–0	0–0–0	———
Buchberger	0–0–0	0–2–2	0–0–0	1–0–1	0–1–1	0–1–1	1–1–2	0–1–1	0–1–1
Byakin	———	0–0–0	0–1–1	1–2–3	0–0–0	0–3–3	1–2–3	0–0–0	0–3–3
Chychrun	———	———	———	0–0–0	———	———	———	———	———
Cierny	———	———	———	———	———	———	———	———	———
Ciger	1–1–2	0–2–2	3–3–6	1–2–3	1–0–1	0–4–4	2–1–3	3–0–3	1–4–5
Corson	1–1–2	0–0–0	0–1–1	1–2–3	———	3–0–3	2–5–7	1–1–2	3–4–7
DeBrusk	0–0–0	0–0–0	0–0–0	1–1–2	———	———	0–1–1	———	0–0–0
Elik	———	———	0–0–0	———	———	———	———	———	———
Grieve	1–0–1	1–0–1	1–0–1	———	1–0–1	0–0–0	1–2–3	0–0–0	1–0–1
Herbers	———	———	0–1–1	0–0–0	———	0–0–0	0–0–0	0–0–0	0–0–0
Joseph	———	———	0–0–0	———	———	———	0–0–0	———	———
Kerch	———	———	———	0–0–0	———	———	———	———	———
Kravchuk	0–0–0	2–3–5	1–2–3	0–3–3	0–0–0	0–4–4	0–4–4	0–1–1	1–4–5
Laforge	———	———	0–0–0	———	———	———	———	0–0–0	———
MacTavish	0–0–0	2–0–2	0–1–1	1–2–3	1–0–1	2–1–3	1–0–1	0–0–0	1–1–2
Maltby	1–0–1	0–0–0	2–0–2	0–0–0	0–0–0	0–1–1	0–1–1	0–0–0	1–0–1
Manson	0–1–1	1–1–2	0–1–1	0–0–0	0–0–0	0–0–0	0–1–1	0–0–0	0–0–0
Marchant	0–0–0	———	———	———	———	———	———	———	———
Mark	0–1–1	———	———	———	———	———	———	———	0–0–0
Martini	0–0–0	———	———	0–0–0	———	———	———	———	———
McAmmond	0–1–1	0–1–1	0–0–0	0–1–1	0–4–4	1–0–1	0–0–0	0–0–0	1–0–1
Mironov	0–0–0	0–0–0	0–0–0	———	0–0–0	———	———	———	0–0–0
Oksiuta	———	———	0–0–0	———	———	———	0–0–0	———	1–0–1
Olausson	1–0–1	0–0–0	0–2–2	1–1–2	0–1–1	1–0–1	1–4–5	0–0–0	1–0–1
Pearson	1–1–2	1–0–1	2–0–2	1–1–2	1–2–3	0–0–0	1–2–3	0–0–0	1–0–1
Podein	———	———	0–1–1	0–0–0	2–1–3	0–1–1	0–0–0	0–0–0	———
Rice	1–1–2	1–1–2	1–0–1	1–0–1	———	0–0–0	4–2–6	0–0–0	0–1–1
Richardson	0–0–0	0–0–0	0–0–0	0–0–0	0–0–0	1–1–2	1–0–1	0–0–0	0–0–0
Smith	———	———	0–0–0	0–0–0	———	0–0–0	0–1–1	0–0–0	0–0–0
Stapleton	0–1–1	1–0–1	0–0–0	———	0–0–0	1–2–3	0–2–2	———	0–2–2
Thornton	0–0–0	0–1–1	0–0–0	0–0–0	0–1–1	0–1–1	1–0–1	0–0–0	0–0–0
Vujtek	———	0–1–1	0–2–2	0–0–0	———	0–3–3	0–1–1	0–1–1	0–0–0
Weight	1–1–2	1–0–1	3–3–6	0–4–4	0–0–0	3–1–4	3–7–10	0–1–1	0–4–4
Werenka	———	0–1–1	0–0–0	———	———	———	———	0–0–0	0–1–1
White	0–0–0	———	0–0–0	0–0–0	———	0–0–0	2–1–3	0–0–0	0–1–1
Wright	———	———	———	0–0–0	———	———	———	———	———
Zavisha	———	———	———	———	———	———	———	0–0–0	———

1993–94 Goaltender Records vs. Opposition

	GP	*Min.*	*GA*	*EN*	*SO*	*Ave.*	*W–L–T*	*Opposition*
Fred Brathwaite	4	220	10	0	0	2.73	1–3–0	Anaheim
	2	31	2	0	0	3.87	0–0–0	Calgary
	1	60	3	0	0	3.00	0–1–0	Chicago
	1	60	3	0	0	3.00	1–0–0	Detroit
	1	65	4	0	0	3.69	0–0–1	Florida
	1	60	5	0	0	5.00	0–1–0	Hartford
	3	147	9	0	0	3.67	0–1–1	Los Angeles
	1	33	2	0	0	3.64	0–1–0	N.Y. Rangers
	2	125	5	0	0	2.40	0–1–1	San Jose
	1	60	6	0	0	6.00	0–1–0	St. Louis
	2	120	9	0	0	4.50	1–1–0	Winnipeg
Wayne Cowley	1	57	3	0	0	3.16	0–1–0	New Jersey
Bill Ranford	4	140	12	1	0	5.14	0–2–0	Anaheim
	2	118	6	2	0	3.05	0–2–0	Boston
	2	125	7	0	0	3.36	0–1–1	Buffalo
	6	327	25	2	0	4.59	1–5–0	Calgary
	3	178	8	0	0	2.70	1–2–0	Chicago
	4	242	20	0	0	4.96	0–4–0	Dallas
	3	180	9	0	0	3.00	2–1–0	Detroit
	1	60	5	0	0	5.00	0–1–0	Florida

GP	*Min.*	*GA*	*EN*	*SO*	*Ave.*	*W–L–T*	*Opposition*
1	65	4	0	0	3.69	0–0–1	Hartford
5	290	19	0	0	3.93	2–1–2	Los Angeles
2	120	5	1	0	2.50	1–1–0	Montreal
2	68	5	0	0	4.41	0–0–1	New Jersey
2	125	5	0	0	2.40	1–0–1	N.Y. Islanders
2	92	4	0	0	2.61	0–0–1	N.Y. Rangers
2	121	11	0	0	5.45	0–2–0	Ottawa
2	120	2	0	0	1.00	2–0–0	Philadelphia
2	119	7	0	0	3.53	1–1–0	Pittsburgh
2	120	7	0	0	3.50	2–0–0	Quebec
4	244	12	0	0	2.95	2–1–1	San Jose
3	179	11	2	0	3.69	0–3–0	St. Louis
2	125	6	0	0	2.88	1–0–1	Tampa Bay
4	245	14	0	0	3.43	1–2–1	Toronto
7	420	25	0	0	3.57	3–4–0	Vancouver
2	127	5	0	0	2.36	0–1–1	Washington
2	120	2	0	1	1.00	2–0–0	Winnipeg

1993-94 Schedule Results

Date	Team	Score		Team	Score
Oct. 6	San Jose	2	at	Edmonton	3
Oct. 8	Islanders	1	at	Edmonton	5
Oct. 11	Edmonton	1	at	Vancouver	4
Oct. 13	Edmonton	3	at	Anaheim	4
Oct. 14	Edmonton	4	at	Los Angeles	4 OT
Oct. 16	Vancouver	3	at	Edmonton	2
Oct. 18	Edmonton	3	at	Winnipeg	6
Oct. 20	Calgary	5	at	Edmonton	3
Oct. 22	Boston	3	at	Edmonton	1
Oct. 24	Washington	3	at	Edmonton	2 OT
Oct. 26	Edmonton	1	at	San Jose	3
Oct. 29	Buffalo	6	at	Edmonton	3
Oct. 30	Edmonton	1	at	Calgary	4
Nov. 3	Ottawa	7	at	Edmonton	5
Nov. 6	Edmonton	5	at	St. Louis	6 OT
Nov. 7	Edmonton	0	at	Chicago	3
Nov. 9	Edmonton	4	at	Detroit	2
Nov. 11	Edmonton	1	at	Boston	5
Nov. 13	Edmonton	4	at	Hartford	4 OT
Nov. 15	Edmonton	5	at	Toronto	5 OT
Nov. 17	Edmonton	1	at	Montreal	3
Nov. 20	Toronto	3	at	Edmonton	2
Nov. 21	Anaheim	4	at	Edmonton	2
Nov. 24	Chicago	3	at	Edmonton	1
Nov. 27	Vancouver	1	at	Edmonton	2
Nov. 29	Dallas	6	at	Edmonton	5 OT
Dec. 1	Philadelphia	1	at	Edmonton	3
Dec. 5	Edmonton	3	at	Dallas	4
Dec. 7	Edmonton	4	at	Islanders	4 OT
Dec. 8	Edmonton	1	at	Rangers	1 OT
Dec. 11	Edmonton	2	at	New Jersey	5
Dec. 12	Edmonton	2	at	Philadelphia	1
Dec. 15	Vancouver	2	at	Edmonton	7
Dec. 17	San Jose	2	at	Edmonton	4
Dec. 19	St. Louis	4	at	Edmonton	1
Dec. 21	Edmonton	3	at	Vancouver	6
Dec. 22	Calgary	3	at	Edmonton	7
Dec. 27	Winnipeg	0	at	Edmonton	6
Dec. 29	Montreal	3	at	Edmonton	6
Dec. 30	Edmonton	1	at	Calgary	7
Jan. 2	San Jose	4	at	Edmonton	4 OT
Jan. 7	Quebec	4	at	Edmonton	6
Jan. 9	Edmonton	4	at	Chicago	2
Jan. 11	Edmonton	2	at	Dallas	5
Jan. 13	Edmonton	4	at	St. Louis	6
Jan. 15	Edmonton	3	at	Pittsburgh	4
Jan. 18	Edmonton	3	at	Ottawa	4 OT
Jan. 29	Dallas	5	at	Edmonton	3
Jan. 19	Edmonton	1	at	Buffalo	1 OT
Jan. 24	Edmonton	4		Vancouver	5 OT*
Jan. 26	New Jersey	3	at	Edmonton	3 OT
Jan. 28	St. Louis	3	at	Edmonton	2
Feb. 2	Los Angeles	4	at	Edmonton	6
Feb. 4	Chicago	3	at	Edmonton	1
Feb. 6	Winnipeg	2	at	Edmonton	5
Feb. 7	Edmonton	3	at	Calgary	4
Feb. 9	Calgary	6	at	Edmonton	1
Feb. 12	Hartford	5	at	Edmonton	2
Feb. 13	Anaheim	6	at	Edmonton	3
Feb. 15	Edmonton	2	at	Washington	2 OT
Feb. 18	Edmonton	1	at	Detroit	5
Feb. 19	Edmonton	2	at	Toronto	3
Feb. 23	Toronto	3	at	Edmonton	6
Feb. 25	Los Angeles	5	at	Edmonton	5 OT
Feb. 27	Tampa Bay	2	at	Edmonton	3
Mar. 1	Edmonton	7	at	Vancouver	4
Mar. 3	Edmonton	2	at	San Jose	4
Mar. 4	Edmonton	1	at	Anaheim	4
Mar. 9	Florida	5	at	Edmonton	3
Mar. 11	Detroit	2	at	Edmonton	4
Mar. 16	Edmonton	4	at	Tampa Bay	4 OT
Mar. 18	Edmonton	4	at	Florida	4 OT
Mar. 20	Edmonton	5	at	Quebec	3
Mar. 23	Rangers	5	at	Edmonton	3
Mar. 25	Los Angeles	4	at	Edmonton	3 OT
Mar. 27	Pittsburgh	3	at	Edmonton	5
Mar. 31	Edmonton	3	at	Anaheim	2 OT
April 02	Edmonton	5	at	Los Angeles	3
April 03	Edmonton	1		Los Angeles	6 **
April 06	Edmonton	4	at	Winnipeg	3
April 08	Anaheim	3	at	Edmonton	1
April 10	Detroit	3	at	Edmonton	4
April 13	Edmonton	2	at	San Jose	2 OT
April 14	Edmonton	2	at	Los Angeles	2 OT

*-game played in Saskatoon

**-game played in Sacramento

Record vs. Opponents

Opponent	*Home*	*Road*	*Overall*	*GF-GA*	*Opponent*
Anaheim	0–3–0	1–2–0	1–5–0	13–23	Anaheim
Boston	0–1–0	0–1–0	0–2–0	2–8	Boston
Buffalo	0–1–0	0–0–1	0–1–1	4–7	Buffalo
Calgary	1–2–0	0–3–0	1–5–0	16–29	Calgary
Chicago	0–2–0	1–1–0	1–3–0	6–11	Chicago
Dallas	0–2–0	0–2–0	0–4–0	13–20	Dallas
Detroit	2–0–0	1–1–0	3–1–0	13–12	Detroit
Florida	0–1–0	0–0–1	0–1–1	7–9	Florida
Hartford	0–1–0	0–0–1	0–1–1	6–9	Hartford
Los Angeles	1–1–1	1–1–2	2–2–3	26–28	Los Angeles
Montreal	1–0–0	0–1–0	1–1–0	7–6	Montreal
New Jersey	0–0–1	0–1–0	0–1–1	5–8	New Jersey
Islanders	1–0–0	0–0–1	1–0–1	9–5	Islanders
Rangers	0–1–0	0–0–1	0–1–1	4–6	Rangers
Ottawa	0–1–0	0–1–0	0–2–0	8–11	Ottawa
Philadelphia	1–0–0	1–0–0	2–0–0	5–2	Philadelphia
Pittsburgh	1–0–0	0–1–0	1–1–0	8–7	Pittsburgh
Quebec	1–0–0	1–0–0	2–0–0	11–7	Quebec
San Jose	2–0–1	0–2–1	2–2–2	16–17	San Jose
St. Louis	0–2–0	0–2–0	0–4–0	12–19	St. Louis
Tampa Bay	1–0–0	0–0–1	1–0–1	7–6	Tampa Bay
Toronto	1–1–0	0–1–1	1–2–1	15–14	Toronto
Vancouver	2–2–0	1–2–0	3–4–0	26–25	Vancouver
Washington	0–1–0	0–0–1	0–1–1	4–5	Washington
Winnipeg	2–0–0	1–1–0	3–1–0	18–11	Winnipeg

1994-95

Former Oiler star Wayne Gretzky. (EA340-1760 City of Edmonton Archives.)

George Burnett, a native of Port Perry, Ontario, became the team's fifth head coach, replacing interim coach Glen Sather. After completing a successful collegiate playing career, Burnett quickly rose through the minor league coaching ranks, eventually signing on as head coach of the Oilers' minor league affiliate in Cape Breton. Following his two year coaching stint in the AHL Burnett became at the age of 32 the NHL's youngest head coach. It marked the first time that someone had been brought in from outside of the team to become head coach. Ron Low and Kevin Primeau returned as associate coaches.

At the league's annual entry draft the Oilers had two first round picks. With their first choice, and number four overall, the Oilers chose 6'4", 220 pound center Jason Bonsignore from the Niagara Falls Thunder of the OHL. Bonsignore played only 21 games for the Oilers before being traded to Tampa Bay in December of 1997.

With their second pick, number six overall, the Oilers chose forward Ryan Smyth from the Moose Jaw Warriors of the Western Hockey League. The native of Banff, Alberta, would get off to a slow start in his career, scoring only 11 points in 51 games over parts of two seasons. Right from the start though Smyth would display the determination and hard work which would be characteristic of his game throughout his career. In the 1996-97 season Smyth would become an offensive force, registering 61 points in

82 games, 39 of them goals. The 20 power play goals he scored tied Wayne Gretzky's team record set in 1983-84.

The Oilers were without veteran Craig MacTavish this year as he had been traded to the Rangers late in the 1993-94 season for Todd Marchant. The team got off to a poor start again this season, winning only two of their first seven games. The Oilers were only able to put together two modest winning streaks in this strike shortened season.

George Burnett was replaced as coach in the midst of a nine game losing streak with a record of 12–20–3 and Ron Low took over the coaching duties for the remainder of the season. There was no All-Star break this year but the team was 12–17–3 (.422) two-thirds of the way through the season.

Due in part to the short season, injuries did not play a great part in the team's fortunes although the defense corps was seldom at full strength. Defenseman Igor Kravchuk missed 12 games after undergoing arthroscopy surgery on his damaged left knee. Fredrick Olausson would be out for ten games due to colitis; Boris Mironov missed ten with a lower back strain; while Bryan Marchment missed six games after being suspended by the league. Jason Arnott also was out for a couple of games with a concussion and two more with a knee injury.

The team finished in fifth place in the Pacific Division, 17 points behind division leading Calgary. Their 38 points translated into a .396 winning percentage which was marginally better than last year's record. Edmonton's 136 goals scored tied them for 13th in offense (with New Jersey, Washington and Dallas), while their 183 goals allowed was the worst in the entire league. Doug Weight became only the second player on the team (the other being Wayne Gretzky) to lead the Oilers in scoring in more than one season. Weight recorded 40 points in 48 games. For the third year in succession Edmonton failed to advance to the playoffs.

1994-95 Regular Season Scoring

#		Ht.	Wt.	Age	GP	G	A	Pts	Shots	S%	GW	GT	PP	SH	P/M	PIM
39	Weight	71	191	23	48	7	33	40	104	6.7	1	0	1	0	-17	69
7	Arnott	75	200	20	42	15	22	37	156	9.6	1	0	7	0	-14	128
9	Corson (C)	73	200	28	48	12	24	36	131	9.2	1	0	2	0	-17	86
20	Oliver	72	190	23	44	16	14	30	79	20.3	0	1	10	0	-11	20
26	Marchant	70	170	21	45	13	14	27	95	13.7	2	0	3	2	-3	32
16	Buchberger (A)	74	210	28	48	7	17	24	73	9.6	5	0	2	1	0	82
17	Thornton	74	200	23	47	10	12	22	69	14.5	1	0	0	1	-4	89
21	Kravchuk	73	200	28	36	7	11	18	93	7.5	0	0	3	1	-15	29
25	Stapleton	70	183	28	46	6	11	17	59	10.2	2	0	3	0	-12	21
28	Oksiuta	75	220	24	26	11	2	13	52	21.2	0	0	5	0	-14	8
22	Richardson (A)	76	210	25	46	3	10	13	51	5.9	1	0	1	1	-6	40
18	Maltby	72	190	22	47	8	3	11	73	11.0	1	1	0	2	-11	49
32	Kennedy	74	208	31	40	2	8	10	45	4.4	1	0	0	0	2	25
15	Olausson	74	195	28	33	0	10	10	52	0.0	0	0	0	0	-4	20
2	Mironov	75	200	22	29	1	7	8	48	2.1	0	0	0	0	-9	40
28	Slegr	73	205	23	12	1	5	6	27	3.7	0	0	1	0	-5	14
27	White	71	200	25	9	2	4	6	13	15.4	0	0	2	0	1	0
24	Marchment	73	200	25	40	1	5	6	57	1.8	0	0	0	0	-11	184
34	Esau	75	190	26	14	0	6	6	17	0.0	0	0	0	0	-8	15
33	Pearson	73	205	25	28	1	4	5	21	4.8	0	0	0	0	-11	54
6	Sutton	72	200	25	12	3	1	4	28	10.7	0	0	0	0	-1	12
8	Ciger	73	190	25	5	2	2	4	10	20.0	1	0	1	0	-1	0
38	Fraser	70	175	25	9	3	0	3	5	60.0	0	0	0	0	3	0
29	DeBrusk	74	215	23	34	2	0	2	14	14.3	0	0	0	0	-4	93
6	Mark	76	218	30	18	0	2	2	21	0.0	0	0	0	0	-9	35
30	Ranford	71	185	28	40	0	2	2	0	0.0	0	0	0	0	0	2
23	Bonsignore	76	208	18	1	1	0	1	3	33.3	0	0	0	0	-1	0
14	Nilsson	73	195	38	6	1	0	1	2	50.0	0	0	1	0	-5	0
19	Wright	71	185	21	6	1	0	1	6	16.7	0	0	0	0	1	14
36	Intranuovo	68	185	21	1	0	1	1	1	0.0	0	0	0	0	1	0
1	Gage	72	200	21	2	0	1	1	0	0.0	0	0	0	0	0	0
12	Aivazoff	72	195	25	21	0	1	1	6	0.0	0	0	0	0	-2	2
43	Bonvie	71	210	21	2	0	0	0	0	0.0	0	0	0	0	0	0
10	Smyth	73	185	18	3	0	0	0	2	0.0	0	0	0	0	-1	0
33	Tuomainen	75	203	22	4	0	0	0	5	0.0	0	0	0	0	0	0
37	McAmmond	71	185	21	6	0	0	0	3	0.0	0	0	0	0	-1	0
31	Brathwaite	67	170	22	14	0	0	0	0	0.0	0	0	0	0	0	0
34	McGill	74	210	25	8	0	0	0	6	0.0	0	0	0	0	-4	8

#	Ht.	Wt.	Age	GP	G	A	Pts	Shots	S%	GW	GT	PP	SH	P/M	PIM
Bench															12
	73	197	24	48	136	232	368	1427	9.9	17	2	42	8	-37	1183

1994-95 Goaltender Records

	GP	Min.	GA	W	L	T	Ave.	SA	Pct.	SO	EN
Bill Ranford	40	2203	133	15	20	3	3.62	1134	0.883	2	2
Fred Brathwaite	14	601	40	2	5	1	3.99	292	0.863	0	1
Joaquin Gage	2	99	7	0	2	0	4.24	40	0.825	0	0
	48	2912	183	17	27	4	3.77	1469	0.875	2	3

Coach: George Burnett 12-20-3
Coach: Ron Low 5-7-1

1994-95 Scoring vs. Opposition

	Ana.	Calg.	Chi.	Dall.	Det.	L.A.	S. J.	St.L.	Tor.	Van.	Win.
Aivazoff	———	0–0–0	0–0–0	0–0–0	———	0–0–0	0–0–0	0–0–0	0–0–0	0–1–1	0–0–0
Arnott	0–3–3	3–1–4	0–0–0	0–2–2	0–4–4	3–2–5	2–3–5	2–2–4	2–4–6	2–0–2	1–1–2
Bonsignore	———	1–0–1	———	———	———	———	———	———	———	———	———
Bonvie	———	0–0–0	———	———	———	0–0–0	———	———	———	———	———
Buchberger	2–0–2	0–1–1	0–1–1	0–1–1	1–0–1	1–2–3	1–3–4	1–1–2	1–2–3	0–3–3	0–3–3
Ciger	———	1–0–1	———	———	———	———	———	1–0–1	0–0–0	———	0–2–2
Corson	2–3–5	1–0–1	0–1–1	0–4–4	2–2–4	0–4–4	2–3–5	0–2–2	4–0–4	0–2–2	1–3–4
DeBrusk	0–0–0	1–0–1	0–0–0	0–0–0	0–0–0	0–0–0	0–0–0	0–0–0	1–0–1	0–0–0	0–0–0
Esau	0–0–0	0–1–1	0–1–1	0–0–0	0–0–0	0–0–0	0–1–1	0–0–0	0–3–3	0–1–1	0–0–0
Fraser	———	———	———	0–0–0	1–0–1	0–0–0	0–0–0	1–0–1	———	1–0–1	———
Intranuovo	———	———	———	———	———	———	———	———	0–1–1	———	———
Kennedy	0–1–1	0–0–0	0–0–0	0–0–0	1–1–2	0–0–0	0–2–2	0–0–0	0–1–1	0–2–2	1–1–2
Kravchuk	0–1–1	2–3–5	0–0–0	0–0–0	0–0–0	2–0–2	1–1–2	0–1–1	2–2–4	0–1–1	0–2–2
Maltby	1–0–1	0–1–1	0–0–0	0–0–0	1–0–1	1–1–2	1–0–1	0–0–0	0–1–1	2–0–2	2–0–2
Marchant	0–2–2	0–0–0	0–0–0	2–2–4	1–1–2	2–1–3	1–3–4	1–2–3	1–1–2	3–1–4	2–1–3
Marchment	0–0–0	0–0–0	1–1–2	0–0–0	0–1–1	0–0–0	0–1–1	0–0–0	0–1–1	0–1–1	0–0–0
Mark	0–0–0	0–0–0	0–1–1	0–0–0	0–1–1	0–0–0	0–0–0	———	0–0–0	———	———
McAmmond	0–0–0	———	0–0–0	———	0–0–0	0–0–0	———	———	———	———	———
McGill	0–0–0	0–0–0	———	0–0–0	———	———	0–0–0	0–0–0	0–0–0	0–0–0	———
Mironov	0–0–0	1–0–1	0–0–0	0–1–1	0–1–1	0–0–0	0–3–3	0–0–0	0–0–0	0–1–1	0–1–1
Nilsson	———	0–0–0	0–0–0	0–0–0	0–0–0	1–0–1	0–0–0	———	———	———	———
Oksiuta	2–0–2	1–0–1	1–1–2	0–0–0	1–0–1	———	1–1–2	1–0–1	1–0–1	3–0–3	0–0–0
Olausson	0–0–0	0–1–1	0–0–0	0–0–0	0–0–0	0–2–2	0–2–2	0–1–1	0–2–2	0–0–0	0–2–2
Oliver	2–1–3	1–3–4	0–0–0	5–0–5	2–1–3	1–3–4	2–1–3	1–1–2	0–2–2	0–0–0	2–2–4
Pearson	0–0–0	1–3–4	0–0–0	0–0–0	0–0–0	0–0–0	0–0–0	0–0–0	0–1–1	0–0–0	0–0–0
Richardson	0–0–0	0–0–0	0–3–3	0–1–1	0–1–1	0–1–1	3–1–4	0–2–2	0–0–0	0–0–0	0–1–1
Slegr	———	0–0–0	———	———	———	1–1–2	0–0–0	0–0–0	0–1–1	0–1–1	0–2–2
Smyth	———	0–0–0	———	———	0–0–0	0–0–0	———	———	———	———	———
Stapleton	1–4–5	0–0–0	0–0–0	3–1–4	0–1–1	1–0–1	0–1–1	0–0–0	0–3–3	0–0–0	1–1–2
Sutton	———	0–1–1	———	———	———	0–0–0	0–0–0	1–0–1	0–0–0	1–0–1	1–0–1
Thornton	1–1–2	0–2–2	1–0–1	0–0–0	0–0–0	0–3–3	3–0–3	0–1–1	3–1–4	2–2–4	0–2–2
Tuomainen	———	0–0–0	———	———	———	0–0–0	0–0–0	———	———	0–0–0	———
Weight	0–3–3	1–8–9	1–0–1	0–2–2	0–1–1	1–3–4	0–2–2	1–4–5	1–3–4	0–5–5	2–2–4
White	———	———	———	———	———	0–0–0	———	0–0–0	1–1–2	0–0–0	1–3–4
Wright	———	0–0–0	———	———	———	0–0–0	———	———	———	———	1–0–1

1994–95 Goaltender Records vs. Opposition

	GP	Min.	GA	EN	SO	Ave.	W–L–T	Opposition
Fred Brathwaite	1	60	5	0	0	5.00	0–1–0	Calgary
	3	132	8	0	0	3.64	0–1–0	Chicago
	1	24	0	0	0	0.00	0–0–1	Dallas
	2	90	4	1	0	2.67	0–1–0	Detroit
	1	34	2	0	0	3.53	0–0–0	Los Angeles
	1	22	2	0	0	5.45	0–0–0	San Jose
	3	119	10	0	0	5.04	1–1–0	Toronto

	GP	Min.	GA	EN	SO	Ave.	W–L–T	Opposition
	1	60	4	0	0	4.00	1–0–0	Vancouver
	1	60	5	0	0	5.00	0–1–0	Winnipeg
Joaquin Gage	1	60	5	0	0	5.00	0–1–0	Calgary
	1	39	2	0	0	3.08	0–1–0	Toronto
Bill Ranford	4	248	10	0	1	2.42	2–2–0	Anaheim
	3	179	11	1	0	3.69	1–2–0	Calgary
	3	107	12	1	0	6.73	0–3–0	Chicago
	4	218	12	0	0	3.30	1–2–0	Dallas
	3	148	10	0	0	4.05	1–2–0	Detroit
	5	271	15	0	0	3.32	2–2–1	Los Angeles
	5	278	14	0	0	3.02	3–2–0	San Jose
	4	243	16	0	0	3.95	2–2–0	St. Louis
	2	80	2	0	0	1.50	1–0–0	Toronto
	4	245	20	0	0	4.90	0–3–1	Vancouver
	3	185	11	0	0	3.57	2–0–1	Winnipeg

1994-95 Schedule Results

Jan. 20	Anaheim	1	at	Edmonton	2
Jan. 22	Edmonton	4	at	Los Angeles	3
Jan. 23	Edmonton	4	at	Anaheim	5 OT
Jan. 25	Edmonton	1	at	Chicago	5
Jan. 28	Edmonton	2	at	Detroit	5
Jan. 30	Detroit	4	at	Edmonton	2
Feb. 1	Chicago	7	at	Edmonton	0
Feb. 3	Toronto	3	at	Edmonton	5
Feb. 7	Edmonton	4	at	Vancouver	4 OT
Feb. 8	Winnipeg	3	at	Edmonton	3 OT
Feb. 10	San Jose	1	at	Edmonton	5
Feb. 12	Anaheim	0	at	Edmonton	2
Feb. 15	Edmonton	4	at	Toronto	1
Feb. 17	Edmonton	2	at	Detroit	4
Feb. 19	Edmonton	1	at	Chicago	4
Feb. 20	Edmonton	0	at	St. Louis	4
Feb. 22	Dallas	1	at	Edmonton	2
Feb. 25	Los Angeles	4	at	Edmonton	3
Feb. 28	Edmonton	2	at	Calgary	5
Mar. 1	Dallas	5	at	Edmonton	3
Mar. 3	Chicago	5	at	Edmonton	2
Mar. 5	Detroit	2	at	Edmonton	4
Mar. 8	Edmonton	5	at	San Jose	2
Mar. 12	Vancouver	5	at	Edmonton	2
Mar. 14	St. Louis	5	at	Edmonton	6
Mar. 17	San Jose	3	at	Edmonton	5
Mar. 20	Calgary	2	at	Edmonton	5
Mar. 22	Edmonton	4	at	Dallas	4 OT
Mar. 23	Edmonton	1	at	Dallas	2
Mar. 26	Edmonton	1	at	St. Louis	5
Mar. 27	Edmonton	3	at	Toronto	4
Mar. 31	Calgary	6	at	Edmonton	2
April 1	Vancouver	5	at	Edmonton	1
April 3	Edmonton	2	at	Los Angeles	7
April 5	Edmonton	3	at	Anaheim	4 OT
April 7	Edmonton	0	at	San Jose	5
April 9	San Jose	5	at	Edmonton	2
April 13	Edmonton	6	at	Vancouver	4
April 15	Calgary	4	at	Edmonton	2
April 17	Edmonton	6	at	Winnipeg	5
April 19	Los Angeles	0	at	Edmonton	2
April 21	Edmonton	3	at	Los Angeles	3 OT
April 22	Edmonton	1	at	Vancouver	6
April 25	Edmonton	5	at	Winnipeg	3
April 27	St. Louis	2	at	Edmonton	3 OT
April 29	Winnipeg	5	at	Edmonton	1
May 1	Toronto	6	at	Edmonton	5
May 3	Edmonton	3	at	Calgary	5

Opponent	Home W–L–T	Road W–L–T
Anaheim	2–0–0	0–2–0
Calgary	1–2–0	0–2–0
Chicago	0–2–0	0–2–0
Dallas	1–1–0	0–1–1
Detroit	1–1–0	0–2–0
Los Angeles	1–1–0	1–1–1
San Jose	2–1–0	1–1–0
St. Louis	2–0–0	0–2–0
Toronto	1–1–0	1–1–0
Vancouver	0–2–0	1–1–1
Winnipeg	0–1–1	2–0–0

Opponent	Overall W–L–T	GF–GA
Anaheim	2–2–0	11–10
Calgary	1–4–0	14–22
Chicago	0–4–0	4–21
Dallas	1–2–1	10–12
Detroit	1–3–0	10–15
Los Angeles	2–2–1	14–17
San Jose	3–2–0	17–16
St. Louis	2–2–0	10–16
Toronto	2–2–0	17–14
Vancouver	1–3–1	14–24
Winnipeg	2–1–1	15–16

Table 12. Oilers All Time Penalty Shots

Player	Opponent	Road/Home	Goaltender	Date	Result
Stan Weir	Toronto	R	Mike Palmateer	March 29, 1980	GOAL
Wayne Gretzky	Winnipeg	H	Pierre Hamel	February 6, 1981	No Goal
Dave Lumley	Quebec	R	Dan Bouchard	December 2, 1981	GOAL
Wayne Gretzky	Toronto	R	Michel Larocque	January 16, 1982	No Goal
Wayne Gretzky	Washington	H	Pat Riggin	November 24, 1982	No Goal
Wayne Gretzky	Vancouver	H	Richard Brodeur	January 19, 1983	GOAL
Ken Linseman	Toronto	R	Rick St. Croix	October 26, 1983	No Goal
Wayne Gretzky	Minnesota	R	Don Beaupre	April 28, 1984 (P)	GOAL
Craig MacTavish	Calgary	H	Mike Vernon	December 23, 1988	GOAL
Jeff Beukeboom	Winnipeg	H	Rick Tabaracci	October 6, 1990	No Goal
Petr Klima	Boston	R	Rejean Lemelin	May 18, 1990 (P)	No Goal
Ken Linseman	Detroit	R	Tim Cheveldae	January 9, 1991	No Goal
Scott Pearson	Toronto	H	Damian Rhodes	November 20, 1993	No Goal
Roman Oksiuta	Chicago	H	Ed Belfour	February 4, 1994	No Goal
Doug Weight	Tampa Bay	H	Darren Puppa	January 3, 1996	No Goal
Dean McAmmond	Florida	H	Mark Fitzpatrick	January 5, 1996	No Goal
Todd Marchant	Ottawa	R	Damian Rhodes	November 13, 1996	No Goal
Todd Marchant	Washington	R	Olaf Kolzig	January 26, 1996	No Goal
Doug Weight	N.Y. Rangers	H	Mike Richter	October 8, 1997	GOAL

Table 13 All Time Penalty Shots Against the Oilers

Goaltender	Opponent	Road/Home	Shooter	Date	Result
Ron Low	Detroit	R	Mike Foligno	March 26, 1980	No Goal
Grant Fuhr	Detroit	R	Ron Duguay	January 9, 1984	No Goal
Grant Fuhr	Buffalo	R	Brent Peterson	January 13, 1984	No Goal
Andy Moog	New Jersey	R	Rocky Trottier	December 17, 1984	GOAL
Grant Fuhr	Philadelphia	R	Ron Sutter	May 28, 1985 (P)	No Goal
Grant Fuhr	Philadelphia	R	Dave Poulin	May 30, 1985 (P)	No Goal
Bill Ranford	Quebec	R	Claude Loiselle	October 28, 1989	No Goal
Bill Ranford	Toronto	R	Tom Kurvers	March 10, 1990	No Goal
Bill Ranford	Vancouver	H	Greg Adams	December 1, 1991	No Goal
Bill Ranford	Buffalo	R	Alexander Mogilny	January 10, 1992	No Goal
Bill Ranford	Pittsburgh	R	Mario Lemieux	March 17, 1992	No Goal
Bill Ranford	Minnesota	H	Dave Gagner	October 28, 1992	No Goal
Bill Ranford	Calgary	H	C.J. Young	December 27, 1992	No Goal
Ron Tugnutt	N.Y. Islanders	R	Benoit Hogue	February 16, 1993	GOAL
Bill Ranford	Calgary	R	Robert Reichel	February 7, 1994	GOAL
Bill Ranford	St. Louis	R	Brett Hull	March 26, 1995	No Goal
Curtis Joseph	Colorado	R	Valeri Kamensky	October 26, 1996	GOAL
Bob Essensa	Phoenix	R	Keith Tkachuk	January 24, 1998	No Goal
Curtis Joseph	Anaheim	H	J.F. Jomphe	April 15, 1998	No Goal
Tommy Salo	Tampa Bay	H	Mike Sillinger	January 7, 2000	No Goal
Joaquin Gage	Minnesota	R	Scott Pellerin	October 15, 2000	No Goal
Dominic Roussel	San Jose	R	Jeff Friesen	January 24, 2001	No Goal

(P)=Playoff

1995-96

Ron Low began his first full season behind the bench as head coach of the Edmonton Oilers. Bob McCammon took over the vacant associate coaching position, joining the returning Kevin Primeau. For the first time in history the league's annual entry draft was held in Edmonton. With their first choice, sixth overall, the Oilers chose two-way forward Steve Kelly from the Prince Albert Raiders of the Western Hockey League. Chosen in the second round was Georges Laraque, a 235-pound forward from the St. Jean Lynx of the Quebec League. Laraque would quickly evolve into the most feared fighter in the National Hockey League.

In July Shayne Corson was signed to a free agent contract by the St. Louis Blues, and Kelly Buchberger would take over the duties as team captain when the season started. A week after the loss of Corson, goaltender Curtis Joseph and the rights to forward Mike Grier were acquired from the Blues, for two draft choices. The Blues and Joseph had been unable to come to terms on a new contract.

General Manager Glen Sather made a number of deals during the season in an attempt to improve the team. In January defensemen Igor Kravchuk and Ken Sutton were traded to the now familiar St. Louis Blues for another pair of defensemen, Jeff Norton and Donald Dufresne. Glenn Anderson was picked up on waivers January 25 but the former Oilers star had little interest in playing for his former team and was placed back on waivers in March. He too signed a contract with St. Louis. In a deal which did not involve St. Louis the overworked and now expendable Bill Ranford was traded to Boston for Sean Brown, Mariusz Czerkawski and Boston's first round choice (Matthieu Descoteaux) in the 1996 draft.

Edmonton got off to a slow start, losing their first four games but then won four of their next six. The longest winning streak the team could string together this year was three games, which they managed to do only three times. Unfortunately they also suffered losing streaks of three or more games nine different times and finished the season with 68 points. They were 17–23–6 (.435) at the All-Star break.

A number of players missed games due to injury. Jason Arnott missed seven games with a concussion and nine with an injury to his left knee. Miroslav Satan missed two games with a collapsed lung and four with a separated right shoulder, while defenseman Jeff Norton missed nine games with a strained ligament in his left knee. Also many players such as Bonsignore, de Vries, Dufresne, Intranuovo, McAmmond and Curtis Joseph spent time in the minors, being called up at various times to bolster the roster.

The 68 points the Oilers compiled was only good enough for fifth place in the seven team Pacific Division. This was 36 points behind the division leading Colorado Avalanche. The Oilers missed the playoffs for the fourth year in a row.

Doug Weight again led Edmonton in scoring and became the first Oiler to score more than 100 points since Mark Messier had done it in 1990. Weight ended the season with 104 points.

1995-96 Regular Season Scoring

#		Ht	Wt	Age	GP	G	A	Pts	Shots	S%	GW	GT	PP	SH	P/M	PIM
39	Weight (A)	71	191	23	82	25	79	104	204	12.3	2	1	9	0	-19	95
8	Ciger	73	190	25	78	31	39	70	184	16.8	3	0	12	0	-15	41
7	Arnott (A)	75	200	21	64	28	31	59	244	11.5	5	1	8	0	-6	87
20	Oliver	72	190	23	80	20	19	39	131	15.3	0	0	14	0	-22	34
26	Marchant	70	175	21	81	19	19	38	221	8.6	2	1	2	3	-19	66
32	Satan	73	185	20	62	18	17	35	113	15.9	4	0	6	0	0	22
2	Mironov	75	220	22	78	8	24	32	158	5.1	1	0	7	0	-23	101
37	McAmmond	71	185	21	53	15	15	30	79	19.0	0	0	4	0	6	23
10	Czerkawski	72	195	22	37	12	17	29	79	15.2	1	0	2	0	7	8
16	Buchberger (C)	74	200	28	82	11	14	25	119	9.2	3	0	0	2	-20	184
6	Norton	74	200	29	30	4	16	20	52	7.7	1	0	1	0	5	16
17	Thornton	75	210	23	77	9	9	18	95	9.5	3	0	0	2	-25	149
24	Marchment	73	205	25	78	3	15	18	96	3.1	0	0	0	0	-7	202
28	Jiri Slegr	73	205	23	57	4	13	17	91	4.4	1	0	0	1	-1	74
94	Smyth	73	195	18	48	2	9	11	65	3.1	0	0	1	0	-10	28
22	Richardson (A)	76	210	25	82	2	9	11	61	3.3	0	0	0	0	-27	108
9	Anderson	73	190	34	17	4	6	10	36	11.1	1	0	0	0	0	27
27	White	71	200	25	26	5	3	8	34	14.7	0	0	1	0	-14	0
21	Kravchuk	73	200	28	26	4	4	8	59	6.8	0	0	3	0	-13	10
19	Manderville	75	207	23	37	3	5	8	63	4.8	0	0	0	2	-5	38
18	Maltby	72	190	22	49	2	6	8	51	3.9	1	0	0	0	-16	61
6	Sutton	72	200	25	32	0	8	8	38	0.0	0	0	0	0	-12	39
34	Dufresne	73	206	27	42	1	6	7	20	5.0	0	0	0	0	-2	16
15	Roberts	72	185	24	6	2	4	6	12	16.7	0	0	0	0	0	6
5	Hauer	74	210	23	29	4	2	6	53	7.5	1	0	2	0	-11	30
15	Olausson	74	195	28	20	0	6	6	20	0.0	0	0	0	0	-14	14
29	DeBrusk	74	215	23	38	1	3	4	17	5.9	0	0	0	0	-7	96
27	Intranuovo	68	185	21	13	1	2	3	19	5.3	1	0	0	0	-3	4
25	de Vries	75	218	21	13	1	1	2	8	12.5	0	0	0	0	-2	12
64	Bonsignore	76	220	18	20	0	2	2	13	0.0	0	0	0	0	-6	4
12	Wright	71	185	21	23	1	0	1	18	5.6	0	0	0	0	-7	33
31	Joseph	70	182	27	34	0	1	1	1	0.0	0	0	0	0	0	4
30	Ranford	71	185	28	37	0	1	1	0	0.0	0	0	0	0	0	2
23	Stajduhar	75	200	20	2	0	0	0	1	0.0	0	0	0	0	2	4
35	Muir	76	220	21	5	0	0	0	4	0.0	0	0	0	0	-4	6
40	Brathwaite	67	170	22	7	0	0	0	0	0.0	0	0	0	0	0	2
36	Bonvie	71	205	21	8	0	0	0	0	0.0	0	0	0	0	-3	47

#		Ht	Wt	Age	GP	G	A	Pts	Shots	S%	GW	GT	PP	SH	P/M	PIM
1	Gage	72	200	21	16	0	0	0	0	0.0	0	0	0	0	0	4
	Bench															12
		73	198	23	82	240	405	645	2459	9.8	30	3	72	10	-56	1709

1995-96 Goaltender Records

	GP	Min.	GA	W	L	T	Ave.	SA	Pct.	SO	EN
Fred Brathwaite	7	293	12	0	2	0	2.46	140	0.914	0	1
Curtis Joseph	34	1936	111	15	16	2	3.44	971	0.886	0	4
Joaquin Gage	16	717	45	2	8	1	3.77	350	0.871	0	1
Bill Ranford	37	2015	128	13	18	5	3.81	1024	0.875	1	2
	82	4978	304	30	44	8	3.66	2493	0.878	1	8

Coach: Ron Low 30-44-8

1995-96 Scoring vs. Opposition

	Ana.	Bost.	Buff.	Calg.	Chi.	Col.	Dall.	Det.
Anderson	1–0–1	0–3–3	———	2–0–2	0–0–0	0–0–0	0–0–0	———
Arnott	2–0–2	———	0–1–1	1–3–4	2–3–5	1–4–5	0–2–2	0–2–2
Bonsignore	0–0–0	———	0–0–0	0–1–1	0–0–0	0–1–1	———	0–0–0
Bonvie	———	———	———	0–0–0	———	———	———	0–0–0
Buchberger	0–0–0	1–0–1	1–1–2	0–2–2	0–1–1	0–0–0	0–0–0	1–0–1
Ciger	1–1–2	0–0–0	1–2–3	3–1–4	1–1–2	1–4–5	1–1–2	2–1–3
Czerkawski	0–0–0	1–1–2	0–2–2	0–3–3	1–0–1	0–1–1	1–0–1	———
DeBrusk	0–1–1	0–0–0	0–0–0	1–0–1	0–0–0	0–0–0	0–0–0	0–1–1
de Vries	0–0–0	0–0–0	———	0–0–0	0–0–0	0–0–0	0–0–0	———
Dufresne	0–0–0	0–0–0	0–1–1	0–0–0	0–0–0	0–0–0	0–0–0	———
Hauer	1–0–1	———	1–0–1	0–0–0	0–0–0	0–0–0	0–2–2	0–0–0
Intranuovo	0–0–0	0–1–1	———	———	———	0–1–1	———	———
Kravchuk	0–0–0	———	0–1–1	1–0–1	0–0–0	0–0–0	———	0–0–0
Maltby	1–1–2	———	0–0–0	0–0–0	0–0–0	1–0–1	0–0–0	0–0–0
Manderville	1–2–3	———	0–0–0	0–0–0	0–0–0	0–0–0	0–1–1	———
Marchant	1–1–2	0–0–0	0–1–1	0–1–1	1–1–2	1–0–1	2–2–4	1–1–2
Marchment	0–1–1	1–1–2	0–0–0	0–2–2	0–1–1	0–1–1	1–1–2	0–1–1
McAmmond	0–1–1	0–0–0	0–0–0	1–2–3	0–0–0	0–0–0	2–1–3	0–0–0
Mironov	0–1–1	0–0–0	0–0–0	0–3–3	0–1–1	0–1–1	1–2–3	0–0–0
Muir	———	———	———	0–0–0	———	0–0–0	0–0–0	———
Norton	0–1–1	2–1–3	1–0–1	0–1–1	0–1–1	0–0–0	0–1–1	———
Olausson	———	———	0–0–0	———	———	———	———	0–1–1
Oliver	1–1–2	0–0–0	0–0–0	3–0–3	2–0–2	1–0–1	0–0–0	1–1–2
Richardson	0–2–2	0–1–1	0–0–0	0–0–0	0–0–0	0–2–2	0–0–0	0–0–0
Roberts	———	———	———	———	———	1–0–1	0–1–1	———
Satan	1–0–1	0–0–0	1–0–1	1–0–1	0–1–1	2–2–4	0–0–0	0–0–0
Slegr	0–1–1	0–0–0	0–0–0	0–0–0	0–0–0	0–0–0	0–1–1	1–0–1
Smyth	0–0–0	0–0–0	———	1–0–1	0–0–0	0–0–0	0–1–1	0–0–0
Stajduhar	———	———	———	———	———	———	———	———
Sutton	0–0–0	———	0–0–0	0–2–2	0–1–1	0–0–0	———	0–1–1
Thornton	1–0–1	0–0–0	0–0–0	2–0–2	0–1–1	3–0–3	0–0–0	0–0–0
Weight	0–5–5	3–2–5	1–3–4	0–8–8	1–3–4	4–3–7	2–2–4	1–2–3
White	0–0–0	———	0–0–0	1–0–1	0–1–1	0–0–0	———	0–0–0
Wright	0–0–0	———	———	0–0–0	0–0–0	0–0–0	———	0–0–0

	Flor.	Hart.	L.A.	Mont.	N.J.	NYI.	NYR.	Ott.
Anderson	———	0–0–0	0–2–2	———	———	0–0–0	———	———
Arnott	1–1–2	0–0–0	0–3–3	4–2–6	1–0–1	1–0–1	1–0–1	1–0–1
Bonsignore	0–0–0	———	———	0–0–0	0–0–0	———	———	0–0–0
Bonvie	———	———	———	———	———	———	———	———
Buchberger	0–0–0	0–0–0	0–4–4	0–0–0	0–0–0	0–0–0	———	1–0–1
Ciger	2–1–3	1–2–3	4–3–7	0–1–1	1–2–3	0–0–0	0–1–1	0–0–0
Czerkawski	———	0–0–0	2–1–3	———	———	1–1–2	2–0–2	———
DeBrusk	0–0–0	0–0–0	0–0–0	0–0–0	0–0–0	0–0–0	———	———
de Vries	———	———	1–0–1	———	———	———	———	———

	Flor.	Hart.	L.A.	Mont.	N.J.	NYI.	NYR.	Ott.
Dufresne	0–0–0	0–0–0	1–0–1	0–0–0	———	0–0–0	0–0–0	0–1–1
Hauer	0–0–0	0–0–0	———	———	———	0–0–0	0–0–0	———
Intranuovo	———	———	1–0–1	0–0–0	———	0–0–0	———	0–0–0
Kravchuk	———	———	0–1–1	0–0–0	0–0–0	———	0–0–0	1–0–1
Maltby	0–0–0	0–0–0	0–1–1	0–0–0	0–0–0	0–0–0	0–0–0	0–0–0
Manderville	0–0–0	0–0–0	0–0–0	0–0–0	———	0–0–0	0–0–0	0–1–1
Marchant	0–0–0	0–0–0	3–4–7	1–0–1	1–0–1	0–0–0	0–0–0	1–1–2
Marchment	0–1–1	0–0–0	1–0–1	0–0–0	0–0–0	0–2–2	———	0–0–0
McAmmond	0–0–0	1–0–1	2–1–3	1–2–3	0–0–0	1–1–2	1–2–3	0–0–0
Mironov	0–0–0	1–1–2	0–2–2	0–1–1	0–0–0	0–1–1	2–0–2	0–0–0
Muir	———	———	———	———	———	———	———	———
Norton	0–0–0	0–1–1	1–2–3	0–1–1	———	0–1–1	0–2–2	0–0–0
Olausson	0–0–0	———	0–0–0	———	0–1–1	———	0–1–1	0–0–0
Oliver	0–1–1	1–1–2	0–1–1	0–0–0	2–0–2	1–1–2	0–2–2	1–1–2
Richardson	0–0–0	0–0–0	0–0–0	0–0–0	0–0–0	0–0–0	0–0–0	0–0–0
Roberts	———	———	0–1–1	———	———	———	0–0–0	———
Satan	0–0–0	0–2–2	3–2–5	1–1–2	0–0–0	0–0–0	0–2–2	0–0–0
Slegr	0–0–0	0–0–0	0–0–0	0–0–0	0–0–0	———	0–0–0	1–0–1
Smyth	———	0–0–0	0–1–1	0–1–1	———	0–0–0	0–0–0	0–0–0
Stajduhar	———	———	———	———	———	———	———	———
Sutton	0–0–0	———	0–1–1	0–0–0	0–1–1	———	0–0–0	0–0–0
Thornton	0–0–0	0–0–0	0–2–2	0–0–0	0–1–1	0–0–0	0–0–0	0–0–0
Weight	0–2–2	1–1–2	3–7–10	0–3–3	0–1–1	0–1–1	1–3–4	0–1–1
White	0–0–0	———	———	0–0–0	0–0–0	———	———	———
Wright	0–0–0	0–0–0	0–0–0	———	0–0–0	———	0–0–0	0–0–0

	Phil.	Pitt.	S. J.	St.L.	Tampa	Tor.	Van.	Wash.	Winn.
Anderson	———	0–1–1	———	0–0–0	———	———	———	1–0–1	———
Arnott	0–0–0	1–0–1	2–2–4	1–3–4	1–1–2	4–1–5	2–2–4	0–0–0	2–1–3
Bonsignore	0–0–0	———	0–0–0	0–0–0	0–0–0	0–0–0	———	0–0–0	0–0–0
Bonvie	———	———	0–0–0	0–0–0	———	0–0–0	0–0–0	———	0–0–0
Buchberger	1–1–2	1–0–1	0–0–0	1–1–2	1–0–1	1–0–1	1–3–4	0–1–1	1–0–1
Ciger	0–0–0	1–1–2	4–1–5	4–4–8	———	1–3–4	2–4–6	1–1–2	0–4–4
Czerkawski	———	1–1–2	1–4–5	1–1–2	———	0–0–0	1–2–3	0–0–0	0–0–0
DeBrusk	———	0–0–0	0–0–0	0–0–0	0–1–1	———	0–0–0	———	0–0–0
de Vries	———	———	0–1–1	———	———	0–0–0	0–0–0	———	0–0–0
Dufresne	———	0–0–0	0–2–2	0–1–1	———	0–1–1	0–0–0	0–0–0	0–0–0
Hauer	———	———	0–0–0	1–0–1	1–0–1	———	0–0–0	0–0–0	0–0–0
Intranuovo	———	———	0–0–0	———	———	0–0–0	0–0–0	———	0–0–0
Kravchuk	1–0–1	———	0–1–1	1–0–1	0–0–0	0–0–0	0–0–0	———	0–1–1
Maltby	0–0–0	———	0–0–0	0–0–0	0–0–0	0–1–1	0–2–2	0–0–0	0–1–1
Manderville	0–0–0	0–0–0	1–0–1	0–0–0	0–0–0	0–0–0	0–1–1	1–0–1	0–0–0
Marchant	0–1–1	0–0–0	2–3–5	0–0–0	0–1–1	1–1–2	4–0–4	0–0–0	0–1–1
Marchment	0–0–0	0–1–1	0–2–2	0–0–0	0–0–0	0–0–0	0–1–1	0–0–0	0–0–0
McAmmond	0–0–0	0–1–1	2–2–4	1–0–1	0–0–0	0–2–2	2–0–2	0–0–0	1–0–1
Mironov	0–0–0	0–1–1	0–2–2	0–1–1	0–1–1	2–1–3	2–3–5	0–0–0	0–2–2
Muir	———	———	0–0–0	———	———	0–0–0	———	———	———
Norton	———	0–2–2	0–0–0	0–1–1	———	———	———	0–1–1	———
Olausson	0–0–0	———	0–1–1	0–0–0	0–0–0	0–0–0	0–1–1	0–0–0	0–1–1
Oliver	0–0–0	0–0–0	3–1–4	0–3–3	0–0–0	0–1–1	2–4–6	1–1–2	1–0–1
Richardson	0–0–0	0–0–0	0–0–0	2–1–3	0–1–1	0–0–0	0–0–0	0–1–1	0–1–1
Roberts	———	———	1–2–3	———	———	0–0–0	———	———	———
Satan	1–1–2	3–1–4	0–2–2	0–1–1	0–0–0	0–0–0	2–1–3	———	3–1–4
Slegr	1–1–2	0–3–3	0–2–2	1–0–1	0–0–0	0–1–1	0–3–3	0–0–0	0–1–1
Smyth	———	0–1–1	1–1–2	0–1–1	0–0–0	0–0–0	0–3–3	0–0–0	0–0–0
Stajduhar	———	———	———	0–0–0	0–0–0	———	———	———	———
Sutton	0–0–0	———	0–0–0	0–0–0	0–0–0	0–0–0	0–0–0	———	0–2–2
Thornton	0–0–0	0–0–0	1–0–1	0–1–1	0–0–0	0–3–3	1–1–2	0–0–0	1–0–1
Weight	0–1–1	1–0–1	2–4–6	1–8–9	0–2–2	1–3–4	1–6–7	0–3–3	2–5–7
White	0–1–1	———	0–0–0	0–0–0	1–0–1	0–0–0	1–1–2	———	2–0–2
Wright	0–0–0	———	0–0–0	0–0–0	———	0–0–0	0–0–0	———	1–0–1

1995-96 Goaltender Records vs. Opposition

	GP	Min.	GA	EN	SO	Ave.	W-L-T	Opposition
Fred Brathwaite	1	59	3	0	0	3.05	0-1-0	Florida
	1	40	2	0	0	3.00	0-0-0	Hartford
	1	30	0	0	0	0.00	0-0-0	Pittsburgh
	1	43	0	1	0	0.00	0-0-0	San Jose
	1	34	3	0	0	2.65	0-0-0	Tampa Bay
	1	60	3	0	0	3.00	0-1-0	Vancouver
	1	27	1	0	0	2.22	0-0-0	Washington
Joaquin Gage	2	119	2	0	0	1.01	1-1-0	Anaheim
	1	60	4	0	0	4.00	0-1-0	Buffalo
	2	118	6	1	0	3.05	0-2-0	Calgary
	1	45	1	0	0	1.33	0-0-1	Chicago
	1	45	3	0	0	4.00	0-0-0	Colorado
	1	20	3	0	0	9.00	0-0-0	Detroit
	1	20	3	0	0	9.00	0-1-0	Hartford
	1	16	4	0	0	15.00	0-1-0	San Jose
	1	18	0	0	0	0.00	0-0-0	St. Louis
	1	42	3	0	0	4.29	0-1-0	Toronto
	2	110	4	0	0	2.18	1-0-0	Vancouver
	2	104	12	0	0	6.92	0-1-0	Winnipeg
Curtis Joseph	1	60	2	0	0	2.00	1-0-0	Anaheim
	2	124	9	1	0	4.25	1-1-0	Boston
	1	65	4	0	0	5.54	1-0-0	Buffalo
	2	122	5	0	0	2.46	1-1-0	Calgary
	2	120	8	0	0	4.00	0-2-0	Chicago
	2	74	12	0	0	9.73	0-2-0	Colorado
	4	239	16	2	0	4.02	1-3-0	Dallas
	1	65	4	0	0	3.69	0-0-1	Hartford
	4	244	10	0	0	2.46	2-1-1	Los Angeles
	1	60	5	0	0	5.00	1-0-0	Montreal
	2	119	3	0	0	1.51	1-1-0	N.Y. Islanders
	1	60	1	0	0	1.00	1-0-0	N.Y. Rangers
	1	60	2	0	0	2.00	1-0-0	Ottawa
	2	89	10	0	0	6.74	0-2-0	Pittsburgh
	2	120	5	0	0	2.50	2-0-0	San Jose
	2	119	5	0	0	2.52	1-1-0	St. Louis
	2	76	6	1	0	4.74	0-1-0	Toronto
	1	60	2	0	0	2.00	0-1-0	Washington
	2	76	6	0	0	4.74	1-0-0	Winnipeg
Bill Ranford	2	120	1	0	1	0.50	2-0-0	Anaheim
	2	120	10	0	0	5.00	1-1-0	Calgary
	2	80	8	0	0	6.00	0-1-0	Chicago
	3	184	10	0	0	3.26	1-1-1	Colorado
	4	219	17	1	0	4.66	0-4-0	Detroit
	1	60	2	0	0	2.00	0-1-0	Florida
	1	64	4	0	0	3.75	1-0-0	Los Angeles
	1	59	3	1	0	3.05	0-1-0	Montreal
	2	120	2	0	0	1.00	2-0-0	New Jersey
	1	60	8	0	0	8.00	0-1-0	N.Y. Rangers
	1	60	1	0	0	1.00	1-0-0	Ottawa
	2	120	9	0	0	4.50	1-1-0	Philadelphia
	2	125	3	0	0	1.44	1-0-1	San Jose
	2	102	12	0	0	7.06	0-2-0	St. Louis
	2	88	5	0	0	3.41	1-1-0	Tampa Bay
	2	125	9	0	0	4.32	0-1-1	Toronto
	4	200	13	0	0	3.90	1-1-2	Vancouver
	1	33	5	0	0	9.09	0-1-0	Washington
	2	76	6	0	0	4.74	1-1-0	Winnipeg

1995-96 Schedule Results

Oct. 8	Detroit	3	at	Edmonton	1	Oct. 13	Edmonton	0	at	Detroit	9
Oct. 10	Edmonton	3	at	St. Louis	5	Oct. 15	Edmonton	1	at	Philadelphia	7

Oct. 17	Edmonton	3	at	New Jersey	1	Jan. 13	Buffalo	4	at	Edmonton	5 OT
Oct. 18	Edmonton	1	at	Buffalo	4	Jan. 16	Edmonton	5	at	St. Louis	1
Oct. 21	Vancouver	4	at	Edmonton	6	Jan. 17	Edmonton	4	at	Dallas	3
Oct. 22	San Jose	1	at	Edmonton	1 OT	Jan. 24	Edmonton	3	at	Dallas	5
Oct. 27	Winnipeg	5	at	Edmonton	7	Jan. 26	Islanders	1	at	Edmonton	4
Oct. 31	New Jersey	1	at	Edmonton	2	Jan. 30	Edmonton	2	at	Calgary	3 OT
Nov. 1	Edmonton	3	at	Vancouver	3 OT	Jan. 31	Chicago	4	at	Edmonton	0
Nov. 4	Toronto	3	at	Edmonton	3 OT	Feb. 7	Washington	2	at	Edmonton	1
Nov. 7	Edmonton	2	at	Detroit	4	Feb. 9	Vancouver	3	at	Edmonton	2 OT
Nov. 9	Edmonton	1	at	Florida	2	Feb. 11	Calgary	2	at	Edmonton	4
Nov. 10	Edmonton	4	at	Tampa Bay	3 OT	Feb. 14	Anaheim	2	at	Edmonton	3
Nov. 12	Edmonton	4	at	Chicago	4 OT	Feb. 16	Edmonton	1	at	Dallas	6
Nov. 14	Edmonton	2	at	Calgary	4	Feb. 18	Edmonton	1	at	Chicago	4
Nov. 15	Montreal	4	at	Edmonton	1	Feb. 19	Edmonton	5	at	Colorado	7
Nov. 17	Detroit	5	at	Edmonton	4	Feb. 21	Los Angeles	2	at	Edmonton	7
Nov. 20	Colorado	3	at	Edmonton	3 OT	Feb. 23	Boston	7	at	Edmonton	4
Nov. 22	Anaheim	0	at	Edmonton	2	Feb. 25	Edmonton	0	at	Islanders	2
Nov. 24	Edmonton	5	at	Calgary	2	Feb. 27	Edmonton	4	at	Boston	3 OT
Nov. 26	Edmonton	0	at	Winnipeg	4	Feb. 28	Edmonton	4	at	Hartford	4 OT
Nov. 28	Chicago	5	at	Edmonton	3	Mar. 1	Pittsburgh	5	at	Edmonton	4
Dec. 1	Calgary	8	at	Edmonton	2	Mar. 3	St. Louis	4	at	Edmonton	3
Dec. 2	St. Louis	7	at	Edmonton	3	Mar. 6	Edmonton	2	at	Los Angeles	3
Dec. 5	Edmonton	2	at	Vancouver	6	Mar. 8	San Jose	2	at	Edmonton	4
Dec. 7	Edmonton	5	at	Colorado	3	Mar. 13	Edmonton	8	at	San Jose	3
Dec. 9	Edmonton	4	at	San Jose	2	Mar. 16	Edmonton	5	at	Los Angeles	2
Dec. 10	Edmonton	3	at	Anaheim	1	Mar. 17	Edmonton	1	at	Colorado	8
Dec. 13	Vancouver	2	at	Edmonton	2 OT	Mar. 19	Edmonton	4	at	Rangers	1
Dec. 15	Edmonton	4	at	Winnipeg	9	Mar. 21	Edmonton	4	at	Pittsburgh	5
Dec. 18	Ottawa	1	at	Edmonton	3	Mar. 23	Edmonton	6	at	Montreal	5
Dec. 20	Colorado	4	at	Edmonton	1	Mar. 24	Edmonton	3	at	Ottawa	2
Dec. 22	Edmonton	3	at	Washington	6	Mar. 27	Los Angeles	3	at	Edmonton	3 OT
Dec. 23	Edmonton	1	at	Toronto	6	Mar. 29	Winnipeg	2	at	Edmonton	3
Dec. 27	Philadelphia	2	at	Edmonton	3	Mar. 30	Toronto	4	at	Edmonton	3
Dec. 29	Los Angeles	4	at	Edmonton	5 OT	April 1	Edmonton	6	at	Vancouver	2
Dec. 30	Rangers	8	at	Edmonton	3	April 3	Edmonton	0	at	Anaheim	1
Jan. 3	Tampa Bay	5	at	Edmonton	0	April 4	Edmonton	3	at	San Jose	5
Jan. 5	Florida	3	at	Edmonton	2	April 8	Calgary	3	at	Edmonton	2
Jan. 7	Anaheim	1	at	Edmonton	3	April 10	Dallas	4	at	Edmonton	2
Jan. 9	Hartford	5	at	Edmonton	1	April 13	Edmonton	3	at	Toronto	6

Overall Record vs. Opponents

Opponent	*Home*	*Road*	*Overall*	*GF-GA*	*Opponent*
Anaheim	3–0–0	1–1–0	4–1–0	11–5	Anaheim
Boston	0–1–0	1–0–0	1–1–0	8–10	Boston
Buffalo	1–0–0	0–1–0	1–1–0	6–8	Buffalo
Calgary	1–2–0	1–2–0	2–4–0	17–22	Calgary
Chicago	0–2–0	0–1–1	0–3–1	8–17	Chicago
Colorado	0–1–1	1–2–0	1–3–1	15–25	Colorado
Dallas	0–2–0	1–1–0	1–3–0	10–18	Dallas
Detroit	0–2–0	0–2–0	0–4–0	7–21	Detroit
Florida	0–1–0	0–1–0	0–2–0	3–5	Florida
Hartford	0–1–0	0–0–1	0–1–1	5–9	Hartford
Los Angeles	2–0–1	1–1–0	3–1–1	22–14	Los Angeles
Montreal	0–1–0	1–0–0	1–1–0	7–9	Montreal
New Jersey	1–0–0	1–0–0	2–0–0	5–2	New Jersey
Islanders	1–0–0	0–1–0	1–1–0	4–3	Islanders
Rangers	0–1–0	1–0–0	1–1–0	7–9	Rangers
Ottawa	1–0–0	1–0–0	2–0–0	6–3	Ottawa
Philadelphia	1–0–0	0–1–0	1–1–0	4–9	Philadelphia
Pittsburgh	0–1–0	0–1–0	0–2–0	8–10	Pittsburgh
San Jose	1–0–1	2–1–0	3–1–1	20–13	San Jose
St. Louis	0–2–0	1–1–0	1–3–0	14–17	St. Louis
Tampa Bay	0–1–0	1–0–0	1–1–0	4–8	Tampa Bay
Toronto	0–1–1	0–2–0	0–3–1	10–19	Toronto
Vancouver	1–1–1	1–1–1	2–2–2	21–20	Vancouver
Washington	0–1–0	0–1–0	0–2–0	4–8	Washington
Winnipeg	2–0–0	0–2–0	2–2–0	14–20	Winnipeg

1996-97

Ron Low began his second full season as coach, again with Primeau and McCammon assisting him. In an off-season deal goaltender Bob Essensa was acquired by the Oilers to provide a more than adequate backup for Curtis Joseph. Also picked up in the off-season was the "Russian Tank" Andrei Kovalenko. The nickname could refer either to his build (only 5'10" but 215 pounds) or his habit of "going into the tank" and playing in somewhat of a fog for long stretches at a time. This latter characteristic had prompted Montreal to trade him to the Oilers for Scott Thornton. Kovalenko would end up having a fine first season with the team, scoring 32 goals in 74 games.

Glen Sather had two first round draft picks this year. Chosen first (sixth overall) was Boyd Devereaux, a 6'2" center from Seaforth, Ontario. Devereaux had recorded 58 points in 66 games with the Kitchener Rangers of the Ontario Hockey League. With their second choice, acquired from Boston in the Bill Ranford trade, the Oilers chose Matthieu Descoteaux. Descoteaux, a 6'3" defenseman out of Shawinigan of the QMJHL, had accumulated 129 penalty minutes in 69 games for the Cataractes.

In September Sather signed the team's former first ever draft choice and former captain, Kevin Lowe, to a free agent contract. Sather also acquired the likes of Petr Klima, Michel Petit, Ralph Intranuovo, Drew Bannister and Craig Millar in various trades throughout the season.

The Oilers got off to a good start, winning four of their first six games. The team put together three-four- and five-game winning streaks this season, and from December 28 to February 5, won 11 games while losing three and tying one. At the All-Star break the team was 21–21–4 (.500).

Several key players missed games this season due to injury. Andrei Kovalenko missed five games with a hip pointer, while Jason Arnott missed nine games with an ankle injury and four with a back strain. Hard shooting defenseman Boris Mironov missed a total of 22 games due to an abdominal strain. Dean McAmmond, who was just starting to get his game in shape, would miss the last 18 contests with a disc problem in his back. Defenseman Bryan Marchment also missed eight games, due to cracked ribs suffered in a game against the Calgary Flames. Veteran Kevin Lowe, who had returned to the Oilers this season and would have a settling effect on the blueline, missed nine games with a neck strain.

The team finished third in the Pacific Division with 81 points, 26 less than division leading Colorado. Doug Weight led the team in scoring with 82 points. This was quite a respectable total as only two players in the entire league recorded more than 100 points. This was the lowest number of players to reach the 100 point plateau (except during the strike shortened 1994-95 season) since 1970.

For the first time in five years the team qualified for the postseason. In the first playoff round they met the Dallas Stars, a team which had registered the second highest point total in the league during the regular season and had finished 23 points ahead of the Oilers. In an exciting and memorable seven game series the Oilers defeated the Stars four games to three. Three of the Oilers' four victories were in overtime; the last one, at 12:26 in game seven by Todd Marchant, was one of the most memorable goals in franchise history.

After their victory over Dallas, the team met defending Stanley Cup champion Colorado Avalanche. Edmonton, just coming off his exhausting series with Dallas, was no match for the high flying Avalanche and was defeated four games to one.

1996-97 Regular Season Scoring

#		*Ht.*	*Wt.*	*Age*	*GP*	*G*	*A*	*Pts*	*Shots*	*S%*	*GW*	*GT*	*PP*	*SH*	*P/M*	*PIM*
39	Weight (A)	71	191	25	80	21	61	82	235	8.9	2	0	4	0	1	80
94	Smyth	73	195	20	82	39	22	61	265	14.7	4	0	20	0	-7	76
51	Kovalenko	70	200	26	74	32	27	59	163	19.6	2	0	14	0	-5	81
7	Arnott (A)	75	200	22	67	19	38	57	248	7.7	2	1	10	1	-21	92
21	Czerkawski	72	195	24	76	26	21	47	182	14.3	3	0	4	0	0	16
16	Buchberger (C)	74	200	30	81	8	30	38	78	10.3	3	0	0	0	4	159
26	Marchant	70	175	23	79	14	19	33	202	6.9	3	0	0	4	11	44
25	Grier	73	232	21	79	15	17	32	89	16.9	2	0	4	0	7	45
2	Mironov	75	220	24	55	6	26	32	147	4.1	1	0	2	0	2	85
17	Murray	74	195	24	82	11	20	31	85	12.9	2	0	1	0	9	16
37	McAmmond	71	185	23	57	12	17	29	106	11.3	6	0	4	0	-15	28
18	Satan	73	185	22	64	17	11	28	90	18.9	2	0	5	0	-4	22
14	Lindgren	74	200	22	69	11	14	25	71	15.5	1	0	2	3	-7	12
23	McGillis	74	220	24	73	6	16	22	139	4.3	2	0	2	1	2	52
24	Marchment	73	205	27	71	3	13	16	89	3.4	0	0	1	0	13	132
4	Lowe	74	190	37	64	1	13	14	46	2.2	0	0	0	0	-1	50
6	Norton	74	200	31	62	2	11	13	68	2.9	0	0	0	0	-7	42
22	Richardson (A)	76	210	27	82	1	11	12	67	1.5	0	0	0	0	9	91

#		*Ht.*	*Wt.*	*Age*	*GP*	*G*	*A*	*Pts*	*Shots*	*S%*	*GW*	*GT*	*PP*	*SH*	*P/M*	*PIM*
85	Klima	72	190	32	16	1	5	6	22	4.5	0	0	0	0	-1	6
8	Petit	73	205	32	18	2	4	6	30	6.7	0	0	0	0	-13	20
5	deVries	75	218	23	37	0	4	4	31	0.0	0	0	0	0	-2	52
20	Oliver	72	190	25	17	1	2	3	22	4.5	0	0	0	0	-8	4
29	DeBrusk	74	215	25	32	2	0	2	10	20.0	0	0	0	0	-6	94
31	Joseph	68	182	29	72	0	2	2	0	0.0	0	0	0	0	0	20
55	Bannister	74	205	22	1	0	1	1	2	0.0	0	0	0	0	-2	0
9	Intranuovo	68	185	23	5	1	0	1	2	50.0	0	0	0	0	0	0
10	Kelly	73	190	18	8	1	0	1	6	16.7	1	0	0	0	-1	6
34	Dufresne	73	206	29	22	0	1	1	10	0.0	0	0	0	0	-1	15
18	Moore	71	175	21	4	0	0	0	1	0.0	0	0	0	0	0	0
35	Millar	74	200	20	1	0	0	0	1	0.0	0	0	0	0	0	2
8	S. Brown	74	205	18	5	0	0	0	2	0.0	0	0	0	0	-1	4
12	Belanger	73	190	27	6	0	0	0	8	0.0	0	0	0	0	-3	0
15	Hulbig	75	215	23	6	0	0	0	4	0.0	0	0	0	0	-1	0
30	Essensa	72	185	31	19	0	0	0	0	0.0	0	0	0	0	0	4
	Bench															18
		73	199	25	82	252	406	658	2521	10.0	36	1	73	9	-9	1368

1996-97 Goaltender Records

	GP	*Min.*	*GA*	*W*	*L*	*T*	*Ave.*	*SA*	*Pct.*	*SO*	*EN*
Bob Essensa	19	868	41	4	8	0	2.83	406	0.899	1	3
Curtis Joseph	72	4100	200	32	29	9	2.93	2144	0.907	6	3
	82	4982	247	36	37	9	2.97	2556	0.903	7	6

Coach: Ron Low 36-37-9

1996-97 Scoring vs. Opposition

	Ana.	*Bost.*	*Buff.*	*Calg.*	*Chi.*	*Col.*	*Dall.*	*Det.*
Arnott	0–2–2	0–1–1	0–1–1	2–0–2	1–3–4	1–1–2	0–0–0	0–2–2
Belanger	———	———	0–0–0	———	———	0–1–1	———	0–0–0
Brown	0–0–0	———	———	———	———	0–0–0	0–0–0	———
Buchberger	0–2–2	0–3–3	0–0–0	1–0–1	1–0–1	1–2–3	0–0–0	0–1–1
Czerkawski	2–0–2	3–2–5	0–0–0	3–0–3	0–1–1	1–1–2	1–0–1	0–0–0
DeBrusk	0–0–0	———	0–0–0	1–0–1	0–0–0	0–0–0	0–0–0	———
de Vries	0–1–1	0–0–0	0–0–0	0–0–0	0–0–0	0–0–0	0–0–0	0–0–0
Dufresne	0–0–0	0–0–0	———	0–0–0	0–0–0	0–0–0	0–0–0	0–0–0
Grier	1–0–1	0–1–1	0–0–0	0–3–3	2–0–2	1–0–1	1–0–1	0–0–0
Hulbig	———	———	———	———	———	———	0–0–0	———
Intranuovo	———	———	———	———	0–0–0	———	———	0–0–0
Kelly	———	———	———	———	0–0–0	———	0–0–0	0–0–0
Klima	0–1–1	———	———	———	———	———	0–1–1	———
Kovalenko	2–0–2	0–0–0	1–2–3	3–1–4	1–2–3	3–1–4	0–2–2	1–1–2
Lindgren	1–0–1	0–0–0	0–0–0	1–1–2	2–0–2	0–1–1	0–0–0	0–0–0
Lowe	0–0–0	———	0–1–1	0–0–0	0–1–1	1–1–2	0–0–0	0–0–0
Marchant	1–1–2	2–1–3	0–2–2	2–1–3	0–0–0	0–2–2	0–1–1	0–1–1
Marchment	0–0–0	0–1–1	0–0–0	1–3–4	1–0–1	0–0–0	0–0–0	———
McAmmond	1–1–2	0–1–1	1–1–2	1–5–6	0–0–0	1–2–3	0–0–0	0–0–0
McGillis	0–0–0	0–0–0	1–2–3	1–1–2	0–0–0	0–1–1	1–0–1	0–0–0
Mironov	0–0–0	0–1–1	0–0–0	0–3–3	0–4–4	0–1–1	1–1–2	1–1–2
Moore	———	———	———	———	———	———	0–0–0	———
Murray	0–1–1	1–0–1	1–0–1	0–3–3	1–2–3	0–0–0	0–0–0	0–0–0
Norton	0–1–1	0–0–0	0–0–0	0–2–2	0–0–0	0–1–1	0–0–0	1–0–1
Oliver	0–0–0	0–0–0	0–1–1	0–0–0	0–0–0	0–0–0	———	0–0–0
Petit	———	1–0–1	———	———	0–0–0	1–2–3	———	0–0–0
Richardson	0–0–0	0–0–0	0–1–1	0–4–4	0–1–1	0–0–0	0–0–0	0–0–0
Satan	0–0–0	2–0–2	1–0–1	2–3–5	0–0–0	0–0–0	0–0–0	0–0–0
Smyth	0–0–0	1–1–2	2–0–2	2–1–3	1–0–1	1–1–2	1–2–3	1–0–1
Weight	0–2–2	0–3–3	0–2–2	3–4–7	1–2–3	0–2–2	1–2–3	1–0–1

	Flor.	*Hart.*	*L.A.*	*Mont.*	*N.J.*	*NYI.*	*NYR.*	*Ott.*
Arnott	0–3–3	1–0–1	2–6–8	2–0–2	1–1–2	0–1–1	0–3–3	0–1–1
Bannister	———	———	———	———	———	———	———	———
Belanger	———	———	———	———	———	———	———	———
Brown	———	———	0–0–0	0–0–0	———	———	———	———
Buchberger	0–1–1	0–2–2	0–2–2	0–0–0	0–0–0	0–0–0	0–1–1	0–0–0
Czerkawski	1–0–1	0–0–0	3–1–4	0–0–0	0–0–0	0–1–1	0–2–2	2–1–3
DeBrusk	0–0–0	0–0–0	0–0–0	0–0–0	0–0–0	0–0–0	0–0–0	0–0–0
de Vries	———	0–0–0	0–1–1	0–0–0	0–0–0	0–0–0	———	———
Dufresne	———	———	0–0–0	———	———	0–1–1	———	———
Grier	1–0–1	0–1–1	1–0–1	1–0–1	0–0–0	0–0–0	0–0–0	0–1–1
Hulbig	———	0–0–0	0–0–0	———	0–0–0	———	———	———
Intranuovo	———	———	———	———	———	———	———	———
Kelly	———	———	———	———	———	———	———	———
Klima	———	0–0–0	0–0–0	1–2–3	0–0–0	———	———	———
Kovalenko	0–1–1	0–0–0	6–1–7	0–1–1	0–1–1	1–0–1	2–0–2	0–1–1
Lindgren	0–1–1	2–1–3	0–0–0	0–0–0	0–1–1	0–0–0	0–0–0	0–2–2
Lowe	0–2–2	0–0–0	0–1–1	0–0–0	0–0–0	0–0–0	0–0–0	0–0–0
Marchant	1–0–1	0–0–0	1–1–2	0–1–1	0–0–0	0–0–0	0–0–0	1–0–1
Marchment	0–0–0	0–1–1	0–1–1	0–0–0	0–0–0	0–0–0	0–1–1	0–0–0
McAmmond	0–0–0	0–0–0	0–1–1	1–0–1	———	1–0–1	0–0–0	0–0–0
McGillis	1–0–1	0–0–0	0–0–0	0–1–1	0–0–0	0–0–0	0–0–0	0–0–0
Mironov	0–1–1	0–1–1	0–1–1	0–0–0	0–1–1	———	0–2–2	0–3–3
Moore	———	———	———	———	———	———	———	———
Murray	0–1–1	1–0–1	3–2–5	0–2–2	0–0–0	0–0–0	0–1–1	1–0–1
Norton	0–0–0	0–0–0	0–1–1	0–0–0	0–0–0	0–0–0	0–0–0	0–0–0
Oliver	———	0–0–0	———	———	0–1–1	———	———	———
Petit	0–0–0	———	0–1–1	———	0–0–0	———	———	0–0–0
Richardson	0–0–0	0–0–0	1–1–2	0–0–0	0–0–0	0–0–0	0–0–0	0–1–1
Satan	1–0–1	0–1–1	1–2–3	0–0–0	1–0–1	0–0–0	2–0–2	1–1–2
Smyth	2–1–3	0–1–1	1–3–4	1–0–1	1–0–1	0–0–0	2–1–3	2–2–4
Weight	0–2–2	2–1–3	1–7–8	0–3–3	0–1–1	0–1–1	1–3–4	2–0–2

	Phil.	*Phoe.*	*Pitt.*	*S.J.*	*St.L.*	*Tampa*	*Tor.*	*Van.*	*Wash.*
Arnott	0–0–0	2–3–5	1–1–2	1–0–1	1–1–2	0–1–1	1–3–4	2–4–6	1–0–1
Bannister	———	———	———	———	———	———	———	0–1–1	———
Belanger	———	0–0–0	———	———	———	———	0–0–0	0–0–0	———
Brown	———	———	———	———	———	———	———	———	———
Buchberger	1–1–2	0–3–3	0–0–0	2–4–6	1–0–1	1–0–1	0–3–3	0–5–5	0–0–0
Czerkawski	1–0–1	1–2–3	0–2–2	2–1–3	0–0–0	1–1–2	4–1–5	0–3–3	1–2–3
DeBrusk	0–0–0	0–0–0	0–0–0	0–0–0	1–0–1	0–0–0	0–0–0	0–0–0	0–0–0
de Vries	0–0–0	0–0–0	0–1–1	0–0–0	0–1–1	0–0–0	0–0–0	0–0–0	0–0–0
Dufresne	———	0–0–0	———	0–0–0	0–0–0	———	0–0–0	0–0–0	———
Grier	1–1–2	0–1–1	0–1–1	0–1–1	2–2–4	2–1–3	1–1–2	0–2–2	1–1–2
Hulbig	0–0–0	———	———	———	0–0–0	———	———	———	———
Intranuovo	———	0–0–0	———	———	———	———	———	1–0–1	———
Kelly	———	1–0–1	———	0–0–0	———	———	———	0–0–0	———
Klima	0–0–0	0–0–0	———	0–0–0	0–0–0	0–0–0	———	0–1–1	———
Kovalenko	1–0–1	3–1–4	1–1–2	2–4–6	2–1–3	0–1–1	0–4–4	3–1–4	0–0–0
Lindgren	1–1–2	1–0–1	0–1–1	2–2–4	0–0–0	0–1–1	0–1–1	1–0–1	0–1–1
Lowe	0–0–0	0–0–0	0–0–0	0–0–0	0–1–1	0–1–1	0–1–1	0–2–2	0–2–2
Marchant	0–0–0	1–0–1	0–0–0	2–3–5	0–0–0	0–1–1	1–2–3	1–2–3	1–0–1
Marchment	0–0–0	0–3–3	1–0–1	0–0–0	0–1–1	0–0–0	0–1–1	0–0–0	0–0–0
McAmmond	0–0–0	2–1–3	0–1–1	0–0–0	0–1–1	0–0–0	1–2–3	3–1–4	0–0–0
McGillis	0–2–2	0–0–0	0–0–0	0–5–5	0–0–0	0–1–1	0–1–1	0–2–2	2–0–2
Millar	———	———	———	———	———	0–0–0	———	———	———
Mironov	0–1–1	1–0–1	0–1–1	0–0–0	0–0–0	0–0–0	2–2–4	1–2–3	———
Moore	———	0–0–0	———	0–0–0	———	———	———	———	———
Murray	1–0–1	0–1–1	0–1–1	1–1–2	0–2–2	0–1–1	0–1–1	1–0–1	0–1–1
Norton	0–1–1	0–0–0	0–0–0	0–2–2	0–0–0	0–0–0	1–2–3	0–0–0	0–1–1
Oliver	———	0–0–0	———	———	1–0–1	———	0–0–0	0–0–0	———
Petit	———	0–0–0	0–0–0	0–0–0	0–0–0	0–0–0	0–0–0	0–1–1	———
Richardson	0–1–1	0–0–0	0–0–0	0–1–1	0–0–0	0–0–0	0–0–0	0–1–1	0–0–0
Satan	1–1–2	0–0–0	1–0–1	2–1–3	0–2–2	0–0–0	2–0–2	0–0–0	0–0–0
Smyth	1–2–3	3–1–4	2–0–2	5–2–7	0–2–2	1–0–1	4–0–4	4–1–5	1–1–2
Weight	0–1–1	0–7–7	1–2–3	2–4–6	4–3–7	0–1–1	0–4–4	2–1–3	0–3–3

1996–97 Goaltender Records vs. Opposition

	GP	*Min.*	*GA*	*EN*	*SO*	*Ave.*	*W–L–T*	*Opposition*
Bob Essensa	1	20	0	2	0	0.00	0–0–0	Anaheim
	1	62	3	0	0	2.90	0–1–0	Calgary
	1	60	3	1	0	3.00	0–1–0	Chicago
	1	20	2	0	0	6.00	0–0–0	Colorado
	1	49	0	0	0	0.00	0–0–0	Dallas
	2	71	1	1	0	0.85	0–1–0	Detroit
	1	49	3	0	0	3.67	0–1–0	Florida
	3	180	13	0	0	4.33	1–2–0	Los Angeles
	1	49	3	0	0	3.67	0–0–0	New Jersey
	1	17	3	0	0	10.59	0–0–0	N.Y. Islanders
	1	59	4	1	0	4.07	0–1–0	Pittsburgh
	1	60	3	0	0	3.00	1–0–0	San Jose
	1	26	1	0	0	2.31	0–0–0	Toronto
	2	87	1	0	1	0.69	1–1–0	Vancouver
	1	60	1	0	0	1.00	1–0–0	Washington
Curtis Joseph	5	285	17	1	0	3.58	0–4–1	Anaheim
	2	120	3	0	1	1.50	2–0–0	Boston
	2	120	4	0	0	2.00	2–0–0	Buffalo
	4	240	11	1	0	2.75	3–1–0	Calgary
	3	184	10	0	0	3.26	1–1–1	Chicago
	5	286	17	2	0	3.57	0–4–1	Colorado
	4	189	18	0	0	5.71	0–4–0	Dallas
	3	178	9	0	1	3.03	0–1–2	Detroit
	2	71	3	0	1	2.54	1–0–0	Florida
	2	122	3	0	0	1.48	2–0–0	Hartford
	3	185	4	0	0	1.30	2–0–1	Los Angeles
	2	122	8	0	0	3.93	0–2–0	Montreal
	2	70	6	0	0	5.14	0–2–0	New Jersey
	2	103	5	0	1	2.91	1–1–0	N.Y. Islanders
	1	125	6	0	0	2.88	1–0–1	N.Y. Rangers
	2	120	2	0	1	1.00	2–0–0	Ottawa
	2	124	11	0	0	5.32	0–2–0	Philadelphia
	4	240	11	0	0	2.75	3–1–0	Phoenix
	1	60	2	0	0	2.00	1–0–0	Pittsburgh
	5	299	10	0	0	2.01	3–2–0	San Jose
	4	239	9	0	0	2.26	2–2–0	St. Louis
	2	125	3	0	0	1.44	1–0–1	Tampa Bay
	4	214	16	0	0	4.49	3–1–0	Toronto
	4	218	11	0	1	3.03	1–1–1	Vancouver
	1	60	1	0	0	1.00	1–0–0	Washington

Overall Record vs. Opponents

Opponent	*Home*	*Road*	*Overall*	*GF-GA*	*Opponent*
Anaheim	0–2–0	0–2–1	0–4–1	8–18	Anaheim
Boston	1–0–0	1–0–0	2–0–0	10–3	Boston
Buffalo	1–0–0	1–0–0	2–0–0	7–4	Buffalo
Calgary	2–0–0	1–2–0	3–2–0	23–14	Calgary
Chicago	1–0–1	0–2–0	1–2–1	11–14	Chicago
Colorado	0–2–1	0–2–0	0–4–1	11–21	Colorado
Dallas	0–2–0	0–2–0	0–4–0	6–18	Dallas
Detroit	0–1–1	0–1–1	0–2–2	5–11	Detroit
Florida	1–0–0	0–1–0	1–1–0	7–6	Florida
Hartford	1–0–0	1–0–0	2–0–0	6–3	Hartford
Los Angeles	2–1–0	1–1–1	3–2–1	20–17	Los Angeles
Montreal	0–1–0	0–1–0	0–2–0	6–8	Montreal
New Jersey	0–1–0	0–1–0	0–2–0	3–9	New Jersey
Islanders	1–0–0	0–1–0	1–1–0	2–8	Islanders
Rangers	1–0–0	0–0–1	1–0–1	7–6	Rangers
Ottawa	1–0–0	1–0–0	2–0–0	9–2	Ottawa
Philadelphia	0–1–0	0–1–0	0–2–0	8–11	Philadelphia
Phoenix	1–1–0	2–0–0	3–1–0	15–11	Phoenix

Opponent	*Home*	*Road*	*Overall*	*GF-GA*	*Opponent*
Pittsburgh	1–0–0	0–1–0	1–1–0	7–7	Pittsburgh
San Jose	2–1–0	2–1–0	4–2–0	21–13	San Jose
St. Louis	0–2–0	2–0–0	2–2–0	12–9	St. Louis
Tampa Bay	1–0–0	0–0–1	1–0–1	5–3	Tampa Bay
Toronto	2–0–0	1–1–0	3–1–0	17–17	Toronto
Vancouver	1–1–1	1–1–0	2–2–1	19–12	Vancouver
Washington	1–0–0	1–0–0	2–0–0	7–2	Washington

1996-97 Schedule Results

Oct. 4	Buffalo	3	at	Edmonton	4
Oct. 6	Vancouver	0	at	Edmonton	2
Oct. 8	Edmonton	4	at	Toronto	2
Oct. 9	Edmonton	0	at	Detroit	2
Oct. 11	St. Louis	3	at	Edmonton	1
Oct. 14	Edmonton	6	at	Phoenix	3
Oct. 15	Edmonton	2	at	Colorado	7
Oct. 20	Edmonton	3	at	Calgary	6
Oct. 22	Pittsburgh	2	at	Edmonton	5
Oct. 24	Edmonton	8	at	Los Angeles	2
Oct. 26	Colorado	4	at	Edmonton	2
Oct. 30	Phoenix	1	at	Edmonton	4
Nov. 1	Vancouver	5	at	Edmonton	4 OT
Nov. 3	Edmonton	2	at	Chicago	4
Nov. 6	Edmonton	2	at	Pittsburgh	5
Nov. 7	Edmonton	6	at	Boston	0
Nov. 9	Edmonton	3	at	Toronto	7
Nov. 11	Edmonton	2	at	Montreal	3 OT
Nov. 13	Edmonton	4	at	Ottawa	0
Nov. 17	Dallas	7	at	Edmonton	3
Nov. 19	Chicago	4	at	Edmonton	4 OT
Nov. 21	Rangers	2	at	Edmonton	3
Nov. 23	Calgary	2	at	Edmonton	3
Nov. 26	Edmonton	10	at	Calgary	1
Nov. 27	Los Angeles	5	at	Edmonton	1
Nov. 29	Edmonton	4	at	San Jose	2
Dec. 1	Edmonton	2	at	Anaheim	4
Dec. 4	Edmonton	0	at	Colorado	2
Dec. 6	Ottawa	2	at	Edmonton	5
Dec. 8	St. Louis	3	at	Edmonton	2
Dec. 10	Edmonton	0	at	Detroit	0 OT
Dec. 12	Edmonton	2	at	Tampa Bay	2 OT
Dec. 15	Edmonton	3	at	Florida	6
Dec. 18	Colorado	4	at	Edmonton	4 OT
Dec. 20	New Jersey	3	at	Edmonton	2
Dec. 22	Detroit	6	at	Edmonton	2
Dec. 23	Edmonton	7	at	Vancouver	0
Dec. 27	Philadelphia	6	at	Edmonton	4
Dec. 28	San Jose	3	at	Edmonton	5
Dec. 30	Los Angeles	1	at	Edmonton	2
Jan. 3	Toronto	3	at	Edmonton	4
Jan. 7	Edmonton	5	at	St. Louis	2
Jan. 8	Edmonton	1	at	Chicago	4
Jan. 11	San Jose	2	at	Edmonton	1
Jan. 12	Hartford	1	at	Edmonton	2 OT
Jan. 15	Florida	0	at	Edmonton	4
Jan. 21	Edmonton	4	at	Rangers	4 OT
Jan. 22	Edmonton	1	at	Islanders	8
Jan. 24	Edmonton	3	at	Buffalo	1
Jan. 26	Edmonton	3	at	Washington	1
Jan. 29	San Jose	1	at	Edmonton	3
Jan. 31	Islanders	0	at	Edmonton	1
Feb. 5	Calgary	2	at	Edmonton	5
Feb. 8	Anaheim	2	at	Edmonton	1 OT
Feb. 9	Washington	1	at	Edmonton	4
Feb. 12	Boston	3	at	Edmonton	4
Feb. 13	Edmonton	2	at	Calgary	3 OT
Feb. 15	Edmonton	2	at	Los Angeles	2 OT
Feb. 17	Edmonton	1	at	Anaheim	5
Feb. 19	Toronto	5	at	Edmonton	6
Feb. 21	Colorado	4	at	Edmonton	3 OT
Feb. 23	Edmonton	1	at	Dallas	6
Feb. 26	Edmonton	3	at	Anaheim	3 OT
Feb. 27	Edmonton	3	at	Los Angeles	6
Mar. 1	Montreal	5	at	Edmonton	4
Mar. 4	Los Angeles	1	at	Edmonton	4
Mar. 7	Edmonton	1	at	Dallas	2
Mar. 9	Edmonton	4	at	St. Louis	1
Mar. 11	Edmonton	1	at	New Jersey	6
Mar. 13	Edmonton	4	at	Philadelphia	5 OT
Mar. 15	Edmonton	4	at	Hartford	2
Mar. 19	Tampa Bay	1	at	Edmonton	3
Mar. 23	Anaheim	4	at	Edmonton	1
Mar. 24	Edmonton	5	at	San Jose	1
Mar. 28	Edmonton	3	at	San Jose	4
Mar. 29	Edmonton	3	at	Phoenix	1
Mar. 31	Dallas	3	at	Edmonton	1
April 3	Chicago	2	at	Edmonton	4
April 5	Vancouver	2	at	Edmonton	2 OT
April 9	Detroit	3	at	Edmonton	3 OT
April 11	Phoenix	6	at	Edmonton	6
April 12	Edmonton	4	at	Vancouver	5

1996-97 Playoff Scoring

#		*GP*	*G*	*A*	*Pts*	*Shots*	*S%*	*GW*	*OT*	*PP*	*SH*	*P/M*	*PIM*
39	Doug Weight	12	3	8	11	54	5.6	0	0	0	0	0	8
94	Ryan Smyth	12	5	5	10	48	10.4	2	1	1	0	-4	12
2	Boris Mironov	12	2	8	10	31	6.5	0	0	2	0	-6	16
7	Jason Arnott	12	3	6	9	27	11.1	0	0	1	0	-3	18
16	Kelly Buchberger	12	5	2	7	19	26.3	1	1	0	0	-1	16
51	Andrei Kovalenko	12	4	3	7	35	11.4	0	0	3	0	1	6
26	Todd Marchant	12	4	2	6	40	10.0	1	1	0	3	2	12
23	Dan McGillis	12	0	5	5	20	0.0	0	0	0	0	8	24
25	Mike Grier	12	3	1	4	21	14.3	1	0	1	0	-2	4

#		GP	G	A	Pts	Shots	S%	GW	OT	PP	SH	P/M	PIM
14	Mats Lindgren	12	0	4	4	22	0.0	0	0	0	0	-2	0
21	Mariusz Czerkawski	12	2	1	3	19	10.5	0	0	0	0	-2	10
17	Rem Murray	12	1	2	3	7	14.3	0	0	0	0	-1	4
22	Luke Richardson	12	0	2	2	6	0.0	0	0	0	0	-4	14
15	Joe Hulbig	6	0	1	1	5	0.0	0	0	0	0	2	2
5	Greg de Vries	12	0	1	1	16	0.0	0	0	0	0	4	8
4	Kevin Lowe	1	0	0	0	0	0.0	0	0	0	0	-1	0
34	Donald Dufresne	3	0	0	0	0	0.0	0	0	0	0	0	0
24	Bryan Marchment	3	0	0	0	2	0.0	0	0	0	0	-3	4
35	Bryan Muir	5	0	0	0	7	0.0	0	0	0	0	-2	4
85	Petr Klima	6	0	0	0	2	0.0	0	0	0	0	0	4
29	Louie DeBrusk	6	0	0	0	1	0.0	0	0	0	0	0	4
10	Steve Kelly	6	0	0	0	2	0.0	0	0	0	0	1	2
31	Curtis Joseph	12	0	0	0	0	0.0	0	0	0	0	0	2
55	Drew Bannister	12	0	0	0	9	0.0	0	0	0	0	-4	30
		12	32	51	83	393	8.1	5	3	8	3	-3	204

1996-97 Playoff Goaltending

	GP	Min.	GA	W	L	Ave.	SA	Pct.	SO	EN
Curtis Joseph	12	767	36	5	7	3.00	405	0.911	2	1
	12	771	37	5	7	3.08	406	0.909	2	1

Date			Result			Winning Goaltender	Winning Goal
April 16, 1997	Edmonton	3	at	Dallas	5	Andy Moog	Mike Modano
April 18, 1997	Edmonton	4	at	Dallas	0	Curtis Joseph	Mike Grier
April 20, 1997	Dallas	3	at	Edmonton	4	Curtis Joseph	Kelly Buchberger[1]
April 22, 1997	Dallas	4	at	Edmonton	3	Andy Moog	Jamie Langenbruner
April 25, 1997	Edmonton	1	at	Dallas	0	Curtis Joseph	Ryan Smyth[2]
April 27, 1997	Dallas	3	at	Edmonton	2	Andy Moog	Mike Modano
April 29, 1997	Edmonton	4	at	Dallas	3	Curtis Joseph	Todd Marchant[3]
May 2, 1997	Edmonton	1	at	Colorado	5	Patrick Roy	Claude Lemieux
May 4, 1997	Edmonton	1	at	Colorado	4	Patrick Roy	Valeri Kamensky
May 7, 1997	Colorado	3	at	Edmonton	4	Curtis Joseph	Ryan Smyth
May 9, 1997	Colorado	3	at	Edmonton	2	Patrick Roy	Claude Lemieux[4]
May 11, 1997	Edmonton	3	at	Colorado	4	Patrick Roy	Adam Deadmarsh

[1]9:15 of overtime [3]12:26 of overtime
[2]20:22 of overtime [4]8:35 of overtime

Table 14. Oilers All-Time Playoff Record

	Home					Road					Overall				
Season	*GP*	*W*	*L*	*GF*	*GA*	*GP*	*W*	*L*	*GF*	*GA*	*GP*	*W*	*L*	*GF*	*GA*
2000-01	*3*	*1*	*2*	*5*	*7*	*3*	*1*	*2*	*8*	*9*	*6*	*2*	*4*	*13*	*16*
1999-00	*2*	*1*	*1*	*8*	*6*	*3*	*0*	*3*	*3*	*8*	*5*	*1*	*4*	*11*	*14*
1998-99	*2*	*0*	*2*	*4*	*6*	*2*	*0*	*2*	*3*	*5*	*4*	*0*	*4*	*7*	*11*
1997-98	*5*	*1*	*4*	*8*	*12*	*7*	*4*	*3*	*16*	*13*	*12*	*5*	*7*	*24*	*25*
1996-97	*5*	*2*	*3*	*15*	*16*	*7*	*3*	*4*	*17*	*21*	*12*	*5*	*7*	*32*	*37*
1991-92	*8*	*5*	*3*	*25*	*20*	*8*	*3*	*5*	*24*	*34*	*16*	*8*	*8*	*49*	*54*
1990-91	*9*	*6*	*3*	*32*	*23*	*9*	*3*	*6*	*25*	*37*	*18*	*9*	*9*	*57*	*60*
1989-90	*11*	*8*	*3*	*47*	*26*	*11*	*8*	*3*	*46*	*34*	*22*	*16*	*6*	*93*	*60*
1988-89	*3*	*2*	*1*	*9*	*7*	*4*	*1*	*3*	*11*	*18*	*7*	*3*	*4*	*20*	*25*
*1987-88**	*11*	*11*	*0*	*55*	*28*	*8*	*5*	*2*	*32*	*28*	*19*	*16*	*2*	*87*	*56*
1986-87	*12*	*9*	*3*	*52*	*33*	*9*	*7*	*2*	*37*	*24*	*21*	*16*	*5*	*89*	*57*
1985-86	*6*	*3*	*3*	*22*	*20*	*4*	*3*	*1*	*19*	*10*	*10*	*6*	*4*	*41*	*30*
1984-85	*11*	*11*	*0*	*69*	*29*	*7*	*4*	*3*	*29*	*28*	*18*	*15*	*3*	*98*	*57*
1983-84	*11*	*9*	*2*	*65*	*33*	*8*	*6*	*2*	*29*	*23*	*19*	*15*	*4*	*94*	*56*
1982-83	*9*	*6*	*3*	*48*	*30*	*7*	*4*	*3*	*31*	*25*	*16*	*10*	*6*	*79*	*55*
1981-82	*3*	*1*	*2*	*15*	*19*	*2*	*1*	*1*	*8*	*8*	*5*	*2*	*3*	*23*	*27*
1980-81	*4*	*2*	*2*	*17*	*14*	*5*	*3*	*2*	*18*	*21*	*9*	*5*	*4*	*35*	*35*
1979-80	*1*	*0*	*1*	*2*	*3*	*2*	*0*	*2*	*4*	*9*	*3*	*0*	*3*	*6*	*12*
	116	*78*	*38*	*498*	*332*	*106*	*56*	*49*	*360*	*355*	*222*	*134*	*87*	*858*	*687*

*The above win-loss totals do not include the game of May 24, 1988 which was abandoned with 3:23 remaining in the third period due to a power failure. However the total number of games played and the total number of goals scored and allowed are included in the above totals.

Table 15. Oilers All-Time Playoff Special Teams

	Powerplay				Penalty Killing			
Year	*Adv*	*PPGF*	*%*	*SHGA*	*Dis*	*PPGA*	*%*	*SHGF*
2001	31	5	16.1	0	26	4	84.6	0
2000	25	3	12.0	0	26	2	92.3	1
1999	17	2	11.8	0	22	2	90.9	0
1998	71	8	11.3	1	67	7	89.6	0
1997	55	8	14.5	1	61	10	83.6	3
1992	78	14	17.9	0	90	17	81.1	1
1991	91	12	13.2	2	95	21	77.9	0
1990	99	21	21.2	2	98	14	85.7	4
1989	32	6	18.8	1	36	11	69.4	1
1988	113	30	26.5	5	111	19	82.9	2
1987	91	17	18.7	1	84	14	83.3	5
1986	39	8	20.5	2	51	8	84.3	4
1985	78	15	19.2	4	90	16	82.2	6
1984	76	17	22.4	3	89	20	77.5	3
1983	72	14	19.4	2	74	18	75.7	10
1982	18	3	16.7	0	26	9	65.4	3
1981	43	9	20.9	2	45	15	66.7	1
1980	16	1	6.3	0	11	2	81.8	0

1997-98

Ron Low returned behind the bench as the Oilers head coach with Bob McCammon and Ted Green as associate coaches. Green took over the position left vacant by Kevin Primeau, who had left for Europe to coach.

The Oilers' top draft choice this year was Michel Riesen, the first player ever to be drafted out of the Swiss League. In 1996-97 playing for Biel of that league he scored 32 points in 38 games.

With the Oilers sporting a record of 11–20–9 Sather made a series of deals hoping to improve his club. On December 30, the Oilers traded former first round picks Jason Bonsignore and Steve Kelly along with hard hitting defenseman Bryan Marchment to Tampa Bay for offensive defenseman Roman Hamrlik and Edmonton native Paul Comrie.

Five days later Sather traded another first round draft choice, underachieving Jason Arnott, and defenseman Bryan Muir to New Jersey for Valeri Zelepukin and Bill Guerin. Two days later on January 6, Sather picked up veteran Tony Hrkac on waivers. All three players would add experience and talent to the young team.

In one other deal, which Sather engineered on January 9, prior to a game with Anaheim, Sather traded defenseman Drew Bannister to the Mighty Ducks for defenseman Bobby Dollas. With Kevin Lowe out of the lineup much of the season, Dollas would add much experience to a very young Oiler blueline. Following this flurry of trades the team went on a six game winning streak. The Oilers were 16–22–9 (.436) at the All-Star break.

On March 13, 1998, a group of 17 local investors stalled a bid by Houston investor Les Alexander that would have seen the team moved to Houston in the 1998-99 season. The Alberta Treasury Branches had seized the team from former owner Peter Pocklington and had been accepting bids for the team. The number of individuals in the ownership group would grow to 37 by the end of the season.

At the trading deadline, Glen Sather traded last year's playoff stalwart Dan McGillis to Philadelphia for Janne Niinimaa. He along with Mironov and Hamrlik would give the Oilers three of the league's top offensive defensemen.

The Oilers finished third in the Pacific Division, 15 points behind division leading Colorado. Their 215 goals scored were the lowest in the team's history (excluding the strike shortened season) and they finished 15th in offense. The 223 goals against was a record low for the team (excluding the strike shortened season). Edmonton finished 16th in defense, and Curtis Joseph recorded a team record eight shutouts.

The Oilers suffered through a spate of injuries this season. Mike Grier missed a number of games with a sprained left knee while Ryan Smyth sat out 15 games with a torn ligament in his left knee. The defense was particularly hard hit as Kevin Lowe missed all but seven games with an inner ear infection while Drake Berehowsky was sidelined with a separated right shoulder and Bryan Marchment was suspended for three games before undergoing anal surgery. Rugged winger Bill Huard suffered through three separate injuries. Huard first missed nine games with a sprained right knee, and then after returning to the roster he broke his left hand in a fight, missing 24 more games. After only a few games back he was rammed into the boards and broke his right wrist. Smyth, Berehowsky and Huard did not miss as many games as they might have, thanks to the Olympic break.

Doug Weight led the team in scoring for the fifth consecutive year, with 70 points. Excluding the strike shortened season this was the second lowest point total for the team's scoring leader since 1980. However due to an overall drop in league offense, this was good enough to place him 21st overall in the scoring race. Jaromir Jagr of Pittsburgh was the only player to register over 100 points this season, finishing with 102. Not since the 1969-70 season, when Bobby Orr led the NHL in scoring with 120 points, did the league have only one player score in excess of 100 points, excluding 1994-95 when each team played only 48 games. It might be interesting to note that Jaromir Jagr also led the league in scoring in 1994-95, with 70 points, which was the same total Doug Weight registered in 79 games this year.

In the first round of the playoffs the Oilers met the Colorado Avalanche. In the only series to go seven games in the conference quarterfinals the Oilers fell behind the Avalanche three games to one but then came back to win the last three games—the final two by shutouts—to win the series.

After defeating Colorado the Oilers went up against league champion Dallas, who had been knocked out of the playoffs the previous season by the Oilers. Though the Oilers were an improved team from last year they were no match for the aging but disciplined Stars, losing four games to one, setting a team record for the least number of goals in a five game series with five.

1997-98 Regular Season Scoring

#		Ht.	Wt.	Age	GP	G	A	Pts	Shots	S%	GW	GT	PP	SH	P/M	PIM
39	Weight (A)	71	200	26	79	26	44	70	205	12.7	4	0	9	0	1	69
37	McAmmond	71	185	24	77	19	31	50	128	14.8	3	0	8	0	9	46
2	Mironov (A)	75	220	25	81	16	30	46	203	7.9	1	1	10	1	-8	100
9	Guerin	74	210	27	40	13	16	29	130	10.0	2	0	8	0	1	80
26	Marchant	70	175	24	76	14	21	35	194	7.2	3	0	2	1	9	71
94	Smyth	73	195	21	65	20	13	33	205	9.8	2	2	10	0	-24	44
14	Lindgren	74	200	23	82	13	13	26	131	9.9	3	0	1	3	0	42
22	Hamrlik	74	202	24	41	6	20	26	112	5.4	3	0	4	1	3	48
33	McGillis	74	225	25	67	10	15	25	119	8.4	3	1	5	0	-17	74
18	Fraser	74	206	25	29	12	11	23	61	19.7	2	0	6	0	6	6
51	Kovalenko	70	215	27	59	6	17	23	89	6.7	2	1	1	0	-14	28
16	Buchberger (C)	74	200	31	82	6	17	23	86	7.0	1	0	1	1	-10	122
20	Hrkac	71	170	31	36	8	11	19	43	18.6	1	0	4	0	3	10
17	Murray	74	195	25	61	9	9	18	59	15.3	0	0	2	2	-9	39
7	Arnott	75	220	23	35	5	13	18	100	5.0	0	0	1	0	-16	78
25	Grier	73	225	22	66	9	6	15	90	10.0	1	0	1	0	-3	73
21	Zelepukin	72	200	29	33	2	10	12	47	4.3	0	0	0	0	-2	57
5	de Vries	75	218	24	65	7	4	11	53	13.2	0	0	1	0	-17	80
24	Niinimaa	73	220	22	11	1	8	9	19	5.3	0	0	1	0	7	6
6	Dollas	74	212	32	30	2	5	7	27	7.4	0	0	0	0	6	22
15	Berehowsky	73	211	25	67	1	6	7	58	1.7	1	0	1	0	1	169
19	Devereaux	74	195	19	38	1	4	5	27	3.7	0	0	0	0	-5	6
32	Millar	74	200	20	11	4	0	4	10	40.0	0	0	1	0	-3	8
12	Hulbig	75	215	24	17	2	2	4	8	25.0	1	0	0	0	-1	2
8	Whitney	69	160	25	9	1	3	4	19	5.3	0	0	0	0	-1	0
24	Marchment	73	205	28	27	0	4	4	23	0.0	0	0	0	0	-2	58
9	Watt	74	212	21	14	1	2	3	14	7.1	1	0	0	0	-4	4
8	Musil	75	215	33	17	1	2	3	8	12.5	1	0	0	1	1	8
31	Joseph	70	182	30	71	0	2	2	0	0.0	0	0	0	0	0	4
10	Kelly	73	190	21	23	0	2	2	8	0.0	0	0	0	0	-4	8
55	Bannister	74	200	23	34	0	2	2	27	0.0	0	0	0	0	-7	42
23	Brown	74	205	21	18	0	1	1	9	0.0	0	0	0	0	-1	43
28	Huard	73	215	30	30	0	1	1	12	0.0	0	0	0	0	-5	72
40	Ferguson	73	195	24	1	0	0	0	0	0.0	0	0	0	0	1	0
21	Benysek	74	190	22	2	0	0	0	0	0.0	0	0	0	0	-2	0
29	Bowen	76	215	24	4	0	0	0	3	0.0	0	0	0	0	0	10
36	Bonvie	71	205	24	4	0	0	0	0	0.0	0	0	0	0	0	27
4	Lowe	74	200	38	7	0	0	0	5	0.0	0	0	0	0	-3	22
6	Muir	76	220	24	7	0	0	0	6	0.0	0	0	0	0	0	17
38	Sandwith	76	210	25	8	0	0	0	4	0.0	0	0	0	0	-4	6
27	Laraque	75	235	21	11	0	0	0	4	0.0	0	0	0	0	-4	59
30	Essensa	72	185	32	16	0	0	0	0	0.0	0	0	0	0	0	0

#		Ht.	Wt.	Age	GP	G	A	Pts	Shots	S%	GW	GT	PP	SH	P/M	PIM
8	Friedman	73	195	26	16	0	0	0	8	0.0	0	0	0	0	0	20
	Bench															10
		73	203	25	82	215	345	560	2345	9.2	35	5	87	10	-118	1680

1997-98 Goaltender Records

	GP	Min.	GA	W	L	T	Ave.	SA	Pct.	SO	EN
Bob Essensa	16	825	35	6	6	1	2.55	404	.913	0	2
Curtis Joseph	71	4132	181	29	31	9	2.63	1901	.905	8	6
	82	4957	216	35	37	10	2.61	2305	.903	8	8

Coach: Ron Low 35-37-10

Scoring vs. Opposition

	Ana.	Bost.	Buff.	Calg.	Caro.	Chic.	Col.	Dall.	Detr.
Arnott	0–0–0	0–0–0	0–1–1	0–0–0	0–0–0	0–0–0	0–2–2	0–1–1	1–0–1
Bannister	0–0–0	0–0–0	0–0–0	———	0–0–0	0–0–0	0–0–0	0–0–0	0–0–0
Benysek	———	———	———	0–0–0	———	———	———	———	———
Berehowsky	0–0–0	0–0–0	0–0–0	0–0–0	0–0–0	0–1–1	0–0–0	0–0–0	0–1–1
Bonvie	———	———	———	0–0–0	———	———	———	———	———
Bowen	———	0–0–0	———	———	———	———	———	———	———
Brown	0–0–0	———	———	0–0–0	———	0–0–0	———	0–0–0	0–0–0
Buchberger	0–1–1	0–0–0	0–1–1	0–2–2	0–0–0	0–1–1	0–0–0	0–1–1	1–2–3
Devereaux	0–0–0	0–0–0	0–1–1	0–1–1	0–0–0	0–0–0	0–0–0	0–0–0	0–0–0
de Vries	0–0–0	0–0–0	0–0–0	0–0–0	0–1–1	1–0–1	0–0–0	0–0–0	0–1–1
Dollas	1–0–1	———	0–0–0	0–0–0	———	0–0–0	0–1–1	0–1–1	———
Fraser	2–1–3		0–0–0	1–2–3	1–0–1	0–1–1	2–0–2	0–0–0	0–1–1
Friedman	0–0–0	———	———	———	———	0–0–0	0–0–0	0–0–0	0–0–0
Grier	1–0–1	0–1–1	1–0–1	1–1–2	1–0–1	———	0–0–0	0–0–0	0–0–0
Guerin	2–2–4	———	0–0–0	0–2–2	0–0–0	0–0–0	2–1–3	0–0–0	1–0–1
Hamrlik	0–1–1	———	0–0–0	0–1–1	0–0–0	1–1–2	0–0–0	0–1–1	0–0–0
Hrkac	2–2–4	———	0–0–0	1–0–1	0–0–0	0–1–1	1–0–1	0–0–0	0–0–0
Huard	0–0–0	———	0–0–0	0–0–0	0–0–0	———	0–0–0	0–0–0	0–0–0
Hulbig	0–0–0	———	———	0–0–0	———	0–0–0	———	0–0–0	1–0–1
Kelly	0–0–0	0–0–0	0–0–0	———	0–0–0	0–0–0	0–0–0	0–0–0	0–0–0
Kovalenko	0–1–1	0–1–1	0–0–0	0–0–0	0–2–2	1–0–1	1–0–1	0–0–0	0–0–0
Laraque	———	———	———	0–0–0	———	———	0–0–0	———	0–0–0
Lindgren	0–0–0	0–0–0	0–0–0	1–1–2	0–1–1	1–1–2	0–0–0	2–1–3	3–0–3
Lowe	———	———	———	———	———	———	0–0–0	———	———
Marchant	1–2–3	0–0–0	0–1–1	4–2–6	0–0–0	1–0–1	0–0–0	2–2–4	0–4–4
Marchment	0–0–0	0–0–0	———	———	———	0–0–0	0–0–0	0–1–1	0–1–1
McAmmond	0–4–4	1–0–1	0–2–2	1–2–3	0–1–1	1–1–2	0–0–0	1–0–1	0–2–2
McGillis	1–0–1	0–0–0	1–0–1	0–0–0	0–0–0	0–0–0	0–1–1	1–1–2	1–1–2
Millar	———	0–0–0	0–0–0	0–0–0	0–0–0	———	———	0–0–0	———
Mironov	1–1–2	0–0–0	1–0–1	2–3–5	0–1–1	1–3–4	1–0–1	0–1–1	1–0–1
Muir	———	———	———	———	———	0–0–0	0–0–0	———	0–0–0
Murray	2–0–2	0–0–0	0–0–0	0–0–0	1–0–1	1–2–3	0–1–1	———	0–0–0
Musil	0–0–0	———	0–0–0	1–0–1	0–0–0	———	———	0–0–0	0–0–0
Niinimaa	0–4–4	———	0–0–0	1–2–3	———	———	———	0–0–0	———
Sandwith	———	———	———	———	———	———	0–0–0	———	———
Smyth	1–1–2	0–1–1	1–0–1	0–0–0	1–1–2	1–0–1	2–1–3	1–1–2	1–1–2
Watt	0–0–0	———	———	0–1–1	———	0–1–1	0–0–0	0–0–0	0–0–0
Weight	0–1–1	1–0–1	0–1–1	2–3–5	1–1–2	0–1–1	3–4–7	1–1–2	1–0–1
Whitney	0–0–0	0–0–0	———	———	———	———	0–0–0	———	0–0–0
Zelepukin	0–1–1	———	0–0–0	1–0–1	0–1–1	0–0–0	0–1–1	0–0–0	0–0–0

	Flor.	L.A.	Mont.	N.J.	NYI.	NYR.	Ott.	Phil.
Arnott	———	0–2–2	0–1–1	———	0–0–0	0–0–0	0–1–1	0–0–0
Bannister	———	0–0–0	0–0–0	0–0–0	———	0–0–0	0–0–0	0–0–0
Berehowsky	0–1–1	0–0–0	0–0–0	0–0–0	0–0–0	0–0–0	0–0–0	0–0–0
Bonvie	———	0–0–0	———	———	———	———	———	———
Bowen	———	0–0–0	———	———	———	———	———	———

	Flor.	*L.A.*	*Mont.*	*N.J.*	*NYI.*	*NYR.*	*Ott.*	*Phil.*
Brown	0–0–0	0–0–0	0–0–0	0–0–0	———	———	0–0–0	0–0–0
Buchberger	0–0–0	2–0–2	0–0–0	0–0–0	0–2–2	0–0–0	0–0–0	0–2–2
Devereaux	———	0–0–0	0–0–0	0–0–0	0–0–0	0–1–1	0–0–0	0–0–0
de Vries	1–0–1	0–0–0	0–0–0	0–0–0	0–0–0	0–0–0	0–0–0	–0–1
Dollas	———	0–0–0	———	0–0–0	———	———	0–0–0	———
Fraser	0–1–1	1–1–2	2–0–2	———	0–0–0	———	0–0–0	0–0–0
Friedman	———	———	0–0–0	0–0–0	———	———	———	0–0–0
Grier	0–0–0	1–0–1	0–0–0	0–0–0	0–0–0	0–0–0	0–0–0	0–1–1
Guerin	0–0–0	1–0–1	———	0–0–0	0–1–1	———	1–1–2	———
Hamrlik	0–2–2	1–4–5	0–1–1	0–1–1	0–0–0	———	1–1–2	———
Hrkac	0–3–3	1–0–1	———	0–0–0	1–0–1	———	2–0–2	———
Huard	———	0–0–0	———	0–0–0	———	0–0–0	0–0–0	0–0–0
Hulbig	———	———	0–1–1	1–0–1	———	0–0–0	0–0–0	———
Kelly	———	0–0–0	0–0–0	———	0–1–1	0–0–0	———	———
Kovalenko	0–0–0	0–2–2	0–0–0	0–0–0	0–2–2	0–1–1	0–1–1	0–0–0
Laraque	———	0–0–0	0–0–0	———	———	———	———	0–0–0
Lindgren	1–0–1	0–1–1	0–1–1	0–0–0	1–1–2	0–1–1	0–1–1	1–0–1
Lowe	———	———	———	———	———	0–0–0	———	———
Marchant	0–0–0	2–1–3	0–1–1	0–0–0	0–1–1	0–0–0	0–0–0	0–1–1
Marchment	———	0–0–0	0–0–0	———	0–0–0	1–0–1	———	0–0–0
McAmmond	0–1–1	1–2–3	0–0–0	1–0–1	1–1–2	0–0–0	0–3–3	0–1–1
McGillis	0–1–1	0–1–1	0–0–0	0–1–1	0–0–0	0–1–1	0–1–1	0–0–0
Millar	———	———	———	———	2–0–2	0–0–0	———	1–0–1
Mironov	1–0–1	1–2–3	1–1–2	0–0–0	0–0–0	0–1–1	0–0–0	0–0–0
Muir	———	———	———	———	———	———	———	———
Murray	0–0–0	0–1–1	0–1–1	0–1–1	0–0–0	1–0–1	0–0–0	0–0–0
Musil	0–0–0	0–0–0	———	———	0–0–0	———	———	———
Niinimaa	———	0–1–1	———	———	———	———	———	———
Sandwith	———	0–0–0	———	———	———	———	———	———
Smyth	2–1–3	2–0–2	1–1–2	1–0–1	0–1–1	1–0–1	0–0–0	0–0–0
Watt	———	———	———	0–1–1	———	———	1–0–1	———
Weight	2–1–3	1–5–6	2–2–4	0–1–1	0–0–0	2–1–0	1–1–2	0–0–0
Whitney	———	0–0–0	———	———	———	0–1–1	———	———
Zelepukin	0–0–0	0–1–1	———	0–0–0	0–0–0	———	0–1–1	———

	Phoe.	*Pitt.*	*S.J.*	*St.L.*	*Tamp.*	*Tor.*	*Van.*	*Was.*
Arnott	0–2–2	0–1–1	4–1–5	0–0–0	———	0–2–2	0–0–0	0–0–0
Bannister	0–0–0	0–0–0	0–2–2	0–0–0	———	0–0–0	0–0–0	0–0–0
Berehowsky	0–1–1	0–0–0	1–0–1	0–0–0	0–0–0	0–1–1	0–1–1	0–0–0
Bonvie	———	———	———	———	———	———	0–0–0	———
Bowen	———	0–0–0	———	———	———	———	———	———
Brown	0–0–0	———	0–0–0	0–0–0	———	———	———	———
Buchberger	0–1–1	1–0–1	0–0–0	1–1–2	1–1–2	0–1–1	0–0–0	0–0–0
Devereaux	1–0–1	0–0–0	0–0–0	0–0–0	0–0–0	0–1–1	0–0–0	0–0–0
de Vries	1–0–1	1–0–1	0–0–0	0–0–0	0–1–1	2–1–3	0–0–0	0–0–0
Dollas	0–0–0	———	0–0–0	0–1–1	———	0–1–1	0–1–1	1–0–1
Ferguson	———	———	———	———	0–0–0	———	———	———
Fraser	———	0–0–0	0–0–0	0–1–1	1–0–1	1–1–2	0–1–1	0–1–1
Friedman	———	———	0–0–0	0–0–0	———	0–0–0	———	———
Grier	1–2–3	1–1–2	0–0–0	1–0–1	0–0–0	1–0–1	0–0–0	0–0–0
Guerin	2–2–4	0–0–0	1–2–3	0–0–0	0–3–3	0–2–2	2–0–2	1–0–1
Hamrlik	1–0–1	0–0–0	1–2–3	0–1–1	1–0–1	0–0–0	0–4–4	0–0–0
Hrkac	0–2–2	0–0–0	0–1–1	0–0–0	0–1–1	0–0–0	0–2–2	0–0–0
Huard	0–0–0	0–1–1	0–0–0	0–0–0	0–0–0	0–0–0	0–0–0	0–0–0
Hulbig	———	———	0–0–0	0–0–0	———	———	———	———
Kelly	0–0–0	0–1–1	———	0–0–0	———	———	———	0–0–0
Kovalenko	0–1–1	———	1–3–4	0–1–1	———	0–1–1	2–0–2	1–1–2
Laraque	0–0–0	———	0–0–0	———	———	0–0–0	———	———
Lindgren	0–0–0	0–0–0	0–0–0	1–1–2	0–0–0	2–1–3	0–1–1	0–0–0
Lowe	———	———	0–0–0	———	———	0–0–0	0–0–0	———
Marchant	1–1–2	0–0–0	0–1–1	0–1–1	0–1–1	1–1–2	0–0–0	0–0–0
Marchment	0–1–1	0–0–0	0–1–1	1–1–2	———	0–0–0	0–0–0	———
McAmmond	2–1–3	1–0–1	3–1–4	0–0–0	1–1–2	1–2–3	3–2–5	0–3–3
McGillis	0–3–3	1–0–1	1–1–2	3–0–3	0–2–2	0–1–1	1–0–1	0–0–0
Millar	———	———	———	———	0–0–0	———	———	1–0–1

	Phoe.	*Pitt.*	*S.J.*	*St.L.*	*Tamp.*	*Tor.*	*Van.*	*Was.*
Mironov	3–5–8	1–1–2	0–3–3	1–2–3	1–0–1	0–1–1	1–4–5	0–1–1
Muir	———	———	0–0–0	0–0–0	———	———	———	———
Murray	0–0–0	1–0–1	2–1–3	1–1–2	0–0–0	0–0–0	0–0–0	0–0–0
Musil	———	0–1–1	———	0–0–0	0–0–0	———	0–0–0	0–1–1
Niinimaa	———	———	———	———	———	0–0–0	0–1–1	0–0–0
Sandwith	———	0–0–0	0–0–0	———	0–0–0	0–0–0	———	———
Smyth	1–0–1	0–1–1	1–3–4	0–0–0	0–0–0	1–0–1	2–0–2	0–0–0
Watt	———	———	0–0–0	0–0–0	———	———	———	———
Weight	3–1–4	0–2–2	2–6–8	2–3–5	1–1–2	1–2–3	0–2–2	1–2–3
Whitney	———	———	0–2–2	———	———	1–0–1	0–0–0	———
Zelepukin	1–1–2	0–0–0	0–0–0	0–1–1	0–1–1	0–0–0	0–2–2	0–0–0

Goaltender Record vs. Opposition

	GP	*Min.*	*GA*	*EN*	*SO*	*Ave.*	*W–L–T*	*Opposition*
Bob Essensa	2	119	6	1	0	2.52	0–2–0	Anaheim
	1	53	1	1	0	1.13	0–1–0	Calgary
	1	23	0	0	0	0.00	1–0–0	Colorado
	1	35	0	0	0	0.00	0–0–0	Dallas
	4	213	10	0	0	2.82	2–1–0	Detroit
	1	65	3	0	0	2.77	0–0–1	Montreal
	1	60	2	0	0	2.00	1–0–0	Ottawa
	1	60	2	0	0	2.00	1–0–0	Phoenix
	1	60	6	0	0	6.00	0–1–0	Philadelphia
	1	60	3	0	0	3.00	1–0–0	Toronto
	2	80	3	0	0	2.25	0–1–0	Vancouver
Curtis Joseph	4	240	8	1	0	2.00	2–2–0	Anaheim
	2	118	4	1	0	2.03	0–2–0	Boston
	2	120	5	0	0	2.50	0–1–1	Buffalo
	5	251	11	0	0	2.63	3–1–0	Calgary
	2	119	10	1	0	5.04	0–2–0	Carolina
	4	259	8	0	1	1.85	1–0–3	Chicago
	6	340	24	0	0	4.24	0–5–0	Colorado
	4	205	10	0	0	2.93	1–3–0	Dallas
	1	27	5	0	0	11.11	0–1–0	Detroit
	2	120	2	0	1	1.00	2–0–0	Florida
	5	303	8	0	2	1.58	4–1–0	Los Angeles
	1	59	4	1	0	4.07	0–1–0	Montreal
	2	125	4	1	0	1.92	0–1–1	New Jersey
	2	125	7	0	0	3.36	0–1–1	N.Y. Islanders
	2	130	5	0	0	2.31	0–0–2	N.Y. Rangers
	1	60	0	0	1	0.00	1–0–0	Ottawa
	1	59	3	0	0	3.05	0–1–0	Philadelphia
	3	179	9	1	0	3.02	2–1–0	Phoenix
	2	120	7	0	0	3.50	1–1–0	Pittsburgh
	5	299	11	0	0	2.21	3–2–0	San Jose
	4	240	2	0	2	0.50	4–0–0	St. Louis
	2	120	2	0	1	1.00	2–0–0	Tampa Bay
	3	179	10	0	0	3.35	1–2–0	Toronto
	4	219	17	0	0	4.66	1–3–0	Vancouver
	2	119	4	0	0	2.02	1–1–0	Washington

1997-98 Schedule Results

Date	Visitor	Score		Home	Score
Oct. 1	Edmonton	5	at	San Jose	3
Oct. 3	Detroit	8	at	Edmonton	2
Oct. 5	Colorado	3	at	Edmonton	0
Oct. 8	Rangers	3	at	Edmonton	3 OT
Oct. 11	Toronto	1	at	Edmonton	2
Oct. 13	Edmonton	0	at	Vancouver	3
Oct. 15	Colorado	6	at	Edmonton	2
Oct. 17	Edmonton	1	at	Anaheim	2
Oct. 19	Edmonton	3	at	Los Angeles	2 OT
Oct. 21	Boston	2	at	Edmonton	1
Oct. 24	Pittsburgh	3	at	Edmonton	4
Oct. 29	Phoenix	2	at	Edmonton	3
Nov. 1	Edmonton	1	at	Boston	3
Nov. 3	Edmonton	2	at	Rangers	2 OT
Nov. 5	Edmonton	4	at	Islanders	4 OT
Nov. 6	Edmonton	2	at	Philadelphia	6
Nov. 8	Edmonton	1	at	Washington	2
Nov. 10	Edmonton	4	at	Buffalo	4 OT

Nov. 12	Carolina	6	at	Edmonton	4
Nov. 15	Calgary	2	at	Edmonton	2 OT
Nov. 17	Edmonton	3	at	Phoenix	6
Nov. 19	Edmonton	2	at	Dallas	3
Nov. 20	Edmonton	3	at	St. Louis	0
Nov. 22	Edmonton	1	at	Ottawa	0
Nov. 25	Chicago	2	at	Edmonton	2 OT
Nov. 28	Anaheim	3	at	Edmonton	1
Nov. 30	San Jose	1	at	Edmonton	6
Dec. 2	Edmonton	2	at	Colorado	4
Dec. 3	Edmonton	1	at	Dallas	4
Dec. 5	Detroit	1	at	Edmonton	3
Dec. 7	Edmonton	3	at	Chicago	3 OT
Dec. 10	Edmonton	2	at	New Jersey	4
Dec. 12	Edmonton	3	at	Detroit	2
Dec. 13	Edmonton	4	at	St. Louis	1
Dec. 17	Chicago	0	at	Edmonton	0 OT
Dec. 20	Dallas	2	at	Edmonton	1 OT
Dec. 22	Edmonton	3	at	Montreal	3 OT
Dec. 23	Edmonton	4	at	Toronto	5
Dec. 27	Colorado	5	at	Edmonton	1
Dec. 30	Philadelphia	3	at	Edmonton	1
Jan. 2	Montreal	5	at	Edmonton	3
Jan. 4	Los Angeles	3	at	Edmonton	2
Jan. 7	Florida	2	at	Edmonton	3
Jan. 9	Edmonton	5	at	Anaheim	1
Jan. 10	Edmonton	4	at	Los Angeles	3
Jan. 12	St. Louis	1	at	Edmonton	2
Jan. 14	Calgary	2	at	Edmonton	5
Jan. 20	Phoenix	2	at	Edmonton	6
Jan. 23	Edmonton	2	at	San Jose	3
Jan. 24	Edmonton	5	at	Phoenix	2
Jan. 26	Edmonton	1	at	Colorado	2 OT
Jan. 28	New Jersey	1	at	Edmonton	1 OT
Jan. 31	Vancouver	6	at	Edmonton	3
Feb. 2	Los Angeles	0	at	Edmonton	1
Feb. 4	San Jose	3	at	Edmonton	0
Feb. 6	Edmonton	4	at	Vancouver	5
Feb. 7	Edmonton	2	at	Calgary	4
Feb. 25	Ottawa	2	at	Edmonton	5
Feb. 27	Anaheim	4	at	Edmonton	0
Feb. 28	San Jose	1	at	Edmonton	4
Mar. 2	Edmonton	5	at	Colorado	4 OT
Mar. 4	Tampa Bay	2	at	Edmonton	4
Mar. 7	Edmonton	1	at	Toronto	4
Mar. 9	Edmonton	4	at	Chicago	3 OT
Mar. 11	Edmonton	2	at	Tampa Bay	0
Mar. 13	Edmonton	4	at	Florida	0
Mar. 15	Edmonton	1	at	Carolina	4
Mar. 17	Edmonton	3	at	Detroit	4
Mar. 18	Edmonton	2	at	Pittsburgh	4
Mar. 21	St. Louis	0	at	Edmonton	2
Mar. 22	Islanders	3	at	Edmonton	1
Mar. 25	Washington	2	at	Edmonton	4
Mar. 27	Buffalo	1	at	Edmonton	0
Mar. 30	Calgary	1	at	Edmonton	3
April 1	Edmonton	2	at	Vancouver	4
April 3	Dallas	1	at	Edmonton	4
April 6	Vancouver	2	at	Edmonton	3
April 8	Edmonton	2	at	Anaheim	4
April 9	Edmonton	4	at	Los Angeles	0
April 11	Edmonton	5	at	Calgary	4
April 15	Anaheim	3	at	Edmonton	5
April 18	Toronto	3	at	Edmonton	4

Overall Record vs. Opponents

Opponent	*Home*	*Road*	*Overall*	*GF-GA*	*Opponent*
Anaheim	1–2–0	1–2–0	2–4–0	14–17	Anaheim
Boston	0–1–0	0–1–0	0–2–0	2–5	Boston
Buffalo	0–1–0	0–0–1	0–1–1	4–5	Buffalo
Calgary	1–0–1	2–1–0	3–1–1	17–13	Calgary
Carolina	0–1–0	0–1–0	0–2–0	5–10	Carolina
Chicago	0–0–2	1–0–1	1–0–3	9–8	Chicago
Colorado	0–3–0	1–2–0	1–5–0	11–24	Colorado
Dallas	1–1–0	0–2–0	1–3–0	8–10	Dallas
Detroit	1–1–0	1–1–0	2–2–0	11–15	Detroit
Florida	1–0–0	1–0–0	2–0–0	7–2	Florida
Los Angeles	1–1–0	3–0–0	4–1–0	14–8	Los Angeles
Montreal	0–1–0	0–0–1	0–1–1	6–8	Montreal
New Jersey	0–0–1	0–1–0	0–1–1	3–5	New Jersey
Islanders	0–1–0	0–0–1	0–1–1	5–7	Islanders
Rangers	0–0–1	0–0–1	0–0–2	5–5	Rangers
Ottawa	1–0–0	1–0–0	2–0–0	6–2	Ottawa
Philadelphia	0–1–0	0–1–0	0–2–0	3–9	Philadelphia
Phoenix	2–0–0	1–1–0	2–1–0	17–12	Phoenix
Pittsburgh	1–0–0	0–1–0	1–1–0	6–7	Pittsburgh
San Jose	2–1–0	1–1–0	3–2–0	17–11	San Jose
St. Louis	2–0–0	2–0–0	4–0–0	11–3	St. Louis
Tampa Bay	1–0–0	1–0–0	2–0–0	6–2	Tampa Bay
Toronto	2–0–0	0–2–0	2–2–0	11–13	Toronto
Vancouver	1–1–0	0–3–0	1–4–0	12–20	Vancouver
Washington	1–0–0	0–1–0	1–0–0	5–4	Washington

1997-98 Playoff Scoring

#		*GP*	*G*	*A*	*Pts*	*Shots*	*S%*	*GW*	*OT*	*PP*	*SH*	*P/M*	*PIM*
39	Doug Weight	12	2	7	9	26	7.7	1	0	2	0	-4	14

#		GP	G	A	Pts	Shots	S%	GW	OT	PP	SH	P/M	PIM
9	Bill Guerin	12	7	1	8	47	14.9	0	0	4	0	-6	17
2	Boris Mironov	12	3	3	6	26	11.5	1	0	1	0	-3	27
22	Roman Hamrlik	12	0	6	6	19	0.0	0	0	0	0	-4	12
17	Rem Murray	11	1	4	5	15	6.7	0	0	0	0	-1	2
37	Dean McAmmond	12	1	4	5	22	4.5	0	0	0	0	0	12
25	Mike Grier	12	2	2	4	14	14.3	1	0	0	0	4	13
94	Ryan Smyth	12	1	3	4	24	4.2	0	0	1	0	-2	16
21	Valeri Zelepukin	8	1	2	3	8	12.5	0	0	0	0	3	2
15	Drake Berehowsky	12	1	2	3	4	25.0	1	0	0	0	1	14
16	Kelly Buchberger	12	1	2	3	13	7.7	0	0	0	0	0	25
20	Tony Hrkac	12	0	3	3	11	0.0	0	0	0	0	2	2
18	Scott Fraser	11	1	1	2	17	5.9	0	0	0	0	0	0
24	Janne Niinimaa	11	1	1	2	20	5.0	1	0	0	0	3	12
14	Mats Lindgren	12	1	1	2	16	6.3	0	0	0	0	0	10
26	Todd Marchant	12	1	1	2	17	5.9	0	0	0	0	0	10
8	Frantisek Musil	7	0	0	0	0	0.0	0	0	0	0	1	6
5	Greg de Vries	7	0	0	0	2	0.0	0	0	0	0	-4	21
6	Bobby Dollas	11	0	0	0	10	0.0	0	0	0	0	2	16
4	Kevin Lowe	1	0	0	0	0	0.0	0	0	0	0	0	4
28	Bill Huard	4	0	0	0	3	0.0	0	0	0	0	0	2
51	Andrei Kovalenko	1	0	0	0	2	0.0	0	0	0	0	0	2
31	Curtis Joseph	12	0	0	0	0	0.0	0	0	0	0	0	2
		12	24	43	67	316	7.6	5	0	8	0	-8	241

1997-98 Playoff Goaltending

	GP	Min.	GA	W	L	Ave.	SA	Pct.	SO	EN
Bob Essensa	1	27	1	0	0	0.00	11	0.909	0	0
Curtis Joseph	12	716	23	5	7	1.93	320	0.928	3	0
	12	743	24	5	7	1.94	331	0.927	3	0

Date			Result			Winning Goaltender	Winning Goal
April 22, 1998	Edmonton	3	at	Colorado	2	Curtis Joseph	Boris Mironov
April 24, 1998	Edmonton	2	at	Colorado	5	Patrick Roy	Joe Sakic
April 26, 1998	Colorado	5	at	Edmonton	4	Patrick Roy	Joe Sakic[1]
April 28, 1998	Colorado	3	at	Edmonton	1	Patrick Roy	Claude Lemieux
April 30, 1998	Edmonton	3	at	Colorado	1	Curtis Joseph	Mike Grier
May 2, 1998	Colorado	0	at	Edmonton	2	Curtis Joseph	Drake Berehowsky
May 4, 1998	Edmonton	4	at	Colorado	0	Curtis Joseph	Janne Niinimaa
May 7, 1998	Edmonton	1	at	Dallas	3	Ed Belfour	Sergei Zubov
May 9, 1998	Edmonton	2	at	Dallas	0	Curtis Joseph	Doug Weight
May 11, 1998	Dallas	1	at	Edmonton	0	Ed Belfour	Benoit Hogue[2]
May 13, 1998	Dallas	3	at	Edmonton	1	Ed Belfour	Benoit Hogue
May 16, 1998	Edmonton	1	at	Dallas	2	Ed Belfour	Greg Adams

[1]15:25 of overtime [2]13:07 of overtime

Table 16. Oilers Shutouts

Date		Goaltender	Opponent	Score	Saves
December 9, 1979	*Home*	*Eddie Mio (1)*	*Hartford*	*3–0*	*30*
February 27, 1983	*Home*	*Andy Moog (1)*	*Winnipeg*	*3–0*	*25*
November 18, 1983	*Home*	*Andy Moog (2)*	*Buffalo*	*7–0*	*29*
December 30, 1983	*Home*	*Grant Fuhr (1)*	*Boston*	*2–0*	*36*
May 10, 1984 (P)	*Road*	*Grant Fuhr (2)*	*N.Y. Islanders*	*1–0*	*34*
October 30, 1984	*Home*	*Andy Moog (3)*	*Vancouver*	*7–0*	*25*
November 17, 1984	*Home*	*Grant Fuhr (3)*	*Vancouver*	*7–0*	*20*
January 8, 1985	*Road*	*Fuhr/Moog*	*Quebec*	*4–0*	*18/10*
November 8, 1985	*Home*	*Andy Moog (4)*	*Vancouver*	*13–0*	*29*
November 7, 1987	*Home*	*Grant Fuhr (4)*	*Buffalo*	*5–0*	*26*
December 9, 1987	*Home*	*Grant Fuhr (5)*	*Winnipeg*	*2–0*	*28*
December 30, 1987	*Home*	*Grant Fuhr (6)*	*Philadelphia*	*6–0*	*23*
March 7, 1988	*Road*	*Grant Fuhr (7)*	*Winnipeg*	*6–0*	*21*
March 1, 1989	*Home*	*Grant Fuhr (8)*	*Montreal*	*3–0*	*23*

Date		*Goaltender*	*Opponent*	*Score*	*Saves*
April 8, 1989 (P)	*Home*	*Grant Fuhr (9)*	*Los Angeles*	*4–0*	*26*
January 8, 1989	*Home*	*Bill Ranford (1)*	*Calgary*	*6–0*	*35*
November 17, 1989	*Home*	*Grant Fuhr (10)*	*Buffalo*	*3–0*	*30*
December 19, 1989	*Road*	*Bill Ranford (2)*	*Minnesota*	*5–0*	*22*
April 18, 1990 (P)	*Home*	*Bill Ranford (3)*	*Los Angeles*	*7–0*	*25*
February 18, 1991	*Road*	*Grant Fuhr (11)*	*New Jersey*	*4–0*	*27*
December 1, 1991	*Home*	*Bill Ranford (4)*	*Vancouver*	*7–0*	*33*
April 28, 1992 (P)	*Home*	*Bill Ranford (5)*	*Los Angeles*	*3–0*	*26*
May 12, 1992 (P)	*Home*	*Bill Ranford (6)*	*Vancouver*	*3–0*	*26*
February 12, 1993	*Home*	*Bill Ranford (7)*	*San Jose*	*6–0*	*28*
December 27, 1993	*Home*	*Bill Ranford (8)*	*Winnipeg*	*6–0*	*24*
February 12, 1995	*Home*	*Bill Ranford (9)*	*Anaheim*	*2–0*	*29*
April 19, 1995	*Home*	*Bill Ranford (10)*	*Los Angeles*	*2–0*	*28*
November 22, 1995	*Home*	*Bill Ranford (11)*	*Anaheim*	*2–0*	*31*
October 6, 1996	*Home*	*Curtis Joseph (1)*	*Vancouver*	*2–0*	*35*
November 7, 1996	*Road*	*Curtis Joseph (2)*	*Boston*	*6–0*	*25*
November 13, 1996	*Road*	*Curtis Joseph (3)*	*Ottawa*	*4–0*	*28*
December 10, 1996	*Road*	*Curtis Joseph (4)*	*Detroit*	*0–0 (OT)*	*52*
December 23, 1996	*Road*	*Bob Essensa (1)*	*Vancouver*	*7–0*	*26*
January 15, 1997	*Home*	*Curtis Joseph (5)*	*Florida*	*4–0*	*40*
January 31, 1997	*Home*	*Curtis Joseph (6)*	*N.Y. Islanders*	*1–0*	*24*
April 18, 1997 (P)	*Road*	*Curtis Joseph (7)*	*Dallas*	*4–0*	*25*
April 25, 1997 (P)	*Road*	*Curtis Joseph (8)*	*Dallas*	*1–0 (OT)*	*43*
November 20, 1997	*Road*	*Curtis Joseph (9)*	*St. Louis*	*3–0*	*22*
November 22, 1997	*Road*	*Curtis Joseph (10)*	*Ottawa*	*1–0*	*26*
December 17, 1997	*Home*	*Curtis Joseph (11)*	*Chicago*	*0–0 (OT)*	*28*
February 2, 1998	*Home*	*Curtis Joseph (12)*	*Los Angeles*	*1–0*	*30*
March 11, 1998	*Road*	*Curtis Joseph (13)*	*Tampa Bay*	*2–0*	*20*
March 13, 1998	*Road*	*Curtis Joseph (14)*	*Florida*	*4–0*	*23*
March 21, 1998	*Home*	*Curtis Joseph (15)*	*St. Louis*	*2–0*	*20*
April 9, 1998	*Road*	*Curtis Joseph (16)*	*Los Angeles*	*4–0*	*14*
May 2, 1998 (P)	*Home*	*Curtis Joseph (17)*	*Colorado*	*2–0*	*31*
May 4, 1998 (P)	*Road*	*Curtis Joseph (18)*	*Colorado*	*4–0*	*31*
May 9, 1998 (P)	*Road*	*Curtis Joseph (19)*	*Dallas*	*2–0*	*15*
November 25, 1998	*Home*	*M. Shtalenkov (1)*	*Colorado*	*3–0*	*26*
December 27, 1998	*Home*	*M. Shtalenkov (2)*	*Vancouver*	*3–0*	*25*
January 30, 1999	*Home*	*M. Shtalenkov (3)*	*Anaheim*	*1–0*	*22*
January 19, 2000	*Home*	*Tommy Salo (1)*	*Calgary*	*7–0*	*24*
March 13, 2000	*Road*	*Tommy Salo (2)*	*Atlanta*	*3–0*	*24*
November 3, 2000	*Home*	*Tommy Salo (3)*	*Minnesota*	*3–0*	*20*
November 14, 2000	*Home*	*Tommy Salo (4)*	*St. Louis*	*3–0*	*29*
November 19, 2000	*Home*	*Tommy Salo (5)*	*Calgary*	*2–0*	*23*
December 6, 2000	*Home*	*Tommy Salo (6)*	*Nashville*	*4–0*	*18*
February 20, 2001	*Home*	*Tommay Salo (7)*	*Los Angeles*	*5–0*	*21*
March 7, 2001	*Home*	*Tommy Salo (8)*	*Toronto*	*4–0*	*25*
March 9, 2001	*Road*	*Tommy Salo (9)*	*Buffalo*	*4–0*	*28*
March 21, 2001	*Road*	*Tommy Salo (10)*	*Los Angeles*	*7–0*	*28*
Total 61 games	*40 Home 21 Road*			*232–0*	*1638*

P—indicates playoff game.

1998-99

Ron Low began his fifth season as head coach of the Oilers with Ted Green and veteran defenseman Kevin Lowe as his assistants. Lowe had replaced Bob McCammon, who was released by the team.

Glen Sather continued his tradition of signing players that had worn out their welcome with other teams. Former first round draft pick Pat Falloon was signed as a free agent and would have a fine season, finishing fourth in team scoring, while returning veteran Marty McSorley added some much needed experience to a young blue line corps. Also returning to the Oilers this year would be Josef Beranek, who spent much of the season as the team's first line center due to the absence of Doug Weight. Beranek would finish second in team scoring.

The injury bug hit the team hard this season. Doug Weight, who had led the team in scoring the last five seasons, sat out the first four games due to a contract dispute, then assisted on five goals in four games before being felled by a knee injury. Weight would miss 34 games before returning to the lineup for the final 43 games.

Team captain and inspirational leader Kelly Buchberger sat out 31 games due to a broken forearm, while sniper Ryan Smyth missed 11 games with a broken jaw, and Josef Beranek missed 16 games with an assortment of injuries. Defensive workhorse Roman Hamrlik also missed six games with a broken toe. Neither Weight nor Buchberger played at the top of their game for the remainder of the season. Smyth, after a very slow start, would be the team's most effective forward during the last month of the season.

All was not doom and gloom however. Bill Guerin scored 30 goals, while Beranek, Falloon, Mike Grier and Rem Murray would all have fine years offensively. Two rookies would also contribute much to the team's fortunes. At 240 pounds Georges Laraque would quickly become one of the league's most feared fighters and was almost impossible to knock off of the puck once he gained control of it inside of the opposition zone.

Perhaps the most pleasant surprise of all was big rookie defenseman Tom Poti. Instantly recognizable on the ice wielding his 63-inch shiny aluminum Easton hockey stick, Poti played with the poise of a veteran, was gifted both offensively and defensively, and often would carry the puck deep into the opposition's end. Although he started slowly Poti blossomed with the trade of Boris Mironov to Chicago. Poti would be named to the league's All-Rookie team.

Bill Guerin replaced Buchberger as captain while "Bucky" was recuperating and then Doug Weight took over the duties when he returned to action. Weight, Guerin, Mironov and even Mike Grier would spend time wearing the "A" (assistant captain) this season.

The Oilers had one of their best starts in years, and after the first couple of weeks the team was first overall in offense and was sitting on top of the league. The team then came crashing back to reality and was 18–19–7 (.489) at the All-Star break.

With the team floundering near the bottom of the league, Sather again performed some magic at the trading deadline. Traded to the Oilers from the New York Islanders for Mats Lindgren was Swedish netminder Tommy Salo. Salo would win eight and tie two of the twelve games he played during the regular season. That same day, Sather traded talented but error prone defenseman Boris Mironov and underachieving winger Dean McAmmond to Chicago for Ethan Moreau, Christian Laflamme and Chad Kilger. All three players would add size, toughness and enthusiasm to the team. Three days later Sather obtained hard hitting, stay at home defenseman Jason Smith from Toronto for a future draft choice. With these five new players in the lineup the team compiled a record of 9–3–2 in the last 14 games of the season and edged out Calgary for the final playoff spot.

Edmonton scored 230 goals during the regular season, good enough for tenth overall and allowed 226, which was only eighteenth best in the league. The Oilers then went on to meet the number one overall, Dallas Stars in the postseason. Although Edmonton lost all four games, they gave Dallas a good run, losing every game by just one goal. Included was the team's longest ever game on April 27, when they lost to the Stars by a score of 3–2 after 57:34 of overtime.

1998-99 Regular Season Scoring

#		Ht.	Wt.	Age	GP	G	A	Pts	Shots	S%	GW	GT	PP	SH	P/M	PIM
9	Guerin (A)	74	210	28	80	30	34	64	261	11.5	2	1	13	0	7	133
20	Beranek	74	195	29	66	19	30	49	160	11.9	2	0	7	0	6	23
25	Grier	73	227	23	82	20	24	44	143	14.0	1	0	3	2	5	54
2	Mironov (A)	75	223	26	63	11	29	40	138	8.0	4	1	5	0	6	104
10	Falloon	71	190	26	82	17	23	40	152	11.2	2	0	8	0	-4	20
17	Murray	74	195	26	78	21	18	39	116	18.1	4	1	4	1	4	20
39	Weight (A)	71	200	27	43	6	31	37	79	7.6	0	1	1	0	-8	12
26	Marchant	70	178	25	82	14	22	36	183	7.7	2	0	3	1	3	65
22	Hamrlik	74	215	24	75	8	24	32	172	4.7	0	0	3	0	9	70
94	Smyth	73	195	22	71	13	18	31	161	8.1	2	2	6	0	0	62
44	Niinimaa	74	220	23	81	4	24	28	142	2.8	1	0	2	0	7	88
51	Kovalenko	70	215	28	43	13	14	27	75	17.3	3	1	2	0	-4	30
37	McAmmond	71	200	25	65	9	16	25	122	7.4	0	0	1	0	5	36
5	Poti	75	215	21	73	5	16	21	94	5.3	3	0	2	0	10	42
14	Lindgren	74	202	24	48	5	12	17	53	9.4	0	0	0	1	4	22
28	Selivanov	72	206	27	29	8	6	14	57	14.0	1	0	1	0	0	24
19	Devereaux	74	195	20	61	6	8	14	39	15.4	4	1	0	1	2	23
16	Buchberger (C)	74	210	32	52	4	4	8	29	13.8	1	0	0	2	-6	68
23	Brown, S.	75	205	22	51	0	7	7	27	0.0	0	0	0	0	1	188
42	Brown, K.	73	212	24	12	4	2	6	13	30.8	0	0	2	0	-2	0
18	Moreau	74	205	23	14	1	5	6	16	6.3	1	0	0	0	2	8
46	Reirden	77	220	27	17	2	3	5	26	7.7	0	0	0	0	-1	20

#		Ht.	Wt.	Age	GP	G	A	Pts	Shots	S%	GW	GT	PP	SH	P/M	PIM
27	Laraque	75	230	22	39	3	2	5	17	17.6	0	0	0	0	-1	57
33	McSorley	73	235	35	46	2	3	5	29	6.9	0	0	0	0	-5	101
8	Musil	75	215	34	39	0	3	3	9	0.0	0	0	0	0	0	34
34	Vorobiev	72	185	26	2	2	0	2	5	40.0	0	0	0	0	1	2
21	Smith	75	205	25	12	1	1	2	15	6.7	0	0	0	0	0	11
15	Kilger	75	204	22	13	1	1	2	13	7.7	0	0	0	0	-3	4
32	Millar	74	205	22	24	0	2	2	18	0.0	0	0	0	0	-6	19
29	Passmore	69	165	25	6	0	1	1	0	0.0	0	0	0	0	0	2
30	Essensa	72	188	33	39	0	1	1	0	0.0	0	0	0	0	0	0
38	Ferraro	70	185	25	2	1	0	1	1	100.0	0	0	0	0	1	0
24	Laflamme	73	202	22	11	0	1	1	15	0.0	0	0	0	0	-3	0
34	Dowd	73	190	30	1	0	0	0	1	0.0	0	0	0	0	0	0
12	Hulbig	75	215	25	1	0	0	0	2	0.0	0	0	0	0	1	2
28	Huard	73	215	31	3	0	0	0	2	0.0	0	0	0	0	0	0
15	LaCouture	75	210	21	3	0	0	0	0	0.0	0	0	0	0	1	0
21	Lacroix	74	205	29	4	0	0	0	5	0.0	0	0	0	0	0	13
7	Lindquist	72	190	25	8	0	0	0	6	0.0	0	0	0	0	-2	2
35	Salo	71	173	27	13	0	0	0	0	0.0	0	0	0	0	0	0
35	Shtalenkov	74	185	33	34	0	0	0	0	0.0	0	0	0	0	0	2
	Bench															12
		73	203	26	82	230	385	615	2396	9.6	33	8	63	8	30	1373

1998-99 Goaltender Records

	GP	Min.	GA	W	L	T	Ave.	SA	Pct.	SO	EN
Tommy Salo	13	702	27	8	2	2	2.31	279	0.903	0	0
M. Shtalenkov	34	1819	81	12	17	3	2.67	782	0.896	3	2
Bob Essensa	39	2091	96	12	14	6	2.75	974	0.901	0	2
S. Passmore	6	362	17	1	4	1	2.82	183	0.907	0	1
	82	4974	221	33	37	12	2.71	2218	0.900	3	5

Coach: Ron Low 33-37-12

Scoring vs. Opposition

	Ana.	Bost.	Buff.	Calg.	Caro.	Chic.	Col.	Dall.	Detr.
Beranek	0–1–1	0–0–0	0–1–1	0–3–3	0–0–0	1–1–2	2–2–4	1–1–2	0–2–2
Brown, K.	———	———	———	———	———	———	1–0–1	———	———
Brown, S.	0–0–0	———	0–1–1	0–2–2	0–0–0	0–0–0	0–1–1	0–0–0	0–0–0
Buchberger	0–0–0	———	———	0–0–0	0–0–0	0–0–0	0–0–0	0–0–0	0–0–0
Devereaux	0–0–0	0–0–0	———	0–0–0	———	0–0–0	0–1–1	0–0–0	1–0–1
Dowd	———	———	———	———	———	———	———	0–0–0	———
Falloon	1–0–1	0–0–0	0–0–0	0–3–3	0–0–0	2–1–3	0–1–1	0–0–0	2–2–4
Ferraro	———	———	1–0–1	———	0–0–0	———	———	———	———
Grier	2–0–2	0–0–0	0–3–3	5–2–7	0–1–1	0–0–0	2–5–7	0–0–0	0–0–0
Guerin	0–7–7	0–0–0	2–1–3	0–3–3	0–0–0	2–0–2	2–4–6	1–3–4	0–1–1
Hamrlik	0–1–1	0–0–0	0–0–0	2–3–5	0–0–0	0–2–2	0–2–2	0–2–2	0–1–1
Hulbig	———	———	———	———	———	———	0–0–0	———	———
Kilger	———	———	———	0–0–0	———	———	0–0–0	———	———
Kovalenko	2–0–2	———	———	1–0–1	0–0–0	1–0–1	1–1–2	0–1–1	2–1–3
Lacouture	———	———	0–0–0	———	0–0–0	———	———	———	———
Lacroix	———	———	———	———	———	———	———	0–0–0	———
Laflamme	———	———	———	0–0–0	———	———	0–0–0	———	———
Laraque	0–0–0	0–0–0	0–0–0	0–0–0	0–0–0	———	0–0–0	1–0–1	0–1–1
Lindgren	0–1–1	———	0–0–0	0–0–0	0–0–0	0–0–0	1–0–1	2–1–3	0–1–1
Lindquist	———	———	———	———	0–0–0	0–0–0	———	———	0–0–0
Marchant	0–2–2	0–0–0	3–1–4	0–3–3	0–1–1	0–0–0	2–1–3	1–0–1	0–0–0
McAmmond	1–2–3	0–0–0	1–1–2	0–0–0	1–0–1	0–0–0	0–1–1	0–0–0	0–0–0
McSorley	0–0–0	0–0–0	0–0–0	0–0–0	0–0–0	0–1–1	0–0–0	0–1–1	0–0–0
Millar	0–0–0	———	———	———	0–0–0	0–0–0	0–0–0	0–0–0	0–0–0
Mironov	0–3–3	0–0–0	3–2–5	0–0–0	1–0–1	0–4–4	2–1–3	0–0–0	0–0–0
Moreau	———	———	———	1–0–1	———	———	0–0–0	———	———
Murray	1–2–3	0–0–0	0–2–2	2–3–5	0–1–1	1–1–2	4–0–4	0–1–1	1–2–3
Musil	0–0–0	———	0–0–0	0–0–0	———	0–0–0	0–0–0	0–0–0	0–0–0

	Ana.	*Bost.*	*Buff.*	*Calg.*	*Caro.*	*Chic.*	*Col.*	*Dall.*	*Detr.*
Niinimaa	1–2–3	0–0–0	1–0–1	0–1–1	0–0–0	1–1–2	0–0–0	0–2–2	0–1–1
Poti	0–0–0	0–0–0	0–1–1	1–0–1	0–0–0	0–0–0	0–2–2	0–1–1	1–2–3
Reirden	1–1–2	0–0–0	———	0–0–0	———	0–0–0	———	0–1–1	0–0–0
Selivanov	3–0–3	0–0–0	0–0–0	0–2–2	0–0–0	———	1–0–1	0–0–0	0–0–0
Smith	———	———	———	0–0–0	———	———	0–0–0	———	———
Smyth	0–1–1	0–0–0	0–1–1	2–2–4	0–0–0	1–1–2	1–1–2	1–0–1	1–0–1
Vorobiev	———	———	———	1–0–1	———	———	1–0–1	———	———
Weight	0–2–2	0–0–0	0–3–3	2–1–3	0–1–1	0–1–1	0–3–3	1–1–2	1–1–2

	Flor.	*L.A.*	*Mont.*	*Nash.*	*N.J.*	*NYI.*	*NYR.*	*Ott.*	*Phil.*
Beranek	0–1–1	0–0–0	1–1–2	3–2–5	0–2–2	———	1–1–2	1–0–1	1–1–2
Brown, K.	———	1–0–1	0–0–0	0–0–0	0–0–0	0–0–0	———	———	———
Brown, S.	0–0–0	0–1–1	0–0–0	0–0–0	———	0–0–0	0–1–1	0–0–0	0–0–0
Buchberger	0–0–0	0–1–1	0–0–0	1–0–1	0–0–0	0–2–2	0–0–0	0–0–0	0–0–0
Devereaux	———	0–2–2	0–2–2	0–0–0	0–0–0	2–0–2	0–0–0	0–0–0	0–0–0
Falloon	0–0–0	0–0–0	0–0–0	1–0–1	0–0–0	1–0–1	0–0–0	0–1–1	0–0–0
Grier	0–0–0	0–1–1	0–1–1	2–0–2	0–1–1	0–1–1	1–0–1	0–0–0	0–0–0
Guerin	0–1–1	1–1–2	2–0–2	2–0–2	2–1–3	1–0–1	1–0–1	1–0–1	1–1–2
Hamrlik	0–0–0	0–0–0	0–0–0	0–1–1	0–0–0	0–1–1	0–1–1	0–0–0	0–1–1
Huard	———	———	0–0–0	———	———	———	———	0–0–0	———
Kilger	———	———	0–0–0	———	———	———	———	———	———
Kovalenko	0–0–0	0–1–1	0–0–0	1–1–2	1–1–2	0–1–1	0–1–1	1–0–1	0–1–1
Laflamme	———	———	0–0–0	———	———	———	———	———	———
Laraque	———	0–0–0	0–0–0	0–0–0	0–0–0	———	0–0–0	0–0–0	———
Lindgren	0–0–0	0–0–0	0–0–0	0–0–0	0–0–0	———	0–0–0	0–0–0	0–1–1
Lindquist	0–0–0	0–0–0	———	0–0–0	———	———	———	———	0–0–0
Marchant	0–0–0	1–0–1	0–0–0	0–2–2	1–0–1	0–0–0	0–0–0	0–0–0	0–0–0
McAmmond	0–0–0	0–0–0	0–0–0	0–2–2	0–0–0	0–0–0	0–1–1	0–0–0	0–0–0
McSorley	0–0–0	0–0–0	0–0–0	———	0–0–0	0–0–0	0–0–0	0–0–0	1–0–1
Millar	———	0–0–0	———	0–0–0	0–0–0	0–0–0	———	0–0–0	0–0–0
Mironov	0–0–0	0–3–3	0–2–2	0–2–2	0–0–0	———	0–0–0	0–1–1	1–2–3
Moreau	———	———	0–0–0	———	———	———	———	———	———
Murray	0–0–0	0–0–0	3–0–3	0–0–0	0–1–1	0–1–1	0–0–0	0–0–0	0–1–1
Musil	———	———	0–0–0	1–0–1	0–0–0	———	0–0–0	———	———
Niinimaa	0–0–0	0–0–0	0–1–1	0–0–0	0–0–0	0–0–0	0–0–0	0–1–1	0–0–0
Passmore	———	———	———	———	0–1–1	———	———	———	———
Poti	1–0–1	0–0–0	0–0–0	0–1–1	0–0–0	0–0–0	0–0–0	0–1–1	0–0–0
Reirden	———	0–0–0	———	0–1–1	———	———	———	0–0–0	———
Selivanov	———	2–0–2	———	0–2–2	0–0–0	———	0–0–0	0–0–0	———
Smith	———	———	0–0–0	———	———	———	———	———	———
Smyth	0–0–0	1–2–3	0–0–0	0–0–0	1–0–1	0–0–0	0–0–0	0–0–0	0–0–0
Weight	———	0–0–0	0–0–0	0–1–1	0–0–0	0–2–2	0–1–1	0–1–1	———

	Phoe.	*Pitt.*	*S.J.*	*St.L.*	*Tamp.*	*Tor.*	*Van.*	*Was.*
Beranek	0–2–2	0–0–0	0–3–3	1–2–3	0–1–1	0–1–1	2–2–4	2–1–3
Brown, K.	———	1–0–1	———	———	———	0–0–0	1–1–2	0–1–1
Brown, S.	0–0–0	0–0–0	0–0–0	———	0–0–0	0–0–0	0–0–0	0–0–0
Buchberger	1–0–1	0–0–0	0–1–1	0–0–0	0–0–0	0–0–0	0–0–0	1–0–1
Devereaux	1–2–3	1–0–1	0–0–0	0–0–0	0–0–0	0–0–0	0–0–0	0–1–1
Essensa	———	———	———	———	———	———	———	0–1–1
Falloon	1–5–6	1–1–2	2–0–2	0–3–3	1–1–2	0–0–0	4–1–5	0–2–2
Grier	2–3–5	1–0–1	1–5–6	0–0–0	0–1–1	0–1–1	3–1–4	1–0–1
Guerin	1–0–1	0–1–1	4–0–4	2–2–4	1–1–2	1–1–2	1–3–4	2–2–4
Hamrlik	1–2–3	1–0–1	0–0–0	2–2–4	0–0–0	0–0–0	0–4–4	1–0–1
Huard	———	———	———	———	0–0–0	———	———	———
Kilger	0–0–0	———	1–0–1	0–0–0		0–0–0	0–0–0	———
Kovalenko	1–0–1	1–1–2	0–1–1	———	0–1–1	1–0–1	0–1–1	0–1–1
Lacroix	———	———	———	0–0–0	———	0–0–0	———	0–0–0
Laflamme	———	———	0–0–0	0–0–0	———	0–0–0	0–0–0	———
Laraque	2–0–2	0–0–0	0–0–0	0–0–0		0–0–0	0–0–0	0–1–1
Lindgren	0–3–3	0–0–0	0–0–0	0–2–2	0–1–1	0–1–1	1–1–2	0–1–1
Lindquist	———	———	0–0–0	———	———	———	———	———
Marchant	1–4–5	0–1–1	2–1–3	0–0–0	1–2–3	0–0–0	1–3–4	0–1–1
McAmmond	2–2–4	0–0–0	1–2–3	0–2–2	1–0–1	0–0–0	1–3–4	0–1–1

	Phoe.	*Pitt.*	*S.J.*	*St.L.*	*Tamp.*	*Tor.*	*Van.*	*Was.*
McSorley	0–0–0	———	0–0–0	0–0–0	0–0–0	0–1–1	0–0–0	1–0–1
Millar	0–1–1	0–1–1	———	———	———	0–0–0	0–0–0	0–0–0
Mironov	0–0–0	0–0–0	0–1–1	0–2–2	0–0–0	0–1–1	2–4–6	2–1–3
Moreau	0–1–1	———	0–1–1	0–0–0	———	0–0–0	0–3–3	———
Murray	2–1–3	0–0–0	1–1–2	2–0–2	0–0–0	2–0–2	0–1–1	0–1–1
Musil	0–1–1	0–0–0	0–0–0	0–0–0	0–0–0	0–0–0	0–0–0	0–0–0
Niinimaa	0–1–1	0–1–1	0–3–3	1–0–1	0–0–0	0–0–0	0–5–5	0–3–3
Poti	0–1–1	0–0–0	1–2–3	0–1–1	0–0–0	0–0–0	1–1–2	0–0–0
Reirden	0–0–0	———	0–0–0	1–0–1	———	———	0–0–0	———
Selivanov	———	0–1–1	1–1–2	0–0–0	———	———	0–0–0	1–0–1
Smith	0–0–0	———	0–1–1	0–0–0	———	1–0–1	0–0–0	———
Smyth	1–2–3	0–1–1	0–0–0	3–1–4	1–0–1	0–1–1	0–1–1	0–1–1
Weight	1–0–1	0–1–1	0–5–5	0–5–5	———	0–1–1	1–0–1	0–1–1

Goaltender Record vs. Opposition

	GP	*Min.*	*GA*	*EN*	*SO*	*Ave.*	*W–L–T*	*Opposition*
Bob Essensa	1	31	1	0	0	1.94	0–0–0	Anaheim
	1	60	3	0	0	3.00	1–0–0	Buffalo
	1	60	2	0	0	2.00	0–1–0	Calgary
	1	65	4	0	0	3.69	0–1–0	Chicago
	4	220	13	2	0	3.55	1–3–0	Colorado
	4	177	14	0	0	4.75	0–2–1	Dallas
	4	240	14	0	0	3.50	1–3–0	Detroit
	3	127	2	0	0	1.26	0–0–1	Los Angeles
	1	34	0	0	0	0.00	0–0–0	Montreal
	2	120	4	0	0	2.00	2–0–0	Nashville
	2	130	3	0	0	1.38	0–0–2	Ottawa
	2	112	5	0	0	2.68	1–1–0	Phoenix
	2	115	3	0	0	1.57	1–0–1	Pittsburgh
	2	121	5	0	0	2.48	0–2–0	Rangers
	2	86	6	0	0	4.19	0–0–1	San Jose
	2	120	8	0	0	4.00	1–1–0	St. Louis
	1	60	1	0	0	1.00	1–0–0	Tampa
	1	40	2	0	0	3.00	0–0–0	Toronto
	2	120	4	0	0	2.00	2–0–0	Vancouver
	1	60	2	0	0	2.00	1–0–0	Washington
Steve Passmore	1	60	2	0	0	2.00	0–1–0	Anaheim
	1	60	3	0	0	3.00	1–0–0	Buffalo
	1	65	2	0	0	1.85	0–0–1	Carolina
	1	60	2	1	0	2.00	0–1–0	Nashville
	1	60	4	0	0	4.00	0–1–0	New Jersey
	1	60	4	0	0	4.00	0–1–0	Washington
Tommy Salo	4	245	7	0	0	1.71	3–0–1	Calgary
	1	60	1	0	0	1.00	1–0–0	Colorado
	1	60	2	0	0	2.00	0–1–0	Montreal
	1	8	3	0	0	22.50	0–0–0	Phoenix
	2	124	6	0	0	2.90	2–0–0	San Jose
	1	60	1	0	0	1.00	1–0–0	St. Louis
	1	20	3	0	0	9.00	0–1–0	Toronto
	2	125	4	0	0	1.92	1–0–1	Vancouver
Mikhail Shtalenkov	4	210	9	0	1	2.57	3–1–0	Anaheim
	1	60	2	0	0	2.00	0–1–0	Boston
	1	60	2	0	0	2.00	1–0–0	Calgary
	1	60	3	0	0	3.00	0–1–0	Carolina
	3	181	8	0	0	2.65	1–2–0	Chicago
	2	80	4	0	1	3.00	1–0–0	Colorado
	2	68	5	0	0	4.41	0–1–0	Dallas
	1	60	3	0	0	3.00	0–1–0	Florida
	1	60	2	0	0	2.00	1–0–0	Islanders
	3	119	8	0	0	4.03	0–3–0	Los Angeles
	2	86	5	1	0	3.49	1–1–0	Montreal
	1	65	3	0	0	2.77	0–0–1	Nashville
	1	60	2	0	0	2.00	1–0–0	New Jersey

	GP	Min.	GA	EN	SO	Ave.	W–L–T	Opposition
Mikhail Shtalenkov	2	130	5	0	0	2.31	0–0–2	Philadelphia
	2	124	6	0	0	1.45	1–1–0	Phoenix
	1	39	1	1	0	1.54	0–1–0	San Jose
	1	61	4	0	0	3.93	0–1–0	St. Louis
	1	60	2	0	0	2.00	0–1–0	Tampa
	2	120	6	0	0	3.00	0–2–0	Toronto
	2	120	1	0	1	0.50	2–0–0	Vancouver

1998–99 Schedule Results

Date	Visitor			Home	
Oct. 10	Los Angeles	2	at	Edmonton	1
Oct. 13	Toronto	3	at	Edmonton	2
Oct. 14	Edmonton	4	at	Vancouver	1
Oct. 17	Edmonton	4	at	New Jersey	2
Oct. 20	Edmonton	2	at	Rangers	3
Oct. 21	Edmonton	4	at	Islanders	2
Oct. 24	Edmonton	4	at	Colorado	6
Oct. 28	Washington	2	at	Edmonton	8
Oct. 31	Pittsburgh	1	at	Edmonton	4
Nov. 2	Vancouver	3	at	Edmonton	5
Nov. 4	Nashville	2	at	Edmonton	3
Nov. 6	Colorado	5	at	Edmonton	2
Nov. 8	Edmonton	3	at	Chicago	2 (OT)
Nov. 11	Edmonton	2	at	Toronto	3
Nov. 12	Edmonton	1	at	Ottawa	1 (OT)
Nov. 14	Edmonton	4	at	Montreal	1
Nov. 18	Detroit	6	at	Edmonton	2
Nov. 20	Edmonton	3	at	Anaheim	2 (OT)
Nov. 21	Phoenix	3	at	Edmonton	2 (OT)
Nov. 25	Colorado	0	at	Edmonton	3
Nov. 27	Edmonton	3	at	Calgary	2
Nov. 29	Chicago	3	at	Edmonton	2
Dec. 2	Phoenix	3	at	Edmonton	4
Dec. 4	Tampa Bay	2	at	Edmonton	1
Dec. 6	Dallas	6	at	Edmonton	2
Dec. 8	Edmonton	3	at	Nashville	3 (OT)
Dec. 9	Edmonton	1	at	Chicago	3
Dec. 11	Edmonton	2	at	Detroit	3
Dec. 13	Edmonton	2	at	Philadelphia	2 (OT)
Dec. 15	Edmonton	0	at	Carolina	3
Dec. 18	Edmonton	4	at	Tampa Bay	1
Dec. 19	Edmonton	1	at	Florida	3
Dec. 23	San Jose	5	at	Edmonton	3
Dec. 27	Vancouver	0	at	Edmonton	3
Dec. 29	Montreal	5	at	Edmonton	2
Jan. 3	Philadelphia	3	at	Edmonton	3 (OT)
Jan. 5	Los Angeles	4	at	Edmonton	3 (OT)
Jan. 7	Edmonton	7	at	Phoenix	1
Jan. 9	Edmonton	1	at	Los Angeles	1 (OT)
Jan. 10	Edmonton	4	at	Anaheim	6
Jan. 12	Dallas	2	at	Edmonton	2 (OT)
Jan. 14	Edmonton	3	at	Vancouver	1
Jan. 17	Detroit	1	at	Edmonton	4
Jan. 21	Edmonton	3	at	San Jose	3 (OT)
Jan. 27	Chicago	4	at	Edmonton	3 (OT)
Jan. 30	Anaheim	0	at	Edmonton	1
Feb. 1	St. Louis	4	at	Edmonton	3 (OT)
Feb. 3	Ottawa	2	at	Edmonton	2 (OT)
Feb. 5	Nashville	2	at	Edmonton	4
Feb. 8	Edmonton	1	at	Calgary	2
Feb. 9	Boston	2	at	Edmonton	0
Feb. 11	Edmonton	2	at	Detroit	4
Feb. 13	Edmonton	3	at	St. Louis	2
Feb. 15	Edmonton	1	at	Dallas	4
Feb. 17	Edmonton	6	at	Anaheim	2
Feb. 18	Edmonton	2	at	Los Angeles	3
Feb. 21	Rangers	2	at	Edmonton	1 (OT)
Feb. 24	Anaheim	2	at	Edmonton	1
Feb. 26	Buffalo	3	at	Edmonton	6
Feb. 27	Carolina	2	at	Edmonton	2 (OT)
Mar. 1	Edmonton	4	at	Colorado	3
Mar. 3	Edmonton	5	at	Buffalo	3
Mar. 5	Edmonton	2	at	Pittsburgh	2 (OT)
Mar. 6	Edmonton	3	at	Washington	4
Mar. 10	Edmonton	4	at	Dallas	7
Mar. 13	Edmonton	4	at	St. Louis	6
Mar. 14	Edmonton	1	at	Washington	3
Mar. 17	New Jersey	4	at	Edmonton	1
Mar. 20	Vancouver	3	at	Edmonton	4
Mar. 22	Calgary	2	at	Edmonton	2 (OT)
Mar. 24	Montreal	2	at	Edmonton	0
Mar. 26	St. Louis	1	at	Edmonton	2
Mar. 28	San Jose	2	at	Edmonton	5
Mar. 30	Phoenix	7	at	Edmonton	4
Apr. 1	Toronto	5	at	Edmonton	1
Apr. 3	Edmonton	2	at	Colorado	5
Apr. 7	Calgary	2	at	Edmonton	4
Apr. 9	Edmonton	4	at	Calgary	1
Apr. 10	Edmonton	1	at	Vancouver	1 (OT)
Apr. 11	Edmonton	5	at	San Jose	4 (OT)
Apr. 16	Colorado	1	at	Edmonton	5
Apr. 17	Calgary	2	at	Edmonton	3

Overall Record vs. Opponents

Opponent	*Home*	*Road*	*Overall*	*GF–GA*	*Opponent*
Anaheim	1–1–0	2–1–0	3–2–0	15–12	Anaheim
Boston	0–1–0	0–0–0	0–1–0	0–2	Boston
Buffalo	1–0–0	1–0–0	2–0–0	11–6	Buffalo
Calgary	2–0–1	2–1–0	4–1–1	17–11	Calgary
Carolina	0–0–1	0–1–0	0–1–1	2–5	Carolina
Chicago	0–2–0	1–1–0	1–3–0	9–12	Chicago
Colorado	2–1–0	1–2–0	3–3–0	20–20	Colorado
Dallas	0–1–1	0–2–0	0–3–1	9–19	Dallas
Detroit	1–1–0	0–2–0	1–3–0	10–14	Detroit

Opponent	Home	Road	Overall	GF–GA	Opponent
Florida	0–0–0	0–1–0	0–1–0	1–3	Florida
Los Angeles	0–2–0	0–1–1	0–3–1	7–10	Los Angeles
Montreal	0–2–0	1–0–0	1–2–0	6–8	Montreal
Nashville	2–0–0	0–1–1	2–1–1	11–10	Nashville
New Jersey	0–1–0	1–0–0	1–1–0	5–6	New Jersey
Islanders	0–0–0	1–0–0	1–0–0	4–2	Islanders
Rangers	0–1–0	0–1–0	0–2–0	3–5	Rangers
Ottawa	0–0–1	0–0–1	0–0–2	3–3	Ottawa
Philadelphia	0–0–1	0–0–1	0–0–2	5–5	Philadelphia
Phoenix	1–1–0	1–1–0	2–2–0	17–14	Phoenix
Pittsburgh	1–0–0	0–0–1	1–0–1	6–3	Pittsburgh
San Jose	1–1–0	1–0–1	2–1–1	16–14	San Jose
St. Louis	1–1–0	1–1–0	2–2–0	12–13	St. Louis
Tampa Bay	0–0–1	1–0–0	1–0–1	5–3	Tampa Bay
Toronto	0–2–0	0–1–0	0–3–0	5–11	Toronto
Vancouver	3–0–0	2–0–1	5–0–1	20–9	Vancouver
Washington	1–0–0	0–1–0	1–1–0	11–6	Washington

1998-99 Playoff Scoring

#		GP	G	A	Pts	Shots	S%	GW	OT	PP	SH	P/M	PIM
94	Ryan Smyth	3	3	0	3	7	42.9	0	0	2	0	-1	0
18	Ethan Moreau	4	0	3	3	6	0.0	0	0	0	0	3	6
39	Doug Weight	4	1	1	2	4	25.0	0	0	0	0	-3	15
17	Rem Murray	4	1	1	2	6	16.7	0	0	0	0	-1	2
26	Todd Marchant	4	1	1	2	10	10.0	0	0	0	0	2	12
25	Mike Grier	4	1	1	2	9	11.1	0	0	0	0	3	6
9	Bill Guerin	3	0	2	2	8	0.0	0	0	0	0	-4	2
28	Alex Selivanov	2	0	1	1	3	0.0	0	0	0	0	0	2
10	Pat Falloon	4	0	1	1	6	0.0	0	0	0	0	0	4
21	Jason Smith	4	0	1	1	1	0.0	0	0	0	0	0	4
24	Christian Laflamme	4	0	1	1	5	0.0	0	0	0	0	-4	2
5	Tom Poti	4	0	1	1	9	0.0	0	0	0	0	-3	2
8	Frank Musil	1	0	0	0	2	0.0	0	0	0	0	-1	2
34	Vladimir Vorobiev	1	0	0	0	1	0.0	0	0	0	0	-1	0
23	Sean Brown	1	0	0	0	0	0.0	0	0	0	0	0	10
19	Boyd Devereaux	1	0	0	0	3	0.0	0	0	0	0	0	0
20	Josef Beranek	1	0	0	0	0	0.0	0	0	0	0	-1	4
33	Marty McSorley	3	0	0	0	3	0.0	0	0	0	0	1	2
22	Roman Hamrlik	3	0	0	0	1	0.0	0	0	0	0	1	2
16	Kelly Buchberger	4	0	0	0	2	0.0	0	0	0	0	-4	0
44	Janne Niinimaa	4	0	0	0	5	0.0	0	0	0	0	-2	2
35	Tommy Salo	4	0	0	0	0	0.0	0	0	0	0	0	0
15	Chad Kilger	4	0	0	0	1	0.0	0	0	0	0	-2	4
27	Georges Laraque	4	0	0	0	1	0.0	0	0	0	0	-2	2
		4	7	14	21	93	7.5	0	0	2	0	-19	85

1998-99 Playoff Goaltending

	GP	Min.	GA	W	L	Ave.	SA	Pct.	SO	EN
Tommy Salo	4	296	11	0	4	2.21	149	0.926	0	0

Date	Result					Winning Goaltender	Winning Goal
April 21, 1999	Edmonton	1	at	Dallas	2	Ed Belfour	Guy Carbonneau
April 23, 1999	Edmonton	2	at	Dallas	3	Ed Belfour	Jamie Langenbrunner
April 25, 1999	Dallas	3	at	Edmonton	2	Ed Belfour	Joe Nieuwendyk
April 27, 1999	Dallas	3	at	Edmonton	2	Ed Belfour	Joe Nieuwendyk[1]

[1]57:34 of overtime

Table 17. Opposition Shutouts

Date		Goaltender	Opponent	Score	Shots
November 17, 1979	*Road*	*Al Smith (1)*	*Hartford*	*0–4*	*23*
April 1, 1980	*Road*	*Gary Bromley (1)*	*Vancouver*	*0–5*	*22*

Date		*Goaltender*	*Opponent*	*Score*	*Shots*
October 15, 1980	*Road*	*Bob Sauve (1)*	*Buffalo*	*0–2*	*15*
January 12, 1981	*Road*	*Richard Sevigny (1)*	*Montreal*	*0–5*	*20*
March 12, 1981	*Home*	*Billy Smith (1)*	*N.Y. Islanders*	*0–5*	*36*
May 10, 1983 (P)	*Home*	*Billy Smith (2)*	*N.Y. Islanders*	*0–2*	*35*
February 12, 1984	*Road*	*Greg Millen (1)*	*Hartford*	*0–11*	*28*
November 1, 1985	*Home*	*Daren Puppa (1)*	*Buffalo*	*0–2*	*37*
March 11, 1986	*Road*	*Don Beaupre (1)*	*Minnesota*	*0–4*	*27*
October 27, 1987	*Road*	*Mario Gosselin (1)*	*Quebec*	*0–5*	*21*
January 2, 1988	*Road*	*Clint Malarchuk (1)*	*Washington*	*0–2*	*28*
January 15, 1989	*Road*	*Sean Burke (1)*	*New Jersey*	*0–1*	*26*
March 16, 1989	*Road*	*Kirk McLean (1)*	*Vancouver*	*0–3*	*22*
October 19, 1989	*Home*	*Andy Moog (1)*	*Boston*	*0–3*	*11*
October 28, 1990	*Home*	*Don Beaupre (2)*	*Washington*	*0–1*	*31*
October 31, 1990	*Home*	*Bob Essensa (1)*	*Winnipeg*	*0–1 (OT)*	*34*
January 2, 1991	*Home*	*Andre Racicot (1)*	*Montreal*	*0–3*	*24*
March 23, 1991	*Home*	*Bob Essensa (2)*	*Winnipeg*	*0–3*	*26*
March 26, 1991	*Road*	*Kelly Hrudey (1)*	*Los Angeles*	*0–2*	*33*
November 18, 1991	*Road*	*Patrick Roy (1)*	*Montreal*	*0–1*	*12*
November 23, 1991	*Home*	*Bob Essensa (3)*	*Winnipeg*	*0–4*	*36*
May 5, 1992 (P)	*Road*	*Kirk McLean (2)*	*Vancouver*	*0–4*	*14*
October 25, 1992	*Home*	*Jeff Reese (1)*	*Calgary*	*0–4*	*21*
November 21, 1992	*Road*	*Kirk McLean (3)*	*Vancouver*	*0–9*	*27*
January 10, 1993	*Road*	*T. Soderstrom (1)*	*Philadelphia*	*0–4*	*29*
February 27, 1993	*Home*	*Mike Richter (1)*	*N.Y. Rangers*	*0–1*	*29*
April 15, 1993	*Road*	*Bob Essensa (4)*	*Winnipeg*	*0–3*	*31*
November 7, 1993	*Road*	*Ed Belfour (1)*	*Chicago*	*0–3*	*23*
February 1, 1995	*Home*	*Ed Belfour (2)*	*Chicago*	*0–7*	*22*
February 20, 1995	*Road*	*Curtis Joseph (1)*	*St. Louis*	*0–4*	*21*
April 7, 1995	*Road*	*Wade Flaherty (1)*	*San Jose*	*0–5*	*26*
October 13, 1995	*Road*	*Chris Osgood (1)*	*Detroit*	*0–9*	*17*
November 26, 1995	*Road*	*N. Khabibulin (1)*	*Winnipeg*	*0–4*	*34*
January 3, 1996	*Home*	*Daren Puppa (2)*	*Tampa Bay*	*0–5*	*28*
January 31, 1996	*Home*	*Ed Belfour (3)*	*Chicago*	*0–4*	*35*
February 25, 1996	*Road*	*T. Soderstrom (2)*	*N.Y. Islanders*	*0–2*	*25*
April 3, 1996	*Road*	*Guy Hebert (1)*	*Anaheim*	*0–1*	*27*
October 9, 1996	*Road*	*Chris Osgood (2)*	*Detroit*	*0–2*	*18*
December 4, 1996	*Road*	*Patrick Roy (2)*	*Colorado*	*0–2*	*36*
December 10, 1996	*Road*	*Chris Osgood (3)*	*Detroit*	*0–0 (OT)*	*21*
October 5, 1997	*Road*	*Patrick Roy (3)*	*Colorado*	*0–3*	*34*
October 13, 1997	*Road*	*Kirk McLean (4)*	*Vancouver*	*0–3*	*33*
December 17, 1997	*Home*	*Jeff Hackett (1)*	*Chicago*	*0–0 (OT)*	*30*
February 4, 1998	*Home*	*Mike Vernon (1)*	*San Jose*	*0–3*	*21*
February 27, 1998	*Home*	*M. Shtalenkov (1)*	*Anaheim*	*0–4*	*26*
March 27, 1998	*Home*	*Dominik Hasek (1)*	*Buffalo*	*0–1*	*20*
May 11, 1998 (P)	*Home*	*Ed Belfour (4)*	*Dallas*	*0–1 (OT)*	*28*
December 15, 1998	*Road*	*Arturs Irbe (1)*	*Carolina*	*0–3*	*29*
February 9, 1999	*Home*	*Byron Dafoe (1)*	*Boston*	*0–2*	*31*
March 24, 1999	*Home*	*Jeff Hackett (2)*	*Montreal*	*0–2*	*32*
March 7, 2000	*Home*	*Curtis Joseph (2)*	*Toronto*	*0–2*	*33*
April 3, 2000	*Home*	*Steve Shields (1)*	*San Jose*	*0–1*	*20*
April 13, 2000 (P)	*Road*	*Ed Belfour (5)*	*Dallas*	*0–3*	*17*
November 9, 2000	*Road*	*R. Cechmanek (1)*	*Philadelphia*	*0–2*	*28*
December 16, 2000	*Road*	*Olaf Kolzig (1)*	*Washington*	*0–4*	*14*
February 9, 2001	*Road*	*Sean Burke (2)*	*Phoenix*	*0–2*	*38*
Total 56 games	*33 road 23 home*			*0–178*	*1465*

P—indicates playoff game

1999–2000

Former Oiler star Kevin Lowe became the team's head coach, taking over from Ron Low and Craig MacTavish, became an assistant coach, joining Ted Green.

Two players of note to come out of this year's draft, were Mike Comrie and Tomas Groschl. Comrie, a native of Edmonton and the brother of Oiler's Paul Comrie spent two seasons at the University of Michigan and half a season in the Western Hockey League before making the big team for the 2000-01 season. Groschl, who played for the Leksands team in the Swedish league, was the first Hungarian born player ever chosen in the entry draft.

Doug Weight who had led the team in scoring for five of the previous six seasons, took over duties as team captain, replacing Kelly Buchberger. Jason Smith, Todd Marchant, Roman Hamrlik and Bill Guerin rotated as assistant captains.

On October 1st the Oilers and the New York Rangers became the first two NHL teams to be involved in the new four on four overtime format. The game ended in a 1-1 tie. This same night the team officially retired Wayne Gretzky's jersey in a quiet pre game ceremony.

The Oilers did not play their first game against a divisional opponent until December 1st but had played all three of their matches against St. Louis by November 12th.

Eight of the team's first seventeen games went into overtime. Their record was three losses and five ties during those eight games. The Oilers did not win in overtime until their twenty first overtime game of the season.

Following a successful road trip in February in which the team won three and tied two of five games the Oilers took over top spot in the Northwest Division a spot which they were in contention for until near the end of the season. This was one of the best road trips in franchise history. The Oilers were 18-22-13-.462 at the All-Star break.

Kevin Lowe and Craig MacTavish developed a stingy defensive system while still maintaining the wide open offensive style for which the Oilers have traditionally been known.

Edmonton scored 226 goals, good enough for fourteenth in the league while allowing 212 which was twelfth best.

This Oiler team was probably the most talented one since the last Stanley Cup winning squad. Georges Laraque became one of the league's top enforcers. Combined with a decent scoring touch Laraque was a major force in the opponents zone. Sophomore defenseman Tom Poti continued his fine play while goaltender Tommy Salo turned in the best goals against average of any Oiler netminder in team history. Most of the regular roster had fine seasons. Glen Sather had only to tweak the team this year obtaining Igor Ulanov and German Titov near the trading deadline. Alex Selivanov got off to a fast start scoring 17 goals (on 42 shots) in 19 games. He then went into an extended slump scoring ten goals in the remaining 48 games.

Injuries plagued the team all year. Mike Grier missed four games with a chipped clavicle as well as the final twelve with a hyperextended elbow. Ethan Moreau missed eight games with a rib injury and Doug Weight missed five games for the same reason. After playing the first three games Rem Murray missed the next twenty eight with a knee injury. Boyd Devereaux missed the final four regular season games as well as the playoffs with a concussion.

In the previous couple of seasons the Oilers had put on late spurts which enabled them to enter the post season but this year they did the opposite. After challenging Colorado for first place in the Northwest Division for much of the season they won only nine of the final twenty games just clinching a playoff spot in the second last game of the season.

For the fourth straight year the Oilers met the Dallas Stars in the playoffs and in a rather uninspired series lost to the Stars in five games.

On May 19th, the sixteenth anniversary of the team's first Stanley Cup victory, long time coach and general manager, Glen Sather tendered his resignation. Citing differences with team owners and a wish to spend more time with his family, "Slats" ended a twenty four year association with the club which saw him elected to the Hockey Hall of Fame and the Oilers win five Stanley Cups. On June 1st the New York Rangers announced that they had signed Sather as their new President and General Manager.

On June 9th, Kevin Lowe whose name perhaps more than any is intrinsically linked with the Oilers, was named as the team's new General Manager. On June 22nd, Edmonton named Craig MacTavish as head coach.

1999-2000 Regular Season Scoring

#		*Ht.*	*Wt.*	*Age*	*GP*	*G*	*A*	*Pts*	*Shots*	*S%*	*GW*	*GT*	*PP*	*SH*	*P/M*	*PIM*
39	Weight (C)	71	200	28	77	21	51	72	167	12.6	4	0	3	1	6	54
94	Smyth	73	195	23	82	28	26	54	238	11.8	4	1	11	0	-2	58
29	Selivanov	72	208	28	67	27	20	47	122	22.1	5	0	10	0	2	46
9	Guerin (A)	74	210	29	70	24	22	46	188	12.8	2	0	11	0	4	123
22	Hamrlik (A)	74	215	25	80	8	37	45	180	4.4	0	1	5	0	1	68
26	Marchant (A)	70	178	26	82	17	23	40	170	10.0	0	2	0	1	7	70
5	Poti	75	215	22	76	9	26	35	125	7.2	1	0	2	1	8	65
44	Niinimaa	74	220	24	81	8	25	33	133	6.0	0	0	2	2	14	89
25	Grier	73	227	24	65	9	22	31	115	7.8	2	0	0	3	9	68
18	Moreau	74	211	24	73	17	10	27	106	16.0	3	0	1	0	8	62
19	Devereaux	74	195	21	76	8	19	27	108	7.4	2	1	0	1	7	20
34	Dowd	73	190	31	69	5	18	23	103	4.9	1	1	2	0	10	45

#		Ht.	Wt.	Age	GP	G	A	Pts	Shots	S%	GW	GT	PP	SH	P/M	PIM
10	Falloon	71	190	27	33	5	13	18	51	9.8	0	0	1	0	6	4
20	Beranek	74	195	30	58	9	8	17	107	8.4	1	0	3	0	-6	39
27	Laraque	75	230	23	76	8	8	16	56	14.3	0	0	0	0	5	123
17	Murray	74	195	27	44	9	5	14	65	13.8	3	0	2	0	-2	8
21	Smith (A)	75	210	26	80	3	11	14	96	3.1	1	0	0	0	16	60
23	Brown, S.	75	205	23	72	4	8	12	36	11.1	2	0	0	0	1	192
37	Cleary	72	203	21	17	3	2	5	18	16.7	1	0	0	0	-1	8
15	Kilger	75	215	23	40	3	2	5	32	9.4	0	0	0	0	-6	18
24	Laflamme	73	210	23	50	0	5	5	18	0.0	0	0	0	0	-4	32
13	Titov	73	201	34	7	0	4	4	11	0.0	0	0	0	0	2	4
14	Robertsson	75	205	25	52	0	4	4	31	0.0	0	0	0	0	-3	34
47	Comrie	71	192	22	15	1	2	3	11	9.1	0	0	0	0	-2	4
2	Ulanov	75	211	30	14	0	3	3	6	0.0	0	0	0	0	-3	10
2	Hauer	74	200	28	5	0	2	2	8	0.0	0	0	0	0	-2	2
35	Salo	71	173	28	70	0	1	1	0	0.0	0	0	0	0	0	8
1	Minard	75	205	23	1	0	0	0	0	0.0	0	0	0	0	0	0
12	Picard	71	190	30	2	0	0	0	2	0.0	0	0	0	0	0	2
33	LaCouture	75	210	22	5	0	0	0	2	0.0	0	0	0	0	0	10
10	Brown, K.	73	212	25	7	0	0	0	5	0.0	0	0	0	0	0	0
30	Ranford	71	185	33	16	0	0	0	0	0.0	0	0	0	0	0	2
	Bench															12
		73	203	26	82	226	377	603	2310	9.8	32	6	53	9	75	1340

1999-2000 Goaltender Records

	GP	Min.	GA	W	L	T	Ave.	SA	Pct.	SO	EN
Tommy Salo	70	4164	162	27	28	13	2.33	1871	0.913	2	0
Mike Minard	1	60	3	1	0	0	3.00	36	0.917	0	0
Bill Ranford	16	785	47	4	6	3	3.59	407	0.885	0	0
	82	5009	212	32	34	16	2.54	2314	0.908	2	0

Coach: Kevin Lowe 32-34-16-.488

Scoring vs. Opposition

	Ana.	Atl.	Bost.	Buff.	Calg.	Caro.	Chic.	Col.	Dall.
Beranek	0-0-0	1-0-1	0-0-0	0-0-0	0-0-0	0-0-0	0-0-0	0-1-1	0-0-0
Brown, K.	———	0-0-0	———	———	0-0-0	0-0-0	———	0-0-0	———
Brown, S.	0-0-0	0-1-1	1-0-1	0-0-0	1-2-3	0-0-0	0-0-0	0-0-0	0-0-0
Cleary	0-0-0	0-0-0	0-0-0	———	1-0-1	———	———	0-0-0	0-0-0
Comrie	———	———	———	———	———	0-0-0	0-0-0	———	———
Devereaux	0-0-0	1-1-2	0-0-0	0-0-0	0-0-0	0-0-0	1-0-1	0-3-3	0-2-2
Dowd	1-1-2	0-1-1	0-0-0	0-0-0	0-2-2	0-1-1	0-0-0	0-4-4	0-2-2
Falloon	0-2-2	———	0-0-0	———	0-0-0	0-0-0	———	0-1-1	0-0-0
Grier	0-1-1	0-1-1	0-1-1	1-0-1	1-0-1	1-0-1	1-2-3	0-1-1	0-1-1
Guerin	1-1-2	1-1-2	2-0-2	0-1-1	3-2-5	0-0-0	0-0-0	1-2-3	1-0-1
Hamrlik	0-1-1	0-2-2	0-0-0	0-0-0	1-4-5	0-0-0	0-2-2	2-0-2	0-2-2
Hauer	———	———	———	———	———	———	0-1-1	0-0-0	———
Kilger	0-0-0	0-0-0	0-0-0	———	0-0-0	0-0-0	1-0-1	0-0-0	———
LaCouture	———	———	———	———	0-0-0	———	———	0-0-0	———
Laflamme	0-0-0	0-0-0	0-0-0	———	0-0-0	0-0-0	0-0-0	———	0-0-0
Laraque	0-0-0	0-1-1	0-0-0	0-0-0	0-0-0	0-0-0	0-0-0	1-0-1	1-0-1
Marchant	2-1-3	1-0-1	1-2-3	0-1-1	1-4-5	0-0-0	0-1-1	0-0-0	0-1-1
Moreau	1-0-1	0-0-0	1-1-2	0-1-1	0-0-0	0-1-1	1-2-3	0-0-0	0-0-0
Murray	0-0-0	0-0-0	0-0-0	0-0-0	1-3-4	1-0-1	0-0-0	1-0-1	0-0-0
Niinimaa	0-1-1	0-0-0	0-0-0	0-0-0	1-3-4	0-0-0	2-2-4	0-1-1	0-0-0
Picard	———	———	0-0-0	———	———	———	———	———	———
Poti	1-0-1	0-1-1	0-1-1	0-0-0	1-2-3	0-0-0	0-0-0	0-1-1	1-1-2
Robertsson	———	0-0-0	0-0-0	0-0-0	0-1-1	0-0-0	0-1-1	0-0-0	0-0-0
Salo	0-0-0	0-0-0	0-0-0	0-0-0	———	0-0-0	0-0-0	0-1-1	0-0-0
Selivanov	1-1-2	———	0-2-2	0-0-0	4-1-5	1-0-1	4-1-5	4-1-5	0-0-0
Smith	0-1-1	0-0-0	0-0-0	0-0-0	0-2-2	0-2-2	0-0-0	0-0-0	0-1-1
Smyth	0-2-2	3-1-4	0-1-1	1-0-1	3-1-4	1-1-2	0-4-4	1-3-4	1-0-1
Titov	0-0-0	———	———	———	0-3-3	0-0-0	———	———	———

	Ana.	*Atl.*	*Bost.*	*Buff.*	*Calg.*	*Caro.*	*Chic.*	*Col.*	*Dall.*
Ulanov	0-0-0	———	———	———	0-0-0	0-0-0	———	0-2-2	———
Weight	1-4-5	1-4-5	1-1-2	0-1-1	2-2-4	1-1-2	2-3-5	4-1-5	0-0-0

	Det.	*Flor.*	*L.A.*	*Mont.*	*Nash.*	*NJ.*	*NYI.*	*NYR.*	*Ott.*
Beranek	0-1-1	0-1-1	0-1-1	0-0-0	1-1-2	1-0-1	0-0-0	0-0-0	0-0-0
Brown, K.	———	———	———	———	———	———	———	———	0-0-0
Brown, S.	0-0-0	0-0-0	0-0-0	1-0-1	0-0-0	0-0-0	0-0-0	0-0-0	0-1-1
Cleary	———	———	2-0-2	0-1-1	0-0-0	———	———	———	———
Comrie	0-0-0	———	———	0-1-1	1-0-1	———	0-0-0	0-0-0	———
Devereaux	0-0-0	0-0-0	0-2-2	0-2-2	1-0-1	1-1-2	0-1-1	0-0-0	4-0-4
Dowd	1-0-1	0-0-0	0-3-3	0-1-1	0-1-1	———	———	0-0-0	1-0-1
Falloon	0-0-0	0-0-0	0-2-2	———	0-0-0	0-0-0	1-0-1	0-0-0	0-1-1
Grier	0-1-1	1-0-1	1-0-1	0-1-1	2-1-3	0-1-1	1-0-1	0-0-0	0-0-0
Guerin	1-1-2	0-2-2	1-0-1	1-1-2	0-0-0	0-0-0	1-2-3	0-0-0	0-0-0
Hamrlik	1-0-1	0-0-0	0-3-3	0-1-1	1-2-3	0-0-0	0-2-2	0-0-0	0-0-0
Hauer	———	———	———	———	———	———	———	0-0-0	———
Kilger	0-0-0	———	0-0-0	0-0-0	0-0-0	———	1-0-1	0-0-0	0-1-1
Laflamme	0-1-1	0-1-1	0-0-0	0-0-0	0-0-0	0-1-1	0-0-0	0-1-1	0-1-1
Laraque	0-0-0	0-0-0	3-0-3	1-1-2	0-1-1	0-1-1	0-0-0	0-0-0	0-3-3
Marchant	0-1-1	0-0-0	0-1-1	1-0-1	1-2-3	0-0-0	0-1-1	0-1-1	0-0-0
Moreau	2-0-2	0-0-0	1-0-1	0-1-1	0-1-1	1-0-1	0-1-1	0-0-0	1-1-2
Murray	0-0-0	2-0-2	0-0-0	0-0-0	2-0-2	———	———	0-1-1	0-0-0
Niinimaa	0-1-1	0-1-1	1-1-2	0-1-1	1-1-2	0-0-0	1-0-1	0-0-0	0-0-0
Picard	———	———	———	———	———	———	———	0-0-0	———
Poti	0-0-0	0-1-1	1-1-2	1-0-1	0-0-0	0-0-0	0-1-1	0-0-0	1-2-3
Robertsson	0-0-0	0-0-0	———	———	0-1-1	0-1-1	0-0-0	0-0-0	0-0-0
Selivanov	1-2-3	0-0-0	1-1-2	1-0-1	3-1-4	0-0-0	2-1-3	0-0-0	0-1-1
Smith	0-0-0	0-0-0	0-0-0	1-0-1	0-2-2	0-1-1	0-0-0	0-0-0	0-0-0
Smyth	2-1-3	0-0-0	1-3-4	0-0-0	1-1-2	0-0-0	1-1-2	2-0-2	0-0-0
Titov	———	———	———	———	———	———	———	———	0-0-0
Ulanov	———	———	———	———	0-0-0	———	———	———	0-1-1
Weight	0-4-4	0-0-0	1-4-5	0-2-2	0-2-2	0-0-0	0-2-2	0-1-1	0-0-0

	Phil.	*Phoe.*	*Pitt.*	*S.J.*	*St.L.*	*Tamp.*	*Tor.*	*Van.*	*Was.*
Beranek	0-1-1	1-1-2	0-1-1	1-0-1	0-0-0	2-0-2	1-0-1	0-0-0	0-0-0
Brown, K.	———	———	———	0-0-0	———	———	0-0-0	———	———
Brown, S.	1-1-2	0-0-0	0-0-0	0-0-0	0-0-0	0-1-1	0-0-0	0-1-1	0-0-0
Cleary	———	0-0-0	———	0-0-0	0-0-0	———	———	0-1-1	———
Comrie	———	0-0-0	———	0-0-0	0-1-1	———	———	———	———
Devereaux	0-0-0	0-1-1	0-0-0	0-0-0	0-0-0	0-2-2	0-0-0	0-3-3	0-1-1
Dowd	0-0-0	0-1-1	0-0-0	0-1-1	0-0-0	0-0-0	0-1-1	1-0-1	1-1-2
Falloon	———	0-2-2	———	0-1-1	0-1-1	1-1-2	0-0-0	1-0-1	0-2-2
Grier	0-0-0	0-3-3	0-1-1	0-0-0	0-0-0	0-3-3	0-1-1	0-2-2	0-0-0
Guerin	2-0-2	1-0-1	0-1-1	0-0-0	1-1-2	2-1-3	1-1-2	2-3-5	2-0-2
Hamrlik	0-1-1	1-2-3	1-0-1	0-1-1	0-1-1	0-3-3	0-0-0	2-4-6	0-2-2
Hauer	———	———	———	———	———	———	———	0-0-0	———
Kilger	———	0-0-0	———	0-0-0	0-0-0	———	0-0-0	0-0-0	0-1-1
LaCouture	———	0-0-0	———	0-0-0	———	———	———	0-0-0	———
Laflamme	———	0-0-0	0-0-0	0-0-0	0-0-0	0-0-0	0-0-0	0-0-0	0-0-0
Laraque	0-0-0	0-0-0	1-0-1	0-0-0	0-0-0	1-0-1	0-0-0	0-1-1	———
Marchant	0-0-0	1-1-2	1-0-1	1-1-2	0-1-1	1-1-2	1-2-3	3-2-5	1-0-1
Moreau	0-0-0	4-1-5	0-0-0	1-0-1	0-0-0	1-0-1	0-0-0	2-0-2	0-0-0
Murray	0-0-0	0-0-0	0-0-0	0-1-1	———	1-0-1	0-0-0	1-0-1	———
Niinimaa	0-0-0	0-1-1	0-1-1	0-0-0	1-1-2	0-2-2	0-0-0	0-4-4	0-1-1
Poti	0-1-1	1-2-3	0-1-1	0-2-2	0-2-2	1-3-4	0-1-1	0-2-2	1-1-2
Robertsson	0-0-0	0-0-0	0-0-0	0-0-0	0-0-0	0-0-0	0-0-0	0-0-0	0-0-0
Selivanov	0-1-1	2-3-5	1-0-1	1-1-2	1-0-1	0-0-0	0-0-0	0-2-2	0-0-0
Smith	0-0-0	0-0-0	0-0-0	0-0-0	1-1-2	0-0-0	0-0-0	0-0-0	0-1-1
Smyth	0-1-1	2-1-3	0-0-0	0-0-0	1-2-3	2-2-4	1-0-1	3-2-5	1-0-1
Titov	———	———	———	———	———	———	———	0-1-1	———
Ulanov	———	0-0-0	———	0-0-0	———	———	———	0-0-0	———
Weight	0-0-0	2-6-8	0-2-2	0-1-1	2-2-4	0-2-2	0-2-2	4-4-8	———

Goaltender Record vs. Opposition

	GP	Min.	GA	EN	SO	Ave.	W-L-T	Opposition
Mike Minard	1	60	3	0	0	3.00	1-0-0-0	Calgary
Bill Ranford	1	60	3	0	0	3.00	0-1-0-0	Anaheim
	2	125	4	0	0	2.00	1-0-1-0	Boston
	1	65	3	0	0	3.00	1-0-1-0	Carolina
	1	20	1	0	0	3.00	0-0-0-0	Chicago
	1	20	0	0	0	0.00	0-0-0-0	Colorado
	1	60	5	0	0	5.00	0-1-0-0	Detroit
	1	60	8	0	0	8.00	0-1-0-0	Los Angeles
	2	120	8	0	0	4.00	0-2-0-0	Nashville
	1	60	1	0	0	1.00	1-0-0-0	New Jersey
	1	40	4	0	0	6.00	0-0-1-0	NY Islanders
	1	64	3	0	0	3.00	0-1-0-0	San Jose
	1	60	3	0	0	3.00	1-0-0-0	Tampa
	1	16	3	0	0	11.25	0-0-0-0	Vancouver
	1	20	1	0	0	3.00	1-0-0-0	Washington
Tommy Salo	3	179	5	0	0	1.68	2-1-0-0	Anaheim
	2	120	4	0	1	2.00	2-0-0-0	Atlanta
	1	65	2	0	0	2.00	0-0-1-0	Buffalo
	5	301	12	0	1	2.39	1-4-0-0	Calgary
	1	65	2	0	0	2.00	1-0-1-0	Carolina
	4	220	11	0	0	3.00	2-2-0-0	Chicago
	6	344	14	0	0	2.44	2-3-1-0	Colorado
	4	243	9	0	0	2.22	0-3-1-0	Dallas
	3	185	8	0	0	2.59	1-1-1-0	Detroit
	2	125	4	0	0	1.92	0-1-1-0	Florida
	3	185	8	0	0	2.59	2-0-1-0	Los Angeles
	2	123	5	0	0	2.44	2-0-0-1	Montreal
	3	181	6	0	0	1.99	2-1-0-0	Nashville
	2	85	2	0	0	1.41	1-0-0-0	NY Islanders
	2	128	3	0	0	1.41	0-0-1-1	NY Rangers
	2	125	5	0	0	2.40	1-0-1-0	Ottawa
	1	60	2	0	0	2.00	1-0-0-0	Philadelphia
	4	245	13	0	0	3.18	3-1-0-0	Phoenix
	2	124	5	0	0	2.42	0-1-1-0	Pittsburgh
	3	184	3	0	0	0.97	1-1-1-0	San Jose
	4	250	11	0	0	2.64	0-2-1-1	St. Louis
	1	60	1	0	0	1.00	1-0-0-0	Tampa
	3	182	10	0	0	3.30	0-3-0-0	Toronto
	6	359	16	0	0	2.67	3-1-1-1	Vancouver
	1	40	1	0	0	1.50	0-0-0-0	Washington

1999-2000 Schedule Results

Oct. 1	Rangers	1	at	Edmonton	1 (OT)
Oct. 6	Montreal	1	at	Edmonton	2
Oct. 7	Edmonton	2	at	San Jose	3 (OT)
Oct. 9	St. Louis	4	at	Edmonton	2
Oct. 13	Carolina	3	at	Edmonton	3 (OT)
Oct. 16	Los Angeles	4	at	Edmonton	5
Oct. 20	Edmonton	1	at	Dallas	2
Oct. 21	Edmonton	2	at	St. Louis	3 (OT)
Oct. 23	Edmonton	3	at	Nashville	4
Oct. 26	Phoenix	1	at	Edmonton	3
Oct. 31	Nashville	2	at	Edmonton	4
Nov. 3	Florida	2	at	Edmonton	2 (OT)
Nov. 5	St. Louis	2	at	Edmonton	1
Nov. 7	Edmonton	1	at	Anaheim	3
Nov. 9	Edmonton	1	at	Los Angeles	1 (OT)
Nov. 10	Edmonton	4	at	Phoenix	5 (OT)
Nov. 12	Edmonton	2	at	St. Louis	2 (OT)
Nov. 14	Edmonton	6	at	Chicago	3
Nov. 20	Detroit	1	at	Edmonton	2
Nov. 21	Islanders	4	at	Edmonton	4 (OT)
Nov. 24	Chicago	3	at	Edmonton	2
Nov. 26	Edmonton	2	at	Detroit	4
Nov. 27	Edmonton	2	at	Toronto	5
Dec. 1	Colorado	1	at	Edmonton	3
Dec. 2	Edmonton	2	at	Vancouver	3 (OT)
Dec. 4	Vancouver	2	at	Edmonton	3
Dec. 6	Edmonton	1	at	Chicago	5
Dec. 8	Edmonton	1	at	Rangers	2 (OT)
Dec. 9	Edmonton	2	at	Boston	2 (OT)
Dec. 11	Edmonton	3	at	New Jersey	1
Dec. 14	Edmonton	4	at	Islanders	2
Dec. 15	Edmonton	1	at	Detroit	5
Dec. 17	Dallas	2	at	Edmonton	2 (OT)
Dec. 19	Ottawa	3	at	Edmonton	3 (OT)
Dec. 21	Washington	2	at	Edmonton	6
Dec. 23	Edmonton	1	at	Calgary	2

Dec. 27	Anaheim	1	at	Edmonton	4	Feb. 19	Calgary	3	at	Edmonton	2 (OT)
Dec. 30	Edmonton	2	at	Los Angeles	8	Feb. 21	Los Angeles	3	at	Edmonton	6
Jan. 1	Edmonton	5	at	Phoenix	4	Feb. 23	Boston	2	at	Edmonton	4
Jan. 3	Edmonton	2	at	Colorado	2 (OT)	Feb. 25	Atlanta	4	at	Edmonton	5
Jan. 5	San Jose	1	at	Edmonton	1 (OT)	Feb. 27	Edmonton	2	at	Anaheim	3
Jan. 7	Tampa Bay	1	at	Edmonton	5	Feb. 29	Edmonton	3	at	Colorado	1
Jan. 11	Dallas	3	at	Edmonton	2	Mar. 4	Pittsburgh	3	at	Edmonton	2
Jan. 14	Toronto	3	at	Edmonton	2 (OT)	Mar. 7	Toronto	2	at	Edmonton	0
Jan. 16	Detroit	3	at	Edmonton	3 (OT)	Mar. 10	Colorado	4	at	Edmonton	0
Jan. 19	Calgary	0	at	Edmonton	7	Mar. 12	Edmonton	3	at	Nashville	4
Jan. 22	Vancouver	3	at	Edmonton	3 (OT)	Mar. 13	Edmonton	3	at	Atlanta	0
Jan. 24	Nashville	3	at	Edmonton	2 (OT)	Mar. 15	Edmonton	2	at	Carolina	2 (OT)
Jan. 25	Edmonton	5	at	Vancouver	4 (OT)	Mar. 17	Ottawa	2	at	Edmonton	4
Jan. 28	Edmonton	7	at	Tampa Bay	3	Mar. 19	Calgary	3	at	Edmonton	2
Jan. 29	Edmonton	1	at	Florida	2	Mar. 22	Anaheim	1	at	Edmonton	2
Jan. 31	Edmonton	1	at	Dallas	2	Mar. 25	Vancouver	3	at	Edmonton	2
Feb. 2	Chicago	1	at	Edmonton	4	Mar. 27	Edmonton	2	at	San Jose	1
Feb. 8	Edmonton	5	at	Montreal	4 (OT)	Mar. 29	Edmonton	2	at	Colorado	3
Feb. 10	Edmonton	3	at	Philadelphia	2	Apr. 1	Phoenix	3	at	Edmonton	4 (OT)
Feb. 11	Edmonton	2	at	Pittsburgh	2 (OT)	Apr. 3	San Jose	1	at	Edmonton	0
Feb. 13	Edmonton	2	at	Buffalo	2 (OT)	Apr. 5	Colorado	3	at	Edmonton	2
Feb. 15	Edmonton	2	at	Nashville	1	Apr. 7	Edmonton	5	at	Vancouver	4 (OT)
Feb. 18	Edmonton	2	at	Calgary	4	Apr. 8	Edmonton	6	at	Calgary	3

Overall Record vs. Opponents

Opponent	*Home*	*Road*	*Overall*	*GF-GA*	*Opponent*
Anaheim	2-0-0-0	0-2-0-0	2-2-0-0	9-8	Anaheim
Atlanta	1-0-0-0	1-0-0-0	2-0-0-0	8-4	Atlanta
Boston	1-0-0-0	0-0-1-0	1-0-1-0	6-4	Boston
Buffalo	0-0-0-0	0-0-1-0	0-0-1-0	2-2	Buffalo
Calgary	1-2-0-0	1-2-0-0	2-4-0-0	20-15	Calgary
Carolina	0-0-1-0	0-0-1-0	0-0-2-0	5-5	Carolina
Chicago	1-1-0-0	1-1-0-0	2-2-0-0	13-12	Chicago
Colorado	1-2-0-0	1-1-1-0	2-3-1-0	14-14	Colorado
Dallas	0-1-1-0	0-2-0-0	0-3-1-0	6-9	Dallas
Detroit	1-0-1-0	0-2-0-0	1-2-1-0	8-13	Detroit
Florida	0-0-1-0	0-1-0-0	0-1-1-0	3-4	Florida
Los Angeles	2-0-0-0	0-1-1-0	2-1-1-0	14-16	Los Angeles
Montreal	1-0-0-0	1-0-0-1	2-0-0-1	7-5	Montreal
Nashville	1-1-0-0	1-2-0-0	2-3-0-0	14-14	Nashville
New Jersey	0-0-0-0	1-0-0-0	1-0-0-0	3-1	New Jersey
Islanders	0-0-1-0	1-0-0-0	1-0-1-0	8-6	Islanders
Rangers	0-0-1-0	0-0-0-1	0-0-1-1	2-3	Rangers
Ottawa	1-0-1-0	0-0-0-0	1-0-1-0	7-5	Ottawa
Philadelphia	0-0-0-0	1-0-0-0	1-0-0-0	3-2	Philadelphia
Phoenix	2-0-0-0	1-0-1-0	3-0-1-0	16-13	Phoenix
Pittsburgh	0-1-0-0	0-0-1-0	0-1-1-0	4-5	Pittsburgh
San Jose	0-1-1-0	1-1-0-0	1-2-1-0	5-6	San Jose
St. Louis	0-2-0-0	0-1-1-1	0-3-1-1	7-11	St. Louis
Tampa Bay	1-0-0-0	1-0-0-0	2-0-0-0	12-4	Tampa Bay
Toronto	0-2-0-0	0-0-0-1	0-2-0-1	4-10	Toronto
Vancouver	1-1-1-0	2-1-0-0	3-2-1-0	20-19	Vancouver
Washington	1-0-0-0	0-0-0-0	1-0-0-0	6-2	Washington

1999-2000 Playoff Scoring

#		*GP*	*G*	*A*	*Pts*	*Shots*	*S%*	*GW*	*OT*	*PP*	*SH*	*P/M*	*PIM*
39	Doug Weight	5	3	2	5	8	37.5	1	0	2	0	-3	4
9	Bill Guerin	5	3	2	5	12	25.0	0	0	1	0	-1	9
34	Jim Dowd	5	2	1	3	6	33.3	0	0	0	0	-2	4
13	German Titov	5	1	1	2	3	33.3	0	0	0	0	-2	0
44	Janne Niinimaa	5	0	2	2	8	0.0	0	0	0	0	1	2
26	Todd Marchant	3	1	0	1	6	16.7	0	0	0	0	-1	2
94	Ryan Smyth	5	1	0	1	13	7.7	0	0	0	1	-2	6

#		GP	G	A	Pts	Shots	S%	GW	OT	PP	SH	P/M	PIM
37	Daniel Cleary	4	0	1	1	3	0.0	0	0	0	0	1	2
22	Roman Hamrlik	5	0	1	1	10	0.0	0	0	0	0	-4	4
5	Tom Poti	5	0	1	1	7	0.0	0	0	0	0	-3	0
21	Jason Smith	5	0	1	1	5	0.0	0	0	0	0	0	4
17	Rem Murray	5	0	1	1	9	0.0	0	0	0	0	-1	2
27	Georges Laraque	5	0	1	1	5	0.0	0	0	0	0	-1	6
18	Ethan Moreau	5	0	1	1	5	0.0	0	0	0	0	0	0
33	Dan LaCouture	1	0	0	0	0	0.0	0	0	0	0	0	0
10	Kevin Brown	1	0	0	0	0	0.0	0	0	0	0	0	0
23	Sean Brown	3	0	0	0	0	0.0	0	0	0	0	-1	23
15	Chad Kilger	3	0	0	0	1	0.0	0	0	0	0	0	0
35	Tommy Salo	5	0	0	0	0	0.0	0	0	0	0	0	0
14	Bert Robertsson	5	0	0	0	2	0.0	0	0	0	0	-1	0
29	Alex Selivanov	5	0	0	0	6	0.0	0	0	0	0	0	8
55	Igor Ulanov	5	0	0	0	4	0.0	0	0	0	0	-1	6
		5	11	15	26	113	9-7	1	0	3	1	-21	82

1999-2000 Playoff Goaltending

	GP	Min.	GA	W	L	Ave.	SA	Pct.	SO	EN
Tommy Salo	5	300	13	1	4	2.60	133	0.902	0	0

Date	Result					Winning Goaltender	Winning Goal
April 12, 2000	Edmonton	1	at	Dallas	2	Ed Belfour	Roman Lyashenko
April 13, 2000	Edmonton	0	at	Dallas	3	Ed Belfour	Kirk Muller
April 16, 2000	Dallas	2	at	Edmonton	5	Tommy Salo	Doug Weight
April 18, 2000	Dallas	4	at	Edmonton	3	Ed Belfour	Guy Carbonneau
April 21, 2000	Edmonton	2	at	Dallas	3	Ed Belfour	Brett Hull

2000-2001

The Oilers for the first time in 20 years had a new face in the front office. Kevin Lowe became the team's general manager, replacing Glen Sather who had been lured by the Rangers to New York.

Craig MacTavish replaced Lowe behind the team's bench while former U. of A. Golden Bear coach Billy Moores and longtime Oiler defenseman Charlie Huddy became the assistant coaches. In a reversal of the trend which had seen many former Oilers move to "The Big Apple," all three Oiler coaches had been assistants with the Rangers in the late 1990s.

Joaquin Gage returned to the team as the number two goaltender. Gage had not appeared in an NHL game since the 1995-96 season. Defenseman Frank Musil also rejoined the team this season. Musil had missed the complete 1999-2000 season with a spinal cord injury. Both of these feel-good stories ended prematurely though. Gage only appeared in five games before being sent to the farm team in favor of Dominic Roussel, whom the Oilers had picked up on waivers from Anaheim in January. Musil started the season well but then suffered a reoccurrence of the injury that had sidelined him the previous year. The injury probably ended Musil's career but not before he was named as the team's nominee for the Masterton Trophy.

The line of Brian Swanson, Daniel Cleary and Michel Riesen made it through training camp and began the season with the team. This "Bulldog Line" was the top scoring unit on the Oilers' farm team the previous year. Only Cleary remained with the Oilers for the balance of the season. In an economic move Bill Guerin was traded to Boston in November for Anson Carter who was having trouble coming to terms with the Bruins.

The team began to jell as the season progressed. The hard hitting duo of Jason Smith and Igor Ulanov were near the top of the league all season in hits and blocked shots and made opposition forwards pay a heavy toll in front of the Oilers' net. Young Eric Brewer started slow but then showed a fine offensive flair while not neglecting his defensive duties, and defenseman Janne Niinimaa was one of two Oilers to play in the league's annual All-Star game.

The offense also improved from last year with the addition of rookie Mike Comrie, who was signed to a contract in January. Comrie scored 21 points in 41 games, but more importantly he gave the Oilers a legitimate second line center, taking some of the pressure off of Doug Weight.

Eric Brewer missed four games with a strained gluteus muscle, Ethan Moreau missed the first 13 games due to shoulder surgery, and Mike Grier missed eight games with a shoulder injury. Igor Ulanov missed six games with complications from an eye injury suffered in a game against

Calgary. Defensive specialist Todd Marchant was out for 11 games with a shoulder injury, thus ending his 234 game iron man streak. At the time of the injury this was the league's third longest consecutive game streak. The Oilers allowed 8 goals on 42 powerplay opportunities (81 percent) while Marchant was out. With him in the lineup the Oilers penalty killers were effective on 84 percent of their penalty kills. All five players returned in time to have fine seasons with the team.

Forward Josh Green, who had come to the Oilers in the Roman Hamrlik trade in June, missed the first 40 games of the season due to a shoulder injury. After recovery he went to Hamilton for conditioning. In his second game with the Bulldogs he hurt his other shoulder and was out for the season. The 1 stands for overtime loss which was introduced last year.

The Oilers were 25–21–8–1 (.536) at the All-Star break. The line of Doug Weight, former Oiler Bill Guerin and Tony Amonte accounted for 13 of Team North America's 34 points in the league's annual All-Star game.

Edmonton finished 9th in offense during the regular season with 243 goals. Even with Tommy Salo playing spectacularly and the defense near the top of the league in blocked shots and hits the Oilers finished only 15th in defense with 222 goals against. Doug Weight, with 90 points, again led the team in scoring and finished fourth in the league in assists.

Clinching a playoff spot on the second to last game of the season, the Oilers for the fifth straight year met Dallas in the postseason. In a series in which Edmonton lost only one game in regulation time the Stars defeated the Oilers in six games. In the final game of the series, Mike Grier played half of the game with a dislocated shoulder while Ethan Moreau played the game with a broken foot.

On June 14 it was announced that Jari Kurri was elected to the Hockey Hall of Fame in his first year of eligibility.

2000-2001 Regular Season Scoring

#		*Ht.*	*Wt.*	*Age*	*GP*	*G*	*A*	*Pts*	*Shots*	*S%*	*GW*	*GT*	*PP*	*SH*	*P/M*	*PIM*
39	Weight (C)	71	200	29	82	25	65	90	188	13.3	3	2	8	0	12	91
94	Smyth (A)	73	195	24	82	31	39	70	245	12.7	6	1	11	0	10	56
44	Niinimaa	74	220	25	82	12	33	45	122	9.8	1	0	8	0	6	90
22	Carter	73	200	26	61	16	26	42	102	15.7	4	0	7	1	1	23
26	Marchant (A)	70	178	27	71	13	26	39	113	11.5	2	1	0	4	0	51
25	Grier (A)	73	227	25	74	20	16	36	124	16.1	2	1	2	3	11	20
17	Murray (A)	74	195	28	82	15	20	35	122	12.3	3	1	1	3	5	24
7	Cleary	72	203	22	81	14	20	34	107	13.1	2	1	2	0	5	37
5	Poti	75	215	23	81	12	20	32	161	7.5	3	0	6	0	-4	60
27	Laraque	75	230	24	82	13	16	29	73	17.8	1	1	1	0	5	148
55	Ulanov	75	211	31	67	3	21	24	74	4.1	0	1	1	0	15	90
9	Guerin (A)	74	210	30	21	12	10	22	64	18.7	1	0	4	0	11	18
89	Comrie, M.	69	172	20	41	8	13	21	62	12.9	1	0	3	0	6	14
2	Brewer	75	220	21	77	7	13	20	91	7.7	2	0	2	0	15	53
21	Smith (A)	75	210	27	82	5	15	20	140	3.6	0	0	1	1	14	120
34	Zholtok	74	191	28	37	4	16	20	61	6.6	0	0	1	0	8	22
18	Moreau	74	211	25	68	9	10	19	97	9.3	3	0	0	1	-6	90
36	Horcoff	73	202	22	49	9	7	16	42	21.4	2	0	0	0	8	10
14	Pittis	71	190	26	47	4	5	9	42	9.5	2	0	0	0	-5	49
15	Kilger	75	215	24	34	5	2	7	28	17.9	0	0	1	0	-7	17
33	LaCouture	75	210	23	37	2	4	6	22	9.1	1	0	0	0	-2	29
23	Brown, S.	75	205	24	62	2	3	5	30	6.7	0	0	0	0	2	110
19	Butenschon	76	215	24	7	1	1	2	3	33.3	0	0	0	0	2	2
37	Swanson	70	180	24	16	1	1	2	8	12.5	0	0	0	0	-1	6
8	Musil	75	215	36	13	0	2	2	0	0.0	0	0	0	0	-2	4
34	Riesen	74	190	21	12	0	1	1	16	0.0	0	0	0	0	2	4
32	Ferguson	73	202	27	20	0	1	1	8	0.0	0	0	0	0	2	13
20	Chimera	72	180	21	1	0	0	0	0	0.0	0	0	0	0	0	0
19	Hajt	75	206	22	1	0	0	0	0	0.0	0	0	0	0	-1	0
29	Cote	75	220	25	6	0	0	0	0	0.0	0	0	0	0	-2	18
35	Salo	71	173	29	73	0	1	1	0	0.0	0	0	0	0	0	4
31	Gage	72	200	27	5	0	0	0	0	0.0	0	0	0	0	0	0
30	Roussel	74	200	30	8	0	0	0	0	0.0	0	0	0	0	0	2
	Bench															10
		73	203	25	82	243	407	650	2145	11.3	39	9	59	13	110	1275

2000-2001 Goaltender Records

	GP	Min.	GA	W	L	T	Ave.	SA	Pct.	SO	EN
Tommy Salo	73	4364	179	36	25	12	2.46	1856	.904	8	5
Joaquin Gage	5	260	15	2	2	0	3.46	125	.880	0	1
D. Roussel	8	348	21	1	4	0	3.62	151	.861	0	1
	82	4972	222	39	31	12	2.68	2139	.896	8	7

Coach: Craig MacTavish

Scoring vs. Opposition

	Ana.	Atl.	Bost.	Buff.	Calg.	Caro.	Chic.
Brewer	0–1–1	0–0–0	0–0–0	0–1–1	1–2–3	1–0–1	0–0–0
Brown	0–0–0	0–1–1	0–0–0	0–0–0	0–0–0	———	0–0–0
Butenschon	———	———	———	———	———	———	0–0–0
Carter	2–1–3	———	———	0–1–1	2–1–3	0–0–0	0–2–2
Cleary	1–1–2	0–0–0	0–1–1	0–0–0	0–5–5	1–1–2	0–1–1
Comrie	0–1–1	———	———	0–0–0	0–0–0	0–0–0	1–0–1
Cote	———	———	———	———	0–0–0	———	0–0–0
Ferguson	———	———	———	0–0–0	0–0–0	0–0–0	0–0–0
Grier	1–0–1	0–0–0	0–0–0	0–0–0	1–0–1	0–0–0	0–3–3
Guerin	2–1–3	0–0–0	2–1–3	1–1–2	0–0–0	———	———
Horcoff	0–0–0	———	———	0–0–0	1–1–2	0–0–0	1–0–1
Kilger	1–0–1	0–0–0	0–1–1	0–0–0	0–0–0	———	0–1–1
LaCouture	0–0–0	0–0–0	1–0–1	0–0–0	0–0–0	———	0–0–0
Laraque	0–0–0	0–1–1	0–1–1	2–0–2	1–0–1	1–0–1	0–0–0
Marchant	0–0–0	0–0–0	1–0–1	1–0–1	0–4–4	0–0–0	3–2–5
Moreau	0–0–0	———	———	0–1–1	1–0–1	0–0–0	1–0–1
Murray	0–2–2	0–0–0	1–1–2	0–2–2	3–0–3	0–0–0	1–0–1
Musil	———	———	———	0–1–1	0–0–0	———	0–0–0
Niinimaa	1–2–3	0–0–0	0–1–1	0–1–1	0–4–4	0–0–0	1–0–1
Pittis	0–0–0	———	———	———	1–0–1	———	0–0–0
Poti	1–2–3	0–0–0	0–1–1	1–0–1	2–1–3	0–0–0	1–0–1
Riesen	0–0–0	0–0–0	0–0–0	0–0–0	———	———	———
Salo	0–0–0	———	———	0–0–0	0–0–0	0–0–0	0–0–0
Smith	1–1–2	0–0–0	0–0–0	0–0–0	0–1–1	0–0–0	0–1–1
Smyth	0–4–4	0–0–0	0–0–0	1–2–3	0–1–1	0–0–0	1–2–3
Swanson	0–0–0	0–0–0	1–0–1	0–0–0	0–0–0	———	———
Ulanov	0–2–2	0–0–0	0–1–1	0–1–1	0–0–0	0–0–0	0–2–2
Weight	2–3–5	1–0–0	0–1–1	1–2–3	0–3–3	0–1–1	1–2–3
Zholtok	1–0–1	———	———	0–0–0	1–0–1	0–2–2	0–2–2

	Cmb.	Col.	Dall.	Det.	Flor.	L.A.	Min.
Brewer	1–0–1	0–2–2	0–2–2	0–0–0	0–0–0	1–2–3	0–0–0
Brown, S.	0–0–0	0–0–0	1–0–1	0–0–0	———	0–1–1	0–0–0
Butenschon	0–0–0	0–0–0	0–0–0	———	———	———	———
Carter	2–0–2	0–2–2	0–0–0	0–0–0	0–0–0	1–4–5	0–1–1
Chimera	———	————	———	———	———	0–0–0	———
Cleary	2–1–3	1–1–2	0–2–2	0–1–1	0–1–1	0–0–0	2–2–4
Comrie, M.	0–0–0	0–2–2	0–0–0	1–0–1	0–0–0	3–0–3	0–1–1
Cote	———	0–0–0	———	———	———	———	———
Ferguson	0–0–0	0–0–0	0–0–0	0–0–0	0–0–0	0–1–1	0–0–0
Grier	1–2–3	1–2–3	1–0–1	0–2–2	0–0–0	1–0–1	1–2–3
Guerin	2–0–2	0–1–1	———	3–0–3	———	———	1–4–5
Hajt	———	———	———	0–0–0	———	———	———
Horcoff	1–0–1	0–0–0	2–1–3	1–0–1	0–0–0	2–0–2	0–1–1
Kilger	0–0–0	0–0–0	0–0–0	0–0–0	———	0–0–0	1–0–1
LaCouture	0–0–0	0–0–0	0–0–0	0–0–0	———	———	0–1–1
Laraque	0–1–1	0–0–0	2–2–4	1–0–1	0–1–1	0–4–4	0–0–0
Marchant	0–1–1	1–3–4	0–1–1	0–1–1	0–0–0	0–1–1	0–2–2
Moreau	2–1–3	1–1–2	0–0–0	0–1–1	0–0–0	0–1–1	0–0–0
Murray	0–0–0	0–1–1	1–2–3	2–1–3	0–0–0	2–3–5	2–0–2
Musil	———	0–0–0	———	0–0–0	———	———	0–0–0
Niinimaa	0–2–2	2–0–2	1–3–4	2–2–4	0–0–0	1–2–3	3–3–6

	Cmb.	Col.	Dall.	Det.	Flor.	L.A.	Min.
Pittis	0–0–0	0–1–1	0–0–0	0–0–0	———	0–0–0	0–1–1
Poti	0–3–3	0–1–1	1–2–3	0–0–0	0–0–0	1–2–3	1–2–3
Riesen	———	0–0–0	———	0–0–0	———	———	0–1–1
Smith	0–1–1	1–0–0	0–1–1	0–1–1	0–0–0	0–0–0	0–0–0
Smyth	3–2–5	3–2–5	0–1–1	1–2–3	0–1–1	3–4–7	4–3–7
Swanson	———	0–0–0	———	0–0–0	———	———	0–1–1
Ulanov	0–2–2	1–2–3	0–0–0	0–1–1	0–0–0	0–1–1	0–1–1
Weight	0–8–8	0–3–3	1–2–3	0–5–5	2–0–2	5–2–7	3–7–10
Zholtok	0–0–0	1–0–1	1–0–1	0–0–0	0–1–1	0–4–4	0–1–1

	Mont.	Nash.	N.J.	NYI	NYR	Ott.	Phil.
Brewer	0–0–0	0–0–0	0–0–0	0–0–0	1–0–1	0–0–0	0–0–0
Brown	0–0–0	0–0–0	0–0–0	0–0–0	0–0–0	0–0–0	0–0–0
Carter	0–0–0	1–2–3	0–1–1	0–0–0	0–0–0	1–3–4	1–1–2
Cleary	1–0–1	0–2–2	0–0–0	1–0–1	0–0–0	0–0–0	0–0–0
Comrie, M.	———	0–1–1	1–1–2	0–1–1	———	0–1–1	0–2–2
Gage	———	———	———	———	———	———	———
Grier	2–1–3	0–0–0	1–1–2	0–0–0	1–0–1	2–0–2	0–0–0
Guerin	0–0–0	———	———	———	1–0–1	———	———
Hajt	———	———	———	———	———	———	———
Horcoff	———	2–1–3	0–0–0	0–0–0	———	———	0–0–0
Kilger	1–0–1	0–1–1	———	———	0–0–0	———	———
LaCouture	0–1–1	1–0–1	———	———	0–0–0	0–0–0	———
Laraque	0–1–1	0–2–2	0–1–1	0–0–0	0–0–0	1–0–1	0–0–0
Marchant	0–1–1	0–2–2	1–1–2	0–0–0	0–1–1	1–0–1	0–0–0
Moreau	0–0–0	3–1–4	0–1–1	0–0–0	0–0–0	0–0–0	0–0–0
Murray	1–1–2	0–1–1	0–0–0	0–0–0	0–0–0	0–2–2	0–0–0
Musil	0–0–0	0–0–0	———	———	———	———	———
Niinimaa	0–0–0	1–1–2	0–0–0	0–1–1	0–1–1	0–0–0	0–0–0
Pittis	0–0–0	1–1–2	———	———	0–1–1	0–0–0	———
Poti	0–0–0	2–1–3	1–0–1	0–0–0	0–1–1	0–1–1	0–0–0
Riesen	0–0–0	———	———	———	———	———	———
Roussel	———	———	———	0–0–0	———	0–0–0	0–0–0
Salo	0–0–0	0–1–1	0–0–0	———	0–0–0	———	———
Smith	0–1–1	1–2–3	1–0–1	0–0–0	0–0–0	0–1–1	0–0–0
Smyth	0–0–0	2–2–4	0–2–2	1–0–1	0–0–0	3–1–4	1–1–2
Swanson	0–0–0	———	———	———	———	———	———
Ulanov	1–3–4	0–0–0	0–1–1	0–0–0	0–0–0	0–1–1	0–0–0
Weight	1–3–4	1–4–5	0–0–0	0–1–1	0–0–0	1–4–5	0–0–0
Zholtok	0–1–1	0–0–0	0–0–0	0–0–0	———	0–0–0	0–0–0

	Phoe.	Pitt.	S.J.	St.L.	T.B.	Tor.	Van.	Wash
Brewer	0–0–0	0–0–0	0–0–0	0–0–0	1–0–1	0–0–0	0–4–4	0–0–0
Brown	0–0–0	———	1–1–2	0–0–0	———	0–0–0	0–0–0	0–0–0
Butenschon	0–1–1	———	———	———	———	———	1–0–1	———
Carter	1–1–2	———	2–2–4	0–1–1	0–1–1	0–1–1	2–1–3	0–0–0
Cleary	1–0–1	0–0–0	1–1–2	1–0–1	0–1–1	1–0–1	0–1–1	0–0–0
Comrie, M.	0–0–0	———	0–0–0	0–1–1	1–1–2	1–0–1	0–0–0	———
Cote	———	———	———	0–0–0	———	0–0–0	0–0–0	———
Ferguson	0–0–0	———	———	0–0–0	0–0–0	0–0–0	———	0–0–0
Gage	———	———	———	0–0–0	———	———	———	0–0–0
Grier	1–0–1	1–0–1	1–1–2	1–0–1	0–1–1	1–1–2	2–0–2	———
Guerin	0–1–1	0–0–0	———	0–0–0	———	0–1–1	———	———
Horcoff	0–0–0	———	0–0–0	1–0–1	0–1–1	0–0–0	0–0–0	0–0–0
Kilger	0–0–0	1–0–1	1–0–1	0–0–0	———	0–0–0	0–0–0	0–0–0
LaCouture	0–0–0	0–0–0	0–1–1	0–0–0	———	0–0–0	0–1–1	0–0–0
Laraque	1–0–1	0–1–1	0–0–0	0–0–0	0–1–1	0–0–0	3–0–3	0–0–0
Marchant	1–1–2	0–1–1	0–0–0	0–0–0	0–0–0	2–1–3	1–2–3	0–0–0
Moreau	0–0–0	0–0–0	0–0–0	0–1–1	0–0–0	1–0–1	0–1–1	0–0–0
Murray	0–0–0	0–0–0	0–0–0	0–1–1	1–0–1	0–2–2	1–1–2	0–0–0
Musil	0–0–0	0–1–1	0–0–0	———	———	———	————	———
Niinimaa	0–2–2	0–0–0	0–1–1	0–1–1	0–1–1	0–2–2	0–5–5	0–0–0
Pittis	0–0–0	0–0–0	1–1–2	0–0–0	———	0–0–0	1–0–1	0–0–0
Poti	0–1–1	0–0–0	1–0–1	1–0–1	0–0–0	0–1–1	0–2–2	0–0–0

	Phoe.	Pitt.	S.J.	St.L.	T.B.	Tor.	Van.	Wash
Riesen	0–0–0	———	———	———	———	0–0–0	———	———
Rousell	0–0–0	———	———	0–0–0	———	———	0–0–0	———
Salo	0–0–0	0–0–0	0–0–0	0–0–0	0–0–0	0–0–0	0–0–0	———
Smith	1–1–2	0–0–0	0–0–0	0–3–3	0–1–1	0–0–0	0–0–0	0–0–0
Smyth	2–1–3	0–0–0	0–2–2	4–1–5	1–0–1	1–2–3	0–1–1	0–0–0
Swanson	0–0–0	———	0–0–0	———	———	0–0–0	———	———
Ulanov	0–0–0	0–1–1	0–0–0	0–0–0	0–0–0	0–0–0	1–2–3	———
Weight	0–1–1	0–0–0	0–3–3	2–3–5	0–1–1	1–1–2	3–5–8	0–0–0
Zholtok	0–0–0	———	0–0–0	0–1–1	1–0–1	0–1–1	0–2–2	———

Goaltender Record vs. Opposition

	GP	Min.	GA	EN	SO	Ave.	W–L–T	Opposition
Joaquin Gage	1	59	2	1	0	1.97	0–1–0–0	Atlanta
	2	121	7	0	0	3.47	2–0–0–0	Minnesota
	1	20	2	0	0	6.00	0–0–0–0	St. Louis
	1	60	4	0	0	4.00	0–1–0–0	Washington
Tommy Salo	4	240	11	0	0	2.75	2–1–1–0	Anaheim
	1	60	1	0	0	1.00	1–0–0–0	Boston
	2	120	2	0	1	1.00	2–0–0–0	Buffalo
	5	305	7	0	1	1.38	4–0–1–0	Calgary
	1	60	2	0	0	2.00	1–0–0–0	Carolina
	4	250	9	0	0	2.16	2–0–2–0	Chicago
	5	304	13	1	0	2.57	1–3–1–0	Colorado
	4	239	9	1	0	2.26	3–1–0–0	Columbus
	4	239	15	0	0	3.77	1–3–0–0	Dallas
	4	243	9	0	0	2.22	3–1–0–0	Detroit
	1	60	2	0	0	2.00	0–0–1–0	Florida
	4	239	7	0	2	1.76	3–1–0–0	Los Angeles
	3	185	3	0	1	0.97	2–0–1–0	Minnesota
	3	181	10	0	0	3.31	1–2–0–0	Montreal
	4	240	7	1	1	1.75	3–1–0–0	Nashville
	1	65	6	0	0	5.54	0–0–0–1	New Jersey
	1	60	4	0	0	4.00	0–1–0–0	NY Rangers
	1	60	3	0	0	3.00	1–0–0–0	Ottawa
	4	228	11	0	0	2.89	0–2–2–0	Phoenix
	1	59	4	1	0	3.93	0–1–0–0	Pittsburgh
	3	195	7	0	0	2.15	0–0–3–0	San Jose
	3	160	6	0	0	2.25	2–1–0–0	St. Louis
	1	61	4	0	0	3.93	1–0–0–0	Tampa
	3	179	8	0	0	2.68	1–2–0–0	Toronto
	5	274	17	0	0	3.72	2–3–0–0	Vancouver
Dominic Roussel	1	0	0	0	0	0.00	0–0–0–0	Minnesota
	1	59	3	1	0	3.05	0–1–0–0	N.Y. Islanders
	1	60	1	0	0	1.00	1–0–0–0	Ottawa
	1	58	4	0	0	4.14	0–1–0–0	Philadelphia
	1	22	2	0	0	5.45	0–0–0–0	Phoenix
	1	60	6	0	0	6.00	0–1–0–0	San Jose
	1	60	4	0	0	4.00	0–1–0–0	St. Louis
	1	29	1	0	0	2.07	0–0–0–0	Vancouver

2000-2001 Schedule Results

Oct. 6	Detroit	1	at	Edmonton	2
Oct. 7	Colorado	1	at	Edmonton	1 (OT)
Oct. 10	Edmonton	2	at	Montreal	5
Oct. 11	Edmonton	4	at	Detroit	3
Oct. 13	Buffalo	2	at	Edmonton	3
Oct. 15	Edmonton	5	at	Minnesota	3
Oct. 17	Boston	1	at	Edmonton	6
Oct. 19	Toronto	4	at	Edmonton	1
Oct. 22	Phoenix	3	at	Edmonton	3 (OT)
Oct. 25	Atlanta	3	at	Edmonton	1
Oct. 27	Edmonton	2	at	Anaheim	3
Oct. 28	Edmonton	2	at	Colorado	4
Oct. 30	Anaheim	3	at	Edmonton	5
Nov. 1	Calgary	2	at	Edmonton	3
Nov. 3	Minnesota	0	at	Edmonton	3
Nov. 5	Edmonton	4	at	Columbus	2
Nov. 7	Edmonton	3	at	Rangers	4
Nov. 9	Edmonton	0	at	Philadelphia	2
Nov. 11	Edmonton	2	at	Pittsburgh	5
Nov. 12	Edmonton	5	at	Minnesota	4 (OT)

Nov. 14	St. Louis	0	at	Edmonton	3
Nov. 18	Chicago	3	at	Edmonton	3 (OT)
Nov. 19	Calgary	0	at	Edmonton	2
Nov. 22	Edmonton	3	at	Toronto	4
Nov. 23	Edmonton	5	at	Ottawa	3
Nov. 25	Anaheim	2	at	Edmonton	3
Nov. 29	Montreal	3	at	Edmonton	2
Dec. 2	Edmonton	2	at	Vancouver	5
Dec. 3	San Jose	3	at	Edmonton	3 (OT)
Dec. 6	Nashville	0	at	Edmonton	4
Dec. 9	Los Angeles	4	at	Edmonton	2
Dec. 13	Edmonton	2	at	Dallas	5
Dec. 14	Edmonton	6	at	Nashville	2
Dec. 16	Edmonton	0	at	Washington	4
Dec. 18	Edmonton	3	at	Detroit	4 (OT)
Dec. 20	Vancouver	2	at	Edmonton	3 (OT)
Dec. 22	Edmonton	1	at	Calgary	1 (OT)
Dec. 27	Edmonton	2	at	Colorado	3
Dec. 28	Edmonton	2	at	San Jose	2 (OT)
Dec. 30	Montreal	2	at	Edmonton	3 (OT)
Jan. 1	Edmonton	2	at	St. Louis	5
Jan. 3	Edmonton	2	at	Columbus	5
Jan. 5	Edmonton	2	at	Chicago	1
Jan. 7	Columbus	2	at	Edmonton	4
Jan. 10	Nashville	5	at	Edmonton	2
Jan. 12	Vancouver	3	at	Edmonton	2
Jan. 14	Ottawa	1	at	Edmonton	4
Jan. 16	Edmonton	2	at	Nashville	1
Jan. 18	Edmonton	1	at	St. Louis	4
Jan. 20	Detroit	1	at	Edmonton	2
Jan. 22	San Jose	2	at	Edmonton	2 (OT)
Jan. 24	Edmonton	1	at	San Jose	6
Jan. 26	Phoenix	1	at	Edmonton	1 (OT)
Jan. 30	Edmonton	5	at	Calgary	3
Jan. 31	Chicago	2	at	Edmonton	3
Feb. 7	Edmonton	2	at	Dallas	3
Feb. 9	Edmonton	0	at	Phoenix	2
Feb. 12	Edmonton	6	at	Los Angeles	3
Feb. 14	Edmonton	3	at	Anaheim	3 (OT)
Feb. 16	Islanders	4	at	Edmonton	2
Feb. 17	Vancouver	6	at	Edmonton	5 (OT)
Feb. 20	Los Angeles	0	at	Edmonton	5
Feb. 24	Edmonton	3	at	Calgary	1
Feb. 25	Dallas	2	at	Edmonton	3 (OT)
Feb. 28	St. Louis	3	at	Edmonton	5
Mar. 2	Minnesota	1	at	Edmonton	3
Mar. 7	Toronto	0	at	Edmonton	4
Mar. 9	Edmonton	4	at	Buffalo	0
Mar. 11	Edmonton	3	at	Carolina	2
Mar. 13	Edmonton	5	at	Tampa Bay	4 (OT)
Mar. 14	Edmonton	2	at	Florida	2 (OT)
Mar. 17	New Jersey	6	at	Edmonton	5 (OT)
Mar. 19	Philadelphia	4	at	Edmonton	2
Mar. 21	Edmonton	7	at	Los Angeles	0
Mar. 24	Edmonton	4	at	Phoenix	7
Mar. 26	Columbus	2	at	Edmonton	4
Mar. 28	Colorado	1	at	Edmonton	4
Mar. 30	Dallas	5	at	Edmonton	4
Apr. 1	Edmonton	3	at	Chicago	3 (OT)
Apr. 2	Edmonton	3	at	Colorado	5
Apr. 4	Minnesota	2	at	Edmonton	2 (OT)
Apr. 7	Edmonton	4	at	Vancouver	2

Overall Record vs. Opponents

Opponent	*Home*	*Road*	*Overall*	*GF-GA*	*Opponent*
Anaheim	2–0–0–0	0–1–1–0	2–1–1–0	13–11	Anaheim
Atlanta	0–1–0–0	0–0–0–0	0–1–0–0	1–3	Atlanta
Boston	1–0–0–0	0–0–0–0	1–0–0–0	6–1	Boston
Buffalo	1–0–0–0	1–0–0–0	2–0–0–0	7–2	Buffalo
Calgary	2–0–0–0	2–0–1–0	4–0–1–0	14–7	Calgary
Carolina	0–0–0–0	1–0–0–0	1–0–0–0	3–2	Carolina
Chicago	1–0–1–0	1–0–1–0	2–0–2–0	11–9	Chicago
Colorado	1–0–1–0	0–3–0–0	1–3–1–0	12–14	Colorado
Columbus	2–0–0–0	1–1–0–0	3–1–0–0	14–11	Columbus
Dallas	1–1–0–0	0–2–0–0	1–3–0–0	11–15	Dallas
Detroit	2–0–0–0	1–0–0–1	3–0–0–1	11–9	Detroit
Florida	0–0–0–0	0–0–1–0	0–0–1–0	2–2	Florida
Los Angeles	1–1–0–0	2–0–0–0	3–1–0–0	22–5	Los Angeles
Minnesota	2–0–1–0	2–0–0–0	4–0–1–0	18–10	Minnesota
Montreal	1–1–0–0	0–1–0–0	1–2–0–0	7–10	Montreal
Nashville	1–1–0–0	2–0–0–0	3–1–0–0	14–8	Nashville
New Jersey	0–0–0–1	0–0–0–0	0–0–0–1	5–6	New Jersey
Islanders	0–1–0–0	0–0–0–0	0–1–0–0	2–4	Islanders
Rangers	0–0–0–0	0–1–0–0	0–1–0–0	3–4	Rangers
Ottawa	1–0–0–0	1–0–0–0	2–0–0–0	9–4	Ottawa
Philadelphia	0–1–0–0	0–0–0–0	0–1–0–0	2–4	Philadelphia
Phoenix	0–0–2–0	0–2–0–0	0–2–2–0	8–13	Phoenix
Pittsburgh	0–0–0–0	0–1–0–0	0–1–0–0	2–5	Pittsburgh
San Jose	0–0–2–0	0–1–1–0	0–1–3–0	8–13	San Jose
St. Louis	2–0–0–0	0–2–0–0	2–2–0–0	11–12	St. Louis
Tampa Bay	0–0–0–0	1–0–0–0	1–0–0–0	5–4	Tampa Bay
Toronto	1–1–0–0	0–1–0–0	1–2–0–0	8–8	Toronto
Vancouver	1–2–0–0	1–1–0–0	2–3–0–0	16–18	Vancouver
Washington	0–0–0–0	0–1–0–0	0–1–0–0	0–4	Washington

2000–2001 Playoff Scoring

#		GP	G	A	Pts	Shots	S%	GW	OT	PP	SH	P/M	PIM
94	Ryan Smyth	6	3	4	7	22	13.6	0	0	0	0	0	4
39	Doug Weight	6	1	5	6	18	5.6	0	0	0	0	0	17
2	Eric Brewer	6	1	5	6	11	9.1	0	0	1	0	−3	2
22	Anson Carter	6	3	1	4	13	23.1	1	0	1	0	1	4
89	Mike Comrie	6	1	2	3	7	14.3	1	1	1	0	0	0
17	Rem Murray	6	2	0	2	15	13.3	0	0	1	0	−2	6
27	Georges Laraque	6	1	1	2	5	20.0	0	0	0	0	2	8
37	Daniel Cleary	6	1	1	2	6	16.7	0	0	1	0	−2	8
21	Jason Smith	6	0	2	2	6	0.0	0	0	0	0	−3	6
44	Janne Niinimaa	6	0	2	2	11	0.0	0	0	0	0	−1	6
5	Tom Poti	6	0	2	2	7	0.0	0	0	0	0	2	2
34	Sergei Zholtok	3	0	0	0	3	0.0	0	0	0	0	−1	0
12	Josh Green	3	0	0	0	1	0.0	0	0	0	0	1	0
14	Domenic Pittis	3	0	0	0	1	0.0	0	0	0	0	−1	2
18	Ethan Moreau	4	0	0	0	5	0.0	0	0	0	0	−2	2
36	Sean Horcoff	5	0	0	0	2	0.0	0	0	0	0	0	0
26	Todd Marchant	6	0	0	0	7	0.0	0	0	0	0	−3	4
25	Mike Grier	6	0	0	0	6	0.0	0	0	0	0	−2	8
55	Igor Ulanov	6	0	0	0	4	0.0	0	0	0	0	−6	4
32	Scott Ferguson	6	0	0	0	2	0.0	0	0	0	0	2	0
35	Tommy Salo	6	0	0	0	0	0.0	0	0	0	0	0	0
		6	13	25	38	152	8.6	2	1	5	0	-18	83

2000-2001 Playoff Goaltending

	GP	Min.	GA	W	L	Ave.	SA	Pct.	SO	EN
Tommy Salo	6	406	15	2	4	2.22	186	.919	0	1

Date	Result					Winning Goaltender	Winning Goal
April 11, 2001	Edmonton	1	at	Dallas	2	Ed Belfour	Jamie Langenbrunner [1]
April 14, 2001	Edmonton	4	at	Dallas	3	Tommy Salo	Anson Carter
April 15, 2001	Dallas	3	at	Edmonton	2	Ed Belfour	Benoit Hogue[2]
April 17, 2001	Dallas	1	at	Edmonton	2	Tommy Salo	Mike Comrie[3]
April 19, 2001	Edmonton	3	at	Dallas	4	Ed Belfour	Kirk Muller[4]
April 21, 2001	Dallas	3	at	Edmonton	1	Ed Belfour	Joe Nieuwendyk

[1]2:08 of overtime
[2]19:48 of overtime
[3]17:19 of overtime
[4]8:01 of overtime

Part Two
The Players

As of the conclusion of the 2000-01 season, 323 professional hockey players have dressed in the uniform of the Edmonton Oilers in the regular season and playoffs during the team's NHL existence. Of these players, 231 were born in Canada, 31 have been born in the U.S., 15 in Czechoslovakia, 15 in the Soviet Union (or former Soviet republics), 12 in Finland, 10 in Sweden, 2 in West Germany, and 1 each in Brazil, Venezuela, Poland, Denmark, Scotland, England and Switzerland.

Of the 231 Canadian born players on the team, 93 have been from the province of Ontario, 44 from Alberta, 31 from British Columbia, 22 from Quebec, 21 from Saskatchewan, 13 from Manitoba, 2 from Nova Scotia, 2 from New Brunswick, and 1 each from Prince Edward Island, Newfoundland and the Yukon Territory. No player on the Oilers has hailed from the Northwest Territories or Nunavut.

Of the 44 players born in Alberta, 21 have been born in Edmonton, 6 in Calgary, 2 in Camrose and 1 each in Banff, Barrhead, Bonnyville, Cold Lake, Fort Saskatchewan, Grand Cache, Hines Creek, Hythe, Jasper, Pincher Creek, Ponoka, Red Deer, Spruce Grove, Two Hills, and Vermilion.

The Oilers have been built largely through trades with other NHL teams. Of the 323 players on the team, 154 have been acquired through trades. Of the Oilers' 233 draft choices, 72 have seen service with the Oilers. The Oilers have also been fairly active in the free agent market, signing 57 players to free agent contracts. Of the remaining players; 13 joined the team from the WHA, 10 were chosen in the Expansion Draft when the team joined the NHL, 9 were claimed in various waiver drafts, 6 were claimed on waivers, and 2 were purchased.

Of the 154 players obtained in trades, the Oilers have obtained 15 from the Rangers, 12 from the Bruins, 11 from Pittsburgh, 10 from Chicago, 8 each from Detroit, Minnesota North Stars, Montreal and Toronto, 7 each from Buffalo, St. Louis, New Jersey, and Philadelphia, 6 each from Vancouver, Quebec and the Islanders, 5 each from Los Angeles, Hartford, Winnipeg, and Tampa Bay, 3 from Nashville, 2 from Washington, and 1 each from the Colorado Rockies, Anaheim, and Ottawa.

Of the 72 Oiler draft choices who have played with the team, 21 were chosen from the Western Hockey League, 16 from the Ontario Hockey League, 3 from the Quebec Major Junior Hockey League, 13 from major U.S. colleges (6-CCHA, 4-WCHA, 2-ECAC, 1-HE), 6 from Czechoslovakia, 3 from Finland, 2 from the USSR, 2 from Tier II, 1 each from the Canadian Olympic Team, Sweden, the CIS, Germany, a US high school, and Switzerland.

Of the 72 players drafted who went on to appear in a game for the Oilers 57 were from North American junior or collegiate teams. Of these 57 players 4 were drafted from the Sault Ste. Marie Greyhounds, 3 each were drafted from the Prince Albert Raiders, Regina Pats and the Michigan State University Spartans, 2 each from the Kamloops Blazers, Kamloops Jr. Oilers, Kingston Canadians, Kitchener Rangers, London Knights, Moose Jaw Warriors, Portland Winter Hawks, Saskatoon Blades, Swift Current Broncos and the University of Michigan Wolverines, and 1 each from the Billings Bighorns, Chilliwack, Granby Bisons, Hamilton Steelhawks, Medicine Hat Tigers, Oshawa Generals, Owen Sound Platers, Quebec Remparts, Saint Albert Saints, St. Jean Beavers, Sudbury Wolves, Victoria Cougars, Windsor Spitfires, Boston University Terriers, Canadian Olympic Team, Clarkson University Golden Knights, Cushing Academy, Lake Superior State Lakers, Michigan Tech, Northern Michigan University Wildcats, Providence College Friars, University of Minnesota-Duluth, the University of South Dakota Fighting Sioux and the Guelph Storm.

Of the 323 players, 39 were born in January, 35 in March, 32 in May, 30 in April, 29 in October, 29 in June, 27 in February, 24 in September, 23 in August, 19 in December, 18 in July, and 18 in November.

The youngest player to suit up for the Oilers in the NHL was Martin Gelinas, who was 18 years, 4 months and 2 days old when he played in his first Oilers game. The oldest Oiler was Kevin Lowe, who was 39 years and 9 days old when he appeared in a 1997-1998 playoff game.

Wayne Gretzky was 17 years and 10 months old when he first played for the Oilers in the WHA, and goaltender Jacques Plante was over 45 years of age when he played 31

This last edition of the WHA Oilers includes many players who would go on to star with the team in the NHL. (A85-4 City of Edmonton Archives)

games in goal for the Oilers during the 1974-75 season in the World Hockey Association.

Of the 323 players, 64 are listed as being taller than 6'2", 169 players are shown as being 6'0" to 6'2" in height, and the remaining 90 players were shorter than 6 feet in height. The tallest Oilers were Jeff Beukeboom, Dave Brown, Francois Leroux, Mike Ware, and Todd Reirden, each listed at 6'5" in height; the two shortest Oilers—goaltenders Lindsay Middlebrook and Fred Brathwaite—were 5'7" in height.

While an individual player's weight will vary from year to year or in fact from day to day the weight shown for each player is his listed weight in the Oiler media guides or the *NHL Guide* and *Record Book*. Of the 323 players to play on the Oilers 140 are shown to weigh over 200 pounds. Georges Laraque has been the heaviest Oiler weighing in at 240 pounds, while diminutive goalie Ron Tugnutt weighed only 155 pounds and was the lightest Oiler. Of these 323 men, 33 of them have been goaltenders (31 caught left handed, 2 right handed), 96 of them have been defensemen (61 shot left handed, 35 right handed), 81 have been centers (57 shot left handed and 24 right handed) and 113 have been listed as wingers (73 left handed shots and 40 right handed shots).

The most common first names used by players were Mike (Michael) with 14 and Dave (David) with 13, Tom or Tommy with 9, and Jim (Jimmy) and Dan (Danny, Daniel), with 7. Six players each had the names Bill (William), Don (Donald), Ron (Ronald), Steve and Scott.

The most popular sweater number worn has been 15. Twenty-four players have worn that number. Sweater number 20 has been worn 20 times; following in frequency are number 23 (19 times), numbers 8 and 34 (18 times), number 26 (17 times), numbers 19, 28, and 33 (14 times), numbers 6, 12, and 18 (13 times), number 29 (12 times), numbers 25 and 32 (11 times), numbers 10, 14, 21, 27, and 35 (10 times), number 1 (9 times), numbers 2, 9, 24, and 36 (8 times), numbers 5 and 7 (7 times), numbers 22, 30, and 37 (6 times), numbers 16 and 31 (5 times), number 17 (4 times), numbers 13, 38, 40, and 42 (3 times), numbers 41 and 47 (2 times), numbers 3, 4, 11, 39, 43, 44, 46, 51, 55, 64, 65, 77, 85, 89, 94, and 99 (1 time).

An additional 129 players played for the team in the World Hockey Association only.

Players listed as retired played their last NHL game for the Oilers.

ACTON, KEITH EDWARD SWEATER # 23 # 20 CENTER SL

Born: Stouffville, Ontario April 15, 1958 5'8"-170

Last Amateur Club: Peterborough Petes (OHA)

How the Oilers Got Him: Montreal's 8th choice, 103rd overall in the 1978 draft. Traded to the Oilers by the Minnesota North Stars for Moe Mantha, January 22, 1988.

First Game as an Oiler: January 23, 1988

First Assist as an Oiler: January 25, 1988

First Goal as an Oiler: January 30, 1988

First Penalty as an Oiler: January 23, 1988

Where He Went: Traded to Philadelphia with the Oilers' sixth round choice (Dimitri Yushkevich) in the 1991 draft for Dave Brown, February 7, 1989.

Season	*GP*	*G*	*A*	*Pts*	*Shots*	*S%*	*GW*	*GT*	*PP*	*SH*	*P/M*	*PIM*
1987-88	26	3	6	9	26	11.5	1	0	1	0	-10	21
Playoffs	*7*	*2*	*0*	*2*	*10*	*20.0*	*2*	*0*	*0*	*0*	*4*	*16*
1988-89	46	11	15	26	74	14.9	1	0	0	1	9	47
2 years	72	14	21	35	100	14.0	2	0	1	1	-1	68
Playoffs	*7*	*2*	*0*	*2*	*10*	*20.0*	*2*	*0*	*0*	*0*	*4*	*16*

ADAMS, GREGORY CHARLES SWEATER # 25 LEFT WING SL

Born: Duncan, British Columbia May 31, 1960 6'1"-190

Last Amateur Club: Victoria Cougars (WHL)

How the Oilers Got Him: Traded to the Oilers by the Washington Capitals for the rights to Geoff Courtnall, July 22, 1988.

First Game as an Oiler: October 7, 1988 *First Assist as an Oiler:* November 4, 1988

First Goal as an Oiler: October 16, 1988 *First Penalty as an Oiler:* October 7, 1988

Where He Went: Traded to Vancouver with Doug Smith for Jean LeBlanc and the Canucks' fifth round choice (Peter White) in the 1989 draft, March 7, 1989.

Season	*GP*	*G*	*A*	*Pts*	*Shots*	*S%*	*GW*	*GT*	*PP*	*SH*	*P/M*	*PIM*
1988-89	49	4	5	9	49	8.2	1	0	0	0	1	72

AITKEN, BRADLEY SWEATER # 24 LEFT WING SL

Born: Scarborough, Ontario October 30, 1967 6'2"-200

Last Amateur Club: Sault Ste. Marie Greyhounds (OHA)

How the Oilers Got Him: Pittsburgh's 3rd choice, 46th overall in the 1986 draft. Traded to the Oilers by the Penguins for Kim Issel, March 5, 1991.

First Game as an Oiler: March 6, 1991 *First Assist as an Oiler:* March 10, 1991

First Goal as an Oiler: None Recorded *First Penalty as an Oiler*: None Recorded

Where He Went: Signed as a free agent by the Leafs, July 30, 1991.

Season	*GP*	*G*	*A*	*Pts*	*Shots*	*S%*	*GW*	*GT*	*PP*	*SH*	*P/M*	*PIM*
1990-91	3	0	1	1	0	0.0	0	0	0	0	-1	0

AIVAZOFF, MICAH SWEATER # 12 CENTER SL

Born: Powell River, British Columbia May 4, 1969 6'0"-195

Last Amateur Club: Victoria Cougars (WHL)

How the Oilers Got Him: Los Angeles' 6th choice, 109th overall in the 1988 draft. Claimed by the Oilers from the Pittsburgh Penguins in the NHL Waiver Draft, January 18, 1995.

First Game as an Oiler: January 25, 1995 *First Assist as an Oiler:* April 13, 1995

First Goal as an Oiler: None Recorded *First Penalty as an Oiler:* February 22, 1995

Where He Went: Signed as a free agent by the Islanders, August 23, 1995.

Season	*GP*	*G*	*A*	*Pts*	*Shots*	*S%*	*GW*	*GT*	*PP*	*SH*	*P/M*	*PIM*
1994-95	21	0	1	1	6	0.0	0	0	0	0	-2	2

ANDERSON, GLENN CHRIS SWEATER # 9 RIGHT WING SL

Born: Vancouver, British Columbia October 2, 1960 5'11"-175

Last Amateur Club: Canadian Olympic Team

How the Oilers Got Him: Edmonton's 3rd choice, 69th overall in 1979 draft.

First Game as an Oiler: October 10, 1980 *First Assist as an Oiler*: October 12, 1980

First Goal as an Oiler: October 12, 1980 *First Penalty as an Oiler:* October 12, 1980

Where He Went: Traded to the Leafs with Craig Berube and Grant Fuhr, for Vincent Damphousse, Peter Ing, Luke Richardson, Scott Thornton, future considerations and cash, September 19, 1991. Claimed on waivers by the Oilers January 25, 1996. Claimed on waivers by St. Louis, March 12, 1996.

Season	*GP*	*G*	*A*	*Pts*	*Shots*	*S%*	*GW*	*GT*	*PP*	*SH*	*P/M*	*PIM*
1980-81	58	30	23	53	160	18.8	5	2	10	3	4	24
Playoffs	*9*	*5*	*7*	*12*			*0*	*0*	*3*	*0*		*12*
1981-82	80	38	67	105	252	15.1	8	2	9	0	46	71
Playoffs	*5*	*2*	*5*	*7*			*1*	*0*	*0*	*0*		*8*
1982-83	72	48	56	104	243	19.8	10	3	11	0	41	70
Playoffs	*16*	*10*	*10*	*20*	*49*	*20.4*	*2*	*0*	*1*	*0*	*4*	*32*
1983-84	80	54	45	99	277	19.5	11	1	11	4	41	65
Playoffs	*19*	*6*	*11*	*17*	*68*	*8.8*	*1*	*0*	*1*	*0*	*6*	*33*
1984-85	80	42	39	81	258	16.3	6	0	12	1	24	69
Playoffs	*18*	*10*	*16*	*26*	*47*	*21.3*	*1*	*1*	*2*	*0*	*11*	*38*

Season	GP	G	A	Pts	Shots	S%	GW	GT	PP	SH	P/M	PIM
1985-86	72	54	48	102	243	22.2	9	0	18	2	38	90
Playoffs	*10*	*8*	*3*	*11*	*38*	*21.1*	*2*	*1*	*1*	*0*	*2*	*14*
1986-87	80	35	38	73	188	18.6	6	0	7	1	27	65
Playoffs	*21*	*14*	*13*	*27*	*62*	*22.6*	*2*	*1*	*4*	*0*	*13*	*59*
1987-88	80	38	50	88	255	14.9	3	0	16	1	5	58
Playoffs	*19*	*9*	*16*	*25*	*43*	*20.9*	*1*	*0*	*4*	*0*	*5*	*49*
1988-89	79	16	48	64	212	7.5	3	0	7	0	-16	93
Playoffs	*7*	*1*	*2*	*3*	*16*	*6.3*	*0*	*0*	*1*	*0*	*-1*	*8*
1989-90	73	34	38	72	204	16.6	7	1	17	1	-1	107
Playoffs	*22*	*10*	*12*	*22*	*46*	*21.7*	*2*	*0*	*2*	*0*	*12*	*20*
1990-91	74	24	31	55	193	12.4	4	0	8	0	-7	59
Playoffs	*18*	*6*	*7*	*13*	*43*	*14.0*	*0*	*0*	*3*	*0*	*-2*	*41*
1995-96	17	4	6	10	36	11.1	1	0	0	0	0	27
12 years	845	417	489	906	2521	16.5	73	9	126	13	202	798
Playoffs	*164*	*81*	*102*	*183*			*12*	*3*	*22*	*0*		*314*

ARESHENKOFF, RONALD SWEATER # 10 CENTER SL

Born: Grand Forks, British Columbia June 13, 1957 6'0"-175

Last Amateur Club: Medicine Hat Tigers (WHL)

How the Oilers Got Him: Buffalo's 2nd choice, 32nd overall in the 1977 draft. Claimed from the Sabres by the Oilers in the Expansion Draft, June 13, 1979.

First Game as an Oiler: October 1979

First Goal as an Oiler: None Recorded

First Assist as an Oiler: None Recorded

First Penalty as an Oiler: None Recorded

Where He Went: Traded to the Flyers along with the Oilers' tenth round choice (Bob O'Brien) for Barry Dean, June 11, *1980.*

Season	GP	G	A	Pts	Shots	S%	GW	GT	PP	SH	P/M	PIM
1979-80	4	0	0	0	3	0.0	0	0	0	0	-4	0

ARNOTT, JASON WILLIAM SWEATER # 7 CENTER SR

Born: Collingwood, Ontario October 11, 1974 6'3"-220

Last Amateur Club: Oshawa Generals (OHL)

How the Oilers Got Him: Oilers' 1st choice, 7th overall in the 1993 draft.

First Game as an Oiler: October 6, 1993

First Goal as an Oiler: October 6, 1993

First Assist as an Oiler: October 8, 1993

First Penalty as an Oiler: October 6, 1993

Where He Went: Traded to New Jersey with Bryan Muir for Valeri Zelepukin and Bill Guerin, January 4, 1998.

Season	GP	G	A	Pts	Shots	S%	GW	GT	PP	SH	P/M	PIM
1993-94	78	33	35	68	194	17.0	4	1	10	0	1	104
1994-95	42	15	22	37	156	9.6	1	0	7	0	-14	128
1995-96	64	28	31	59	244	11.5	5	1	8	0	-6	87
1996-97	67	19	38	57	248	7.7	2	1	10	1	-21	92
Playoffs	*12*	*3*	*6*	*9*	*27*	*11.1*	*0*	*0*	*1*	*0*	*-3*	*18*
1997-98	35	5	13	18	100	5.0	0	0	1	0	-16	78
5 years	286	100	139	239	942	10.6	12	3	36	1	-56	489
Playoffs	*12*	*3*	*6*	*9*	*27*	*11.1*	*0*	*0*	*1*	*0*	*-3*	*18*

ASHBY, DONALD ALAN SWEATER # 19 CENTER SL

Born: Kamloops, British Columbia March 8, 1955 Died: May 30, 1981 6'1"-185

Last Amateur Club: Calgary Centennials (WCHL)

How the Oilers Got Him: Toronto's 1st choice, 6th overall in the 1975 draft. Obtained from Colorado for Bobby Schmautz, February 25, 1980.

First Game as an Oiler: March 4, 1980

First Goal as an Oiler: March 4, 1980

First Assist as an Oiler: March 4, 1980

First Penalty as an Oiler: November 16, 1980

Where He Went: Deceased

Season	GP	G	A	Pts	Shots	S%	GW	GT	PP	SH	P/M	PIM
1979-80	18	10	9	19	31	32.3	1	0	3	0	1	0
Playoffs	*3*	*0*	*0*	*0*			*0*	*0*	*0*	*0*		*0*
1980-81	6	2	3	5	13	15.4	1	0	1	0	-1	2
2 years	24	12	12	24	44	27.3	2	0	4	0	0	2
Playoffs	*3*	*0*	*0*	*0*			*0*	*0*	*0*	*0*		*0*

BALTIMORE, BRYON DON SWEATER # 33 DEFENSE SR
Born: Whitehorse, Yukon Territory August 26, 1952 6'2"-200
Last Amateur Club: University of Alberta (CWUAA)
How the Oilers Got Him: Claimed in the WHA dispersal draft, June 9, 1979.
First Game as an Oiler: November 13, 1979
First Assist as an Oiler: None Recorded
First Goal as an Oiler: None Recorded
First Penalty as as Oiler: November 13, 1979
Where He Went: Retired

Season	GP	G	A	Pts	Shots	S%	GW	GT	PP	SH	P/M	PIM
1979-80	2	0	0	0	2	0.0	0	0	0	0	4	4

BANNISTER, DREW SWEATER # 55 DEFENSE SR
Born: Belleville, Ontario September 4, 1974 6'2"-200
Last Amateur Club: Sault Ste. Marie Greyhounds (OHL)
How the Oilers Got Him: Tampa Bay's 2nd choice, 26th overall in the 1992 draft. Traded to the Oilers by the Lightning with Tampa Bay's 6th round choice (Peter Sarno) in the 1997 draft, for Jeff Norton, March 18, 1997.
First Game as an Oiler: April 12, 1997
First Assist as an Oiler: April 12, 1997
First Goal as an Oiler: None Recorded
First Penalty as an Oiler: April 18, 1997
Where He Went: Traded to Anaheim for Bobby Dollas, January 9, 1998.

Season	GP	G	A	Pts	Shots	S%	GW	GT	PP	SH	P/M	PIM
1996-97	1	0	1	1	2	0.0	0	0	0	0	-2	0
Playoffs	*12*	*0*	*0*	*0*	*9*	*0.0*	*0*	*0*	*0*	*0*	*-4*	*30*
1997-98	34	0	2	2	27	0.0	0	0	0	0	-7	42
2 years	35	0	3	3	29	0.0	0	0	0	0	-9	42
Playoffs	*12*	*0*	*0*	*0*	*9*	*0.0*	*0*	*0*	*0*	*0*	*-4*	*30*

BARON, MARCO JOSEPH SWEATER # 33 GOALTENDER CL
Born: Montreal, Quebec April 8, 1959 5'11"-180
Last Amateur Club: Montreal Juniors (QMJHL)
How the Oilers Got Him: Boston's 6th choice, 99th overall in the 1979 draft. Signed as a free agent by the Oilers February 21, 1985.
First Game as an Oiler: March 1, 1985
First Assist as an Oiler: None Recorded
First Goal as an Oiler: None Recorded
First Penalty as an Oiler: None Recorded
Where He Went: Retired

Season	GP	Min	GA	W	L	T	Ave	SA	S%	SO	EN	PIM	Ast.
1984-85	1	33	2	0	1	0	3.64	9	0.778	0	0	0	0

BEDNARSKI, JOHN SEVERN SWEATER # 33 DEFENSE SL
Born: Thunder Bay, Ontario July, 4, 1952 5'10"-195
Last Amateur Club: Winnipeg Jets (JRS)
How the Oilers Got Him: Signed as a free agent by the Oilers, July 15, 1979.
First Game as an Oiler: November 7, 1979
First Assist as an Oiler: None Recorded
First Goal as an Oiler: None Recorded
First Penalty as an Oiler: None Recorded
Where He Went: Signed as a free agent by Buffalo, June 26, 1980.

Season	GP	G	A	Pts	Shots	S%	GW	GT	PP	SH	P/M	PIM
1979-80	1	0	0	0	2	0.0	0	0	0	0	0	0

BEERS, ROBERT CHARLES SWEATER # 2 DEFENSE SR
Born: Pittsburgh, Pennsylvania May 20, 1967 6'2"-200
Last Amateur Club: University of Maine Black Bears (H.E.)
How the Oilers Got Him: Boston's 10th choice, 210th overall in the 1985 draft. Traded to the Oilers from the Tampa Bay Lightning for Chris Joseph, November 11, 1993.
First Game as an Oiler: November 13, 1993
First Assist as an Oiler: November 13, 1993
First Goal as an Oiler: December 8, 1993
First Penalty as an Oiler: November 24, 1993
Where He Went: Signed as a free agent by the Islanders, August 29, 1994.

Season	GP	G	A	Pts	Shots	S%	GW	GT	PP	SH	P/M	PIM
1993-94	66	10	27	37	152	6.6	0	1	5	0	-11	74

BELANGER, JESSE SWEATER # 12 CENTER SR
Born: St. Georges de Beauce, Quebec, June 15, 1969 6'1"-190
Last Amateur Club: Granby Bisons (QMJHL)
How the Oilers Got Him: Signed as a free agent by the Oilers, September 16, 1996.
First Game as an Oiler: October 4, 1996
First Assist as an Oiler: None Recorded
First Goal as an Oiler: None Recorded
First Penalty as an Oiler: None Recorded
Where He Went: Signed as a free agent by Tampa Bay, August 18, 1998.

Season	GP	G	A	Pts	Shots	S%	GW	GT	PP	SH	P/M	PIM
1996-97	6	0	0	0	8	0.0	0	0	0	0	-3	0

BELL, BRUCE SWEATER # 36 DEFENSE SL
Born: Toronto, Ontario February 15, 1965 6'0"-190
Last Amateur Club: Brantford Alexanders (OHL)
How the Oilers Got Him: Quebec's 2nd choice, 52nd overall in the 1983 draft. Signed as a free agent by the Oilers, February 1, 1990.
First Game as an Oiler: February 2, 1990
First Assist as an Oiler: None Recorded
First Goal as an Oiler: None Recorded
First Penalty as an Oiler: None Recorded
Where He Went: Traded to Minnesota for Kari Takko November 22, 1990.

Season	GP	G	A	Pts	Shots	S%	GW	GT	PP	SH	P/M	PIM
1989-90	1	0	0	0	1	0.0	0	0	0	0	0	0

BENNETT, ADAM SWEATER # 35 DEFENSE SR
Born: Georgetown, Ontario March 30, 1971 6'4"-205
Last Amateur Club: Sudbury Wolves (OHL)
How the Oilers Got Him: Chicago's 1st choice, 6th overall in the 1989 draft. Traded to the Oilers from the Black Hawks for Kevin Todd, October 7, 1993.
First Game as an Oiler: October 19, 1993
First Assist as an Oiler: November 3, 1993
First Goal as an Oiler: November 6, 1993
First Penalty as an Oiler: November 7, 1993
Where He Went: Retired.

Season	GP	G	A	Pts	Shots	S%	GW	GT	PP	SH	P/M	PIM
1993-94	48	3	6	9	57	5.3	0	0	1	0	-8	49

BENNING, BRIAN SWEATER # 19 DEFENSE SL
Born: Edmonton, Alberta June 10, 1966 6'0"-195
Last Amateur Club: Kamloops Junior Oilers (WHL)
How the Oilers Got: St. Louis' 1st choice, 26th overall in the 1984 draft. Traded to the Oilers from the Philadelphia Flyers for Greg Hawgood and Josef Beranek, January 16, 1993.
First Game as an Oiler: January 19, 1993
First Assist as an Oiler: February 12, 1993
First Goal as an Oiler: February 12, 1993
First Penalty as an Oiler: February 12, 1993
Where He Went: Signed as a free agent by Florida , July 13, 1993.

Season	GP	G	A	Pts	Shots	S%	GW	GT	PP	SH	P/M	PIM
1992-93	18	1	7	8	28	3.6	0	0	0	0	-1	59

BENYSEK, LADISLAV SWEATER # 21 DEFENSE SL
Born: Olomouc, Czechoslovakia March 24, 1975 6'2"-190
Last Amateur Club: Sparta Praha (Czech)
How the Oilers Got Him: Oilers' 16th pick, 266th overall in the 1994 draft.
First Game as an Oiler: November 15, 1997
First Assist as an Oiler: None Recorded
First Goal as an Oiler: None Recorded
First Penalty as an Oiler: None Recorded
Where He Went: Claimed in the Waiver Draft by Anaheim, September 27, 1999.

Season	GP	G	A	Pts	Shots	S%	GW	GT	PP	SH	P/M	PIM
1997-98	2	0	0	0	0	0.0	0	0	0	0	-2	0

BERANEK, JOSEF SWEATER # 42, # 29, #20 RIGHT WING SL
Born: Litvinov, Czechoslovakia October 25, 1969 6'2"-185
Last Amateur Club: CHZ Litvinov (Czech)
How the Oilers Got Him: Edmonton's 3rd choice, 78th overall in the 1989 draft.
First Game as an Oiler: October 6, 1991
First Assist as an Oiler: October 20, 1991
First Goal as an Oiler: October 6, 1991
First Penalty as an Oiler: October 26, 1991

Where He Went: Traded to the Flyers with Greg Hawgood for Brian Benning, January 16, 1993. Reacquired by the Oilers, from Pittsburgh for Bobby Dollas and Tony Hrkac, June 16, 1998. Traded to Pittsburgh for German Titov, March 14, *2000.*

Season	*GP*	*G*	*A*	*Pts*	*Shots*	*S%*	*GW*	*GT*	*PP*	*SH*	*P/M*	*PIM*
1991-92	58	12	16	28	79	15.2	1	0	0	0	-2	18
Playoffs	*12*	*2*	*1*	*3*	*17*	*11.8*	*1*	*0*	*1*	*0*	*-6*	*0*
1992-93	26	2	6	8	44	4.5	0	0	0	0	-7	28
1998-99	66	19	30	49	160	11.9	2	0	7	0	6	23
Playoffs	*1*	*0*	*0*	*0*	*0*	*0.0*	*0*	*0*	*0*	*0*	*-1*	*4*
1999-00	58	9	8	17	107	8.4	1	0	3	0	-6	39
4 years	208	42	60	102	390	10.8	4	0	10	0	-9	108
Playoffs	*13*	*2*	*1*	*3*	*17*	*11.8*	*1*	*0*	*1*	*0*	*-7*	*4*

BEREHOWSKY, DRAKE SWEATER # 15 DEFENSE SR

Born: Toronto, Ontario January 3, 1972 6'1"-210

Last Amateur Club: North Bay Centennials (OHL)

How the Oilers Got Him: Toronto's 1st choice, 10th overall in 1990 draft. Signed as a free agent September 29, 1997.

First Game as an Oiler: October 1, 1997 *First Assist as an Oiler:* October 11, 1997

First Goal as an Oiler: October 1, 1997 *First Penalty as an Oiler*: October 3, 1997

Where He Went: Traded to Nashville with Greg de Vries and Eric Fichaud for Jim Dowd and Mikhail Shtalenkov, October 1, 1998.

Season	*GP*	*G*	*A*	*Pts*	*Shots*	*S%*	*GW*	*GT*	*PP*	*SH*	*P/M*	*PIM*
1997-98	67	1	6	7	58	1.7	1	0	1	0	1	169
Playoffs	*12*	*1*	*2*	*3*	*4*	*25.0*	*1*	*0*	*0*	*0*	*1*	*14*

BERRY, KENNETH EDWARD SWEATER # 19, # 18 LEFT WING SL

Born: New Westminster, British Columbia June 21, 1960 5'9"-160

Last Amateur Club: University of Denver Pioneers (WCHA)

How the Oilers Got Him: Vancouver's 5th choice, 112th overall in 1980 draft. Traded by the Canucks to the Oilers with Garry Lariviere for Blair MacDonald and Lars Gunnar Petersson, March 10, 1981.

First Game as an Oiler: October 9, 1981 *First Assist as an Oiler:* December 7, 1981

First Goal as an Oiler: December 27, 1981 *First Penalty as an Oiler*: December 9, 1981

Where He Went: Signed as a free agent by Vancouver, March 1, 1988.

Season	*GP*	*G*	*A*	*Pts*	*Shots*	*S%*	*GW*	*GT*	*PP*	*SH*	*P/M*	*PIM*
1981-82	15	2	3	5	9	22.2	0	0	0	0	-6	9
1983-84	13	2	3	5	18	11.1	0	0	0	1	6	10
2 years	28	4	6	10	27	14.8	0	0	0	1	0	19

BEUKEBOOM, JEFF SWEATER # 6 DEFENSE SR

Born: Ajax, Ontario March 28, 1965 6'5"-230

Last Amateur Club: Sault Ste. Marie Greyhounds (OHL)

How the Oilers Got Him: Oilers' 1st choice, 19th overall in the 1983 draft.

First Game as an Oiler: April 10, 1986 *First Assist as an Oiler:* Oct. 17, 1986

First Goal as an Oiler: December 30, 1986 *First Penalty as an Oiler:* April 10, 1986

Where He Went: Traded to the Rangers for David Shaw, November 12, 1991.

Season	*GP*	*G*	*A*	*Pts*	*Shots*	*S%*	*GW*	*GT*	*PP*	*SH*	*P/M*	*PIM*
Playoffs(85-86)	*1*	*0*	*0*	*0*	*1*	*0.0*	*0*	*0*	*0*	*0*	*1*	*4*
1986-87	44	3	8	11	24	12.5	1	0	1	0	7	124
1987-88	73	5	20	25	76	6.6	1	0	1	0	27	201
Playoffs	*7*	*0*	*0*	*0*	*2*	*0.0*	*0*	*0*	*0*	*0*	*-1*	*16*
1988-89	36	0	5	5	26	0.0	0	0	0	0	2	94
Playoffs	*1*	*0*	*0*	*0*	*0*	*0.0*	*0*	*0*	*0*	*0*	*0*	*2*
1989-90	46	1	12	13	36	2.8	0	0	0	0	5	86
Playoffs	*2*	*0*	*0*	*0*	*0*	*0.0*	*0*	*0*	*0*	*0*	*2*	*0*
1990-91	67	3	7	10	48	6.3	0	0	0	0	6	150
Playoffs	*18*	*1*	*3*	*4*	*15*	*6.7*	*0*	*0*	*0*	*0*	*-5*	*28*
1991-92	18	0	5	5	7	0.0	0	0	0	0	4	78
6 years	284	12	57	69	217	5.6	2	0	2	0	51	733
Playoffs	*29*	*1*	*3*	*4*	*18*	*5.6*	*0*	*0*	*0*	*0*	*-3*	*50*

BIANCHIN, WAYNE RICHARD SWEATER # 15 LEFT WING SL

Born: Nanaimo, British Columbia September 6, 1953 5'10"-180

Last Amateur Club: Flin Flon Bombers (WCHL)

How the Oilers Got Him: Pittsburgh's 2nd choice, 23rd overall in the 1973 draft. Claimed from the Penguins by the Oilers in the Expansion Draft, June 13, 1979.

First Game as an Oiler: October 14, 1979
First Assist as an Oiler: None Recorded
First Goal as an Oiler: None Recorded
First Penalty as an Oiler: October 24, 1979
Where He Went : Retired

Season	*GP*	*G*	*A*	*Pts*	*Shots*	*S%*	*GW*	*GT*	*PP*	*SH*	*P/M*	*PIM*
1979-80	11	0	0	0	7	0.0	0	0	0	0	-4	7

BLADON, THOMAS GEORGE SWEATER # 23 DEFENSE SR

Born: Edmonton, Alberta December 29, 1952 6'1"-195

Last Amateur Club: Edmonton Oil Kings (WCHL)

How the Oilers Got Him: Philadelphia's 2nd choice, 23rd overall in the 1972 draft. Signed as a free agent by the Oilers, July 10, 1980.

First Game as an Oiler: October 12, 1980
First Assist as an Oiler: None Recorded
First Goal as an Oiler: None Recorded
First Penalty as an Oiler: None Recorded
Where He Went: Signed as a free agent by Winnipeg, December 13, 1980.

Season	*GP*	*G*	*A*	*Pts*	*Shots*	*S%*	*GW*	*GT*	*PP*	*SH*	*P/M*	*PIM*
1980-81	1	0	0	0	0	0.0	0	0	0	0	-1	0

BLUM, JOHN JOSEPH SWEATER # 28 DEFENSE SR

Born: Detroit, Michigan October 8, 1959 6'3"-205

Last Amateur Club: University of Michigan Wolverines (WCHA)

How the Oilers Got Him: Signed as a free agent by the Oilers May 5, 1981.

First Game as an Oiler: October 5, 1982
First Assist as an Oiler: October 5, 1982
First Goal as an Oiler: None Recorded
First Penalty as an Oiler: October 5, 1982
Where He Went: Traded to the Bruins for Larry Melnyk, March 6, 1984.

Season	*GP*	*G*	*A*	*Pts*	*Shots*	*S%*	*GW*	*GT*	*PP*	*SH*	*P/M*	*PIM*
1982-83	5	0	3	3	0	0.0	0	0	0	0	2	24
1983-84	4	0	1	1	3	0.0	0	0	0	0	0	2
2 years	9	0	4	4	3	0.0	0	0	0	0	2	26

BONSIGNORE, JASON SWEATER # 23, # 64 CENTER SR

Born: Rochester, New York April 15, 1976 6'4"-220

Last Amateur Club: Sudbury Wolves (OHL)

How the Oilers Got Him: Oilers 1st choice, 4th overall in the 1994 draft.

First Game as an Oiler: May 3, 1995
First Assist as an Oiler: December 1, 1995
First Goal as an Oiler: May 3, 1995
First Penalty as an Oiler: October 18, 1995
Where He Went: Traded to Tampa Bay with Steve Kelly and Bryan Marchment, for Roman Hamrlik and Paul Comrie, December 30, 1997.

Season	*GP*	*G*	*A*	*Pts*	*Shots*	*S%*	*GW*	*GT*	*PP*	*SH*	*P/M*	*PIM*
1994-95	1	1	0	1	3	33.3	0	0	0	0	-1	0
1995-96	20	0	2	2	13	0.0	0	0	0	0	-6	4
2 years	21	1	2	3	16	6.3	0	0	0	0	-7	4

BONVIE, DENNIS KEVIN SWEATER # 43, # 36 RIGHT WING/DEFENSE SR

Born: Antigonish, Nova Scotia July 23, 1973 5'11"-205

Last Amateur Club: North Bay Centennials (OHL)

How the Oilers Got Him: Signed as a free agent by the Oilers, August 25, 1994.

First Game as an Oiler: April 19, 1995
First Assist as an Oiler: None Recorded
First Goal as an Oiler: None Recorded
First Penalty as an Oiler: October 8, 1995
Where He Went: Claimed on waivers by Chicago October 5, 1998.

Season	*GP*	*G*	*A*	*Pts*	*Shots*	*S%*	*GW*	*GT*	*PP*	*SH*	*P/M*	*PIM*
1994-95	2	0	0	0	0	0.0	0	0	0	0	0	0
1995-96	8	0	0	0	0	0.0	0	0	0	0	-3	47
1997-98	4	0	0	0	0	0.0	0	0	0	0	0	27
3 years	14	0	0	0	0	0.0	0	0	0	0	-3	74

BOSCHMAN, LAURIE JOSEPH SWEATER # 14 CENTER SL
Born: Major, Saskatchewan June 4, 1960 6'0"-185
Last Amateur Club: Brandon Wheat Kings (WHL)
How the Oilers Got Him: Toronto's 1st choice, 9th overall in the 1979 draft. Traded by the Maple Leafs to the Oilers, for Walt Podubny and Phil Drouilliard, March 8, 1982.
First Game as an Oiler: March 10, 1982 *First Assist as an Oiler*: March 17, 1982
First Goal as an Oiler: March 13, 1982 *First Penalty as an Oiler*: March 25, 1982
Where He Went: Traded to Winnipeg for Willy Lindstrom, March 7, 1983.

Season	GP	G	A	Pts	Shots	S%	GW	GT	PP	SH	P/M	PIM
1981-82	11	2	3	5	4	50.0	0	0	0	0	2	37
Playoffs	*3*	*0*	*1*	*1*			*0*	*0*	*0*	*0*		*4*
1982-83	62	8	12	20	59	13.6	0	1	0	0	3	183
2 years	73	10	15	25	63	15.9	0	1	0	0	5	220
Playoffs	*3*	*0*	*1*	*1*			*0*	*0*	*0*	*0*		*4*

BOWEN, JASON SWEATER # 29 LEFT WING SL
Born: Port Alice, British Columbia November 9, 1973 6'4"-215
Last Amateur Club: Tri-City Americans (WHL)
How the Oilers Got Him: Philadelphia's 2nd choice, 15th overall in the 1992 draft. Traded by the Flyers to the Oilers for Brantt Myhres, October 15, 1997.
First Game as an Oiler: October 19, 1997 *First Assist as an Oiler:* None Recorded
First Goal as an Oiler: None Recorded *First Penalty as an Oiler:* October 21, 1997

Season	GP	G	A	Pts	Shots	S%	GW	GT	PP	SH	P/M	PIM
1997-98	4	0	0	0	3	0.0	0	0	0	0	0	10

BRACKENBURY, JOHN CURTIS SWEATER # 15 RIGHT WING SR
Born: Kapuskasing, Ontario January 31, 1952 5'10"-197
Last Amateur Club: Jersey Devils (EHL)
How the Oilers Got Him: Claimed from the Quebec Nordiques by the Oilers in the Waiver Draft, on October 10. 1980.
First Game as an Oiler: October 12, 1980 *First Assist as an Oiler:* November 3, 1980
First Goal as an Oiler: December 14, 1980 *First Penalty as an Oiler*: October 12, 1980
Where He Went: Signed as a free agent by St. Louis, October 1, 1982.

Season	GP	G	A	Pts	Shots	S%	GW	GT	PP	SH	P/M	PIM
1980-81	58	2	7	9	20	10.0	0	0	0	0	-3	153
Playoffs	*2*	*0*	*0*	*0*			*0*	*0*	*0*	*0*		*0*
1981-82	14	0	2	2	2	0.0	0	0	0	0	2	12
2 years	72	2	9	11	22	9.1	0	0	0	0	-1	165
Playoffs	*2*	*0*	*0*	*0*			*0*	*0*	*0*	*0*		*0*

BRATHWAITE, FRED SWEATER # 31, # 40 GOALTENDER CL
Born: Ottawa, Ontario November 24, 1972 5'7"-170
Last Amateur Club: Detroit Jr. Red Wings (OHL)
How the Oilers Got Him: Signed as a free agent by the Oilers, October 6, 1993.
First Game as an Oiler: October 13, 1993 *First Assist as an Oiler:* None Recorded
First Goal as an Oiler: None Recorded *First Penalty as an Oiler*: January 9, 1996
Where He Went: Signed as a free agent by the Calgary Flames, January 6, 1999.

Season	GP	Min	GA	W	L	T	Ave	SA	S%	SO	EN	PIM	Ast.
1993-94	19	982	58	3	10	3	3.54	523	0.889	0	0	0	0
1994-95	14	601	40	2	5	1	3.99	292	0.863	0	1	0	0
1995-96	7	293	12	0	2	0	2.46	140	0.914	0	1	2	0
3 years	40	1876	110	5	17	4	3.52	955	0.885	0	2	2	0

BREWER, ERIC SWEATER # 2 DEFENSE SL
Born: Vernon, British Columbia April 17, 1979 6'3"-220
Last Amateur Club: Prince George Cougars (WHL)
How the Oilers Got Him: Islanders 2nd choice, 5th overall in the 1997 draft. Traded to the Oilers by the Islanders with Josh Green and the Islanders 2nd choice (Brad Winchester) in the 2000 draft for Roman Hamrlik, June 24th 2000.
First Game as an Oiler: October 6, 2000 *First Assist as an Oiler:* October 30, 2000
First Goal as an Oiler: November 7, 2000 *First Penalty as an Oiler:* October 17, 2000

Season	GP	G	A	Pts	Shots	S%	GW	GT	PP	SH	P/M	PIM
2000-01	77	7	13	20	91	7.7	2	0	2	0	15	53
Playoffs	*6*	*1*	*5*	*6*	*11*	*9.1*	*0*	*0*	*1*	*0*	*-3*	*2*

BROWN, DAVID JAMES SWEATER # 32 RIGHT WING SR
Born: Saskatoon, Saskatchewan October 12, 1962 6'5"-205
Last Amateur Club: Saskatoon Blades (WHL)
How the Oilers Got Him: Philadelphia's 7th choice, 40th overall in the 1982 draft. Traded to the Oilers by Philadelphia for Keith Acton and the Oilers 6th round choice (Dimitri Yushkevich) in the 1991 draft, February 7th, 1989.
First Game as an Oiler: February 9, 1989
First Assist as an Oiler: February 25, 1989
First Goal as an Oiler: October 21, 1990
First Penalty as an Oiler: February 9, 1989
Where He Went: Traded to Philadelphia with Corey Foster and Jari Kurri for Craig Fisher, Craig Berube and Scott Mellanby, May 30, 1991.

Season	GP	G	A	Pts	Shots	S%	GW	GT	PP	SH	P/M	PIM
1988-89	22	0	2	2	14	0.0	0	0	0	0	-4	56
Playoffs	*7*	*0*	*0*	*0*	*5*	*0.0*	*0*	*0*	*0*	*0*	*-2*	*6*
1989-90	60	0	6	6	32	0.0	0	0	0	0	-3	145
Playoffs	*3*	*0*	*0*	*0*	*2*	*0.0*	*0*	*0*	*0*	*0*	*0*	*0*
1990-91	58	3	4	7	32	9.4	0	0	0	0	-7	160
Playoffs	16	0	1	1	11	0.0	0	0	0	0	-2	30
3 years	140	3	12	15	78	3.8	0	0	0	0	-14	361
Playoffs	*26*	*0*	*1*	*1*	*18*	*0.0*	*0*	*0*	*0*	*0*	*-4*	*36*

BROWN, KEVIN SWEATER # 42, #10 RIGHT WING SR
Born: Birmingham, England May 11, 1974 6'1"-212
Last Amateur Club: Detroit Jr. Red Wings (OHL)
How the Oilers Got Him: Los Angeles' 3rd choice, 87th overall in the 1992 draft. Signed as a free agent by the Oilers July 22, 1998. Signed as a free agent by the Oilers, March 7, 2000.
First Game as an Oiler: October 10, 1998
First Assist as an Oiler: October 28, 1998
First Goal as an Oiler: October 10, 1998
First Penalty as an Oiler: None Recorded
Where He Went: Traded to the Rangers' for Vladimir Vorobiev, March 23, 1999.

Season	GP	G	A	Pts	Shots	S%	GW	GT	PP	SH	P/M	PIM
1998-99	12	4	2	6	13	30.8	0	0	2	0	-2	0
1999-00	7	0	0	0	5	0.0	0	0	0	0	0	0
Playoffs	*1*	*0*	*0*	*0*	*0*	*0.0*	*0*	*0*	*0*	*0*	*0*	*0*
2 years	19	4	2	6	18	22.2	0	0	2	0	-2	0
Playoffs	*1*	*0*	*0*	*0*	*0*	*0.0*	*0*	*0*	*0*	*0*	*0*	*0*

BROWN, SEAN SWEATER # 8, #23 DEFENSE SL
Born: Oshawa, Ontario November 5, 1976 6'2"-205
Last Amateur Club: Sarnia Sting (OHL)
How the Oilers Got Him: Boston's 2nd choice, 21st overall in the 1995 draft. Traded to the Oilers by the Bruins with Mariusz Czerkawski and Boston's 1st round choice (Matthieu Descoteaux) in the 1996 draft for Bill Ranford, January 11, 1996.
First Game as an Oiler: February 21, 1997
First Assist as an Oiler: November 17, 1997
First Goal as an Oiler: October 6, 1999
First Penalty as an Oiler: February 27, 1997

Season	GP	G	A	Pts	Shots	S%	GW	GT	PP	SH	P/M	PIM
1996-97	5	0	0	0	2	0.0	0	0	0	0	-1	4
1997-98	18	0	1	1	9	0.0	0	0	0	0	-1	43
1998-99	51	0	7	7	27	0.0	0	0	0	0	1	188
Playoffs	*1*	*0*	*0*	*0*	*0*	*0.0*	*0*	*0*	*0*	*0*	*0*	*10*
1999-00	72	4	8	12	36	11.1	2	0	0	0	1	192
Playoffs	*3*	*0*	*0*	*0*	*0*	*0.0*	*0*	*0*	*0*	*0*	*-1*	*23*
2000-01	62	2	3	5	30	6.7	0	0	0	0	2	110
5 years	208	6	19	25	104	5.8	2	0	0	0	2	537
Playoffs	*4*	*0*	*0*	*0*	*0*	*0.0*	*0*	*0*	*0*	*0*	*-1*	*33*

BRUBAKER, JEFFREY JOSEPH SWEATER # 15 LEFT WING SL
Born: Frederick, Maryland February, 24, 1958 6'2"-210
Last Amateur Club: Peterborough Petes (OHL)
How the Oilers Got Him: Boston's 6th choice, 102nd overall in the 1978 draft. Signed as a free agent by the Oilers, June 21, 1984.

First Game as an Oiler: December 15, 1985
First Goal as an Oiler: December 18, 1985
First Assist as an Oiler: None Recorded
First Penalty as an Oiler: December 15, 1985
Where He Went: Claimed by the Leafs in the Waiver Draft, October 9, 1984. Claimed on waivers by the Oilers, December 5, 1985. Traded to Philadelphia for Dom Campedelli, March 9, 1987.

Season	*GP*	*G*	*A*	*Pts*	*Shots*	*S%*	*GW*	*GT*	*PP*	*SH*	*P/M*	*PIM*
1985-86	4	1	0	1	4	25.0	0	0	0	0	1	12

Buchberger, Kelly — Sweater # 16 — Right Wing — SL
Born: Langenburg, Saskatchewan — December 2, 1966 — 6'2"-200
Last Amateur Club: Moose Jaw Warriors (WHL)
How the Oilers Got Him: Oilers' 8th choice, 188th overall in the 1985 draft.
First Game as an Oiler: May 17, 1987
First Goal as an Oiler: January 19, 1988
First Assist as an Oiler: December 7, 1988
First Penalty as an Oiler: May 17, 1987
Where He Went: Claimed in the Expansion Draft by the Atlanta Thrashers, June 25, 1999.

Season	*GP*	*G*	*A*	*Pts*	*Shots*	*S%*	*GW*	*GT*	*PP*	*SH*	*P/M*	*PIM*
Playoffs (86-87)	*3*	*0*	*0*	*0*	*1*	*0.0*	*0*	*0*	*0*	*0*	*0*	*5*
1987-88	19	1	0	1	10	10.0	0	1	0	0	-1	81
1988-89	66	5	9	14	57	8.8	1	0	1	0	-14	234
1989-90	55	2	6	8	35	5.7	2	0	0	0	-8	168
Playoffs	*19*	*0*	*5*	*5*	*15*	*0.0*	*0*	*0*	*0*	*0*	*2*	*13*
1990-91	64	3	1	4	54	5.6	2	0	0	0	-6	160
Playoffs	*12*	*2*	*1*	*3*	*12*	*16.7*	*0*	*0*	*0*	*0*	*-3*	*25*
1991-92	79	20	24	44	90	22.2	3	1	0	4	9	157
Playoffs	*16*	*1*	*4*	*5*	*12*	*8.3*	*0*	*0*	*0*	*0*	*2*	*32*
1992-93	83	12	18	30	92	13.0	3	0	1	2	-27	133
1993-94	84	3	18	21	93	3.2	0	0	0	0	-20	199
1994-95	48	7	17	24	73	9.6	5	0	2	1	0	82
1995-96	82	11	14	25	119	9.2	3	0	0	2	-20	184
1996-97	81	8	30	38	78	10.3	3	0	0	0	4	159
Playoffs	*12*	*5*	*2*	*7*	*19*	*26.3*	*1*	*1*	*0*	*0*	*-1*	*16*
1997-98	82	6	17	23	86	7.0	1	0	1	1	-10	122
Playoffs	*12*	*1*	*2*	*3*	*13*	*7.7*	*0*	*0*	*0*	*0*	*0*	*25*
1998-99	52	4	4	8	29	13.8	1	0	0	2	-6	68
Playoffs	*4*	*0*	*0*	*0*	*2*	*0.0*	*0*	*0*	*0*	*0*	*-4*	*0*
12 years	795	82	158	240	816	10.0	24	2	5	12	-99	1747
Playoffs	*78*	*9*	*14*	*23*	*74*	*12.2*	*1*	*1*	*0*	*0*	*-4*	*116*

Butenschon, Sven — Sweater # 19 — Defense — SL
Born: Itzehoe, West Germany — March 22, 1976 — 6'4"-215
Last Amateur Club: Brandon Wheat Kings (WHL)
How the Oilers Got Him: Pittsburgh's 3rd choice, 57th overall in the 1994 draft. Traded to the Oilers by Pittsburgh for Dan LaCouture, March 13, 2001.
First Game as an Oiler: March 24, 2001
First Goal as an Oiler: April 7, 2001
First Assist as an Oiler: March 24, 2001
First Penalty as an Oiler: March 26, 2001

Season	*GP*	*G*	*A*	*Pts*	*Shots*	*S%*	*GW*	*GT*	*PP*	*SH*	*P/M*	*PIM*
2000-01	7	1	1	2	3	33.3	0	0	0	0	2	2

Byakin, Ilya — Sweater # 10 — Defense — SL
Born: Sverdlovsk, USSR — February 2, 1963 — 5'9"-185
Last Amateur Club: Eislauf-Verein Landshut (Ger)
How the Oilers Got Him: Oilers' 11th choice, 267th overall in the 1993 draft.
First Game as an Oiler: November 6, 1993
First Goal as an Oiler: November 6, 1993
First Assist as an Oiler: November 6, 1993
First Penalty as an Oiler: November 13, 1993
Where He Went: Signed as a free agent by San Jose, September 18, 1994.

Season	*GP*	*G*	*A*	*Pts*	*Shots*	*S%*	*GW*	*GT*	*PP*	*SH*	*P/M*	*PIM*
1993-94	44	8	20	28	51	15.7	3	0	6	0	-3	30

Callighen, Brett Charles — Sweater # 18 — Center — SL
Born: Toronto, Ontario — May 15, 1953 — 5'11"-180
Last Amateur Club: Centennial College

How the Oilers Got Him: While still a part of the WHA, the Oilers traded Louis Levasseur to the New England Whalers in exchange for Callighen, Dave Dryden and a fourth round draft choice, September 1977.
First Game as an Oiler: October 10, 1979
First Assist as an Oiler: October 10, 1979
First Goal as an Oiler: October 19, 1979
First Penalty as an Oiler: October, 13, 1979
Where He Went: Retired

Season	GP	G	A	Pts	Shots	S%	GW	GT	PP	SH	P/M	PIM
1979-80	59	23	35	58	159	14.5	0	2	8	0	-1	72
Playoffs	*3*	*0*	*2*	*2*			*0*	*0*	*0*	*0*		*0*
1980-81	55	25	35	60	127	19.7	1	1	6	0	13	32
Playoffs	*9*	*4*	*4*	*8*			*1*	*0*	*1*	*0*		*6*
1981-82	46	8	19	27	87	9.2	1	0	3	0	16	28
Playoffs	*2*	*0*	*0*	*0*			*0*	*0*	*0*	*0*		*2*
3 years	160	56	89	145	373	15.0	2	3	17	0	28	132
Playoffs	*14*	*4*	*6*	*10*			*1*	*0*	*1*	*0*		*8*

CAMPBELL, COLIN JOHN SWEATER # 6 DEFENSE SL
Born: London, Ontario January, 28, 1953 5'9"-190
Last Amateur Club: Peterborough Petes (OHL)
How the Oilers Got Him: Pittsburgh's 3rd choice, 27th overall in 1973 draft. Claimed by the Oilers in the Expansion Draft, June 13, 1979.
First Game as an Oiler: October 10, 1979
First Assist as an Oiler: November 13, 1979
First Goal as an Oiler: February 17, 1980
First Penalty as an Oiler: October 10, 1979
Where He Went: Claimed by the Canucks in the Waiver Draft, October 10, 1980.

Season	GP	G	A	Pts	Shots	S%	GW	GT	PP	SH	P/M	PIM
1979-80	72	2	11	13	80	2.5	0	0	0	0	-18	196
Playoffs	*3*	*0*	*0*	*0*			*0*	*0*	*0*	*0*		*11*

CARROLL, WILLIAM ALLAN SWEATER # 20 CENTER SL
Born: Toronto, Ontario January 19, 1959 5'10"-190
Last Amateur Club: London Knights (OHA)
How the Oilers Got Him: New York Islanders' 3rd choice, 38th overall in the 1979 draft. Claimed from the Islanders in the Waiver Draft, October 9, 1984.
First Game as an Oiler: October 11, 1984
First Assist as an Oiler: October 12, 1984
First Goal as an Oiler: October 14, 1984
First Penalty as an Oiler: November 9, 1984
Where He Went: Traded to Detroit for Bruce Eakin, December 28, 1985.

Season	GP	G	A	Pts	Shots	S%	GW	GT	PP	SH	P/M	PIM
1984-85	65	8	9	17	44	18.2	1	0	0	0	0	22
Playoffs	*9*	*0*	*0*	*0*	*4*	*0.0*	*0*	*0*	*0*	*0*	*3*	*4*
1985-86	5	0	2	2	0	0.0	0	0	0	0	2	0
2 years	70	8	11	19	44	18.2	1	0	0	0	2	22
Playoffs	*9*	*0*	*0*	*0*	*4*	*0.0*	*0*	*0*	*0*	*0*	*3*	*4*

CARSON, JAMES CHARLES SWEATER # 12 CENTER SR
Born: Southfield, Michigan July 20, 1968 6'0"-185
Last Amateur Club: Verdun Junior Canadians (QMJHL)
How the Oilers Got Him: Los Angeles' 1st choice, 2nd overall in the 1985 draft. Traded to the Oilers from Los Angeles with Martin Gelinas, the Kings' 1st round draft choices in 1989 (Jason Miller, the pick was acquired by New Jersey on June 17, 1989), 1991 (Martin Rucinsky), 1993 (Nick Stajduhar) and cash for Wayne Gretzky, Mike Krushelnyski and Marty McSorley, August 9, 1988.
First Game as an Oiler: October 7, 1988
First Assist as an Oiler: October 17, 1988
First Goal as an Oiler: October 7, 1988
First Penalty as an Oiler: October 19, 1988
Where He Went: Traded to Detroit with Kevin McClelland and the Oilers' fifth round choice in the 1991 draft (later traded to Montreal, the Habs chose Brad Layzell), for Adam Graves, Petr Klima, Joe Murphy and Jeff Sharples, November 2, 1989.

Season	GP	G	A	Pts	Shots	S%	GW	GT	PP	SH	P/M	PIM
1988-89	80	49	51	100	240	20.4	5	1	19	0	3	36
Playoffs	*7*	*2*	*1*	*3*	*15*	*13.3*	*1*	*0*	*1*	*0*	*0*	*6*
1989-90	4	1	2	3	11	9.1	0	0	1	0	-2	0
2 years	84	50	53	103	251	19.9	5	1	20	0	1	36
Playoffs	*7*	*2*	*1*	*3*	*15*	*13.3*	*1*	*0*	*1*	*0*	*0*	*6*

Carter, Anson — Sweater # 22 — Right Wing — SR

Born: Toronto, Ontario — June 6, 1974 — 6'1"-200

Last Amateur Club: Michigan State University Spartans (CCHA)

How the Oilers Got Him: Quebec's 11th choice, 220th overall in 1992 draft. Traded to the Oilers for Bill Guerin, the Bruins 2nd choice in the 2001 draft, the right to switch 1st round draft choices with the Bruins in the 2001 or 2002 draft and future considerations, November 15th, 2000.

First Game as an Oiler: November 17, 2000 — *First Assist as an Oiler:* November 23, 2000

First Goal as an Oiler: November 23, 2000 — *First Penalty as an Oiler:* November 19, 2000

Season	*GP*	*G*	*A*	*Pts*	*Shots*	*S%*	*GW*	*GT*	*PP*	*SH*	*P/M*	*PIM*
2000-01	61	16	26	42	102	15.7	4	0	7	1	1	23
Playoffs	*6*	*3*	*1*	*4*	*13*	*23.1*	*1*	*0*	*1*	*0*	*1*	*4*

Carter, Ronald — Sweater # 22 — Right Wing — SL

Born: Montreal, Quebec — March 14, 1958 — 6'1"-205

Last Amateur Club: Sherbrooke Beavers (QMJHL)

How the Oilers Got Him: Montreal's 4th choice, 36th overall in 1978 draft. Signed as a free agent July 1978.

First Game as an Oiler: February 27, 1980 — *First Assist as an Oiler:* None Recorded

First Goal as an Oiler: None Recorded — *First Penalty as an Oiler:* None Recorded

Where He Went: Retired

Season	*GP*	*G*	*A*	*Pts*	*Shots*	*S%*	*GW*	*GT*	*PP*	*SH*	*P/M*	*PIM*
1979-80	2	0	0	0	0	0.0	0	0	0	0	0	0

Chartraw, Raymond Richard — Sweater # 6 — Defense/ Right Wing — SR

Born: Caracas, Venezuela — July 13, 1954 — 6'2"-210

Last Amateur Club: Kitchener Rangers (OHL)

How the Oilers Got Him: Montreal's 3rd choice, 10th overall in the 1974 draft. Traded by the New York Rangers to the Oilers for Edmonton's 9th round choice (Heinz Ehlers) in the 1984 draft, January 20, 1984.

First Game as an Oiler: January 21, 1984 — *First Assist as an Oiler:* February 3, 1984

First Goal as an Oiler: January 25, 1984 — *First Penalty as an Oiler*: February 21, 1984

Where He Went: Retired.

Season	*GP*	*G*	*A*	*Pts*	*Shots*	*S%*	*GW*	*GT*	*PP*	*SH*	*P/M*	*PIM*
1983-84	24	2	6	8	23	8.7	0	0	0	0	5	21
Playoffs	*1*	*0*	*0*	*0*	*0*	*0.0*	*0*	*0*	*0*	*0*	*-1*	*2*

Chimera, Jason — Sweater # 20 — Center — SL

Born: Edmonton, Alberta — May 2, 1979 — 6'0"-180

Last Amateur Club: Brandon Wheat Kings (WHL)

How the Oilers Got Him: Oilers' 5th choice, 121st overall in the 1997 draft.

First Game as an Oiler: December 9, 2000 — *First Assist as an Oiler:* None Recorded

First Goal as an Oiler: None Recorded — *First Penalty as an Oiler:* None Recorded

Season	*GP*	*G*	*A*	*Pts*	*Shots*	*S%*	*GW*	*GT*	*PP*	*SH*	*P/M*	*PIM*
2000-01	1	0	0	0	0	0.0	0	0	0	0	0	0

Chipperfield, Ronald James — Sweater # 7 — Center — SR

Born: Brandon, Manitoba — March 28, 1954 — 5'11"-185

Last Amateur Club: Brandon Wheat Kings (WHL)

How the Oilers Got Him: California's 2nd choice, 17th overall in 1974 draft. Acquired from the WHA's Calgary Cowboys May 31, 1977.

First Game as an Oiler: October 10, 1979 — *First Assist as an Oiler:* October 19, 1979

First Goal as an Oiler: October 30, 1979 — *First Penalty as an Oiler:* November 11, 1979

Where He Went: Traded to Quebec for Ron Low, March 11, 1980.

Season	*GP*	*G*	*A*	*Pts*	*Shots*	*S%*	*GW*	*GT*	*PP*	*SH*	*P/M*	*PIM*
1979-80	67	18	19	37	129	14.0	1	1	2	1	-15	24

Chychrun, Jeff — Sweater # 20 — Defense — SR

Born: LaSalle, Quebec — May 3, 1966 — 6'4"-215

Last Amateur Club: Kingston Canadians (OHL)

How the Oilers Got Him: Philadelphia's 3rd choice, 37th overall in the 1984 draft. Traded to the Oilers from the Los Angeles Kings for a conditional draft choice in the 1995 draft, November 2, 1993.

First Game as an Oiler: January 11, 1994
First Assist as an Oiler: None Recorded
First Goal as an Oiler: None Recorded
First Penalty as an Oiler: None Recorded
Where He Went: Signed as a free agent by Hartford, May 27, 1994.

Season	*GP*	*G*	*A*	*Pts*	*Shots*	*S%*	*GW*	*GT*	*PP*	*SH*	*P/M*	*PIM*
1993-94	2	0	0	0	2	0.0	0	0	0	0	1	0

CIERNY, JOZEF SWEATER # 20 LEFT WING SL
Born: Zvolen, Czechoslovakia October 19, 1969 6'2"-185
Last Amateur Club: ZTK Zvolen (Czech 2)
How the Oilers Got Him: Buffalo's 2nd choice, 35th overall in the 1992 draft. Traded to the Oilers from the Sabres with Buffalo's 4th round choice (Jussi Tarvainen) in the 1994 draft for Craig Simpson, September 1, 1993.
First Game as an Oiler: January 18, 1994
First Assist as an Oiler: None Recorded
First Goal as an Oiler: None Recorded
First Penalty as an Oiler: None Recorded

Season	*GP*	*G*	*A*	*Pts*	*Shots*	*S%*	*GW*	*GT*	*PP*	*SH*	*P/M*	*PIM*
1993-94	1	0	0	0	0	0.0	0	0	0	0	-1	0

CIGER, ZDENO SWEATER # 8 LEFT WING SL
Born: Martin, Czechoslovakia October 19, 1969 6'1"-190
Last Amateur Club: Dukla Trencin (Czech)
How the Oilers Got Him: New Jersey's 3rd choice, 54th overall in the 1988 draft. Traded to the Oilers from the Devils with Kevin Todd for Bernie Nicholls, January 13, 1993.
First Game as an Oiler: January 15, 1993
First Assist as an Oiler: January 19, 1993
First Goal as an Oiler: January 17, 1993
First Penalty as an Oiler: February 14, 1993
Where He Went: Claimed on waivers by Nashville October 5, 1998

Season	*GP*	*G*	*A*	*Pts*	*Shots*	*S%*	*GW*	*GT*	*PP*	*SH*	*P/M*	*PIM*
1992-93	37	9	15	24	67	13.4	1	0	0	0	-5	6
1993-94	84	22	35	57	158	13.9	1	2	8	0	-11	8
1994-95	5	2	2	4	10	20.0	1	0	1	0	-1	0
1995-96	78	31	39	70	184	16.8	3	0	12	0	-15	41
4 years	204	64	91	155	419	15.3	6	2	21	0	-32	55

CLARK, DEAN SWEATER # 6 DEFENSE SL
Born: Edmonton, Alberta January 10, 1964 6'1"-180
Last Amateur Club: Kamloops Junior Oilers (WHL)
How the Oilers Got Him: Edmonton's 8th choice, 167th overall in the 1982 draft.
First Game as an Oiler: January 7, 1994
First Assist as an Oiler: None Recorded
First Goal as an Oiler: None Recorded
First Penalty as an Oiler: None Recorded
Where He Went: Retired.

Season	*GP*	*G*	*A*	*Pts*	*Shots*	*S%*	*GW*	*GT*	*PP*	*SH*	*P/M*	*PIM*
1983-84	1	0	0	0	0	0.0	0	0	0	0	0	0

CLEARY, DANIEL MICHAEL T. SWEATER # 37, #7 LEFT WING SL
Born: Carbonear, Newfoundland December 18, 1978 6'0"-203
Last Amateur Club: Belleville Bulls (OHL)
How the Oilers Got Him: Chicago's 1st choice, 13th overall in the 1997 draft. Traded to the Oilers by Chicago with Chad Kilger, Ethan Moreau, and Christian Laflamme for Boris Mironov, Dean McAmmond and Jonas Elofsson, March 20, 1999.
First Game as an Oiler: October 16, 1999
First Assist as an Oiler: February 8, 2000
First Goal as an Oiler: October 16, 1999
First Penalty as an Oiler: October 16, 1999

Season	*GP*	*G*	*A*	*Pts*	*Shots*	*S%*	*GW*	*GT*	*PP*	*SH*	*P/M*	*PIM*
1999-00	17	3	2	5	18	16.7	1	0	0	0	-1	8
Playoffs	*4*	*0*	*1*	*1*	*3*	*0.0*	*0*	*0*	*0*	*0*	*1*	*2*
2000-01	81	14	20	34	107	13.1	2	1	2	0	5	37
Playoffs	*6*	*1*	*1*	*2*	*6*	*16.7*	*0*	*0*	*1*	*0*	*-2*	*8*
2 years	98	17	22	39	125	13.6	3	1	2	0	4	45
Playoffs	*10*	*1*	*2*	*3*	*9*	*11.1*	*0*	*0*	*1*	*0*	*-1*	*10*

Cochrane, Glen MacLeod Sweater # 34 Center SR

Born: Cranbrook, British Columbia January 29, 1958 6'2"-205

Last Amateur Club: Victoria Cougars (WHL)

How the Oilers Got Him: Philadelphia's 6th choice, 50th overall in the 1978 draft. Claimed on waivers by the Oilers from Chicago, November 7, 1988.

First Game as an Oiler: November 8, 1988 *First Assist as an Oiler:* None Recorded

First Goal as an Oiler: None Recorded *First Penalty as an Oiler:* November 8, 1988

Where He Went: Retired.

Season	*GP*	*G*	*A*	*Pts*	*Shots*	*S%*	*GW*	*GT*	*PP*	*SH*	*P/M*	*PIM*
1988-89	12	0	0	0	3	0.0	0	0	0	0	-2	52

Coffey, Paul Douglas Sweater # 7 Defense SL

Born: Weston, Ontario June 1, 1961 6'0"-190

Last Amateur Club: Kitchener Rangers (OHL)

How the Oilers Got Him: Oilers' 1st choice, 6th overall in the 1980 draft.

First Game as an Oiler: October 10, 1980 *First Assist as an Oiler:* October 19, 1980

First Goal as an Oiler: October 22, 1980 *First Penalty as an Oiler:* October 10, 1980

Where He Went: Traded to the Penguins with Dave Hunter and Wayne Van Dorp for Dave Hannan, Chris Joseph, Moe Mantha and Craig Simpson, November 24, 1987.

Season	*GP*	*G*	*A*	*Pts*	*Shots*	*S%*	*GW*	*GT*	*PP*	*SH*	*P/M*	*PIM*
1980-81	74	9	23	32	113	8.0	0	0	2	0	4	130
Playoffs	*9*	*4*	*3*	*7*			*0*	*0*	*1*	*0*		*22*
1981-82	80	29	60	89	234	12.4	1	0	13	0	35	106
Playoffs	*5*	*1*	*1*	*2*			*0*	*0*	*1*	*0*		*6*
1982-83	80	29	67	96	259	11.2	2	0	9	1	52	87
Playoffs	*16*	*7*	*7*	*14*	*42*	*16.7*	*0*	*0*	*2*	*2*	*15*	*14*
1983-84	80	40	86	126	258	15.5	4	1	14	1	52	104
Playoffs	*19*	*8*	*14*	*22*	*66*	*12.1*	*1*	*0*	*2*	*0*	*21*	*21*
1984-85	80	37	84	121	284	13.0	6	0	12	2	55	97
Playoffs	*18*	*12*	*25*	*37*	*66*	*18.2*	*4*	*0*	*3*	*1*	*26*	*44*
1985-86	79	48	90	138	307	15.6	3	1	9	9	61	120
Playoffs	*10*	*1*	*9*	*10*	*33*	*3.0*	*0*	*0*	*1*	*0*	*0*	*30*
1986-87	59	17	50	67	165	10.3	3	0	10	2	12	49
Playoffs	*17*	*3*	*8*	*11*	*45*	*6.7*	*1*	*0*	*1*	*0*	*7*	*30*
7 years	532	209	460	669	1620	12.9	19	2	69	15	271	693
Playoffs	*94*	*36*	*67*	*103*			*6*	*0*	*11*	*3*		*167*

Comrie, Mike Sweater # 89 Center SL

Born: Edmonton, Alberta September 11, 1980 5'9"-172

Last Amateur Club: Kootenay Ice (WHL)

How the Oilers Got Him: Oilers' 5th choice, 91st overall in the 1999 draft.

First Game as an Oiler: December 30, 2000 *First Assist as an Oiler:* January 10, 2000

First Goal as an Oiler: January 20, 2001 *First Penalty as an Oiler:* January 24, 2001

Season	*GP*	*G*	*A*	*Pts*	*Shots*	*S%*	*GW*	*GT*	*PP*	*SH*	*P/M*	*PIM*
2000-01	41	8	13	21	62	12.9	1	0	3	0	6	14
Playoffs	*6*	*1*	*2*	*3*	*7*	*14.3*	*1*	*0*	*1*	*0*	*0*	*0*

Comrie, Paul Sweater # 47 Center SL

Born: Edmonton, Alberta February 7, 1977 5'11"-192

Last Amateur Club: University of Denver Pioneers (WCHA)

How the Oilers Got Him: Tampa Bay's 12th choice, 224th overall in the 1997 draft. Traded to Edmonton by the Lightning with Roman Hamrlik, for Bryan Marchment, Steve Kelly and Jason Bonsignore, December 30, 1997.

First Game as an Oiler: October 1, 1999 *First Assist as an Oiler:* October 6, 1999

First Goal as an Oiler: October 23, 1999 *First Penalty as an Oiler:* November 14, 1999

Season	*GP*	*G*	*A*	*Pts*	*Shots*	*S%*	*GW*	*GT*	*PP*	*SH*	*P/M*	*PIM*
1999-00	15	1	2	3	11	9.1	0	0	0	0	-2	4

Conacher, Patrick John Sweater # 15 Center SL
Born: Edmonton, Alberta May 1, 1959 5'8"-185
Last Amateur Club: Saskatoon Blades (WHL)
How the Oilers Got Him: New York Rangers' 4th choice, 76th overall in the 1979 draft. Signed as a free agent by Edmonton, October 4, 1983.
First Game as an Oiler: October 26, 1983
First Assist as an Oiler: October 30, 1983
First Goal as an Oiler: November 2, 1983
First Penalty as an Oiler: November 2, 1983
Where He Went: Signed as a free agent by New Jersey, August 14, 1985.

Season	GP	G	A	Pts	Shots	S%	GW	GT	PP	SH	P/M	PIM
1983-84	45	2	8	10	18	11.1	0	0	0	0	-2	31
Playoffs	*3*	*1*	*0*	*1*	*3*	*33.3*	*0*	*0*	*0*	*0*	*1*	*2*

Connor, Cameron Duncan Sweater # 17 Right Wing SR
Born: Winnipeg, Manitoba August 10, 1954 6'2"-200
Last Amateur Club: Flin Flon Bombers (WCHL)
How the Oilers Got Him: Montreal's 1st choice, 5th overall in 1974 draft. Claimed by the Oilers in the 1979 Expansion Draft, June 13th, 1979.
First Game as an Oiler: November 28, 1979
First Assist as an Oiler: January 7, 1980
First Goal as an Oiler: January 11, 1980
First Penalty as an Oiler: November 28, 1979
Where He Went: Traded to the Rangers along with the Oilers third choice in the 1981 draft (Peter Sundstrum) for Don Murdoch, March 11, 1980.

Season	GP	G	A	Pts	Shots	S%	GW	GT	PP	SH	P/M	PIM
1979-80	38	7	13	20	44	15.9	0	0	0	0	2	136

Corsi, James Sweater # 35 Goaltender CL
Born: Montreal, Quebec June 19, 1954 5'10"-180
Last Amateur Club: Concordia University Stingers
How the Oilers Got Him: Signed as a free agent by the Oilers, October 4, 1979.
First Game as an Oiler: December 26, 1979
First Assist as an Oiler: January 7, 1980
First Goal as an Oiler: None Recorded
First Penalty as an Oiler: January 7, 1980
Where He Went: Traded to Minnesota for future considerations, March 11, 1980.

Season	GP	Min	GA	W	L	T	Ave	SA	S%	SO	EN	PIM	Ast.
1979-80	26	1366	83	8	14	3	3.65	644	.871	0	3	6	3

Corson, Shayne Sweater # 21, # 9 Left Wing SL
Born: Midland, Ontario August 13, 1966 6'1"-200
Last Amateur Club: Hamilton Steelhawks (OHL)
How the Oilers Got Him: Montreal's 2nd choice, 8th overall in the 1984 draft. Traded to the Oilers by the Canadiens with Brent Gilchrist and Vladimir Vujtek for Vincent Damphousse and the Oilers' 4th round pick (Adam Wiesel) in the 1993 draft, August 27, 1992.
First Game as an Oiler: October 6, 1992
First Assist as an Oiler: October 6, 1992
First Goal as an Oiler: October 15, 1992
First Penalty as an Oiler: October 11, 1992
Where He Went: Signed as a free agent by St. Louis, July 28, 1995.

Season	GP	G	A	Pts	Shots	S%	GW	GT	PP	SH	P/M	PIM
1992-93	80	16	31	47	164	9.8	1	0	9	2	-19	209
1993-94	64	25	29	54	171	14.6	3	1	11	0	-8	118
1994-95	48	12	24	36	131	9.2	1	0	2	0	-17	86
3 years	192	53	84	137	466	11.4	5	1	22	2	-44	413

Cote, Patrick Sweater # 29 Left Wing SL
Born: Lasalle, Quebec January 24, 1975 6'3"-220
Last Amateur Club: Beauport Harfangs (QMJHL)
How the Oilers Got Him: Dallas' 2nd choice, 37th overall in the 1995 draft. Traded to Edmonton by Nashville for Phoenix' 5th choice (previously acquired by Edmonton, the Predators selected Matt Koalska) in the 2000 draft, June 12th, 2000.
First Game as an Oiler: October 28, 2000
First Assist as an Oiler: None Recorded
First Goal as an Oiler: None Recorded
First Penalty as an Oiler: October 28, 2000

Season	GP	G	A	Pts	Shots	S%	GW	GT	PP	SH	P/M	PIM
2000-01	6	0	0	0	0	0.0	0	0	0	0	-2	18

COTE, RAYMOND SWEATER # 14 CENTER SR

Born: Pincher Creek, Alberta May 31, 1961 5'11"-170

Last Amateur Club: Calgary Wranglers (WHL)

How the Oilers Got Him: Signed as a free agent by the Oilers, October 6, 1981.

First Game as an Oiler: April 9, 1983 *First Assist as an Oiler:* April 26, 1983

First Goal as an Oiler: April 17, 1983 *First Penalty as an Oiler:* April 20, 1983

Where He Went: Retired

Season	GP	G	A	Pts	Shots	S%	GW	GT	PP	SH	P/M	PIM
Playoffs(82-83)	*14*	*3*	*2*	*5*	*17*	*17.6*	*0*	*0*	*0*	*0*	*6*	*4*
1983-84	13	0	0	0	12	0.0	0	0	0	0	-5	2
1984-85	2	0	0	0	1	0.0	0	0	0	0	0	2
2 years	15	0	0	0	13	0.0	0	0	0	0	-5	4
Playoffs	*14*	*3*	*2*	*5*	*17*	*17.6*	*0*	*0*	*0*	*0*	*6*	*4*

COURTNALL, GEOFF LAWTON SWEATER # 15 LEFT WING SL

Born: Duncan, British Columbia August 18, 1962 6'1"-195

Last Amateur Club: Victoria Cougars (WHL)

How the Oilers Got Him: Traded by the Bruins to the Oilers with Bill Ranford and future considerations for Andy Moog, March 8, 1988.

First Game as an Oiler: March 9, 1988 *First Assist as an Oiler*: March 20, 1988

First Goal as an Oiler: March 14, 1988 *First Penalty as an Oiler*: March 15, 1988

Where He Went: Traded to Washington for Greg Adams, July 22, 1988.

Season	GP	G	A	Pts	Shots	S%	GW	GT	PP	SH	P/M	PIM
1987-88	12	4	4	8	32	12.5	1	0	0	0	1	15
Playoffs	*19*	*0*	*3*	*3*	*33*	*0.0*	*0*	*0*	*0*	*0*	*2*	*23*

COWLEY, WAYNE SWEATER # 1 GOALTENDER CL

Born: Scarborough, Ontario December 4, 1964 6'0"-185

Last Amateur Club: Colgate University Red Raiders (ECAC)

How the Oilers Got Him: Signed as a free agent by the Oilers, September 13, 1993.

First Game as an Oiler: December 11, 1993 *First Assist as an Oiler:* None Recorded

First Goal as an Oiler: None Recorded *First Penalty as an Oiler:* None Recorded

Where He Went: Retired

Season	GP	Min	GA	W	L	T	Ave	SA	S%	SO	EN	PIM	Ast.
1993-94	1	57	3	0	1	0	3.16	35	0.914	0	0	0	0

CURRIE, DAN SWEATER # 15, # 23, # 24, # 26 LEFT WING SL

Born: Burlington, Ontario March 15, 1968 6'2"-195

Last Amateur Club: Sault Ste. Marie Greyhounds (OHA)

How the Oilers Got Him: Edmonton's 4th choice, 84th overall in the 1986 draft.

First Game as an Oiler: February 22, 1991 *First Assist as an Oiler*: None Recorded

First Goal as an Oiler: March 24, 1992 *First Penalty as an Oiler:* January 3, 1993

Where He Went: Signed as a free agent by Los Angeles, July 16, 1993.

Season	GP	G	A	Pts	Shots	S%	GW	GT	PP	SH	P/M	PIM
1990-91	5	0	0	0	5	0.0	0	0	0	0	0	0
1991-92	7	1	0	1	3	33.3	0	0	0	0	-1	0
1992-93	5	0	0	0	11	0.0	0	0	0	0	-4	4
3 years	17	1	0	1	19	5.3	0	0	0	0	-5	4

CUTTS, DONALD EDWARD SWEATER # 1 GOALTENDER CL

Born: Edmonton, Alberta February 24, 1953 6'3"-190

Last Amateur Club: R.P.I. University Engineers (ECAC)

How the Oilers Got Him: New York Islanders 6th choice, 97th overall in 1973 draft. Signed as a free agent by the Oilers January 12, 1980.

First Game as an Oiler: February 8, 1980 *First Assist as an Oiler:* None Recorded

First Goal as an Oiler: None Recorded *First Penalty as an Oiler:* February 13, 1980

Where He Went: Retired.

Season	GP	Min	GA	W	L	T	Ave	SA	S%	SO	EN	PIM	Ast.
1979-80	6	269	16	1	2	1	3.57	142	0.887	0	1	6	0

CZERKAWSKI, MARIUSZ SWEATER # 10, # 21 RIGHT WING SL
Born: Radomsko, Poland April 13, 1972 6'0"-195
Last Amateur Club: Djurgardens IF (Sweden)
How the Oilers Got Him: Boston's 5th choice, 106th overall in the 1991 draft. Traded to the Oilers by the Bruins with Sean Brown and the Bruins' 1st round choice (Matthieu Descoteaux) in the 1996 draft for Bill Ranford, January 11, 1996.
First Game as an Oiler: January 13, 1996 *First Assist as an Oiler:* January 13, 1996
First Goal as an Oiler: January 16, 1996 *First Penalty as an Oiler:* March 27, 1996
Where He Went: Traded to the Islanders for Dan Lacouture, August 25, 1997.

Season	*GP*	*G*	*A*	*Pts*	*Shots*	*S%*	*GW*	*GT*	*PP*	*SH*	*P/M*	*PIM*
1995-96	37	12	17	29	79	15.2	1	0	2	0	7	8
1996-97	76	26	21	47	182	14.3	3	0	4	0	0	16
Playoffs	*12*	*2*	*1*	*3*	*19*	*10.5*	*0*	*0*	*0*	*0*	*-2*	*10*
2 years	113	38	38	76	261	14.6	4	0	6	0	7	24
Playoffs	*12*	*2*	*1*	*3*	*19*	*10.5*	*0*	*0*	*0*	*0*	*-2*	*10*

DAMPHOUSSE, VINCENT SWEATER # 21 LEFT WING SL
Born: Montreal, Quebec December 17, 1967 6'1"-190
Last Amateur Club: Laval Titans (QMJHL)
How the Oilers Got Him: Toronto's 1st choice, 6th overall in the 1986 draft. Traded to the Oilers from the Maple Leafs with Peter Ing, Scott Thornton, Luke Richardson, future considerations and cash, for Glenn Anderson, Craig Berube and Grant Fuhr, September 19, 1991.
First Game as an Oiler: October 4, 1991 *First Assist as an Oiler:* October 4, 1991
First Goal as an Oiler: October 20, 1991 *First Penalty as an Oiler:* October 8, 1991
Where He Went: Traded to Montreal with the Oilers' fourth round choice (Adam Wiesel) in the 1993 draft for Shayne Corson, Brent Gilchrist and Vladimir Vujtek, August 27, 1992.

Season	*GP*	*G*	*A*	*Pts*	*Shots*	*S%*	*GW*	*GT*	*PP*	*SH*	*P/M*	*PIM*
1991-92	80	38	51	89	247	15.4	8	1	12	1	10	53
Playoffs	*16*	*6*	*8*	*14*	*45*	*13.3*	*0*	*0*	*1*	*0*	*5*	*8*

DEBRUSK, LOUIE DENNIS SWEATER # 29 LEFT WING SL
Born: Cambridge, Ontario March 19, 1971 6'2"-215
Last Amateur Club: London Knights (OHA)
How the Oilers Got Him: New York Rangers' 4th choice, 49th overall in the 1989 draft. Traded to the Oilers by the Rangers with Bernie Nicholls, and Steve Rice for Mark Messier and future considerations, October 4, 1991.
First Game as an Oiler: October 8, 1991 *First Assist as an Oiler:* January 28, 1992
First Goal as an Oiler: October 27, 1991 *First Penalty as an Oiler*: October 8, 1991
Where He Went: Signed as a free agent by Tampa Bay, August 26, 1997.

Season	*GP*	*G*	*A*	*Pts*	*Shots*	*S%*	*GW*	*GT*	*PP*	*SH*	*P/M*	*PIM*
1991-92	25	2	1	3	7	28.6	1	0	0	0	4	124
1992-93	51	8	2	10	33	24.2	1	0	0	0	-16	205
1993-94	48	4	6	10	27	14.8	0	0	0	0	-9	185
1994-95	34	2	0	2	14	14.3	0	0	0	0	-4	93
1995-96	38	1	3	4	17	5.9	0	0	0	0	-7	96
1996-97	32	2	0	2	10	20.0	0	0	0	0	-6	94
Playoffs	*6*	*0*	*0*	*0*	*1*	*0.0*	*0*	*0*	*0*	*0*	*0*	*4*
6 years	228	19	12	31	108	17.6	2	0	0	0	-38	797
Playoffs	*6*	*0*	*0*	*0*	*1*	*0.0*	*0*	*0*	*0*	*0*	*0*	*4*

DEVEREAUX, BOYD FLETCHER SWEATER # 19 CENTER SL
Born: Seaforth, Ontario April 16, 1978 6'2"-195
Last Amateur Club: Kitchener Rangers (OHL)
How the Oilers Got Him: Oilers' 1st choice, 6th overall in the 1996 draft.
First Game as an Oiler: October 5, 1997 *First Assist as an Oiler:* November 3, 1997
First Goal as an Oiler: January 2, 1998 *First Penalty as an Oiler:* October 21, 1997
Where He Went: Signed as a free agent by the Detroit Red Wings, August 23rd, 2000.

Season	*GP*	*G*	*A*	*Pts*	*Shots*	*S%*	*GW*	*GT*	*PP*	*SH*	*P/M*	*PIM*
1997-98	38	1	4	5	27	3.7	0	0	0	0	-5	6
1998-99	61	6	8	14	39	15.4	4	1	0	1	2	23
Playoffs	*1*	*0*	*0*	*0*	*3*	*0.0*	*0*	*0*	*0*	*0*	*0*	*0*
1999-00	76	8	19	27	108	7.4	2	1	0	1	7	20
3 years	175	15	31	46	174	8.6	6	2	0	2	4	49
Playoffs	*1*	*0*	*0*	*0*	*3*	*0.0*	*0*	*0*	*0*	*0*	*0*	*0*

de Vries, Greg Sweater # 25, # 5 Defense SL
Born: Sundridge, Ontario January 4, 1973 6'3"-220
Last Amateur Club: Niagara Falls Thunder (OHL)
How the Oilers Got Him: Signed as a free agent by the Oilers, March 20, 1994.
First Game as an Oiler: January 17, 1996 *First Assist as an Oiler:* April 4, 1996
First Goal as an Oiler: February 21, 1996 *First Penalty as an Oiler:* February 9, 1996
Where He Went: Traded to Nashville with Eric Fichaud and Drake Berehowsky for Jim Dowd and Mikhail Shtalenkov October 1, 1998.

Season	*GP*	*G*	*A*	*Pts*	*Shots*	*S%*	*GW*	*GT*	*PP*	*SH*	*P/M*	*PIM*
1995-96	13	1	1	2	8	12.5	0	0	0	0	-2	12
1996-97	37	0	4	4	31	0.0	0	0	0	0	-2	52
Playoffs	*12*	*0*	*1*	*1*	*16*	*0.0*	*0*	*0*	*0*	*0*	*4*	*8*
1997-98	65	7	4	11	53	13.2	0	0	1	0	-17	80
Playoffs	*7*	*0*	*0*	*0*	*2*	*0.0*	*0*	*0*	*0*	*0*	*-4*	*21*
3 years	115	8	9	17	92	8.7	0	0	1	0	-21	144
Playoffs	*19*	*0*	*1*	*1*	*18*	*0.0*	*0*	*0*	*0*	*0*	*0*	*29*

Dollas, Bobby Sweater # 6 Defense SL
Born: Montreal, Quebec January 31, 1965 6'2"-212
Last Amateur Club: Laval Titans (QMJHL)
How the Oilers Got Him: Winnipeg's 2nd choice 14th overall in the 1983 draft. Traded to the Oilers from Anaheim for Drew Bannister, January 9, 1998.
First Game as an Oiler: January 9, 1998 *First Assist as an Oiler:* January 12, 1998
First Goal as an Oiler: March 25, 1998. *First Penalty as an Oiler*: January 10, 1998
Where He Went: Traded to Pittsburgh with Tony Hrkac for the rights to Josef Beranek, June 16, 1998.

Season	*GP*	*G*	*A*	*Pts*	*Shots*	*S%*	*GW*	*GT*	*PP*	*SH*	*P/M*	*PIM*
1997-98	30	2	5	7	27	7.4	0	0	0	0	6	22
Playoffs	*11*	*0*	*0*	*0*	*10*	*0.0*	*0*	*0*	*0*	*0*	*2*	*16*

Donnelly, David Sweater # 34 Center SL
Born: Edmonton, Alberta February 2, 1962 5'11"-185
Last Amateur Club: Canadian Olympic Team
How the Oilers Got Him: Traded to the Oilers by Chicago for future considerations, October 19, 1987.
First Game as an Oiler: October 23, 1987 *First Assist as an Oiler:* None Recorded
First Goal as an Oiler: None Recorded *First Penalty as an Oiler:* October 23, 1987
Where He Went: Retired

Season	*GP*	*G*	*A*	*Pts*	*Shots*	*S%*	*GW*	*GT*	*PP*	*SH*	*P/M*	*PIM*
1987-88	4	0	0	0	3	0.0	0	0	0	0	0	4

Dowd, James Thomas Sweater # 34 Center SR
Born: Brick, New Jersey December 25, 1968 6'1"-190
Last Amateur Club: Lake Superior State
How the Oilers Got Him: New Jersey's 7th choice 149th overall in the 1987 draft. Traded to the Oilers by Nashville with Mikhail Shtalenkov for Greg de Vries and Eric Fichaud, October 1, 1998.
First Game as an Oiler: January 12, 1999 *First Assist as an Oiler:* October 20, 1999
First Goal as an Oiler: December 19, 1999 *First Penalty as an Oiler:* October 26, 1999
Where He Went: Taken in the Expansion Draft by the Minnesota Wild, June 23rd 2000.

Season	*GP*	*G*	*A*	*Pts*	*Shots*	*S%*	*GW*	*GT*	*PP*	*SH*	*P/M*	*PIM*
1998-99	1	0	0	0	1	0.0	0	0	0	0	0	0
1999-00	69	5	18	23	103	4.9	1	1	2	0	10	45
Playoffs	*5*	*2*	*1*	*3*	*6*	*33.3*	*0*	*0*	*0*	*0*	*-2*	*4*
2 years	70	5	18	23	104	4.8	1	1	2	0	10	45
Playoffs	*5*	*2*	*1*	*3*	*6*	*33.3*	*0*	*0*	*0*	*0*	*-2*	*4*

Driscoll, Peter John Sweater # 24 Left Wing SL
Born: Kingston, Ontario October, 27, 1954 6'1"-190
Last Amateur Club: Kingston Canadians (OHL)
How the Oilers Got Him: Toronto's 4th choice., 67th overall in the 1974 draft. Traded to the Oilers with Wayne Gretzky, and Ed Mio for $850,000 and other considerations, November 3, 1978.
First Game as an Oiler: October 10, 1979 *First Assist as an Oiler:* October 26, 1979

First Goal as an Oiler: October 23, 1979
First Penalty as an Oiler: October 10, 1979
Where He Went: Retired

Season	*GP*	*G*	*A*	*Pts*	*Shots*	*S%*	*GW*	*GT*	*PP*	*SH*	*P/M*	*PIM*
1979-80	39	1	5	6	23	4.3	0	1	0	0	-11	54
Playoffs	*3*	*0*	*0*	*0*			*0*	*0*	*0*	*0*		*0*
1980-81	21	2	3	5	17	11.8	0	0	1	0	1	43
2 years	60	3	8	11	40	7.5	0	1	1	0	-10	97
Playoffs	*3*	*0*	*0*	*0*			*0*	*0*	*0*	*0*		*0*

DRYDEN, DAVID MURRAY SWEATER # 28 GOALTENDER CL
Born: Hamilton, Ontario September 5, 1941 6'1"-186
Last Amateur Club: Galt Hornets (SR. A OHA)
How the Oilers Got Him: Signed to a WHA contract prior to the 1975-76 season. Reclaimed by the Buffalo Sabres from the Oilers prior to the Expansion Draft, June 9, 1979 and reclaimed as a priority selection by the Oilers on the same date.
First Game as an Oiler: October 10, 1979
First Assist as an Oiler: None Recorded
First Goal as an Oiler: None Recorded
First Penalty as an Oiler: None Recorded
Where He Went: Retired

Season	*GP*	*Min*	*GA*	*W*	*L*	*T*	*Ave*	*SA*	*S%*	*SO*	*EN*	*PIM*	*Ast.*
1979-80	14	744	53	2	7	3	4.27	350	0.849	0	2	0	0

DUFRESNE, DONALD SWEATER # 34 DEFENSE SR
Born: Quebec City, Quebec April 10, 1967 6'1"-205
Last Amateur Club: Longueuil Chevaliers (QMJHL)
How the Oilers Got Him: Montreal's 8th choice, 117th overall in the 1985 draft. Traded to the Oilers from the St. Louis Blues with Jeff Norton for Igor Kravchuk and Ken Sutton, January 4, 1996.
First Game as an Oiler: January 5, 1996
First Assist as an Oiler: January 13, 1996
First Goal as an Oiler: February 21, 1996.
First Penalty as an Oiler: February 7, 1996
Where He Went: Retired

Season	*GP*	*G*	*A*	*Pts*	*Shots*	*S%*	*GW*	*GT*	*PP*	*SH*	*P/M*	*PIM*
1995-96	42	1	6	7	20	5.0	0	0	0	0	-2	16
1996-97	22	0	1	1	10	0.0	0	0	0	0	-1	15
Playoffs	*3*	*0*	*0*	*0*	*0*	*0.0*	*0*	*0*	*0*	*0*	*0*	*0*
2 years	64	1	7	8	30	3.3	0	0	0	0	-3	31
Playoffs	*3*	*0*	*0*	*0*	*0*	*0.0*	*0*	*0*	*0*	*0*	*0*	*0*

DUPUIS, ROBERT SWEATER # 33 GOALTENDER CL
Born: North Bay, Ontario August 26, 1952 5'11"-167
Last Amateur Club: Canadian Olympic Team
How the Oilers Got Him: Signed as a free agent by the Oilers, March 1980.
First Game as an Oiler: February 11, 1980
First Assist as an Oiler: None Recorded
First Goal as an Oiler: None Recorded
First Penalty as an Oiler: None Recorded
Where He Went: Retired

Season	*GP*	*Min*	*GA*	*W*	*L*	*T*	*Ave*	*SA*	*S%*	*SO*	*EN*	*PIM*	*Ast.*
1979-80	1	60	4	0	1	0	4.00	36	.914	0	1	0	0

DYKSTRA, STEVEN SWEATER # 20 DEFENSE SL
Born: Edmonton, Alberta December 1, 1962 6'2"-210
Last Amateur Club: Seattle Breakers (WHL)
How the Oilers Got Him: Traded by Buffalo to the Oilers along with the Sabres 7th round choice (Dave Payne) in the 1989 draft for Scott Metcalfe and the Oilers 9th round draft (Donald Audette) in the 1989 draft, February 11, 1988.
First Game as an Oiler: February 11, 1988
First Assist as an Oiler: February 14, 1988
First Goal as an Oiler: March 22, 1988
First Penalty as an Oiler: February 11, 1988
Where He Went: Claimed by Pittsburgh in the Waiver Draft, October 3, 1988.

Season	*GP*	*G*	*A*	*Pts*	*Shots*	*S%*	*GW*	*GT*	*PP*	*SH*	*P/M*	*PIM*
1987-88	15	2	3	5	15	13.3	0	0	0	0	1	39

EDWARDS, GARY WILLIAM SWEATER # 33 GOALTENDER CL
Born: Toronto, Ontario October 5, 1947 5'9"-165
Last Amateur Club: Toronto Marlboros (OHL)
How the Oilers Got Him: St. Louis Blues' 1st choice, 6th overall in 1968 draft. Traded to the Oilers by Minnesota for Edmonton's third choice in 1982 draft, February 2, 1981.
First Game as an Oiler: February 8, 1981 *First Assist as an Oiler:* April 4, 1981
First Goal as an Oiler: None Recorded *First Penalty as an Oiler:* None Recorded
Where He Went: Claimed in the Waiver Draft by St. Louis, October 8, 1981.

Season	GP	Min	GA	W	L	T	Ave	SA	S%	SO	EN	PIM	Ast.
1980-81	17	729	44	5	3	4	3.62	326	0.865	0	0	0	2
Playoffs	*1*	*20*	*2*	*0*	*0*		*6.00*	*6*	*0.667*	*0*	*0*	*0*	*0*

ELIK, TODD SLOAN SWEATER # 34, # 27 CENTER SL
Born: Brampton, Ontario April 15, 1966 6'2"-195
Last Amateur Club: University of Regina Cougars (CWUAA)
How the Oilers Got Him: Traded to the Oilers from the Minnesota North Stars for Brent Gilchrist, March 5, 1993.
First Game as an Oiler: March 6, 1993 *First Assist as an Oiler:* March 7, 1993
First Goal as an Oiler: March 12, 1993 *First Penalty as an Oiler:* March 6, 1993
Where He Went: Claimed on waivers by San Jose, October 26, 1993.

Season	GP	G	A	Pts	Shots	S%	GW	GT	PP	SH	P/M	PIM
1992-93	14	1	9	10	28	3.6	0	0	0	0	1	8
1993-94	4	0	0	0	5	0.0	0	0	0	0	0	6
2 years	18	1	9	10	33	3.0	0	0	0	0	1	14

ENNIS, JIM SWEATER #2 DEFENSE SL
Born: Edmonton, Alberta July 10, 1967 6'0"-200
Last Amateur Club: Boston University Terriers (ECAC)
How the Oilers Got Him: Oilers' 6th choice, 126th overall in the 1986 draft.
First Game as an Oiler: October 9, 1987 *First Assist as an Oiler:* None Recorded
First Goal as an Oiler: October 11, 1987 *First Penalty as an Oiler*: October 11, 1987
Where He Went: Traded to Hartford Whalers for Norm Maciver October 10, 1989.

Season	GP	G	A	Pts	Shots	S%	GW	GT	PP	SH	P/M	PIM
1987-88	5	1	0	1	9	11.1	0	0	1	0	0	10

ERIKSSON, PETER KESSLER SWEATER # 26 LEFT WING SL
Born: Kramfors, Sweden July 12, 1965 6'4"-225
Last Amateur Club: HV 71 (Sweden)
How the Oilers Got Him: Oilers' 4th choice, 64th overall in the 1987 draft.
First Game as an Oiler: October 11, 1989 *First Assist as an Oiler:* October 29, 1989
First Goal as an Oiler: October 11, 1989 *First Penalty as an Oiler:* October 22, 1989
Where He Went: Retired

Season	GP	G	A	Pts	Shots	S%	GW	GT	PP	SH	P/M	PIM
1989-90	20	3	3	6	23	13.0	0	0	1	0	-1	24

ESAU, LEONARD SWEATER # 34 DEFENSE SR
Born: Meadow Lake, Saskatchewan June 3, 1968 6'3"-190
Last Amateur Club: St. Cloud (NCAA)
How the Oilers Got Him: Toronto's 5th choice, 86th overall in the 1988 draft. Claimed by the Oilers from the Calgary Flames in the Waiver Draft, January 18, 1995.
First Game as an Oiler: January 25, 1995 *First Assist as an Oiler:* February 3, 1995
First Goal as an Oiler: None Recorded *First Penalty as an Oiler:* February 12, 1995
Where He Went: Claimed on waivers by Calgary, March 7, 1995.

Season	GP	G	A	Pts	Shots	S%	GW	GT	PP	SH	P/M	PIM
1994-95	14	0	6	6	17	0.0	0	0	0	0	-8	15

ESSENSA, ROBERT EARLE SWEATER # 30 GOALTENDER CL
Born: Toronto, Ontario, January 14, 1965 6'0"-185
Last Amateur Club: Michigan State University Spartans (CCHA)

How the Oilers Got Him: Winnipeg's 5th choice, 69th overall in the 1983 draft. Traded to the Oilers by the Detroit Red Wings for future considerations, June 14, 1996.
First Game as an Oiler: October 9, 1996
First Assist as an Oiler: October 28, 1998
First Goal as an Oiler: None Recorded
First Penalty as an Oiler: February 13, 1997
Where He Went: Signed as a free agent by the Phoenix Coyotes, September 5, 1999.

Season	*GP*	*Min*	*GA*	*W*	*L*	*T*	*Ave*	*SA*	*S%*	*SO*	*EN*	*PIM*	*Ast.*
1996-97	19	868	41	4	8	0	2.83	406	0.899	1	3	4	0
1997-98	16	825	35	6	6	1	2.55	404	0.913	0	2	0	0
Playoffs	*1*	*27*	*1*	*0*	*0*		*0.00*	*11*	*0.909*	*0*	*0*	*0*	*0*
1998-99	39	2091	96	12	14	6	2.75	974	0.901	0	2	0	1
3 years	74	3784	172	22	28	7	2.73	1784	0.904	1	7	4	1
Playoffs	*1*	*27*	*1*	*0*	*0*		*0.00*	*11*	*0.909*	*0*	*0*	*0*	*0*

EXELBY, RANDY

SWEATER # 35 — GOALTENDER — CL
Born: Toronto, Ontario — August 13, 1965 — 5'9"-170
Last Amateur Club: Lake Superior State Lakers (CCHA)
How the Oilers Got Him: Montreal's 1st choice, 20th overall in the 1986 Supplemental Draft. Traded to the Oilers by the Canadiens for future considerations, October 2, 1989.
First Game as an Oiler: February 2, 1990
First Assist as an Oiler: None Recorded
First Goal as an Oiler: None Recorded
First Penalty as an Oiler: None Recorded
Where He Went: Retired

Season	*GP*	*Min*	*GA*	*W*	*L*	*T*	*Ave*	*SA*	*S%*	*SO*	*EN*	*PIM*	*Ast.*
1989-90	1	60	5	0	1	0	5.00	30	0.833	0	1	0	0

FALLOON, PATRICK

SWEATER # 10 — RIGHT WING — SR
Born: Foxwarren, Manitoba — September 22, 1972 — 5'11"-200
Last Amateur Club: Spokane Chiefs (WHL)
How the Oilers Got Him: San Jose's 1st choice 2nd overall in the 1991 draft. Signed as a free agent by the Oilers, August 21, 1998.
First Game as an Oiler: October 10, 1998
First Assist as an Oiler: October 31, 1998
First Goal as an Oiler: October 14, 1998
First Penalty as an Oiler: November 2, 1998
Where He Went: Acquired on waivers by the Pittsburgh Penguins, February 4, 2000.

Season	*GP*	*G*	*A*	*Pts*	*Shots*	*S%*	*GW*	*GT*	*PP*	*SH*	*P/M*	*PIM*
1998-99	82	17	23	40	152	11.2	2	0	8	0	-4	20
Playoffs	*4*	*0*	*1*	*1*	*6*	*0.0*	*0*	*0*	*0*	*0*	*0*	*4*
1999-00	33	5	13	18	51	9.8	0	0	1	0	6	4
2 years	115	22	36	58	203	10.8	2	0	9	0	2	24
Playoffs	*4*	*0*	*1*	*1*	*6*	*0.0*	*0*	*0*	*0*	*0*	*0*	*4*

FERGUSON, SCOTT

SWEATER # 40, #32 — DEFENSE — SL
Born: Camrose, Alberta — January 6, 1973 — 6'1"-195
Last Amateur Club: Kamloops Blazers (WHL)
How the Oilers Got Him: Signed as a free agent by the Oilers, June 2, 1994. Re-signed as a free agent by the Oilers, July 5th, 2000.
First Game as an Oiler: March 4, 1998
First Assist as an Oiler: February 20, 2001
First Goal as an Oiler: None Recorded
First Penalty as an Oiler: February 20, 2001
Where He Went: Traded to Ottawa for Frantisek Musil, March 9, 1998.

Season	*GP*	*G*	*A*	*Pts*	*Shots*	*S%*	*GW*	*GT*	*PP*	*SH*	*P/M*	*PIM*
1997-98	1	0	0	0	0	0.0	0	0	0	0	1	0
2000-01	20	0	1	1	8	0.0	0	0	0	0	2	13
Playoffs	*6*	*0*	*0*	*0*	*2*	*0.0*	*0*	*0*	*0*	*0*	*2*	*0*
2 years	21	0	1	1	8	0.0	0	0	0	0	3	13
Playoffs	*6*	*0*	*0*	*0*	*2*	*0.0*	*0*	*0*	*0*	*0*	*2*	*0*

FERRARO, CHRIS

SWEATER # 38 — CENTER — SR
Born: Port Jefferson, New York — January 24, 1973 — 5'10"-185
Last Amateur Club: US National Team
How the Oilers Got Him: Rangers' 4th choice, 85th overall in the 1992 draft. Signed as a free agent by the Oilers, August 13, 1998.
First Game as an Oiler: February 26, 1999
First Assist as an Oiler: None Recorded

First Goal as an Oiler: February 26, 1999 *First Penalty as an Oiler:* None Recorded
Where He Went: Signed as a free agent by the New York Islanders, July 7, 1999.

Season	*GP*	*G*	*A*	*Pts*	*Shots*	*S%*	*GW*	*GT*	*PP*	*SH*	*P/M*	*PIM*
1998-99	2	1	0	1	1	100.0	0	0	0	0	1	0

Flett, William Myer Sweater # 19 Right Wing SR
Born: Vermilion, Alberta July 21, 1943 Died: July 13, 1999 6'1"-205
Last Amateur Club: Victoria Maple Leafs (WHL)
How the Oilers Got Him: After playing 24 games for Atlanta of the NHL in 1976-77, Flett signed a WHA contract with the Oilers and played the rest of the 1976-77 season with Edmonton.
First Game as an Oiler: October 10, 1979 *First Assist as an Oiler:* October 30, 1979
First Goal as an Oiler: October 23, 1979 *First Penalty as an Oiler:* October 14, 1979
Where He Went: Retired

Season	*GP*	*G*	*A*	*Pts*	*Shots*	*S%*	*GW*	*GT*	*PP*	*SH*	*P/M*	*PIM*
1979-80	20	5	2	7	26	19.2	0	0	1	0	-17	2

Fogolin, Lee Joseph Sweater # 2 Defense SR
Born: Chicago, Illinois February 7, 1955 6'0"-200
Last Amateur Club: Oshawa Generals (OHL)
How the Oilers Got Him: Chosen by the Oilers from Buffalo in the Expansion Draft, June 13, 1979.
First Game as an Oiler: October 10, 1979 *First Assist as an Oiler:* November 13, 1979
First Goal as an Oiler: January 16, 1980 *First Penalty as an Oiler:* October 10, 1979
Where He Went: Traded to Buffalo with Mark Napier for Normand Lacombe, Wayne Van Dorp and future considerations, March 6, 1987.

Season	*GP*	*G*	*A*	*Pts*	*Shots*	*S%*	*GW*	*GT*	*PP*	*SH*	*P/M*	*PIM*
1979-80	80	5	10	15	90	5.6	0	0	0	0	-8	104
Playoffs	*3*	*0*	*0*	*0*			*0*	*0*	*0*	*0*		*4*
1980-81	80	13	17	30	89	14.6	1	1	0	4	2	139
Playoffs	*9*	*0*	*0*	*0*			*0*	*0*	*0*	*0*		*12*
1981-82	80	4	25	29	98	4.1	0	0	0	0	40	154
Playoffs	*5*	*1*	*1*	*2*			*0*	*0*	*0*	*0*		*14*
1982-83	72	0	18	18	66	0.0	0	0	0	0	24	92
Playoffs	*16*	*0*	*5*	*5*	*15*	*0.0*	*0*	*0*	*0*	*0*	*8*	*36*
1983-84	80	5	16	21	73	6.8	0	0	0	0	33	125
Playoffs	*19*	*1*	*4*	*5*	*22*	*4.5*	*0*	*0*	*0*	*0*	*10*	*23*
1984-85	79	4	13	17	63	6.3	1	0	0	1	17	126
Playoffs	*18*	*3*	*1*	*4*	*10*	*30.0*	*1*	*1*	*0*	*0*	*8*	*16*
1985-86	80	4	22	26	71	5.6	0	0	0	0	48	129
Playoffs	*8*	*0*	*2*	*2*	*7*	*0.0*	*0*	*0*	*0*	*0*	*3*	*10*
1986-87	35	1	3	4	37	2.7	0	0	0	0	-2	17
8 years	586	36	124	160	587	6.1	2	1	0	5	154	886
Playoffs	*78*	*5*	*13*	*18*			*1*	*1*	*0*	*0*		*115*

Forbes, Michael D. Sweater # 23, # 26 Defense SR
Born: Brampton, Ontario September 20, 1957 6'2"-200
Last Amateur Club: St. Catherines Fincups (OHL)
How the Oilers Got Him: Boston's 3rd choice, 52nd overall in the 1977 draft. Claimed by the Oilers in the Expansion Draft, June 13, 1979.
First Game as an Oiler: October 16, 1981 *First Assist as an Oiler:* October 18, 1981
First Goal as an Oiler: December 5, 1981 *First Penalty as an Oiler:* October 16, 1981
Where He Went: Retired

Season	*GP*	*G*	*A*	*Pts*	*Shots*	*S%*	*GW*	*GT*	*PP*	*SH*	*P/M*	*PIM*
1979-80	2	0	0	0	3	0.0	0	0	0	0	-4	0
1981-82	16	1	7	8	14	7.1	0	0	0	0	14	26
2 years	18	1	7	8	17	5.9	0	0	0	0	10	26

Foster, Norman Richard Sweater # 33 Goaltender CL
Born: Vancouver, British Columbia February 10, 1965 5'9"-175
Last Amateur Club: Michigan State University Spartans (CCHA)
How the Oilers Got Him: Boston's 11th choice, 222nd overall in the 1983 draft. Traded to the Oilers from the Bruins for future considerations, September 11, 1991.

First Game as an Oiler: January 4, 1992
First Assist as an Oiler: None Recorded
First Goal as an Oiler: None Recorded
First Penalty as an Oiler: January 31, 1992
Where He Went: Signed as a free agent by Philadelphia, August 4, 1993.

Season	GP	Min	GA	W	L	T	Ave	SA	S%	SO	EN	PIM	Ast.
1991-92	10	439	20	5	3	0	2.73	183	0.891	0	0	2	0

FOTIU, NICHOLAS EVLAMPIOS SWEATER # 32 LEFT WING SL
Born: Staten Island, New York May 25, 1952 6'2"-200
Last Amateur Club: New Hyde Park Arrows (New York MJHA)
How the Oilers Got Him: Signed to a 20 game option contract, October 10, 1988.
First Game as an Oiler: October 14, 1988
First Assist as an Oiler: None Recorded
First Goal as an Oiler: None Recorded
First Penalty as an Oiler: None Recorded
Where He Went: Retired

Season	GP	G	A	Pts	Shots	S%	GW	GT	PP	SH	P/M	PIM
1988-89	1	0	0	0	0	0.0	0	0	0	0	1	0

FRASER, IAIN JAMES SWEATER # 38 CENTER SL
Born: Scarborough, Ontario August 10, 1969 5'10"-175
Last Amateur Club: Oshawa Generals (OHL)
How the Oilers Got Him: New York Islanders' 12th choice, 233rd overall in the 1989 draft. Claimed on waivers from the Dallas Stars, March 3, 1995.
First Game as an Oiler: March 5, 1995
First Assist as an Oiler: None Recorded
First Goal as an Oiler: March 5, 1995
First Penalty as an Oiler: None Recorded
Where He Went: Signed as a free agent by Winnipeg, October 11, 1995.

Season	GP	G	A	Pts	Shots	S%	GW	GT	PP	SH	P/M	PIM
1994-95	9	3	0	3	5	60.0	0	0	0	0	3	0

FRASER, SCOTT SWEATER # 18 CENTER SR
Born: Moncton, New Brunswick May 3, 1972 6'2"-206
Last Amateur Club: Canadian National Team
How the Oilers Got Him: Montreal's 12th choice, 193rd overall in the 1991 draft. Signed as a free agent July 23, 1997.
First Game as an Oiler: January 2, 1998
First Assist as an Oiler: March 9, 1998
First Goal as an Oiler: January 2, 1998
First Penalty as an Oiler: March 2, 1998
Where He Went: Signed as a free agent by the Rangers, July 2, 1998.

Season	GP	G	A	Pts	Shots	S%	GW	GT	PP	SH	P/M	PIM
1997-98	29	12	11	23	61	19.7	2	0	6	0	6	6
Playoffs	*11*	*1*	*1*	*2*	*17*	*5.9*	*0*	*0*	*0*	*0*	*0*	*0*

FRIEDMAN, DOUGLAS SWEATER # 8 LEFT WING SL
Born: Cape Elizabeth, Maine September 1, 1971 6'1"-195
Last Amateur Club: Boston University Terriers (H.E.)
How the Oilers Got Him: Quebec's 11th choice, 222nd overall in the 1991 draft. Signed as a free agent by the Oilers, July 14, 1997.
First Game as an Oiler: November 25, 1997
First Assist as an Oiler: None Recorded
First Goal as an Oiler: None Recorded
First Penalty as an Oiler: December 2, 1997
Where He Went: Chosen by the Nashville Predators in the Expansion Draft, June 26, 1998.

Season	GP	G	A	Pts	Shots	S%	GW	GT	PP	SH	P/M	PIM
1997-98	16	0	0	0	8	0.0	0	0	0	0	0	20

FRYCER, MIROSLAV OPAVA SWEATER # 15 RIGHT WING SR
Born: Ostrava, Czechoslovakia September 27, 1959 6'0"-200
Last Amateur Club: Vitkovice (Czech)
How the Oilers Got Him: Traded to the Oilers by Detroit for Edmonton's 10th round choice (Rick Judson) in the 1989 draft, January 3, 1989.
First Game as an Oiler: January 4, 1989
First Assist as an Oiler: January 8, 1989
First Goal as an Oiler: January 4, 1989
First Penalty as an Oiler: January 7, 1989
Where He Went: Retired

Season	GP	G	A	Pts	Shots	S%	GW	GT	PP	SH	P/M	PIM
1988-89	14	5	5	10	33	15.2	0	0	2	0	2	18

FUHR, GRANT SWEATER # 1, # 31 GOALTENDER CR
Born: Spruce Grove, Alberta September 28, 1962 5'10"-185
Last Amateur Club: Victoria Cougars (WHL)
How the Oilers Got Him: Edmonton's 1st choice, 8th overall in 1981 draft.
First Game as an Oiler: October 14, 1981 *First Assist as an Oiler:* October 23, 1989
First Goal as an Oiler: None Recorded *First Penalty as an Oiler:* November 25, 1981
Where He Went: Traded to Toronto with Glenn Anderson and Craig Berube for Vincent Damphousse, Peter Ing, Luke Richardson, Scott Thornton, future considerations and cash, September 19, 1991.

Season	*GP*	*Min*	*GA*	*W*	*L*	*T*	*Ave*	*SA*	*S%*	*SO*	*EN*	*PIM*	*Ast.*
1981-82	48	2845	157	28	5	14	3.31	1545	0.898	0	2	6	6
Playoffs	*5*	*309*	*26*	*2*	*3*		*5.05*	*177*	*0.853*	*0*	*1*	*0*	*0*
1982-83	32	1803	129	13	12	5	4.29	974	0.867	0	4	6	0
Playoffs	*1*	*11*	*0*	*0*	*0*		*0.00*	*4*	*1.000*	*0*	*0*	*0*	*0*
1983-84	45	2625	171	30	10	4	3.91	1463	0.883	1	2	6	14
Playoffs	*16*	*883*	*44*	*11*	*4*		*2.99*	*491*	*0.910*	*1*	*0*	*4*	*3*
1984-85	46	2559	165	26	8	7	3.87	1426	0.884	1.5	1	6	3
Playoffs	*18*	*1064*	*55*	*15*	*3*		*3.10*	*522*	*0.894*	*0*	*2*	*2*	*3*
1985-86	40	2184	143	29	8	0	3.93	1296	0.890	0	1	0	2
Playoffs	*9*	*541*	*28*	*5*	*4*		*3.11*	*273*	*0.897*	*0*	*1*	*0*	*1*
1986-87	44	2388	137	22	13	3	3.44	1149	0.881	0	1	6	2
Playoffs	*19*	*1148*	*47*	*14*	*5*		*2.46*	*511*	*0.908*	*0*	*2*	*0*	*1*
1987-88	75	4304	246	40	24	9	3.43	2066	0.881	4	5	16	8
Playoffs	*19*	*1136*	*55*	*16*	*2*		*2.90*	*471*	*0.883*	*0*	*1*	*6*	*1*
1988-89	59	3341	213	23	26	6	3.83	1714	0.875	1	4	6	1
Playoffs	*7*	*417*	*24*	*3*	*4*		*3.43*	*227*	*0.894*	*1*	*1*	*0*	*0*
1989-90	21	1081	70	9	7	3	3.88	532	0.868	1	0	2	0
1990-91	13	778	39	6	4	3	3.01	380	0.897	1	0	0	0
Playoffs	*17*	*1019*	*51*	*8*	*7*		*3.00*	*488*	*0.895*	*0*	*1*	*2*	*2*
10 years	423	23908	1470	226	117	54	3.69	12545	0.883	9.5	20	54	36
Playoffs	*111*	*6528*	*330*	*74*	*32*		*3.03*	*3164*	*0.896*	*2*	*9*	*14*	*11*

GAGE, JOAQUIN JESSE SWEATER # 1, #31 GOALTENDER CL
Born: Vancouver, British Columbia October 19, 1973 6'0"-200
Last Amateur Club: Prince Albert Raiders (WHL)
How the Oilers Got Him: Oilers' 6th choice, 109th overall in the 1992 draft.
First Game as an Oiler: May 1, 1995 *First Assist as an Oiler:* May 1, 1995
First Goal as an Oiler: None Recorded *First Penalty as an Oiler:* January 7, 1995

Season	*GP*	*Min*	*GA*	*W*	*L*	*T*	*Ave*	*SA*	*S%*	*SO*	*EN*	*PIM*	*Ast.*
1994-95	2	99	7	0	2	0	4.24	40	0.825	0	0	0	1
1995-96	16	717	45	2	8	1	3.77	350	0.871	0	1	4	0
2000-01	5	260	15	2	2	0	3.46	125	0.880	0	1	0	0
3 years	23	1076	67	4	12	1	3.74	515	0.870	0	2	4	1

GARE, DANIEL MIRL SWEATER # 18, # 19 RIGHT WING SR
Born: Nelson, British Columbia May 14, 1954 5'9"-175
Last Amateur Club: Calgary Centennials (WHL)
How the Oilers Got Him: Buffalo's 2nd choice, 29th overall in the 1974 draft. Signed as a free agent by the Oilers September 1986.
First Game as an Oiler: October 11, 1986 *First Assist as an Oiler:* November 8, 1986
First Goal as an Oiler: January 28, 1987 *First Penalty as an Oiler*: October 15, 1986
Where He Went: Retired

Season	*GP*	*G*	*A*	*Pts*	*Shots*	*S%*	*GW*	*GT*	*PP*	*SH*	*P/M*	*PIM*
1986-87	18	1	3	4	22	4.5	0	0	0	0	2	6

GELINAS, MARTIN SWEATER # 20, # 7 CENTER SL
Born: Shawinigan, Quebec June 5, 1970 5'11"-195
Last Amateur Club: Hull Olympiques (QMJHL)
How the Oilers Got Him: Los Angeles' 1st choice, 7th overall in the 1988 draft. Traded to the Oilers, with Jimmy Carson, and the Kings' 1st round choice in 1989 draft (acquired by New Jersey-the Devils selected Jason Miller), 1991 draft (Martin Rucinsky), 1993 draft (Nick Stajduhar) and cash, for Wayne Gretzky, Marty McSorley and Mike Krushelnyski, August 9th, 1988.
First Game as an Oiler: October 7, 1988 *First Assist as an Oiler:* October 7, 1988
First Goal as an Oiler: October 17, 1988 *First Penalty as an Oiler*: October 7, 1989

Where He Went: Traded to Quebec with the Oilers' 6th choice (Nicholas Checco) in the 1993 draft for Scott Pearson, June 20, 1993.

Season	*GP*	*G*	*A*	*Pts*	*Shots*	*S%*	*GW*	*GT*	*PP*	*SH*	*P/M*	*PIM*
1988-89	6	1	2	3	14	7.1	0	0	0	0	-1	0
1989-90	46	17	8	25	71	23.9	2	2	5	0	0	30
Playoffs	*20*	*2*	*3*	*5*	*24*	*8.3*	*0*	*0*	*0*	*0*	*0*	*6*
1990-91	73	20	20	40	124	16.1	2	1	4	0	-7	34
Playoffs	*18*	*3*	*6*	*9*	*29*	*10.3*	*1*	*0*	*0*	*0*	*4*	*25*
1991-92	68	11	18	29	94	11.7	0	0	1	0	14	62
Playoffs	*15*	*1*	*3*	*4*	*15*	*6.7*	*0*	*0*	*0*	*0*	*-3*	*10*
1992-93	65	11	12	23	93	11.8	1	0	0	0	3	30
5 years	258	60	60	120	396	15.2	5	3	10	0	9	156
Playoffs	*53*	*6*	*12*	*18*	*68*	*8.8*	*1*	*0*	*0*	*0*	*1*	*41*

GILCHRIST, BRENT SWEATER # 41 LEFT WING SL

Born: Moose Jaw, Saskatchewan April 3, 1967 5'11"-180

Last Amateur Club: Spokane Chiefs (WHL)

How the Oilers Got Him: Montreal's 6th choice, 79th overall in the 1985 draft. Traded to the Oilers by the Canadiens with Shayne Corson and Vladimir Vujtek for Vincent Damphousse and the Oilers' 4th round pick (Adam Wiesel) in the 1993 draft, August 27th, 1992.

First Game as an Oiler: October 6, 1992
First Assist as an Oiler: October 6, 1992
First Goal as an Oiler: October 6, 1992
First Penalty as an Oiler: October 6, 1992
Where He Went: Traded to Minnesota for Todd Elik, March 5, 1993.

Season	*GP*	*G*	*A*	*Pts*	*Shots*	*S%*	*GW*	*GT*	*PP*	*SH*	*P/M*	*PIM*
1992-93	60	10	10	20	94	10.6	0	0	2	0	-10	47

GLYNN, BRIAN SWEATER # 6 DEFENSE SL

Born: Iserlohn, West Germany November 23, 1967 6'4"-215

Last Amateur Club: Saskatoon Blades (WHL)

How the Oilers Got Him: Calgary's 2nd choice, 37th overall in the 1986 draft. Traded to the Oilers from the Minnesota North Stars for David Shaw, January 21, 1992.

First Game as an Oiler: January 23, 1992
First Assist as an Oiler: February 7, 1992
First Goal as an Oiler: February 7, 1992
First Penalty as an Oiler: January 25, 1992
Where He Went: Traded to Ottawa for the Senators' 8th round choice (Rob Quinn) in the 1994 draft, September 15, 1993.

Season	*GP*	*G*	*A*	*Pts*	*Shots*	*S%*	*GW*	*GT*	*PP*	*SH*	*P/M*	*PIM*
1991-92	25	2	6	8	29	6.9	0	0	0	1	11	6
Playoffs	*16*	*4*	*1*	*5*	*13*	*30.8*	*1*	*0*	*1*	*0*	*1*	*12*
1992-93	64	4	12	16	80	5.0	0	0	2	0	-13	60
2 years	89	6	18	24	109	5.5	0	0	2	1	-2	66
Playoffs	*16*	*4*	*1*	*5*	*13*	*30.8*	*1*	*0*	*1*	*0*	*1*	*12*

GORENCE, THOMAS J. SWEATER # 26 RIGHT WING SR

Born: St. Paul, Minnesota March 11, 1957 6'0"-190

Last Amateur Club: University of Minnesota Gophers (WCHA)

How the Oilers Got Him: Philadelphia's 2nd choice, 35th overall in the 1977 draft. Signed as a free agent by the Oilers, November 1, 1983.

First Game as an Oiler: January 11, 1984
First Assist as an Oiler: January 11, 1984
First Goal as an Oiler: January 28, 1984
First Penalty as an Oiler: None Recorded
Where He Went: Signed as a free agent by New Jersey, March 5, 1985.

Season	*GP*	*G*	*A*	*Pts*	*Shots*	*S%*	*GW*	*GT*	*PP*	*SH*	*P/M*	*PIM*
1983-84	12	1	1	2	7	14.3	0	0	0	0	0	0

GRAVES, ADAM SWEATER # 12 CENTER SL

Born: Toronto, Ontario April 12, 1968 6'0"-210

Last Amateur Club: Windsor Compuware Spitfires (OHL)

How the Oilers Got Him: Detroit's 2nd choice, 22nd overall in the 1986 draft. Traded to the Oilers by Detroit, with Petr Klima, Joe Murphy, and Jeff Sharples for Jimmy Carson, Kevin McClelland, and the Oilers' 5th round choice (later acquired by Montreal in exchange for Rick Green; the Canadiens chose Brad Layzell) in the 1991 draft, November 2, 1989.

First Game as an Oiler: November 3, 1989
First Assist as an Oiler: November 3, 1989
First Goal as an Oiler: December 17, 1989
First Penalty as an Oiler: November 11, 1989
Where He Went: Signed as a free agent by the Rangers', September 3, 1991.

Season	*GP*	*G*	*A*	*Pts*	*Shots*	*S%*	*GW*	*GT*	*PP*	*SH*	*P/M*	*PIM*
1989-90	63	9	12	21	84	10.7	1	0	1	0	5	123
Playoffs	*22*	*5*	*6*	*11*	*46*	*10.9*	*1*	*0*	*0*	*0*	*1*	*17*
1990-91	76	7	18	25	126	5.6	1	0	2	0	-21	127
Playoffs	*18*	*2*	*4*	*6*	*48*	*4.2*	*0*	*0*	*0*	*0*	*7*	*22*
2 years	139	16	30	46	210	7.6	2	0	3	0	-16	250
Playoffs	*40*	*7*	*10*	*17*	*94*	*7.4*	*1*	*0*	*0*	*0*	*8*	*39*

GRAVES, STEVE SWEATER # 8 # 15 CENTER SL
Born: Trenton, Ontario April 7, 1964 5'10"-175
Last Amateur Club: Sault Ste. Marie Greyhounds (OHL)
How the Oilers Got Him: Edmonton's 2nd choice, 41st overall in the 1982 draft.
First Game as an Oiler: January 7, 1984 *First Assist as an Oiler:* November 1, 1987
First Goal as an Oiler: December 5, 1986 *First Penalty as an Oiler:* October 11, 1987
Where He Went: Signed as a free agent by Los Angeles, July 16, 1990.

Season	*GP*	*G*	*A*	*Pts*	*Shots*	*S%*	*GW*	*GT*	*PP*	*SH*	*P/M*	*PIM*
1983-84	2	0	0	0	2	0.0	0	0	0	0	0	0
1986-87	12	2	0	2	12	16.7	1	0	0	0	-2	0
1987-88	21	3	4	7	21	14.3	0	0	0	0	13	10
3 years	35	5	4	9	35	14.3	1	0	0	0	11	10

GREEN, JOSH SWEATER # 12 LEFT WING SL
Born: Camrose, Alberta November 16, 1977 6'4"-212
Last Amateur Club: Portland Winter Hawks (WHL)
How the Oilers Got Him: Los Angeles' 1st choice, 30th overall in the 1996 draft.
First Game as an Oiler: April 15, 2001 *First Assist as an Oiler:* None Recorded
First Goal as an Oiler: None Recorded *First Penalty as an Oiler:* None Recorded

Season	*GP*	*G*	*A*	*Pts*	*Shots*	*S%*	*GW*	*GT*	*PP*	*SH*	*P/M*	*PIM*
Playoffs (00-01)	3	0	0	0	1	0.0	0	0	0	0	1	0

GREENLAY, MIKE SWEATER # 35 GOALTENDER CL
Born: Vitoria, Brazil September 15, 1968 6'3"-200
Last Amateur Club: Lake Superior State Lakers (CCHA)
How the Oilers Got Him: Oilers' 9th choice, 189th overall in the 1986 draft.
First Game as an Oiler: February 25, 1990 *First Assist as an Oiler:* February 25, 1990
First Goal as an Oiler: None Recorded *First Penalty as an Oiler:* None Recorded
Where He Went: Signed as a free agent by Tampa Bay, July 29, 1992.

Season	*GP*	*Min*	*GA*	*W*	*L*	*T*	*Ave*	*SA*	*S%*	*SO*	*EN*	*PIM*	*Ast.*
1989-90	2	20	4	0	0	0	12.00	17	0.765	0	0	0	1

GREGG, RANDALL JOHN SWEATER # 21 DEFENSE SL
Born: Edmonton Alberta February 19, 1956 6'4"-215
Last Amateur Club: Kokudo Bunnies (Japan)
How the Oilers Got Him: Signed as a free agent by the Oilers, October 18, 1982.
First Game as an Oiler: April 8, 1982 *First Assist as an Oiler:* April 10, 1982
First Goal as an Oiler: October 24, 1982 *First Penalty as an Oiler:* April 10, 1982
Where He Went: Claimed as a free agent by the Canucks in the Waiver Draft, October 1, 1990.

Season	*GP*	*G*	*A*	*Pts*	*Shots*	*S%*	*GW*	*GT*	*PP*	*SH*	*P/M*	*PIM*
Playoffs(81-82)	*4*	*0*	*2*	*2*			*0*	*0*	*0*	*0*		*12*
1982-83	80	6	22	28	94	6.4	2	0	0	2	15	54
Playoffs	*16*	*2*	*4*	*6*	*16*	*12.5*	*1*	*0*	*0*	*1*	*13*	*13*
1983-84	80	13	27	40	91	14.3	2	0	2	1	40	56
Playoffs	*19*	*3*	*7*	*10*	*32*	*9.4*	*1*	*1*	*0*	*0*	*16*	*21*
1984-85	57	3	20	23	58	5.2	0	0	0	0	28	32
Playoffs	*17*	*0*	*6*	*6*	*17*	*0.0*	*0*	*0*	*0*	*0*	*19*	*12*
1985-86	64	2	26	28	55	3.6	0	0	0	0	30	47
Playoffs	*10*	*1*	*0*	*1*	*6*	*16.7*	*0*	*0*	*0*	*0*	*3*	*12*
1986-87	52	8	16	24	59	13.6	2	0	0	0	36	42
Playoffs	*18*	*3*	*6*	*9*	*29*	*10.3*	*1*	*0*	*1*	*0*	*8*	*17*
1987-88	15	1	2	3	20	5.0	0	0	0	0	4	8

Season	GP	G	A	Pts	Shots	S%	GW	GT	PP	SH	P/M	PIM
Playoffs	*19*	*1*	*8*	*9*	*22*	*4.5*	*1*	*0*	*0*	*0*	*17*	*24*
1988-89	57	3	15	18	42	7.1	1	0	1	0	-9	28
Playoffs	*7*	*1*	*0*	*1*	*8*	*12.5*	*0*	*0*	*0*	*0*	*4*	*4*
1989-90	48	4	20	24	41	9.8	0	0	0	0	24	42
Playoffs	*20*	*2*	*6*	*8*	*17*	*11.8*	*0*	*0*	*1*	*0*	*1*	*16*
8 years	453	40	148	188	460	8.7	7	0	3	3	168	309
Playoffs	*130*	*13*	*39*	*52*			*4*	*1*	*2*	*1*		*131*

GRETZKY, WAYNE DOUGLAS SWEATER # 99 CENTER SL

Born: Brantford, Ontario January, 26, 1961 6'0"-170

Last Amateur Club: Sault Ste. Marie Greyhounds (OHL)

How the Oilers Got Him: While still a part of the WHA the Oilers obtained Gretzky, Ed Mio and Peter Driscoll in exchange for $850,000 and other considerations, November 3, 1978.

First Game as an Oiler: October 10, 1979 *First Assist as an Oiler:* October 10, 1979

First Goal as an Oiler: October 14, 1979 *First Penalty as an Oiler:* October 10, 1979

Where He Went: Traded to Los Angeles with Mike Krushelnyski and Marty McSorley, for Jimmy Carson, Martin Gelinas, the Kings' 1st round choice (later acquired by New Jersey, the Devils selected Jason Miller) in the 1989 draft, 1st round choice in the 1991 draft (Martin Rucinsky) and 1st round choice (Nick Stajduhar) in the 1993 draft and cash, August 9, 1988.

Season	GP	G	A	Pts	Shots	S%	GW	GT	PP	SH	P/M	PIM
1979-80	79	51	86	137	284	18.0	6	4	13	1	15	21
Playoffs	*3*	*2*	*1*	*3*			*0*	*0*	*0*	*0*		*0*
1980-81	80	55	109	164	261	21.1	3	2	15	4	41	28
Playoffs	*9*	*7*	*14*	*21*			*1*	*0*	*2*	*1*		*4*
1981-82	80	92	120	212	369	24.9	12	4	18	6	81	26
Playoffs	*5*	*5*	*7*	*12*			*1*	*1*	*1*	*1*		*8*
1982-83	80	71	125	196	348	20.4	9	1	18	6	60	59
Playoffs	*16*	*12*	*26*	*38*	*76*	*15.8*	*3*	*0*	*2*	*3*	*19*	*4*
1983-84	74	87	118	205	324	26.9	11	0	20	12	76	39
Playoffs	*19*	*13*	*22*	*35*	*86*	*15.1*	*3*	*0*	*2*	*0*	*18*	*12*
1984-85	80	73	135	208	358	20.4	7	2	8	11	98	52
Playoffs	*18*	*17*	*30*	*47*	*67*	*25.4*	*3*	*0*	*4*	*2*	*28*	*4*
1985-86	80	52	163	215	350	14.9	6	1	11	3	71	46
Playoffs	*10*	*8*	*11*	*19*	*42*	*19.0*	*2*	*0*	*4*	*1*	*0*	*2*
1986-87	79	62	121	183	288	21.5	4	0	13	7	70	28
Playoffs	*21*	*5*	*29*	*34*	*55*	*9.1*	*0*	*0*	*2*	*0*	*10*	*6*
1987-88	64	40	109	149	211	19.0	3	0	9	5	39	24
Playoffs	*19*	*12*	*31*	*43*	*62*	*19.4*	*3*	*1*	*5*	*1*	*9*	*16*
9 years	696	583	1086	1669	2793	20.87	61	14	125	55	551	323
Playoffs	*120*	*81*	*171*	*252*			*16*	*2*	*22*	*9*		*52*

GRIER, MICHAEL JAMES SWEATER # 25 RIGHT WING SR

Born: Detroit, Michigan January 5, 1975 6'1"-225

Last Amateur Club: Boston University Terriers (H.E.)

How the Oilers Got Him: St. Louis' 7th choice, 219th overall in the 1993 draft. Rights were traded to the Oilers from the St. Louis Blues, with Curtis Joseph for the Blues' former 1st round choices in the 1996 draft previously acquired by the Oilers (Marty Reasoner) and the 1997 draft, later traded to Los Angeles (the Kings chose Matt Zultek), August 4, 1995.

First Game as an Oiler: October 4, 1996 *First Assist as an Oiler:* October 20, 1996

First Goal as an Oiler: October 26, 1996 *First Penalty as an Oiler:* October 20, 1996

Season	GP	G	A	Pts	Shots	S%	GW	GT	PP	SH	P/M	PIM
1996-97	79	15	17	32	89	16.9	2	0	4	0	7	45
Playoffs	*12*	*3*	*1*	*4*	*21*	*14.3*	*1*	*0*	*1*	*0*	*-2*	*4*
1997-98	66	9	6	15	90	10.0	1	0	1	0	-3	73
Playoffs	*12*	*2*	*2*	*4*	*14*	*14.3*	*1*	*0*	*0*	*0*	*4*	*13*
1998-99	82	20	24	44	143	14.0	1	0	3	2	5	54
Playoffs	*4*	*1*	*1*	*2*	*9*	*11.1*	*0*	*0*	*0*	*0*	*3*	*6*
1999-00	65	9	22	31	115	7.8	2	0	0	3	9	68
2000-01	74	20	16	36	124	16.1	2	1	2	3	11	20
Playoffs	*6*	*0*	*0*	*0*	*6*	*0.0*	*0*	*0*	*0*	*0*	*-2*	*8*
5 years	366	73	85	158	561	13.0	8	0	10	8	29	260
Playoffs	*34*	*6*	*4*	*10*	*50*	*12.0*	*2*	*0*	*1*	*0*	*3*	*31*

GRIEVE, BRENT SWEATER # 34 LEFT WING SL
Born: Oshawa, Ontario May 9, 1969 6'1"-200
Last Amateur Club: Oshawa Generals (OHL)
How the Oilers Got Him: New York Islanders' 4th choice, 65th overall in the 1989 draft. Traded to the Oilers from the Islanders for Marc Laforge, December 15, 1993.
First Game as an Oiler: February 12, 1994
First Assist as an Oiler: February 12, 1994
First Goal as an Oiler: February 18, 1994
First Penalty as an Oiler: February 18, 1994
Where He Went: Signed as a free agent by Chicago, July 7, 1994.

Season	*GP*	*G*	*A*	*Pts*	*Shots*	*S%*	*GW*	*GT*	*PP*	*SH*	*P/M*	*PIM*
1993-94	24	13	5	18	53	24.5	0	1	4	0	4	14

GUERIN, WILLIAM ROBERT SWEATER # 9 RIGHT WING SR
Born: Wilbraham, Massachusetts November 9, 1970 6'2"-210
Last Amateur Club: U.S. National Team
How the Oilers Got Him: New Jersey's 1st choice, 5th overall in the 1989 draft. Traded to the Oilers with Valeri Zelepukin for Jason Arnott and Bryan Muir, January 4, 1998.
First Game as an Oiler: January 7, 1998
First Assist as an Oiler: January 9, 1998
First Goal as an Oiler: January 9, 1998
First Penalty as an Oiler: January 9, 1998
Where He Went: Traded to Boston for Anson Carter, the Bruins 2nd choice in the 2001 draft (Doug Lynch), the right to switch 1st round draft choices with the Bruins in the 2001 or 2002 draft and future considerations, November 15th, 2000.

Season	*GP*	*G*	*A*	*Pts*	*Shots*	*S%*	*GW*	*GT*	*PP*	*SH*	*P/M*	*PIM*
1997-98	40	13	16	29	130	10.0	2	0	8	0	1	80
Playoffs	*12*	*7*	*1*	*8*	*47*	*14.9*	*0*	*0*	*4*	*0*	*-6*	*17*
1998-99	80	30	34	64	261	11.5	2	1	13	0	7	133
Playoffs	*3*	*0*	*2*	*2*	*8*	*0.0*	*0*	*0*	*0*	*0*	*-4*	*2*
1999-00	70	24	22	46	188	12.8	2	0	11	0	4	123
Playoffs	*5*	*3*	*2*	*5*	*12*	*25.0*	*0*	*0*	*1*	*0*	*-1*	*9*
2000-01	21	12	10	22	64	18.7	1	0	4	0	11	18
3 years	211	79	82	161	643	12.3	7	1	36	0	23	354
Playoffs	*20*	*10*	*5*	*15*	*67*	*16.4*	*0*	*0*	*5*	*0*	*-11*	*28*

HAAS, DAVID SWEATER # 15, # 26 LEFT WING SL
Born: Toronto, Ontario June 23, 1968 6'2"-195
Last Amateur Club: Windsor Spitfires (OHA)
How the Oilers Got Him: Oilers 5th choice, 105th overall in the 1986 draft.
First Game as an Oiler: November 6, 1990
First Assist as an Oiler: None Recorded
First Goal as an Oiler: November 8, 1990
First Penalty as an Oiler: None Recorded
Where He Went: Signed as a free agent by Calgary, August 10, 1993.

Season	*GP*	*G*	*A*	*Pts*	*Shots*	*S%*	*GW*	*GT*	*PP*	*SH*	*P/M*	*PIM*
1990-91	5	1	0	1	4	25.0	0	0	0	0	-2	0

HABSCHEID, MARC JOSEPH SWEATER # 23 CENTER SR
Born: Swift Current, Saskatchewan March 1, 1963 5'10"-170
Last Amateur Club: Saskatoon Blades (WHL)
How the Oilers Got Him: Edmonton's 6th choice, 113th overall in the 1981 draft.
First Game as an Oiler: November 25, 1981
First Assist as an Oiler: November 25, 1981
First Goal as an Oiler: November 29, 1981
First Penalty as an Oiler: November 25, 1981
Where He Went: Traded to Minnesota with Don Barber and Emanuel Viveiros for Gord Sherven and Don Biggs, December 20, 1985.

Season	*GP*	*G*	*A*	*Pts*	*Shots*	*S%*	*GW*	*GT*	*PP*	*SH*	*P/M*	*PIM*
1981-82	7	1	3	4	7	14.3	0	0	1	0	5	2
1982-83	32	3	10	13	19	15.8	0	0	0	0	14	14
1983-84	9	1	0	1	6	16.7	0	0	0	0	-3	6
1984-85	26	5	3	8	30	16.7	0	0	2	0	-2	4
4 years	74	10	16	26	62	16.1	0	0	3	0	14	26

HAGMAN, MATTI RISTO TAPIO SWEATER # 10 CENTER SL
Born: Helsinki, Finland September 21, 1955 6'1"-185
Last Amateur Club: Finland IFK (Fin)
How the Oilers Got Him: Boston's 6th choice, 104th overall in the 1975 draft. Signed as a free agent by the Oilers September 11, 1980.

First Game as an Oiler: October 10, 1980
First Goal as an Oiler: October, 26, 1980
Where He Went: Retired
First Assist as an Oiler: October 18, 1980
First Penalty as an Oiler: November 5, 1980

Season	*GP*	*G*	*A*	*Pts*	*Shots*	*S%*	*GW*	*GT*	*PP*	*SH*	*P/M*	*PIM*
1980-81	75	20	33	53	96	20.8	0	0	2	0	4	16
Playoffs	*9*	*4*	*1*	*5*			*2*	*0*	*0*	*0*		*6*
1981-82	72	21	38	59	94	22.3	2	0	5	0	15	18
Playoffs	*3*	*1*	*0*	*1*			*0*	*0*	*0*	*0*		*0*
2 years	147	41	71	112	190	21.6	2	0	7	0	19	34
Playoffs	*12*	*5*	*1*	*6*			*2*	*0*	*0*	*0*		*6*

HAJT, CHRIS SWEATER # 19 DEFENSE SL
Born: Saskatoon, Saskatchewan July 5, 1978 6'3"-206
Last Amateur Club: Guelph Storm (OHL)
How the Oilers Got Him: Oilers' 3rd choice, 32nd overall in the 1996 draft.
First Game as an Oiler: October 11, 2000
First Goal as an Oiler: None Recorded
First Assist as an Oiler: None Recorded
First Penalty as an Oiler: None Recorded

Season	*GP*	*G*	*A*	*Pts*	*Shots*	*S%*	*GW*	*GT*	*PP*	*SH*	*P/M*	*PIM*
2000-01	1	0	0	0	0	0.0	0	0	0	0	-1	0

HALWARD, DOUGLAS ROBERT SWEATER # 37 DEFENSE SL
Born: Toronto, Ontario November 1, 1955 6'1"-200
Last Amateur Club: Peterborough Petes (OHA)
How the Oilers Got Him: Traded to the Oilers by the Detroit Red Wings for Edmonton's 12th choice (Jason Glickman) in the 1989 draft, January 23, 1989.
First Game as an Oiler: January 25, 1989
First Goal as an Oiler: None Recorded
Where He Went: Retired
First Assist as an Oiler: January 25, 1989
First Penalty as an Oiler: February 12, 1989

Season	*GP*	*G*	*A*	*Pts*	*Shots*	*S%*	*GW*	*GT*	*PP*	*SH*	*P/M*	*PIM*
1988-89	24	0	7	7	8	0.0	0	0	0	0	-3	25
Playoffs	*2*	*0*	*0*	*0*	*0*	*0.0*	*0*	*0*	*0*	*0*	*-2*	*0*

HAMILTON, ALLAN GUY SWEATER # 3 DEFENSE SR
Born: Flin Flon, Manitoba August 20, 1946 6'2"-210
Last Amateur Club: Edmonton Oil Kings (WCHL)
How the Oilers Got Him: Signed to a WHA contract before the 1972-73 season.
First Game as an Oiler: October 14, 1979
First Goal as an Oiler: October 24, 1979
Where He Went: Retired
First Assist as an Oiler: October 14, 1979
First Penalty as an Oiler: October 24, 1979

Season	*GP*	*G*	*A*	*Pts*	*Shots*	*S%*	*GW*	*GT*	*PP*	*SH*	*P/M*	*PIM*
1979-80	31	4	15	19	34	11.8	0	0	1	0	-2	20
Playoffs	*1*	*0*	*0*	*0*			*0*	*0*	*0*	*0*		*0*

HAMMOND, KEN PAUL SWEATER # 26 DEFENSE SL
Born: Port Credit, Ontario August 22, 1963 6'1"-190
Last Amateur Club: RPI Engineers (ECAC)
How the Oilers Got Him: Los Angeles' 8th choice, 152nd overall in the 1983 draft. Claimed by the Oilers in the Waiver Draft, October 3, 1988.
First Game as an Oiler: October 9, 1988
First Goal as an Oiler: None Recorded
Where He Went: Claimed on waivers by the Rangers, November 1, 1988.
First Assist as an Oiler: October 12, 1988
First Penalty as an Oiler: October 9, 1988

Season	*GP*	*G*	*A*	*Pts*	*Shots*	*S%*	*GW*	*GT*	*PP*	*SH*	*P/M*	*PIM*
1988-89	5	0	1	1	1	0.0	0	0	0	0	-2	8

HAMRLIK, ROMAN SWEATER # 22 DEFENSE SL
Born: Gottwaldov, Czechoslovakia April 12, 1974 6'2"-202
Last Amateur Club: ZPS Zlin (Czech)
How the Oilers Got Him: Tampa Bay's 1st choice, 1st overall in the 1992 draft. Obtained from Tampa Bay with Paul Comrie for Bryan Marchment, Steve Kelly and Jason Bonsignore, December 30, 1997.

First Game as an Oiler: January 2, 1998
First Assist as an Oiler: January 2, 1998
First Goal as an Oiler: January 4, 1998.
First Penalty as an Oiler: January 7, 1998
Where He Went: Traded to the Islanders for Josh Green, Eric Brewer and the Islanders' third choice in the 2000 draft (the Oilers chose Brad Winchester), June 24th, 2000.

Season	GP	G	A	Pts	Shots	S%	GW	GT	PP	SH	P/M	PIM
1997-98	41	6	20	26	112	5.4	3	0	4	1	3	48
Playoffs	*12*	*0*	*6*	*6*	*19*	*0.0*	*0*	*0*	*0*	*0*	*-4*	*12*
1998-99	75	8	24	32	172	4.7	0	0	3	0	9	70
Playoffs	*3*	*0*	*0*	*0*	*1*	*0.0*	*0*	*0*	*0*	*0*	*1*	*2*
1999-00	80	8	37	45	180	4.4	0	1	5	0	1	68
Playoffs	*5*	*0*	*1*	*1*	*10*	*0.0*	*0*	*0*	*0*	*0*	*-4*	*4*
3 years	196	22	81	103	464	4.7	3	0	12	1	13	186
Playoffs	*20*	*0*	*7*	*7*	*30*	*0.0*	*0*	*0*	*0*	*0*	*-7*	*18*

HANNAN, DAVID PATRICK — SWEATER # 12 — CENTER — SL

Born: Sudbury, Ontario — November 26, 1961 — 5'10"-175
Last Amateur Club: Brantford Alexanders (OHA)
How the Oilers Got Him: Pittsburgh's 9th choice, 196th overall in the 1981 draft. Traded by the Pittsburgh Penguins to the Oilers with Craig Simpson, Moe Mantha, and Chris Joseph for Paul Coffey, Dave Hunter and Wayne Van Dorp, November 24, 1987.
First Game as an Oiler: November 25, 1987
First Assist as an Oiler: December 19, 1987
First Goal as an Oiler: December 12, 1987
First Penalty as a Oiler: November 27, 1987
Where He Went: Claimed in the Waiver Draft by the Penguins, October 3, 1988.

Season	GP	G	A	Pts	Shots	S%	GW	GT	PP	SH	P/M	PIM
1987-88	51	9	11	20	62	14.5	2	1	0	2	12	43
Playoffs	*12*	*1*	*1*	*2*	*11*	*9.1*	*1*	*0*	*0*	*0*	*-3*	8

HARRISON, JAMES DAVID — SWEATER # 9 — CENTER — SR

Born: Bonnyville, Alberta — July 9, 1947 — 5'11"-185
Last Amateur Club: Estevan Bruins (WCHL)
How the Oilers Got Him: Rights transferred to Edmonton by Chicago, September 24, 1979.
First Game as an Oiler: October 19, 1979
First Assist as an Oiler: None Recorded
First Goal as an Oiler: None Recorded
First Penalty as an Oiler: None Recorded
Where He Went: Retired

Season	GP	G	A	Pts	Shots	S%	GW	GT	PP	SH	P/M	PIM
1979-80	3	0	0	0	3	0.0	0	0	0	0	-1	0

HAUER, BRETT — SWEATER # 5, #2 — DEFENSE — SR

Born: Richfield, Minnesota — July 11, 1971 — 6'2"-200
Last Amateur Club: AIK Solna (Swe)
How the Oilers Got Him: Vancouver's 3rd choice, 71st overall in the 1989 draft. Traded to the Oilers by the Canucks for a conditional draft choice, August 24, 1995.
First Game as an Oiler: November 7, 1995
First Assist as an Oiler: January 17, 1996
First Goal as an Oiler: November 10, 1995
First Penalty as an Oiler: November 9, 1995

Season	GP	G	A	Pts	Shots	S%	GW	GT	PP	SH	P/M	PIM
1995-96	29	4	2	6	53	7.5	1	0	2	0	-11	30
1999-00	5	0	2	2	8	0.0	0	0	0	0	-2	2
2 years	34	4	4	8	61	6.6	1	0	2	0	-13	32

HAWGOOD, GREG — SWEATER # 23, # 15, # 34 — DEFENSE — SL

Born: Edmonton, Alberta — August 10, 1968 — 5'8"-175
Last Amateur Club: Kamloops Blazers (WHL)
How the Oilers Got Him: Boston's 9th choice, 202nd overall in the 1986 draft. Traded to the Oilers from the Bruins for Vladimir Ruzicka, October 22, 1990.
First Game as an Oiler: October 24, 1990
First Assist as an Oiler: November 3, 1990
First Goal as an Oiler: February 19, 1992
First Penalty as an Oiler: October 25, 1990
Where He Went: Traded to Philadelphia with Josef Beranek for Brian Benning, January 16, 1993.

Season	GP	G	A	Pts	Shots	S%	GW	GT	PP	SH	P/M	PIM
1990-91	6	0	1	1	9	0.0	0	0	0	0	-2	6
1991-92	20	2	11	13	24	8.3	0	0	0	0	19	22

Season	GP	G	A	Pts	Shots	S%	GW	GT	PP	SH	P/M	PIM
Playoffs	*13*	*0*	*3*	*3*	*19*	*0.0*	*0*	*0*	*0*	*0*	*-4*	*23*
1992-93	29	5	13	18	47	10.6	0	0	2	0	-1	35
3 years	55	7	25	32	80	8.8	0	0	2	0	16	63
Playoffs	*13*	*0*	*3*	*3*	*19*	*0.0*	*0*	*0*	*0*	*0*	*-4*	*23*

HERBERS, IAN SWEATER # 6 DEFENSE SL

Born: Jasper, Alberta July 18, 1967 6'4"-225

Last Amateur Club: University of Alberta Golden Bears (CWUAA)

How the Oilers Got Him: Buffalo's 11th choice, 190th overall in the 1987 draft. Signed as a free agent by the Oilers, September 9, 1992.

First Game as an Oiler: October 6, 1993 *First Assist as an Oiler:* October 6, 1993

First Goal as an Oiler: None Recorded *First Penalty as an Oiler:* October 8, 1993

Where He Went: Signed as a free agent by Tampa Bay, September 1999.

Season	GP	G	A	Pts	Shots	S%	GW	GT	PP	SH	P/M	PIM
1993-94	22	0	2	2	16	0.0	0	0	0	0	-6	32

HICKS, DOUGLAS ALLAN SWEATER # 5 DEFENSE SL

Born: Cold Lake, Alberta May 29, 1955 6'0"-185

Last Amateur Club: Flin Flon Bombers (WHL)

How the Oilers Got Him: Minnesota's 1st choice, 6th overall in 1974 draft. Chosen from the Chicago Black Hawks in the 1979 Expansion Draft, June 13, 1979.

First Game as an Oiler: October 10, 1979 *First Assist as an Oiler:* October 19, 1979

First Goal as an Oiler: October 19, 1979 *First Penalty as an Oiler:* October 28, 1979

Where He Went: Traded to Washington for Todd Bidner, March 9, 1982.

Season	GP	G	A	Pts	Shots	S%	GW	GT	PP	SH	P/M	PIM
1979-80	78	9	31	40	122	7.4	1	0	5	2	18	52
Playoffs	*3*	*0*	*0*	*0*			*0*	*0*	*0*	*0*		*2*
1980-81	59	5	16	21	109	4.6	0	0	1	1	21	76
Playoffs	*9*	*1*	*1*	*2*			*0*	*0*	*0*	*0*		*4*
1981-82	49	3	20	23	44	6.8	0	0	1	0	6	55
3 years	186	17	67	84	275	6.2	1	0	7	3	45	183
Playoffs	*12*	*1*	*1*	*2*			*0*	*0*	*0*	*0*		*6*

HOPKINS, DEAN ROBERT SWEATER # 34 RIGHT WING SR

Born: Cobourg, Ontario June 6, 1959 6'1"-210

Last Amateur Club: London Knights (OHA)

How the Oilers Got Him: Los Angeles' 2nd choice, 29th overall in the 1979 draft. Traded to the Oilers by Los Angeles for cash, November 27, 1984.

First Game as an Oiler: November 18, 1985 *First Assist as an Oiler:* None Recorded

First Goal as an Oiler: None Recorded *First Penalty as an Oiler:* None Recorded

Where He Went: Traded to Los Angeles for future considerations, May 31, 1985.

Season	GP	G	A	Pts	Shots	S%	GW	GT	PP	SH	P/M	PIM
1985-86	1	0	0	0	0	0.0	0	0	0	0	0	0

HORCOFF, SHAWN SWEATER # 36 CENTER SL

Born: Trail, British Columbia September 17, 1978 6'1"-202

Last Amateur Club: Michigan State University Spartans (CCHA)

How the Oilers Got Him: Edmonton's 3rd choice, 99th overall in the 1998 draft.

First Game as an Oiler: December 6, 2000 *First Assist as an Oiler:* December 6, 2000

First Goal as an Oiler: December 13, 2000 *First Penalty as an Oiler:* January 31, 2001

Season	GP	G	A	Pts	Shots	S%	GW	GT	PP	SH	P/M	PIM
2000-01	49	9	7	16	42	21.4	2	0	0	0	8	10
Playoffs	*5*	*0*	*0*	*0*	*2*	*0.0*	*0*	*0*	*0*	*0*	*0*	*0*

HRKAC, ANTHONY SWEATER # 20 CENTER SL

Born: Thunder Bay, Ontario July 7, 1966 5'11"-170

Last Amateur Club: North Dakota Fighting Sioux (WCHA)

How the Oilers Got Him: St. Louis' 2nd choice, 32nd overall in the 1984 draft. Claimed on waivers by the Oilers, January 6, 1998.

First Game as an Oiler: January 7, 1998
First Goal as an Oiler: January 9, 1998
First Assist as an Oiler: January 9, 1998
First Penalty as an Oiler: January 31, 1998
Where He Went: Traded to Pittsburgh with Bobby Dollas for the rights to Josef Beranek, June 16, 1998.

Season	GP	G	A	Pts	Shots	S%	GW	GT	PP	SH	P/M	PIM
1997-98	36	8	11	19	43	18.6	1	0	4	0	3	10
Playoffs	*12*	*0*	*3*	*3*	*11*	*0.0*	*0*	*0*	*0*	*0*	*2*	*2*

HUARD, WILLIAM JOHN

SWEATER # 28 — LEFT WING — SL

Born: Welland, Ontario — June 24, 1967 — 6'1"-215
Last Amateur Club: Peterborough Petes (OHL)
How the Oilers Got Him: Signed as a free agent by the Oilers, July 22, 1997.
First Game as an Oiler: October 1, 1997
First Goal as an Oiler: None Recorded
First Assist as an Oiler: March 18, 1998
First Penalty as an Oiler: October 3, 1997
Where He Went: Signed as a free agent by Los Angeles, July 19, 1999.

Season	GP	G	A	Pts	Shots	S%	GW	GT	PP	SH	P/M	PIM
1997-98	30	0	1	1	12	0.0	0	0	0	0	-5	72
Playoffs	*4*	*0*	*0*	*0*	*3*	*0.0*	*0*	*0*	*0*	*0*	*0*	*2*
1998-99	3	0	0	0	2	0.0	0	0	0	0	0	0
2 years	33	0	1	1	14	0.0	0	0	0	0	-5	72

HUDDY, CHARLES WILLIAM

SWEATER # 22 — DEFENSE — SL

Home: Toronto, Ontario — June 2, 1959 — 6'0"-200
Last Amateur Club: Oshawa Generals (OHL)
How the Oilers Got Him: Signed as a free agent by the Oilers, September 14, 1979.
First Game as an Oiler: November 15, 1980
First Goal as an Oiler: November 16, 1980
First Assist as an Oiler: November 15, 1980
First Penalty as an Oiler: November 28, 1980
Where He Went: Claimed by Minnesota in the Expansion Draft, May 30, 1991.

Season	GP	G	A	Pts	Shots	S%	GW	GT	PP	SH	P/M	PIM
1980-81	12	2	5	7	23	8.7	0	0	1	0	1	6
1981-82	41	4	11	15	84	4.8	0	1	0	0	17	46
Playoffs	*5*	*1*	*2*	*3*			*0*	*0*	*0*	*1*		*14*
1982-83	76	20	37	57	151	13.2	2	0	7	0	62	58
Playoffs	*15*	*1*	*6*	*7*	*47*	*2.1*	*0*	*0*	*0*	*0*	*12*	*10*
1983-84	75	8	34	42	161	5.0	0	0	3	0	50	43
Playoffs	*12*	*1*	*9*	*10*	*35*	*2.9*	*0*	*0*	*0*	*0*	*18*	*8*
1984-85	80	7	44	51	146	4.8	1	1	3	0	50	46
Playoffs	*18*	*3*	*17*	*20*	*50*	*6.0*	*0*	*0*	*1*	*0*	*20*	*17*
1985-86	76	6	35	41	151	4.0	0	0	1	0	30	55
Playoffs	*7*	*0*	*2*	*2*	*5*	*0.0*	*0*	*0*	*0*	*0*	*3*	*0*
1986-87	58	4	15	19	75	5.3	0	0	0	0	27	35
Playoffs	*21*	*1*	*7*	*8*	*34*	*2.9*	*0*	*0*	*0*	*0*	*12*	*21*
1987-88	77	13	28	41	163	8.0	2	1	2	0	23	71
Playoffs	*13*	*4*	*5*	*9*	*33*	*12.1*	*0*	*0*	*2*	*0*	*2*	*10*
1988-89	76	11	33	44	178	6.2	0	0	5	2	0	52
Playoffs	*7*	*2*	*0*	*2*	*17*	*11.8*	*0*	*0*	*1*	*0*	*-2*	*4*
1989-90	70	1	23	24	119	0.8	1	0	1	0	-13	56
Playoffs	*22*	*0*	*6*	*6*	*35*	*0.0*	*0*	*0*	*0*	*0*	*11*	*10*
1990-91	53	5	22	27	90	5.6	0	0	2	0	4	32
Playoffs	*18*	*3*	*7*	*10*	*35*	*8.6*	*0*	*0*	*1*	*0*	*9*	*10*
11 years	694	81	287	368	1341	6.0	6	3	25	2	251	500
Playoffs	*138*	*16*	*61*	*77*			*0*	*0*	*5*	*1*		*104*

HUDSON, MIKE

SWEATER # 20 — CENTER/LEFT WING — SL

Born: Guelph, Ontario — February 6, 1967 — 6'1"-205
Last Amateur Club: Sudbury Wolves (OHL)
How the Oilers Got Him: Chicago's 6th choice, 140th overall in the 1986 draft. Traded to Edmonton from the Chicago Black Hawks for Craig Muni, March 22, 1993.
First Game as an Oiler: March 26, 1993
First Goal as an Oiler: None Recorded
First Assist as an Oiler: April 7, 1993
First Penalty as an Oiler: April 15, 1993
Where He Went: Claimed by the Rangers in the Waiver Draft, October 3, 1993.

Season	GP	G	A	Pts	Shots	S%	GW	GT	PP	SH	P/M	PIM
1992-93	5	0	1	1	2	0.0	0	0	0	0	-1	2

HUGHES, JOHN SPENCER SWEATER # 6 DEFENSE SL
Born: Charlottetown, Prince Edward Island March 18, 1954 5'11"-200
Last Amateur Club: Toronto Marlboros (OHL)
How the Oilers Got Him: Vancouver Canucks' 2nd choice, 41st overall in the 1974 draft. Signed to a WHA contract by the Oilers for the 1978-79 season. Reclaimed by the Canucks prior to the Expansion Draft June 9, 1979. Claimed on waivers by the Oilers, December 15, 1980.
First Game as an Oiler: October 18, 1980
First Assist as an Oiler: October 18, 1980
First Goal as an Oiler: None Recorded
First Penalty as an Oiler: October 24, 1980
Where He Went: Traded to the Rangers for Ray Markham, March 10, 1981.

Season	*GP*	*G*	*A*	*Pts*	*Shots*	*S%*	*GW*	*GT*	*PP*	*SH*	*P/M*	*PIM*
1980-81	18	0	3	3	9	0.0	0	0	0	0	-6	30

HUGHES, PATRICK JAMES SWEATER # 16 RIGHT WING SR
Born: Calgary, Alberta March 25, 1955 6'1"-180
Last Amateur Club: University of Michigan Wolverines (WCHA)
How the Oilers Got Him: Montreal's 6th choice, 52nd overall in 1975 draft. Traded to the Oilers by the Pittsburgh Penguins for Pat Price, March 10, 1981.
First Game as an Oiler: March 12, 1981
First Assist as an Oiler: October 7, 1981
First Goal as an Oiler: October 7, 1981
First Penalty as an Oiler: April 22, 1981
Where He Went: Traded to Pittsburgh for Mike Moller, October 4, 1985.

Season	*GP*	*G*	*A*	*Pts*	*Shots*	*S%*	*GW*	*GT*	*PP*	*SH*	*P/M*	*PIM*
1980-81	2	0	0	0	3	0.0	0	0	0	0	-3	0
Playoffs	*5*	*0*	*5*	*5*			*0*	*0*	*0*	*0*		*16*
1981-82	68	24	22	46	167	14.4	0	1	4	2	21	99
Playoffs	*5*	*2*	*1*	*3*			*0*	*0*	*0*	*0*		*6*
1982-83	80	25	20	45	144	17.4	7	1	2	5	0	85
Playoffs	*16*	*2*	*5*	*7*	*31*	*6.5*	*1*	*0*	*0*	*0*	*10*	*14*
1983-84	77	27	28	55	164	16.5	3	0	2	3	18	61
Playoffs	*19*	*2*	*11*	*13*	*44*	*4.5*	*0*	*0*	*0*	*0*	*14*	*12*
1984-85	73	12	13	25	98	12.2	0	0	1	1	-7	85
Playoffs	*10*	*1*	*1*	*2*	*3*	*33.3*	*0*	*0*	*0*	*0*	*1*	*4*
5 years	300	88	83	171	576	15.3	10	2	9	11	29	330
Playoffs	*55*	*7*	*23*	*30*			*1*	*0*	*0*	*0*		*52*

HULBIG, JOSEPH ALLAN SWEATER # 15, #12 LEFT WING SL
Born: Norwood, Massachusetts September 29, 1973 6'3"-215
Last Amateur Club: Providence College Friars (H.E.)
How the Oilers Got Him: Edmonton's 1st choice, 13th overall in the 1992 draft.
First Game as an Oiler: March 4, 1997
First Assist as an Oiler: April 29, 1997
First Goal as an Oiler: December, 5 1997
First Penalty as an Oiler: May 7, 1997
Where He Went: Signed as a free agent by the Boston Bruins, July 23, 1999.

Season	*GP*	*G*	*A*	*Pts*	*Shots*	*S%*	*GW*	*GT*	*PP*	*SH*	*P/M*	*PIM*
1996-97	6	0	0	0	4	0.0	0	0	0	0	-1	0
Playoffs	*6*	*0*	*1*	*1*	*5*	*0.0*	*0*	*0*	*0*	*0*	*2*	*2*
1997-98	17	2	2	4	8	25.0	1	0	0	0	-1	2
1998-99	1	0	0	0	2	0.0	0	0	0	0	1	2
3 years	24	2	2	4	14	14.3	1	0	0	0	-1	4
Playoffs	*6*	*0*	*1*	*1*	*5*	*0.0*	*0*	*0*	*0*	*0*	*2*	*2*

HUNTER, DAVID SWEATER # 12, # 27, # 37 LEFT WING SL
Born: Petrolia, Ontario January 1, 1958 5'11"-195
Last Amateur Club: Sudbury Wolves (OHL)
How the Oilers Got Him: Montreal's 2nd choice, 17th overall in 1978 draft. Signed to a WHA contract by the Oilers.
First Game as an Oiler: October 10, 1979
First Assist as an Oiler: October 21, 1979
First Goal as an Oiler: October 10, 1979
First Penalty as an Oiler: October 14, 1979
Where He Went: Traded to the Penguins with Paul Coffey and Wayne Van Dorp for Dave Hannan, Chris Joseph, Moe Mantha and Craig Simpson, November 24, 1987.

Season	*GP*	*G*	*A*	*Pts*	*Shots*	*S%*	*GW*	*GT*	*PP*	*SH*	*P/M*	*PIM*
1979-80	80	12	31	43	109	11.0	3	0	1	2	7	103
Playoffs	*3*	*0*	*0*	*0*			*0*	*0*	*0*	*0*		*7*
1980-81	78	12	16	28	104	11.5	3	3	0	0	-12	98

Season	GP	G	A	Pts	Shots	S%	GW	GT	PP	SH	P/M	PIM
Playoffs	*9*	*0*	*0*	*0*			*0*	*0*	*0*	*0*		*28*
1981-82	63	16	22	38	124	12.9	3	1	0	0	33	63
Playoffs	*5*	*0*	*1*	*1*		*0*	*0*	*0*	*0*	*0*		*26*
1982-83	80	13	18	31	113	11.5	0	0	0	1	12	120
Playoffs	*16*	*4*	*7*	*11*	*16*	*25.0*	*0*	*0*	*0*	*0*	*8*	*60*
1983-84	80	22	26	48	117	18.8	3	0	1	1	25	90
Playoffs	*17*	*5*	*5*	*10*	*25*	*20.0*	*0*	*0*	*1*	*1*	*10*	*14*
1984-85	80	17	19	36	119	14.3	1	0	1	1	0	122
Playoffs	*18*	*2*	*5*	*7*	*31*	*6.5*	*0*	*0*	*0*	*0*	*5*	*33*
1985-86	62	15	22	37	110	13.6	1	0	0	0	37	77
Playoffs	*10*	*2*	*3*	*5*	*18*	*11.1*	*0*	*0*	*0*	*0*	*7*	*23*
1986-87	77	6	9	15	84	7.1	1	0	0	1	1	79
Playoffs	*21*	*3*	*3*	*6*	*27*	*11.1*	*0*	*0*	*0*	*0*	*4*	*20*
1987-88	21	3	3	6	18	16.7	0	0	0	0	1	6
1988-89	32	3	5	8	44	6.8	0	0	0	0	-5	22
Playoffs	*6*	*0*	*0*	*0*	*5*	*0.0*	*0*	*0*	*0*	*0*	*-2*	*0*
10 years	653	119	171	290	942	12.6	15	4	3	6	99	780
Playoffs	*105*	*16*	*24*	*40*			*0*	*0*	*1*	*1*		*211*

ING, PETER SWEATER # 1 GOALTENDER CL

Born: Toronto, Ontario April 28, 1969 6'2"-170

Last Amateur Club: London Knights (OHL)

How the Oilers Got Him: Toronto's 3rd choice, 48th overall in the 1988 draft. Traded to the Oilers from Toronto with Vincent Damphousse, Luke Richardson, Scott Thornton, future considerations and cash for Glenn Anderson, Craig Berube, and Grant Fuhr, September 19, 1991.

First Game as an Oiler: October 4, 1991 *First Assist as an Oiler:* November 6, 1991

First Goal as an Oiler: None Recorded *First Penalty as an Oiler:* None Recorded

Where He Went: Traded to Detroit for the Red Wings' 7th round choice (Chris Wickenheiser) in the 1994 draft and future considerations, August 30, 1993.

Season	GP	Min	GA	W	L	T	Ave	SA	S%	SO	EN	PIM	Ast.
1991-92	12	463	33	3	4	0	4.27	252	0.869	0	1	0	3

INTRANUOVO, RALPH SWEATER # 36, # 27, # 9 CENTER SL

Born: East York, Ontario December 11, 1973 5'8"-185

Last Amateur Club: Sault Ste. Marie Greyhounds (OHL)

How the Oilers Got Him: Edmonton's 5th choice, 96th overall in the 1992 draft.

First Game as an Oiler: March 27, 1995 *First Assist as an Oiler:* March 27, 1995

First Goal as an Oiler: February 21, 1996 *First Penalty as an Oiler*: March 30, 1996

Where He Went: Claimed by Toronto in the Waiver Draft, September 30, 1996. Claimed on waivers by the Oilers, October 25, 1996.

Season	GP	G	A	Pts	Shots	S%	GW	GT	PP	SH	P/M	PIM
1994-95	1	0	1	1	1	0.0	0	0	0	0	1	0
1995-96	13	1	2	3	19	5.3	1	0	0	0	-3	4
1996-97	5	1	0	1	2	50.0	0	0	0	0	0	0
3 years	19	2	3	5	22	9.1	1	0	0	0	-2	4

ISSEL, KIM SWEATER # 27, # 33 RIGHT WING SR

Born: Regina, Saskatchewan September 25, 1967 6'4"-200

Last Amateur Club: Prince Albert Raiders (WHL)

How the Oilers Got Him: Oilers' 1st choice, 21st overall in the 1986 draft.

First Game as an Oiler: December 23, 1988 *First Assist as an Oiler:* None Recorded

First Goal as an Oiler: None Recorded *First Penalty as an Oiler:* None Recorded

Where He Went: Traded to Pittsburgh for Brad Aitken, March 5, 1991.

Season	GP	G	A	Pts	Shots	S%	GW	GT	PP	SH	P/M	PIM
1988-89	4	0	0	0	1	0.0	0	0	0	0	-1	0

JACKSON, DONALD CLINTON SWEATER # 25, # 29 DEFENSE SL

Born: Minneapolis Minnesota September 2, 1956 6'3"-210

Last Amateur Club: University of Notre Dame (WCHA)

How the Oilers Got Him: Minnesota's 3rd choice, 39th overall in the 1976 draft. Traded from the North Stars with Edmonton's 3rd round choice, previously owned by Minnesota (Wally Chapman), August 21, 1981, for the rights to Don Murdoch.
First Game as an Oiler: November 11, 1981 *First Assist as an Oiler:* December 26, 1982
First Goal as an Oiler: January 15, 1983 *First Penalty as an Oiler:* November 11, 1981
Where He Went: Traded to the Rangers with Mike Golden and Miloslav Horava for Clark Donatelli, Ville Kentala, Reijo Ruotsalainen and Jim Wiemer, October 2, 1986.

Season	*GP*	*G*	*A*	*Pts*	*Shots*	*S%*	*GW*	*GT*	*PP*	*SH*	*P/M*	*PIM*
1981-82	8	0	0	0	4	0.0	0	0	0	0	0	18
1982-83	71	2	8	10	72	2.8	1	0	0	1	12	136
Playoffs	*16*	*3*	*3*	*6*	*16*	*18.8*	*0*	*0*	*0*	*0*	*9*	*30*
1983-84	60	8	12	20	57	14.0	2	0	0	1	28	120
Playoffs	*19*	*1*	*2*	*3*	*16*	*6.3*	*0*	*0*	*0*	*0*	*9*	*32*
1984-85	78	3	17	20	47	6.4	0	0	0	0	28	141
Playoffs	*9*	*0*	*0*	*0*	*6*	*0.0*	*0*	*0*	*0*	*0*	*4*	*64*
1985-86	45	2	8	10	34	5.9	0	0	0	0	2	93
Playoffs	*8*	*0*	*0*	*0*	*7*	*0.0*	*0*	*0*	*0*	*0*	*3*	*21*
5 years	262	15	45	60	214	7.0	3	0	0	2	70	508
Playoffs	*52*	*4*	*5*	*9*	*45*	*8.9*	*0*	*0*	*0*	*0*	*25*	*147*

JALO, RISTO SWEATER # 13 CENTER SL
Born: Tampere, Finland July 18, 1962 5'11"-185
Last Amateur Club: Ilves Tampere (Fin)
How the Oilers Got Him: Washington's 7th choice, 131st overall in 1981 draft. Traded by the Washington Capitals to Edmonton for the Oilers' 4th round choice (Larry Shaw) in the 1985 draft, March 6, 1984.
First Game as an Oiler: March 14, 1986 *First Assist as an Oiler:* March 14, 1986
First Goal as an Oiler: None Recorded *First Penalty as an Oiler:* None Recorded
Where He Went: Retired.

Season	*GP*	*G*	*A*	*Pts*	*Shots*	*S%*	*GW*	*GT*	*PP*	*SH*	*P/M*	*PIM*
1985-86	3	0	3	3	3	0.0	0	0	0	0	2	0

JALONEN, KARI SWEATER # 8 CENTER SL
Born: Oulu, Finland January 6, 1960 6'3"-190
Last Amateur Club: Karpat, (Fin)
How the Oilers Got Him: Signed as a free agent by the Oilers, December 1983.
First Game as an Oiler: December 18, 1983 *First Assist as an Oiler:* None Recorded
First Goal as an Oiler: None Recorded *First Penalty as an Oiler:* None Recorded
Where He Went: Retired.

Season	*GP*	*G*	*A*	*Pts*	*Shots*	*S%*	*GW*	*GT*	*PP*	*SH*	*P/M*	*PIM*
1983-84	3	0	0	0	0	0.0	0	0	0	0	-2	0

JONSSON, TOMAS SWEATER # 23 DEFENSE SL
Born: Falun, Sweden April 12, 1960 5'10"-175
Last Amateur Club: MoDo AIK (Swe)
How the Oilers Got Him: New York Islanders' 2nd choice, 25th overall in the 1979 draft. Traded by the Islanders to the Oilers for future considerations, February 15, 1989.
First Game as an Oiler: February 17, 1989 *First Assist as an Oiler:* February 19, 1989
First Goal as an Oiler: March 12, 1989 *First Penalty as an Oiler:* February 17, 1989
Where He Went: Retired

Season	*GP*	*G*	*A*	*Pts*	*Shots*	*S%*	*GW*	*GT*	*PP*	*SH*	*P/M*	*PIM*
1988-89	20	1	10	11	46	2.2	0	0	1	0	-12	22
Playoffs	*4*	*2*	*0*	*2*	*6*	*33.3*	*0*	*0*	*2*	*0*	*1*	*6*

JOSEPH, CHRISTOPHER Sweater # 2 Defense SR
Born: Burnaby, British Columbia September 10, 1969 6'1"-195
Last Amateur Club: Seattle Thunderbirds (WHL)
How the Oilers Got Him: Pittsburgh's 1st choice, 5th overall in the 1987 draft. Traded by the Penguins to the Oilers, with Craig Simpson, Dave Hannan, and Moe Mantha for Paul Coffey, Dave Hunter and Wayne Van Dorp, November 24, 1987.
First Game as an Oiler: November 25, 1987 *First Assist as an Oiler:* November 25, 1987
First Goal as an Oiler: October 19, 1988 *First Penalty as an Oiler:* November 29, 1987
Where He Went: Traded to Tampa Bay by the Oilers for Bob Beers, November 11, 1993.

Season	*GP*	*G*	*A*	*Pts*	*Shots*	*S%*	*GW*	*GT*	*PP*	*SH*	*P/M*	*PIM*
1987-88	7	0	4	4	1	0.0	0	0	0	0	-3	6
1988-89	44	4	5	9	36	11.1	0	0	0	0	-9	54
1989-90	4	0	2	2	5	0.0	0	0	0	0	-2	2
1990-91	49	5	17	22	74	6.8	0	0	2	0	3	59
1991-92	7	0	0	0	5	0.0	0	0	0	0	-1	8
Playoffs	*5*	*1*	*3*	*4*	*6*	*16.7*	*0*	*0*	*0*	*0*	*2*	*2*
1992-93	33	2	10	12	49	4.1	0	0	1	0	-9	48
1993-94	10	1	1	2	25	4.0	0	0	1	0	-8	28
7 years	154	12	39	51	195	6.2	0	0	4	0	-29	205
Playoffs	*5*	*1*	*3*	*4*	*6*	*16.7*	*0*	*0*	*0*	*0*	*2*	*2*

JOSEPH, CURTIS — SWEATER # 31 — GOALTENDER — CL

Born: Keswick, Ontario — April 29, 1967 — 5'10"-185

Last Amateur Club: University of Wisconsin Badgers (WCHA)

How the Oilers Got Him: Traded to the Oilers by the St. Louis Blues with the rights to Mike Grier for St. Louis' 1st round choice, previously acquired by Edmonton, (Marty Reasoner) in the 1996 draft, and 1997 draft, later traded to the Los Angeles Kings (Matt Zultek), August 4, 1995.

First Game as an Oiler: January 13, 1996 — *First Assist as an Oiler:* March 24, 1996

First Goal as an Oiler: None Recorded — *First Penalty as an Oiler:* November 29, 1987

Where He Went: Signed as a free agent by Toronto July 15, 1998.

Season	*GP*	*Min*	*GA*	*W*	*L*	*T*	*Ave*	*SA*	*S%*	*SO*	*EN*	*PIM*	*Ast.*
1995-96	34	1936	111	15	16	2	3.44	971	0.886	0	4	4	1
1996-97	72	4100	200	32	29	9	2.93	2144	0.907	6	3	20	2
Playoffs	*12*	*767*	*36*	*5*	*7*		*3.00*	*405*	*0.911*	*2*	*1*	*2*	*0*
1997-98	71	4132	181	29	31	9	2.63	1901	0.905	8	6	4	2
Playoffs	*12*	*716*	*23*	*5*	*7*		*1.93*	*320*	*0.928*	*3*	*0*	*0*	*2*
3 years	177	10168	492	76	76	20	2.90	5016	0.902	14	13	28	5
Playoffs	*24*	*1483*	*59*	*10*	*14*		*2.39*	*725*	*0.919*	*5*	*1*	*2*	*2*

KELLY, STEVE — SWEATER # 10 — CENTER — SL

Born: Vancouver, British Columbia — October 26, 1976 — 6'1"-190

Last Amateur Club: Prince Albert Raiders (WHL)

How the Oilers Got Him: Edmonton's 1st choice, 6th overall in the 1995 draft.

First Game as an Oiler: March 24, 1997 — *First Assist as an Oiler:* October 24, 1997

First Goal as an Oiler: March 29, 1997 — *First Penalty as an Oiler:* March 24, 1997

Where He Went: Traded to Tampa Bay with Jason Bonsignore and Bryan Marchment for Roman Hamrlik and Paul Comrie, December 30, 1997.

Season	*GP*	*G*	*A*	*Pts*	*Shots*	*S%*	*GW*	*GT*	*PP*	*SH*	*P/M*	*PIM*
1996-97	8	1	0	1	6	16.7	1	0	0	0	-1	6
Playoffs	*6*	*0*	*0*	*0*	*2*	*0.0*	*0*	*0*	*0*	*0*	*1*	*2*
1997-98	23	0	2	2	8	0.0	0	0	0	0	-4	8
2 years	31	1	2	3	14	7.1	1	0	0	0	-5	14
Playoffs	*6*	*0*	*0*	*0*	*2*	*0.0*	*0*	*0*	*0*	*0*	*1*	*2*

KENNEDY, EDWARD DEAN — SWEATER # 32 — DEFENSE — SR

Born: Redvers, Saskatchewan — January 18, 1963 — 6'2"-208

Last Amateur Club: Saskatoon Blades (WHL)

How the Oilers Got Him: Los Angeles' 2nd choice, 39th overall in the 1981 draft. Claimed by the Oilers from the Winnipeg Jets in the Waiver Draft, January 18, 1995.

First Game as an Oiler: January 20, 1995 — *First Assist as an Oiler:* January 23, 1995

First Goal as an Oiler: January 30, 1995 — *First Penalty as an Oiler:* January 28, 1995

Where He Went: Retired.

Season	*GP*	*G*	*A*	*Pts*	*Shots*	*S%*	*GW*	*GT*	*PP*	*SH*	*P/M*	*PIM*
1994-95	40	2	8	10	45	4.4	1	0	0	0	2	25

KERCH, ALEXANDER — SWEATER # 34 — LEFT WING — SR

Born: Arkangelsk, USSR — March 16, 1967 — 5'10"-190

Last Amateur Club: Riga (CIS)

How the Oilers Got Him: Oilers' 5th choice, 60th overall in the 1993 draft.

First Game as an Oiler: October 29, 1993 — *First Assist as an Oiler:* None Recorded

First Goal as an Oiler: None Recorded *First Penalty as an Oiler:* November 3, 1993
Where He Went: Retired.

Season	GP	G	A	Pts	Shots	S%	GW	GT	PP	SH	P/M	PIM
1993-94	5	0	0	0	4	0.0	0	0	0	0	-8	2

KERR, REGINALD JOHN SWEATER # 8, # 25 LEFT WING/ CENTER SL
Born: Oxbow, Saskatchewan October 16, 1957 5'10"-180
Last Amateur Club: Kamloops Chiefs (WHL)
How the Oilers Got Him: Signed as a free agent by the Oilers, November 9, 1983.
First Game as an Oiler: November 9, 1983 *First Assist as an Oiler:* None Recorded
First Goal as an Oiler: None Recorded *First Penalty as an Oiler:* None Recorded
Where He Went: Retired.

Season	GP	G	A	Pts	Shots	S%	GW	GT	PP	SH	P/M	PIM
1983-84	3	0	0	0	3	0.0	0	0	0	0	-3	0

KILGER, CHAD WILLIAM L. SWEATER # 15 CENTER SL
Born: Cornwall, Ontario November 27, 1976 6'3"-204
Last Amateur Club: Kingston Frontenacs (OHL)
How the Oilers Got Him: Anaheim's 1st choice, 4th overall in the 1995 draft. Traded to the Oilers by Chicago with Ethan Moreau, Christian Laflamme and Daniel Cleary for Boris Mironov, Dean McAmmond and Jonas Elofsson, March 20, 1999.
First Game as an Oiler: March 20, 1999 *First Assist as an Oiler:* April 12, 1999
First Goal as an Oiler: March 28, 1999 *First Penalty as an Oiler:* April 1, 1999
Where He Went: Traded to Montreal for Sergei Zholtok, December 18, 2000.

Season	GP	G	A	Pts	Shots	S%	GW	GT	PP	SH	P/M	PIM
1998-99	13	1	1	2	13	7.7	0	0	0	0	-3	4
Playoffs	*4*	*0*	*0*	*0*	*1*	*0.0*	*0*	*0*	*0*	*0*	*-2*	*4*
1999-00	40	3	2	5	32	9.4	0	0	0	0	-6	18
Playoffs	*3*	*0*	*0*	*0*	*1*	*0.0*	*0*	*0*	*0*	*0*	*0*	*0*
2000-01	34	5	2	7	28	17.9	0	0	1	0	-7	17
2 years	87	9	5	14	73	12.3	0	0	1	0	-16	39
Playoffs	*3*	*0*	*0*	*0*	*1*	*0.0*	*0*	*0*	*0*	*0*	*0*	*0*

KLIMA, PETR SWEATER # 85 RIGHT/LEFT WING SR
Born: Chomutov, Czechoslovakia December 23, 1964 6'0"-190
Last Amateur Club: Dukla Jihlava (Czech)
How the Oilers Got Him: Detroit's 5th choice, 86th overall in the 1983 draft. Traded to the Oilers by Detroit, with Joe Murphy, Adam Graves and Jeff Sharples for Jimmy Carson, Kevin McClelland, and the Oilers 5th round choice (later acquired by Montreal in exchange for Rick Green; the Canadiens chose Brad Layzell) in the 1991 draft, November 2, 1989.
First Game as an Oiler: November 3, 1989 *First Assist as an Oiler*: November 3, 1989
First Goal as an Oiler: November 27, 1989 *First Penalty as an Oiler:* November 3, 1989
Where He Went: Traded to Tampa Bay for the Lightnings' 3rd round choice (Brad Symes) in the 1994 draft, June 16, 1993. Signed as a free agent by the Oilers, February 26, 1997. Signed as a free agent by Detroit, January 11, 1999.

Season	GP	G	A	Pts	Shots	S%	GW	GT	PP	SH	P/M	PIM
1989-90	63	25	28	53	149	16.8	3	0	7	0	-1	66
Playoffs	*21*	*5*	*0*	*5*	*25*	*20.0*	*1*	*1*	*1*	*0*	*-2*	*8*
1990-91	70	40	28	68	204	19.6	5	0	7	1	24	113
Playoffs	*18*	*7*	*6*	*13*	*51*	*13.7*	*3*	*1*	*1*	*0*	*-1*	*16*
1991-92	57	21	13	34	107	19.6	0	0	5	0	-18	52
Playoffs	*15*	*1*	*4*	*5*	*22*	*4.5*	*0*	*0*	*0*	*0*	*-1*	*8*
1992-93	68	32	16	48	175	18.3	2	0	13	0	-15	100
1996-97	16	1	5	6	22	4.5	0	0	0	0	-1	6
Playoffs	*6*	*0*	*0*	*0*	*2*	*0.0*	*0*	*0*	*0*	*0*	*0*	*4*
5 years	274	119	90	209	657	18.1	10	0	32	1	-11	337
Playoffs	*60*	*13*	*10*	*23*	*100*	*13.0*	*4*	*2*	*2*	*0*	*-4*	*36*

KOVALENKO, ANDREI SWEATER # 51 RIGHT WING SL
Born: Balakovo, USSR June 7, 1970 5'10"-215
Last Amateur Club: CSKA Moscow (CIS)
How the Oilers Got Him: Quebec's 6th choice, 148th overall in the 1990 draft. Traded to the Oilers by the Montreal Canadiens for Scott Thornton, September 6, 1996.

First Game as an Oiler: October 4, 1996
First Assist as an Oiler: October 8, 1996
First Goal as an Oiler: October 14, 1996
First Penalty as an Oiler: October 4, 1996
Where He Went: Traded to Philadelphia for Alexandre Daigle, who was then traded to Tampa Bay for Alex Selivanov, January 29, 1999.

Season	*GP*	*G*	*A*	*Pts*	*Shots*	*S%*	*GW*	*GT*	*PP*	*SH*	*P/M*	*PIM*
1996-97	74	32	27	59	163	19.6	2	0	14	0	-5	81
Playoffs	*12*	*4*	*3*	*7*	*35*	*11.4*	*0*	*0*	*3*	*0*	*1*	*6*
1997-98	59	6	17	23	89	6.7	2	1	1	0	-14	28
Playoffs	*1*	*0*	*0*	*0*	*2*	*0.0*	*0*	*0*	*0*	*0*	*0*	*2*
1998-99	43	13	14	27	75	17.3	3	1	2	0	-4	30
3 years	176	51	58	109	327	15.6	7	2	17	0	-23	139
Playoffs	*13*	*4*	*3*	*7*	*37*	*10.8*	*0*	*0*	*3*	*0*	*1*	*8*

KRAVCHUK, IGOR SWEATER # 21 DEFENSE SL
Born: Ufa, USSR September 13, 1966 6'1"-200
Last Amateur Club: CSKA Moscow (CIS)
How the Oilers Got Him: Chicago's 5th choice, 71st overall in the 1991 draft. Traded to the Oilers from the Black Hawks with Dean McAmmond for Joe Murphy, February 24, 1993.
First Game as an Oiler: February 27, 1993
First Assist as an Oiler: February 28, 1993
First Goal as an Oiler: March 4, 1993
First Penalty as an Oiler: March 27, 1993
Where He Went: Traded to St. Louis with Ken Sutton for Donald Dufresne and Jeff Norton, January 4, 1996.

Season	*GP*	*G*	*A*	*Pts*	*Shots*	*S%*	*GW*	*GT*	*PP*	*SH*	*P/M*	*PIM*
1992-93	17	4	8	12	42	9.5	0	0	1	0	-8	2
1993-94	81	12	38	50	197	6.1	2	0	5	0	-12	16
1994-95	36	7	11	18	93	7.5	0	0	3	1	-15	29
1995-96	26	4	4	8	59	6.8	0	0	3	0	-13	10
4 years	160	27	61	88	391	6.9	2	0	12	1	-48	57

KRUSHELNYSKI, MICHAEL SWEATER # 26 CENTER SL
Born: Montreal, Quebec April 27, 1960 6'2"-200
Last Amateur Club: Montreal Juniors (QMJHL)
How the Oilers Got Him: Boston's 7th choice, 120th overall in the 1979 draft. Traded by the Bruins to the Oilers for Ken Linseman, June 21, 1984.
First Game as an Oiler: October 11, 1984
First Assist as an Oiler: October 12, 1984
First Goal as an Oiler: October 14, 1984
First Penalty as an Oiler: October 11, 1984
Where He Went: Traded to Los Angeles with Wayne Gretzky, and Marty McSorley for Jimmy Carson, Martin Gelinas, the Kings' 1st round choice (later acquired by New Jersey; the Devils chose Jason Miller) in the 1989 draft, 1st round choice in the 1991 draft (Martin Rucinsky), 1st round choice in the 1993 draft (Nick Stajduhar) and cash, August 9, 1988.

Season	*GP*	*G*	*A*	*Pts*	*Shots*	*S%*	*GW*	*GT*	*PP*	*SH*	*P/M*	*PIM*
1984-85	80	43	45	88	187	23.0	4	1	13	0	56	60
Playoffs	*18*	*5*	*8*	*13*	*37*	*13.5*	*2*	*0*	*2*	*0*	*9*	*22*
1985-86	54	16	24	40	98	16.3	1	1	3	0	11	22
Playoffs	*10*	*4*	*5*	*9*	*15*	*26.7*	*2*	*0*	*1*	*0*	*3*	*16*
1986-87	80	16	35	51	89	18.0	2	0	4	1	26	67
1987-88	76	20	27	47	124	16.1	0	0	4	0	26	64
Playoffs	*19*	*4*	*6*	*10*	*18*	*22.2*	*0*	*0*	*0*	*0*	*4*	*12*
4 years:	290	95	131	226	498	19.1	7	2	24	1	119	213
Playoffs	*68*	*16*	*23*	*39*	*99*	*16.2*	*5*	*0*	*3*	*0*	*20*	*68*

KULAK, STUART SWEATER # 8 RIGHT WING SR
Born: Edmonton, Alberta March 10, 1963 5'10"-180
Last Amateur Club: Victoria Cougars (WHL)
How the Oilers Got Him: Vancouver's 5th choice, 115th overall in the 1981 draft. Sold to the Oilers by the Canucks, December 11, 1986.
First Game as an Oiler: December 12, 1986
First Assist as an Oiler: January 23, 1987
First Goal as an Oiler: December 20, 1987
First Penalty as an Oiler: December 14, 1986
Where He Went: Acquired by the Rangers to complete the Reijo Ruotsalainen deal, March 10, 1987.

Season	*GP*	*G*	*A*	*Pts*	*Shots*	*S%*	*GW*	*GT*	*PP*	*SH*	*P/M*	*PIM*
1986-87	23	3	1	4	30	10.0	1	0	0	0	3	41

KURRI, JARI SWEATER # 17 RIGHT WING SR

Born: Helsinki, Finland May 18, 1960 6'1"-190

Last Amateur Club: Jokerit (Fin)

How the Oilers Got Him: Edmonton's 3rd choice, 69th overall in the 1980 draft.

First Game as an Oiler: October 10, 1980 *First Assist as an Oiler:* October 10, 1980

First Goal as an Oiler: October 18, 1980 *First Penalty as an Oiler:* November 5, 1980

Where He Went: Traded to Philadelphia with Dave Brown and Corey Foster for Craig Berube, Craig Fisher, and Scott Mellanby, May 30, 1991.

Season	GP	G	A	Pts	Shots	S%	GW	GT	PP	SH	P/M	PIM
1980-81	75	32	43	75	202	15.8	1	2	9	0	26	40
Playoffs	*9*	*5*	*7*	*12*			*0*	*0*	*0*	*0*		*4*
1981-82	71	32	54	86	211	15.2	5	1	6	1	38	32
Playoffs	*5*	*2*	*5*	*7*			*0*	*0*	*0*	*0*		*10*
1982-83	80	45	59	104	218	20.6	3	1	10	1	47	22
Playoffs	*16*	*8*	*15*	*23*	*31*	*25.8*	*0*	*0*	*2*	*2*	*15*	*8*
1983-84	64	52	61	113	194	26.8	4	1	10	5	38	14
Playoffs	*19*	*14*	*14*	*28*	*60*	*23.3*	*0*	*0*	*4*	*0*	*9*	*13*
1984-85	73	71	64	135	261	27.2	13	3	14	3	77	30
Playoffs	*18*	*19*	*12*	*31*	*89*	*21.3*	*2*	*0*	*1*	*2*	*24*	*6*
1985-86	78	68	63	131	236	28.8	9	1	16	6	45	22
Playoffs	*10*	*2*	*10*	*12*	*25*	*8.0*	*0*	*0*	*0*	*1*	*1*	*4*
1986-87	79	54	54	108	211	25.6	10	0	12	5	35	41
Playoffs	*21*	*15*	*10*	*25*	*52*	*28.8*	*5*	*1*	*4*	*1*	*11*	*20*
1987-88	80	43	53	96	207	20.8	5	1	10	3	25	30
Playoffs	*19*	*14*	*17*	*31*	*57*	*24.6*	*3*	*1*	*5*	*0*	*15*	*12*
1988-89	76	44	58	102	214	20.6	8	1	10	5	19	69
Playoffs	*7*	*3*	*5*	*8*	*17*	*17.6*	*0*	*0*	*0*	*1*	*-2*	*6*
1989-90	78	33	60	93	201	16.4	2	1	10	2	18	48
Playoffs	*22*	*10*	*15*	*25*	*58*	*17.2*	*3*	*0*	*6*	*0*	*13*	*18*
10 years	754	474	569	1043	2155	22.0	60	12	107	31	368	348
Playoffs	*146*	*92*	*110*	*202*			*13*	*2*	*22*	*7*		*101*

LACOMBE, NORMAND SWEATER # 19 RIGHT WING SR

Born: Pierrefonds, Quebec October 18, 1964 5'11"-205

Last Amateur Club: New Hampshire Wildcats (ECAC)

How the Oilers Got Him: Buffalo's 2nd choice, 10th overall in the 1983 draft. Traded to the Oilers by Buffalo with Wayne Van Dorp and future considerations for Mark Napier and Lee Fogolin, March 6, 1987.

First Game as an Oiler: March 23, 1987 *First Assist as an Oiler:* November 10, 1987

First Goal as an Oiler: October 11, 1987 *First Penalty as an Oiler:* March 23, 1987

Where He Went: Traded to Philadelphia for future considerations, January 5, 1990.

Season	GP	G	A	Pts	Shots	S%	GW	GT	PP	SH	P/M	PIM
1986-87	1	0	0	0	0	0.0	0	0	0	0	-1	2
1987-88	53	8	9	17	44	18.2	2	0	1	0	-3	36
Playoffs	*19*	*3*	*0*	*3*	*17*	*17.6*	*1*	*0*	*0*	*0*	*0*	*28*
1988-89	64	17	11	28	71	23.9	1	0	2	0	2	57
Playoffs	*7*	*2*	*1*	*3*	*10*	*20.0*	*0*	*0*	*0*	*0*	*3*	*21*
1989-90	15	5	2	7	15	33.3	0	0	0	0	4	21
4 years	133	30	22	52	130	23.1	3	0	3	0	2	116
Playoffs	*26*	*5*	*1*	*6*	*27*	*18.5*	*1*	*0*	*0*	*0*	*3*	*49*

LACOUTURE, DANIEL SCOTT SWEATER # 15, #33 LEFT WING SL

Born: Hyannis, Massachusetts April 18, 1977 6'3"-210

Last Amateur Club: Boston University Terriers (H.E.)

How the Oilers Got Him: Islanders' 2nd choice, 29th overall in the 1996 draft. Obtained from the Islanders for Mariusz Czerkawski, August 25, 1997.

First Game as an Oiler: February 24, 1999 *First Assist as an Oiler:* October 10, 2000

First Goal as an Oiler: October 17, 2000 *First Penalty as an Oiler:* April 1, 2000

Where He Went: Traded to the Pittsburgh Penguins for Sven Butenschon, March 13, 2001.

Season	GP	G	A	Pts	Shots	S%	GW	GT	PP	SH	P/M	PIM
1998-99	3	0	0	0	0	0.0	0	0	0	0	1	0
1999-00	5	0	0	0	2	0.0	0	0	0	0	0	10
Playoffs	*1*	*0*	*0*	*0*	*0*	*0.0*	*0*	*0*	*0*	*0*	*0*	*0*

Season	GP	G	A	Pts	Shots	S%	GW	GT	PP	SH	P/M	PIM
2000-01	37	2	4	6	22	9.1	1	0	0	0	-2	29
2 years	45	2	4	6	24	8.3	1	0	0	0	-1	39
Playoffs	*1*	*0*	*0*	*0*	*0*	*0.0*	*0*	*0*	*0*	*0*	*0*	*0*

LACROIX, DANIEL SWEATER # 21 LEFT WING SL

Born: Montreal, Quebec March 11, 1969 6'2"-205

Last Amateur Club: Granby Bisons (QMJHL)

How the Oilers Got Him: Rangers' 2nd choice, 31st overall in the 1987 draft. Traded to the Oilers from the Flyers for Valeri Zelepukin, October 5th 1998.

First Game as an Oiler: October 13, 1998

First Assist as an Oiler: None Recorded

First Goal as an Oiler: None Recorded

First Penalty as an Oiler: March 10, 1999

Where He Went: Signed as a free agent by the Islanders, August 11, 1999.

Season	GP	G	A	Pts	Shots	S%	GW	GT	PP	SH	P/M	PIM
1998-99	4	0	0	0	5	0.0	0	0	0	0	0	13

LAFLAMME, CHRISTIAN SWEATER # 24 DEFENSE SR

Born: St. Charles, Quebec March 11, 1969 6'1"-202

Last Amateur Club: Beauport Harfangs (QMJHL)

How the Oilers Got Him: Chicago's 2nd choice, 45th overall in the 1995 draft. Traded to the Oilers by Chicago with Ethan Moreau, Chad Kilger and Daniel Cleary for Boris Mironov, Dean McAmmond and Jonas Elofsson, March 20, 1999.

First Game as an Oiler: March 22, 1999

First Assist as an Oiler: April 7, 1999

First Goal as an Oiler: None Recorded

First Penalty as an Oiler: April 27, 1999

Where He Went: Traded to Montreal with Matthieu Descoteaux for Igor Ulanov and Alain Nasreddine, March 9, 2000.

Season	GP	G	A	Pts	Shots	S%	GW	GT	PP	SH	P/M	PIM
1998-99	11	0	1	1	15	0.0	0	0	0	0	-3	0
1999-00	50	0	5	5	18	0.0	0	0	0	0	-4	32
2 years	61	0	6	6	33	0.0	0	0	0	0	-7	32

LAFORGE, MARC SWEATER # 20 LEFT WING SL

Born: Sudbury, Ontario January 3, 1968 6'2"-210

Last Amateur Club: Sudbury Wolves (OHL)

How the Oilers Got Him: Hartford's 2nd choice, 32nd overall in the 1986 draft. Traded to the Oilers from the Whalers for the rights to Cam Brauer, March 6th 1990.

First Game as an Oiler: October 24, 1993

First Assist as an Oiler: None Recorded

First Goal as an Oiler: None Recorded

First Penalty as an Oiler: October 24, 1993

Where He Went: Traded to the Islanders for Brent Grieve, December 15, 1993.

Season	GP	G	A	Pts	Shots	S%	GW	GT	PP	SH	P/M	PIM
1993-94	5	0	0	0	0	0.0	0	0	0	0	-2	21

LAMB, MARK SWEATER # 18, # 7 CENTER SL

Born: Ponteix, Saskatchewan August 3, 1964 5'9"-180

Last Amateur Club: Medicine Hat Tigers (WHL)

How the Oilers Got Him: Calgary's 5th choice, 72nd overall in the 1982 draft. Claimed from Calgary by the Oilers in the Waiver Draft, October 5, 1987.

First Game as an Oiler: October 16, 1987

First Assist as an Oiler: February 21, 1989

First Goal as an Oiler: January 18, 1989

First Penalty as an Oiler: January 21, 1989

Where He Went: Claimed by Ottawa in the Expansion Draft, June 18, 1992.

Season	GP	G	A	Pts	Shots	S%	GW	GT	PP	SH	P/M	PIM
1987-88	2	0	0	0	0	0.0	0	0	0	0	0	0
1988-89	20	2	8	10	20	10.0	0	0	1	0	4	14
Playoffs	*6*	*0*	*2*	*2*	*8*	*0.0*	*0*	*0*	*0*	*0*	*1*	*8*
1989-90	58	12	16	28	81	14.8	2	0	2	0	10	42
Playoffs	*22*	*6*	*11*	*17*	*34*	*17.6*	*2*	*1*	*1*	*0*	*12*	*2*
1990-91	37	4	8	12	41	9.8	1	0	1	0	-2	25
Playoffs	*15*	*0*	*5*	*5*	*14*	*0.0*	*0*	*0*	*0*	*0*	*-4*	*20*
1991-92	59	6	22	28	61	9.8	1	0	2	0	4	46
Playoffs	*16*	*1*	*1*	*2*	*13*	*7.7*	*0*	*0*	*0*	*0*	*-5*	*10*
5 years	176	24	54	78	203	11.8	4	0	6	0	16	127
Playoffs	*61*	*7*	*19*	*26*	*69*	*10.1*	*2*	*1*	*1*	*0*	*4*	*40*

Laraque, Georges Sweater # 27 Right Wing SR
Born: Montreal, Quebec December 7, 1976 6'3"-240
Last Amateur Club: Granby Bisons (QMJHL)
How the Oilers Got Him: Oilers' 2nd choice, 31st overall in the 1995 draft.
First Game as an Oiler: November 15, 1997
First Assist as an Oiler: January 17, 1999
First Goal as an Oiler: January 7, 1999
First Penalty as an Oiler: November 15, 1997

Season	*GP*	*G*	*A*	*Pts*	*Shots*	*S%*	*GW*	*GT*	*PP*	*SH*	*P/M*	*PIM*
1997-98	11	0	0	0	4	0.0	0	0	0	0	-4	59
1998-99	39	3	2	5	17	17.6	0	0	0	0	-1	57
Playoffs	*4*	*0*	*0*	*0*	*1*	*0.0*	*0*	*0*	*0*	*0*	*-2*	*2*
1999-00	76	8	8	16	56	14.3	0	0	0	0	5	123
Playoffs	*5*	*0*	*1*	*1*	*5*	*0.0*	*0*	*0*	*0*	*0*	*-1*	*6*
2000-01	82	13	16	29	73	17.8	1	1	1	0	5	148
Playoffs	*6*	*1*	*1*	*2*	*5*	*20.1*	*0*	*0*	*0*	*0*	*2*	*8*
4 years	208	24	26	50	150	16.0	1	1	1	0	5	387
Playoffs	*15*	*1*	*2*	*3*	*11*	*9.1*	*0*	*0*	*0*	*0*	*-1*	*16*

Lariviere, Garry Joseph Sweater # 6 Defense SR
Born: St. Catherines, Ontario December 6, 1954 6'0"-190
Last Amateur Club: St. Catherines Black Hawks (OHL)
How the Oilers Got Him: Buffalo Sabres' 5th choice, 83rd overall in the 1974 draft. Traded by the Vancouver Canucks to the Oilers with the rights to Lars Gunnar Pettersson for Blair MacDonald and the rights to Ken Berry, March 10, 1981.
First Game as an Oiler: March 15, 1981
First Assist as an Oiler: March 16, 1981
First Goal as an Oiler: March 17, 1982
First Penalty as an Oiler: March 25, 1981
Where He Went: Retired.

Season	*GP*	*G*	*A*	*Pts*	*Shots*	*S%*	*GW*	*GT*	*PP*	*SH*	*P/M*	*PIM*
1980-81	13	0	2	2	8	0.0	0	0	0	0	9	6
Playoffs	*9*	*0*	*3*	*3*			*0*	*0*	*0*	*0*		*8*
1981-82	62	1	21	22	46	2.2	0	0	0	0	27	41
Playoffs	*4*	*0*	*1*	*1*			*0*	*0*	*0*	*0*		*0*
1982-83	17	0	2	2	15	0.0	0	0	0	0	13	14
Playoffs	*1*	*0*	*1*	*1*	*0*	*0.0*	*0*	*0*	*0*	*0*	*2*	*0*
3 years	92	1	25	26	69	1.4	0	0	0	0	49	61
Playoffs	*14*	*0*	*5*	*5*			*0*	*0*	*0*	*0*		*8*

Larson, Reed David Sweater # 27 Defense SR
Born: Minneapolis, Minnesota July 30, 1956 6'0"-195
Last Amateur Club: University of Minnesota Gophers (WCHA)
How the Oilers Got Him: Detroit's 2nd choice, 22nd overall in the 1976 draft. Signed as a free agent by the Oilers September 30, 1988.
First Game as an Oiler: October 14, 1988
First Assist as an Oiler: November 12, 1988
First Goal as an Oiler: October 19, 1988
First Penalty as an Oiler: October 14, 1988
Where He Went: Traded to the Islanders for future considerations, December 6, 1988.

Season	*GP*	*G*	*A*	*Pts*	*Shots*	*S%*	*GW*	*GT*	*PP*	*SH*	*P/M*	*PIM*
1988-89	10	2	7	9	19	10.5	0	0	0	1	1	15

LeBlanc, Jean Glenn Sweater # 8 Left Wing SL
Born: Campbelltown, New Brunswick January 21, 1964 6'1"-195
Last Amateur Club: University of New Brunswick Red Devils (AUAA)
How the Oilers Got Him: Traded to the Oilers, by Vancouver with the Canucks' 5th round choice (Peter White) in the 1989 draft for Doug Smith and Greg Adams, March 7, 1989.
First Game as an Oiler: March 16, 1989
First Assist as an Oiler: None Recorded
First Goal as an Oiler: March 23, 1989
First Penalty as an Oiler: None Recorded
Where He Went: Traded to Winnipeg with the Oilers' 10th round choice (Teemu Numminen) in the 1992 draft for the Jets' 5th round choice (Ryan Haggerty) in the 1991 draft, June 12, 1991.

Season	*GP*	*G*	*A*	*Pts*	*Shots*	*S%*	*GW*	*GT*	*PP*	*SH*	*P/M*	*PIM*
1988-89	2	1	0	1	5	20.0	0	0	0	0	0	0
Playoffs	*1*	*0*	*0*	*0*	*2*	*0.0*	*0*	*0*	*0*	*0*	*0*	*0*

LEHMANN, TOMMY SWEATER # 23 CENTER SL
Born: Solna, Sweden February 3, 1964 6'1"-185
Last Amateur Club: AIK Solna (Swe)
How the Oilers Got Him: Boston's 11th choice, 228th overall in the 1982 draft. Traded to the Oilers by the Bruins for Edmonton's 3rd choice (Wes Walz) in the 1989 draft, June 17, 1989.
First Game as an Oiler: October 18, 1989
First Assist as an Oiler: None Recorded
First Goal as an Oiler: None Recorded
First Penalty as an Oiler: None Recorded
Where He Went: Retired.

Season	GP	G	A	Pts	Shots	S%	GW	GT	PP	SH	P/M	PIM
1989-90	1	0	0	0	0	0.0	0	0	0	0	1	0

LEMAY, MAURICE (MOE) SWEATER # 23 LEFT WING SL
Born: Saskatoon, Saskatchewan February 18, 1962 5'11"-185
Last Amateur Club: Ottawa 67's (OHL)
How the Oilers Got Him: Vancouver's 4th choice, 105th overall in the 1981 draft. Traded by the Canucks to the Oilers for Raimo Summanen, March 10, 1987.
First Game as an Oiler: March 14, 1987
First Assist as an Oiler: March 14, 1987
First Goal as an Oiler: April 2, 1987
First Penalty as an Oiler: March 17, 1987
Where He Went: Traded to the Bruins for Alan May, March 8, 1988.

Season	GP	G	A	Pts	Shots	S%	GW	GT	PP	SH	P/M	PIM
1986-87	10	1	2	3	7	14.3	0	0	0	0	2	36
Playoffs	*9*	*2*	*1*	*3*	*7*	*28.6*	*1*	*0*	*0*	*0*	*1*	*11*
1987-88	4	0	0	0	5	0.0	0	0	0	0	-1	2
2 years	14	1	2	3	12	8.3	0	0	0	0	1	38

LEROUX, FRANCOIS SWEATER # 35 DEFENSE SL
Born: Ste. Adele, Quebec April 18, 1970 6'5"-220
Last Amateur Club: St. Jean Beavers (QMJHL)
How the Oilers Got Him: Edmonton's 1st choice, 19th overall in the 1988 draft.
First Game as an Oiler: January 21, 1989
First Assist as an Oiler: October 11, 1989
First Goal as an Oiler: None Recorded
First Penalty as an Oiler: March 24, 1992
Where He Went: Claimed on waivers by Ottawa, October 6, 1993.

Season	GP	G	A	Pts	Shots	S%	GW	GT	PP	SH	P/M	PIM
1988-89	2	0	0	0	0	0.0	0	0	0	0	1	0
1989-90	3	0	1	1	0	0.0	0	0	0	0	-2	0
1990-91	1	0	2	2	1	0.0	0	0	0	0	1	0
1991-92	4	0	0	0	0	0.0	0	0	0	0	-1	7
1992-93	1	0	0	0	0	0.0	0	0	0	0	0	4
5 years	11	0	3	3	1	0.0	0	0	0	0	-1	11

LINDGREN, MATS SWEATER # 14 CENTER SL
Born: Skelleftea, Sweden October 1, 1974 6'2"-200
Last Amateur Club: Farjestads BK (Swe)
How the Oilers Got Him: Winnipeg's 1st choice, 15th overall in the 1993 draft. Traded to the Oilers from the Winnipeg Jets with Boris Mironov, Winnipeg's 1st round choice in the 1994 draft (Jason Bonsignore), and the Florida Panthers' 4th round choice in the same draft, which had previously been acquired by the Jets (the Oilers selected Adam Copeland) for Dave Manson and the St. Louis Blues' 6th round choice, which had previously been acquired by Edmonton (Winnipeg selected Chris Kibermanis) in the 1994 draft, March 15, 1994.
First Game as an Oiler: November 3, 1996
First Assist as an Oiler: November 6, 1996
First Goal as an Oiler: November 3, 1996
First Penalty as an Oiler: January 11, 1997
Where He Went: Traded to the Islanders with an 8th round choice (Radek Martinek) in the 1999 draft for Tommy Salo, March 20, 1999.

Season	GP	G	A	Pts	Shots	S%	GW	GT	PP	SH	P/M	PIM
1996-97	69	11	14	25	71	15.5	1	0	2	3	-7	12
Playoffs	*12*	*0*	*4*	*4*	*22*	*0.0*	*0*	*0*	*0*	*0*	*-2*	*0*
1997-98	82	13	13	26	131	9.9	3	0	1	3	0	42
Playoffs	*12*	*1*	*1*	*2*	*16*	*6.3*	*0*	*0*	*0*	*0*	*0*	*10*
1998-99	48	5	12	17	53	9.4	0	0	0	1	4	22
3 years	199	29	39	68	255	11.4	4	0	3	7	-3	76
Playoffs	*24*	*1*	*5*	*6*	*38*	*2.6*	*0*	*0*	*0*	*0*	*-2*	*10*

LINDQUIST, FREDRIK SWEATER # 7 RIGHT WING SL
Born: Sodertalje, Sweden June 21, 1973 6'0"-190
Last Amateur Club: Djurgarden (Swe)
How the Oilers Got Him: New Jersey's 4th choice, 55th overall in the 1991 draft. Traded to the Oilers from the Devils with New Jersey's fifth (Oleg Smirnov) and sixth (Trevor Ettinger) choices in the 1998 draft for Edmonton's second choice in the third round (Brian Gionta) in the 1998 draft, June 27, 1998.
First Game as an Oiler: October 10, 1998
First Assist as an Oiler: None Recorded
First Goal as an Oiler: None Recorded
First Penalty as an Oiler: December 9, 1998

Season	GP	G	A	Pts	Shots	S%	GW	GT	PP	SH	P/M	PIM
1998-99	8	0	0	0	6	0.0	0	0	0	0	-2	2

LINDSTROM, BO MORGAN WILLY Sweater # 19 Right Wing SL
Born: Grunns, Sweden May 5, 1951 6'0"-180
Last Amateur Club: Swedish National Team
How the Oilers Got Him: Traded by the Winnipeg Jets to the Oilers for Laurie Boschman, March 8, 1983.
First Game as an Oiler: March 11, 1983
First Assist as an Oiler: March 13, 1983
First Goal as an Oiler: March 13, 1983
First Penalty as an Oiler: March 13, 1983
Where He Went: Claimed by Pittsburgh in the Waiver Draft, October 7, 1985.

Season	GP	G	A	Pts	Shots	S%	GW	GT	PP	SH	P/M	PIM
1982-83	10	6	5	11	21	28.6	0	0	0	0	5	2
Playoffs	*16*	*2*	*11*	*13*	*31*	*6.5*	*0*	*0*	*1*	*0*	*12*	*4*
1983-84	73	22	16	38	116	19.0	3	1	2	0	17	38
Playoffs	*19*	*5*	*5*	*10*	*30*	*16.7*	*0*	*0*	*3*	*0*	*7*	*10*
1984-85	80	12	20	32	98	12.2	1	0	1	0	5	18
Playoffs	*18*	*5*	*1*	*6*	*20*	*25.0*	*1*	*0*	*0*	*0*	*4*	*8*
3 years	163	40	41	81	235	17.0	4	1	3	0	27	58
Playoffs	*53*	*12*	*17*	*29*	*81*	*14.8*	*1*	*0*	*4*	*0*	*23*	*22*

LINSEMAN, KEN SWEATER # 13 CENTER SL
Born: Kingston, Ontario August 11, 1958 5'11"-175
Last Amateur Club: Kingston Canadians (OHL)
How the Oilers Got Him: Philadelphia's 2nd choice, 7th overall in 1978 draft. Traded by Hartford to the Oilers with Don Nachbaur for Risto Siltanen and Brent Loney, August 19, 1982.
First Game as an Oiler: October 5, 1982
First Assist as an Oiler: October 16, 1982
First Goal as an Oiler: October 5, 1982
First Penalty as an Oiler: October 5, 1982
Where He Went: Traded to Boston for Mike Krushelnyski, June 21, 1984. Signed as a free agent by the Oilers, August 31, 1990. Sold to Toronto for cash, October 7, 1991.

Season	GP	G	A	Pts	Shots	S%	GW	GT	PP	SH	P/M	PIM
1982-83	72	33	42	75	141	23.4	3	0	10	4	16	181
Playoffs	*16*	*6*	*8*	*14*	*31*	*19.4*	*1*	*0*	*1*	*0*	*7*	*22*
1983-84	72	18	49	67	105	17.1	2	0	5	1	30	119
Playoffs	*19*	*10*	*4*	*14*	*44*	*22.7*	*4*	*0*	*3*	*1*	*5*	*65*
1990-91	56	7	29	36	49	14.3	0	0	2	1	15	94
Playoffs	*2*	*0*	*1*	*1*	*1*	*0.0*	*0*	*0*	*0*	*0*	*1*	*0*
3 years	200	58	120	178	295	19.7	5	0	17	6	61	394
Playoffs	*37*	*16*	*13*	*29*	*76*	*21.1*	*5*	*0*	*4*	*1*	*13*	*87*

LOPRESTI, PETER JON SWEATER # 1 GOALTENDER CL
Born: Virginia, Minnesota May 23, 1954 6'1"-195
Last Amateur Club: Denver University Pioneers (WCHA)
How the Oilers Got Him: Minnesota's 3rd choice, 42nd overall in the 1974 draft. Claimed from the North Stars by Edmonton in the Expansion Draft, June 13, 1979.
First Game as an Oiler: October 10, 1980
First Assist as an Oiler: None Recorded
First Goal as an Oiler: None Recorded
First Penalty as an Oiler: None Recorded
Where He Went: Retired.

Season	GP	Min	GA	W	L	T	Ave	SA	S%	SO	EN	PIM	Ast.
1980-81	2	105	8	0	1	0	4.57	46	0.826	0	1	0	0

LOW, RONALD ALBERT SWEATER # 30 GOALTENDER CL
Born: Birtle, Manitoba June 21, 1950 6'1"-205
Last Amateur Club: Jacksonville Rockets (EHL)
How the Oilers Got Him: Toronto's 8th choice, 103rd overall in 1970 draft. Traded by Quebec to the Oilers for Ron Chipperfield, March 11, 1980.
First Game as an Oiler: March 12, 1980
First Assist as an Oiler: October 19, 1980
First Goal as an Oiler: None Recorded
First Penalty as an Oiler: March 3, 1982
Where He Went: Traded to New Jersey with Jim McTaggert for Lindsay Middlebrook and Paul Miller, February 19, 1983.

Season	*GP*	*Min*	*GA*	*W*	*L*	*T*	*Ave*	*SA*	*S%*	*SO*	*EN*	*PIM*	*Ast.*
1979-80	11	650	37	8	2	1	3.42	804	0.891	0	0	0	1
Playoffs	*3*	*212*	*12*	*0*	*3*		*3.40*	*127*	*0.906*	*0*	*0*	*0*	*0*
1980-81	24	1260	93	5	13	3	4.43	661	0.859	0	2	0	3
1981-82	29	1556	100	17	7	1	3.86	790	0.873	0	2	2	0
1982-83	3	104	10	0	1	0	5.78	55	0.815	0	1	0	0
4 years	67	3570	240	30	23	5	4.03	2310	0.896	0	5	2	4
Playoffs	*3*	*212*	*12*	*0*	*3*		*3.40*	*127*	*0.906*	*0*	*0*	*0*	*0*

LOWE, KEVIN HUGH SWEATER # 4 DEFENSE SL
Born: Lachute, Quebec April 15, 1959 6'2"-200
Last Amateur Club: Quebec Remparts (QMJHL)
How the Oilers Got Him: Oilers' 1st choice, 21st overall in the 1979 draft. Oilers' first ever draft pick.
First Game as an Oiler: October 10, 1979
First Assist as an Oiler: November 30, 1979
First Goal as an Oiler: October 10, 1979
First Penalty as an Oiler: October 10, 1979
Where He Went: Traded to the Rangers for Roman Oksiuta and the Rangers' 3rd choice (Alexander Kerch) in the 1993 draft, December 11, 1992. Signed as a free agent by the Oilers, September 28, 1996. Retired

Season	*GP*	*G*	*A*	*Pts*	*Shots*	*S%*	*GW*	*GT*	*PP*	*SH*	*P/M*	*PIM*
1979-80	64	2	19	21	86	2.3	0	0	2	0	1	70
Playoffs	*3*	*0*	*1*	*1*			*0*	*0*	*0*	*0*		*0*
1980-81	79	10	24	34	115	8.7	2	0	4	0	-10	94
Playoffs	*9*	*0*	*2*	*2*			*0*	*0*	*0*	*0*		*11*
1981-82	80	9	31	40	110	8.2	2	0	1	1	46	63
Playoffs	*5*	*0*	*3*	*3*			*0*	*0*	*0*	*0*		*0*
1982-83	80	6	34	40	92	6.5	0	0	1	0	39	43
Playoffs	*16*	*1*	*8*	*9*	*19*	*5.3*	*0*	*0*	*0*	*0*	*8*	*10*
1983-84	80	4	42	46	81	4.9	1	0	1	0	37	59
Playoffs	*19*	*3*	*7*	*10*	*19*	*15.8*	*0*	*0*	*0*	*0*	*13*	*16*
1984-85	80	4	21	25	83	4.8	1	0	1	0	11	104
Playoffs	*16*	*0*	*5*	*5*	*20*	*0.0*	*0*	*0*	*0*	*0*	*5*	*8*
1985-86	74	2	16	18	57	3.5	0	0	0	0	24	90
Playoffs	*10*	*1*	*3*	*4*	*16*	*6.3*	*0*	*0*	*0*	*0*	*6*	*15*
1986-87	77	8	29	37	99	8.1	1	0	2	2	41	94
Playoffs	*21*	*2*	*4*	*6*	*21*	*9.5*	*1*	*0*	*0*	*2*	*8*	*22*
1987-88	70	9	15	24	82	11.0	2	0	2	1	18	89
Playoffs	*19*	*0*	*2*	*2*	*9*	*0.0*	*0*	*0*	*0*	*0*	*2*	*26*
1988-89	76	7	18	25	85	8.2	1	0	0	0	26	98
Playoffs	*7*	*1*	*2*	*3*	*11*	*9.1*	*0*	*0*	*0*	*0*	*-1*	*4*
1989-90	78	7	26	33	74	9.4	0	0	2	1	18	140
Playoffs	*20*	*0*	*2*	*2*	*11*	*0.0*	*0*	*0*	*0*	*0*	*3*	*10*
1990-91	73	3	13	16	51	5.9	0	0	0	0	-9	113
Playoffs	*14*	*1*	*1*	*2*	*5*	*20.0*	*0*	*0*	*0*	*0*	*-1*	*14*
1991-92	55	2	8	10	33	6.1	0	0	0	0	-4	107
Playoffs	*11*	*0*	*3*	*3*	*7*	*0.0*	*0*	*0*	*0*	*0*	*-2*	*16*
1996-97	64	1	13	14	46	2.2	0	0	0	0	-1	50
Playoffs	*1*	*0*	*0*	*0*	*0*	*0.0*	*0*	*0*	*0*	*0*	*-1*	*0*
1997-98	7	0	0	0	5	0.0	0	0	0	0	-3	22
Playoffs	*1*	*0*	*0*	*0*	*0*	*0.0*	*0*	*0*	*0*	*0*	*0*	*4*
15 years	1037	74	309	383	1099	6.7	10	0	16	5	234	1236
Playoffs	*172*	*9*	*43*	*52*			*1*	*0*	*0*	*2*		*156*

LUMLEY, DAVID SWEATER # 20, # 8 RIGHT WING SR
Born: Toronto, Ontario September 1, 1954 6'0"-185
Last Amateur Club: University of New Hampshire Wildcats (ECAC)

How the Oilers Got Him: Montreal's 17th choice, 199th overall in 1974 draft. Chosen from the Canadiens in the 1979 Expansion Draft, June 13, 1979.
First Game as an Oiler: October 10, 1979 *First Assist as an Oiler:* October 21, 1979
First Goal as an Oiler: October 26, 1979 *First Penalty as an Oiler:* October 10, 1979
Where He Went: Claimed by Hartford in the Waiver Draft, October 9, 1984. Reacquired by the Oilers on waivers, February 6, 1985.

Season	*GP*	*G*	*A*	*Pts*	*Shots*	*S%*	*GW*	*GT*	*PP*	*SH*	*P/M*	*PIM*
1979-80	80	20	38	58	145	13.8	6	0	1	0	15	138
Playoffs	*3*	*1*	*0*	*1*			*0*	*0*	*1*	*0*		*12*
1980-81	53	7	9	16	54	13.0	1	0	0	0	-15	74
Playoffs	*7*	*1*	*0*	*1*			*0*	*0*	*0*	*0*		*4*
1981-82	66	32	42	74	148	21.6	6	3	4	1	12	96
Playoffs	*5*	*2*	*1*	*3*			*0*	*0*	*0*	*0*		*21*
1982-83	72	13	24	37	96	13.5	1	0	2	0	19	158
Playoffs	*16*	*0*	*0*	*0*	*4*	*0.0*	*0*	*0*	*0*	*0*	*-1*	*19*
1983-84	56	6	15	21	44	13.6	0	1	0	0	14	68
Playoffs	*19*	*2*	*5*	*7*	*21*	*9.5*	*0*	*0*	*0*	*0*	*6*	*44*
1984-85	12	1	3	4	10	10.0	0	0	0	0	-1	13
Playoffs	*8*	*0*	*0*	*0*	*2*	*0.0*	*0*	*0*	*0*	*0*	*-5*	*29*
1985-86	46	11	9	20	33	33.3	1	0	1	0	13	35
Playoffs	*3*	*0*	*2*	*2*	*1*	*0.0*	*0*	*0*	*0*	*0*	*0*	*2*
1986-87	1	0	0	0	0	0.0	0	0	0	0	0	0
8 years	386	90	140	230	530	17.0	15	4	8	1	57	582
Playoffs	*61*	*6*	*8*	*14*			*0*	*0*	*1*	*1*		*131*

MacDonald, Blair Joseph

Sweater # 14 — Right Wing — SR

Born: Cornwall, Ontario November 17, 1953 5'10"-180
Last Amateur Club: Cornwall Royals (OHL)
How the Oilers Got Him: Los Angeles' 4th choice, 86th overall in 1973 draft. Signed to a WHA contract by the Oilers. Traded to Indianapolis of the WHA in the 1975-76 season. Reacquired by the Oilers in 1977-78 season.
First Game as an Oiler: October 10, 1979 *First Assist as an Oiler:* October 14, 1979
First Goal as an Oiler: October 13, 1979 *First Penalty as an Oiler:* November 24, 1979
Where He Went: Traded to Vancouver with the rights to Ken Berry for Garry Lariviere and the rights to Lars Gunnar Petterson, March 10, 1981.

Season	*GP*	*G*	*A*	*Pts*	*Shots*	*S%*	*GW*	*GT*	*PP*	*SH*	*P/M*	*PIM*
1979-80	80	46	48	94	266	17.3	6	1	13	2	1	6
Playoffs	*3*	*0*	*3*	*3*			*0*	*0*	*0*	*0*		*0*
1980-81	51	19	24	43	134	14.2	1	0	5	0	-8	27
2 years	131	65	72	137	400	16.3	7	1	18	2	-7	33
Playoffs	*3*	*0*	*3*	*3*			*0*	*0*	*0*	*0*		*0*

MacIver, Norm

Sweater # 36 — Defense — SL

Born: Thunder Bay, Ontario September 1, 1964 5'11"-180
Last Amateur Club: University of Minnesota-Duluth Bulldogs (WCHA)
How the Oilers Got Him: Traded to the Oilers from the Hartford Whalers for Jim Ennis, October 10, 1989.
First Game as an Oiler: October 28, 1989 *First Assist as an Oiler:* February 24, 1991
First Goal as an Oiler: March 24, 1991 *First Penalty as an Oiler:* February 22, 1991
Where He Went: Claimed by Ottawa in the Waiver Draft, October 4, 1992.

Season	*GP*	*G*	*A*	*Pts*	*Shots*	*S%*	*GW*	*GT*	*PP*	*SH*	*P/M*	*PIM*
1989-90	1	0	0	0	0	0.0	0	0	0	0	-1	0
1990-91	21	2	5	7	25	8.0	0	0	1	0	1	14
Playoffs	*18*	*0*	*4*	*4*	*18*	*0.0*	*0*	*0*	*0*	*0*	*10*	*8*
1991-92	57	6	34	40	69	8.7	3	0	2	0	20	38
Playoffs	*13*	*1*	*2*	*3*	*17*	*5.9*	*0*	*0*	*0*	*0*	*3*	*10*
3 years	79	8	39	47	94	8.5	3	0	3	0	20	52
Playoffs	*31*	*1*	*6*	*7*	*35*	*2.9*	*0*	*0*	*0*	*0*	*13*	*18*

MacTavish, Craig

Sweater # 14 — Center — SL

Born: London, Ontario August 15, 1958 6'0"-185
Last Amateur Club: University of Lowell Chiefs (ECAC)
How the Oilers Got Him: Boston's 9th choice, 153rd overall in 1984 draft. Signed as a free agent by the Oilers, February 1, 1985.

First Game as an Oiler: October 10, 1985
First Goal as an Oiler: October 10, 1985
First Assist as an Oiler: October 16, 1985
First Penalty as an Oiler: October 16, 1985
Where He Went: Traded to the Rangers for Todd Marchant, March 21, 1994.

Season	GP	G	A	Pts	Shots	S%	GW	GT	PP	SH	P/M	PIM
1985-86	74	23	24	47	121	19.0	5	0	4	1	17	70
Playoffs	*10*	*4*	*4*	*8*	*17*	*23.5*	*0*	*0*	*1*	*0*	*6*	*11*
1986-87	79	20	19	39	140	14.3	2	0	1	4	9	55
Playoffs	*21*	*1*	*9*	*10*	*35*	*2.9*	*0*	*0*	*0*	*0*	*1*	*16*
1987-88	80	15	17	32	90	16.7	5	0	0	3	-3	47
Playoffs	*19*	*0*	*1*	*1*	*12*	*0.0*	*0*	*0*	*0*	*0*	*0*	*31*
1988-89	80	21	31	52	120	17.5	2	2	2	4	10	55
Playoffs	*7*	*0*	*1*	*1*	*10*	*0.0*	*0*	*0*	*0*	*0*	*1*	*8*
1989-90	80	21	22	43	109	19.2	5	0	1	6	13	89
Playoffs	*22*	*2*	*6*	*8*	*21*	*9.5*	*0*	*0*	*0*	*0*	*6*	*29*
1990-91	80	17	15	32	113	15.0	1	0	2	6	-1	76
Playoffs	*18*	*3*	*3*	*6*	*24*	*12.5*	*1*	*1*	*0*	*0*	*-3*	*20*
1991-92	80	12	18	30	86	14.0	1	0	0	2	-1	98
Playoffs	*16*	*3*	*0*	*3*	*27*	*11.1*	*1*	*0*	*0*	*1*	*4*	*28*
1992-93	82	10	20	30	101	9.9	3	0	0	3	-16	110
1993-94	66	16	10	26	97	16.5	1	0	0	0	-20	80
9 years	701	155	176	331	977	15.9	25	2	10	26	8	680
Playoffs	*113*	*13*	*24*	*37*	*146*	*8.9*	*2*	*1*	*1*	*1*	*15*	*143*

MAKKONEN, KARI SWEATER # 9 RIGHT WING SR
Born: Pori, Finland January 20, 1955 6'0"-190
Last Amateur Club: Finnish Nationals
How the Oilers Got Him: New York Islanders' 12th choice, 194th overall in 1975 draft. Signed as a free agent by the Oilers, June 23rd, 1979.
First Game as an Oiler: November 7, 1979
First Goal as an Oiler: December 12, 1979
First Assist as an Oiler: December 7, 1979
First Penalty as an Oiler: None Recorded
Where He Went: Retired

Season	GP	G	A	Pts	Shots	S%	GW	GT	PP	SH	P/M	PIM
1979-80	9	2	2	4	11	18.2	0	0	0	0	-2	0

MALEY, DAVID JOSEPH SWEATER # 12 LEFT WING SL
Born: Beaver Dam, Wisconsin April 24, 1963 6'2"-195
Last Amateur Club: University of Wisconsin Badgers (WCHA)
How the Oilers Got Him: Montreal's 4th choice, 33rd overall in the 1982 draft. Traded to the Oilers from the New Jersey Devils for Troy Mallette, January 12, 1992.
First Game as an Oiler: January 13, 1992
First Goal as an Oiler: January 23, 1992
First Assist as an Oiler: January 13, 1992
First Penalty as an Oiler: January 13, 1992
Where He Went: Claimed on waivers by the San Jose Sharks, January 1, 1993.

Season	GP	G	A	Pts	Shots	S%	GW	GT	PP	SH	P/M	PIM
1991-92	23	3	6	9	31	9.7	1	0	0	0	8	46
Playoffs	*10*	*1*	*1*	*2*	*6*	*16.7*	*0*	*0*	*0*	*0*	*-4*	*4*
1992-93	13	1	1	2	9	11.1	0	0	0	0	-3	29
2 years	36	4	7	11	40	10.0	1	0	0	0	5	75
Playoffs	*10*	*1*	*1*	*2*	*6*	*16.7*	*0*	*0*	*0*	*0*	*-4*	*4*

MALLETTE, TROY MATTHEW SWEATER # 12 LEFT WING SL
Born: Sudbury, Ontario February 25, 1970 6'2"-210
Last Amateur Club: Sault Ste. Marie Greyhounds (OHA)
How the Oilers Got Him: New York Rangers' 1st choice, 22nd overall in the 1988 draft. Acquired by the Oilers as compensation for the Rangers' signing of free agent Adam Graves, September 12, 1991.
First Game as an Oiler: October 4, 1991
First Goal as an Oiler: December 1, 1991
First Assist as an Oiler: November 16, 1991
First Penalty as an Oiler: October 4, 1991
Where He Went: Traded to New Jersey for David Maley, January 12, 1992.

Season	GP	G	A	Pts	Shots	S%	GW	GT	PP	SH	P/M	PIM
1991-92	15	1	3	4	9	11.1	0	0	0	0	-1	36

Maltby, Kirk — Sweater # 18 — Right Wing — SR
Born: Guelph, Ontario — December 22, 1972 — 6'0"-180
Last Amateur Club: Owen Sound Platers (OHL)
How the Oilers Got Him: Edmonton's 4th choice, 65th overall in the 1992 draft.
First Game as an Oiler: October 8, 1993
First Assist as an Oiler: November 20, 1993
First Goal as an Oiler: October 8, 1993
First Penalty as an Oiler: October 11, 1993
Where He Went: Traded to Detroit for Daniel McGillis, March 20, 1996.

Season	*GP*	*G*	*A*	*Pts*	*Shots*	*S%*	*GW*	*GT*	*PP*	*SH*	*P/M*	*PIM*
1993-94	68	11	8	19	89	12.4	1	0	0	1	-2	74
1994-95	47	8	3	11	73	11.0	1	1	0	2	-11	49
1995-96	49	2	6	8	51	3.9	1	0	0	0	-16	61
3 years	164	21	17	38	213	9.9	3	1	0	3	-29	184

Manderville, Kent — Sweater # 19 — Left Wing — SL
Born: Edmonton, Alberta — April 12, 1971 — 6'3"-210
Last Amateur Club: Canadian Olympic Team
How the Oilers Got Him: Calgary's 1st choice, 24th overall in the 1989 draft. Traded to the Oilers by the Maple Leafs for Peter White and the Oilers' 4th round choice (Jason Sessa) in the 1996 draft, December 4, 1995.
First Game as an Oiler: December 5, 1995
First Assist as an Oiler: December 10, 1995
First Goal as an Oiler: December 10, 1995
First Penalty as an Oiler: December 5, 1995
Where He Went: Signed as a free agent by Hartford, October 2, 1996.

Season	*GP*	*G*	*A*	*Pts*	*Shots*	*S%*	*GW*	*GT*	*PP*	*SH*	*P/M*	*PIM*
1995-96	37	3	5	8	63	4.8	0	0	0	2	-5	38

Manson, Dave — Sweater # 24 # 23 — Defense — SL
Born: Prince Albert, Saskatchewan — January 27, 1967 — 6'2"-205
Last Amateur Club: Prince Albert Raiders (WHL)
How the Oilers Got Him: Chicago's 1st choice, 11th overall in the 1985 draft. Traded to the Oilers from the Black Hawks for Steve Smith, October 2, 1991.
First Game as an Oiler: October 4, 1991
First Assist as an Oiler: October 23, 1991
First Goal as an Oiler: October 26, 1991
First Penalty as an Oiler: October 4, 1991
Where He Went: Traded to Winnipeg with St. Louis' 6th round choice (previously acquired by the Oilers; Winnipeg selected Chris Kibermanis) in the 1994 draft for Mats Lindgren, Boris Mironov, the Jets' 1st found choice in the 1994 draft (Jason Bonsignore) and Florida's 4th round choice (previously acquired by Winnipeg; the Oilers selected Adam Copeland) in the 1994 draft, March 15, 1994.

Season	*GP*	*G*	*A*	*Pts*	*Shots*	*S%*	*GW*	*GT*	*PP*	*SH*	*P/M*	*PIM*
1991-92	79	15	32	47	206	7.3	2	0	7	0	9	220
Playoffs	*16*	*3*	*9*	*12*	*47*	*6.4*	*0*	*0*	*1*	*0*	*-2*	*44*
1992-93	83	15	30	45	244	6.1	1	1	9	1	-28	210
1993-94	57	3	13	16	144	2.1	0	0	0	0	-4	140
3 years	219	33	75	108	594	5.6	3	1	16	1	-23	570
Playoffs	*16*	*3*	*9*	*12*	*47*	*6.4*	*0*	*0*	*1*	*0*	*-2*	*44*

Mantha, Maurice William — Sweater # 20 — Defense — SR
Born: Lakewood, Ohio — January 21, 1961 — 6'2"-195
Last Amateur Club: Toronto Marlboros (OHA)
How the Oilers Got Him: Winnipeg's 2nd choice, 23rd overall in the 1980 draft. Traded to the Oilers by Pittsburgh with Dave Hannan, Craig Simpson and Chris Joseph for Dave Hunter, Paul Coffey and Wayne Van Dorp, November 24, 1987.
First Game as an Oiler: November 25, 1987
First Assist as an Oiler: November 25, 1987
First Goal as an Oiler: None Recorded
First Penalty as an Oiler: November 29, 1987
Where He Went: Traded to Minnesota for Keith Acton, January 22, 1988.

Season	*GP*	*G*	*A*	*Pts*	*Shots*	*S%*	*GW*	*GT*	*PP*	*SH*	*P/M*	*PIM*
1987-88	25	0	6	6	18	16.7	0	0	0	0	1	26

Marchant, Todd Michael — Sweater # 36, # 26 — Center — SL
Born: Buffalo, New York — August 12, 1973 — 5'10"-175
Last Amateur Club: U.S. Olympic Team
How the Oilers Got Him: New York Rangers' 8th choice, 164th overall in the 1993 draft. Traded to the Oilers by the Rangers for Craig MacTavish, March 21, 1994.

First Game as an Oiler: March 23, 1994
First Goal as an Oiler: January 28, 1995
First Assist as an Oiler: March 25, 1994
First Penalty as an Oiler: March 25, 1994

Season	GP	G	A	Pts	Shots	S%	GW	GT	PP	SH	P/M	PIM
1993-94	3	0	1	1	5	0.0	0	0	0	0	-1	2
1994-95	45	13	14	27	95	13.7	2	0	3	2	-3	32
1995-96	81	19	19	38	221	8.6	2	1	2	3	-19	66
1996-97	79	14	19	33	202	6.9	3	0	0	4	11	44
Playoffs	*12*	*4*	*2*	*6*	*40*	*10.0*	*1*	*1*	*0*	*3*	*2*	*12*
1997-98	76	14	21	35	194	7.2	3	0	2	1	9	71
Playoffs	*12*	*1*	*1*	*2*	*17*	*5.9*	*0*	*0*	*0*	*0*	*0*	*10*
1998-99	82	14	22	36	183	7.7	2	0	3	1	3	65
Playoffs	*4*	*1*	*1*	*2*	*10*	*10.0*	*0*	*0*	*0*	*0*	*2*	*12*
1999-00	82	17	23	40	170	10.0	0	2	0	1	7	70
Playoffs	*3*	*1*	*0*	*1*	*6*	*16.7*	*0*	*0*	*0*	*0*	*-1*	*2*
2000-01	71	13	26	39	113	11.5	2	1	0	4	0	51
Playoffs	6	0	0	0	7	0.0	0	0	0	0	-3	4
8 years	519	104	145	249	1183	8.8	14	4	10	16	0	401
Playoffs	*37*	*7*	*4*	*11*	*80*	*8.8*	*1*	*1*	*0*	*3*	*0*	*40*

MARCHMENT, BRYAN WILLIAM — SWEATER # 24 — DEFENSE — SL

Born: Scarborough, Ontario — May 1, 1969 — 6'1"-205
Last Amateur Club: Belleville Bulls (OHL)
How the Oilers Got Him: Chicago's 1st choice, 16th overall in the 1987 draft. Acquired by the Oilers from the Hartford Whalers as compensation for the Whalers signing Steve Rice, August 30, 1994.
First Game as an Oiler: January 20, 1995
First Goal as an Oiler: February 19, 1995
First Assist as an Oiler: January 15, 1995
First Penalty as an Oiler: January 20, 1995
Where He Went: Traded to Tampa Bay with Jason Bonsignore and Steve Kelly for Roman Hamrlik and Paul Comrie, December 30, 1997.

Season	GP	G	A	Pts	Shots	S%	GW	GT	PP	SH	P/M	PIM
1994-95	40	1	5	6	57	1.8	0	0	0	0	-11	184
1995-96	78	3	15	18	96	3.1	0	0	0	0	-7	202
1996-97	71	3	13	16	89	3.4	0	0	1	0	13	132
Playoffs	*3*	*0*	*0*	*0*	*2*	*0.0*	*0*	*0*	*0*	*0*	*-3*	*4*
1997-98	27	0	4	4	23	0.0	0	0	0	0	-2	58
3 years	216	7	37	44	265	2.6	0	0	1	0	-7	576
Playoffs	*3*	*0*	*0*	*0*	*2*	*0.0*	*0*	*0*	*0*	*0*	*-3*	*4*

MARK, GORDON — SWEATER # 32, # 6, # 34 — DEFENSE — SR

Born: Edmonton, Alberta — September 10, 1964 — 6'4"-218
Last Amateur Club: Stony Plain Eagles (SR.)
How the Oilers Got Him: Signed as a free agent by the Oilers, February 1, 1994.
First Game as an Oiler: February 2, 1994
First Goal as an Oiler: None Recorded
First Assist as an Oiler: March 27, 1994
First Penalty as an Oiler: February 2, 1994
Where He Went: Retired

Season	GP	G	A	Pts	Shots	S%	GW	GT	PP	SH	P/M	PIM
1993-94	12	0	1	1	8	0.0	0	0	0	0	-2	43
1994-95	18	0	2	2	21	0.0	0	0	0	0	-9	35
2 years	30	0	3	3	29	0.0	0	0	0	0	-11	78

MARTIN, TERRY GEORGE — SWEATER # 18 — LEFT WING — SL

Born: Barrie, Ontario — October 25, 1955 — 5'11"-195
Last Amateur Club: London Knights (OHA)
How the Oilers Got Him: Buffalo's 3rd choice, 44th overall in the 1975 draft. Claimed by the Oilers in the Waiver Draft, from the Leafs, October 9, 1984.
First Game as an Oiler: October 14, 1984
First Goal as an Oiler: None Recorded
First Assist as an Oiler: October 14, 1984
First Penalty as an Oiler: None Recorded
Where He Went: Traded to Minnesota with Gord Sherven for Mark Napier, January 24, 1985.

Season	GP	G	A	Pts	Shots	S%	GW	GT	PP	SH	P/M	PIM
1984-85	4	0	2	2	6	0.0	0	0	0	0	3	0

MARTINI, DARCY SWEATER # 34 DEFENSE SL
Born: Castlegar, British Columbia January 30, 1969 6'4"-210
Last Amateur Club: Michigan Tech Huskies (WCHA)
How the Oilers Got Him: Oilers' 8th choice, 162nd overall in the 1989 draft.
First Game as an Oiler: January 13, 1994
First Assist as an Oiler: None Recorded
First Goal as an Oiler: None Recorded
First Penalty as an Oiler: None Recorded
Where He Went: Retired

Season	*GP*	*G*	*A*	*Pts*	*Shots*	*S%*	*GW*	*GT*	*PP*	*SH*	*P/M*	*PIM*
1993-94	2	0	0	0	0	0.0	0	0	0	0	-1	0

MAY, ALAN RANDY SWEATER # 32 RIGHT WING SR
Born: Barrhead, Alberta January 14, 1965 6'1"-200
Last Amateur Club: New Westminster Bruins (WHL)
How the Oilers Got Him: Traded to the Oilers from Boston, for Moe Lemay, March 8, 1988.
First Game as an Oiler: December 23, 1988
First Assist as an Oiler: None Recorded
First Goal as an Oiler: December 23, 1988
First Penalty as an Oiler: December 23, 1988
Where He Went: Traded to Los Angeles with Jim Wiemer for Brian Wilks and John English, March 7, 1989.

Season	*GP*	*G*	*A*	*Pts*	*Shots*	*S%*	*GW*	*GT*	*PP*	*SH*	*P/M*	*PIM*
1988-89	3	1	0	1	3	33.3	1	0	0	0	0	7

MCAMMOND, DEAN SWEATER # 37 CENTER SL
Born: Grand Cache, Alberta, June 15, 1973 5'11"-185
Last Amateur Club: Swift Current Broncos (WHL)
How the Oilers Got Him: Chicago's 1st choice, 22nd overall in the 1991 draft. Traded to Edmonton by the Chicago Black Hawks with Igor Kravchuk, for Joe Murphy, February 24, 1993.
First Game as an Oiler: October 6, 1993
First Assist as an Oiler: October 8, 1993
First Goal as an Oiler: October 18, 1993
First Penalty as an Oiler: October 20, 1993
Where He Went: Traded to Chicago by the Oilers with Boris Mironov and Jonas Elofsson for Ethan Moreau, Chad Kilger, Christian Laflamme, and Daniel Cleary, March 20, 1999.

Season	*GP*	*G*	*A*	*Pts*	*Shots*	*S%*	*GW*	*GT*	*PP*	*SH*	*P/M*	*PIM*
1993-94	45	6	21	27	52	11.5	0	0	2	0	12	16
1994-95	6	0	0	0	3	0.0	0	0	0	0	-1	0
1995-96	53	15	15	30	79	19.0	0	0	4	0	6	23
1996-97	57	12	17	29	106	11.3	6	0	4	0	-15	28
1997-98	77	19	31	50	128	14.8	3	0	8	0	9	46
Playoffs	*12*	*1*	*4*	*5*	*22*	*4.5*	*0*	*0*	*0*	*0*	*0*	*12*
1998-99	65	9	16	25	122	7.4	0	0	1	0	5	36
6 years	303	61	100	161	490	12.4	9	0	19	0	16	149
Playoffs	*12*	*1*	*4*	*5*	*22*	*4.5*	*0*	*0*	*0*	*0*	*0*	*12*

MCCLELLAND, KEVIN WILLIAM SWEATER # 24 CENTER SR
Born: Oshawa, Ontario July 4, 1962 6'0"-190
Last Amateur Club: Niagara Falls Flyers (OHL)
How the Oilers Got Him: Traded to the Oilers by Pittsburgh with the Penguins' 6th round choice (Emanuel Viveiros) in 1984 draft for Tom Roulston, December 5, 1983.
First Game as an Oiler: December 7, 1983
First Assist as an Oiler: December 13, 1983
First Goal as an Oiler: December 14, 1983
First Penalty as an Oiler: December 13, 1983
Where He Went: Traded to Detroit with Jimmy Carson and the Oilers' 5th choice (later traded to Montreal for Rick Green; the Canadiens selected Brad Layzell) in the 1991 draft for Adam Graves, Petr Klima, Joe Murphy and Jeff Sharples, November 2, 1989.

Season	*GP*	*G*	*A*	*Pts*	*Shots*	*S%*	*GW*	*GT*	*PP*	*SH*	*P/M*	*PIM*
1983-84	52	8	20	28	65	12.3	2	0	0	2	9	127
Playoffs	*18*	*4*	*6*	*10*	*32*	*12.5*	*1*	*0*	*0*	*0*	*13*	*42*
1984-85	62	8	15	23	96	8.3	3	0	0	0	-11	205
Playoffs	*18*	*1*	*3*	*4*	*22*	*4.5*	*0*	*0*	*0*	*0*	*4*	*75*
1985-86	79	11	25	36	104	10.6	1	0	0	0	9	266
Playoffs	*10*	*1*	*0*	*1*	*7*	*14.3*	*0*	*0*	*0*	*0*	*-1*	*32*
1986-87	72	12	13	25	76	15.8	1	0	0	0	-4	238
Playoffs	*21*	*2*	*3*	*5*	*24*	*8.3*	*0*	*0*	*0*	*0*	*-6*	*43*
1987-88	74	10	6	16	61	16.4	0	0	0	0	1	281
Playoffs	*19*	*2*	*3*	*5*	*13*	*15.4*	*0*	*0*	*0*	*0*	*-1*	*68*

Season	GP	G	A	Pts	Shots	S%	GW	GT	PP	SH	P/M	PIM
1988-89	79	6	14	20	43	14.0	0	0	0	0	-10	161
Playoffs	*7*	*0*	*2*	*2*	*7*	*0.0*	*0*	*0*	*0*	*0*	*3*	*16*
1989-90	10	1	1	2	7	14.3	0	0	0	0	-1	13
7 years	428	56	94	150	452	12.4	7	0	0	2	-7	1291
Playoffs	*93*	*10*	*17*	*27*	*105*	*9.5*	*1*	*0*	*0*	*0*	*12*	*276*

McDOUGALL, WILLIAM HENRY SWEATER # 41 CENTER SR

Born: Mississauga, Ontario August 10, 1966 6'0"-185

Last Amateur Club: Pt. Basques (SR.)

How the Oilers Got Him: Traded to the Oilers from the Detroit Red Wings for Max Middendorf, February 22, 1992.

First Game as an Oiler: March 17, 1993 *First Assist as an Oiler:* March 17, 1993

First Goal as an Oiler: March 18, 1993 *First Penalty as an Oiler:* March 18, 1993

Where He Went: Signed as a free agent by Tampa Bay , August 13, 1993

Season	GP	G	A	Pts	Shots	S%	GW	GT	PP	SH	P/M	PIM
1992-93	4	2	1	3	8	25.0	0	0	0	0	2	4

McGILL, RYAN CLIFFORD SWEATER # 34 DEFENSE SR

Born: Prince Albert, Saskatchewan February 28, 1969 6'2"-210

Last Amateur Club: Medicine Hat Tigers (WHL)

How the Oilers Got Him: Chicago's 2nd choice, 29th overall in the 1987 draft. Traded to the Oilers from the Philadelphia Flyers for Brad Zavisha and the Oilers' 6th choice (Jamie Sololosky) in the 1995 draft, March 13, 1995.

First Game as an Oiler: March 14, 1995 *First Assist as an Oiler:* None Recorded

First Goal as an Oiler: None Recorded *First Penalty as an Oiler:* March 14, 1995

Where He Went: Retired.

Season	GP	G	A	Pts	Shots	S%	GW	GT	PP	SH	P/M	PIM
1994-95	8	0	0	0	6	0.0	0	0	0	0	-4	8

McGILLIS, DANIEL SWEATER # 18, # 23, #33 DEFENSE SL

Born: Hawksebury, Ontario July 1, 19 6'2"-225

Last Amateur Club: Northeastern University Wildcats (H.E.)

How the Oilers Got Him: Detroit's 10th choice, 238th overall in the 1992 draft. Traded to the Oilers from the Red Wings for Kirk Maltby, March 20, 1996.

First Game as an Oiler: October 4, 1996 *First Assist as an Oiler:* October 4, 1996

First Goal as an Oiler: November 26, 1996 *First Penalty as an Oiler:* October 4, 1996

Where He Went: Traded to Philadelphia with the Oilers' 2nd choice (Jason Beckett) in the 1998 draft for Janne Niinimaa, March 24, 1998.

Season	GP	G	A	Pts	Shots	S%	GW	GT	PP	SH	P/M	PIM
1996-97	73	6	16	22	139	4.3	2	0	2	1	2	52
Playoffs	*12*	*0*	*5*	*5*	*20*	*0.0*	*0*	*0*	*0*	*0*	*8*	*24*
1997-98	67	10	15	25	119	8.4	3	1	5	0	-17	74
2 years	140	16	31	47	258	6.2	5	1	7	1	-15	126
Playoffs	*12*	*0*	*5*	*5*	*20*	*0.0*	*0*	*0*	*0*	*0*	*8*	*24*

McMURCHY, THOMAS SWEATER # 37 RIGHT WING SL

Born: New Westminster, British Columbia December 2, 1963 5'9"-165

Last Amateur Club: Brandon Wheat Kings (WHL)

How the Oilers Got Him: Chicago's 3rd choice, 49th overall in the 1982 draft. Signed as a free agent by the Oilers, August 18, 1986.

First Game as an Oiler: October 31, 1987 *First Assist as an Oiler:* November 1, 1987

First Goal as an Oiler: October 31, 1987 *First Penalty as an Oiler:* November 1, 1987

Where He Went: Retired.

Season	GP	G	A	Pts	Shots	S%	GW	GT	PP	SH	P/M	PIM
1987-88	9	4	1	5	11	36.4	1	0	0	0	2	8

McSORLEY, MARTIN JAMES SWEATER # 33 DEFENSE SR

Born: Hamilton, Ontario May 18, 1963 6'2"-220

Last Amateur Club: Belleville Bulls (OHL)

How the Oilers Got Him: Traded to Edmonton by the Pittsburgh Penguins with Tim Hrynewich for Gilles Meloche, and future considerations (Craig Muni), September 12, 1985. Signed as a free agent October 1, 1998.

First Game as an Oiler: October 10, 1985 *First Assist as an Oiler:* December 10, 1985
First Goal as an Oiler: December 3, 1985 *First Penalty as an Oiler:* October 10, 1985
Where He Went: Traded to Los Angeles with Wayne Gretzky and Mike Krushelnyski for Jimmy Carson, Martin Gelinas, the Kings' 1st choice in the 1989 draft (later acquired by New Jersey; the Devils selected Jason Miller), 1st choice in the 1991 draft (Martin Rucinsky), 1st choice in the 1993 draft (Nick Stajduhar) and cash, August 9, 1988.

Season	*GP*	*G*	*A*	*Pts*	*Shots*	*S%*	*GW*	*GT*	*PP*	*SH*	*P/M*	*PIM*
1985-86	59	11	12	23	72	15.3	2	0	0	0	9	265
Playoffs	*8*	*0*	*2*	*2*	*4*	*0.0*	*0*	*0*	*0*	*0*	*3*	*50*
1986-87	41	2	4	6	32	6.3	0	0	0	0	-4	159
Playoffs	*21*	*4*	*3*	*7*	*21*	*19.0*	*1*	*0*	*0*	*0*	*8*	*65*
1987-88	60	9	17	26	66	13.6	1	0	0	0	23	223
Playoffs	*16*	*0*	*3*	*3*	*15*	*0.0*	*0*	*0*	*0*	*0*	*2*	*67*
1998-99	46	2	3	5	29	6.9	0	0	0	0	-5	101
Playoffs	*3*	*0*	*0*	*0*	*3*	*0.0*	*0*	*0*	*0*	*0*	*1*	*2*
4 years	206	24	36	60	199	12.1	3	0	0	0	23	748
Playoffs	*48*	*4*	*8*	*12*	*43*	*9.3*	*1*	*0*	*0*	*0*	*14*	*184*

MELLANBY, SCOTT SWEATER # 27 RIGHT WING SR
Born: Montreal, Quebec June 11, 1966 6'1"-200
Last Amateur Club: University of Wisconsin Badgers (WCHA)
How the Oilers Got Him: Philadelphia's 2nd choice, 27th overall in the 1984 draft. Traded to the Oilers from Philadelphia with Craig Berube and Craig Fisher for Dave Brown, Corey Foster and Jari Kurri, May 30, 1991.
First Game as an Oiler: October 4, 1991 *First Assist as an Oiler:* October 17, 1991
First Goal as an Oiler: October 4, 1991 *First Penalty as an Oiler:* October 4, 1991
Where He Went: Claimed by Florida in the Expansion Draft, June 24, 1993.

Season	*GP*	*G*	*A*	*Pts*	*Shots*	*S%*	*GW*	*GT*	*PP*	*SH*	*P/M*	*PIM*
1991-92	80	23	27	50	159	14.5	5	0	7	0	5	197
Playoffs	*16*	*2*	*1*	*3*	*26*	*7.7*	*1*	*0*	*1*	*0*	*-3*	*29*
1992-93	69	15	17	32	114	13.2	3	1	6	0	-4	147
2 years	149	38	44	82	273	13.9	8	1	13	0	1	344
Playoffs	*16*	*2*	*1*	*3*	*26*	*7.7*	*1*	*0*	*1*	*0*	*-3*	*29*

MELNYK, LARRY JOSEPH SWEATER # 28 DEFENSE SL
Born: New Westminster, British Columbia February 21, 1960 6'0"-180
Last Amateur Club: New Westminster Bruins (WHL)
How the Oilers Got Him: Boston's 5th choice, 78th overall in the 1979 draft. Traded to the Oilers from Boston for John Blum, March 6, 1984.
First Game as an Oiler: April 26, 1984 *First Assist as an Oiler:* April 26, 1984
First Goal as an Oiler: November 3, 1985 *First Penalty as an Oiler:* April 28, 1984
Where He Went: Traded to the Rangers with Todd Strueby for Mike Rogers, December 20, 1985.

Season	*GP*	*G*	*A*	*Pts*	*Shots*	*S%*	*GW*	*GT*	*PP*	*SH*	*P/M*	*PIM*
Playoffs(83-84)	*6*	*0*	*1*	*1*	*1*	*0.0*	*0*	*0*	*0*	*0*	*1*	*2*
1984-85	28	0	11	11	8	0.0	0	0	0	0	12	25
Playoffs	*12*	*1*	*3*	*4*	*15*	*6.7*	*0*	*0*	*0*	*0*	*10*	*26*
1985-86	6	2	3	5	4	50.0	0	0	0	0	8	11
2 years	34	2	14	16	12	16.7	0	0	0	0	20	36
Playoffs	*18*	*1*	*4*	*5*	*16*	*6.3*	*0*	*0*	*0*	*0*	*11*	*28*

MESSIER, MARK DOUGLAS SWEATER # 11 CENTER/LEFT WING SR
Born: Edmonton, Alberta January 18, 1961 6'1"-200
Last Amateur Club: Saint Albert Saints (Tier II)
How the Oilers Got Him: Signed to a WHA contract by the Oilers after playing the 1978-79 season with Indianapolis and Cincinnati. Oilers' 2nd choice, 48th overall in 1979 entry draft.
First Game as an Oiler: October 10, 1979 *First Assist as an Oiler:* October 19, 1979
First Goal as an Oiler: October 13, 1979 *First Penalty as an Oiler:* October 14, 1979
Where He Went: Traded to the Rangers with future considerations for Louie DeBrusk, Bernie Nicholls, and Steven Rice, October 4, 1991.

Season	*GP*	*G*	*A*	*Pts*	*Shots*	*S%*	*GW*	*GT*	*PP*	*SH*	*P/M*	*PIM*
1979-80	75	12	21	33	113	10.6	1	1	1	1	-10	120
Playoffs	*3*	*1*	*2*	*3*			*0*	*0*	*0*	*1*		*2*
1980-81	72	23	40	63	179	12.8	1	1	4	0	-12	102

Season	GP	G	A	Pts	Shots	S%	GW	GT	PP	SH	P/M	PIM
Playoffs	*9*	*2*	*5*	*7*			*0*	*0*	*0*	*0*		*13*
1981-82	78	50	38	88	235	21.3	3	2	10	0	21	119
Playoffs	*5*	*1*	*2*	*3*			*0*	*0*	*0*	*0*		*8*
1982-83	77	48	58	106	237	20.3	2	5	12	1	19	72
Playoffs	*15*	*15*	*6*	*21*	*50*	*30.0*	*2*	*0*	*4*	*2*	*10*	*14*
1983-84	73	37	64	101	219	16.9	7	0	7	4	40	165
Playoffs	*19*	*8*	*18*	*26*	*63*	*12.7*	*2*	*0*	*1*	*1*	*9*	*19*
1984-85	55	23	31	54	136	16.9	1	0	4	5	9	57
Playoffs	*18*	*12*	*13*	*25*	*56*	*21.4*	*1*	*0*	*1*	*1*	*13*	*12*
1985-86	63	35	49	84	201	17.4	7	0	10	5	36	68
Playoffs	*10*	*4*	*6*	*10*	*23*	*17.4*	*0*	*0*	*0*	*2*	*1*	*18*
1986-87	77	37	70	107	208	17.8	5	0	7	4	21	73
Playoffs	*21*	*12*	*16*	*28*	*62*	*19.4*	*1*	*0*	*1*	*2*	*13*	*16*
1987-88	77	37	74	111	182	20.3	7	2	12	3	21	103
Playoffs	*19*	*11*	*23*	*34*	*42*	*26.2*	*0*	*0*	*7*	*1*	*9*	*29*
1988-89	72	33	61	94	164	20.1	4	1	6	6	-5	130
Playoffs	*7*	*1*	*11*	*12*	*23*	*4.3*	*0*	*0*	*0*	*0*	*-1*	*8*
1989-90	79	45	84	129	211	21.3	3	2	13	6	19	79
Playoffs	*22*	*9*	*22*	*31*	*47*	*19.1*	*1*	*0*	*1*	*1*	*5*	*20*
1990-91	53	12	52	64	109	11.0	2	0	3	1	15	34
Playoffs	*18*	*4*	*11*	*15*	*41*	*9.8*	*0*	*0*	*1*	*0*	*2*	*16*
12 years	851	392	642	1034	2194	17.9	43	14	89	36	174	1122
Playoffs	*166*	*80*	*135*	*215*			*7*	*0*	*16*	*11*		*175*

Metcalfe, Scott Sweater # 20, # 34 Left Wing SL

Born: Toronto, Ontario January 6, 1967 6'0"-200

Last Amateur Club: Kingston Canadians (OHA)

How the Oilers Got Him: Edmonton's 1st choice, 20th overall in the 1985 draft.

First Game as an Oiler: January 4, 1988 *First Assist as an Oiler:* None Recorded

First Goal as an Oiler: None Recorded *First Penalty as an Oiler:* None Recorded

Where He Went: Traded to the Sabres with the Oilers' 9th choice in the 1989 draft (Donald Audette) for Steve Dykstra and the Sabres' 7th choice in the 1989 draft (David Payne), February 11, 1988.

Season	GP	G	A	Pts	Shots	S%	GW	GT	PP	SH	P/M	PIM
1987-88	2	0	0	0	0	0.0	0	0	0	0	-1	0

Middendorf, Max Sweater # 26 Right Wing SR

Born: Syracuse, New York August 18, 1967 6'4"-210

Last Amateur Club: Kitchener Rangers (OHA)

How the Oilers Got Him: Quebec's 3rd choice, 57th overall in the 1985 draft. Traded to the Oilers by the Quebec Nordiques for the Oilers' 9th round choice (Brent Brekke) in the 1991 draft, November 10, 1990.

First Game as an Oiler: November 16, 1990 *First Assist as an Oiler:* None Recorded

First Goal as an Oiler: November 18, 1990 *First Penalty as an Oiler*: November 20, 1990

Where He Went: Traded to Detroit for Bill McDougall, February 22, 1992.

Season	GP	G	A	Pts	Shots	S%	GW	GT	PP	SH	P/M	PIM
1990-91	3	1	0	1	1	100.0	0	0	0	0	0	2

Middlebrook, Lindsay Sweater # 33 Goaltender CR

Born: Collingwood, Ontario September 7, 1955 5'7"-160

Last Amateur Club: St. Louis Billekins (CCHA)

How the Oilers Got Him: Traded to the Oilers by New Jersey Devils, with Paul Miller for Ron Low and Jim McTaggert, February 19, 1983.

First Game as an Oiler: March 1, 1983 *First Assist as an Oiler:* None Recorded

First Goal as an Oiler: None Recorded *First Penalty as an Oiler:* None Recorded

Where He Went: Retired

Season	GP	Min	GA	W	L	T	Ave	SA	S%	SO	EN	PIM	Ast.
1982-83	1	60	3	1	0	0	3.00	33	0.909	0	0	0	0

MILLAR, CRAIG SWEATER # 35, # 32 DEFENSE SL
Born: Winnipeg, Manitoba May 10, 1977 6'2"-200
Last Amateur Club: Swift Current Broncos (WHL)
How the Oilers Got Him: Buffalo's 10th choice, 225th overall in the 1994 draft. Traded to the Oilers from the Sabres with Barrie Moore for Miroslav Satan, March 18, 1997.
First Game as an Oiler: March 19, 1997 *First Assist as an Oiler:* October 31, 1998
First Goal as an Oiler: November 5, 1997 *First Penalty as an Oiler:* March 19, 1997
Where He Went: Traded to Nashville for Detroit's third round choice (previously acquired by the Predators; the Oilers chose Mike Comrie) in the 1999 Entry Draft, June 26, 1999.

Season	GP	G	A	Pts	Shots	S%	GW	GT	PP	SH	P/M	PIM
1996-97	1	0	0	0	1	0.0	0	0	0	0	0	2
1997-98	11	4	0	4	10	40.0	0	0	1	0	-3	8
1998-99	24	0	2	2	18	0.0	0	0	0	0	-6	19
3 years	36	4	2	6	29	13.8	0	0	1	0	-9	29

MINARD, MICHAEL SWEATER # 1 GOALTENDER CL
Born: Owen Sound, Ontario November 1, 1976 6'3"-205
Last Amateur Club: Detroit Whalers (OHL)
How the Oilers Got Him: Oilers' 4th choice, 83rd overall in the 1995 draft.
First Game as an Oiler: April 7, 2000 *First Assist as a Oiler:* None Recorded
First Goal as an Oiler: None Recorded *First Penalty as an Oiler:* None Recorded

Season	GP	Min	GA	W	L	T	Ave	SA	S%	SO	EN	PIM	Ast.
1999-00	1	60	3	1	0	0	3.00	36	.917	0	0	0	0

MINER, JOHN SWEATER # 8 DEFENSE SR
Born: Moose Jaw, Saskatchewan August 28, 1965 5'10"-180
Last Amateur Club: Regina Pats (WHL)
How the Oilers Got Him: Oilers' 10th choice, 229th overall in the 1983 draft.
First Game as an Oiler: October 11, 1987 *First Assist as a Oiler:* October 11, 1987
First Goal as an Oiler: October 16, 1987 *First Penalty as an Oiler:* October 11, 1987
Where He Went: Traded to Los Angeles for Craig Redmond, August 10, 1988.

Season	GP	G	A	Pts	Shots	S%	GW	GT	PP	SH	P/M	PIM
1987-88	14	2	3	5	16	12.5	0	0	0	0	-4	16

MIO, EDWARD DARIO SWEATER # 31 GOALTENDER CL
Born: Windsor, Ontario January 31, 1954 5'10"-180
Last Amateur Club: Colorado College Tigers (WCHA)
How the Oilers Got Him: Chicago's 7th choice, 124th overall in 1974 draft. Traded with Wayne Gretzky and Ed Mio from Indianapolis to the Oilers for $850,000 and other considerations. Reclaimed by Minnesota North Stars prior to the Expansion Draft on June 9, 1979, and then reclaimed by the Oilers as a priority selection on the same date.
First Game as an Oiler: October 13, 1979 *First Assist as an Oiler:* December 19, 1979
First Goal as an Oiler: None Recorded *First Penalty as an Oiler:* November 7, 1979
Where He Went: Traded to the Rangers for Lance Nethery, December 11, 1981.

Season	GP	Min	GA	W	L	T	Ave	SA	S%	SO	EN	PIM	Ast.
1979-80	34	1711	120	9	13	5	4.21	915	.869	1	2	4	1
1980-81	43	2393	155	16	15	9	3.89	1115	.861	0	4	6	5
2 years	77	4104	275	25	28	14	4.02	2030	.865	1	6	10	6

MIRONOV, BORIS SWEATER # 20, # 2 DEFENSE SR
Born: Moscow, USSR March 21, 1972 6'3"-220
Last Amateur Club: CSKA Moscow (CIS)
How the Oilers Got Him: Winnipeg's 2nd choice, 27th overall in the 1992 draft. Traded to the Oilers by the Winnipeg Jets with Mats Lindgren, the Jets' 1st round choice in the 1994 draft (Jason Bonsignore) and the Florida Panthers' 4th pick, previously acquired by Winnipeg (Oilers selected Adam Copeland), in the 1994 draft for Dave Manson and the St. Louis Blues' 6th choice, previously acquired by Edmonton (Winnipeg selected Chris Kibermanis) in 1994 draft, March 15, 1994.
First Game as an Oiler: March 16, 1994 *First Assist as an Oiler:* March 23, 1994
First Goal as an Oiler: May 3, 1995 *First Penalty as an Oiler:* March 16, 1994
Where He Went: Traded to Chicago by the Oilers with Dean McAmmond and Jonas Elofsson for Ethan Moreau, Chad Kilger, Christian Laflamme, and Daniel Cleary, March 20, 1999.

Season	GP	G	A	Pts	Shots	S%	GW	GT	PP	SH	P/M	PIM
1993-94	14	0	2	2	23	0.0	0	0	0	0	-4	14
1994-95	29	1	7	8	48	2.1	0	0	0	0	-9	40
1995-96	78	8	24	32	158	5.1	1	0	7	0	-23	101
1996-97	55	6	26	32	147	4.1	1	0	2	0	2	85
Playoffs	*12*	*2*	*8*	*10*	*31*	*6.5*	*0*	*0*	*2*	*0*	*-6*	*16*
1997-98	81	16	30	46	203	7.9	1	1	10	1	-8	100
Playoffs	*12*	*3*	*3*	*6*	*26*	*11.5*	*1*	*0*	*1*	*0*	*-3*	*27*
1998-99	63	11	29	40	138	8.0	4	1	5	0	6	104
6 years	320	42	118	160	717	5.9	7	2	24	1	-36	444
Playoffs	*24*	*5*	*11*	*16*	*57*	*8.8*	*1*	*0*	*3*	*0*	*-9*	*43*

MOLLER, MICHAEL JOHN SWEATER # 15, # 25 RIGHT WING SR

Born: Calgary, Alberta June 16, 1962 6'0"-190

Last Amateur Club: Lethbridge Broncos (WHL)

How the Oilers Got Him: Buffalo's 2nd choice, 41st overall in the 1980 draft. Traded to Edmonton by the Pittsburgh Penguins for Pat Hughes, October 4, 1985

First Game as an Oiler: October 15, 1985

First Assist as an Oiler: March 23, 1987

First Goal as an Oiler: March 23, 1987

First Penalty as an Oiler: None Recorded

Where He Went: Retired

Season	GP	G	A	Pts	Shots	S%	GW	GT	PP	SH	P/M	PIM
1985-86	1	0	0	0	2	0.0	0	0	0	0	0	0
1986-87	6	2	1	3	10	20.0	0	0	0	0	2	0
2 years	7	2	1	3	12	16.7	0	0	0	0	2	0

MOOG, DONALD ANDREW SWEATER # 35 GOALTENDER CL

Born: Penticton, British Columbia February 18, 1960 5'8"-160

Last Amateur Club: Billings Bighorns (WHL)

How the Oilers Got Him: The Oilers' 6th choice, 132nd overall, in the 1980 draft.

First Game as an Oiler: December 23, 1980

First Assist as an Oiler: November 7, 1981

First Goal as an Oiler: None Recorded

First Penalty as an Oiler: October 18, 1981

Where He Went: Traded to Boston for Geoff Courtnall, Bill Ranford and the Bruins' 2nd choice in the 1988 draft (Petro Koivunen), March 8, 1988.

Season	GP	Min	GA	W	L	T	Ave	SA	S%	SO	EN	PIM	Ast.
1980-81	7	313	20	3	3	0	3.83	206	0.903	0	0	0	1
Playoffs	*9*	*526*	*32*	*5*	*4*		*3.65*	*271*	*0.882*	*0*	*1*	*0*	*0*
1981-82	8	399	32	3	5	0	4.81	197	0.838	0	2	2	1
1982-83	50	2833	167	33	8	7	3.54	1531	0.891	1	1	16	4
Playoffs	*16*	*949*	*48*	*11*	*5*		*3.00*	*463*	*0.896*	*0*	*2*	*2*	*1*
1983-84	38	2212	139	27	8	1	3.77	1179	0.882	1	2	4	1
Playoffs	*7*	*263*	*12*	*4*	*0*		*2.74*	*110*	*0.891*	*0*	*0*	*2*	*0*
1984-85	39	2019	111	22	9	3	3.30	1050	0.894	1.5	1	8	0
Playoffs	*2*	*20*	*0*	*0*	*0*		*0.00*	*3*	*1.000*	*0*	*0*	*0*	*0*
1985-86	47	2664	164	27	9	7	3.69	1480	0.889	1	2	8	2
Playoffs	*1*	*60*	*1*	*1*	*0*		*1.00*	*27*	*0.963*	*0*	*0*	*0*	*0*
1986-87	46	2461	144	28	11	3	3.51	1218	0.882	0	2	8	2
Playoffs	*2*	*120*	*8*	*2*	*0*		*4.00*	*37*	*0.784*	*0*	*0*	*0*	*0*
7 years	235	12901	777	143	53	21	3.61	6861	0.887	6.5	8	46	11
Playoffs	*37*	*1938*	*101*	*23*	*9*		*3.13*	*911*	*0.889*	*0*	*3*	*4*	*1*

MOORE, BARRIE SWEATER # 20, # 18 LEFT WING SL

Born: London, Ontario May 22, 1975 5'11"-175

Last Amateur Club: Sudbury Wolves (OHL)

How the Oilers Got Him: Buffalo's 7th choice, 220th overall in the 1993 draft. Traded to the Oilers from the Sabres with Craig Millar for Miroslav Satan, March 18, 1997.

First Game as an Oiler: March 24, 1997

First Assist as an Oiler: None Recorded

First Goal as an Oiler: None Recorded

First Penalty as an Oiler: None Recorded

Where He Went: Rights traded to Washington for Brad Church February 3, 1999.

Season	GP	G	A	Pts	Shots	S%	GW	GT	PP	SH	P/M	PIM
1996-97	4	0	0	0	1	0.0	0	0	0	0	0	0

MOREAU, ETHAN BYRON SWEATER # 18 LEFT WING SL
Born: Huntsville, Ontario September 22, 1975 6'2"-205
Last Amateur Club: Sudbury Wolves (OHL)
How the Oilers Got Him: Chicago's 1st choice, 14th overall in the 1994 draft. Traded to the Oilers by Chicago with Christian Laflamme, Chad Kilger and Daniel Cleary for Boris Mironov, Dean McAmmond and Jonas Elofsson, March 20, 1999.
First Game as an Oiler: March 20, 1999 *First Assist as an Oiler:* March 20, 1999
First Goal as an Oiler: April 9, 1999 *First Penalty as an Oiler:* March 20, 1999

Season	GP	G	A	Pts	Shots	S%	GW	GT	PP	SH	P/M	PIM
1998-99	14	1	5	6	16	6.3	1	0	0	0	2	8
Playoffs	*4*	*0*	*3*	*3*	*6*	*0.0*	*0*	*0*	*0*	*0*	*3*	*6*
1999-00	73	17	10	27	106	16.0	3	0	1	0	8	62
Playoffs	*5*	*0*	*1*	*1*	*5*	*0.0*	*0*	*0*	*0*	*0*	*0*	*0*
2000-01	68	9	10	19	97	9.3	3	0	0	1	-6	90
Playoffs	*4*	*0*	*0*	*0*	*5*	*0.0*	*0*	*0*	*0*	*0*	*-2*	*2*
3 years	155	27	25	52	219	12.3	7	0	1	1	4	160
Playoffs	*13*	*0*	*4*	*4*	*16*	*0.0*	*0*	*0*	*0*	*0*	*1*	*8*

MUIR, BRYAN SWEATER # 35, # 6 DEFENSE SL
Born: Winnipeg, Manitoba June 8, 1973 6'4"-220
Last Amateur Club: Canadian National Team
How the Oilers Got Him: Signed as a free agent by the Oilers, April 30, 1996.
First Game as an Oiler: March 8, 1996 *First Assist as an Oiler:* None Recorded
First Goal as an Oiler: None Recorded *First Penalty as an Oiler:* April 10, 1996
Where He Went: Traded to New Jersey with Jason Arnott for Bill Guerin and Valeri Zelepukin, January 4, 1998.

Season	GP	G	A	Pts	Shots	S%	GW	GT	PP	SH	P/M	PIM
1995-96	5	0	0	0	4	0.0	0	0	0	0	-4	6
Playoffs (96-97)	*5*	*0*	*0*	*0*	*7*	*0.0*	*0*	*0*	*0*	*0*	*-2*	*4*
1997-98	7	0	0	0	6	0.0	0	0	0	0	0	17
2 years	12	0	0	0	10	0.0	0	0	0	0	-4	23
Playoffs	*5*	*0*	*0*	*0*	*7*	*0.0*	*0*	*0*	*0*	*0*	*-2*	*4*

MUNI, CRAIG DOUGLAS SWEATER # 28 DEFENSE SL
Born: Toronto, Ontario July 19, 1962 6'3"-210
Last Amateur Club: Windsor Spitfires (OHL)
How the Oilers Got Him: Toronto's 1st choice, 25th overall in the 1980 draft. Signed as a free agent by the Oilers, August 18, 1986.
First Game as an Oiler: October 9, 1986 *First Assist as an Oiler:* October 19, 1986
First Goal as an Oiler: November 8, 1986 *First Penalty as an Oiler:* October 12, 1986
Where He Went: Sold to Buffalo October 2, 1986. Traded to the Oilers from Pittsburgh, October 6, 1986 to complete September 11, 1985 trade which sent Gilles Meloche to the Penguins for Tim Hrynewich, Marty McSorley and future considerations. Traded to Chicago for Mike Hudson, March 22, 1993.

Season	GP	G	A	Pts	Shots	S%	GW	GT	PP	SH	P/M	PIM
1986-87	79	7	22	29	69	10.1	2	0	0	0	45	85
Playoffs	*14*	*0*	*2*	*2*	*11*	*0.0*	*0*	*0*	*0*	*0*	*2*	*17*
1987-88	72	4	15	19	56	7.1	0	0	0	1	32	77
Playoffs	*19*	*0*	*4*	*4*	*11*	*0.0*	*0*	*0*	*0*	*0*	*7*	*31*
1988-89	69	5	13	18	40	12.5	1	0	0	0	43	71
Playoffs	*7*	*0*	*3*	*3*	*4*	*0.0*	*0*	*0*	*0*	*0*	*-1*	*8*
1989-90	71	5	12	17	42	11.9	0	0	0	2	22	81
Playoffs	*22*	*0*	*3*	*3*	*13*	*0.0*	*0*	*0*	*0*	*0*	*7*	*16*
1990-91	76	1	9	10	47	2.1	0	0	0	0	10	77
Playoffs	*18*	*0*	*3*	*3*	*10*	*0.0*	*0*	*0*	*0*	*0*	*5*	*20*
1991-92	54	2	5	7	38	5.3	0	0	0	0	11	34
Playoffs	*3*	*0*	*0*	*0*	*3*	*0.0*	*0*	*0*	*0*	*0*	*-4*	*2*
1992-93	72	0	11	11	51	0.0	0	0	0	0	-15	67
7 years	493	24	87	111	343	7.0	3	0	0	3	148	492
Playoffs	*83*	*0*	*15*	*15*	*52*	*0.0*	*0*	*0*	*0*	*0*	*16*	*94*

MURDOCH, DONALD WALTER SWEATER # 47 RIGHT WING SR
Born: Cranbrook, British Columbia October, 25, 1956 5'11"-180
Last Amateur Club: Medicine Hat Tigers (WCHL)

How the Oilers Got Him: Rangers' 1st choice, 6th overall in the 1976 draft. Traded by New York to Edmonton for Cam Connor and the Oilers' 3rd choice (Peter Sundstrum) in the 1981 Entry Draft, March 11, 1980.
First Game as an Oiler: March 12, 1980 *First Assist as an Oiler:* March 21, 1980
First Goal as an Oiler: March 14, 1980 *First Penalty as an Oiler*: March 12, 1980
Where He Went: Rights traded to Minnesota for Don Jackson August 21, 1981.

Season	*GP*	*G*	*A*	*Pts*	*Shots*	*S%*	*GW*	*GT*	*PP*	*SH*	*P/M*	*PIM*
1979-80	10	5	2	7	35	14.3	0	0	1	0	0	4
Playoffs	*3*	*2*	*0*	*2*			*0*	*0*	*0*	*0*		*0*
1980-81	40	10	9	19	102	9.8	2	0	4	0	-16	18
2 years	50	15	11	26	135	11.1	2	0	5	0	-16	22
Playoffs	*3*	*2*	*0*	*2*			*0*	*0*	*0*	*0*		*0*

Murphy, Joseph Patrick Sweater # 8 Center SL
Born: London, Ontario October 16, 1967 6'1"-190
Last Amateur Club: Michigan State University Spartans (CCHA)
How the Oilers Got Him: Detroit's 1st choice, 1st overall in the 1986 draft. Traded to the Oilers by Detroit with Adam Graves, Petr Klima, and Jeff Sharples for Jimmy Carson, Kevin McClelland and the Oilers' 5th choice (later traded to Montreal in exchange for Rick Green; Montreal selected Brad Layzell) in the 1991 draft, November 2, 1989.
First Game as an Oiler: November 3, 1989 *First Assist as an Oiler:* November 3, 1989
First Goal as an Oiler: November 19, 1989 *First Penalty as an Oiler:* November 24, 1989
Where He Went: Traded to Chicago for Igor Kravchuk and Dean McAmmond, February 24, 1993.

Season	*GP*	*G*	*A*	*Pts*	*Shots*	*S%*	*GW*	*GT*	*PP*	*SH*	*P/M*	*PIM*
1989-90	62	7	18	25	101	6.9	0	0	2	0	1	56
Playoffs	*22*	*6*	*8*	*14*	*29*	*20.7*	*2*	*1*	*0*	*0*	*1*	*16*
1990-91	80	27	35	62	141	19.1	4	1	4	1	2	35
Playoffs	*15*	*2*	*5*	*7*	*22*	*9.1*	*1*	*0*	*1*	*0*	*3*	*14*
1991-92	80	35	47	82	193	18.1	2	2	10	2	17	52
Playoffs	*16*	*8*	*16*	*24*	*32*	*25.0*	*2*	*1*	*4*	*0*	*2*	*12*
3 years	222	69	100	169	435	15.9	6	3	16	3	20	143
Playoffs	*53*	*16*	*29*	*45*	*83*	*19.2*	*5*	*2*	*5*	*0*	*6*	*42*

Murray, Raymond (Rem) Sweater # 17 Left Wing SL
Born: Stratford, Ontario October 9, 1972 6'2"-195
Last Amateur Club: Michigan State University Spartans (CCHA)
How the Oilers Got Him: Los Angeles' 5th choice, 135th overall in the 1992 draft. Signed as a free agent by Edmonton, September 19, 1995.
First Game as an Oiler: October 4, 1996 *First Assist as an Oiler:* October 8, 1996
First Goal as an Oiler: October 4, 1996 *First Penalty as an Oiler:* November 7, 1996

Season	*GP*	*G*	*A*	*Pts*	*Shots*	*S%*	*GW*	*GT*	*PP*	*SH*	*P/M*	*PIM*
1996-97	82	11	20	31	85	12.9	2	0	1	0	9	16
Playoffs	*12*	*1*	*2*	*3*	*7*	*14.3*	*0*	*0*	*0*	*0*	*-1*	*4*
1997-98	61	9	9	18	59	15.3	0	0	0	0	-2	89
Playoffs	*11*	*1*	*4*	*5*	*15*	*6.7*	*0*	*0*	*0*	*0*	*-1*	*2*
1998-99	78	21	18	39	116	18.1	4	1	4	1	4	20
Playoffs	*4*	*1*	*1*	*2*	*6*	*16.7*	*0*	*0*	*0*	*0*	*-1*	*2*
1999-00	44	9	5	14	65	13.8	3	0	2	0	-2	8
Playoffs	*5*	*0*	*1*	*1*	*9*	*0.0*	*0*	*0*	*0*	*0*	*-1*	*2*
2000-01	82	15	20	35	122	12.3	3	1	1	3	5	24
Playoffs	*6*	*2*	*0*	*2*	*15*	*13.3*	*0*	*1*	*1*	*0*	*-2*	*6*
5 years	347	65	72	137	447	14.5	12	2	8	4	14	157
Playoffs	*38*	*5*	*8*	*13*	*52*	*9.6*	*0*	*1*	*1*	*0*	*-6*	*16*

Musil, Frantisek Sweater # 8 Defense SL
Born: Pardubice, Czechoslovakia December 17, 1964 6'3"-215
Last Amateur Club: Dukla Jihlava (Czech)
How the Oilers Got Him: Traded to the Oilers from Ottawa for Scott Ferguson, March 9, 1998.
First Game as an Oiler: March 11, 1998 *First Assist as an Oiler:* March 18, 1998
First Goal as an Oiler: April 11, 1998 *First Penalty as an Oiler:* March 11, 1998

Season	*GP*	*G*	*A*	*Pts*	*Shots*	*S%*	*GW*	*GT*	*PP*	*SH*	*P/M*	*PIM*
1997-98	17	1	2	3	8	12.5	1	0	0	1	1	8
Playoffs	*7*	*0*	*0*	*0*	*0*	*0.0*	*0*	*0*	*0*	*0*	*1*	*6*

Season	GP	G	A	Pts	Shots	S%	GW	GT	PP	SH	P/M	PIM
1998-99	39	0	3	3	9	0.0	0	0	0	0	0	34
Playoffs	*1*	*0*	*0*	*0*	*2*	*0.0*	*0*	*0*	*0*	*0*	*-1*	*2*
2000-01	13	0	2	2	0	0.0	0	0	0	0	-2	4
3 years	69	1	7	8	17	5.9	1	0	0	1	-1	46
Playoffs	*8*	*0*	*0*	*0*	*2*	*0.0*	*0*	*0*	*0*	*0*	*0*	*8*

NACHBAUR, DONALD KENNETH SWEATER # 26 CENTER SL
Born: Kitimat, British Columbia January 30, 1959 6'2"-200
Last Amateur Club: Billings Bighorns (WHL)
How the Oilers Got Him: Hartford's 3rd choice, 60th overall in 1979 draft. Traded by the Hartford Whalers to the Oilers with Ken Linseman for Risto Siltanen and the rights to Brent Loney, August 19, 1982.
First Game as an Oiler: October 9, 1982 *First Assist as an Oiler:* None Recorded
First Goal as an Oiler: None Recorded *First Penalty as an Oiler:* October 9, 1982
Where He Went: Claimed by Los Angeles in the Waiver Draft, October 3, 1983.

Season	GP	G	A	Pts	Shots	S%	GW	GT	PP	SH	P/M	PIM
1982-83	4	0	0	0	0	0.0	0	0	0	0	-1	17
Playoffs	*2*	*0*	*0*	*0*	*0*	*0.0*	*0*	*0*	*0*	*0*	*-1*	*7*

NAPIER, ROBERT MARK SWEATER # 18, # 65 RIGHT WING SL
Born: Toronto, Ontario January 28, 1957 5'10"-185
Last Amateur Club: Toronto Marlboros (OHL)
How the Oilers Got Him: Montreal's 1st choice, 10th overall in the 1977 draft. Traded to the Oilers by Minnesota for Gord Sherven and Terry Martin, January 24, 1985.
First Game as an Oiler: January 21, 1985 *First Assist as an Oiler:* January 25, 1985
First Goal as an Oiler: January 26, 1985 *First Penalty as an Oiler:* January 29, 1985
Where He Went: Traded to Buffalo with Lee Fogolin for Normand Lacombe, Wayne Van Dorp and future considerations, March 6, 1987.

Season	GP	G	A	Pts	Shots	S%	GW	GT	PP	SH	P/M	PIM
1984-85	33	9	26	35	50	18.0	0	1	3	0	12	19
Playoffs	*18*	*5*	*5*	*10*	*20*	*25.0*	*0*	*0*	*1*	*0*	*8*	*7*
1985-86	80	24	32	56	117	20.5	4	1	3	1	13	14
Playoffs	*10*	*1*	*4*	*5*	*14*	*7.1*	*0*	*0*	*0*	*0*	*6*	*0*
1986-87	62	8	13	21	88	9.1	0	0	0	1	3	2
3 years	175	41	71	112	255	16.1	4	2	6	2	28	35
Playoffs	*28*	*6*	*9*	*15*	*34*	*17.6*	*0*	*0*	*1*	*0*	*14*	*7*

NETHERY, LANCE SWEATER # 28 CENTER SL
Born: Toronto, Ontario June 28, 1957 6'1"-185
Last Amateur Club: Cornell University Big Red (ECAC)
How the Oilers Got Him: New York Rangers' 9th choice, 131st overall in 1977 draft. Traded to the Oilers for Ed Mio, December 11, 1981.
First Game as an Oiler: December 27, 1981 *First Assist as an Oiler:* December 27, 1981
First Goal as an Oiler: None Recorded *First Penalty as an Oiler:* December 31, 1981
Where He Went: Retired.

Season	GP	G	A	Pts	Shots	S%	GW	GT	PP	SH	P/M	PIM
1981-82	3	0	2	2	1	0.0	0	0	0	0	1	2

NEWMAN, DANIEL KENNETH SWEATER # 16 LEFT WING SL
Born: Windsor, Ontario January 26, 1952 6'1"-195
Last Amateur Club: Port Huron Flags (IHL)
How the Oilers Got Him: Traded to the Oilers by Montreal with Dave Lumley for the Oilers' 2nd round choice (Ric Nattress) in the 1980 entry draft, June 13, 1979.
First Game as an Oiler: October 30, 1979 *First Assist as an Oiler:* November 8, 1979
First Goal as an Oiler: November 2, 1979 *First Penalty as an Oiler:* None Recorded
Where He Went: Traded to Boston for Bobby Schmautz, December 10, 1979.

Season	GP	G	A	Pts	Shots	S%	GW	GT	PP	SH	P/M	PIM
1979-80	10	3	1	4	16	18.8	0	0	0	0	-1	0

NICHOLLS, BERNIE IRVINE SWEATER # 9 CENTER SR
Born: Haliburton, Ontario June 24, 1961 6'0"-185
Last Amateur Club: Kingston Canadians (OHA)
How the Oilers Got Him: Los Angeles' 6th choice, 73rd overall in the 1980 draft. Traded to the Oilers by the New York Rangers with Louie DeBrusk and Steve Rice for Mark Messier and future considerations, October 4, 1991.
First Game as an Oiler: December 10, 1991
First Assist as an Oiler: December 10, 1991
First Goal as an Oiler: December 12, 1991
First Penalty as an Oiler: December 18, 1991
Where He Went: Traded to New Jersey for Zdeno Ciger and Kevin Todd, January 13, 1993.

Season	*GP*	*G*	*A*	*Pts*	*Shots*	*S%*	*GW*	*GT*	*PP*	*SH*	*P/M*	*PIM*
1991-92	49	20	29	49	115	17.4	2	0	7	0	5	60
Playoffs	*16*	*8*	*11*	*19*	*32*	*25.0*	*1*	*0*	*4*	*0*	*2*	*25*
1992-93	46	8	32	40	86	9.3	1	0	4	0	-16	40
2 years	95	28	61	89	201	13.9	3	0	11	0	-11	100
Playoffs	*16*	*8*	*11*	*19*	*32*	*25.0*	*1*	*0*	*4*	*0*	*2*	*25*

NIINIMAA, JANNE HENRIK SWEATER # 24, #44 DEFENSE SL
Born: Raahe, Finland May 22, 1975 6'1"-220
Last Amateur Club: Jokerit (Fin)
How the Oilers Got Him: Traded to the Oilers for Dan McGillis and the Oilers' 2nd round choice (Jason Beckett) in the 1998 draft, March 24, 1998.
First Game as an Oiler: March 25, 1998
First Assist as an Oiler: April 1, 1998
First Goal as an Oiler: April 11, 1998
First Penalty as an Oiler: April 3, 1998

Season	*GP*	*G*	*A*	*Pts*	*Shots*	*S%*	*GW*	*GT*	*PP*	*SH*	*P/M*	*PIM*
1997-98	11	1	8	9	19	5.3	0	0	1	0	7	6
Playoffs	*11*	*1*	*1*	*2*	*20*	*5.0*	*1*	*0*	*0*	*0*	*3*	*12*
1998-99	81	4	24	28	142	2.8	1	0	2	0	7	88
Playoffs	*4*	*0*	*0*	*0*	*5*	*0.0*	*0*	*0*	*0*	*0*	*-2*	*2*
1999-00	81	8	25	33	133	6.0	0	0	2	2	14	89
Playoffs	*5*	*0*	*2*	*2*	*8*	*0.0*	*0*	*0*	*0*	*0*	*1*	*2*
2000-01	82	12	33	45	122	9.8	1	0	8	0	6	90
Playoffs	*6*	*0*	*2*	*2*	*11*	*0.0*	*0*	*0*	*0*	*0*	*-1*	*6*
4 years	255	25	90	115	416	6.0	2	0	13	2	34	273
Playoffs	*26*	*1*	*5*	*6*	*44*	*3.0*	*1*	*0*	*0*	*0*	*1*	*22*

NILSSON, KENT SWEATER # 15, # 14 CENTER SL
Born: Nynashamn, Sweden August 31, 1956 6'1"-195
Last Amateur Club: MoDo AIK (Swe)
How the Oilers Got Him: Atlanta's 5th choice, 64th overall in the 1976 draft. Traded to the Oilers by Minnesota, for future considerations, on March 2, 1987.
First Game as an Oiler: March 4, 1987
First Assist as an Oiler: March 4, 1987
First Goal as an Oiler: March 15, 1987
First Penalty as an Oiler: March 4, 1987
Where He Went: Retired.

Season	*GP*	*G*	*A*	*Pts*	*Shots*	*S%*	*GW*	*GT*	*PP*	*SH*	*P/M*	*PIM*
1986-87	17	5	12	17	25	20.0	0	0	1	0	10	4
Playoffs	*21*	*6*	*13*	*19*	*46*	*13.0*	*0*	*0*	*2*	*0*	*11*	*6*
1994-95	6	1	0	1	2	50.0	0	0	1	0	-5	0
2 years	23	6	12	18	27	22.2	0	0	2	0	5	4
Playoffs	*21*	*6*	*13*	*19*	*46*	*13.0*	*0*	*0*	*2*	*0*	*11*	*6*

NORTON, JEFFREY THOMAS SWEATER # 6 DEFENSE SL
Born: Acton, Massachusetts November 25, 1965 6'2"-200
Last Amateur Club: US Olympic Team
How the Oilers Got Him: New York Islanders' 3rd choice, 62nd overall in the 1984 draft. Traded to the Oilers from the St. Louis Blues with Donald Dufresne for Igor Kravchuk and Ken Sutton, January 4, 1996.
First Game as an Oiler: January 5, 1996
First Assist as an Oiler: January 9, 1996
First Goal as an Oiler: January 13, 1996
First Penalty as an Oiler: January 7, 1996
Where He Went: Traded to Tampa Bay for Drew Bannister and the Lightnings' 6th choice in the 1997 draft (Peter Sarno), March 18, 1997.

Season	*GP*	*G*	*A*	*Pts*	*Shots*	*S%*	*GW*	*GT*	*PP*	*SH*	*P/M*	*PIM*
1995-96	30	4	16	20	52	7.7	1	0	1	0	5	16
1996-97	62	2	11	13	68	2.9	0	0	0	0	-7	42
2 years	92	6	27	33	120	5.0	1	0	1	0	-2	58

ODELEIN, SELMAR SWEATER # 16, # 36 DEFENSE SR
Born: Quill Lake, Saskatchewan April 11, 1966 6'0"-195
Last Amateur Club: Regina Pats (WHL)
How the Oilers Got Him: Edmonton's 1st choice, 21st overall in the 1984 draft.
First Game as an Oiler: February 14, 1986
First Assist as an Oiler: January 19, 1988
First Goal as an Oiler: None Recorded
First Penalty as an Oiler: January 23, 1988
Where He Went: Retired.

Season	GP	G	A	Pts	Shots	S%	GW	GT	PP	SH	P/M	PIM
1985-86	4	0	0	0	2	0.0	0	0	0	0	1	0
1987-88	12	0	2	2	17	0.0	0	0	0	0	-2	33
1988-89	2	0	0	0	0	0.0	0	0	0	0	-1	2
3 years	18	0	2	2	19	0.0	0	0	0	0	-2	35

OKSIUTA, ROMAN SWEATER # 28 RIGHT WING SL
Born: Murmansk, USSR August 21, 1970 6'3"-230
Last Amateur Club: Khimik Voskresensk (CIS)
How the Oilers Got Him: New York Rangers' 11th choice, 202nd overall in the 1989 draft. Traded to the Oilers, with the Rangers' 3rd round choice (Alexander Kerch) in the 1993 draft, for Kevin Lowe, December 11, 1992.
First Game as an Oiler: October 6, 1993
First Assist as an Oiler: October 8, 1993
First Goal as an Oiler: February 6, 1994
First Penalty as an Oiler: October 30, 1993
Where He Went: Traded to Vancouver for Jiri Slegr, April 7, 1995.

Season	GP	G	A	Pts	Shots	S%	GW	GT	PP	SH	P/M	PIM
1993-94	10	1	2	3	18	5.6	0	0	0	0	-1	4
1994-95	26	11	2	13	52	21.2	0	0	5	0	-14	8
2 years	36	12	4	16	70	17.1	0	0	5	0	-15	12

OLAUSSON, FREDRICK SWEATER # 15 DEFENSE SR
Born: Dadesjo, Sweden October 5, 1966 6'2"-195
Last Amateur Club: Farjestads BK (Swe)
How the Oilers Got Him: Winnipeg's 4th choice, 81st overall in the 1985 draft. Traded to the Oilers from the Winnipeg Jets, with the Jets' 7th round pick (Curtis Sheptak) in the 1994 draft, for the Oilers' 3rd round choice (Tavis Hansen) in the 1994 draft, December 6, 1993.
First Game as an Oiler: December 7, 1993
First Assist as an Oiler: December 11, 1993
First Goal as an Oiler: January 13, 1993
First Penalty as an Oiler: December 12, 1993
Where He Went: Claimed on waivers by Anaheim, January 16, 1996.

Season	GP	G	A	Pts	Shots	S%	GW	GT	PP	SH	P/M	PIM
1993-94	55	9	19	28	85	10.6	1	0	6	0	-4	20
1994-95	33	0	10	10	52	0.0	0	0	0	0	-4	20
1995-96	20	0	6	6	20	0.0	0	0	0	0	-14	14
3 years	108	9	35	44	157	5.7	1	0	6	0	-22	54

OLIVER, DAVID LEE SWEATER # 20 RIGHT WING SR
Born: Sechelt, British Columbia April 17, 1971 6'0"-190
Last Amateur Club: University of Michigan Wolverines (CCHA)
How the Oilers Got Him: Edmonton's 7th choice, 144th overall in the 1991 draft.
First Game as an Oiler: January 20, 1995
First Assist as an Oiler: January 20, 1995
First Goal as an Oiler: January 20, 1995
First Penalty as an Oiler: January 30, 1995
Where He Went: Claimed on waivers by the New York Rangers, February 21, 1997.

Season	GP	G	A	Pts	Shots	S%	GW	GT	PP	SH	P/M	PIM
1994-95	44	16	14	30	79	20.3	0	1	10	0	-11	20
1995-96	80	20	19	39	131	15.3	0	0	14	0	-22	34
1996-97	17	1	2	3	22	4.5	0	0	0	0	-8	4
3 years	141	37	35	72	232	15.9	0	1	24	0	-41	58

PASSMORE, STEVE SWEATER # 29 GOALTENDER CL
Born: Thunder Bay, Ontario January 29, 1973 5'9"-165
Last Amateur Club: Kamloops Blazers (WHL)
How the Oilers Got Him: Quebec's 10th choice, 196th overall in the 1992 draft. Traded to the Oilers by the Nordiques for Brad Werenka, March 21, 1994.
First Game as an Oiler: February 24, 1999
First Assist as an Oiler: March 17, 1999

First Goal as an Oiler: None Recorded *First Penalty as an Oiler:* March 17, 1999
Where He Went: Signed as a free agent by Chicago July 8, 1999.

Season	*GP*	*Min*	*GA*	*W*	*L*	*T*	*Ave*	*SA*	*S%*	*SO*	*EN*	*PIM*	*Ast.*
1998-99	6	362	17	1	4	1	2.82	183	0.907	0	1	2	1

PEARSON, SCOTT SWEATER # 33 LEFT WING SL
Born: Cornwall, Ontario December 19, 1969 6'1"-205
Last Amateur Club: Niagara Falls Thunder (OHL)
How the Oilers Got Him: Toronto's 1st choice, 6th overall in the 1988 draft. Traded to the Oilers by the Quebec Nordiques for Martin Gelinas and the Oilers' 6th pick (Nicholas Checco) in the 1993 draft, June 20, 1993.
First Game as an Oiler: October 6, 1993 *First Assist as an Oiler:* October 20, 1993
First Goal as an Oiler: October 8, 1993 *First Penalty as an Oiler:* October 6, 1993
Where He Went: Traded to Buffalo for Ken Sutton, April 7, 1995.

Season	*GP*	*G*	*A*	*Pts*	*Shots*	*S%*	*GW*	*GT*	*PP*	*SH*	*P/M*	*PIM*
1993-94	72	19	18	37	160	11.9	7	0	3	0	-4	165
1994-95	28	1	4	5	21	4.8	0	0	0	0	-11	54
2 years	100	20	22	42	181	11.0	7	0	3	0	-15	219

PETIT, MICHEL SWEATER # 8 DEFENSE SR
Born: St. Malo, Quebec February 12, 1964 6'1"-205
Last Amateur Club: Canadian National Team
How the Oilers Got Him: Vancouver's 1st choice, 11th overall in the 1982 draft. Signed as a free agent by the Oilers, October 24, 1996.
First Game as an Oiler: October 24, 1996 *First Assist as an Oiler:* October 24, 1996
First Goal as an Oiler: November 7, 1997 *First Penalty as an Oiler:* October 24, 1996
Where He Went: Claimed on waivers by Philadelphia, January 17, 1997.

Season	*GP*	*G*	*A*	*Pts*	*Shots*	*S%*	*GW*	*GT*	*PP*	*SH*	*P/M*	*PIM*
1996-97	18	2	4	6	30	6.7	0	0	0	0	-13	20

PICARD, MICHEL SWEATER # 12 LEFT WING SL
Born: Beauport, Quebec November 7, 1969 5'11"-190
Last Amateur Club: Trois Rivieres Draveurs (QMJHL)
How the Oilers Got Him: Hartford's 8th choice, 178th overall in the 1989 draft. Signed as a free agent by the Oilers, December 2, 1999.
First Game as an Oiler: December 8, 1999 *First Assist as an Oiler:* None Recorded
First Goal as an Oiler: None Recorded *First Penalty as an Oiler:* December 9, 1999
Where He Went: Signed as a free agent by Philadelphia, August 14, 2000.

Season	*GP*	*G*	*A*	*Pts*	*Shots*	*S%*	*GW*	*GT*	*PP*	*SH*	*P/M*	*PIM*
1999-00	2	0	0	0	2	0.0	0	0	0	0	0	2

PITTIS, DOMENIC SWEATER # 14 CENTER SL
Born: Calgary, Alberta October 1, 1974 5'11"-190
Last Amateur Club: Lethbridge Broncos (WHL)
How the Oilers Got Him: Pittsburgh's 2nd choice, 52nd overall in the 1993 draft. Signed as a free agent by the Oilers, July 25, 2000.
First Game as an Oiler: October 30, 2000 *First Assist as an Oiler:* November 3, 2000
First Goal as an Oiler: November 1, 2000 *First Penalty as an Oiler:* November 1, 2000

Season	*GP*	*G*	*A*	*Pts*	*Shots*	*S%*	*GW*	*GT*	*PP*	*SH*	*P/M*	*PIM*
2000-01	47	4	5	9	42	9.5	2	0	0	0	-5	49
Playoffs	*3*	*0*	*0*	*0*	*1*	*0.0*	*0*	*0*	*0*	*0*	*-1*	*2*

PLAYFAIR, JAMES SWEATER # 5, # 29 DEFENSE SL
Born: Fort St. James, British Columbia May 22, 1964 6'4"-200
Last Amateur Club: Portland Winter Hawks (WHL)
How the Oilers Got Him: Oilers' 1st choice, 20th overall in the 1982 draft.
First Game as an Oiler: November 19, 1983 *First Assist as an Oiler:* November 19, 1983
First Goal as an Oiler: November 19, 1983 *First Penalty as an Oiler:* January 4, 1984
Where He Went: Signed as a free agent by Chicago, July 31, 1987.

Season	*GP*	*G*	*A*	*Pts*	*Shots*	*S%*	*GW*	*GT*	*PP*	*SH*	*P/M*	*PIM*
1983-84	2	1	1	2	2	50.0	0	0	0	0	4	2

PODEIN, SHJON SWEATER # 26 LEFT WING SL
Born: Rochester, Minnesota March 5, 1968 6'2"-200
Last Amateur Club: University of Minnesota-Duluth Bulldogs (WCHA)
How the Oilers Got Him: Edmonton's 9th choice, 166th overall in the 1988 draft.
First Game as an Oiler: January 9, 1993 *First Assist as an Oiler:* January 22, 1993
First Goal as an Oiler: January 9, 1993 *First Penalty as an Oiler:* January 13, 1993
Where He Went: Signed as a free agent by Philadelphia, July 27, 1994.

Season	*GP*	*G*	*A*	*Pts*	*Shots*	*S%*	*GW*	*GT*	*PP*	*SH*	*P/M*	*PIM*
1992-93	40	13	6	19	64	20.3	1	0	2	1	-2	25
1993-94	28	3	5	8	26	11.5	0	0	0	0	3	8
2 years	68	16	11	27	90	17.8	1	0	2	1	1	33

PODDUBNY, WALTER MICHAEL SWEATER # 14 CENTER SL
Born: Thunder Bay, Ontario February 14, 1960 6'1"-205
Last Amateur Club: Kingston Canadians (OHL)
How the Oilers Got Him: Edmonton's 4 th choice, 90th overall in 1980 draft.
First Game as an Oiler: October 7, 1981 *First Assist as an Oiler:* None Recorded
First Goal as an Oiler: None Recorded *First Penalty as an Oiler:* None Recorded
Where He Went: Traded to Toronto with Phil Drouilliard for Laurie Boschman, March 28, 1982.

Season	*GP*	*G*	*A*	*Pts*	*Shots*	*S%*	*GW*	*GT*	*PP*	*SH*	*P/M*	*PIM*
1981-82	4	0	0	0	2	0.0	0	0	0	0	-1	0

POPIEL, POUL PETER SWEATER # 22 DEFENSE SL
Born: Sollested, Denmark February 28, 1943 5'8"-170
Last Amateur Club: St. Catherines Black Hawks (OHL)
How the Oilers Got Him: Signed as a free agent by the Oilers, November 2, 1979.
First Game as an Oiler: November 4, 1979 *First Assist as an Oiler:* None Recorded
First Goal as an Oiler: None Recorded *First Penalty as an Oiler:* None Recorded
Where He Went: Retired.

Season	*GP*	*G*	*A*	*Pts*	*Shots*	*S%*	*GW*	*GT*	*PP*	*SH*	*P/M*	*PIM*
1979-80	10	0	0	0	12	0.0	0	0	0	0	-5	0

POTI, THOMAS EMILIO SWEATER # 5 DEFENSE SL
Born: Worcester, Massachusetts March 22, 1977 6'3"-215
Last Amateur Club: Boston University Terriers (HE)
How the Oilers Got Him: Oilers' fourth choice, 59th overall in the 1996 draft.
First Game as an Oiler: October 10, 1998 *First Assist as an Oiler:* November 29, 1998
First Goal as an Oiler: November 18, 1998 *First Penalty as an Oiler:* October 13, 1998

Season	*GP*	*G*	*A*	*Pts*	*Shots*	*S%*	*GW*	*GT*	*PP*	*SH*	*P/M*	*PIM*
1998-99	73	5	16	21	94	5.3	3	0	2	0	10	42
Playoffs	*4*	*0*	*1*	*1*	*9*	*0.0*	*0*	*0*	*0*	*0*	*-3*	*2*
1999-00	76	9	26	35	125	7.2	1	0	2	1	8	65
Playoffs	*5*	*0*	*1*	*1*	*7*	*0.0*	*0*	*0*	*0*	*0*	*-3*	*0*
2000-01	81	12	20	32	161	7.5	3	0	6	0	-4	60
Playoffs	*6*	*0*	*2*	*2*	*7*	*0.0*	*0*	*0*	*0*	*0*	*2*	*2*
3 years	230	26	62	88	380	6.8	7	0	10	1	14	167
Playoffs	*15*	*0*	*4*	*4*	*23*	*0.0*	*0*	*0*	*0*	*0*	*-4*	*4*

POUZAR, JAROSLAV SWEATER # 10, # 20 LEFT WING SL
Born: Cakovec, Czechoslovakia January 23, 1952 5'11"-200
Last Amateur Club: Ceske Budejovice (Czech)
How the Oilers Got Him: Oilers' 4th choice, 83rd overall in 1982 draft.
First Game as an Oiler: October 5, 1982 *First Assist as an Oiler:* October 5, 1982
First Goal as an Oiler: October 5, 1982 *First Penalty as an Oiler*: October 8, 1982
Where He Went: Retired.

Season	*GP*	*G*	*A*	*Pts*	*Shots*	*S%*	*GW*	*GT*	*PP*	*SH*	*P/M*	*PIM*
1982-83	74	15	18	33	86	17.4	2	0	2	0	17	57
Playoffs	*1*	*2*	*0*	*2*	*2*	*100.0*	*1*	*0*	*1*	*0*	*1*	*0*
1983-84	67	13	19	32	87	14.9	0	0	2	0	17	44

Season	GP	G	A	Pts	Shots	S%	GW	GT	PP	SH	P/M	PIM
Playoffs	*14*	*1*	*2*	*3*	*14*	*7.1*	*1*	*0*	*0*	*0*	*0*	*12*
1984-85	33	4	8	12	36	11.1	1	0	0	0	3	28
Playoffs	*9*	*2*	*1*	*3*	*12*	*16.7*	*0*	*0*	*0*	*0*	*2*	*2*
1986-87	12	2	3	5	11	18.2	1	0	0	0	3	6
Playoffs	*5*	*1*	*1*	*2*	*9*	*11.1*	*0*	*0*	*0*	*0*	*4*	*2*
4 years	186	34	48	82	220	15.5	4	0	4	0	40	135
Playoffs	*29*	*6*	*4*	*10*	*37*	*16.2*	*2*	*0*	*1*	*0*	*7*	*16*

PRICE, SHAUN PATRICK SWEATER # 26 DEFENSE SL

Born: Nelson, British Columbia March 24, 1955 6'2"-200

Last Amateur Club: Saskatoon Blades (WHL)

How the Oilers Got Him: New York Islanders' 1st choice, 11th overall in 1975 draft. Chosen by the Oilers from the Islanders in the 1979 Expansion Draft, June 13th, 1979.

First Game as an Oiler: October 10, 1979 *First Assist as an Oiler:* October 24, 1979

First Goal as an Oiler: October 28, 1979 *First Penalty as an Oiler:* October 10, 1979

Where He Went: Traded to Pittsburgh for Pat Hughes, March 10, 1981.

Season	GP	G	A	Pts	Shots	S%	GW	GT	PP	SH	P/M	PIM
1979-80	75	11	21	32	95	11.6	0	1	2	0	4	134
Playoffs	*3*	*0*	*0*	*0*			*0*	*0*	*0*	*0*		*11*
1980-81	59	8	24	32	90	8.9	0	1	0	0	-7	193
2 years	134	19	45	64	185	10.3	0	2	2	0	-3	327
Playoffs	*3*	*0*	*0*	*0*			*0*	*0*	*0*	*0*		*11*

RANFORD, WILLIAM EDWARD SWEATER # 30 GOALTENDER CL

Born: Brandon, Manitoba December 14, 1966 5'10"-170

Last Amateur Club: New Westminster Bruins (WHL)

How the Oilers Got Him: Boston's 2nd choice, 52nd overall in the 1985 draft. Traded from the Bruins to the Oilers with Geoff Courtnall, in exchange for Andy Moog, March 7, 1988. Re-signed as a free agent by the Oilers, August 4, 1999.

First Game as an Oiler: March 12, 1988 *First Assist as an Oiler:* March 28, 1988

First Goal as an Oiler: None Recorded *First Penalty as an Oiler:* November 2, 1988

Where He Went: Traded to Boston for Mariusz Czerkawski, Sean Brown and the Bruins' 1st round choice in the 1996 draft (Matthieu Descoteaux), January 11, 1996. Retired.

Season	GP	Min	GA	W	L	T	Ave	SA	S%	SO	EN	PIM	Ast.
1987-88	6	325	16	3	0	2	2.95	159	0.889	0	0	0	2
1988-89	29	1509	88	15	8	2	3.50	718	0.877	1	1	2	0
1989-90	56	3107	165	24	16	9	3.19	1463	0.887	1	5	18	2
Playoffs	*22*	*1401*	*59*	*16*	*6*		*2.68*	*672*	*0.912*	*1*	*1*	*4*	*2*
1990-91	60	3415	182	27	27	3	3.20	1705	0.893	0	5	6	4
Playoffs	*3*	*135*	*8*	*1*	*2*		*2.66*	*78*	*0.897*	*0*	*0*	*0*	*0*
1991-92	67	3822	228	27	26	10	3.58	1971	0.884	1	5	4	3
Playoffs	*16*	*909*	*51*	*8*	*8*		*3.19*	*484*	*0.895*	*2*	*0*	*0*	*0*
1992-93	67	3753	240	17	38	6	3.84	2065	0.884	1	2	10	3
1993-94	71	4070	236	22	34	11	3.48	2325	0.898	1	8	2	2
1994-95	40	2203	133	15	20	3	3.62	1134	0.883	2	2	2	2
1995-96	37	2015	128	13	18	5	3.81	1024	0.875	1	2	2	1
1999-00	16	785	47	4	6	3	3.59	407	0.885	0	0	2	0
9 years	449	25004	1463	167	193	54	3.51	12971	0.887	8	30	48	19
Playoffs	*41*	*2445*	*118*	*25*	*16*		*2.90*	*1234*	*0.904*	*3*	*1*	*4*	*2*

REAUGH, DARYL SWEATER # 32, # 29 GOALTENDER CL

Born: Prince George, British Columbia February 13, 1965 6'4"-190

Last Amateur Club: Kamloops Junior Oilers (WHL)

How the Oilers Got Him: Oilers' 2nd choice, 42nd overall in the 1984 draft.

First Game as an Oiler: March 3, 1985 *First Assist as an Oiler:* None Recorded

First Goal as an Oiler: None Recorded *First Penalty as an Oiler:* None Recorded

Where He Went: Signed as a free agent by Hartford, October 9, 1989.

Season	GP	Min	GA	W	L	T	Ave	SA	S%	SO	EN	PIM	Ast.
1984-85	1	60	5	0	1	0	5.00	35	0.853	0	1	0	0
1987-88	6	176	14	1	1	0	4.78	114	0.870	0	0	0	0
2 years	7	236	19	1	2	0	4.83	149	0.872	0	1	0	0

Reddick, Eldon Wade Sweater # 33 Goaltender CL
Born: Halifax, Nova Scotia October 6, 1964 5'8"-170
Last Amateur Club: Brandon Wheat Kings (WHL)
How the Oilers Got Him: Traded to the Oilers by the Winnipeg Jets for future considerations, September 28, 1989.
First Game as an Oiler: February 6, 1990 *First Assist as an Oiler:* None Recorded
First Goal as an Oiler: None Recorded *First Penalty as an Oiler:* None Recorded
Where He Went: Signed as a free agent by Florida, July 12, 1993.

Season	GP	Min	GA	W	L	T	Ave	SA	S%	SO	EN	PIM	Ast.
1989-90	11	604	31	5	4	2	3.08	283	0.890	0	2	0	0
Playoffs	*1*	*2*	*0*	*0*	*0*		*0.00*	*1*	*1.000*	*0*	*0*	*0*	*0*
1990-91	2	120	9	0	2	0	4.50	59	0.847	0	0	0	0
2 years	13	724	40	5	6	2	3.31	342	0.883	0	2	0	0
Playoffs	*1*	*2*	*0*	*0*	*0*		*0.00*	*1*	*1.000*	*0*	*0*	*0*	*0*

Redmond, Craig Sanford Sweater # 26 Defense SL
Born: Dawson Creek, British Columbia September 22, 1965 5'11"-190
Last Amateur Club: Canadian Olympic Team
How the Oilers Got Him: Los Angeles' 1st choice, 6th overall in the 1984 draft. Traded to the Oilers for John Miner August 10, 1988.
First Game as an Oiler: January 4, 1989 *First Assist as an Oiler:* January 4, 1989
First Goal as an Oiler: January 7, 1989 *First Penalty as an Oiler:* January 4, 1989
Where He Went: Claimed by the Rangers in the Waiver Draft, October 3, 1988, claimed on waiver by the Oilers November. 1, 1988. Retired.

Season	GP	G	A	Pts	Shots	S%	GW	GT	PP	SH	P/M	PIM
1988-89	21	3	10	13	29	10.3	0	0	3	0	-10	12

Reirden, Todd Sweater # 46 Defense SL
Born: Deerfield, Illinois June 25, 1971 6'5"-220
Last Amateur Club: Bowling Green University Falcons (CCHA)
How the Oilers Got Him: New Jersey's 14th choice, 242nd overall in the 1990 draft. Signed as a free agent by the Oilers, May 31, 1998.
First Game as an Oiler: January 7, 1999 *First Assist as an Oiler:* January 10, 1999
First Goal as an Oiler: January 10, 1999 *First Penalty as an Oiler:* January 7, 1999
Where He Went: Claimed on waivers by the St. Louis Blues, September 30, 1999.

Season	GP	G	A	Pts	Shots	S%	GW	GT	PP	SH	P/M	PIM
1998-99	17	2	3	5	26	7.7	0	0	0	0	-1	20

Rice, Steven Sweater # 15, # 12 Right Wing SR
Born: Kitchener, Ontario May 26, 1971 6'0"-215
Last Amateur Club: Kitchener Rangers (OHL)
How the Oilers Got Him: New York Rangers' 1st choice, 20th overall in the 1989 draft. Traded to the Oilers from the Rangers with Louie DeBrusk, and Bernie Nicholls for Mark Messier and future considerations, October 4, 1991.
First Game as an Oiler: November 18, 1991 *First Assist as an Oiler:* February 28, 1993
First Goal as an Oiler: January 2, 1993 *First Penalty as an Oiler:* December 12, 1991
Where He Went: Signed as a free agent by Hartford, August 18, 1994.

Season	GP	G	A	Pts	Shots	S%	GW	GT	PP	SH	P/M	PIM
1991-92	3	0	0	0	2	0.0	0	0	0	0	-2	2
1992-93	28	2	5	7	29	6.9	0	0	0	0	-4	28
1993-94	63	17	15	32	129	13.2	1	1	6	0	-10	36
3 years	94	19	20	39	160	11.9	1	1	6	0	-16	66

Richardson, Luke Glen Sweater # 22 Defense SL
Born: Ottawa, Ontario March 26, 1969 6'4"-210
Last Amateur Club: Peterborough Petes (OHA)
How the Oilers Got Him: Toronto's 1st choice, 7th overall in the 1987 draft. Traded to the Oilers from Toronto with Vincent Damphousse, Peter Ing, Scott Thornton, future considerations and cash for Glenn Anderson, Craig Berube and Grant Fuhr, September 19, 1991.
First Game as an Oiler: October 4, 1991 *First Assist as an Oiler:* October 6, 1991
First Goal as an Oiler: December 12, 1991 *First Penalty as an Oiler:* October 4, 1991
Where He Went: Signed as a free agent by Philadelphia, July 23, 1997.

Season	*GP*	*G*	*A*	*Pts*	*Shots*	*S%*	*GW*	*GT*	*PP*	*SH*	*P/M*	*PIM*
1991-92	75	2	19	21	85	2.4	0	0	0	0	-9	118
Playoffs	*16*	*0*	*5*	*5*	*11*	*0.0*	*0*	*0*	*0*	*0*	*-2*	*45*
1992-93	82	3	10	13	78	3.8	0	0	0	2	-18	142
1993-94	69	2	6	8	92	2.2	0	0	0	0	-13	131
1994-95	46	3	10	13	51	5.9	1	0	1	1	-6	40
1995-96	82	2	9	11	61	3.3	0	0	0	0	-27	108
1996-97	82	1	11	12	67	1.5	0	0	0	0	9	91
Playoffs	*12*	*0*	*2*	*2*	*6*	*0.0*	*0*	*0*	*0*	*0*	*-4*	*14*
6 years	436	13	65	78	434	3.0	1	0	1	3	-64	630
Playoffs	*28*	*0*	*7*	*7*	*17*	*0.0*	*0*	*0*	*0*	*0*	*-6*	*59*

RIESEN, MICHEL — SWEATER # 34 — RIGHT WING — SR

Born: Oberbalm, Switzerland — April 11, 1979 — 6'2"-190

Last Amateur Club: EHC Biel (Swiss)

How the Oilers Got Him: Oilers' 1st choice, 14th overall in the 1997 draft.

First Game as an Oiler: October 6, 2000 — *First Assist as an Oiler:* October 15, 2000

First Goal as an Oiler: None Recorded — *First Penalty as an Oiler:* October 11, 2000

Season	*GP*	*G*	*A*	*Pts*	*Shots*	*S%*	*GW*	*GT*	*PP*	*SH*	*P/M*	*PIM*
2000-01	12	0	1	1	16	0.0	0	0	0	0	2	4

ROBERTS, DAVID — SWEATER # 15 — LEFT WING — SL

Born: Alameda, California — May 28, 1970 — 6'0"-185

Last Amateur Club: US Olympic Team

How the Oilers Got Him: St. Louis' 5th choice, 114th overall in the 1989 draft. Traded to the Oilers by the Blues for future considerations, March 12, 1996.

First Game as an Oiler: March 13, 1996 — *First Assist as an Oiler:* March 13, 1996

First Goal as an Oiler: March 13, 1996 — *First Penalty as an Oiler:* March 17, 1996

Where He Went: Signed as a free agent by Vancouver, July 31, 1996.

Season	*GP*	*G*	*A*	*Pts*	*Shots*	*S%*	*GW*	*GT*	*PP*	*SH*	*P/M*	*PIM*
1995-96	6	2	4	6	12	16.7	0	0	0	0	0	6

ROBERTSSON, BERT — SWEATER # 14 — LEFT WING/DEFENSE — SL

Born: Sodertalje, Sweden — June 30, 1974 — 6'3"-210

Last Amateur Club: Sodertalje SK (Swe)

How the Oilers Got Him: Vancouver's 8th choice, 254th overall in the 1993 draft. Signed as a free agent by the Oilers August 19, 1999.

First Game as an Oiler: October 26, 1999 — *First Assist as an Oiler:* December 11, 1999

First Goal as an Oiler: None Recorded — *First Penalty as an Oiler:* December 2, 1999

Where He Went: Choosen by the Columbus Blue Jackets in the Expansion Draft, June 23rd, 2000.

Season	*GP*	*G*	*A*	*Pts*	*Shots*	*S%*	*GW*	*GT*	*PP*	*SH*	*P/M*	*PIM*
1999-00	52	0	4	4	31	0.0	0	0	0	0	-3	34
Playoffs	*5*	*0*	*0*	*0*	*2*	*0.0*	*0*	*0*	*0*	*0*	*-1*	*0*

ROGERS, MICHAEL — SWEATER # 19 — CENTER — SL

Born: Calgary, Alberta — October 24, 1954 — 5'9"-170

Last Amateur Club: Calgary Centennials (WHL)

How the Oilers Got Him: Vancouver's 4th choice, 77th overall in the 1974 draft. Traded to the Oilers by the New York Rangers, for Larry Melnyk and Todd Strueby, December 20, 1985.

First Game as an Oiler: December 20, 1985 — *First Assist as an Oiler:* None Recorded

First Goal as an Oiler: December 20, 1985 — *First Penalty as an Oiler:* None Recorded

Where He Went: Retired.

Season	*GP*	*G*	*A*	*Pts*	*Shots*	*S%*	*GW*	*GT*	*PP*	*SH*	*P/M*	*PIM*
1985-86	8	1	0	1	6	16.7	0	0	0	0	-2	0

ROULSTON, THOMAS IRWIN — SWEATER # 23, # 24 — CENTER/RIGHT WING — SR

Born: Winnipeg, Manitoba — November 20, 1957 — 6'1"-185

Last Amateur Club: Winnipeg Monarchs (WCHL)

How the Oilers Got Him: St. Louis' 3rd choice, 45th overall in the 1977 draft. Traded to Edmonton by St. Louis with Risto Siltanen, for Joe Micheletti, August 7, 1979.

First Game as an Oiler: December 13, 1980
First Goal as an Oiler: December 16, 1980
First Assist as an Oiler: December 23, 1980
First Penalty as an Oiler: December 23, 1980
Where He Went: Traded to Pittsburgh for Kevin McClelland and the Penguins' 6th choice in the 1984 draft (Emanuel Viveiros) December 5, 1983.

Season	GP	G	A	Pts	Shots	S%	GW	GT	PP	SH	P/M	PIM
1980-81	11	1	1	2	9	11.1	0	0	0	0	-3	2
1981-82	35	11	3	14	54	20.4	0	0	0	1	-6	22
Playoffs	*5*	*1*	*0*	*1*			*0*	*0*	*0*	*0*		*2*
1982-83	67	19	21	40	107	17.8	2	0	2	0	29	24
Playoffs	*16*	*1*	*2*	*3*	*13*	*7.7*	*0*	*0*	*0*	*0*	*-1*	*0*
1983-84	24	5	7	12	38	13.2	0	0	1	0	0	16
4 years	137	36	32	68	208	17.3	2	0	3	1	20	64
Playoffs	*21*	*2*	*2*	*4*			*0*	*0*	*0*	*0*		*2*

ROUSSEL, DOMINIC — SWEATER # 30 — GOALTENDER — CL

Born: Hull, Quebec — February 22, 1970 — 6'2"-200
Last Amateur Club: Shawinigan Cataractes (QMJHL)
How the Oilers Got Him: Philadelphia's 4th choice, 63rd overall in the 1988 draft. Picked up on waivers from Anaheim January 10th, 2001.
First Game as an Oiler: January 14, 2001
First Goal as an Oiler: None Recorded
First Assist as an Oiler: None Recorded
First Penalty as an Oiler: None Recorded

Season	GP	Min	GA	W	L	T	Ave	SA	S%	SO	EN	PIM	Ast.
2000-01	8	348	21	1	4	0	3.62	151	0.861	0	1	0	0

RUCINSKY, MARTIN — SWEATER # 23 — LEFT WING — SL

Born: Most, Czechoslovakia — March 11, 1971 — 5'11"-180
Last Amateur Club: CHZ Litvinov (Czech)
How the Oilers Got Him: Oilers' 2nd choice, 20th overall in the 1991 draft.
First Game as an Oiler: January 10, 1992
First Goal as an Oiler: None Recorded
First Assist as an Oiler: None Recorded
First Penalty as an Oiler: None Recorded
Where He Went: Traded to Quebec for Ron Tugnutt and Brad Zavisha, March 10, 1992.

Season	GP	G	A	Pts	Shots	S%	GW	GT	PP	SH	P/M	PIM
1991-92	2	0	0	0	1	0.0	0	0	0	0	-3	0

RUOTSALAINEN, REIJO JUHANI — SWEATER # 29, # 26 — DEFENSE — SR

Born: Oulu, Finland — April 1, 1960 — 5'8"-170
Last Amateur Club: Karpat (Fin)
How the Oilers Got Him: New York Rangers' 5th choice, 119th overall in the 1980 draft. Traded by the Rangers to Edmonton, with Clark Donatelli, Ville Kentala, and Jim Wiemer for Mike Golden, Don Jackson, and Miloslav Horava, October 2, 1986.
First Game as an Oiler: March 6, 1987
First Goal as an Oiler: March 6, 1987
First Assist as an Oiler: March 7, 1987
First Penalty as an Oiler: March 7, 1987
Where He Went: Claimed by New Jersey in the Waiver Draft, October 5, 1987. Traded to the Oilers, by New Jersey for Jeff Sharples, March 6, 1990. Retired.

Season	GP	G	A	Pts	Shots	S%	GW	GT	PP	SH	P/M	PIM
1986-87	16	5	8	13	52	9.6	1	0	3	0	8	6
Playoffs	*21*	*2*	*5*	*7*	*46*	*4.3*	*1*	*0*	*1*	*0*	*8*	*10*
1989-90	10	1	7	8	28	3.6	0	0	0	0	-1	6
Playoffs	*22*	*2*	*11*	*13*	*55*	*3.6*	*0*	*0*	*1*	*0*	*13*	*12*
2 years	26	6	15	21	80	7.5	1	0	3	0	7	12
Playoffs	*43*	*4*	*16*	*20*	*101*	*4.0*	*1*	*0*	*2*	*0*	*21*	*22*

RUZICKA, VLADIMIR — SWEATER # 29 — CENTER — SL

Born: Most, Czechoslovakia — June 6, 1963 — 6'3"-212
Last Amateur Club: Dukla Trencin (Czech)
How the Oilers Got Him: Toronto's 5th choice, 73rd overall in the 1982 draft. Traded by the Leafs to the Oilers for Edmonton's 4th round choice (Greg Walters) in the 1990 draft, September 21, 1989.
First Game as an Oiler: January 17, 1990
First Goal as an Oiler: January 25, 1990
First Assist as an Oiler: January 25, 1990
First Penalty as an Oiler: January 25, 1990
Where He Went: Traded to Boston, for Greg Hawgood, October 22, 1990.

Season	GP	G	A	Pts	Shots	S%	GW	GT	PP	SH	P/M	PIM
1989-90	25	11	6	17	52	21.2	1	0	4	0	-21	10

SALO, TOMAS MIKAEL SWEATER # 35 GOALTENDER CL
Born: Surahammar, Sweden February 1, 1971 5'11"-173
Last Amateur Club: Vasteras IK (Swe)
How the Oilers Got Him: Islanders' 5th choice, 118th overall in the 1993 draft. Traded to the Oilers by the Islanders for Mats Lindgren and an 8th round choice (Radek Martinek) in the 1999 draft, March 20, 1999.
First Game as an Oiler: March 20, 1999 *First Assist as an Oiler:* February 29, 2000
First Goal as an Oiler: None Recorded *First Penalty as an Oiler:* November 14, 1999

Season	GP	Min	GA	W	L	T	Ave	SA	S%	SO	EN	PIM	Ast.
1998-99	13	702	27	8	2	2	2.31	279	0.903	0	0	0	0
Playoffs	*4*	*298*	*11*	*0*	*4*	*0*	*2.21*	*149*	*0.926*	*0*	*0*	*0*	*0*
1999-00	70	4164	162	27	28	13	2.33	1871	0.913	2	0	8	1
Playoffs	*5*	*300*	*13*	*1*	*4*	*0*	*2.60*	*133*	*0.902*	*0*	*0*	*0*	*0*
2000-01	73	4364	179	36	25	12	2.46	1856	0.904	8	5	4	1
Playoffs	*6*	*406*	*15*	*2*	*4*	*0*	*2.22*	*186*	*0.919*	*0*	*1*	*0*	*0*
3 years	156	9230	368	71	55	27	2.39	4006	0.908	10	5	12	2
Playoffs	*15*	*1004*	*39*	*3*	*12*	*0*	*2.33*	*468*	*0.917*	*0*	*1*	*0*	*0*

SANDWITH, TERRAN SWEATER # 38 DEFENSE SL
Born: Edmonton, Alberta April 17, 1972 6'4"-210
Last Amateur Club: Canadian National Team
How the Oilers Got Him: Flyers' 4th choice 42nd overall in the 1990 draft. Signed as a free agent April 10, 1996.
First Game as an Oiler: February 2, 1998 *First Assist as an Oiler:* None Recorded
First Goal as an Oiler: None Recorded *First Penalty as an Oiler:* February 28, 1998
Where He Went: Signed as a free agent by Anaheim July 13, 1998.

Season	GP	G	A	Pts	Shots	S%	GW	GT	PP	SH	P/M	PIM
1997-98	8	0	0	0	4	0.0	0	0	0	0	-4	6

SATAN, MIROSLAV SWEATER # 32, #18 CENTER SL
Born: Topolcany, Czechoslovakia December 22, 1974 6'1"-195
Last Amateur Club: Dukla Trencin (Czech)
How the Oilers Got Him: Edmonton's 6th choice, 111th overall in the 1993 draft.
First Game as an Oiler: October 15, 1995 *First Assist as an Oiler:* October 15, 1995
First Goal as an Oiler: October 21, 1995 *First Penalty as an Oiler*: October 31, 1995
Where He Went: Traded to Buffalo for Barrie Moore and Craig Millar, March 18, 1997.

Season	GP	G	A	Pts	Shots	S%	GW	GT	PP	SH	P/M	PIM
1995-96	62	18	17	35	113	15.9	4	0	6	0	0	22
1996-97	64	17	11	28	90	18.9	2	0	5	0	-4	22
2 years	126	35	28	63	203	17.2	6	0	11	0	-4	44

SCHMAUTZ, ROBERT JAMES SWEATER # 16 RIGHT WING SR
Born: Saskatoon, Saskatchewan March 28, 1945 5'9"-175
Last Amateur Club: Saskatoon Blades (WCHL)
How the Oilers Got Him: Traded to the Oilers from Boston for Dan Newman, December 10, 1979.
First Game as an Oiler: December 16, 1979 *First Assist as an Oiler:* December 21, 1979
First Goal as an Oiler: December 28, 1979 *First Penalty as an Oiler:* December 21, 1979
Where He Went: Traded to Colorado for Don Ashby, February 25, 1980.

Season	GP	G	A	Pts	Shots	S%	GW	GT	PP	SH	P/M	PIM
1979-80	29	8	8	16	46	17.4	0	0	2	0	-4	20

SELIVANOV, ALEX SWEATER # 28, #29 RIGHT WING SL
Born: Moscow, USSR March 23, 1971 6'0"-206
Last Amateur Club: Spartak (CIS)
How the Oilers Got Him: Philadelphia's 4th choice, 140th overall in the 1994 draft. Traded to the Oilers by Tampa Bay for Alexandre Daigle, who had been obtained from Philadelphia for Andrei Kovalenko, January 29, 1999.
First Game as an Oiler: January 30, 1999 *First Assist as an Oiler:* February 5, 1999
First Goal as an Oiler: February 17, 1999 *First Penalty as an Oiler:* February 5, 1999
Where He Went: Signed as a free agent by Columbus, November 22, 2000.

Season	GP	G	A	Pts	Shots	S%	GW	GT	PP	SH	P/M	PIM
1998-99	29	8	6	14	57	14.0	1	0	1	0	0	24
Playoffs	*2*	*0*	*1*	*1*	*3*	*0.0*	*0*	*0*	*0*	*0*	*0*	*2*

Season	GP	G	A	Pts	Shots	S%	GW	GT	PP	SH	P/M	PIM
1999-00	67	27	20	47	122	22.1	5	0	10	0	2	46
Playoffs	*5*	*0*	*0*	*0*	*6*	*0.0*	*0*	*0*	*0*	*0*	*0*	*8*
2 years	96	35	26	61	179	19.6	6	0	11	0	2	70
Playoffs	*5*	*0*	*0*	*0*	*6*	*0.0*	*0*	*0*	*0*	*0*	*0*	*8*

SEMENKO, DAVID JOHN SWEATER # 27 LEFT WING SL

Born: Winnipeg, Manitoba July 12, 1957 6'3"-200

Last Amateur Club: Brandon Wheat Kings (WCHL)

How the Oilers Got Him: Signed to a WHA contract by the Oilers for the 1977-78 season. Reclaimed by Minnesota North Stars, June 9, 1979 prior to the Expansion Draft. Traded back to the Oilers by the North Stars for the Oilers' second (Neal Broten) and third (Kevin Maxwell) picks in the 1979 entry draft, August 17, 1979.

First Game as an Oiler: October 10, 1979 *First Assist as an Oiler:* October 13, 1979

First Goal as an Oiler: October 26, 1979 *First Penalty as an Oiler:* October 21, 1979

Where He Went: Traded to Hartford for the Whalers' 3rd choice in the 1988 draft (Trevor Sim), December 12, 1986.

Season	GP	G	A	Pts	Shots	S%	GW	GT	PP	SH	P/M	PIM
1979-80	67	6	7	13	43	14.0	1	0	1	0	-13	135
Playoffs	*3*	*0*	*0*	*0*			*0*	*0*	*0*	*0*		*2*
1980-81	58	11	8	19	42	26.2	2	0	4	0	-4	80
Playoffs	*8*	*0*	*0*	*0*			*0*	*0*	*0*	*0*		*5*
1981-82	59	12	12	24	54	22.2	1	0	4	0	7	194
Playoffs	*4*	*0*	*0*	*0*			*0*	*0*	*0*	*0*		*2*
1982-83	75	12	15	27	69	17.4	1	0	0	0	19	141
Playoffs	*15*	*1*	*1*	*2*	*13*	*7.7*	*0*	*0*	*0*	*0*	*-1*	*69*
1983-84	52	6	11	17	39	15.4	2	0	0	0	9	118
Playoffs	*19*	*5*	*5*	*10*	*25*	*20.0*	*1*	*0*	*0*	*0*	*11*	*44*
1984-85	69	6	12	18	50	12.0	1	0	0	0	5	172
Playoffs	*14*	*0*	*0*	*0*	*5*	*0.0*	*0*	*0*	*0*	*0*	*2*	*39*
1985-86	69	6	12	18	51	11.8	0	0	0	0	0	141
Playoffs	*6*	*0*	*0*	*0*	*1*	*0.0*	*0*	*0*	*0*	*0*	*0*	*32*
1986-87	5	0	0	0	1	0.0	0	0	0	0	0	0
8 years	454	59	77	136	349	16.9	8	0	9	0	23	981
Playoffs	*69*	*6*	*6*	*12*			*1*	*0*	*0*	*0*		*193*

SEMENOV, ANATOLI SWEATER # 19 CENTER/LEFT WING SL

Born: Moscow, Soviet Union March 5, 1962 6'2"-190

Last Amateur Club: Moscow Dinamo (USSR)

How the Oilers Got Him: Edmonton's 5th choice, 120th overall in the 1989 draft.

First Game as an Oiler: May 8, 1990 *First Assist as an Oiler:* October 11, 1990

First Goal as an Oiler: October 11, 1990 *First Penalty as an Oiler:* October 14, 1990

Where He Went: Claimed by Tampa Bay in the Expansion Draft, June 18, 1992.

Season	GP	G	A	Pts	Shots	S%	GW	GT	PP	SH	P/M	PIM
Playoffs (89-90)	*2*	*0*	*0*	*0*	*0*	*0.0*	*0*	*0*	*0*	*0*	*-1*	*0*
1990-91	57	15	16	31	101	14.9	1	0	3	1	17	26
Playoffs	*12*	*5*	*5*	*10*	*28*	*17.9*	*0*	*0*	*0*	*0*	*7*	*6*
1991-92	59	20	22	42	105	19.0	3	0	3	0	12	16
Playoffs	*8*	*1*	*1*	*2*	*12*	*8.3*	*0*	*0*	*0*	*0*	*3*	*6*
2 years	116	35	38	73	206	17.0	4	0	6	1	29	42
Playoffs	*22*	*6*	*6*	*12*	*40*	*15.0*	*0*	*0*	*0*	*0*	*9*	*12*

SHAW, DAVID SWEATER # 26 DEFENSE SR

Born: St. Thomas, Ontario May 25, 1964 6'1"-190

Last Amateur Club: Kitchener Rangers (OHL)

How the Oilers Got Him: Quebec's 1st choice, 13th overall in the 1982 draft. Traded to the Oilers from the New York Rangers for Jeff Beukeboom, November 12, 1991.

First Game as an Oiler: November 13, 1991 *First Assist as an Oiler:* November 13, 1991

First Goal as an Oiler: November 13, 1991 *First Penalty as an Oiler*: November 13, 1991

Where He Went: Traded to Minnesota for Brian Glynn, January 21, 1992.

Season	GP	G	A	Pts	Shots	S%	GW	GT	PP	SH	P/M	PIM
1991-92	12	1	1	2	15	6.7	0	0	0	0	-8	8

SHERVEN, GORD SWEATER # 28, # 8 CENTER SR
Born: Mankota, Saskatchewan August 21, 1963 6'0"-185
Last Amateur Club: University of South Dakota Fighting Sioux (WCHA)
How the Oilers Got Him: Edmonton's 9th round choice, 197th overall in the 1981 draft.
First Game as an Oiler: October 5, 1983 *First Assist as an Oiler:* October 21, 1983
First Goal as an Oiler: March 31, 1984 *First Penalty as an Oiler:* October 30, 1984
Where He Went: Traded to Minnesota with Terry Martin for Mark Napier, January 24, 1985, traded back to the Oilers with Don Biggs for Dan Barber, Marc Habscheid, and Emanuel Viveiros, December 20, 1985. Claimed by Hartford in the Waiver Draft, October 6, 1986.

Season	*GP*	*G*	*A*	*Pts*	*Shots*	*S%*	*GW*	*GT*	*PP*	*SH*	*P/M*	*PIM*
1983-84	2	1	0	1	5	20.0	0	0	0	0	1	0
1984-85	37	9	7	16	49	18.4	1	0	1	0	-2	10
1985-86	5	1	1	2	3	33.3	0	0	0	0	2	4
3 years	44	11	8	19	57	19.3	1	0	1	0	1	10

SHTALENKOV, MIKHAIL SWEATER # 35 GOALTENDER CL
Born: Moscow, USSR October 20, 1965 6'2"-185
Last Amateur Club: Moscow Dinamo(CIS)
How the Oilers Got Him: Anaheim's 5th choice, 108th overall in the 1993 draft. Traded to the Oilers from Nashville with Jim Dowd for Drake Berehowsky, Greg de Vries and Eric Fichaud, October 1, 1998.
First Game as an Oiler: October 10, 1998 *First Assist as an Oiler:* None Recorded
First Goal as an Oiler: None Recorded *First Penalty as an Oiler:* January 10, 1999
Where He Went: Traded to Phoenix for a fifth round draft choice in the 2000 draft, March 11, 1999.

Season	*GP*	*Min*	*GA*	*W*	*L*	*T*	*Ave*	*SA*	*S%*	*SO*	*EN*	*PIM*	*Ast.*
1998-99	34	1819	81	12	17	3	2.67	782	0.896	3	2	2	0

SHUDRA, RONALD SWEATER # 27 DEFENSE/RIGHT WING SL
Born: Winnipeg, Manitoba November 28, 1967 6'1"-180
Last Amateur Club: Kamloops Blazers (WHL)
How the Oilers Got Him: Edmonton's 3rd choice, 63rd overall in the 1986 draft.
First Game as an Oiler: November 1, 1987 *First Assist as an Oiler:* November 7, 1987
First Goal as an Oiler: None Recorded *First Penalty as an Oiler:* November 7, 1987
Where He Went: Traded to the Rangers for Jeff Crossman, October 27, 1988.

Season	*GP*	*G*	*A*	*Pts*	*Shots*	*S%*	*GW*	*GT*	*PP*	*SH*	*P/M*	*PIM*
1987-88	10	0	5	5	8	0.0	0	0	0	0	5	6

SILTANEN, RISTO SWEATER # 8 DEFENSE SL
Born: Tampere, Finland October 31, 1958 5'8"-185
Last Amateur Club: Ilves Tampere (Fin)
How the Oilers Got Him: St. Louis' 13th choice, 173rd overall in 1978 draft. Signed to a WHA contract late in 1978-79 season. St. Louis reclaimed him prior to the 1979 expansion draft. Acquired from St. Louis with Tom Roulston for Joe Micheletti, on August 7th, 1979.
First Game as an Oiler: November 10, 1979 *First Assist as an Oiler:* October 21, 1979
First Goal as an Oiler: October 14, 1979 *First Penalty as an Oiler:* October 13, 1979
Where He Went: Traded to Hartford with Brent Loney for Ken Linseman and Don Nachbaur, August 19, 1982.

Season	*GP*	*G*	*A*	*Pts*	*Shots*	*S%*	*GW*	*GT*	*PP*	*SH*	*P/M*	*PIM*
1979-80	64	6	29	35	116	5.2	0	0	1	0	-9	26
Playoffs	*2*	*0*	*0*	*0*			*0*	*0*	*0*	*0*		*2*
1980-81	79	17	36	53	209	8.1	3	2	7	1	5	54
Playoffs	*9*	*2*	*0*	*2*			*1*	*0*	*2*	*0*		*8*
1981-82	63	15	48	63	143	10.5	1	0	6	0	13	26
Playoffs	*5*	*3*	*2*	*5*			*0*	*0*	*1*	*0*		*10*
3 years	206	38	113	151	468	8.1	4	2	14	1	9	106
Playoffs	*16*	*5*	*2*	*7*			*1*	*0*	*3*	*0*		*20*

SIM, TREVOR SWEATER # 15 CENTER SR
Born: Calgary, Alberta June 9, 1970 6'2"-195
Last Amateur Club: Swift Current Broncos (WHL)
How the Oilers Got Him: Edmonton's 2nd choice, 53rd overall in the 1988 draft.
First Game as an Oiler: October 18, 1989 *First Assist as an Oiler:* October 18, 1989

First Goal as an Oiler: None Recorded
First Penalty as an Oiler: October 18, 1989
Where He Went: Retired.

Season	GP	G	A	Pts	Shots	S%	GW	GT	PP	SH	P/M	PIM
1989-90	3	0	1	1	0	0.0	0	0	0	0	0	2

SIMPSON, CRAIG ANDREW SWEATER # 18 CENTER SR
Born: London, Ontario February 15, 1967 6'2"-195
Last Amateur Club: Michigan State University Spartans (CCHA)
How the Oilers Got Him: Pittsburgh's 1st choice, 2nd overall in the 1985 draft. Traded to the Oilers, with Chris Joseph, Moe Mantha, and Dave Hannan, for Paul Coffey, Dave Hunter and Wayne Van Dorp, November 24, 1987.
First Game as an Oiler: November 25, 1987
First Assist as an Oiler: November 27, 1987
First Goal as an Oiler: November 29, 1987
First Penalty as an Oiler: November 25, 1987
Where He Went: Traded to Buffalo for Jozef Cierny and the Sabres' 4th round choice (Jussi Tarvainen) in the 1994 draft, September 1, 1993.

Season	GP	G	A	Pts	Shots	S%	GW	GT	PP	SH	P/M	PIM
1987-88	59	43	21	64	118	36.4	5	0	18	0	15	43
Playoffs	*19*	*13*	*6*	*19*	*33*	*39.4*	*3*	*0*	*3*	*0*	*4*	*26*
1988-89	66	35	41	76	121	28.9	4	0	17	0	-3	80
Playoffs	*7*	*2*	*0*	*2*	*10*	*20.0*	*1*	*0*	*1*	*0*	*-3*	*10*
1989-90	80	29	32	61	129	22.4	2	1	7	0	-2	180
Playoffs	*22*	*16*	*15*	*31*	*42*	*38.1*	*3*	*0*	*6*	*0*	*11*	*8*
1990-91	75	30	27	57	143	21.0	5	0	15	0	-8	66
Playoffs	*18*	*5*	*11*	*16*	*21*	*23.8*	*0*	*0*	*1*	*0*	*1*	*12*
1991-92	79	24	37	61	128	18.8	2	0	6	0	8	80
Playoffs	*1*	*0*	*0*	*0*	*1*	*0.0*	*0*	*0*	*0*	*0*	*0*	*0*
1992-93	60	24	22	46	91	26.4	3	0	12	0	-14	36
6 years	419	185	180	365	730	25.3	21	1	75	0	-4	485
Playoffs	*67*	*36*	*32*	*68*	*107*	*33.6*	*7*	*0*	*11*	*0*	*13*	*56*

SKORODENSKI, WARREN SWEATER # 30 GOALTENDER CL
Born: Winnipeg, Manitoba March 22, 1960 6'1"-180
Last Amateur Club: Calgary Wranglers (WHL)
How the Oilers Got Him: Signed as a free agent by the Oilers, October 8, 1987.
First Game as an Oiler: February 6, 1988
First Assist as an Oiler: None Recorded
First Goal as an Oiler: None Recorded
First Penalty as an Oiler: None Recorded
Where He Went: Retired.

Season	GP	Min	GA	W	L	T	Ave	SA	S%	SO	EN	PIM	Ast.
1987-88	3	61	7	0	0	0	6.86	25	0.720	0	0	0	0

SLEGR, JIRI SWEATER # 28 DEFENSE SL
Born: Jihlava, Czechoslovakia May 30, 1971 6'1"-205
Last Amateur Club: CHZ Litvinov (Czech)
How the Oilers Got Him: Vancouver's 3rd choice, 23rd overall in the 1990 draft. Traded to the Oilers from the Vancouver Canucks for Roman Oksiuta, April 7, 1995.
First Game as an Oiler: April 9, 1995
First Assist as an Oiler: April 13, 1995
First Goal as an Oiler: April 21, 1995
First Penalty as an Oiler: April 9, 1995
Where He Went: Traded to Pittsburgh for the Penguins' 3rd choice in the 1998 draft, August 12, 1997.

Season	GP	G	A	Pts	Shots	S%	GW	GT	PP	SH	P/M	PIM
1994-95	12	1	5	6	27	3.7	0	0	1	0	-5	14
1995-96	57	4	13	17	91	4.4	1	0	0	1	-1	74
2 years	69	5	18	23	118	4.2	1	0	1	1	-6	88

SMITH, DOUGLAS ERIC SWEATER # 8 CENTER SR
Born: Ottawa, Ontario May 17, 1963 5'11"-185
Last Amateur Club: Ottawa 67's (OHA)
How the Oilers Got Him: Claimed by the Oilers in the Waiver Draft, October 3, 1988.
First Game as an Oiler: October 7, 1988
First Assist as an Oiler: November 26, 1988
First Goal as an Oiler: October 12, 1988
First Penalty as an Oiler: November 8, 1988
Where He Went: Traded to Vancouver with Greg Adams for Jean LeBlanc and the Canucks' 5th choice (Peter White) in the 1989 draft, March 7, 1989.

Season	GP	G	A	Pts	Shots	S%	GW	GT	PP	SH	P/M	PIM
1988-89	19	1	1	2	15	6.7	0	0	0	0	-1	9

SMITH, GEOFFREY ARTHUR SWEATER # 25 DEFENSE SL
Born: Edmonton, Alberta March 7, 1969 6'3"-190
Last Amateur Club: Kamloops Blazers (WHL)
How the Oilers Got Him: Oilers' 3rd choice, 63rd overall in the 1987 draft.
First Game as an Oiler: October 5, 1989 *First Assist as an Oiler:* October 24, 1989
First Goal as an Oiler: October 18, 1989 *First Penalty as an Oiler:* October 5, 1989
Where He Went: Traded to Florida with the Oilers' 4th round choice in the 1994 draft (David Nemirovsky) for the Panthers' 3rd round choice (Corey Neilson) in the 1994 draft and St. Louis' 6th choice (previously acquired by Florida and later traded to Winnipeg; the Jets selected Chris Kibermanis) in the 1994 draft, December 6th 1993.

Season	*GP*	*G*	*A*	*Pts*	*Shots*	*S%*	*GW*	*GT*	*PP*	*SH*	*P/M*	*PIM*
1989-90	74	4	11	15	66	6.1	0	0	1	0	13	52
Playoffs	*3*	*0*	*0*	*0*	*1*	*0.0*	*0*	*0*	*0*	*0*	*0*	*0*
1990-91	59	1	12	13	66	1.5	0	0	0	0	13	55
Playoffs	*4*	*0*	*0*	*0*	*5*	*0.0*	*0*	*0*	*0*	*0*	*5*	*0*
1991-92	74	2	16	18	61	3.3	0	0	0	0	-5	43
Playoffs	*5*	*0*	*1*	*1*	*5*	*0.0*	*0*	*0*	*0*	*0*	*2*	*6*
1992-93	78	4	14	18	67	6.0	0	0	0	1	-11	30
1993-94	21	0	3	3	23	0.0	0	0	0	0	-10	12
5 years	306	11	56	67	283	3.9	0	0	1	1	0	192
Playoffs	*12*	*0*	*1*	*1*	*11*	*0.0*	*0*	*0*	*0*	*0*	*7*	*6*

SMITH, JAMES STEPHEN SWEATER # 5 DEFENSE SR
Born: Glasgow, Scotland April 30, 1963 6'4"-215
Last Amateur Club: London Knights (OHA)
How the Oilers Got Him: Edmonton's 5th choice, 111th overall in 1981 draft.
First Game as an Oiler: December 29, 1984 *First Assist as an Oiler:* October 28, 1985
First Goal as an Oiler: November 20, 1985 *First Penalty as an Oiler:* December 29, 1984
Where He Went: Traded to Chicago for Dave Manson and the Black Hawks' 3rd choice (Kirk Maltby) in the 1992 draft, October 2, 1991.

Season	*GP*	*G*	*A*	*Pts*	*Shots*	*S%*	*GW*	*GT*	*PP*	*SH*	*P/M*	*PIM*
1984-85	2	0	0	0	3	0.0	0	0	0	0	-2	2
1985-86	55	4	20	24	74	5.4	1	0	1	0	30	166
Playoffs	*6*	*0*	*1*	*1*	*5*	*0.0*	*0*	*0*	*0*	*0*	*4*	*14*
1986-87	62	7	15	22	71	9.9	1	0	2	0	11	165
Playoffs	*15*	*1*	*3*	*4*	*17*	*5.9*	*0*	*0*	*0*	*0*	*9*	*45*
1987-88	79	12	43	55	116	10.3	1	0	5	0	40	286
Playoffs	*19*	*1*	*11*	*12*	*26*	*3.8*	*0*	*0*	*1*	*0*	*16*	*55*
1988-89	35	3	19	22	47	6.4	0	0	0	0	5	97
Playoffs	*7*	*2*	*2*	*4*	*6*	*33.3*	*1*	*0*	*0*	*0*	*3*	*20*
1989-90	75	7	34	41	125	5.6	1	0	3	0	6	171
Playoffs	*22*	*5*	*10*	*15*	*35*	*14.3*	*1*	*0*	*0*	*1*	*15*	*37*
1990-91	77	13	41	54	114	11.4	2	0	4	0	14	193
Playoffs	*18*	*1*	*2*	*3*	*30*	*3.3*	*0*	*0*	*1*	*0*	*-8*	*45*
7 years	385	46	172	218	550	8.4	6	0	15	0	104	1080
Playoffs	*87*	*10*	*29*	*39*	*119*	*8.4*	*2*	*0*	*2*	*1*	*39*	*216*

SMITH, JASON MATTHEW SWEATER # 21 DEFENSE SR
Born: Calgary, Alberta November 2, 1973 6'3"-205
Last Amateur Club: Regina Pats (WHL)
How the Oilers Got Him: New Jersey's 1st choice 18 overall in the 1992 draft. Traded to the Oilers by Toronto for a 4th round choice in the 1999 draft (Jonathan Zion) and a 2nd round choice in the 2000 draft (Kris Vernarsky), March 23, 1999.
First Game as an Oiler: March 24, 1999 *First Assist as an Oiler:* April 12, 1999
First Goal as an Oiler: April 1, 1999 *First Penalty as an Oiler:* March 28, 1999

Season	*GP*	*G*	*A*	*Pts*	*Shots*	*S%*	*GW*	*GT*	*PP*	*SH*	*P/M*	*PIM*
1998-99	12	1	1	2	15	6.7	0	0	0	0	0	11
Playoffs	*4*	*0*	*1*	*1*	*1*	*0.0*	*0*	*0*	*0*	*0*	*0*	*4*
1999-00	80	3	11	14	96	3.1	1	0	0	0	16	60
Playoffs	*5*	*0*	*1*	*1*	*5*	*0.0*	*0*	*0*	*0*	*0*	*0*	*4*
2000-01	82	5	15	20	140	3.6	0	0	1	1	14	120
Playoffs	*6*	*0*	*2*	*2*	*6*	*0.0*	*0*	*0*	*0*	*0*	*-3*	*6*
3 years	184	9	27	36	251	3.6	1	0	1	1	30	191
Playoffs	*15*	*0*	*4*	*4*	*12*	*0.0*	*0*	*0*	*0*	*0*	*-3*	*14*

Smyth, Ryan Sweater # 10, # 94 Left Wing SL
Born: Banff, Alberta February 21, 1976 6'1"-195
Last Amateur Club: Moose Jaw Warriors (WHL)
How the Oilers Got Him: Oilers' 2nd choice, 6th overall in the 1994 draft.
First Game as an Oiler: January 22, 1995 *First Assist as an Oiler:* December 5, 1995
First Goal as an Oiler: November 24, 1995 *First Penalty as an Oiler:* November 10, 1995

Season	GP	G	A	Pts	Shots	S%	GW	GT	PP	SH	P/M	PIM
1994-95	3	0	0	0	2	0.0	0	0	0	0	-1	0
1995-96	48	2	9	11	65	3.1	0	0	1	0	-10	28
1996-97	82	39	22	61	265	14.7	4	0	20	0	-7	76
Playoffs	*12*	*5*	*5*	*10*	*48*	*10.4*	*2*	*1*	*1*	*0*	*-4*	*12*
1997-98	65	20	13	33	205	9.8	2	2	10	0	-24	44
Playoffs	*12*	*1*	*3*	*4*	*24*	*4.2*	*0*	*0*	*1*	*0*	*-2*	*16*
1998-99	71	13	18	31	161	8.1	2	2	6	0	0	62
Playoffs	*3*	*3*	*0*	*3*	*7*	*42.9*	*0*	*0*	*2*	*0*	*-1*	*0*
1999-00	82	28	26	54	238	11.8	4	1	11	0	-2	58
Playoffs	*5*	*1*	*0*	*1*	*13*	*7.7*	*0*	*0*	*0*	*1*	*-2*	*6*
2000-01	82	31	39	70	245	12.7	6	1	11	0	10	56
Playoffs	*6*	*3*	*4*	*7*	*22*	*13.6*	*0*	*0*	*0*	*0*	*0*	*4*
7 years	433	133	127	260	1181	11.3	18	6	59	0	-34	324
Playoffs	*38*	*13*	*12*	*25*	*114*	*11.4*	*2*	*1*	*4*	*1*	*-9*	*38*

Solheim, Kenneth Lawrence Sweater # 28 Left Wing SL
Born: Hythe, Alberta March 27, 1961 6'3"-210
Last Amateur Club: Medicine Hat Tigers (WHL)
How the Oilers Got Him: Chicago's 4th choice, 24th overall in the 1980 draft. Signed as a free agent by Edmonton, August 15, 1985.
First Game as an Oiler: February 8, 1986 *First Assist as an Oiler:* None Recorded
First Goal as an Oiler: February 14, 1986 *First Penalty as an Oiler:* February 22, 1986
Where He Went: Retired.

Season	GP	G	A	Pts	Shots	S%	GW	GT	PP	SH	P/M	PIM
1985-86	6	1	0	1	8	12.5	0	0	0	0	-2	5

Sommer, Roy Sweater # 28 Center SL
Born: Oakland, California April 5, 1957 6'0"-180
Last Amateur Club: Calgary Centennials (WCHL)
How the Oilers Got Him: Toronto's 7th choice, 101st overall in the 1977 draft. Signed as a free agent by the Oilers, January 1, 1980.
First Game as an Oiler: January 28, 1981 *First Assist as an Oiler:* None Recorded
First Goal as an Oiler: January 28, 1981 *First Penalty as an Oiler:* January 28, 1981
Where He Went: Retired

Season	GP	G	A	Pts	Shots	S%	GW	GT	PP	SH	P/M	PIM
1980-81	3	1	0	1	1	100.0	0	0	0	0	0	7

Srsen, Tomas Sweater # 15 Left Wing SL
Born: Olomouc, Czechoslovakia August 25, 1966 5'11"-180
Last Amateur Club: Zetor Brno (Czech)
How the Oilers Got Him: Oilers' 7th choice, 147th overall in the 1987 draft.
First Game as an Oiler: October 31, 1990 *First Assist as an Oiler:* None Recorded
First Goal as an Oiler: None Recorded *First Penalty as an Oiler:* None Recorded
Where He Went: Retired.

Season	GP	G	A	Pts	Shots	S%	GW	GT	PP	SH	P/M	PIM
1990-91	2	0	0	0	2	0.0	0	0	0	0	0	0

Stajduhar, Nick Sweater # 23 Defense SL
Born: Kitchener, Ontario December 6, 1974 6'3"-200
Last Amateur Club: London Knights (OHL)
How the Oilers Got Him: Edmonton's 2nd choice, 16th overall in the 1993 draft.
First Game as an Oiler: January 3, 1996 *First Assist as an Oiler:* None Recorded

First Goal as an Oiler: None Recorded
Where He Went: Retired
First Penalty as an Oiler: January 3, 1996

Season	GP	G	A	Pts	Shots	S%	GW	GT	PP	SH	P/M	PIM
1995-96	2	0	0	0	1	0.0	0	0	0	0	2	4

STAPLETON, MIKE SWEATER # 28, # 25 CENTER SR
Born: Sarnia, Ontario May 5, 1966 5'10"-185
Last Amateur Club: Cornwall Royals (OHL)
How the Oilers Got Him: Chicago's 7th choice, 132nd overall in the 1984 draft. Claimed on waivers by the Oilers from the Pittsburgh Penguins, February 19, 1994.
First Game as an Oiler: February 19, 1994
First Goal as an Oiler: February 23, 1994
First Assist as an Oiler: February 23, 1994
First Penalty as an Oiler: February 25, 1994
Where He Went: Signed as a free agent by Winnipeg, August 18, 1995.

Season	GP	G	A	Pts	Shots	S%	GW	GT	PP	SH	P/M	PIM
1993-94	23	5	9	14	43	11.6	0	1	1	0	-1	28
1994-95	46	6	11	17	59	10.2	2	0	3	0	-12	21
2 years	69	11	20	31	102	10.8	2	1	4	0	-13	49

STRUEBY, TODD KENNETH SWEATER # 28, # 25, # 26 LEFT WING SL
Born: Lannigan, Saskatchewan June 15, 1963 6'1"-185
Last Amateur Club: Regina Pats (WHL)
How the Oilers Got Him: Edmonton's 2nd choice, 29th overall in the 1981 draft.
First Game as an Oiler: November 23, 1981
First Goal as an Oiler: None Recorded
First Assist as an Oiler: November 19, 1983
First Penalty as an Oiler: November 19, 1983
Where He Went: Traded to the Rangers with Larry Melnyk for Mike Rogers, December 20, 1985.

Season	GP	G	A	Pts	Shots	S%	GW	GT	PP	SH	P/M	PIM
1981-82	3	0	0	0	1	0.0	0	0	0	0	0	0
1982-83	1	0	0	0	0	0.0	0	0	0	0	0	0
1983-84	1	0	1	1	1	0.0	0	0	0	0	2	2
3 years	5	0	1	1	2	0.0	0	0	0	0	2	2

SUMMANEN, RAIMO SWEATER # 25 LEFT WING SL
Born: Jyvaskyla, Finland March 2, 1962 5'11"-185
Last Amateur Club: Tampere Ilves (Fin)
How the Oilers Got Him: Oilers' 6th choice, 125th overall in 1982 draft.
First Game as an Oiler: March 27, 1984
First Goal as an Oiler: March 31, 1984
First Assist as an Oiler: March 27, 1984
First Penalty as an Oiler: March 31, 1984
Where He Went: Traded to Vancouver for Moe Lemay, March 10, 1987.

Season	GP	G	A	Pts	Shots	S%	GW	GT	PP	SH	P/M	PIM
1983-84	2	1	4	5	3	33.3	0	0	0	0	4	2
Playoffs	*5*	*1*	*4*	*5*	*11*	*9.1*	*0*	*0*	*0*	*0*	*2*	*0*
1984-85	9	0	4	4	5	0.0	0	0	0	0	-1	0
1985-86	73	19	18	37	83	22.9	4	0	1	0	7	16
Playoffs	*5*	*1*	*1*	*2*	*6*	*16.7*	*0*	*0*	*0*	*0*	*2*	*0*
1986-87	48	10	7	17	55	18.2	0	0	0	0	-1	15
4 years	132	30	33	63	146	20.5	4	0	1	0	9	33
Playoffs	*10*	*2*	*5*	*7*	*17*	*11.8*	*0*	*0*	*0*	*0*	*4*	*0*

SUTTON, KENNETH WILLIAM SWEATER # 40, # 6 DEFENSE SL
Born: Edmonton, Alberta November 5, 1969 6'0"-200
Last Amateur Club: Saskatoon Blades (WHL)
How the Oilers Got Him: Buffalo's 4th choice, 98th overall in the 1989 draft. Traded to the Oilers by the Sabres for Scott Pearson, April 7, 1995.
First Game as an Oiler: April 9, 1995
First Goal as an Oiler: April 13, 1995
First Assist as an Oiler: May 3, 1995
First Penalty as an Oiler: April 17, 1995
Where He Went: Traded to St. Louis with Igor Kravchuk for Jeff Norton and Donald Dufresne, January 4, 1996.

Season	GP	G	A	Pts	Shots	S%	GW	GT	PP	SH	P/M	PIM
1994-95	12	3	1	4	28	10.7	0	0	0	0	-1	12
1995-96	32	0	8	8	38	0.0	0	0	0	0	-12	39
2 years	44	3	9	12	66	4.5	0	0	0	0	-13	51

SWANSON, BRIAN SWEATER # 37 CENTER SL
Born: Eagle River, Alaska March 24, 1976 5'10"-185
Last Amateur Club: Colorado College Tigers (WCHA)
How the Oilers Got Him: San Jose's 5th choice, 115th overall in the 1994 draft. Signed as a free agent by the Oilers August 20, 1999.
First Game as an Oiler: October 6, 2000
First Assist as an Oiler: October 15, 2000
First Goal as an Oiler: October 17, 2000
First Penalty as an Oiler: October 28, 2000

Season	*GP*	*G*	*A*	*Pts*	*Shots*	*S%*	*GW*	*GT*	*PP*	*SH*	*P/M*	*PIM*
2000-01	16	1	1	2	8	12.5	0	0	0	0	-1	6

TAKKO, KARI SWEATER # 1 GOALTENDER CL
Born: Uusikaupunki, Finland June 23, 1962 6'2"-185
Last Amateur Club: Assat (Fin)
How the Oilers Got Him: Minnesota's 5th choice, 97th overall in the 1984 draft. Traded to the Oilers from the North Stars for Bruce Bell, November 22, 1990.
First Game as an Oiler: November 24, 1990
First Assist as an Oiler: January 23, 1991
First Goal as an Oiler: None Recorded
First Penalty as an Oiler: None Recorded
Where He Went: Retired

Season	*GP*	*Min*	*GA*	*W*	*L*	*T*	*Ave*	*SA*	*S%*	*SO*	*EN*	*PIM*	*Ast.*
1990-91	11	529	37	4	4	0	4.20	279	0.867	0	0	0	1

THORNTON, SCOTT SWEATER # 15, # 17 CENTER SL
Born: London, Ontario January 9, 1971 6'3"-210
Last Amateur Club: Belleville Bulls (OHL)
How the Oilers Got Him: Toronto's 1st choice, 3rd overall in the 1989 draft. Traded to the Oilers by Toronto with Vincent Damphousse, Peter Ing, Luke Richardson, future considerations and cash for Glenn Anderson, Craig Berube, and Grant Fuhr, September 19, 1991.
First Game as an Oiler: October 4, 1991
First Assist as an Oiler: October 10, 1991
First Goal as an Oiler: November 24, 1993
First Penalty as an Oiler: October 4, 1991
Where He Went: Traded to Montreal for Andrei Kovalenko, September 6, 1996.

Season	*GP*	*G*	*A*	*Pts*	*Shots*	*S%*	*GW*	*GT*	*PP*	*SH*	*P/M*	*PIM*
1991-92	15	0	1	1	11	0.0	0	0	0	0	-6	43
Playoffs	*1*	*0*	*0*	*0*	*1*	*0.0*	*0*	*0*	*0*	*0*	*-1*	*0*
1992-93	9	0	1	1	7	0.0	0	0	0	0	-4	0
1993-94	61	4	7	11	65	6.2	0	0	0	0	-15	104
1994-95	47	10	12	22	69	14.5	1	0	0	1	-4	89
1995-96	77	9	9	18	95	9.5	3	0	0	2	-25	149
5 years	209	23	30	53	247	9.3	4	0	0	3	-54	385
Playoffs	*1*	*0*	*0*	*0*	*1*	*0.0*	*0*	*0*	*0*	*0*	*-1*	*0*

TIDEY, ALEX MANSFIELD SWEATER # 15 RIGHT WING SR
Born: Vancouver, British Columbia January 5, 1955 6'0"-180
Last Amateur Club: Lethbridge Broncos (WHL)
How the Oilers Got Him: Buffalo's 9th choice, 143rd overall, in the 1975 draft. Traded by Buffalo to the Oilers for John Gould, November 13, 1979.
First Game as an Oiler: December 5, 1979
First Assist as an Oiler: None Recorded
First Goal as an Oiler: None Recorded
First Penalty as an Oiler: December 9, 1979
Where He Went: Retired.

Season	*GP*	*G*	*A*	*Pts*	*Shots*	*S%*	*GW*	*GT*	*PP*	*SH*	*P/M*	*PIM*
1979-80	5	0	0	0	4	0.0	0	0	0	0	-3	8

TIKKANEN, ESA SWEATER # 14, # 10 LEFT WING SL
Born: Helsinki, Finland January 25, 1965 5'11"-185
Last Amateur Club: IFK Helsinki (Fin)
How the Oilers Got Him: Oilers' 4th choice, 82nd overall in the 1983 draft.
First Game as an Oiler: May 23, 1985
First Assist as an Oiler: October 13, 1985
First Goal as an Oiler: October 13, 1985
First Penalty as an Oiler: May 23, 1985
Where He Went: Traded to the Rangers for Doug Weight, March 17, 1993.

Season	*GP*	*G*	*A*	*Pts*	*Shots*	*S%*	*GW*	*GT*	*PP*	*SH*	*P/M*	*PIM*
Playoffs(84-85)	*3*	*0*	*0*	*0*	*3*	*0.0*	*0*	*0*	*0*	*0*	*-1*	*2*
1985-86	35	7	6	13	44	15.9	2	0	0	0	5	28

Season	GP	G	A	Pts	Shots	S%	GW	GT	PP	SH	P/M	PIM
Playoffs	*8*	*3*	*2*	*5*	*19*	*15.8*	*0*	*0*	*0*	*0*	*1*	*7*
1986-87	76	34	44	78	126	27.0	6	1	7	0	44	120
Playoffs	*21*	*7*	*2*	*9*	*39*	*17.9*	*1*	*0*	*1*	*0*	*1*	*20*
1987-88	80	23	51	74	142	16.2	2	0	6	1	21	153
Playoffs	*19*	*10*	*17*	*27*	*42*	*23.8*	*1*	*0*	*5*	*0*	*2*	*72*
1988-89	67	31	47	78	151	20.5	4	0	6	8	10	92
Playoffs	*7*	*1*	*3*	*4*	*17*	*5.9*	*0*	*0*	*0*	*0*	*-1*	*12*
1989-90	79	30	33	63	199	15.0	6	0	6	4	17	161
Playoffs	*22*	*13*	*11*	*24*	*54*	*24.1*	*0*	*0*	*2*	*2*	*12*	*26*
1990-91	79	27	42	69	235	11.5	6	0	3	2	22	85
Playoffs	*18*	*12*	*8*	*20*	*76*	*15.8*	*3*	*2*	*3*	*0*	*3*	*24*
1991-92	40	12	16	28	117	10.3	1	0	6	2	-8	44
Playoffs	*16*	*5*	*3*	*8*	*37*	*13.5*	*1*	*0*	*1*	*0*	*-1*	*8*
1992-93	66	14	19	33	162	8.6	3	0	2	4	-11	76
8 years	522	178	258	436	1176	15.1	30	1	36	21	100	759
Playoffs	*114*	*51*	*46*	*97*	*287*	*17.8*	*6*	*2*	*12*	*2*	*16*	*171*

TITOV, GERMAN SWEATER # 13 CENTER SL

Born: Moscow, USSR October 16, 1965 6'1"-201

Last Amateur Club: Khimik (CIS)

How the Oilers Got Him: Calgary's 10th choice, 252nd overall in the 1993 draft. Traded to the Oilers from Pittsburgh for Josef Beranek, March 14, 2000.

First Game as an Oiler: March 15, 2000 *First Assist as an Oiler:* April 7, 2000

First Goal as an Oiler: April 12, 2000 *First Penalty as an Oiler:* March 15, 2000

Where He Went: Signed as a free agent by the Anaheim Mighty Ducks July 1st, 2000.

Season	GP	G	A	Pts	Shots	S%	GW	GT	PP	SH	P/M	PIM
1999-00	7	0	4	4	11	0.0	0	0	0	0	2	4
Playoffs	*5*	*1*	*1*	*2*	*3*	*33.3*	*0*	*0*	*0*	*0*	*-2*	*0*

TOAL, MICHAEL JAMES SWEATER # 25 CENTER SR

Born: Red Deer, Alberta March 23, 1959 6'0"-175

Last Amateur Club: Portland Winter Hawks (WHL)

How the Oilers Got Him: Oilers' 5th choice, 105th overall in 1979 draft.

First Game as an Oiler: October 30, 1979 *First Assist as an Oiler:* None Recorded

First Goal as an Oiler: None Recorded *First Penalty as an Oiler:* None Recorded

Where He Went: Retired.

Season	GP	G	A	Pts	Shots	S%	GW	GT	PP	SH	P/M	PIM
1979-80	3	0	0	0	1	0.0	0	0	0	0	0	0

TODD, KEVIN SWEATER # 15 CENTER SL

Born: Winnipeg, Manitoba May 4, 1968 5'10"-180

Last Amateur Club: Prince Albert Raiders (WHL)

How the Oilers Got Him: New Jersey's 7th choice, 129th overall in the 1986 draft. Traded to the Oilers from the Devils with Zdeno Ciger for Bernie Nicholls, January 13, 1993.

First Game as an Oiler: January 15, 1993 *First Assist as an Oiler:* January 23, 1993

First Goal as an Oiler: January 15, 1993 *First Penalty as an Oiler:* January 27, 1993

Where He Went: Traded to Chicago for Adam Bennett, October 7, 1993.

Season	GP	G	A	Pts	Shots	S%	GW	GT	PP	SH	P/M	PIM
1992-93	25	4	9	13	39	10.3	1	0	0	0	-5	10

TUGNUTT, RON SWEATER # 32, # 1 GOALTENDER CL

Born: Scarborough, Ontario October 22, 1967 5'11"-155

Last Amateur Club: Peterborough Petes (OHL)

How the Oilers Got Him: Quebec's 4th choice, 81st overall in the 1986 draft. Traded to the Oilers from the Nordiques with Brad Zavisha for Martin Rucinsky, March 10, 1992.

First Game as an Oiler: March 11, 1992 *First Assist as an Oiler:* None Recorded

First Goal as an Oiler: None Recorded *First Penalty as an Oiler:* March 22, 1992

Where He Went: Claimed by Anaheim in the Expansion Draft, June 24, 1993.

Season	GP	Min	GA	W	L	T	Ave	SA	S%	SO	EN	PIM	Ast.
1991-92	3	124	10	1	1	0	4.83	73	0.863	0	0	2	0
Playoffs	*2*	*60*	*3*	*0*	*0*		*3.00*	*34*	*0.912*	*0*	*0*	*0*	*0*
1992-93	26	1338	93	9	12	2	4.17	767	0.879	0	2	2	0
2 years	29	1462	103	10	13	2	4.23	840	0.877	0	2	4	0
Playoffs	*2*	*60*	*3*	*0*	*0*		*3.00*	*34*	*0.912*	*0*	*0*	*0*	*0*

TUOMAINEN, MARKO — SWEATER # 33 — RIGHT WING — SR

Born: Kuopio, Finland — April 25, 1972 — 6'3"-205
Last Amateur Club: Clarkson University Golden Knights (ECAC)
How the Oilers Got Him: Edmonton's 10th choice, 205th overall in 1992 draft.
First Game as an Oiler: April 9, 1995 — *First Assist as an Oiler:* None Recorded
First Goal as an Oiler: None Recorded — *First Penalty as an Oiler:* None Recorded
Where He Went: Signed as a free agent by the Los Angeles Kings, June 20, 1999.

Season	GP	G	A	Pts	Shots	S%	GW	GT	PP	SH	P/M	PIM
1994-95	4	0	0	0	5	0.0	0	0	0	0	0	0

ULANOV, IGOR — SWEATER # 2, # 55 — DEFENSE — SL

Born: Krasnokamsk, USSR — October 1, 1969 — 6'3"-211
Last Amateur Club: Khimik (CIS)
How the Oilers Got Him: Winnipeg's 8th choice, 203rd overall in 1991 draft. Traded to Edmonton with Alain Nasreddine for Matthieu Descoteaux and Christian LaFlamme, March 9, 2000.
First Game as an Oiler: March 10, 2000 — *First Assist as an Oiler:* March 17, 2000
First Goal as an Oiler: October 7, 2000 — *First Penalty as an Oiler:* March 22, 2000

Season	GP	G	A	Pts	Shots	S%	GW	GT	PP	SH	P/M	PIM
1999-00	14	0	3	3	6	0.0	0	0	0	0	-3	10
Playoffs	*5*	*0*	*0*	*0*	*4*	*0.0*	*0*	*0*	*0*	*0*	*-1*	*6*
2000-01	67	3	21	24	74	4.1	0	1	1	0	15	90
Playoffs	*6*	*0*	*0*	*0*	*4*	*0.0*	*0*	*0*	*0*	*0*	*-6*	*4*
2 years	81	3	24	27	80	3.8	0	1	1	0	12	100
Playoffs	*11*	*0*	*0*	*0*	*8*	*0.0*	*0*	*0*	*0*	*0*	*-7*	*10*

UNGER, GARRY DOUGLAS — SWEATER # 77 — CENTER — SL

Born: Edmonton, Alberta — December 7, 1947 — 6'0"-185
Last Amateur Club: London Nationals (OHA)
How the Oilers Got Him: Traded to the Oilers by Los Angeles for the Oilers' 7th round choice in the 1981 Entry Draft (Craig Hurley), March 10, 1981.
First Game as an Oiler: March 8, 1981 — *First Assist as an Oiler:* October 9, 1981
First Goal as an Oiler: October 7, 1981 — *First Penalty as an Oiler*: March 12, 1981
Where He Went: Retired.

Season	GP	G	A	Pts	Shots	S%	GW	GT	PP	SH	P/M	PIM
1980-81	13	0	0	0	13	0.0	0	0	0	0	-9	6
Playoffs	*8*	*0*	*0*	*0*			*0*	*0*	*0*	*0*		*2*
1981-82	46	7	13	20	62	11.3	2	0	0	0	8	69
Playoffs	*4*	*1*	*0*	*1*			*0*	*0*	*0*	*0*		*23*
1982-83	16	2	0	2	14	14.3	0	0	0	0	1	8
Playoffs	*1*	*0*	*0*	*0*	*0*	*0.0*	*0*	*0*	*0*	*0*	*0*	*0*
3 years	75	9	13	22	89	10.1	2	0	0	0	0	83
Playoffs	*13*	*1*	*0*	*1*			*0*	*0*	*0*	*0*		*25*

VAN ALLEN, SHAUN — SWEATER # 26, # 20 — CENTER — SL

Born: Shaunavon, Saskatchewan — August 29, 1967 — 6'1"-200
Last Amateur Club: Saskatoon Blades (WHL)
How the Oilers Got Him: Oilers' 5th choice, 105th overall in the 1987 draft.
First Game as an Oiler: February 18, 1991 — *First Assist as an Oiler:* December 1, 1992
First Goal as an Oiler: December 10, 1992 — *First Penalty as an Oiler:* December 3, 1992
Where He Went: Signed as a free agent by Anaheim, July 22, 1993.

Season	GP	G	A	Pts	Shots	S%	GW	GT	PP	SH	P/M	PIM
1990-91	2	0	0	0	0	0.0	0	0	0	0	0	0
1992-93	21	1	4	5	19	5.3	0	0	0	0	-2	6
2 years	23	1	4	5	19	5.3	0	0	0	0	-2	6

VAN DORP, WAYNE SWEATER # 8 LEFT WING SL
Born: Vancouver, British Columbia May 19, 1961 6'4"-225
Last Amateur Club: Seattle Breakers (WHL)
How the Oilers Got Him: Signed as a free agent by the Oilers, March 7, 1987.
First Game as an Oiler: March 17, 1987
First Assist as an Oiler: None Recorded
First Goal as an Oiler: None Recorded
First Penalty as an Oiler: March 19, 1987
Where He Went: Traded to Pittsburgh with Paul Coffey and Dave Hunter for Dave Hannan, Chris Joseph, Moe Mantha and Craig Simpson, November 24, 1987.

Season	GP	G	A	Pts	Shots	S%	GW	GT	PP	SH	P/M	PIM
1986-87	3	0	0	0	3	0.0	0	0	0	0	-1	25
Playoffs	*3*	*0*	*0*	*0*	*1*	*0.0*	*0*	*0*	*0*	*0*	*0*	*2*

VOROBIEV, VLADIMIR SWEATER # 34 LEFT WING SR
Born: Cherepovets, USSR October 2, 1972 6'0"-185
Last Amateur Club: Moscow Dinamo (CIS)
How the Oilers Got Him: Traded to the Oilers by the Rangers for Kevin Brown, March 23, 1999.
First Game as an Oiler: April 16, 1999
First Assist as an Oiler: None Recorded
First Goal as an Oiler: April 16, 1999
First Penalty as an Oiler: April 16, 1999

Season	GP	G	A	Pts	Shots	S%	GW	GT	PP	SH	P/M	PIM
1998-99	2	2	0	2	5	40.0	0	0	0	0	1	2
Playoffs	*1*	*0*	*0*	*0*	*1*	*0.0*	*0*	*0*	*0*	*0*	*-1*	*0*

VUJTEK, VLADIMIR SWEATER # 23 LEFT WING SL
Born: Ostrava, Czechoslovakia February 17, 1972 6'1"-190
Last Amateur Club: Tri-City Americans (WHL)
How the Oilers Got Him: Montreal's 4th choice, 73rd overall in the 1991 draft. Traded to the Oilers from Montreal with Shayne Corson and Brent Gilchrist for Vincent Damphousse and the Oilers' 4th round choice in the 1993 draft (Adam Wiesel) August 27, 1992.
First Game as an Oiler: October 6, 1992
First Assist as an Oiler: October 31, 1992
First Goal as an Oiler: October 28, 1992
First Penalty as an Oiler: October 25, 1992
Where He Went: Traded to Tampa Bay with the Oilers' 3rd choice (Dimitry Afanasenkov) in the 1998 draft for Brantt Myhres and a conditional draft choice, July 16, 1997.

Season	GP	G	A	Pts	Shots	S%	GW	GT	PP	SH	P/M	PIM
1992-93	30	1	10	11	49	2.0	0	0	0	0	-1	8
1993-94	40	4	15	19	66	6.1	0	0	1	0	-7	14
2 years	70	5	25	30	115	4.3	0	0	1	0	-8	22

VYAZMIKIN, IGOR SWEATER # 29 RIGHT/LEFT WING SL
Born: Moscow, USSR January 8, 1966 6'1"-195
Last Amateur Club: CSKA Moscow (USSR)
How the Oilers Got Him: Oilers' 13th choice, 252nd overall in the 1987 draft.
First Game as an Oiler: December 12, 1990
First Assist as an Oiler: None Recorded
First Goal as an Oiler: December 18, 1990
First Penalty as an Oiler: None Recorded
Where He Went: Retired.

Season	GP	G	A	Pts	Shots	S%	GW	GT	PP	SH	P/M	PIM
1990-91	4	1	0	1	5	20.0	1	0	0	0	0	0

WARE, MICHAEL SWEATER # 34 DEFENSE SR
Born: York, Ontario March 22, 1967 6'5"-205
Last Amateur Club: Hamilton Steelhawks (OHA)
How the Oilers Got Him: Oilers' 3rd choice, 62nd overall in the 1985 draft.
First Game as an Oiler: January 28, 1989
First Assist as an Oiler: January 31, 1989
First Goal as an Oiler: None Recorded
First Penalty as an Oiler: January 28, 1989
Where He Went: Retired.

Season	GP	G	A	Pts	Shots	S%	GW	GT	PP	SH	P/M	PIM
1988-89	2	0	1	1	0	0.0	0	0	0	0	1	11
1989-90	3	0	0	0	1	0.0	0	0	0	0	-1	4
2 years	5	0	1	1	1	0.0	0	0	0	0	0	15

WATT, MIKE SWEATER # 9 LEFT WING SL

Born: Seaforth, Ontario March 31, 1976 6'2"-210

Last Amateur Club: Michigan State University Spartans (CCHA)

How the Oilers Got Him: Oilers' 3rd choice, 32nd overall in the 1994 draft.

First Game as an Oiler: November 15, 1997 *First Assist as an Oiler:* November 15, 1997

First Goal as an Oiler: November 22, 1997 *First Penalty as an Oiler:* December 12, 1997

Where He Went: Traded to the New York Islanders for Eric Fichaud, June 18, 1998.

Season	*GP*	*G*	*A*	*Pts*	*Shots*	*S%*	*GW*	*GT*	*PP*	*SH*	*P/M*	*PIM*
1997-98	14	1	2	3	14	7.1	1	0	0	0	-4	4

WEIGHT, DOUGLAS DANIEL SWEATER # 42, # 39 CENTER SL

Born: Warren, Michigan January 21, 1971 5'11"-200

Last Amateur Club: Lake Superior State Lakers (CCHA)

How the Oilers Got Him: New York Rangers' 2nd choice, 34th overall in the 1990 draft. Traded to the Oilers from the Rangers for Esa Tikkanen, March 17, 1993.

First Game as an Oiler: March 17, 1993 *First Assist as an Oiler:* March 21, 1993

First Goal as an Oiler: March 20, 1993 *First Penalty as an Oiler:* March 21, 1993

Season	*GP*	*G*	*A*	*Pts*	*Shots*	*S%*	*GW*	*GT*	*PP*	*SH*	*P/M*	*PIM*
1992-93	13	2	6	8	35	5.7	0	0	0	0	-2	10
1993-94	84	24	50	74	188	12.8	1	0	4	1	-22	47
1994-95	48	7	33	40	104	6.7	1	0	1	0	-17	69
1995-96	82	25	79	104	204	12.3	2	1	9	0	-19	95
1996-97	80	21	61	82	235	8.9	2	0	4	0	1	80
Playoffs	*12*	*3*	*8*	*11*	*54*	*5.6*	*0*	*0*	*0*	*0*	*0*	*8*
1997-98	79	26	44	70	205	12.7	4	0	9	0	1	69
Playoffs	*12*	*2*	*7*	*9*	*26*	*7.7*	*1*	*0*	*2*	*0*	*-4*	*14*
1998-99	43	6	31	37	79	7.6	0	1	1	0	-8	12
Playoffs	*4*	*1*	*1*	*2*	*4*	*25.0*	*0*	*0*	*0*	*0*	*-3*	*15*
1999-00	77	21	51	72	167	12.6	4	0	3	1	6	54
Playoffs	*5*	*3*	*2*	*5*	*8*	*37.5*	*1*	*0*	*2*	*0*	*-3*	*4*
2000-01	82	25	65	90	188	13.3	3	2	8	0	12	91
Playoffs	*6*	*1*	*5*	*6*	*18*	*5.6*	*0*	*0*	*0*	*0*	*0*	*17*
9 years	588	157	420	577	1405	11.2	17	4	39	2	-48	527
Playoffs	*39*	*10*	*23*	*33*	*110*	*9.1*	*2*	*0*	*4*	*0*	*-10*	*58*

WEIR, STANLEY BRIAN SWEATER # 21 CENTER SL

Born: Ponoka, Alberta March 17, 1952 6'1"-180

Last Amateur Club: Medicine Hat Tigers (WHL)

How the Oilers Got Him: Signed as a free agent by the WHA Oilers in time for the 1978-79 season.

First Game as an Oiler: October 10, 1979 *First Assist as an Oiler:* October 10, 1979

First Goal as an Oiler: October 14, 1979 *First Penalty as an Oiler:* October 10, 1979

Where He Went: Traded to Colorado for Ed Cooper, March 9, 1982; the rights were then returned to the Oilers for Ed Cooper, July 2, 1982. Traded to Detroit for cash, September 14, 1982.

Season	*GP*	*G*	*A*	*Pts*	*Shots*	*S%*	*GW*	*GT*	*PP*	*SH*	*P/M*	*PIM*
1979-80	79	33	33	66	129	25.6	2	2	3	2	2	40
Playoffs	*3*	*0*	*0*	*0*			*0*	*0*	*0*	*0*		*2*
1980-81	70	12	20	32	84	14.3	2	1	1	0	-7	40
Playoffs	*5*	*0*	*0*	*0*			*0*	*0*	*0*	*0*		*2*
1981-82	51	3	13	16	29	10.3	1	0	1	0	0	13
3 years	200	48	66	114	242	19.8	5	3	5	2	-5	93
Playoffs	*8*	*0*	*0*	*0*			*0*	*0*	*0*	*0*		*4*

WERENKA, BRAD SWEATER # 36, # 5 DEFENSE SL

Born: Two Hills, Alberta February 12, 1969 6'2"-210

Last Amateur Club: Northern Michigan University Wildcats (WCHA)

How the Oilers Got Him: Oilers' 2nd choice, 42nd overall in the 1987 draft.

First Game as an Oiler: January 7, 1993 *First Assist as an Oiler:* January 9, 1993

First Goal as an Oiler: January 9, 1993 *First Penalty as an Oiler:* January 9, 1993

Where He Went: Traded to Quebec for Steve Passmore, March 21, 1994.

Season	GP	G	A	Pts	Shots	S%	GW	GT	PP	SH	P/M	PIM
1992-93	27	5	4	9	38	13.2	1	0	0	1	1	24
1993-94	15	0	4	4	11	0.0	0	0	0	0	-1	14
2 years	42	5	8	13	49	10.2	1	0	0	1	0	38

WHITE, PETER — SWEATER # 27 — CENTER — SL
Born: Montreal, Quebec — March 15, 1969 — 5'11"-200
Last Amateur Club: Michigan State University Spartans (CCHA)
How the Oilers Got Him: Edmonton's 4th choice, 92nd overall in the 1989 draft.
First Game as an Oiler: November 27, 1993 — *First Assist as an Oiler:* December 11, 1993
First Goal as an Oiler: November 29, 1993 — *First Penalty as an Oiler:* January 15, 1994
Where He Went: Traded to Toronto with the Oilers' 4th round choice (Jason Sessa) in the 1996 draft for Kent Manderville, December 4, 1995.

Season	GP	G	A	Pts	Shots	S%	GW	GT	PP	SH	P/M	PIM
1993-94	26	3	5	8	17	17.6	0	0	0	0	1	2
1994-95	9	2	4	6	13	15.4	0	0	2	0	1	0
1995-96	26	5	3	8	34	14.7	0	0	1	0	-14	0
3 years	61	10	12	22	64	15.6	0	0	3	0	-12	2

WHITNEY, RAY — SWEATER # 8 — CENTER — SR
Born: Fort Saskatchewan, Alberta — May 8, 1972 — 5'9"-160
Last Amateur Club: Canadian National Team
How the Oilers Got Him: San Jose's 2nd choice, 23rd overall in the 1991 draft. Signed as a free agent by the Oilers October 1, 1997.
First Game as an Oiler: October 1, 1997 — *First Assist as an Oiler:* October 1, 1997
First Goal as an Oiler: October 11, 1997 — *First Penalty as an Oiler:* None Recorded
Where He Went: Claimed on waivers by Florida November 6, 1997.

Season	GP	G	A	Pts	Shots	S%	GW	GT	PP	SH	P/M	PIM
1997-98	9	1	3	4	19	5.3	0	0	0	0	-1	0

WIEMER, JAMES DUNCAN — SWEATER # 23, # 32 — DEFENSE — SL
Born: Sudbury, Ontario — January 9, 1961 — 6'4"-200
Last Amateur Club: Peterborough Petes (OHA)
How the Oilers Got Him: Buffalo's 5th choice, 83rd overall in the 1980 draft. Traded to the Oilers from the New York Rangers with Clark Donatelli, Ville Kentala and Reijo Ruotsalainen for Mike Golden, Miloslav Horvava, Don Jackson and future considerations, October 2, 1986.
First Game as an Oiler: October 31, 1987 — *First Assist as an Oiler:* November 7, 1987
First Goal as an Oiler: November 10, 1987 — *First Penalty as an Oiler:* November 4, 1987
Where He Went: Traded to Los Angeles with Alan May for Brian Wilks and John English, March 7, 1989.

Season	GP	G	A	Pts	Shots	S%	GW	GT	PP	SH	P/M	PIM
1987-88	12	1	2	3	24	4.2	0	0	0	0	7	15
Playoffs	*2*	*0*	*0*	*0*	*3*	*0.0*	*0*	*0*	*0*	*0*	*-2*	*2*

WRIGHT, TYLER — SWEATER # 19, # 12 — CENTER — SR
Born: Canora, Saskatchewan — April 6, 1973 — 5'11"-175
Last Amateur Club: Swift Current Broncos (WHL)
How the Oilers Got Him: Edmonton's 1st choice, 12th overall in the 1991 draft.
First Game as an Oiler: October 10, 1992 — *First Assist as an Oiler:* October 17, 1992
First Goal as an Oiler: October 10, 1992 — *First Penalty as an Oiler*: October 11, 1992
Where He Went: Traded to Pittsburgh for the Penguins' 7th choice (Brandon Lafrance) in the 1996 draft, June 22, 1996.

Season	GP	G	A	Pts	Shots	S%	GW	GT	PP	SH	P/M	PIM
1992-93	7	1	1	2	7	14.3	0	0	0	0	-4	19
1993-94	5	0	0	0	2	0.0	0	0	0	0	-3	4
1994-95	6	1	0	1	6	16.7	0	0	0	0	1	14
1995-96	23	1	0	1	18	5.6	0	0	0	0	-7	33
4 years	41	3	1	4	33	9.1	0	0	0	0	-13	70

ZANIER, MICHAEL SWEATER # 30 GOALTENDER CL

Born: Trail, British Columbia August 22, 1962 5'11"-183

Last Amateur Club: Calgary Wranglers (WHL)

How the Oilers Got Him: Signed as a free agent October, 4, 1983.

First Game as an Oiler: March 5, 1985

First Goal as an Oiler: None Recorded

First Assist as an Oiler: None Recorded

First Penalty as an Oiler: None Recorded

Where He Went: Retired.

Season	*GP*	*Min*	*GA*	*W*	*L*	*T*	*Ave*	*SA*	*S%*	*SO*	*EN*	*PIM*	*Ast.*
1984-85	3	185	12	1	1	1	3.90	100	0.880	0	0	0	0

ZAVISHA, BRAD SWEATER # 20 LEFT WING SL

Born: Hines Creek, Alberta January 4, 1972 6'2"-205

Last Amateur Club: Lethbridge Broncos (WHL)

How the Oilers Got Him: Quebec's 3rd choice, 43rd overall in the 1990 draft. Traded to the Oilers from the Nordiques with Ron Tugnutt for Martin Rucinsky, March 10, 1992

First Game as an Oiler: February 15, 1994

First Goal as an Oiler: None Recorded

First Assist as an Oiler: None Recorded

First Penalty as an Oiler: None Recorded

Where He Went: Traded to Philadelphia with the Oilers' sixth choice (Jamie Sokolosky) in the 1995 draft for Ryan McGill, March 13, 1995.

Season	*GP*	*G*	*A*	*Pts*	*Shots*	*S%*	*GW*	*GT*	*PP*	*SH*	*P/M*	*PIM*
1993-94	2	0	0	0	1	0.0	0	0	0	0	-2	0

ZELEPUKIN, VALERI SWEATER # 21 LEFT WING SL

Born: Voskresensk, U.S.S.R. September 17, 1968 6'0"-200

Last Amateur Club: Khimik (U.S.S.R.)

How the Oilers Got Him: Traded by New Jersey with Bill Guerin for Jason Arnott and Bryan Muir, January 4, 1998.

First Game as an Oiler: January 7, 1998

First Goal as an Oiler: January 14, 1998

First Assist as an Oiler: January 9, 1998

First Penalty as an Oiler: January 9, 1998

Where He Went: Traded to Philadelphia for Daniel Lacroix October 5, 1998.

Season	*GP*	*G*	*A*	*Pts*	*Shots*	*S%*	*GW*	*GT*	*PP*	*SH*	*P/M*	*PIM*
1997-98	33	2	10	12	47	4.3	0	0	0	0	-2	57
Playoffs	*8*	*1*	*2*	*3*	*8*	*12.5*	*0*	*0*	*0*	*0*	*3*	*2*

ZHOLTOK, SERGEI SWEATER # 34 CENTER SR

Born: Riga, Latvia February 12, 1972 6'2"-191

Last Amateur Club: Dynamo Riga (U.S.S.R.)

How the Oilers Got Him: Traded to the Oilers by Montreal for Chad Kilger, December 18, 2000.

First Game as an Oiler: December 18, 2000

First Goal as an Oiler: Feburary 14, 2001

First Assist as an Oiler: December 30, 2000

First Penalty as an Oiler: December 27, 2000

Season	*GP*	*G*	*A*	*Pts*	*Shots*	*S%*	*GW*	*GT*	*PP*	*SH*	*P/M*	*PIM*
2000-01	37	4	16	20	61	6.6	0	0	1	0	8	22
Playoffs	*3*	*0*	*0*	*0*	*3*	*0.0*	*0*	*0*	*0*	*0*	*-1*	*0*

Part Three: Appendices

Transactions

June 13, 1979	Dan Newman and Dave Lumley traded to Edmonton from Montreal for the Oilers' 2nd round choice (Ric Nattress) in the 1980 entry draft.
August 7, 1979	Oilers traded Joe Micheletti to St. Louis for Risto Siltanen and Tom Roulston.
August 17, 1979	Dave Semenko reacquired by the Oilers from Minnesota for the Oilers' second (Neal Broten) and third (Kevin Maxwell) picks in the 1979 entry draft.
September 14, 1979	Charlie Huddy signed as a free agent by the Oilers.
November 13, 1979	Oilers traded John Gould to Buffalo for Alex Tidey.
December 10, 1979	Oilers traded Dan Newman to Boston for Bobby Schmautz.
February 25, 1980	Oilers traded Bobby Schmautz to the Colorado Rockies for Don Ashby.
March 11, 1980	Oilers traded Ron Chipperfield to Quebec for Ron Low.
March 11, 1980	Oilers traded Jim Corsi to Minnesota for future considerations.
March 11, 1980	Oilers traded Cam Connor plus their third choice in the 1981 draft (Peter Sundstrum) to the Rangers for Don Murdoch.
June 13, 1980	Oilers traded Ron Areshenkoff and the Oilers' tenth round choice (Bob O'Brien) to the Flyers for Barry Dean.
October 10. 1980	Curt Brackenbury claimed from the Quebec Nordiques in the Waiver Draft.
October 10, 1980	Colin Campbell claimed by the Canucks in the Waiver Draft.
February 2, 1981	Gary Edwards traded to the Oilers by Minnesota for Edmonton's third choice in 1982 draft.
March 10, 1981	Oilers traded Blair MacDonald and Ken Berry to Vancouver for Lars Gunnar Petersson and Garry Lariviere.
March 10, 1981	Garry Unger traded to the Oilers by Los Angeles for the Oilers' 7th round choice in the 1981 Entry Draft (Craig Hurley).
March 10, 1981	Oilers traded John Hughes to the Rangers for Ray Markham.
March 10, 1981	Oilers traded Pat Price to the Pittsburgh Penguins for Pat Hughes.
May 5, 1981	John Blum signed as a free agent.
August 21, 1981	Oilers traded the rights to Don Murdoch to Minnesota for Don Jackson and Edmonton's 3rd round draft choice, previously owned by Minnesota (Wally Chapman).
October 6, 1981	Ray Cote signed as a free agent.
December 11, 1981	Oilers traded Ed Mio to the Rangers for Lance Nethery.
March 8, 1982	Oilers traded Walt Poddubny and Phil Drouilliard to Toronto for Laurie Boschman.
March 9, 1982	Oilers traded Doug Hicks to Washington for Todd Bidner.
March 9, 1982	Oilers traded Stan Weir to Colorado Rockies for Ed Cooper.
July 2, 1982	Oilers traded Ed Cooper to Colorado Rockies for Stan Weir.
August 19, 1982	Oilers traded Risto Siltanen and Brent Loney to Hartford for Don Nachbaur and Ken Linseman.
September 14, 1982	Stan Weir sold to Detroit for cash.
October 1, 1982	Curt Brackenbury signed as a free agent by St. Louis.
October 18, 1982	Randy Gregg signed as a free agent.
February 19, 1983	Oilers traded Ron Low and Jim McTaggert to New Jersey for Lindsay Middlebrook and Paul Miller.
March 7, 1983	Oilers traded Laurie Boschman to Winnipeg for Willy Lindstrom.
October 3, 1983	Don Nachbaur claimed by Los Angeles in the Waiver Draft.
October 4, 1983	Pat Conacher signed as a free agent.
October, 4, 1983	Mike Zanier signed as a free agent.
November 1, 1983	Tom Gorence signed as a free agent.
November 9, 1983	Reg Kerr signed as a free agent by the Oilers.
December 5, 1983	Oilers traded Tom Roulston to Pittsburgh for Kevin McClelland and the Penguins' 6th round choice (Emanuel Viveiros) in the 1984 draft.
January 20, 1984	Oilers traded their 9th round choice (Heinz Ehlers) in the 1984 draft to the New York Rangers for Rick Chartraw.
March 6, 1984	Oilers traded John Blum to the Bruins for Larry Melnyk.
March 6, 1984	Risto Jalo traded by the Washington Capitals to Edmonton for the Oilers' 4th round choice (Larry Shaw) in the 1985 draft.
June 21, 1984	Jeff Brubaker signed as a free agent.
June 21, 1984	Oilers traded Ken Linseman to the Boston Bruins for Mike Krushelnyski.
October 9, 1984	Bill Carroll claimed from the New York Islanders in the Waiver Draft.

October 9, 1984	Jeff Brubaker claimed in the Waiver Draft by the Leafs.
October 9, 1984	Terry Martin claimed by the Oilers in the Waiver Draft from Toronto.
October 9, 1984	Dave Lumley claimed by Hartford in the Waiver Draft.
November 27, 1984	Dean Hopkins traded to the Oilers by Los Angeles for cash.
January 24, 1985	Oilers traded Terry Martin and Gord Sherven to Minnesota for Mark Napier.
February 1, 1985	Craig MacTavish signed as a free agent.
February 6, 1985	Dave Lumley claimed by the Oilers on waivers.
February 21, 1985	Marco Baron signed as a free agent.
March 5, 1985	Tom Gorence signed as a free agent by New Jersey.
May 31, 1985	Dean Hopkins traded to Los Angeles for future considerations.
August 14, 1985	Pat Conacher signed as a free agent by New Jersey.
August 15, 1985	Ken Solheim signed as a free agent.
September 12, 1985	Oilers traded Gilles Meloche and future considerations (Craig Muni) to the Pittsburgh Penguins for Tim Hrynewich and Marty McSorley.
October 4, 1985	Oilers traded Pat Hughes to Pittsburgh for Mike Moller.
October 7, 1985	Willy Lindstrom claimed by Pittsburgh in the Waiver Draft.
December 5, 1985	Jeff Brubaker claimed on waivers by the Oilers.
December 20, 1985	Oilers traded Todd Strueby and Larry Melnyk to the Rangers for Mike Rogers.
December 20, 1985	Oilers traded Marc Habscheid, Don Barber and Emanuel Viveiros to Minnesota for Gord Sherven and Don Biggs.
December 28, 1985	Oilers traded Bill Carroll to Detroit for Bruce Eakin.
August 18, 1986	Tom McMurchy signed as a free agent.
August 18, 1986	Craig Muni signed as a free agent.
September 1986	Dan Gare signed as a free agent.
October 2, 1986	Craig Muni sold to Buffalo.
October 2, 1986	Oilers traded Don Jackson, Mike Golden, and Miloslav Horava to the Rangers for Clark Donatelli, Ville Kentala, Reijo Ruotsalainen and Jim Wiemer.
October 6, 1986	Craig Muni traded to the Oilers from Pittsburgh, to complete September 11, 1985 trade which sent Gilles Meloche to the Penguins for Tim Hrynewich, Marty McSorley and future considerations.
October 6, 1986	Gord Sherven claimed by Hartford in the Waiver Draft.
December 11, 1986	Stu Kulak sold to the Oilers by the Canucks.
December 12, 1986	Oilers traded Dave Semenko to Hartford for the Whalers' 3rd choice in the 1988 draft (Trevor Sim).
March 2, 1987	Kent Nilsson traded to the Oilers by Minnesota for future considerations.
March 6, 1987	Oilers traded Lee Fogolin and Mark Napier to Buffalo for Normand Lacombe, Wayne Van Dorp and future considerations.
March 9, 1987	Oilers traded Jeff Brubaker to Philadelphia for Dom Campedelli.
March 10, 1987	Stu Kulak acquired by the Rangers to complete the Reijo Ruotsalainen deal.
March 10, 1987	Oilers traded Raimo Summanen to the Canucks for Moe Lemay.
July 31, 1987	Jim Playfair signed as a free agent by Chicago.
October 5, 1987	Reijo Ruotsalainen claimed by New Jersey in the Waiver Draft.
October 5, 1987	Mark Lamb claimed from Calgary by the Oilers in the Waiver Draft.
October 8, 1987	Warren Skorodenski signed as a free agent.
October 19, 1987	Dave Donnelly traded to the Oilers by Chicago for future considerations.
November 24, 1987	Oilers traded Paul Coffey, Dave Hunter and Wayne Van Dorp to the Penguins for Dave Hannan, Chris Joseph, Moe Mantha and Craig Simpson.
January 22, 1988	Oilers traded Moe Mantha to Minnesota for Keith Acton.
February 11, 1988	Oilers traded Scott Metcalfe and their 9th round choice (Donald Audette) in the 1989 draft, to Buffalo for Steve Dykstra and the Sabres' 7th round choice (Dave Payne) in 1989 draft.
March 1, 1988	Ken Berry signed as a free agent by Vancouver.
March 8, 1988	Oilers traded Andy Moog to the Bruins for Bill Ranford, Geoff Courtnall and future considerations.
March 8, 1988	Oilers traded Moe Lemay to the Bruins for Alan May.
July 22, 1988	Oilers traded the rights to Geoff Courtnall to the Washington Capitals for Greg Adams.
August 9, 1988	Oilers traded Wayne Gretzky, Mike Krushelnyski and Marty McSorley to Los Angeles for Jimmy Carson, Martin Gelinas, the Kings' 1st round draft choices in 1989 (Jason Miller; the pick was acquired by New Jersey on June 17, 1989), 1991 (Martin Rucinsky), 1993 (Nick Stajduhar) and cash.
August 10, 1988	Oilers traded John Miner to Los Angeles for Craig Redmond
September 30, 1988	Reed Larson signed as a free agent by the Oilers.
October 3, 1988	Steve Dykstra claimed by Pittsburgh in the Waiver Draft.
October 3 1988	Dave Hannan claimed in the Waiver Draft by the Penguins.
October 3, 1988	Ken Hammond claimed by the Oilers in the Waiver Draft.
October 3, 1988	Craig Redmond claimed by the Rangers in the Waiver Draft.
October 10, 1988	Nick Fotiu signed to a 20 game option contract.
October 27, 1988	Ron Shudra traded to the Rangers for Jeff Crossman.
November. 1, 1988	Craig Redmond claimed on waiver by the Oilers from the Rangers.
November 1, 1988	Ken Hammond claimed on waivers by the Rangers.
November 7, 1988	Glen Cochrane claimed on waivers by the Oilers from Chicago.
December 6, 1988	Reed Larson traded to the Islanders for future considerations.

January 3, 1989	Miroslav Frycer traded to the Oilers by Detroit for Edmonton's 10th round choice (Rick Judson) in the 1989 draft.
January 23, 1989	Doug Halward traded to the Oilers by the Detroit Red Wings for Edmonton's 12th choice (Jason Glickman) in the 1989 draft.
February 7, 1989	Oilers traded Keith Acton and the Oilers' sixth round choice (Dimitri Yushkevich) in the 1991 draft to Philadelphia for Dave Brown.
February 15, 1989	Tomas Jonsson traded by the Islanders to the Oilers for future considerations.
March 7, 1989	Oilers traded Alan May and Jim Wiemer to Los Angeles for Brian Wilks and John English.
March 7, 1989	Oilers traded Greg Adams and Doug Smith to Vancouver for Jean LeBlanc and the Canucks' fifth round choice (Peter White) in the 1989 draft.
June 17, 1989	Tommy Lehmann traded to the Oilers by the Bruins for Edmonton's 3rd choice (Wes Walz) in the 1989 draft.
September 21, 1989	Vladimir Ruzicka traded by the Leafs to the Oilers for Edmonton's 4th round choice (Greg Walters) in the 1990 draft.
September 28, 1989	Eldon Reddick traded to the Oilers by the Winnipeg Jets for future considerations.
October 2, 1989	Randy Exelby traded to the Oilers by the Canadiens for future considerations.
October 9, 1989	Daryl Reaugh signed as a free agent by Hartford.
October 10, 1989	Oilers traded Jim Ennis to the Hartford Whalers for Norm Maciver
November 2, 1989	Oilers traded Jimmy Carson to Detroit with Kevin McClelland and the Oilers' fifth round choice in the 1991 draft (later traded to Montreal, Montreal chose Brad Layzell), for Adam Graves, Petr Klima, Joe Murphy and Jeff Sharples.
January 5, 1990	Normand Lacombe traded to Philadelphia for future considerations.
February 1, 1990	Bruce Bell signed as a free agent.
March 6 1990	Marc Laforge traded to the Oilers from Hartford for the rights to Cam Brauer.
March 6, 1990	Oilers traded Jeff Sharples to New Jersey for Reijo Ruotsalainen.
July 16, 1990	Steve Graves signed as a free agent by Los Angeles.
August 31, 1990	Mike Krushelnyski signed as a free agent by the Oilers.
October 1, 1990	Randy Gregg claimed as a free agent by the Vancouver Canucks in the Waiver Draft.
October 22, 1990	Oilers traded Vladimir Ruzicka to Boston for Greg Hawgood.
November 10, 1990	Max Middendorf traded to the Oilers by the Quebec Nordiques for the Oilers' 9th round choice (Brent Brekke) in the 1991 draft.
November 22, 1990	Oilers traded Bruce Bell to Minnesota for Kari Takko.
March 5, 1991	Oilers traded Kim Issel to the Pittsburgh Penguins for Brad Aitken.
May 30, 1991	Charlie Huddy claimed by Minnesota in the Expansion Draft.
May 30, 1991	Oilers traded Dave Brown, Corey Foster and Jari Kurri to Philadelphia for Craig Fisher, Craig Berube and Scott Mellanby.
June 12, 1991	Oilers traded Jean LeBlanc plus their 10th round choice (Teemu Numminen) in the 1992 draft to Winnipeg for the Jets' 5th round choice (Ryan Haggerty) in the 1991 draft.
July 30, 1991	Brad Aitken signed as a free agent by the Leafs.
September 3, 1991	Adam Graves signed as a free agent by the New York Rangers.
September 11, 1991	Norm Foster traded to the Oilers from the Bruins for future considerations.
September 12, 1991	Troy Mallette acquired by the Oilers as compensation for the Rangers' signing of free agent Adam Graves.
September 19, 1991	Oilers traded Glenn Anderson, Craig Berube and Grant Fuhr to Toronto for Vincent Damphousse, Peter Ing, Luke Richardson, Scott Thornton, future considerations and cash.
October 2, 1991	Oilers traded Steve Smith to Chicago for Dave Manson.
October 4, 1991	Oilers traded Mark Messier and future considerations, to the Rangers for Bernie Nicholls, Steve Rice and Louie DeBrusk.
November 12, 1991	Oilers traded Jeff Beukeboom to the New York Rangers for David Shaw.
January 12, 1992	Oilers traded David Maley to the New Jersey Devils for Troy Mallette.
January 21, 1992	Oilers traded David Shaw to the Minnesota North Stars for Brian Glynn.
February 22, 1992	Oilers traded Max Middendorf to the Detroit Red Wings for Bill McDougall.
March 10, 1992	Oilers traded Martin Rucinsky to Quebec for Ron Tugnutt and Brad Zavisha.
June 18, 1992	Mark Lamb claimed by Ottawa in the Expansion Draft.
June 18, 1992	Anatoli Semenov claimed by Tampa Bay in the Expansion Draft.
August 27, 1992	Oilers traded Vincent Damphousse plus their 4th round pick (Adam Wiesel) in the 1993 draft, to Montreal for Shayne Corson, Brent Gilchrist and Vladimir Vujtek.
September 9, 1992	Ian Herbers signed as a free agent by the Oilers.
October 4, 1992	Norm Maciver claimed by Ottawa in the Waiver Draft.
December 11, 1992	Oilers traded Kevin Lowe to the Rangers for Roman Oksiuta and the Rangers' 3rd choice (Alexander Kerch) in the 1993 draft.
January 1, 1993	David Maley claimed on waivers by the San Jose Sharks.
January 13, 1993	Oilers traded Bernie Nicholls to the Devils for Kevin Todd and Zdeno Ciger.
January 16, 1993	Oilers traded Greg Hawgood and Josef Beranek to the Philadelphia Flyers for Brian Benning.
February 24, 1993	Oilers traded Joe Murphy to Chicago for Dean McAmmond and Igor Kravchuk.
March 5, 1993	Oilers traded Brent Gilchrist to the Minnesota North Stars for Todd Elik.
March 17, 1993	Oilers traded Esa Tikkanen to the Rangers for Doug Weight.
March 22, 1993	Oilers traded Craig Muni to the Chicago Black Hawks for Mike Hudson.
June 16, 1993	Oilers traded Petr Klima to Tampa Bay for the Lightnings' 3rd round choice (Brad Symes) in the 1994 draft.

June 20, 1993	Oilers traded Martin Gelinas and their 6th choice (Nicholas Checco) in the 1993 draft to Quebec for Scott Pearson.
June 24, 1993	Ron Tugnutt claimed by Anaheim in the Expansion Draft.
June 24, 1993	Scott Mellanby claimed by Florida in the Expansion Draft.
July 13, 1993	Brian Benning signed as a free agent by Florida.
July 16, 1993	Dan Currie signed as a free agent by Los Angeles.
July 22, 1993	Shaun Van Allen signed as a free agent by Anaheim.
August 4, 1993	Norm Foster signed as a free agent by Philadelphia.
August 10, 1993	David Haas signed as a free agent by Calgary.
August 13, 1993	Bill McDougall signed as a free agent by Tampa Bay.
August 30, 1993	Oilers traded Peter Ing to Detroit for the Red Wings' 7th round choice (Chris Wickenheiser) in the 1994 draft and future considerations.
September 1, 1993	Oilers traded Craig Simpson to the Sabres for Jozef Cierny and Buffalo's 4th round choice (Jussi Tarvainen) in the 1994 draft.
September 13, 1993	Wayne Cowley signed as a free agent.
September 15, 1993	Oilers traded Brian Glynn to Ottawa for the Senators' 8th round choice (Rob Quinn) in the 1994 draft.
October 3, 1993	Mike Hudson claimed by the Rangers in the Waiver Draft.
October 6, 1993	Fred Brathwaite signed as a free agent.
October 6, 1993	Francois Leroux claimed on waivers by Ottawa.
October 7, 1993	Oilers traded Kevin Todd to the Chicago Black Hawks for Adam Bennett.
October 26, 1993	Todd Elik claimed on waivers by San Jose.
November 2, 1993	Jeff Chychrun traded to the Oilers from the Los Angeles Kings for a conditional draft choice in the 1995 draft.
November 11, 1993	Oilers traded Chris Joseph to the Tampa Bay Lightning for Bob Beers.
December 6 1993	Geoff Smith traded to Florida with the Oilers' 4th round choice in the 1994 draft (David Nemirovsky) for the Panthers' 3rd round choice (Corey Neilson)in the 1994 draft and St. Louis' 6th choice (previously acquired by Florida and later traded to Winnipeg; the Jets selected Chris Kibermanis) in 1994 draft.
December 6, 1993	Fredrick Olausson traded to the Oilers from Winnipeg with the Jets' 7th round pick (Curtis Sheptak) in the 1994 draft, for the Oilers' 3rd round choice (Tavis Hansen) in the 1994 draft.
December 15, 1993	Oilers traded Marc Laforge to the Islanders for Brent Grieve.
February 1, 1994	Gord Mark signed as a free agent.
February 19, 1994	Mike Stapleton claimed on waivers by the Oilers from the Pittsburgh Penguins.
March 15, 1994	Oilers traded Dave Manson and the St. Louis Blues' 6th round choice, which had previously been acquired by Edmonton (Winnipeg selected Chris Kibermanis) in the 1994 draft to the Winnipeg Jets for Boris Mironov, Mats Lindgren, Winnipeg's 1st round choice in the 1994 draft (Jason Bonsignore), and the Florida Panthers' 4th round choice in the same draft, which had previously been acquired by the Jets (the Oilers selected Adam Copeland).
March 20, 1994	Greg deVries signed as a free agent.
March 21, 1994	Oilers traded Brad Werenka to Quebec for Steve Passmore.
March 21, 1994	Oilers traded Craig MacTavish to the Rangers for Todd Marchant.
May 27, 1994	Jeff Chychrun signed as a free agent by Hartford.
July 7, 1994	Brent Grieve signed as a free agent by Chicago.
July 27, 1994	Shjon Podein signed as a free agent by Philadelphia.
August 18, 1994	Steve Rice signed as a free agent by Hartford.
August 25, 1994	Dennis Bonvie signed as a free agent.
August 29, 1994	Bob Beers signed as a free agent by the Islanders.
August 30, 1994	Bryan Marchment acquired by the Oilers from the Hartford Whalers as compensation for the Whalers signing Steve Rice.
September 18, 1994	Ilya Byakin signed as a free agent by San Jose.
January 18, 1995	Len Esau claimed by the Oilers from the Calgary Flames in the Waiver Draft.
January 18, 1995	Dean Kennedy claimed by the Oilers from the Winnipeg Jets in the Waiver Draft.
March 3, 1995	Iain Fraser claimed on waivers from the Dallas Stars.
March 7, 1995	Len Esau claimed on waivers by Calgary.
March 13, 1995	Ryan McGill traded to the Oilers from the Philadelphia Flyers for Brad Zavisha and the Oilers' 6th choice (Jamie Sololosky) in the 1995 draft.
April 7, 1995	Oilers traded Roman Oksiuta to Vancouver for Jiri Slegr.
April 7, 1995	Oilers traded Scott Pearson to Buffalo for Ken Sutton.
July 28, 1995	Shayne Corson signed as a free agent by St. Louis.
August 4, 1995	Curtis Joseph and the rights to Mike Grier were traded to the Oilers from the St. Louis Blues, for the Blues' former 1st round choices in the 1996 draft previously acquired by the Oilers (Marty Reasoner) and the 1997 draft, later traded to Los Angeles (the Kings chose Matt Zultek).
August 18, 1995	Mike Stapleton signed as a free agent by Winnipeg.
August 23, 1995	Micah Aivazoff signed as a free agent by the Islanders.
August 24, 1995	Brett Hauer traded to the Oilers by the Canucks for a conditional draft choice.
September 19, 1995	Rem Murray signed as a free agent.
October 11, 1995	Iain Fraser signed as a free agent by Winnipeg.
December 4, 1995	Oilers traded Peter White and a 4th round choice (Jason Sessa) in the 1996 draft to Toronto for Kent Manderville.
January 4, 1996	Oilers traded Igor Kravchuk and Ken Sutton to the St. Louis Blues for Jeff Norton and Donald Dufresne.

January 11, 1996	Oilers traded Bill Ranford to the Bruins for Sean Brown, Mariusz Czerkawski and Boston's 1st round choice (Matthieu Descoteaux) in the 1996 draft.
January 16, 1996	Fredrick Olausson claimed on waivers by Anaheim.
January 25, 1996	Glenn Anderson claimed on waivers.
March 12, 1996	Glenn Anderson claimed on waivers by St. Louis.
March 12, 1996	David Roberts traded to the Oilers by the Blues for future considerations.
March 20, 1996	Oilers traded Kirk Maltby to Detroit for Daniel McGillis.
April 10, 1996	Terran Sandwith signed as a free agent.
April 30, 1996	Bryan Muir signed as a free agent.
June 14, 1996	Bob Essensa traded to the Oilers by the Detroit Red Wings for future considerations.
June 22, 1996	Tyler Wright traded to Pittsburgh for the Penguins' 7th choice (Brandon Lafrance) in the 1996 draft.
July 31, 1996	David Roberts signed as a free agent by Vancouver.
September 6, 1996	Oilers traded Scott Thornton to the Montreal Canadiens for Andei Kovalenko.
September 16, 1996	Jesse Belanger signed as a free agent.
September 28, 1996	Kevin Lowe signed as a free agent.
September 30, 1996	Ralph Intranuovo claimed by Toronto in the Waiver Draft.
October 2, 1996	Kent Manderville signed as a free agent by Hartford.
October 24, 1996	Michel Petit signed as a free agent by the Oilers.
October 25, 1996	Ralph Intranuovo claimed on waivers by the Oilers.
January 17, 1997	Michel Petit claimed on waivers by Philadelphia.
February 26, 1997	Petr Klima signed as a free agent.
March 18, 1997	Oilers traded Jeff Norton to the Tampa Bay Lightning for Drew Bannister and Tampa Bay's 6th round choice (Peter Sarno) in the 1997 draft.
March 18, 1997	Oilers traded Miroslav Satan to the Buffalo Sabres for Craig Millar and Barrie Moore.
July 14, 1997	Doug Friedman signed as a free agent.
July 16, 1997	Vladimir Vujtek traded to Tampa Bay with the Oilers' 3rd choice (Dimitri Afanasenkov) in the 1998 draft for Brantt Myhres and a conditional draft choice.
July 22, 1997	Bill Huard signed as a free agent.
July 23, 1997	Scott Fraser signed as a free agent.
July 23, 1997	Luke Richardson signed as a free agent by Philadelphia.
August 12, 1997	Oilers traded Jiri Slegr to Pittsburgh for the Penguins' 3rd choice (acquired by New Jersey; the Devils selected Brian Gionta) in the 1998 draft.
August 25, 1997	Oilers traded Mariusz Czerkawski to the Islanders for Dan Lacouture.
August 26, 1997	Louie DeBrusk signed as a free agent by Tampa Bay.
September 29, 1997	Drake Berehowsky signed as a free agent.
October 1, 1997	Ray Whitney signed as a free agent.
October 15, 1997	Oilers traded Brantt Myhres to the Flyers for Jason Bowen.
November 6, 1997	Ray Whitney claimed on waivers by Florida.
December 30, 1997	Oilers traded Jason Bonsignore, Steve Kelly and Bryan Marchment to Tampa Bay for Roman Hamrlik and Paul Comrie.
January 4, 1998	Oilers traded Jason Arnott and Bryan Muir to New Jersey for Valeri Zelepukin and Bill Guerin.
January 6, 1998	Tony Hrkac claimed on waivers.
March 9, 1998	Scott Ferguson traded to Ottawa for Frantisek Musil.
March 24, 1998	Dan McGillis and the Oilers' 2nd choice (Jason Beckett) in the 1998 draft traded to Philadelphia for Janne Niinimaa.
June 16, 1998	Bobby Dollas and Tony Hrkac traded to Pittsburgh for the rights to Josef Beranek.
June 18, 1998	Mike Watt traded to the New York Islanders for Eric Fichaud.
June 26, 1998	Doug Friedman taken in the Expansion Draft by the Nashville Predators.
July 2, 1998	Scott Fraser signed as a free agent by the Rangers.
July 15, 1998	Curtis Joseph signed as a free agent by Toronto.
August 21, 1998	Pat Falloon signed as a free agent.
October 1, 1998	Drake Berehowsky, Greg de Vries and Eric Fichaud traded to Nashville for Jim Dowd and Mikhail Shtalenkov.
October 5, 1998	Valeri Zelepukin traded to Philadelphia for Daniel Lacroix.
January 29, 1999	Andrei Kovalenko traded to Philadelphia for Alexandre Daigle.
January 29, 1999	Alexandre Daigle traded to Tampa Bay for Alex Selivanov.
February 3, 1999	Rights to Barrie Moore traded to Washington for Brad Church.
March 11, 1999	Mikhail Shtalenkov traded to Phoenix for a fifth round choice in the 2000 draft.
March 20, 1999	Mats Lindgren traded to the Islanders with an 8th round choice in the 1999 draft for Tommy Salo.
March 20, 1999	Boris Mironov traded to Chicago with Dean McAmmond and Jonas Elofsson for Ethan Moreau, Chad Kilger, Christian Laflamme, and Daniel Cleary, March 20, 1999.
March 23, 1999	Jason Smith traded to the Oilers by Toronto for a 4th round choice in the 1999 draft and a 2nd round choice in the 2000 draft.
September 5, 1999	Bob Essensa signed as a free agent by the Phoenix Coyotes.
June 26, 1999	Craig Millar traded to Nashville for Detroit's third round choice (previously acquired by the Predators; the Oilers chose Mike Comrie) in the 1999 Entry Draft.
March 9, 2000	Christian Laflamme and Matthieu Descoteaux traded to Montreal for Igor Ulanov and Alain Nasreddine.

March 14, 2000	Josef Beranek traded to Pittsburgh for German Titov.
June 24, 2000	Roman Hamrlik traded to the Islanders for Josh Green, Eric Brewer and the Islanders' third choice (Edmonton chose Brad Winchester) in the 2000 draft
November 15, 2000	Bill Guerin traded to Boston for Anson Carter, the Bruins' 2nd round choice in the 2001 draft Doug Lynch, the right to switch 1st round picks in the 2001 or 2002 draft and future considerations.
December 18, 2000	Chad Kilger traded to Montreal for Sergei Zholtok.
March 13, 2001	Dan LaCouture traded to Pittsburgh for Sven Butenschon.

The Oilers' Longest Continuous NHL Transaction

August 7 1979, WHA defenseman Joe Micheletti traded for Risto Siltanen; August 19, 1982 Risto Siltanen traded for Ken Linseman; June 21, 1984 Ken Linseman was traded for Mike Krushelnyski; August 9, 1988 Mike Krushelnyski was part of the Wayne Gretzky trade in which the Oilers acquired Jimmy Carson; November 2, 1989 Jimmy Carson was traded for Joe Murphy; February 24, 1993 Joe Murphy traded for Igor Kravchuk; January 4, 1996 Igor Kravchuk was traded for Jeff Norton; March 18, 1997 Jeff Norton traded for Drew Bannister; January 9, 1998 Drew Bannister traded for Bobby Dollas. June 16, 1998 Bobby Dollas and Tony Hrkac traded to Pittsburgh for the rights to Josef Beranek. March 14, 2000 Josef Beranek traded to Pittsburgh for German Titov.

Oilers' first ever draft choice, Kevin Lowe (right) with Wayne Gretzky. (Corporate Communications, City of Edmonton Archives)

The Entry Draft

Rnd.	*#*	*Name*	*Nat.*	*Pos.*	*Drafted From*	*League*	*Record*
1979							
1	21	Kevin Lowe	CAN	D	Quebec Remparts	QMJHL	68-26-60-86-120
3*	48	Mark Messier	CAN	LW	St. Albert Saints	AJHL	54-25-49-74-194
4	69	Glenn Anderson	CAN	RW	U of Denver Pioneers	WCHA	40-26-29-55-58
4	84	Max Kostovich	CAN	LW	Portland Winter Hawks	WHL	64-29-27-56-178
5*	105	Mike Toal	CAN	C	Portland Winter Hawks	WHL	71-38-83-121-32
6	126	Blair Barnes	CAN	RW	Windsor Spitfires	OHL	67-42-76-118-195
1980							
1	6	Paul Coffey	CAN	D	Kitchener Rangers	OHL	75-29-73-102-193
3	48	Shawn Babcock	CAN	RW	Windsor Spitfires	OHL	12-13-25
4	69	Jari Kurri	FIN	RW	Jokerit Helsinki	FIN	33-23-16-39-22
5	90	Walt Podubny	CAN	C/LW	Kingston Canadians	OHL	43-30-17-47-36
6	111	Mike Winther	CAN	C	Brandon Wheat Kings	WHL	36-54-90
7	132	Andy Moog	CAN	G	Billings Big Horns	WHL	46-23-14-1-1-3.67
8	153	R. Polman Tuin	CAN	G	Michigan Tech Huskies	WCHA	
9	174	Lars Petersson	SWE	LW	Lulea H.F.	SWE	
1981							
1*	8	Grant Fuhr	CAN	G	Victoria Cougars	WHL	59-48-9-1-4-2.78
2	29	Todd Strueby	CAN	LW	Regina Pats	WHL	71-18-27-45-99
4	71	Paul Houck	CAN	RW	Kelowna Buckaroos	BCJHL	52-65-51-116-39
5	92	Phil Drouillard	CAN	LW	Niagara Falls Flyers	OHL	62-24-10-34-35
6	111	Steve Smith	SCO	D	London Knights	OHL	62-4-12-16-130
6	113	Marc Habscheid	CAN	C	Saskatoon Blades	WHL	72-34-63-97-50
8	155	Mike Sturgeon	CAN	D	Kelowna Buckaroos	BCJHL	50-6-20-26-71
9	176	Miloslav Horava	CZH	D	Poldi Sonp Kladno	CZH	44-19-25-44
10	197	Gord Sherven	CAN	C	Weyburn Red Wings	SJHL	44-35-34-69
1982							
1	20	Jim Playfair	CAN	D	Portland Winter Hawks	WHL	70-4-13-17-121
2	40	Steve Graves	CAN	LW	Soo Greyhounds	OHL	67-46-73-119-42
3	62	Brent Loney	CAN	LW	Cornwall Royals	OHL	65-13-12-25-57
4	83	Jaroslav Pouzar	CZH	LW	Ceske Budejovice	CZH	34-19-17-36-32
5	104	Dwayne Boettger	CAN	D	Toronto Marlboros	OHL	66-4-21-25-138
6	125	Raimo Summanen	FIN	W	KiekkoReipas Lahti	FIN	36-15-6-21-17
7	146	Brian Small	CAN	RW	Ottawa 67's	OHL	66-18-24-42-72
8*	167	Dean Clark	CAN	D	St. Albert Saints	AJHL	59-21-32-53-146
9	186	Ian Wood	ENG	G	Penticton Knights	BCJHL	
10	209	Grant Dion	CAN	D	Cowichan Valley Capitals	BCJHL	
11	230	Chris Smith	CAN	G	Regina Pats	WHL	10-485-35-4.34
12	251	Jeff Crawford	CAN	LW	Regina Pats	WHL	63-15-22-37-404
1983							
1	19	Jeff Beukeboom	CAN	D	Soo Greyhounds	OHL	70-0-25-25-25
2	40	Mike Golden	USA	C	Reading High School	USHS	
3	61	Mike Flanagan	USA	D	Acton-Boxboro H.S.	USHS	
4	82	Esa Tikkanen	FIN	LW	Helsinki IFK Juniors	FIN	30-34-31-65-104
6	124	Don Barber	CAN	LW	Kelowna Buckaroos	BCJHL	35-26-31-57-54
7	145	Dale Derkatch	CAN	C	Regina Pats	WHL	67-84-95-179-62

Rnd.	#	Name	Nat.	Pos.	Drafted From	League	Record
8	166	Ralph Vos	CAN	LW	Abbotsford Flyers	BCJHL	43 games, 110 pts.
9	180	Dave Roach	CAN	G	New Westminster Royals	BCJHL	
10*	208	W. Yadlowski	CAN	C	Calgary Wranglers	WHL	65-3-11-14-24
11	229	John Miner	CAN	D	Regina Pats	WHL	71-11-23-34-126
12	250	Steve Woodburn	CAN	D	Verdun Juniors	QMJHL	69-5-28-33-202
1984							
1	21	Selmar Odelein	CAN	D	Regina Pats	WHL	71-9-42-51-45
2	42	Daryl Reaugh	CAN	G	Kamloops Oilers	WHL	55-2748-199-4.34
3	63	Todd Norman	USA	C	Hill Murray High School	USHS	
4	84	Rich Novak	CAN	RW	Richmond Sockeyes	BCJHL	
5	105	Richard Lambert		LW	Henry Carr	Jr. B	
6*	106	Emanuel Viveiros	CAN	D	Prince Albert Raiders	WHL	67-15-94-109-48
6	126	Ivan Dornic	CZH	LW	Dukla Trencin	CZH	
7	147	Heikki Riihjarvi	FIN	D	KiekkoReipas Lahti	FIN	
8	168	Todd Ewen	CAN	RW	New Westminster Bruins	WHL	68-11-13-24-176
10	209	Joel Curtis	CAN	LW	Oshawa Generals	OHL	67-8-12-20-68
11	229	Simon Wheeldon	CAN	C	Victoria Cougars	WHL	56-14-24-38-43
12	250	Darren Gani	AUT	D	Belleville Bulls	OHL	67-16-40-56-22
1985							
1	20	Scott Metcalfe	CAN	LW	Kingston Canadians	OHL	58-27-33-60-100
2*	41	Todd Carnelley	CAN	D	Kamloops Blazers	WHL	56-18-29-47-69
3	62	Mike Ware	CAN	D	Hamilton Steelhawks	OHL	57-4-14-18-225
5	104	Thomas Kapusta	CZH	C	Gottwaldov	CZH	
6	125	Brian Tessier	CAN	G	North Bay Centennials	OHL	5-279-20-4.30
7	146	Shawn Tyers	CAN	RW	Kitchener Rangers	OHL	57-13-26-39-26
8*	167	Tony Fairfield	CAN	RW	St. Albert Saints	AJHL	
9	188	Kelly Buchberger	CAN	LW	Moose Jaw Warriors	WHL	51-12-17-29-114
10	209	Mario Barbe	CAN	D	Chicoutimi Sagueneens	QMJHL	64-2-13-15-211
11	230	Peter Headon	CAN	C	Notre Dame High School	SJHL	
12	251	John Haley	USA	G	Hull High School	USHS	
1986							
1	21	Kim Issel	CAN	RW	Prince Albert Raiders	WHL	68-29-39-68-41
2	42	Jamie Nicholls	CAN	LW	Portland Winter Hawks	WHL	65-15-37-52-60
3	63	Ron Shudra	CAN	D	Kamloops Blazers	WHL	72-10-40-50-81
4	84	Dan Currie	CAN	LW	Soo Greyhounds	OHL	66-21-24-45-37
5	105	David Haas	CAN	LW	London Knights	OHL	62-4-13-17-91
6*	126	Jim Ennis	CAN	D	Boston University Terriers	HE	40-1-4-5-22
7	147	Ivan Matulik	CZH	LW	Slovan CHZJD Bratislava	CZH	
8	168	Nicolas Beaulieu	CAN	LW	Drummondville Voltigeurs	QMJHL	70-11-20-31-93
9	189	Mike Greenlay	BRA	G	Calgary Midgets	AAA	
10	210	Matt Lanza	USA	D	Winthrop High School	USHS	
11	231	Majmir Bozik	CZH	D	VSZ Kosice	CZH	
12	252	Tony Hand	SCO	C	Murrayfield Racers	SCO	32-79-85-164-44
1987							
1	21	Peter Soberlak	CAN	LW	Swift Current Broncos	WHL	68-33-42-75-45
2*	42	Brad Werenka	CAN	D	Northern Michigan U.	WCHA	30-4-4-8-35
3*	63	Geoff Smith	CAN	D	St. Albert Saints	AJHL	57-7-28-35-101
4	64	Peter Eriksson	SWE	LW	HV 71 Husqvarna	SWE	36-14-5-19-16
5	105	Shaun Van Allen	CAN	C	Saskatoon Blades	WHL	72-38-59-97-116
6	126	Radek Toupal	CZH	RW	Ceske Motor Budejovice	CZH	
7	147	Tomas Srsen	CZH	LW	Zetor Brno	CZH	40-15-8-23-44
8	168	Age Ellingsen	NOR	D	Storhamer og-Sparta	NOR	
9*	189	Gavin Armstrong	CAN	G	RPI Engineers	ECAC	
10	210	Mike Tinkham	USA	RW	Newburyport High School	USHS	
11	231	Jeff Pauletti		D	U of Minnesota Gophers	WCHA	
12	241	Jesper Duus	DEN	D	Rodovre SK	DEN	
12	252	Igor Viazmikin	USSR	W	Central Red Army	USSR	4-0-0-0-0

Rnd.	#	Name	Nat.	Pos.	Drafted From	League	Record
1988							
1	19	Francois Leroux	CAN	D	St. Jean Castors	QMJHL	58-3-8-11-143
2	39	Petro Koivunen	FIN	C	K Espoo	FIN	32-27-31-58-0
3*	53	Trevor Sim	CAN	C	Seattle Thunderbirds	WHL	67-17-18-35-87
3*	61	Collin Bauer	CAN	D	Saskatoon Blades	WHL	70-9-53-62-66
4*	82	Cam Brauer	CAN	D	RPI Engineers	ECAC	18-0-1-1-4
5	103	Don Martin	CAN	LW	London Knights	OHL	57-30-32-62-190
6	124	Len Barrie	CAN	RW	Victoria Cougars	WHL	70-37-49-86-192
7	145	Mike Glover	CAN	RW	Soo Greyhounds	OHL	63-41-42-83-130
8	166	Shjon Podein	USA	C	U of Minnesota-Duluth	WCHA	30-4-4-8-48
9	187	Tom Cole	USA	G	Woburn High School	USHS	
10	208	Vladimir Zubkov	USSR	D	Central Red Army	USSR	
11*	229	D. MacDonald	CAN	LW	Boston University Terriers	HE	12-1-2-3
12	250	Tim Tisdale	CAN	C	Swift Current Broncos	WHL	32-11-15-26-15
1989							
1	15	Jason Soules	CAN	D	Niagara Falls Thunder	OHL	57-3-8-11-187
2	36	Richard Borgo	CAN	RW	Kitchener Rangers	OHL	66-23-23-46-75
4	78	Josef Beranek	CZH	C	CHZ CSSP Litvinov	CZH	32-18-10-28-47
5	92	Peter White	CAN	LW	Michigan State U. Spartans	CCHA	46-20-33-53-17
6	120	Anatoli Semenov	USSR	C	Moscow Dynamo	USSR	31-9-12-21-24
7	140	Davis Payne	CAN	LW	Michigan Tech Huskies	WCHA	35-5-3-8-39
7	141	Sergei Yashin	USSR	LW	Moscow Dynamo	USSR	44-18-10-28-30
8	162	Darcy Martini	CAN	D	Michigan Tech Huskies	WCHA	35-1-2-3-103
11	225	Roman Bozek	CZH	RW	Motor Ceske Budejovice	CZH	33-16-9-25
1990							
1	17	Scott Allison	CAN	C	Prince Albert Raiders	WHL	66-22-16-38-73
2	38	Alex Legault	CAN	RW	Boston University Terriers	HE	43-9-21-30-54
3	59	Joe Crowley	USA	LW	Lawrence Academy	USHS	10-8-5-13
4	67	Joel Blain	CAN	LW	Hull Olympiques	QMJHL	65-31-47-78-137
5	101	Greg Louder	USA	G	Cushing Academy	USHS	
6	122	Keijo Sailynoja	FIN	LW	Jokerit Helsinki	FIN	41-15-13-28-8
7	143	Mike Power	CAN	G	W. M. U. Broncos	CCHA	24-7-14-1-0-4.83
8	164	Roman Mejzlik	CZH	LW/C	Dukla Jihlava	CZH	44-3-11-14
9	185	Richard Zemlicka	CZH	W	Sparta Praha	CZH	45-15-14-29
10	206	Petr Korinek	CZH	C	Skoda Pizen	CZH	
12	248	Sami Nuutinen	FIN	D	K-Espoo	FIN	40-8-15-23
1991							
1	12	Tyler Wright	CAN	C	Swift Current Broncos	WHL	66-41-51-92-157
1	20	Martin Rucinsky	CZH	LW	CHZ Litvinov	CZH	49-23-18-41-69
2	34	Andrew Verner	CAN	G	Peterborough Petes	OHL	46-22-14-7-0-3.52
3	56	George Breen	USA	RW	Cushing Academy	USHS	20-9-8-17
4	78	Mario Nobili	CAN	LW	Longueuil Chevaliers	QMJHL	70-33-52-85-115
5	93	Ryan Haggerty	USA	C	Westminster	USHS	25-34-38-72-0
7	144	David Oliver	CAN	RW	U of Michigan Wolverines	CCHA	27-13-11-24-34
8	166	Gary Kitching	CAN	C	Thunder Bay	USJHL	46-29-64-93
10	210	Vegar Barlie	NOR	RW	Valerengens Idrettsforening	NOR	36-3-12-15
11	232	E. Belosheiken	USSR	G	Central Red Army	USSR	
12	254	Juha Riihjarvi	FIN	RW	Oulu Karpat	FIN	42-9-17-26-55
1992							
1	13	Joe Hulbig	USA	LW	St. Sebastien's	USHS	17-19-24-43-30
2	37	Martin Reichel	CZH	C	Freiburg	GER	27-15-16-31-8
3	61	Simon Roy	CAN	D	Shawinigan Cataractes	QMJHL	63-3-24-27-24
3	65	Kirk Maltby	CAN	RW	Owen Sound Platers	OHL	66-50-41-91-99
4	96	Ralph Intranuovo	CAN	C	Soo Greyhounds	OHL	65-50-63-113-44
5	109	Joaquin Gage	CAN	G	Portland Winter Hawks	WHL	63-27-30-4-2-4.44
7	157	Steve Gibson	CAN	LW	Windsor Spitfires	OHL	63-49-40-89-41
8*	181	Kyuin Shim	CAN	RW	Sherwood Park Crusaders	AJHL	55-38-38-76-97
8	190	Colin Schmidt	CAN	C	Regina Midgets	MIDG	
9	205	M. Tuomainen	FIN	RW	Clarkson University	ECAC	28-11-12-23-32
11	253	Bryan Rasmussen	USA	LW	St. Louis Park	USHS	

Rnd.	*#*	*Name*	*Nat.*	*Pos.*	*Drafted From*	*League*	*Record*
1993							
1	7	Jason Arnott	CAN	C	Oshawa Generals	OHL	56-41-57-98-74
1	16	Nick Stajduhar	CAN	D	London Knights	OHL	49-15-45-60-58
2	33	David Vyborny	CZH	C	Sparta Praha	CZR	52-20-24-44
3	59	Kevin Paden	USA	C	Detroit Junior Red Wings	OHL	54-14-9-23-41
3	60	Alexander Kerch	USSR	RW	Dynamo Riga	CIS	42-23-14-37-28
5	111	Miroslav Satan	CZH	C	Dukla Trencin	SLO	38-11-6-17
7	163	Alexander Zhurik	USSR	D	Dynamo Minsk Jrs.	CIS	
8	189	Martin Bakula	CZH	D	U of Alaska-Anchorage	WCHA	35-9-15-24-62
9	215	Brad Norton	USA	D	Cushing Academy	USHS	31-10-26-36
10	241	Oleg Maltsev	USSR	LW	Traktor Chelybinsk	CIS	
11	267	Ilya Byakin	USSR	D	Eislaufverein Landshut e.V.	GER	44-12-19-31-43
1994							
1	4	Jason Bonsignore	USA	C	Niagara Falls Thunder	OHL	58-22-64-86-63
1*	6	Ryan Smyth	CAN	LW	Moose Jaw Warriors	WHL	72-50-55-105-88
2	32	Mike Watt	CAN	LW	Stratford	Jr. B	48-34-34-68-165
3	53	Corey Neilson	CAN	D	North Bay Centennials	OHL	62-3-35-38-46
3*	60	Brad Symes	CAN	D	Portland Winter Hawks	WHL	71-7-15-22-170
4	79	Adam Copeland	CAN	RW	Burlington	Jr. B	39-28-44-72-55
4	95	Jussi Tarvainen	FIN	C	KalPA Kuopio	FIN	42-3-4-7-20
5	110	Jon Gaskins	USA	D	Dubuque	USJHL	30-6-13-19-52
6	136	Terry Marchant	USA	LW	Niagara	NAJHL	42-27-40-67-43
7*	160	Curtis Sheptak	CAN	LW	Olds Grizzlies	AJHL	
7	162	Dimitrius Shulga	USSR	RW	Tivali Minsk	CIS	
7*	179	C. Wickenheiser	CAN	G	Red Deer Rebels	WHL	29-11-13-0-0-5.04
8	185	Rob Guinn	CAN	D	Newmarket Royals	OHL	63-2-8-10-135
8	188	Jason Reid	CAN	D	St Andrew's	CHS	
9*	214	Jeremy Jablonski	CAN	G	Victoria Cougars	WHL	6.29
11	266	Ladislav Benysek	CZH	D	HC Olomouc Jrs.	CZR	
1995							
1	6	Steve Kelly	CAN	C	Prince Albert Raiders	WHL	68-31-41-72-153
2	31	Georges Laraque	CAN	RW	St. Jean Lynx	QMJHL	62-19-22-41-259
3	57	Lukas Zib	CZH	D	HC Ceske Budejovice	CZR	13-2-0-2-16
4	83	Mike Minard	CAN	G	Chilliwack Chiefs	BCJHL	3.50
5	109	Jan Snopek	CZH	D	Oshawa Generals	OHL	64-14-30-44-97
7	161	Martin Cerven	CZH	C	Dukla Trencin Jrs.	SLO Jr.	22-8-3-11
8	187	Stephen Douglas	CAN	D	Niagara Falls Thunder	OHL	32-0-2-2-15
9	213	Jiri Antonin	CZH	D	HC Pardubice Jr.	CZR	
1996							
1	6	Boyd Devereaux	CAN	C	Kitchener Rangers	OHL	66-20-38-58-35
1	19	M. Descoteaux	CAN	D	Shawinigan Cataractes	QMJHL	69-2-13-15-129
2	32	Chris Hajt	CAN	D	Guelph Storm	OHL	63-8-27-35-69
3	59	Tom Poti	USA	D	Cushing Academy	USHS	29-14-59-73-18
5	114	Brian Urick	USA	RW	University of Notre Dame	CCHA	36-12-15-27-66
6	141	Bryan Randall	CAN	C	Medicine Hat Tigers	WHL	64-4-5-9-51
7	168	David Bernier	CAN	C	St.-Hyacinthe Laser	QMJHL	65-10-18-28-64
7	170	B. Lafrance	CAN	RW	Ohio State Buckeyes	CCHA	32-11-5-16-34
8*	195	Fernando Pisani	CAN	C	St. Albert Saints	AJHL	58-40-63-103-134
9	221	John Hultberg	USA	G	Kingston Frontenacs	OHL	40-13-15-4-1-3.68
1997							
1	14	Michel Riesen	SWI	C	EHC Biel	SWI 2	38-16-16-32-49
2	41	Patrick Dovigi	CAN	G	Erie Otters	OHL	36-11-14-4-3-3.88
3	68	Sergei Yerkovich	USSR	D	Las Vegas Thunder	IHL	76-6-19-25-167
4	94	Jonas Elofsson	SWE	D	Farjestad Karlstad	SWE	3-0-0-0-0
5*	121	Jason Chimera	CAN	C	Medicine Hat Tigers	WHL	71-16-23-39-64
6	141	Peter Sarno	CAN	C	Windsor Spitfires	OHL	66-20-63-83-59
7	176	Kevin Bolibruck	CAN	D	Peterborough Petes	OHL	46-4-26-30-63
7	187	Chad Hinz	CAN	C	Moose Jaw Warriors	WHL	72-37-47-84-47
8	205	Chris Kerr	CAN	D	Sudbury Wolves	OHL	45-3-10-13-58
9	231	A. Fomitchev	USSR	G	St. Albert Saints	AJHL	2.88

Rnd.	*#*	*Name*	*Nat.*	*Pos.*	*Drafted From*	*League*	*Record†*
1998							
1	13	Michael Henrich	CAN	RW	Barrie Colts	OHL	66-41-22-63-75
3	67	Alex Henry	CAN	D	London Knights	OHL	62-5-9-14-97
4	99	Shawn Horcoff	CAN	C	Michigan State Spartans	CCHA	29-12-11-23-46
4	113	Kristian Antila	FIN	G	Ilves Tampere	FIN	29-2160-2.80
5	128	Paul Elliott	CAN	D	Medicine Hat Tigers	WHL	72-11-27-38-47
5	144	Oleg Smirnov	RUS	F	Kristall Elektrostal	RUS	22-2-8-10-6
6	159	Trevor Ettinger	CAN	D	Cape Breton Scr. Eagles	QMJHL	50-1-2-3-181
7	186	Michael Morrison	USA	G	Exeter	USHS	26-1365-2.26
8	213	Christian Lefebvre	CAN	D	Baie-Comeau Drakkar	QMJHL	8-0-0-0-18
9	241	Maxim Spiridonov	RUS	RW	London Knights	OHL	66-54-44-98-52
1999							
1	13	Jani Rita	FIN	RW	Jokerit Helsinki	FIN	41-3-2-5-39
2	36	Alexei Semenov	RUS	D	Sudbury Wolves	OHL	28-0-3-3-28
2	41	Tony Salmenainen	FIN	LW	IFK Helsinki	FIN Jr.	21-13-10-23
3	81	Adam Hauser	USA	G	U. of Minnesota Gophers	WCHA	37-14-16-7-3.54
3*	91	Mike Comrie	CAN	C	U. of Michigan Wolverines	CCHA	42-19-25-44
5	139	Jonathan Fauteux	CAN	D	Val d'Or Foreurs	QMJHL	59-15-33-48-139
6	171	Chris Legg	CAN	C	London Jr. B.	OHL	52-38-40-78
7	199	Christian Chartier	CAN	D	Saskatoon Blades	WHL	62-2-14-16-71
9	256	Tomas Groschl	HUN	W	Leksands IF	SWE	
2000							
1	17	Alexei Mikhnov	UKR	LW	Torpedo Yaroslavl	RUS	53-24-17-41
2	35	Brad Winchester	USA	LW	U. of Wisconsin Badgers	WCHA	29-8-8-16-48
3	83	Alex Ljubimov	RUS	D	Samara	RUS	21-13-10-23
4	113	Lou Dickenson	CAN	F	Mississauga Ice Dogs	OHL	66-21-25-46
5	152	Paul Flache	CAN	D	Brampton Batallion	OHL	54-1-0-1-59
6*	184	Shaun Norrie	CAN	RW	Calgary Hitmen	WHL	67-12-13-25-94
7	211	Joe Cullen	USA	F	Colorado College Tigers	WCHA	29-4-6-10
7	215	Mat Lombardi	CAN	C	Victoriaville	AMJHL	
8	247	Jason Platt	USA	D	Omaha Lancers	USHL	49-1-6-7-65
9	274	Evgeny Muratov	RUS	LW	Neftecchimik	RUS	

AJHL-Alberta Junior Hockey League, AUT-Australia, BCJHL-British Columbia Junior Hockey League, BRA-Brazil, C-Center, CAN-Canada, CCHA-Central Collegiate Hockey Association, CIS-Commonwealth of Independent States, CZH-Czechoslovakia, CZR-Czech Republic, D-Defense DEN-Denmark, ECAC-Eastern Collegiate Athletic Conference, ENG-England, F-Forward, FIN-Finland, G-Goaltender, GER-Germany, HE-Hockey East, HUN-Hungary, IHL-International Hockey League, LW-Left Wing, MIDG-Midgets, NAJHL-North American Junior Hockey League, NOR-Norway, OHL-Ontario Hockey League, QMJHL-Quebec Major Junior Hockey League, RUS-Russia, RW-Right Wing, SCO-Scotland, SJHL-Saskatchewan Junior Hockey League, SLO-Slovakia, SWE-Sweden, SWI-Swiss, UKR-Ukraine, USA-United States, USHS-United States High School, USJHL-United States Junior Hockey League, USSR-Soviet Union, W-Right Wing and Left Wing, WCHA-Western Collegiate Hockey Association, WHL-Western Hockey League

†Indicates player's record in his draft year. For a goaltender the numbers indicate in order: games played-wins-losses-ties-shutouts-average; for a non goaltender the numbers indicate in order: games played-goals-assists-points-penalty minutes.
*Born in Alberta

Award Winners

ALL-STAR GAME MVP

1982-83 **Wayne Gretzky** scored 4 goals in the All-Star game Feburary 8, 1983 in Long Island.

1986-87 **Grant Fuhr** allowed 0 goals in 31 shots February 4, 1986 in Hartford.

ART ROSS TROPHY

(awarded to the player finishing first in scoring during the regular season)

1979-80 Wayne Gretzky tied Marcel Dionne in the scoring race with 137 points. Dionne won the Art Ross Trophy on the basis of scoring more goals than Gretzky.

1980-81 **Wayne Gretzky** finished first with 164 scoring points. Marcel Dionne of the Kings finished second with 135 points.

1981-82 **Wayne Gretzky** finished first with 212 scoring points. Mike Bossy of the Islanders was runner up with 147 points.

1982-83 **Wayne Gretzky** finished first with 196 scoring points. Peter Stastny of Quebec finished second with 124 points

1983-84 **Wayne Gretzky** finished first with 205 scoring points. Paul Coffey of the Oilers finished second with 126 points.

1984-85 **Wayne Gretzky** finished first with 208 scoring points. Jari Kurri of the Oilers finished second with 135 points.

1985-86 **Wayne Gretzky** finished first with 215 scoring points. Mario Lemieux finished second with 141 scoring points.

1986-87 **Wayne Gretzky** finished first with 183 scoring points. Jari Kurri finished second with 108 points while Mark Messier finished tied for third with Mario Lemieux, both scoring 107 points.

BUDWEISER/NHL MAN OF THE YEAR

(awarded to the player recognized in the local community as a positive role mode both on and off the ice)

1987-88 Wayne Gretzky finished second in voting with 16 votes. Bryan Trottier of the Islanders finished first with 23 votes.

1988-89 Kevin Lowe finished second in voting behind winner Lanny McDonald of Calgary.

1989-90 **Kevin Lowe** won the award after finishing second in the previous year.

CALDER MEMORIAL TROPHY

(awarded to the player voted as the most proficient in his first season of play in the NHL)

1981-82 Grant Fuhr finished third in voting for Rookie of the Year. Dale Hawerchuk finished first in voting with 258 balloting points. Barry Pederson of Boston finished second with 93 voting points. Fuhr collected 87 points. Hawerchuk scored 45 goals and added 58 assists for 103 points in his rookie season while Fuhr won 28, lost 5 and tied 14 and posted a 3.31 average.

1993-94 Jason Arnott was second in voting behind goaltender Martin Brodeur of the New Jersey Devils. Brodeur collected 164 voting points, Arnott had 137 votes. Arnott's regular season statistics were 78-33-35-68-104. Brodeur's regular season statistics were 47-27-11-8-2.40 with three shutouts.

CLARENCE S. CAMPBELL BOWL

(awarded to the team which advances to the playoffs from the Western Conference or the Campbell Conference)

1982-83 **Edmonton Oilers**
1983-84 **Edmonton Oilers**
1984-85 **Edmonton Oilers**
1986-87 **Edmonton Oilers**
1987-88 **Edmonton Oilers**
1989-90 **Edmonton Oilers**

CONN SMYTHE TROPHY

(awarded to the player judged to be the most valuable to his team in the playoffs)

1983-84 **Mark Messier** finished the playoffs with 8 goals, 18 assists and 26 points.

1984-85 **Wayne Gretzky** finished the playoffs with 17 goals, 30 assists and 47 points

1987-88 **Wayne Gretzky** led the playoffs in scoring with 12 goals and 31 assists.

1989-90 **Bill Ranford** led the Oilers to their 5th Stanley Cup, winning 16 games and losing 6 while posting a 2.53 average.

DODGE PERFORMER OF THE YEAR

(presented by Dodge and awarded to the NHL's most outstanding performer)

1986-87 **Wayne Gretzky**

EMERY EDGE TROPHY

(awarded to the player playing in a minimum of 60 games who leads the league in the plus-minus statistic)

1982-83 **Charlie Huddy** won the first Emery Edge Trophy with a +62. Wayne Gretzky finished second with a +60.

1983-84 **Wayne Gretzky** led the league with a +76, Bryan Trottier of the Islanders finished second with a +70.

1984-85 **Wayne Gretzky** led the league with a +98, Jari Kurri finished second with a +76.

1985-86 Wayne Gretzky finished 3rd in the league with a +71. Mark Howe of Philadelphia finished 1st with a +85.

1986-87 **Wayne Gretzky** led the league with a +70. Mark Howe of Philadelphia finished second with a +57.

FRANK J. SELKE TROPHY

(awarded to the forward who best excels in the defensive aspects of the game)

1982-83 Jari Kurri finished second in balloting behind Bobby Clarke of the Flyers. Clarke received 125 points while Kurri was second with 63 voting points.
1988-89 Esa Tikkanen finished second in balloting, tied with Colin Patterson, each accumulating 73 points in postseason balloting. Guy Carbonneau of Montreal finished first with 222 points.
1989-90 Esa Tikkanen finished third in balloting with 81 points. Rick Meagher of St. Louis finished first in voting with 105 points. Guy Cabonneau of Montreal finished second with 100 points.
1990-91 Esa Tikkanen finished second in balloting with 133 voting points. Dirk Graham of Chicago finished first with 157 points.

HART MEMORIAL TROPHY

(awarded to the man who is judged to be the most valuable player to his team)

1979-80 **Wayne Gretzky** won the first of 8 consecutive Hart Trophies polling 211 voting points while Art Ross winner Marcel Dionne finished second with 166 points in the balloting.
1980-81 **Wayne Gretzky** won the award finishing first in balloting with 242 points. Mike Liut, goaltender with the Blues finished as runner up with 237 points.
1981-82 **Wayne Gretzky** finished first with 315 points in balloting. Bryan Trottier finished second with 130 points.
1982-83 **Wayne Gretzky** finished first with 255 points in balloting. Pete Peeters finished second with 159 points.
1983-84 **Wayne Gretzky** finished first with 306 points in balloting. Rod Langway was second with 102 points.
1984-85 **Wayne Gretzky** finished first with 303 points in balloting. Dale Hawerchuk was second with 91 points.
1985-86 **Wayne Gretzky** finished first with 281 balloting points. Mario Lemieux finished second with 163 points.
1986-87 **Wayne Gretzky** finished first with 255 balloting points. Ray Bourque finished second with 95 points.
1987-88 Grant Fuhr finished second with 106 balloting points. Wayne Gretzky finished third with 73 points. Mario Lemieux finished first in balloting with 292 points.
1989-90 **Mark Messier** finished first in balloting with 227 points. Ray Bourque of Boston finished second with 225 points.

JACK ADAMS AWARD

(awarded to the NHL's Coach of the Year as voted on by the NHL's Broadcasters' Association)

1981-82 Glen Sather finished 3rd in voting behind winner Tom Watt of Winnipeg and Herb Brooks of the Rangers.
1985-86 **Glen Sather** finished first in balloting with 80 points. Jacques Demers of St. Louis finished second with 70 points.

JAMES NORRIS MEMORIAL TROPHY

(awarded to the defenseman who demonstrates the greatest all around ability at that position)

1981-82 Paul Coffey finished third in voting with 55 points, behind Doug Wilson (177 points) and Ray Bourque (80 points).Wilson scored 39 goals and added 46 assists while Coffey scored 29 goals and added 60 assists.
1983-84 Paul Coffey finished as runner up to Rod Langway of Washington. Langway collected 227 points in postseason balloting. Coffey collected 126 voting points and scoring points and was a plus 52. Langway finished the regular season with 9 goals, 24 assists, and 33 points and was a plus 14.
1984-85 **Paul Coffey** collected 223 points in balloting while scoring 37 goals, 84 assists and 121 points. Ray Bourque of Boston finished as runner up with 136 balloting points while scoring 20 goals and adding 66 assists.
1985-86 **Paul Coffey** collected 280 points in balloting while scoring 48 goals and adding 90 assists. Mark Howe finished second in balloting with 172 points. Howe scored 24 goals and assisted on 58 more and finished the season with 82 points.

KING CLANCY MEMORIAL TROPHY

(awarded to the player who best shows leadership qualities and makes a significant contribution to his community)

1987-88 Wayne Gretzky finished third in balloting with 13 points. Lanny McDonald of Calgary finished first with 24 points. Bryan Trottier finished second with 14 points.
1988-89 Kevin Lowe finished second in balloting behind winner Bryan Trottier of the Islanders.
1989-90 **Kevin Lowe** won the award after finishing second the previous year.

LADY BYNG MEMORIAL TROPHY

(awarded to the player who best exhibits sportsmanship and gentlemanly conduct and a high standard of play)

1979-80 **Wayne Gretzky** polled 93 points in balloting to win the trophy. Runner up Marcel Dionne polled 85 points in balloting. Gretzky who scored 137 regular season points spent only 21 minutes in the penalty box. Dionne spent 32 minutes in the penalty box.
1980-81 Wayne Gretzky finished second in balloting with 120 points. Rick Kehoe of the Penguins finished first with 138 points. Kehoe who scored 88 points spent only 6 minutes in the sin bin. Gretzky spent 28 minutes in the penalty box while scoring 164 points.
1981-82 Wayne Gretzky finished third in balloting with 105 points. Rick Middleton of the Bruins finished first in balloting with 211 points. Mike Bossy was second with 116 points. Middleton scored 94 points while spending only 12 minutes in the penalty box. Gretzky scored 212 points and had only 26 penalty minutes.
1984-85 **Jari Kurri** finished first in balloting with 128 voting points. Kurri scored 135 points while only amassing 30 minutes in penalties. Joe Mullen finished second with 92 voting points. Mullen scored 92 points in the regular season and 92 points in balloting while only receiving 6 minutes in penalties.
1985-86 Jari Kurri finished second in balloting with 100 points. Mike Bossy of the Islanders finished first with 217 points. Bossy scored 123 points while only serving 14 minutes in penalties. Kurri scored 131 points while only serving 22 penalty minutes.
1986-87 Wayne Gretzky finished second in balloting with 75 points. Joe Mullen of Calgary finished first with 189 points. Mullen scored 87 points while serving only 14 minutes in penalties. Gretzky scored 183 points while accumulating only 28 penalty minutes.
1987-88 Wayne Gretzky finished second in balloting with 155 points. Mats Naslund of Montreal finished first with 170 points. Gretzky scored 149 points while only spending 24 minutes in the penalty box. Naslund also spent only 14 minutes in the penalty box and tallied 83 scoring points.

LESTER B. PEARSON AWARD

(awarded to the league's most outstanding player as voted by members of the NHLPA)

1986-87 **Wayne Gretzky**
1989-90 **Mark Messier**

PRESIDENT'S TROPHY

(awarded annually to the team which finishes first overall during the regular season)

1985-86 The **Oilers** compiled a 56-17-7-119 record to win the first President's Trophy. Philadelphia finished second with 110 points.

1986-87 The **Oilers** compiled a 50-24-6-106 regular season record and finished first in the league. Philadelphia finished second with 100 points.

VEZINA TROPHY

(awarded to the goaltender who is judged to be the best at his position)

1981-82 Grant Fuhr finished second in voting with 31 points. Billy Smith of the Islanders won with 51 balloting points.

1985-86 Grant Fuhr finished third in voting for the Vezina with 32 points. John Vanbiesbrouck finished first with 105 points and Bob Froese finished second with 58 points.

1986-87 Grant Fuhr finished third in voting for the Vezina with 19 points. Ron Hextall of Philadelphia finished first with 65 points. Mike Liut of Hartford finished second with 60 points.

1987-88 **Grant Fuhr** finished first in voting with 78 points. Tom Barrasso of Buffalo finished second with 22 points.

Oilers on the All-Star Teams

Year	*First Team*	*Second Team*	*Rookie Team*
1979-80		Wayne Gretzly (Center)	
1980-81	Wayne Gretzky (Center)		
1981-82	Wayne Gretzky (Center)	Grant Fuhr (Goal)	
	Mark Messier (Left Wing)	Paul Coffey (Defense)	
1982-83	Wayne Grezky (Goal)	Paul Coffey (Defense)	
	Mark Messier (Left Wing)		
1983-84	Wayne Gretzky (Center)	Paul Coffey (Defense)	
	Jari Kurri (Right Wing)		
	Mark Messier (Left Wing)		
1984-85	Paul Coffey (Defense)		
	Wayne Gretzky (Center)		
	Jari Kurri (Right Wing)		
1985-86	Paul Coffey (Defense)	Jari Kurri (Right Wing)	
	Wayne Gretzky (Center)		
1986-87	Wayne Gretzky (Center)		
	Jari Kurri (Right Wing)		
1987-88	Grant Fuhr (Goal)		
	Wayne Gretzky (Center)		

Oilers players won four Conn Smythe Trophies (left) and five Stanley Cups from 1984 to 1990. (Corporate Communications, City of Edmonton Archives)

Year	*First Team*	*Second Team*	*Rookie Team*
1988-89		Jari Kurri (Right Wing)	
1989-90	Mark Messier (Center)		Geoff Smith (Defense)
1993-94			Jason Arnott (Center)
			Boris Mironov (Defense)
1998-99			Tom Poti (Defense)

All-Star Game Appearances

All-Star Game Appearances

Glenn Anderson—1984 (0 points), 1985 (0 points), 1986 (0 points), 1988 (2 assists)
Jason Arnott—1997 (0 points)
Jimmy Carson—1989 (1 goal, 1 assist)
Paul Coffey—1982 (1 assist), 1983 (1 assist), 1984 (0 points), 1985 (0 points), 1986 (2 assists)
Shayne Corson—1994 (0 points)
Vincent Damphousse—1992 (1 assist)
Lee Fogolin—1986 (0 points)
Grant Fuhr—1982 (2 GA), 1984 (1 GA), 1985, 1986 (0 GA, 31 MIN), 1988 (3 GA, 30 MIN), 1989 (3 GA, 30 MIN)
Wayne Gretzky—1980 (0 points), 1981 (1 assist), 1982 (1 goal), 1983 (4 goals), 1984 (1 goal), 1985 (1 goal), 1986 (1 goal), 1988 (1 goal)
Roman Hamrlik—1990 (0 points)
Mike Krushelnyski—1985 (3 assists)
Jari Kurri—1983 (2 assists), 1984 (0 points), 1986 (2 PIM), 1988 (0 points), 1989 (1 goal, 1 assist, 2 PIM), 1990 (1 goal), 1991 (1 assist)
Andy Moog—1985, 1986 (4 GA, 32 MIN)
John Muckler—1991 (coach)
Janne Niinimaa—2001 (0 points)
Bill Ranford—1991 (3 GA in 30 MIN)
Tommy Salo—2000 (2 GA in 20 MIN)
Glen Sather—1984, 1985, 1986, 1988, 1989 (coach)
Steve Smith—1991 (1 assist)
Doug Weight—1996 (0 points), 1998 (2 PIM), 2001 (1 goal, 3 assists)

Individual Milestones

100th Goal (Includes regular season and playoffs)

Scorer	*Assist*	*Assist*	*Date*	*Team*	*Goalie*	*Time*	*Per.*	
Anderson	Messier	Linseman	Jan. 7, 1983	Pittsburgh	Herron	12:42	2	PP
Arnott	Weight	Smyth	Oct. 1, 1997	San Jose	Vernon	18:24	2	ES
Coffey	Anderson	Messier	Jan. 4, 1984	Minnesota	Meloche	7:10	3	ES
Gretzky	Callighen	Kurri	Mar. 7, 1981	Philadelphia	St. Croix	2:40	2	PP
Hunter	Huddy	Coffey	Mar. 29, 1985	Hartford	Weeks	7:54	3	ES
Klima	Nicholls		Oct. 8, 1992	Calgary	Vernon	12:59	1	SH
Krushelnyski	Simpson	S. Smith	Jan. 21, 1988	Philadelphia	Hextall	10:06	3	PP
Kurri	Gretzky		Feb. 4, 1983	Montreal	Wamsley	11:52	1	ES
MacTavish	Messier	Greenlay	Feb. 25, 1990	Calgary	Vernon	4:17	3	SH
Marchant	Grier	Murray	Oct. 28, 2000	Avalanche	Roy	4:16	3	ES
Messier			Nov. 20, 1982	Vancouver	Ellacott	19:51	3	ES
Simpson	Messier	Anderson	Nov. 27, 1989	Detroit	St. Laurent	1:59	2	ES
Smyth	Poti	Weight	Jan. 14, 2000	Toronto	Joseph	15:17	2	PP
Tikkanen			Dec. 4, 1988	Rangers	Froese	2:44	2	ES
Weight	Marchant	Mironov	Jan. 24, 1998	Phoenix	Khabibulin	1:01	2	ES

200th Goal

Anderson	Messier	Lowe	Nov. 2, 1984	Chicago	Bannerman	4:05	2	ES
Coffey	Lumley	Gretzky	Jan. 29, 1986	St. Louis	Millen	14:16	3	ES
Gretzky	Messier	Hagman	Mar. 17, 1982	Pittsburgh	Dion	12:16	1	PP
Kurri	Gretzky	Krushelnyski	Oct. 30, 1984	Vancouver	Brodeur	8:23	2	PP
Messier	Gregg	Lindstrom	Oct. 30, 1984	Vancouver	Brodeur	12:46	3	ES
Simpson	MacTavish		Oct. 17, 1992	Detroit	Cheveldae	4:16	3	ES
Tikkanen			Oct. 15, 1991	Detroit	Cheveldae	6:31	2	SH

300th Goal

Anderson	Messier	Summanen	Apr. 6, 1986	Vancouver	Brodeur	00:38	1	ES
Gretzky	Hunter	Gregg	Oct. 12, 1983	Detroit	Mio	10:06	1	ES
Kurri	Gretzky	Anderson	Dec. 11, 1985	Chicago	Bannerman	14:52	2	ES
Messier	Muni	Anderson	Mar. 4, 1987	Vancouver	Caprice	11:16	1	ES

400th Goal

Anderson	Gretzky	Kurri	May 9, 1988	Detroit	Hanlon	4:03	2	PP
Gretzky	Coffey	Huddy	Oct. 18, 1984	Minnesota	Beaupre	7:11	1	SH
Kurri	Gretzky	Messier	Mar. 17, 1987	New Jersey	Billington	19:31	3	PP
Messier			Mar. 25, 1989	Los Angeles	Hrudey	00:16	3	SH

500th Goal

Gretzky	Messier	Krushelnyski	Nov. 20, 1985	Montreal	Penney	13:41	2	ES
Kurri	Messier	Lowe	Jan. 28, 1989	Los Angeles	Healy	10:06	2	PP

600th Goal

Gretzky	Nilsson	Coffey	Mar. 4, 1987	Vancouver	Caprice	11:33	3	ES

100th Assist

Assist	*Scorer*	*2nd Assist*	*Date*	*Team*	*Goalie*	*Time*	*Per.*	
Anderson	Messier		Apr. 10, 1982	Los Angeles	Lessard	10:39	1	ES
Arnott	Czerkawski	Weight	Nov. 9, 1996	Toronto	Potvin	15:53	1	PP
Buchberger	Thornton	Slegr	Apr. 13, 1995	Vancouver	McLean	15:56	1	ES
Coffey	Messier	Linseman	Nov. 21, 1982	Quebec	Malarchuk	14:02	2	PP
Fogolin	Anderson	Pouzar	Nov. 14, 1984	Montreal	Soetaert	6:21	2	ES
Gregg	Anderson	Messier	Jan. 27, 1986	Chicago	Sauve	18:20	1	SH
Gretzky	Anderson	Hagman	Nov. 5, 1980	Vancouver	Brodeur	18:35	2	ES
Huddy	Hunter	P. Hughes	Apr. 13, 1984	Calgary	D. Edwards	11:08	2	ES
Hughes, P.	Hunter	Gretzky	Feb. 15, 1985	Rangers	Hanlon	7:08	1	ES
Hunter								
Klima	Intranuovo	Bannister	Apr. 12, 1997	Vancouver	McLean	18:55	2	ES
Krushelnyski	Napier	S. Smith	Dec. 30, 1987	Vancouver	Brodeur	9:59	1	ES
Kurri	Gretzky	Huddy	Mar. 15, 1982	Los Angeles	Lessard	15:55	2	ES
Linseman	Semenko	Lindstrom	Apr. 5, 1984	Winnipeg	Behrend	13:14	2	PP
Lowe	P. Hughes	Boschman	Jan. 23, 1983	Los Angeles	Lessard	9:18	2	ES
Lumley	Coffey	Gretzky	Dec. 11, 1982	Minnesota	Beaupre	5:41	1	PP
MacTavish	Lacombe	Hunter	Feb. 3, 1989	Detroit	Hanlon	4:52	2	ES
Marchant	Grier	Moreau	Apr. 23, 1999	Dallas	Belfour	8:32	3	ES
McAmmond	Grier	Marchant	Feb. 5, 1999	Nashville	E.N.G.	19:37	3	ES
McClelland	S. Smith	MacTavish	Dec. 17, 1989	Chicago	Sidorkiewicz	8:34	1	ES
Messier	Coffey	Hagman	Mar. 6, 1982	Colorado	Resch	11:18	1	ES
Mironov	Guerin	Smyth	Apr. 30, 1998	Colorado	Roy	4:25	3	PP
Muni	Todd	Mellanby	Jan. 15, 1993	Hartford	Burke	3:13	1	ES
Siltanen	Anderson	Gretzky	Feb. 17, 1982	Minnesota	Beaupre	8:21	2	ES
Simpson	Murphy		Mar. 27, 1990	Vancouver	McLean	12:01	3	ES
Smith, S.	Anderson	Carson	Nov. 9, 1988	New Jersey	Burke	4:46	OT	ES
Smyth	Weight	Guerin	Oct. 15, 2000	Minnesota	McLennan	16:33	2	ES
Tikkanen	Kurri		Mar. 1, 1988	Los Angeles	Melanson	9:33	3	ES
Weight	Hauer	Arnott	Nov. 10, 1995	Tampa Bay	Wilkinson	12:24	1	ES

200th Assist

Assist	*Scorer*	*2nd Assist*	*Date*	*Team*	*Goalie*	*Time*	*Per.*	
Anderson	Messier	Coffey	Feb. 5, 1984	Washington	Riggin	9:33	2	ES
Coffey	Huddy	Gretzky	Jan. 15, 1984	New Jersey	Resch	1:45	2	PP
Gretzky	Callighen	Lowe	Apr. 8, 1981	Montreal	Sevigny	1:14	3	ES
Huddy	Tikkanen	McSorley	Apr. 26, 1984	Minnesota	Brodeur	00:10	2	ES
Kurri	Gretzky	Huddy	Nov. 8, 1983	Quebec	Malarchuk	13:50	2	ES
Lowe	Gretzky	McClelland	Oct. 10, 1985	Winnipeg	Hayward	9:22	1	ES
MacTavish	Olausson		Mar. 11, 1994	Detroit	E.N.G.	19:55	3	PP
Messier	Anderson	Linseman	Dec. 7, 1983	Vancouver	Garrett	15:58	3	ES
Simpson	Tikkanen	Corson	Dec. 12, 1992	Tampa Bay	Bergeron	18:42	3	ES
Smith, S.	Tikkanen	Simpson	Apr. 10, 1991	Calgary	Vernon	19:00	2	PP
Tikkanen	Klima		Feb. 28, 1990	Los Angeles	Scott	16:18	3	PP
Weight	Kovalenko	Arnott	Jan. 22, 1997	Islanders	Fichaud	3:38	2	PP

300th Assist

Assist	*Scorer*	*2nd Assist*	*Date*	*Team*	*Goalie*	*Time*	*Per.*	
Anderson	Kurri	Gretzky	Dec. 7, 1985	Minnesota	Beaupre	6:34	2	PP
Coffey	Anderson	Krushelnyski	Jan. 18, 1985	Vancouver	Brodeur	19:25	1	ES
Gretzky	Anderson	Kurri	Feb. 19, 1982	Hartford	Millen	12:30	1	ES
Huddy	Messier	S. Smith	Nov. 21, 1989	Vancouver	McLean	3:23	2	ES
Kurri	Coffey	Krushelnyski	Jan. 2, 1985	Philadelphia	Lindbergh	8:34	2	PP
Lowe	Messier	Leroux	Oct. 11, 1989	Vancouver	McLean	5:43	1	ES
Messier	Tikkanen		Oct. 13, 1985	St. Louis	Millen	00:41	3	ES
Tikkanen	Klima	Simpson	Feb. 20, 1993	Hartford	Burke	6:21	2	PP
Weight	Guerin	Poti	Feb. 5, 1999	Nashville	Vokoun	3:30	1	ES

400th Assist

Assist	*Scorer*	*2nd Assist*	*Date*	*Team*	*Goalie*	*Time*	*Per.*	
Anderson	Messier	Simpson	Dec. 22, 1987	Los Angeles	Janecyk	3:27	3	ES
Coffey	Huddy	Napier	Dec. 15, 1985	Vancouver	Brodeur	10:27	1	ES
Gretzky	Kurri	Coffey	Dec. 29, 1982	Chicago	Esposito	3:59	2	ES
Kurri	Hunter	Gretzky	Apr. 12, 1986	Vancouver	Brodeur	10:37	2	ES
Messier	Anderson	Coffey	Jan. 13, 1987	Detroit	Hanlon	5:20	1	ES
Weight	Carter	Smyth	Dec. 3, 2000	Sn Jose	Shields	1:13	2	PP

500th Assist

Assist	*Scorer*	*2nd Assist*	*Date*	*Team*	*Goalie*	*Time*	*Per.*	
Anderson	Simpson	Lowe	Oct. 15, 1989*	Los Angeles	Gosselin	6:35	1	ES
Gretzky	Hughes	Hunter	Oct. 22, 1983	Vancouver	Brodeur	11:32	2	ES
Kurri	Messier	S. Smith	Jan. 8, 1988	Winnipeg	Berthiaume	9:16	1	ES
Messier	Gretzky	Tikkanen	Feb. 28, 1988	Calgary	Vernon	10:14	2	PP

*-ex Oiler Wayne Gretzky became the NHL's all time leading scorer in this same game.

600th Assist

Gretzky	Coffey	Lindstrom	Mar. 17, 1984	Los Angeles	Mattsson	19:48	2	ES
Kurri	Huddy	Messier	Apr. 5, 1989	Los Angeles	Healy	13:58	2	PP
Messier	Jonsson		Apr. 6, 1989	Los Angeles	Hrudey	17:50	2	PP

700th Assist

Gretzky	Kurri	Hunter	Jan. 8, 1985	Quebec	Bouchard	1:50	3	ES
Messier	Graves		Apr. 22, 1990	Los Angeles	Gosselin	15:33	2	ES

800th Assist

Gretzky	Anderson	Kurri	Oct. 20, 1985	Los Angeles	Janecyk	19:39	1	PP

900th Assist

Gretzky	Kurri		Feb. 6, 1986	New Jersey	Resch	5:02	3	ES

1000th Assist

Gretzky	Tikkanen	Lowe	Nov. 24, 1986	Calgary	Vernon	18:50	1	ES

1100th Assist

Gretzky	Tikkanen	Hunter	Apr. 12, 1987	Los Angeles	Melanson	7:49	3	ES

1200th Assist

Gretzky	Simpson	S. Smith	Mar. 7, 1988	Winnipeg	Berthiaume	10:38	2	PP

100th Point

Player	*Goal/Assist*	*Assist*	*Date*	*Team*	*Goalie*	*Time*	*Per*	
Anderson (G)	Forbes		Nov. 29, 1981	Winnipeg	Staniowski	17:53	1	ES
Arnott (A)	Oliver	Kravchuk	April 15, 1995	Calgary	Kidd	13:12	1	PP
Beranek (G)	Smyth		Jan. 28, 2000	Tampa	Hodson	14:38	3	ES
Buchberger (G)	MacTavish	Tikkanen	Jan.31, 1993	Buffalo	Draper	00:46	OT	ES
Callighen (A)	Gretzky	Price	Feb. 25, 1981	Philadelphia	Peeters	18:02	2	ES
Carson (A)	Lacombe	Huddy	Apr. 2, 1989	Calgary	Wamsley	00:40	3	PP
Ciger (G)	Arnott	Weight	Nov. 9, 1995	Florida	Vanbiesbrouck	8:04	1	ES
Coffey (A)	Roulston	Kurri	Jan. 22, 1982	Vancouver	Brodeur	9:04	1	ES
Corson (G)	Beers	Arnott	Feb. 15, 1994	Washington	Beaupre	17:18	2	PP
Damphousse (A)	Murphy	Manson	May 10, 1992	Vancouver	McLean	2:20	2	PP
Fogolin (A)	Gretzky		Oct. 5, 1983	Toronto	St. Croix	2:33	3	SH
Gelinas (G)	Murphy	Richardson	Feb. 2, 1992	Quebec	Tugnutt	3:50	3	ES
Gregg (G)	Hughes	Gretzky	Jan. 4, 1985	Winnipeg	Hayward	2:17	2	ES
Gretzky (A)	Callighen		Feb. 24, 1980	Boston	Gilbert	5:43	2	ES
Grier (G)	Selivanov		Apr. 9, 1999	Calgary	Wregget	18:34	3	ES
Guerin (A)	Smyth	Hamrlik	April 9, 1999	Calgary	Wregget	9:56	3	PP
Hagman (A)	Anderson	Messier	Jan. 2, 1982	Boston	Baron	9:24	3	ES
Hamrlik (A)	Niinimaa	Marchant	Feb. 21, 2000	Los Angeles	E.N.G.	19:31	3	ES
Huddy (G)	Kurri	Gretzky	Dec. 3, 1983	Los Angeles	Laskoski	4:20	2	PP
Hughes (A)	Hunter	Fogolin	Apr. 24, 1983	Chicago	Esposito	1:13	2	ES
Hunter (A)	Fogolin	Gretzky	Feb. 7, 1982	Rangers	Mio	17:38	1	ES
Klima (G)	MacTavish	Ranford	Feb. 1, 1991	Chicago	Belfour	5:10	2	ES
Kovalenko (G)	Guerin	Beranek	Nov. 6, 1998	Colorado	Roy	6:00	2	ES
Krushelnyski (G)	Coffey	Gretzky	May 25, 1985	Philadelphia	Lindbergh	6:58	2	PP
Kurri (A)	Coffey	Gretzky	Oct. 23, 1981	Pittsburgh	Harrison	16:00	3	ES
Lamb (A)	Beranek	Gelinas	Mar. 6, 1992	St. Louis	Jablonski	10:06	1	PP
Lindstrom (A)	Carroll	Semenko	Feb. 15, 1985	Rangers	Hanlon	9:11	1	SH

Player	*Goal/Assist*	*Assist*	*Date*	*Team*	*Goalie*	*Time*	*Per*	
Linseman (A)	Anderson		Nov. 5, 1983	Pittsburgh	Dion	7:14	3	ES
Lowe (A)	P. Hughes	Boschman	Jan. 23, 1983	Los Angeles	Lessard	9:18	2	ES
Lumley (G)	Callighen		Dec. 5, 1981	Vancouver	Hanlon	5:56	3	ES
MacDonald (G)	Anderson	Gretzky	Oct. 12, 1980	Colorado	A. Smith	2:23	1	ES
MacTavish (G)	Ruotsalainen	Fuhr	May 9, 1987	Detroit	Stefan	5:41	1	ES
Manson (G)	McDougall	Rice	Mar. 17, 1993	Rangers	Vanbiesbrouck	4:07	1	ES
Marchant (A)	Kovalenko	Mironov	Apr. 20, 1997	Dallas	Moog	17:44	3	PP
McAmmond (A)	Kovalenko	Murray	Dec. 7, 1997	Chicago	Hackett	7:49	2	ES
McClelland (A)	McSorley	Tikkanen	Mar. 26, 1986	Pittsburgh	Romano	11:51	2	ES
Messier (A)	Gretzky		Apr. 16, 1981	Islanders	B. Smith	8:06	2	PP
Mironov (A)	Weight	Smyth	Dec. 22, 1997	Montreal	Thibault	10:04	1	PP
Muni (A)	Gelinas	Joseph	Jan. 23, 1991	Vancouver	Gamble	10:16	3	PP
Murphy (G)	Messier	Klima	Mar. 28, 1991	Calgary	Vernon	3:26	3	ES
Murray (G)	unassisted		Oct. 31, 1999	Nashville	Vokoun	4:01	2	ES
Napier (A)	MacTavish	Huddy	Mar. 26, 1986	Pittsburgh	Romano	12:25	2	ES
Nicholls (A)	Hawgood	Tikkanen	Dec. 29, 1992	Montreal	Racicot	2:35	1	PP
Semenko G)	Huddy		Mar. 11, 1984	Vancouver	Garrett	8:11	1	ES
Siltanen (A)	Hagman	Anderson	Oct. 21, 1981	Hartford	Garrett	19:01	1	ES
Simpson (G)	Anderson	Messier	Nov. 4, 1988	Buffalo	Barrasso	19:02	2	PP
Smith, S. (A)	Anderson	Messier	Mar. 20, 1988	Minnesota	Casey	13:15	1	ES
Smyth (A)	Kovalenko	Weight	Dec. 2, 1997	Colorado	Roy	3:12	3	PP
Tikkanen (G)	Gretzky	Hunter	Apr. 12, 1987	Los Angeles	Melanson	7:49	3	ES
Weight (G)	Buchberger	Richardson	Mar. 14, 1995	St. Louis	Joseph	1:38	3	ES
Weir (G)	Unger	Siltanen	Oct. 16, 1981	Calgary	Riggin	16:55	3	PP

200th Point

Player	Goal/Assist	Assist	Date	Team	Goalie	Time	Per	
Anderson (G)	Linseman		Nov. 11, 1982	New Jersey	Resch	15:13	3	ES
Arnott (A)	Satan	Czerkawski	Jan. 21, 1997	Rangers	Healy	9:33	3	PP
Buchberger (A)	Lindgren	Smyth	Dec. 27, 1996	Philadelphia	Snow	5:13	2	ES
Coffey (A)	Pouzar	Roulston	Feb. 20, 1983	Buffalo	Sauve	7:32	3	ES
Gregg (A)	Messier	Redmond	Jan. 8, 1989	Calgary	Wamsley	8:13	1	PP
Gretzky (A)	Coffey	Callighen	Jan. 3, 1981	Toronto	Tremblay	7:32	2	ES
Huddy (A)	Coffey		Apr. 20, 1985	Winnipeg	Hayward	14:11	1	PP
Hunter (G)	Hughes	Lowe	Mar. 18, 1984	Buffalo	Barrasso	7:00	2	ES
Klima (G)	Nicholls		Dec. 16, 1992	Vancouver	Whitmore	7:16	3	ES
Krushelnyski (G)	Huddy	S. Smith	Apr. 2, 1987	Calgary	Dadswell	14:18	2	ES
Kurri (A)	Pouzar	Gretzky	Nov. 8, 1982	Quebec	Bouchard	12:04	1	ES
Linseman (A)	Lowe	Klima	Feb. 6, 1991	Hartford	Sidorkiewicz	10:00	1	ES
Lowe (A)	Kurri	Linseman	Apr. 22, 1984	Calgary	Lemelin	18:00	2	ES
Lumley (G)	Fogolin	Lowe	Nov. 23, 1983	Los Angeles	Blake	19:57	1	ES
MacTavish (G)	Beukeboom	Eriksson	Nov. 11, 1989	Washington	Beaupre	7:33	3	PP
Marchant (A)	Grier		Jan. 19, 2000	Calgary	Brathwaite	4:17	3	SH
Messier (A)	Anderson		Oct. 9, 1982	Vancouver	Brodeur	18:15	1	PP
Murphy (A)	Damphousse	Nicholls	Apr. 26, 1992	Los Angeles	Hrudey	2:55	3	ES
Simpson (G)	Klima		Jan. 31, 1990	Detroit	Hanlon	4:48	1	ES
Smith, S. (G)	Messier	Simpson	May 24, 1990	Boston	Moog	6:09	3	ES
Smyth (A)	Weight	Ulanov	Mar. 29, 2000	Colorado	Roy	10:23	3	PP
Tikkanen (G)	Anderson	Gretzky	May 22, 1988	Boston	Lemelin	10:25	2	PP
Weight (A)	Marchment	Anderson	Feb. 23, 1996	Boston	Ranford	16:34	3	ES

300th Point

Player	Goal/Assist	Assist	Date	Team	Goalie	Time	Per	
Anderson (G)	Gretzky	Lowe	May 3, 1983	Chicago	Bannerman	15:01	1	PP
Coffey (A)	P. Hughes	Gretzky	Jan. 13, 1984	Buffalo	Sauve	7:13	3	ES
Gretzky (A)	Lowe		Apr. 4, 1981	Winnipeg	Mattsson	11:42	1	ES
Huddy (G)	Messier	Tikkanen	Jan. 11, 1988	Washington	Malarchuk	5:57	1	PP
Hunter (A)	McClelland	Huddy	Nov. 16, 1986	Rangers	Soetaert	13:08	2	ES
Kurri (G)	Gretzky		Apr. 24, 1983	Chicago	Esposito	14:52	3	ES
Lowe (A)	MacTavish		Jan. 6, 1988	Hartford	Liut	00:33	2	ES
MacTavish (G)	Damphousse	Maciver	Feb. 11, 1992	Minnesota	Casey	00:38	3	ES
Messier (G)	Gretzky	Coffey	Mar. 29, 1983	Vancouver	Brodeur	19:44	1	PP
Simpson (G)	Messier		Feb. 16, 1991	Toronto	Ing	13:43	2	ES
Tikkanen (A)	Lowe	Klima	Nov. 11, 1989	Washington	Beaupre	6:15	2	PP
Weight (A)	Smyth		Mar. 28, 1997	San Jose	Belfour	5:07	1	PP

400th Point

Player	*Goal/Assist*	*Assist*	*Date*	*Team*	*Goalie*	*Time*	*Per*	
Anderson (A)	Gretzky	Coffey	Mar. 25, 1984	Winnipeg	Soetaert	16:56	1	ES
Coffey (G)	Gretzky	Kurri	Oct. 30, 1984	Vancouver	Brodeur	19:41	1	ES
Gretzky (G)	Lowe	Coffey	Dec. 9, 1981	Los Angeles	Keans	8:06	2	PP
Huddy (A)	Messier	Kurri	Mar. 21, 1990	St. Louis	Riendeau	18:23	3	ES
Kurri (A)	Gretzky	Coffey	Feb. 22, 1984	Pittsburgh	Dion	5:34	3	ES
Lowe (A)	Klima		Apr. 24, 1991	Los Angeles	Hrudey	1:49	3	ES
Messier (A)	Lumley	Anderson	Feb. 22, 1984	Pittsburgh	Romano	00:29	1	ES
Simpson (A)	Hawgood	Nicholls	Nov. 10, 1992	St. Louis	Joseph	5:38	1	ES
Tikkanen (G)	Simpson	S. Smith	Dec. 23, 1991	Vancouver	McLean	17:26	3	PP
Weight (A)	Falloon	Hamrlik	Oct. 21, 1998	Islanders	Salo	19:38	1	PP

500th Point

Player	Goal/Assist	Assist	Date	Team	Goalie	Time	Per	
Anderson (G)	Messier	Coffey	Apr. 13, 1985	Los Angeles	Janecyk	00:46	OT	ES
Coffey (G)	Gretzky		Mar. 31, 1985	Chicago	Skorodenski	8:30	3	ES
Gretzky (G)	Messier	Kurri	Feb. 24, 1982	Buffalo	D. Edwards	18:16	3	ES
Kurri (G)	Gretzky		Dec. 5, 1984	Islanders	B. Smith	17:53	3	ES
Messier (A)	Gretzky	Lowe	Mar. 22, 1985	Toronto	Bernhardt	6:32	3	ES
Tikkanen (A)	MacTavish	Lowe	May 16, 1992	Chicago	Belfour	17:24	1	ES
Weight (G)	Niinimaa	Dowd	Mar. 22, 2000	Anaheim	Hebert	17:01	2	ES

600th Point

Player	Goal/Assist	Assist	Date	Team	Goalie	Time	Per	
Anderson (G)	Coffey	Messier	Feb. 11, 1986	Detroit	Laforest	7:13	2	ES
Coffey (A)	Gretzky	Huddy	Dec. 22, 1985	Winnipeg	Hayward	11:23	3	ES
Gretzky (G)	Kurri	P. Hughes	Nov. 21, 1982	Quebec	Malarchuk	12:25	2	PP
Kurri (G)	Coffey	Huddy	May 14, 1985	Chicago	Bannerman	7:52	1	PP
Messier (A)	Coffey	Anderson	Mar. 9, 1986	Los Angeles	Melanson	4:47	1	ES
Weight (G)	Zholtok		April 4, 2001	Minnesota	McLennan	19:12	3	PP

700th Point

Player	Goal/Assist	Assist	Date	Team	Goalie	Time	Per	
Anderson (A)	Muni	Nilsson	Mar. 17, 1987	New Jersey	Billington	00:40	2	ES
Coffey (A)	Kurri	Gretzky	Oct. 17, 1986	Detroit	Stefan	13:07	2	PP
Gretzky (G)	Gregg	Kurri	Feb. 23, 1983	Washington	A. Jensen	1:26	2	SH
Kurri (A)	Solheim	Gretzky	Feb. 14, 1986	Quebec	Malarchuk	10:07	1	ES
Messier (G)	Lowe		Feb. 1, 1987	Chicago	Sauve	17:18	1	ES

800th Point

Player	Goal/Assist	Assist	Date	Team	Goalie	Time	Per	
Anderson (A)	Lowe	Messier	Feb. 19, 1988	Pittsburgh	Pietrangelo	6:30	1	PP
Gretzky (A)	Coffey	Messier	Oct. 16, 1983	Calgary	D. Edwards	10:47	3	PP
Kurri (G)	Gretzky	Tikkanen	Dec. 28, 1986	Philadelphia	Hextall	1:25	2	ES
Messier (A)	S. Graves	S. Smith	Nov. 29, 1987	Buffalo	Puppa	8:45	2	PP

900th Point

Player	Goal/Assist	Assist	Date	Team	Goalie	Time	Per	
Anderson (A)	Corson	Simpson	Feb. 1, 1989	Vancouver	McLean	13:44	2	ES
Gretzky (A)	Kurri	Coffey	Jan. 3, 1984	Calgary	D. Edwards	15:46	3	ES
Kurri (G)	Messier	Anderson	Oct. 24, 1987	Vancouver	Brodeur	11:08	2	ES
Messier (A)	Kurri	Gretzky	May 11, 1988	Detroit	Stefan	18:02	2	PP

1000th Point

Player	Goal/Assist	Assist	Date	Team	Goalie	Time	Per	
Anderson (G)	S. Smith	Messier	May 8, 1990	Chicago	Millen	15:02	1	PP
Gretzky (A)	Pouzar	Kurri	Apr. 15, 1984	Calgary	Lemelin	13:13	3	ES
Kurri (A)	Gretzky	S. Smith	Apr. 21, 1988	Calgary	Vernon	7:54	OT	SH
Messier (A)	Simpson	Anderson	Apr. 5, 1989	Los Angeles	Healy	17:13	3	ES

1100th Point

Player	Goal/Assist	Assist	Date	Team	Goalie	Time	Per	
Gretzky (G)	Kurri	Coffey	Dec. 13, 1984	Los Angeles	Janecyk	18:47	1	ES
Kurri (G)	Messier	Gregg	Mar. 1, 1989	Montreal	Hayward	5:51	1	SH
Messier (A)	Kurri	Klima	Feb. 4, 1990	Washington	Mason	14:57	3	ES

1200th Point

Player	Goal/Assist	Assist	Date	Team	Goalie	Time	Per	
Gretzky (A)	Kurri	Coffey	Mar. 5, 1985	Calgary	Lemelin	13:26	1	PP

Player	*Goal/Assist*	*Assist*	*Date*	*Team*	*Goalie*	*Time*	*Per*	
Kurri (G)	Tikkanen	S. Smith	Feb. 6, 1990	New Jersey	Burke	16:53	1	PP
Messier (A)	Anderson		Jan. 13, 1991	Philadelphia	Hextall	5:25	3	ES
1300th Point								
Gretzky (A)	Anderson	Summanen	Oct. 30, 1985	Winnipeg	Hayward	14:23	2	ES
1400th Point								
Gretzky (G)	Jackson		Jan. 15, 1986	Hartford	Liut	19:45	3	ES
1500th Point								
Gretzky (A)	Anderson	Coffey	Apr. 18, 1986	Calgary	Vernon	19:48	2	PP
1600th Point								
Gretzky (A)	Kurri	Tikkanen	Dec. 28, 1986	Philadelphia	Hextall	1:25	2	ES
1700th Point								
Gretzky (A)	Nilsson	Messier	Apr. 9, 1987	Los Angeles	Eliot	14:05	2	PP
1800th								
Gretzky (A)	Kurri	S. Smith	Dec. 11, 1987	Vancouver	McLean	13:03	2	ES
1900th Point								
Gretzky (A)	Kurri	Tikkanen	May 5, 1988	Detroit	Stefan	1:18	3	ES

Oilers Career Leaders

Seasons

Player	Seasons
Kevin Lowe	15
Glenn Anderson	12
Kelly Buchberger	12
Mark Messier	12
Charlie Huddy	11
Dave Hunter	10
Jari Kurri	10
Grant Fuhr	10
Doug Weight	9
Craig MacTavish	9
Wayne Gretzky	9
Bill Ranford	9

Games

Player	Games
Kevin Lowe	1037
Mark Messier	851
Glenn Anderson	845
Kelly Buchberger	795
Jari Kurri	754
Craig MacTavish	701
Wayne Gretzky	696
Charlie Huddy	694
Dave Hunter	653
Doug Weight	588

Goals

Player	Goals
Wayne Gretzky	583
Jari Kurri	474
Glenn Anderson	417
Mark Messier	392
Paul Coffey	209
Craig Simpson	185
Esa Tikkanen	178
Doug Weight	157
Craig MacTavish	155
Ryan Smyth	133

Assists

Wayne Gretzky	1086
Mark Messier	642
Jari Kurri	569
Glenn Anderson	489
Paul Coffey	460
Doug Weight	420
Kevin Lowe	309
Charlie Huddy	287
Esa Tikkanen	258
Craig Simpson	180

Points

Wayne Gretzky	1669
Jari Kurri	1043
Mark Messier	1034
Glenn Anderson	906
Paul Coffey	669
Doug Weight	577
Esa Tikkanen	436
Kevin Lowe	383
Charlie Huddy	368
Craig Simpson	365

Shots

Player	Shots
Wayne Gretzky	2793
Glenn Anderson	2521
Mark Messier	2194
Jari Kurri	2155
Paul Coffey	1620
Doug Weight	1405
Charlie Huddy	1341
Todd Marchant	1183
Ryan Smyth	1181
Esa Tikkanen	1176

Shooting %
(100 games minimum)

Player	Shooting %
Craig Simpson	25.3
Norm Lacombe	23.1
Jari Kurri	22.0
Matti Hagman	21.6
Wayne Gretzky	20.9
Raimo Summanen	20.5
Stan Weir	19.8
Ken Linseman	19.7
Mike Krushelnyski	19.1
Petr Klima	18.1

Penalty Minutes

Player	Penalty Minutes
Kelly Buchberger	1747
Kevin McClelland	1291
Kevin Lowe	1236
Mark Messier	1122
Steve Smith	1080
Dave Semenko	981
Lee Fogolin	886
Glenn Anderson	798
Louie DeBrusk	797
Dave Hunter	780

Power Play Goals

Player	Power Play Goals
Glenn Anderson	126
Wayne Gretzky	125
Jari Kurri	107
Mark Messier	89
Craig Simpson	75
Paul Coffey	69
Ryan Smyth	59
Doug Weight	39
Jason Arnott	36
Esa Tikkanen	36
Bill Guerin	36

Short Handed Goals

Wayne Grezky	55
Mark Messier	36
Jari Kurri	31
Craig MacTavish	26
Esa Tikkanen	21
Todd Marchant	16
Paul Coffey	15
Glenn Anderson	13
Kelly Buchberger	12
Pat Hughes	11

Game Winning Goals

Player	Game Winning Goals
Glenn Anderson	73
Wayne Gretzky	61
Jari Kurri	60
Mark Messier	43
Esa Tikkanen	30
Craig MacTavish	25
Kelly Buchberger	24
Craig Simpson	21
Paul Coffey	19
Ryan Smyth	18

Game Tying Goals

Player	Game Tying Goals
Mark Messier	14
Wayne Gretzky	14
Jari Kurri	12
Glenn Anderson	9
Ryan Smyth	6
Dave Lumley	4
Doug Weight	4
Dave Hunter	4
Todd Marchant	4
Jason Arnott	3
Joe Murphy	3
Charlie Huddy	3
Stan Weir	3
Martin Gelinas	3
Brett Callighen	3

Minutes by a Goalie

Player	Minutes
Bill Ranford	25004
Grant Fuhr	23908
Andy Moog	12901
Curtis Joseph	10168
Tommy Salo	9230

Most Goals Against

Player	Goals Against
Grant Fuhr	1470
Bill Ranford	1463
Andy Moog	777
Curtis Joseph	492
Tommy Salo	368

Goals Against Average
(minimum 80 games)

Tommy Salo	2.39
Curtis Joseph	2.90
Bill Ranford	3.51
Andy Moog	3.61
Grant Fuhr	3.69

Most Wins

Player	Wins
Grant Fuhr	226
Bill Ranford	167
Andy Moog	143
Curtis Joseph	76
Tommy Salo	71

The Record Book

GAMES, INDIVIDUAL

Most Seasons: 15—Kevin Lowe (1979-80 to 1991-92, 1996-97 to 1997-98).

Most Career Games: 1,037—Kevin Lowe (in 15 seasons, 1979-80 to 1991-92, 1996-97 to 1997-98. 74 goals, 309 assists, 383 points).

Most Career Games in the Playoffs: 172—Kevin Lowe (in 15 seasons, 1979-80 to 1991-92, 1996-97 to 1997-98. 9 goals, 43 assists, 52 points)

Most Career Games Including Playoffs: 1,209—Kevin Lowe (in 15 seasons, 1979-80 to 1991-92, 1996-97 to 1997-98 1,037 regular season, 172 playoff. 83 goals, 352 assists, 435 points).

Most Career Games by a Forward: 851—Mark Messier (1979-80 to 1990-91. 392 goals, 642 assists, 1,034 points).

Most Career Games in the Playoffs by a Forward: 166—Mark Messier (1979-80 to 1990-91. 80 goals, 135 assists, 215 points).

Most Career Games by a Forward Including Playoffs: 1,017—Mark Messier (1979-80 to 1990-91. 851 regular season, 166 playoff games. 472 goals, 777 assists, 1,249 points).

Most Games in One Season: 84—Doug Weight (1993-94 season, 24 goals, 50 assists, 74 points), Zdeno Ciger (1993-94 season, 22 goals, 35 assists, 57 points), Kelly Buchberger (1993-94 season, 3 goals, 18 assists, 21 points).

Most Games in One Playoff Year: 22—Glenn Anderson, Adam Graves, Charlie Huddy, Jari Kurri, Mark Lamb, Craig MacTavish, Mark Messier, Craig Muni, Joe Murphy, Bill Ranford, Reijo Ruotsalainen, Craig Simpson, Steve Smith, Esa Tikkanen (1989-90 playoff year).

Most Games in One Season Including Playoffs: 102—Craig MacTavish (1989-90 season, 80 regular season, 22 playoff), Craig Simpson (1989-90 season, 80 regular season, 22 playoffs).

Most Career Games Appeared in by a Goaltender: 449—Bill Ranford (in 10 seasons, 1987-88 through 1995-96, 1999- 2000. 168 wins, 192 losses, 54 ties, .471 winning percentage).

Most Career Games in the Playoffs by a Goaltender: 111—Grant Fuhr (in 9 seasons, 1981-82 through 1990-91. 74 wins, 32 losses, .667 winning percentage)

Most Career Games Appeared in by a Goaltender Including Playoffs: 534—Grant Fuhr (in 10 seasons, 1981-82 through 1990-91. 300 wins, 149 losses, 54 ties, .612 winning percentage).

Most Games in One Season by a Goaltender: 75—Grant Fuhr (1987-88, 40 wins, 24 losses, 9 ties, .610 winning percentage).

Most Consecutive Games by a Goaltender in One Playoff Year: 22—Bill Ranford (1989-90, 16 wins, 6 losses, .727 winning percentage. Ranford played all but two minutes of the playoffs in 1990).

Most Games in One Season by a Goaltender Including Playoffs: 94—Grant Fuhr (1987-88, 75 regular season, 19 playoffs, 56 wins, 26 losses, 9 ties, .665 winning percentage). *(NHL Record)*

Most Consecutive Complete Games by a Goaltender: 20—Grant Fuhr (December 22, 1987 through February 3, 1988. 11 wins, 5 losses, 4 ties, .650 winning percentage), Bill Ranford (October 6, 1990 through November 23, 1990. 5 wins, 13 losses, 2 ties, .300 winning percentage).

GAMES, TEAM

Most Games Played, One Season: 84—1992-93 (26 wins, 50 losses, 8 ties), and 1993-94 (25 wins, 45 losses, 14 ties)

Most Playoff Games, One Playoff Year: 22—1989-90 (16 wins, 6 losses).

Most Games Including Playoffs, One Year: 102—1989-90 (80 regular season, 22 playoff. (54 wins, 34 losses, 14 ties).

Most Overtime Games, One Year: 28—1999-2000 (in 82 games, 4 wins, 8 losses, 16 ties).

Most Overtime Games, One Playoff Year: 6—1990-91 (in 18 games, 4 wins, 2 losses).

Most Overtime Games Including Playoffs, One Season: 28—1999-2000 (28 regular season, 0 playoff in 87 games).

Longest Overtime Game: 57 minutes, 34 seconds—April 27, 1999 (Joe Nieuwendyk scored with assists from Zubov and Hogue in a 3-2 Dallas win in game four of the Conference Quarter final. Oiler goaltender was Tommy Salo).

Shortest Playoff Overtime Game: 21 seconds—April 5, 1984 (Randy Gregg scored with assists from Mark Messier and Glenn Anderson in a 5-4 win vs. Winnipeg in game two of Division Semi-final. Jets goaltender was Marc Behrend).

GOALS, INDIVIDUAL—CAREER

Most Career Goals: 583—Wayne Gretzky (1979-80 to 1987-88 in 696 games, .838 goals per game).

Most Career Playoff Goals: 92—Jari Kurri (1980-81 to 1989-90 in 146 games, .630 goals per game).

Most Career Goals Including Playoffs: 664—Wayne Gretzky (1979-80 to 1987-88, 583 regular season, 81 playoffs in 816 games, .814 goals per game).

Most Career Goals by a Defenseman: 209—Paul Coffey (1980-81 to 1986-87 in 532 games, .393 goals per game).

Most Career Playoff Goals by a Defenseman: 36—Paul Coffey (1980-81 to 1986-87 in 94 games, .383 goals per game).

Most Career Goals by a Defenseman Including Playoffs: 245—Paul Coffey (1980-81 to 1986-87, 209 regular season, 36 playoffs in 626 games, .391 goals per game).

Most Career Power Play Goals: 126—Glenn Anderson (1980-81 to 1990-91, 1995-96 in 845 games, 30.2% of his regular season goals were scored on the powerplay).

Most Career Power Play Goals in the Playoffs: 22—Wayne Gretzky (1979-80 to 1987-88, in 120 games), Jari Kurri (1980-81 to 1989-90, in 146 games), Glenn Anderson (1980-81 to 1990-91, in 164 games).

Most Career Power Play Goals Including Playoffs: 148—Glenn Anderson (1980-81 to 1990-91, 1995-96 in 1,009 games, 29.7 % of his goals were scored on the powerplay).

Most Career Power Play Goals by a Defenseman: 69—Paul Coffey (1980-81 to 1986-87 in 532 games, 33.0% of his regular season goals were scored on the powerplay).

Most Career Power Play Goals by a Defenseman in the Playoffs: 11—Paul Coffey (1980-81 to 1986-87 in 94 games, 30.6% of his playoff goals were scored on the powerplay).

Most Career Power Play Goals by a Defenseman Including Playoffs: 80—Paul Coffey (1980-81 to 1986-87, 69 regular season, 11 playoff in 626 games, 32.7% of his goals were scored on the powerplay).

Most Career Short Handed Goals: 55—Wayne Gretzky (1979-80 to 1987-88 in 583 games, 9.4% of his regular season goals were scored shorthanded).

Most Career Short Handed Goals in the Playoffs: 11—Mark Messier (1979-80 to 1990-91 in 166 games, 13.8% of his playoff goals were scored shorthanded).

Most Career Short Handed Goals Including Playoffs: 64—Wayne Gretzky (1979-80 to 1987-88, 55 regular season, 9 playoffs, in 816 games, 9.6% of his goals were scored shorthanded).

Most Career Short Handed Goals by a Defenseman: 15—Paul Coffey (1980-81 to 1986-87 in 532 games, 7.2% of his regular season goals were scored shorthanded).

Most Career Short Handed Goals by a Defenseman in the Playoffs: 3—Paul Coffey (1980-81 to 1986-87 in 94 games, 8.3% of his playoff goals were scored shorthanded).

Most Career Short Handed Goals by a Defenseman Including Playoffs: 18—Paul Coffey (1980-81 to 1986-87, 15 regular season, 3 playoffs, in 626 games, 7.3% of his goals were scored shorthanded).

Most Career Game Winning Goals: 73—Glenn Anderson (1980-81 to 1990-91, 1995-96 in 845 games. The Oilers won 500 games while Anderson was on the roster, 17.5% of his regular season goals were game winners).

Most Career Game Winning Goals in the Playoffs: 16—Wayne Gretzky (1979-80 through 1987-88 in 120 games. The Oilers won 85 playoff games with Gretzky on the roster, 19.8% of his playoff goals were game winners).

Most Career Game Winning Goals Including Playoffs: 85—Glenn Anderson (1980-81 to 1990-91, 1995-96, 73 regular season, 12 playoff in 1,009 games. The Oilers won 613 games with Anderson on the roster, 17.1% of his goals were game winners).

Most Career Game Winning Goals by a Defenseman: 19—Paul Coffey (1980-81 to 1986-87 in 532 games. The Oilers won 336 games with Coffey on the roster, 9.1% of his regular season goals were game winners).

Most Career Game Winning Goals in the Playoffs by a Defenseman: 6—Paul Coffey (1980-81 to 1986-87 in 94 games. The Oilers won 68 playoff games with Coffey on the roster, 16.7% of his playoff goals were game winners).

Most Career Game Winning Goals Including Playoffs by a Defenseman: 25—Paul Coffey (1980-81 to 1986-1987. 19 regular season, 6 playoffs, in 626 games. The Oilers won 404 games with Coffey on the roster, 10.2% of his goals were game winners).

Most Career Empty Net Goals: 18—Wayne Gretzky (1979-80 to 1987-88 in 696 games. 5 came against Vancouver.).

Most Career Empty Net Goals in the Playoffs: 4—Wayne Gretzky (1979-80 to 1987-88 in 120 games).

Most Career Empty Net Goals Including Playoffs: 22—Wayne Gretzky (1979-80 to 1987-88 18 regular season, 4 playoffs, in 816 games. 5 came against Vancouver).

Most Career Overtime Goals in the Playoffs: 3—Glenn Anderson (1980-81 through 1990-91, in 164 games, of 23 overtime games played).

Most Games Scoring Three or More Goals: 43—Wayne Gretzky (1979-80 to 1987-88, 147 goals). *(NHL Record)*

Most Games Scoring Three or More Goals in the Playoffs: 7—Wayne Gretzky (1979-80 to 1987-88, 23 goals), Jari Kurri (1980-81 to 1989-90, 23 goals).

Most Games Scoring Three or More Goals Including Playoffs: 50—Wayne Gretzky (1979-80 to 1987-88, 43 regular season, 7 playoffs, 170 goals).

GOALS, INDIVIDUAL—SEASON

Most Goals, Single Season: 92—Wayne Gretzky (80 games, 1981-82 season. 1.15 goals per game). *(NHL Record)*

Most Goals One Playoff Year: 19—Jari Kurri (in 18 games, 1984-85 season, 1.06 goals per game). *(NHL Record)*

Most Goals Including Playoffs, Single Season : 100—Wayne Gretzky (87 regular season, 13 playoff, in 93 games 1983-84 season, 1.08 goals per game). *(NHL Record)*

Most Goals by a Defenseman, Single Season: 48—Paul Coffey (in 79 games, 1985-86 season, .608 goals per game). *(NHL Record)*

Most Goals by a Defenseman One Playoff Year: 12—Paul Coffey (in 18 games, 1984-85 season, .667 goals per game). *(NHL Record)*

Most Goals by a Defenseman Including Playoffs, Single Season: 49—Paul Coffey (48 regular season, 1 playoff, in 89 games, 1985-86 season, .539 goals per game), Paul Coffey (37 regular season, 12 playoff in 98 games, .500 goals per game) *(NHL Record)*

Most Goals by a Rookie, Single Season: 33—Jason Arnott (in 78 games, in 1993-94 season, .423 goals per game).

Most Game Winning Goals, Single Season: 13—Jari Kurri (1984-85 season in 73 games).

First Game Winning Goal at Home—October 19, 1979 vs. Quebec (Blair MacDonald scored at 8:22 of the 2nd period with assists to Brett Callighen and Blair MacDonald vs. Nordiques goaltender Michel Dion).

First Game Winning Goal on the Road—November 13, 1979 in Washington (Wayne Gretzky scored at 12:06 of the 2nd period. with an assist to Lee Fogolin vs. Capitals goaltender Wayne Stephenson).

Most Game Winning Goals One Playoff Year: 5—Jari Kurri (1986-87, 33.3% of his playoff goals were game winners).

First Game Winning Goal in the Playoffs on the Road—April 8, 1981 in Montreal (Brett Callighen scored at 1:14 of the 3rd period with an assist to Wayne Gretzky vs. Montreal goaltender Richard Sevigny).

First Game Winning Goal in the Playoffs at Home—April 11, 1981 vs. Montreal (Wayne Gretzky scored at 8:15 of the 2nd period with assists to Brett Callighen and Paul Coffey vs. Montreal goaltender Richard Sevigny).

Most Game Winning Goals Including Playoffs, Single Season : 15—Jari Kurri (1986-87, 10 regular season, 5 playoff, 21.7% of his goals were game winners)

Most Power Play Goals, Single Season: 20—Wayne Gretzky (1983-84, 23.0% of his goals were on the powerplay), Ryan Smyth (1996-97, 51.3% of his goals were on the powerplay).

First Powerplay Goal on the Road—October 10, 1979 in Chicago (Kevin Lowe with assists to Brett Callighen and Wayne Gretzky at 9:49 of the 1st period, on Chicago goaltender Tony Esposito).

First Powerplay Goal at Home—October 13, 1979 vs. Detroit (Blair MacDonald with assists to Brett Callighen and Wayne Gretzky at 12:06 of the 1st period, on Detroit goaltender Rogatien Vachon).

Most Power Play Goals One Playoff Year: 7—Mark Messier (1987-88, 63.6% of his playoff goals were on the powerplay).

First Powerplay Goal in the Playoffs on the Road—April 8, 1980 in Philadelphia (Dave Lumley scored with assists to Wayne Gretzky and Blair MacDonald at 14:09 of the 1st period, on Flyers' goaltender Pete Peeters).

First Powerplay Goal in the Playoff at Home—April 19, 1981 vs. N.Y. Islanders (Wayne Gretzky scored with assists to Jari Kurri and Paul Coffey at 16:44 of the 2nd period on Islanders' goaltender Billy Smith).

Most Power Play Goals Including Playoffs, Single Season : 22—

Wayne Gretzky (1983-84, 20 regular season, 2 playoffs, 22.% of his goals were scored on the powerplay).

Most Shorthanded Goals, Single Season: 12—Wayne Gretzky (1983-84, 13.8% of his regular season goals were scored shorthanded).

First Shorthanded Goal on the Road—November 15, 1979 in Philadelphia (Doug Hicks at 14:35 of the 3rd period with assists to Stan Weir and Blair MacDonald on Flyers' goaltender Phil Myre).

First Shorthanded Goal at Home—December 12, 1979 vs. Atlanta (Mark Messier scored unassisted at 15:58 of the 2nd period on Flames' goaltender Daniel Bouchard).

Most Shorthanded Goals One Playoff Year: 3—Wayne Gretzky (16 games, 1982-83 season), Todd Marchant (12 games, 1996-97 season).

First Shorthanded Goal in the Playoffs at Home—April 11, 1980 vs. Philadelphia (Mark Messier scored unassisted at 17:16 of the 1st period on Flyers' goaltender Phil Myre).

First Shorthanded Goal in the Playoffs on the Road—April 10, 1982 in Los Angeles (Wayne Gretzky at 19:23 of the 1st period on Kings' goaltender Mario Lessard. The goal was unassisted).

Most Shorthanded Goals Including Playoffs, Single Season: 13—Wayne Gretzky (1984-85 season, 11 regular season, 2 playoffs, 14.4% of his goals were scored shorthanded).

Most Overtime Goals One Playoff Year: 2—Esa Tikkanen (1990-91 season, in 18 games).

First Overtime Goal in the Playoffs—April 8, 1982 vs. Los Angeles (Wayne Gretzky scored at 6:20 of overtime vs. Kings' goaltender Mario Lessard. Charlie Huddy and Dave Lumley assisted on the goal).

First Overtime Goal in the Regular Season—October 9, 1983 vs. Minnesota (Jari Kurri scored at 3:50 of overtime on Minnesota goaltender Gilles Meloche. Wayne Gretzky and Kevin Lowe assisted on the goal).

Most Games Scoring Three or More Goals, Single Season: 10—Wayne Gretzky (80 games, 35 goals, 1981-82 season), Wayne Gretzky (74 games, 34 goals, 1983-84 season). *(NHL Record)*

First Two Goal Game at Home—October 13, 1979 vs. Detroit (Blair MacDonald on Detroit goaltender Rogatien Vachon).

First Two Goal Game on the Road—November 18, 1979 in Buffalo (Blair MacDonald and Stan Weir each scored two goals on Sabres' goaltender Bob Sauve).

First Three Goal Game at Home—October 19, 1979 vs. Quebec (Blair MacDonald on Quebec goaltender Michel Dion).

First Three Goal Game on the Road—January 19, 1980 in Pittsburgh (Blair MacDonald on Penguins' goaltender Greg Millen).

Most Games Scoring Three or More Goals One Playoff Year: 4—Jari Kurri (in 18 games, in 1984-85 season). *(NHL Record)*

First Two Goal Game in the Playoffs on the Road—April 8, 1981 in Montreal (Jari Kurri on Montreal goaltender Richard Sevigny).

First Two Goal Game in the Playoffs at Home—April 11, 1981 vs. Montreal (Wayne Gretzky on Montreal goaltender Richard Sevigny).

First Three Goal Game in the Playoffs at Home—April 11, 1981 vs. Montreal (Wayne Gretzky on Montreal goaltender Richard Sevigny).

First Three Goal Game in the Playoffs on the Road—April 17, 1983 in Calgary (Wayne Gretzky on Calgary goaltenders, Rejean Lemelin and Don Edwards).

Most Goals One Playoff Series: 12—Jari Kurri (1984-85, Conference Final vs. Chicago, 2.00 goals scored per game). *(NHL Record)*

First Oiler to Score 50 goals in a Season—Wayne Gretzky—April 2, 1980 vs. Minnesota North Stars in Edmonton.(Gretzky scored at 9:43 of the 2nd period against goaltender Gary Edwards. Dave Hunter and Colin Campbell received assists on the goal. Gretzky had recorded 50 goals and 84 assists and played in 78 games).

GOALS, INDIVIDUAL—GAME

Most Goals in One Game: 5—Wayne Gretzky (Feb. 18 1981, Edmonton 9 St. Louis 2. Blues goaltenders were Mike Liut [3] and Ed Staniowski [2]), Wayne Gretzky (Dec. 30 1981, Edmonton 7 Philadelphia 5. Flyers goaltender was Pete Peeters [4]. Gretzky also scored one goal into an empty net), Jari Kurri (Nov. 19 1983, Edmonton 13 New Jersey 4. Devils goaltenders were Ron Low and Glenn Resch), Pat Hughes (Feb. 3 1984, Edmonton Oilers 10 Calgary 5. Flames goaltenders were Don Edwards and Rejean Lemelin), Wayne Gretzky (Dec.15 1984, Edmonton 8 St. Louis. 2. Blues goaltender was Rick Wamsley), Wayne Gretzky (Dec. 6 1987, Edmonton 10 Minnesota 4. North Stars goaltenders were Don Beaupre [4] and Kari Takko [1]).

Most Goals One Playoff Game: 4—Wayne Gretzky (Apr. 6 1983, Edmonton 6 Winnipeg 3. Jets goaltender was Brian Hayward), Mark Messier (Apr. 14 1983, Edmonton 6 Calgary 3. Flames goaltender was Don Edwards), Wayne Gretzky (Apr. 17 1983, Edmonton 10 Calgary 2. Flames goaltender was Don Edwards), Glenn Anderson (Apr. 26 1983, Edmonton 8 Chicago 2. Blackhawks goaltender was Murray Bannerman), Jari Kurri (May 16 1985, Edmonton 8 Chicago 2. Blackhawks goaltender was Murray Bannerman), Jari Kurri (Apr. 9 1987, Edmonton 13 Los Angeles 3. Kings goaltenders were Roland Melanson [2] and Darren Eliot [2]).

Most Goals by a Defenseman: 4—Paul Coffey (December 26 1984, Edmonton 6 Calgary 3. Flames goaltender was Rejean Lemelin).

Most Goals One Home Game: 5—Wayne Gretzky (Feb. 18 1981 Edmonton 9 St. Louis 2. Blues goaltenders were Mike Liut [3] and Ed Staniowski [2]) Wayne Gretzky (December 30 1981 Edmonton 7 Philadelphia 5. Flyers goaltender was Pete Peeters [4]. Gretzky also scored one goal into an empty net), Jari Kurri (Nov. 19 1983 Edmonton 13 New Jersey 4. Devils goaltenders were Ron Low and Glenn Resch), Pat Hughes (Feb. 3 1984 Edmonton 10 Calgary 5. Flames goaltenders were Don Edwards and Rejean Lemelin). Wayne Gretzky (December 6 1987 Edmonton 10 Minnesota 4. North Stars goaltenders were Don Beaupre [4] and Kari Takko [1])

First Goal at Home—October 13, 1979 vs. Detroit (Blair MacDonald scored at 12:06 of the 1st period. Detroit goaltender was Rogatien Vachon).

Most Goals One Road Game: 5—Wayne Gretzky (December 15 1984 Edmonton 8 St. Louis 2. Blues goaltender was Rick Wamsley).

First Goal on the Road—October 10, 1979 in Chicago (Kevin Lowe scored at 9:49 of the 1st period. Chicago goaltender was Tony Esposito).

Most Goals One Home Game Playoffs: 4—Mark Messier (Apr. 14 1983 Edmonton 6 Calgary 3. Flames goaltender was was Don Edwards), Glenn Anderson (Apr. 26 1983 Edmonton 8 Chicago 2. Blackhawks goaltender was Murray Bannerman), Jari Kurri (Apr. 9, 1987 Edmonton 13 Los Angeles 3. Kings goaltenders were Roland Melanson [2] and Darren Eliot [2]).

First Playoff Goal Scored at Home—April 11, 1980 vs. Philadelphia (Wayne Gretzky scored at 15:55 of the 1st period. Flyer goaltender was Phil Myre).

Most Goals One Road Game in the Playoffs: 4—Wayne Gretzky (April 17, 1983 Edmonton 10 Calgary 2. Flames goaltender was Don Edwards), Jari Kurri (May 16, 1985 Edmonton 8 Chicago 2. Blackhawks goaltender was Murray Bannerman). *(Ties NHL Record)*

First Playoff Goal Scored on the Road—April 8, 1980 in Philadelphia (Dave Lumley scored at 14:09 of the 1st period. Flyer goaltender was Pete Peeters).

Most Power Play Goals One Game: 3—Glenn Anderson (November 19, 1988 Edmonton 9 Toronto 1. Maple Leafs goaltenders were Ken Wregget and Jeff Reese).

Most Power Play Goals One Playoff Game: 3—Jari Kurri (April 9

1987 Edmonton 13 Los Angeles 3. Kings goaltenders were Roland Melanson [1] and Darren Eliot [2]) *(Ties NHL Record).*

Most Shorthanded Goals One Game: 2—Esa Tikkanen (November 12 1988 Edmonton 6 Toronto 2. Maple Leafs goaltender was Allan Bester).

Most Shorthanded Goals One Playoff Game: 2—Wayne Gretzky (Apr. 6 1983 Edmonton 6 Winnipeg 3. Jets goaltender was Brian Hayward), Jari Kurri (Apr. 24 1983 Edmonton 8 Chicago 4. Blackhawks goaltender was Tony Esposito), Wayne Gretzky (Apr. 25 1985 Edmonton 8 Winnipeg 3. Jets goaltender was Brian Hayward) *(Ties NHL Record).*

GOALS, INDIVIDUAL—PERIOD

Most Goals One Period: 4—Wayne Gretzky (February 18 1981, 3rd period, Edmonton 9 St. Louis 2. Blues goaltenders were Mike Liut [2] and Ed Staniowski [2]).

Most Goals One Period in a Playoff Game: 3—Wayne Gretzky (Apr. 6 1983, 2nd period, Edmonton 6 Winnipeg 3. Jets goaltender was Brian Hayward), Wayne Gretzky (May 25 1985, 1st period, Edmonton 4 Philadelphia 3. Flyers goaltender was Pelle Lindbergh), Glenn Anderson (Apr. 6 1988, 3rd period, Edmonton 7 Winnipeg 4. Jets goaltender was Daniel Berhiaume), Petr Klima (May 4 1991, 1st period, Edmonton 7 Minnesota 2. North Stars goaltender was Jon Casey).

GOALS, INDIVIDUAL—FASTEST

Fastest Opening Goal: 8 seconds—Wayne Gretzky (December 14 1983 vs. N.Y. Rangers goaltender Glen Hanlon).

Fastest Opening Goal in the Playoffs: 10 seconds—Glenn Anderson (May 24 1988 vs. Boston Bruins goaltender Andy Moog).

Fastest Goal From the Start of a Period: 6 seconds—Glenn Anderson (March 17 1984, 3rd period vs. Los Angeles goaltender Markus Mattsson).

Fastest Goal From the Start of a Period in a Playoff Game: 9 seconds—Wayne Gretzky (Apr. 6 1983, 2nd period vs. Winnipeg goaltender Brian Hayward), Mark Messier (Apr. 16 1984, 3rd period vs. Calgary goaltender Rejean Lemelin). *(Ties NHL Record)*

Fastest Two Goals: 9 seconds—Wayne Gretzky (February 18 1981, 5:49 and 5:58 of the 3rd period vs. St. Louis goaltender Ed Staniowski).

Fastest Two Goals in a Playoff Game: 15 seconds—Wayne Gretzky (May 25 1985, 1:10 and 1:25 of 1st period vs. Philadelphia goaltender Pelle Lindbergh).

Fastest Three Goals: 2 minutes 18 seconds—Wayne Gretzky (February 18 1981, 5:49, 5:58 and 8:07 of the 3rd period vs. St. Louis goaltender Ed Staniowski).

Fastest Three Goals in a Playoff Game: 5 minutes 13 seconds—Petr Klima (May 4 1991, 6:14, 8:23, and 11:27 of the 1st period vs. Minnesota goaltender Jon Casey).

Fastest Four Goals: 7 minutes 58 seconds—Wayne Gretzky (February 18 1981, 5:49, 5:58, 8:07, and 13:47 of the 3rd period vs. St. Louis goaltenders Mike Liut [3] and Ed Staniowski [1]).

Fastest Four Goals in a Playoff Game: 16 minutes 50 seconds—Wayne Gretzky (April 6 1983, 15:58 of the 1st period, 0:09, 5:52 and 12:48 of the 2nd period vs. Winnipeg goaltender Brian Hayward).

Fastest Five Goals: 29 minutes 3 seconds—Wayne Gretzky, February 18 1981, 4:44 of the second period, 5:49, 5:58, 8:07 and 13:47 of the 3rd period vs. St. Louis goaltenders Mike Liut [3] and Ed Staniowski [2]).

Fastest Two Shorthanded Goals: 12 seconds—Esa Tikkanen (November 12 1988 vs. Toronto goaltender Allan Bester, at 10:44 and 10:56 of 1st period). *(NHL Record)*

GOALS, TEAM—FASTEST

Fastest Five Goals, One Game: 6 minutes:44 seconds—October 24, 1996 (2nd period vs. Los Angeles. Andrei Kovalenko 2:22, Rem Murray 3:40, Mariusz Czerkawski 4:26, Rem Murray 6:46, and Andrei Kovalenko 9:06. Kings goaltender was Stephane Fiset).

Fastest Five Goals, One Playoff Game: 5 minutes: 44 seconds—April 28, 1984 (3rd period vs. Minnesota. Jari Kurri 4:58, Glenn Anderson 6:06, Ken Linseman 7:05, Mark Messier 10:10, and Wayne Gretzky 10:42. North Star goaltender was Don Beaupre).

Fastest Five Goals, One Game (Both Teams): 3 minutes: 34 seconds—January 20, 1982 (3rd period vs. St. Louis. Tom Roulston 13:57, Dave Lumley 14:17, Wayne Gretzky 15:30, Glenn Anderson 15:38 and the Blues' Tony Currie at 17:31. Oiler goaltender was Grant Fuhr, Blues goaltender was Gary Edwards).

Fastest Five Goals, One Playoff Game (Both Teams): 5 minutes: 12 seconds—April 28, 1984 (2nd period vs. Minnesota. Mark Napier 8:48, Mark Napier 10:22, Neal Broten 12:04, Neal Broten 12:36 and Paul Coffey of the Oilers at 14:00. Oilers won 8-5 Oiler goaltender was Andy Moog, North Star goaltender was Don Beaupre).

Fastest Four Goals, One Game: 1 minute: 41 seconds—January 20, 1982 (3rd period vs. St. Louis. Tom Roulston at 13:57, Dave Lumley at 14:17, Wayne Gretzky at 15:30 and Glenn Anderson at 15:38. Blues goaltender was Gary Edwards).

Fastest Four Goals, One Playoff Game: 4 minutes: 25 seconds—April 20, 1990 (3rd period vs. Los Angeles. Jari Kurri at 13:14, Mark Lamb at 14:29, Esa Tikkanen at 16:38, and Craig MacTavish at 17:39. Oiler goaltender was Bill Ranford).

Fastest Four Goals, One Game (Both Teams): 1 minute: 59 seconds—November 2, 1979 (1st period vs. the Islanders. Stefan Persson of the Islanders at 1:57, Wayne Gretzky at 2:18, Dan Newman at 2:40 and Wayne Gretzky at 3:56. Oiler goaltender was Ed Mio, Islanders goaltender was Glenn Resch).

Fastest Four Goals in One Playoff Game (Both Teams): 2 minutes: 30 seconds—May 12, 1985 (1st period vs. Chicago. Denis Savard at 17:05, Jaroslav Pouzar of the Oilers at 17:20, Curt Fraser at 18:17, Al Secord at 19:35. Oiler goaltender was Grant Fuhr, Blackhawk goaltender was Murray Bannerman).

Fastest Three Goals, One Game: 45 seconds—March 25, 1981. (3rd period vs. Hartford. Wayne Gretzky at 19:04, Mark Messier at 19:18, and Glenn Anderson at 19:49. Oilers won 7-2 and all three goals were scored into an empty net).

Fastest Three Goals, One Playoff Game: 1 minute: 48 seconds—April 6, 1983 (1st period vs. Winnipeg. Ken Linseman at 14:10, Dave Hunter at 14:17 and Wayne Gretzky at 15:58. Jet goaltender was Brian Hayward).

Fastest Three Goals, One Game (Both Teams): 27 seconds—November 2, 1983 (1st period vs. Washington. Don Jackson scored at 17:24, Chris Valentine of the Capitals scored at 17:44 and Glenn Anderson scored at 17:51. Oilers goaltender was Grant Fuhr, Capitals goaltender was Al Jensen).

Fastest Three Goals in One Playoff Game (Both Teams): 31 seconds—May 25, 1985 (1st period vs. Philadelphia. Wayne Gretzky scored at 1:10 and again at 1:25, Derrick Smith of the Flyers scored at 1:41. Oiler goaltender was Grant Fuhr, Flyer goaltender was Pelle Lindbergh).

Fastest Two Goals, One Game: 8 seconds—January 20, 1982 (3rd period vs. St. Louis. Wayne Gretzky scored at 15:30 and Glenn Anderson scored at 15:38. Blues goaltender was Gary Edwards).

Fastest Two Goals in One Playoff Game: 7 seconds—April 6, 1983 (1st period vs. Winnipeg. Ken Linseman scored at 14:10 and Dave Hunter scored at 14:17. Jet goaltender was Brian Hayward).

Fastest Two Goals, One Game (Both Teams): 5 seconds—November 27, 1987 (2nd period vs. Chicago. Wayne Gretzky scored at 18:37 and Chicago's Steve Larmer scored at 18:42. Oiler goaltender was Grant Fuhr, Blackhawk goaltender was Darren Pang).

Fastest Two Goals in One Playoff Game (Both Teams): 11 seconds—April 8, 1991 (1st period vs. Calgary. The Flames' Joe Nieuwendyk scored at 2:03 and Esa Tikkanen scored at 2:14. Oiler goaltender was Grant Fuhr, Flames goaltender was Mike Vernon).

Fastest Three Goals From the Start of a Game: 3 minutes: 25 seconds—December 16, 1981 (Wayne Gretzky scored at 0:59, Garry Unger at 2:46 and Mark Messier at 3:25 vs. Colorado Rockies. Rockies goaltender was Glenn Resch).

Fastest Three Goals From the Start of a Playoff Game: 6 minutes: 26 seconds—April 9, 1987 (Jari Kurri scored at 2:51, Glenn Anderson at 5:17 and Jari Kurri at 6:26 vs. Los Angeles. Kings goaltender was Roland Melanson).

Fastest Three Goals From the Start of a Game (Both Teams): 2 minutes: 40 seconds—November 2, 1979 vs. N.Y. Islanders (Stefan Persson of the Islanders scored at 1:57, Wayne Gretzky scored at 2:18, and Dan Newman at 2:40. Oiler goaltender was Ed Mio, Islander goaltender was Glenn Resch).

Fastest Three Goals From the Start of a Playoff Game (Both Teams): 1 minute: 41 seconds—May 25, 1985 vs. Philadelphia. (Wayne Gretzky scored at 1:10 and 1:25, Derrick Smith of the Flyers scored at 1:41. Oiler goaltender was Grant Fuhr, Flyer goaltender was Pelle Lindbergh).

Fastest Two Goals From the Start of a Game: 24 seconds—March 28, 1982 vs. Los Angeles (Mark Messier scored at 00:14 and Dave Lumley at 00:24. King goaltender was Doug Keans). *(Ties NHL Record)*

Fastest Two Goals From the Start of a Playoff Game: 1 minute: 25 seconds—May 25, 1985 vs. Philadelphia (Wayne Gretzky scored at 1:10 and 1:25. Flyer goaltender was Pelle Lindbergh).

Fastest Two Goals From the Start of a Game (Both Teams): 2 minutes: 6 seconds—October 29, 1980 vs. Toronto (Dave Semenko scored at 1:18, and Dan Maloney of the Leafs scored at 2:06. Oiler goaltender was Ron Low, Leaf goaltender was Jiri Crha).

Fastest Two Goals From the Start of a Playoff Game (Both Teams): 4 minutes: 19 seconds—May 11, 1988 vs. Detroit (Craig Simpson scored at 00:47 and Brent Ashton of Detroit scored at 4:19. Oiler goaltender was Grant Fuhr, Red Wing goaltender was Greg Stefan).

Fastest Three Goals From the Start of a Period: 2 minutes: 27 seconds—December 4, 1982 (3rd period vs. Calgary. Wayne Gretzky scored at 00:33, Jari Kurri at 1:31 and Ken Linseman at 2:27. Flame goaltender was Don Edwards).

Fastest Three Goals From the Start of a Period in a Playoff Game: 5 minutes, 1 second—May 5, 1988 (3rd period vs. Detroit. Mark Messier scored at 00:48, Jari Kurri at 1:18 and Craig Simpson at 5:01. Red Wing goaltender was Greg Stefan).

Fastest Three Goals From the Start of a Period (Both Teams): 2 minutes: 4 seconds—January 3, 1984 (2nd period vs. Calgary. Jim Peplinski of the Flames scored at 00:48, Mark Messier scored at 1:32 and Pat Hughes at 2:04. Oilers goaltender was Andy Moog, Flame goaltender was Mike Vernon).

Fastest Three Goals From the Start of a Period in a Playoff Game (Both Teams): 1 minute: 41 seconds—May 25, 1985. 1st period vs. Philadelphia. Wayne Gretzky scored at 1:10 and 1:25, Derrick Smith of the Flyers scored at 1:41. Oiler goaltender was Grant Fuhr, Flyer goaltender was Pelle Lindbergh).

Fastest Two Goals From the Start of a Period: 24 seconds—March 28, 1982 (1st period vs. Los Angeles. Mark Messier scored at 00:14 and Dave Lumley at 00:24. King goaltender was Doug Keans). *(NHL Record)*

Fastest Two Goals From the Start of a Period in a Playoff Game: 1 minute: 18 seconds—May 5, 1988 (3rd period vs. Detroit. Mark Messier scored at 00:48 and Jari Kurri at 1:18. Red Wing goaltender was Greg Stefan.)

Fastest Two Goals From the Start of a Period (Both Teams): 43 seconds—February 23, 1988 (2nd period vs. St. Louis. The Oilers' Steve Smith scored at 00:23 and Tony McKegney of St. Louis scored at 00:43. Oilers goaltender was Grant Fuhr, Blues goaltender was Greg Millen).

Fastest Two Goals From the Start of a Period in a Playoff Game (Both Teams): 2 minutes: 4 seconds—April 4, 1990 (2nd period vs. Winnipeg. Mark Messier scored at 00:35 and Moe Mantha at 2:04. Oiler goaltender was Bill Ranford, Jets goaltender was Bob Essensa).

GOALS, TEAM

Most Goals Scored, One Season: 446—1983-84 (in 80 games. 5.58 goals per game). *(NHL Record)*

Most Goals Scored, One Playoff Year: 98—1984-85 (in 18 games. 5.44 goals per game).

Most Goals Scored, Three Game Playoff Series: 18—1983-84 (in Division semi-final series vs. Winnipeg. 6.00 goals scored per game).

Most Goals Scored, Three Game Playoff Series (Both Teams): 25—1983-84 (in Division semi-final series vs. Winnipeg. Oilers 18 goals, Winnipeg 7, 8.33 goals scored per game).

Most Goals Scored, Four Game Playoff Series: 25—1982-83 (in Conference final series vs. Chicago. 6.25 goals scored per game).

Most Goals Scored, Four Game Playoff Series (Both Teams): 36—1982-83 (in Conference final series vs. Chicago. Oilers 25 goals, Blackhawks 11, 9.00 goals scored per game).

Most Goals Scored, Five Game Playoff Series: 35—1982-83 (in Division final series vs. Calgary. 7.00 goals scored per game). *(NHL Record)*

Most Goals Scored, Five Game Playoff Series (Both Teams): 52—1986-87 (in Division semi-final series vs. Los Angeles. Oilers 32 goals, Kings 20, 10.4 goals scored per game). *(NHL Record)*

Most Goals Scored, Six Game Playoff Series: 44—1984-85 (in Conference final series vs. Chicago. 7.33 goals scored per game). *(NHL Record)*

Most Goals Scored, Six Game Playoff Series (Both Teams): 69—1984-85 (in Conference final series vs. Chicago, Oilers 44 goals. Blackhawks 25 goals, 11.5 goals scored per game). *(NHL Record)*

Most Goals Scored, Seven Game Playoff Series: 33—1983-84 (in Division final series vs. Calgary. 4.71 goals scored per game).

Most Goals Scored, Seven Game Playoff Series (Both Teams): 60—1983-84 (in Division final series vs. Calgary. Oilers 33 goals, Flames 27, 8.57 goals scored per game).

Most Goals Scored, One Game: 13—November 19, 1983 (13-4 win vs. New Jersey goaltenders Ron Low and Glenn Resch), November 8, 1985 (13-0 win vs. Vancouver goaltender Frank Caprice).

Most Goals Scored, One Game (Both Teams): 21—December 11, 1985 (12-9 win vs. Chicago goaltenders Murray Bannerman and Bob Sauve). *(Ties NHL Record)*

Most Goals Scored, One Playoff Game: 13—April 9, 1987 (13-3 win vs. Los Angeles goaltenders Roland Melanson and Darren Eliot). *(NHL Record)*

Most Goals Scored, One Playoff Game (Both Teams): 18—April 7, 1982 (10-8 loss vs. Los Angeles. Los Angeles goaltender was Mario Lessard, Oiler goaltender was Grant Fuhr). *(NHL Record)*

Most Goals Scored, One Period: 7—October 18, 1983 (3rd period vs. Vancouver goaltender Richard Brodeur, Oilers won 10-7), February 19, 1985 (2nd period vs. Toronto goaltenders Ken Wregget and Tim Bernhardt, Oilers won 9-4), November 8, 1985 (3rd period vs. Vancouver goaltender Frank Caprice, Oilers won 13-0).

Most Goals Scored, One Period (Both Teams): 12—December 11, 1985 (2nd period vs. Chicago. Edmonton 6 goals, Chicago 6 goals. Oiler goaltenders were Andy Moog and Grant Fuhr, Blackhawk goaltender was Murray Bannerman). *(Ties NHL Record)*

Most Goals Scored in One Period, Playoff Game: 6—April 9, 1987 (1st period vs. Los Angeles goaltender Roland Melanson. Oilers won 13-3), April 6, 1988 (3rd period vs. Winnipeg goalie Dan Berthiaume Oilers won 7-4).

Most Goals Scored in One Period, Playoff Game (Both Teams): 8—May 12, 1985 (1st period vs. Chicago. Chicago scored 5 goals, the Oilers 3. Oiler goaltender was Grant Fuhr, Chicago goaltender was Murray Bannerman), April 6, 1988 (3rd period vs. Winnipeg. Oilers scored 6 goals, Winnipeg scored 2. Oiler goaltender was Grant Fuhr, Jet goaltender was Daniel Berthiaume).

Most Consecutive Goals Scored, One Game: 13—November 8, 1985 (13-0 win over Vancouver. Canucks goaltender Frank Caprice).

Most Consecutive Goals Scored, One Playoff Game: 9—May 4, 1985 (11-2 win over Chicago. Blackhawk goaltenders were Murray Bannerman and Warren Skorodenski).

Fewest Goals Scored, One Season (48 games): 136—(1994-95, 2.83 goals per game)

Fewest Goals Scored, One Season (minimum 80 games): 215—(1997-98, 2.62 goals per game)

Fewest Goals Scored, Three Game Playoff Series: 6—1979-80 (in Preliminary round vs. Philadelphia, 2.00 goals per game).

Fewest Goals Scored, Three Game Playoff Series (Both Teams): 18—1979-80 (in Preliminary round vs. Philadelphia. Philadelphia 12 goals, Oilers 6 goals, 6.00 goals scored per game), 1984-85 (in Preliminary round vs. Los Angeles. Oilers 11 goals, Kings 7 goals, 6.00 goals scored per game).

Fewest Goals Scored, Four Game Playoff Series: 6—1982-83 (in Cup final vs. New York Islanders. 1.50 goals per game).

Fewest Goals Scored, Four Game Playoff Series (Both Teams): 18—1998-99 (in Conference Quarterfinal vs. Dallas. Stars scored 11 goals, Oilers 7, 4.50 goals scored per game).

Fewest Goals Scored, Five Game Playoff Series: 5—1997-98 (in Conference semi final series vs. Dallas. 1.00 goals per game).

Fewest Goals Scored, Five Game Playoff Series (Both Teams): 14—1997-98 (in Conference semi final series vs. Dallas. Oilers 5 goals, Dallas 9, 2.80 goals scored per game).

Fewest Goals Scored, Six Game Playoff Series: 18—1991-92 (in Conference semi final series vs. Vancouver. 3.00 goals per game).

Fewest Goals Scored, Six Game Playoff Series (Both Teams): 33—1991-92 (in Conference semi final series vs. Vancouver. Oilers scored 18 goals. Vancouver 15 goals, 5.50 goals scored per game).

Fewest Goals Scored, Seven Game Playoff Series: 19—1997-98 (in Conference quarter final series vs. Colorado. 2.71 goals per game).

Fewest Goals Scored, Seven Game Playoff Series (Both Teams): 35—1997-98 (in Conference quarter final series vs. Colorado. Oilers scored 19 goals, Avalanche 16, 5.00 goals scored per game).

Fewest Goals Scored, One Game (Both Teams): 0—December 10, 1996 (vs. Detroit. Red Wing goaltender was Chris Osgood, Oiler goaltender was Curtis Joseph), December 17, 1997 (vs. Chicago. Blackhawk goaltender was Jeff Hackett, Oiler goaltender was Curtis Joseph).

Fewest Goals Scored, One Playoff Game (Both Teams): 1—May 10, 1984 (1-0 win vs. New York Islanders. Oiler goaltender was Grant Fuhr, New York goaltender was Billy Smith), April 25, 1997 (1-0 win vs. Dallas. Oiler goaltender was Curtis Joseph, Stars goaltender was Andy Moog), May 11, 1998 (1-0 loss vs. Dallas. Oilers goaltender was Curtis Joseph, Stars goaltender was Ed Belfour).

GOALS, POWER PLAY—TEAM

Most Power Play Goals Scored, One Season: 88—1987-88 (in 80 games, powerplay 21.9 %).

Most Power Play Goals Scored, One Playoff Year: 30—1987-88 (in 18 games, powerplay 26.5 %).

Most Power Play Goals Scored Including Playoffs, One Season: 118—in 1987-88 (in 98 games, powerplay 22.9 %).

Most Power Play Goals Scored, One Playoff Series: 10—1987-88 (in 5 games, Division semi-final vs. Winnipeg), 1991-92 (in 6 games, Division semifinal series vs. Los Angeles).

Most Power Play Goals Scored in One Playoff Series (Both Teams): 21—1980-81 Quarter-final series vs. New York Islanders (Islanders had 13 power play goals on 26 opportunities, the Oilers had 8 goals on 34 opportunities). *(Ties NHL Record)*

Most Power Play Goals Scored, One Game: 5—November 26, 1980 vs. Chicago (Blackhawk goaltender was Tony Esposito), October 11, 1987 vs. Los Angeles (Kings goaltender was Roland Melanson), March 4, 1988 vs. Philadelphia (Flyer goaltender was Mark LaForest), November 4, 1988 vs. Buffalo (Sabre goaltender was Tom Barrasso), November 19, 1988 vs. Toronto (Leaf goaltender was Ken Wregget).

Most Power Play Goals Scored in One Game (Both Teams): 8—April 4, 1986 vs. Calgary (Flames had 5 power play goals, Oilers had 3, Flame goaltender was Mike Vernon, Oiler goaltender was Andy Moog), March 4, 1988 vs. Philadelphia (Oilers had 5 power play goals, Philadelphia had 3, Oiler goaltender was Grant Fuhr, Flyer goaltender was Mark LaForest).

Most Power Play Goals Scored, One Playoff Game: 5—April 9, 1987 vs. Los Angeles (King goaltenders were Roland Melanson and Darren Eliot).

Most Power Play Goals Scored in One Playoff Game (Both Teams): 7—April 28, 1984 vs. Minnesota (Minnesota had 4 power play goals, Oilers had 3. Oiler goaltender was Andy Moog, North Star goaltender was Don Beaupre), May 14, 1985 vs. Chicago (Chicago had 4 power play goals, Oilers had 3. Oiler goaltender was Grant Fuhr, Blackhawk goaltender was Murray Bannerman), April 9, 1987 vs. Los Angeles (Oilers had 5 power play goals, Los Angeles had 2. Oiler goaltender was Andy Moog, Kings goaltenders were Roland Melanson and Darren Eliot). *(NHL Record)*

Most Power Play Goals Allowed, One Season: 106—1992-93 (in 84 games, penalty killing 77.2 %).

Most Power Play Goals Allowed, One Playoff Year: 21—1990-91 (in 18 games, penalty killing 77.9%).

Most Power Play Goals Allowed Including Playoffs, One Season: 110—1991-92 (93 regular season 17 playoff, in 96 games, penalty killing 78.6%).

Most Power Play Goals Allowed, One Playoff Series: 13—1980-81 (Quarter-finals series vs. N.Y. Islanders, on 26 opportunities).

Most Power Play Goals Allowed, One Game: 6—February 12, 1984 vs. Hartford (Oilers goaltenders were Andy Moog and Grant Fuhr).

Most Power Play Goals Allowed, One Playoff Game: 4—April 17, 1981 vs. N.Y. Islanders (Oiler goaltender was Andy Moog), April 7, 1982 vs. Los Angeles (Oiler goaltender was Grant Fuhr), April 28, 1984 vs. Minnesota (Oiler goaltender was Andy Moog), May 14, 1985 vs. Chicago (Oiler goaltender was Grant Fuhr).

Fewest Power Play Goals Scored, One Season [48 games]: 42—1994-95 (on 259 opportunities, powerplay 16.2%)

Fewest Power Play Goals Scored, One Season [80 games minimum]: 61—1979-80 (in 80 games, powerplay 21.6%)

GOALS, SHORTHANDED—TEAM

Most Shorthanded Goals Scored, One Season: 36—1983-84 (in 80 games, 386 times shorthanded). *(NHL Record)*

Fewest Shorthanded Goals Scored, One Season: 2—1993-94 (in 84 games, 401 times shorthanded).

ASSISTS, INDIVIDUAL—CAREER

Most Career Assists: 1,086—Wayne Gretzky (1979-80 to 1987-88 in 696 games. 1.56 assists per game).

Most Career Playoff Assists: 171—Wayne Gretzky (1979-80 to 1987-88 in 120 games. 1.43 assists per game).

Most Career Assists Including Playoffs: 1,257—Wayne Gretzky

(1,086 regular season, 171 playoff in 816 games. 1.54 assists per game).

Most Career Assists by a Defenseman: 460—Paul Coffey (1980-81 to 1986-87. .865 assists per game).

Most Career Playoff Assists by a Defenseman: 67—Paul Coffey (1980-81 to 1986-87, .713 assists per game.

Most Career Assists by a Defenseman Including Playoffs: 527—Paul Coffey (1980-81 to 1986-87. 460 regular season, 67 playoff, .842 assists per game).

Most Career Assists by a Goaltender: 36—Grant Fuhr (1981-82 to 1990-91, .085 assists per game).

Most Career Assists by a Goaltender in the Playoffs: 11—Grant Fuhr (1981-81 to 1990-91, .099 assists per game).

Most Career Assists by a Goaltender Including Playoffs: 47—Grant Fuhr (36 regular season, 11 playoff. .088 assists per game).

ASSISTS, INDIVIDUAL—SEASON

Most Assists, Single Season: 163—Wayne Gretzky (1985-86 season, 2.04 assists per game). *(NHL Record)*

Most Assists One Playoff Year: 31 Wayne Gretzky (1987-88 season, 1.63 assists per game). *(NHL Record)*

Most Assists Including Playoffs, Single Season: 174—Wayne Gretzky (1985-86 season, 163 regular season, 11 playoff, 1.93 assists per game) *(NHL Record)*

Most Assists by a Defenseman, Single Season: 90—Paul Coffey (1985-86 season, 1.14 assists per game).

Most Assists by a Defenseman One Playoff Year: 25—Paul Coffey (1984-85 season, 1.39 assists per game). *(NHL Record)*

Most Assists by a Defenseman Including Playoffs, Single Season: 109—Paul Coffey (1984-85 season, 84 regular season, 25 playoff, 1.11 assists per game).

Most Assists by a Rookie, Single Season: 43—Jari Kurri (1980-81 season, .573 assists per game).

Most Assists by a Goaltender, Single Season: 14—Grant Fuhr (1983-84 season, .311 assists per game). *(NHL Record)*

Most Assists by a Goaltender One Playoff Year: 3—Grant Fuhr (in 1983-84 season, .188 assists per game).

Most Assists by a Goaltender Including Playoffs, Single Season: 17—Grant Fuhr (1983-84 season, 14 regular season, 3 playoff. .279 assists per game).

Most Assists One Playoff Series: 14—Wayne Gretzky (in 6 games, in Conference Final vs. Chicago 1984-85 season. 2.33 assists per game). *(NHL Record)*

ASSISTS, INDIVIDUAL—GAME

Most Assists in One Game: 7—Wayne Gretzky-Feb. 15 1980 vs. Washington. (Capitals goaltender was Wayne Stephenson), Dec. 11 1985 vs. Chicago. (Blackhawks goaltenders were Murray Bannerman [5] and Bob Sauve [2]), Feb. 14 1986 vs. Quebec. (Nordiques goaltenders were Clint Malarchuk [3] and Mario Gosselin [4]). *(Ties NHL Record)*

Most Assists One Playoff Game: 6—Wayne Gretzky (April 9 1987 vs. Los Angeles. Kings goaltenders were Roland Melanson [3] and Darren Eliot [3]). *(Ties NHL Record)*

Most Assists by a Defenseman One Game: 6—Paul Coffey (March 14, 1986 vs. Detroit. Red Wing goaltenders were Greg Stefan and Ed Mio). *(Ties NHL Record)*

Most Assists One Home Game: 7—Wayne Gretzky (Feb. 15 1980 vs. Washington. (Capitals goaltender was Wayne Stephenson), Wayne Gretzky (Feb. 14 1986 vs. Quebec. (Nordiques goaltenders were Clint Malarchuk [3] and Mario Gosselin [4]). *(Ties NHL Record)*

First Assist at Home: October 13, 1979 vs. Detroit (Brett Callighen and Wayne Gretzky at 12:06 of the 1st period on the goal by Blair MacDonald. Red Wing goaltender was Rogatien Vachon).

First Assist Against at Home: October 13, 1979 vs. Detroit (Perry Miller and Rogie Vachon at 14:16 of the 2nd period on the goal by Dan Labraaten. Oiler goaltender was Ed Mio).

Most Assists One Road Game: 7—Wayne Gretzky (December 11 1985 vs. Chicago. Blackhawks goaltenders were Murray Bannerman [5] and Bob Sauve [2]),. *(Ties NHL Record)*

First Assists on the Road: October 10, 1979 in Chicago (Brett Callighen and Wayne Gretzky at 9:49 of the 1st period on the goal by Kevin Lowe. Chicago goaltender was Tony Esposito).

First Assists Against on the Road: October 10, 1979 in Chicago (Cliff Koroll and Stan Mikita at 1:26 of the 1st period on the goal by John Marks. Oiler goaltender was Dave Dryden).

Most Assists One Home Game Playoffs: 6—Wayne Gretzky (April 9 1987 vs. Los Angeles. Kings goaltenders were Roland Melanson [3] and Darren Eliot [3]). *(Ties NHL Record)*

First Playoff Assist at Home: April 11, 1980 vs. Philadelphia (Brett Callighen and Blair MacDonald at 15:55 of the 1st period on the goal by Wayne Gretzky. Flyer goaltender was Phil Myre).

Most Assists One Road Game in the Playoffs: 5—Wayne Gretzky (April 8 1981 vs. Montreal. Canadiens goaltender was Richard Sevigny). *(Ties NHL Record)*

First Playoff Assists on the Road: April 8, 1980 in Philadelphia (Wayne Gretzky and Blair MacDonald at 14:09 of the 1st period on the goal by Dave Lumley. Flyer goaltender was Pete Peeters).

First Assists Against in a Playoff Road Game: April 8, 1980 in Philadelphia (Ken Linseman and Bob Dailey at 00:56 of the 1st period on the goal by Paul Holmgren. Oiler goaltender was Ron Low).

ASSISTS, INDIVIDUAL—PERIOD

Most Assists One Period: 4—Wayne Gretzky (Feb. 4, 1983, 1st period vs. Montreal. Canadiens goaltender was Rick Wamsley), Jari Kurri (Oct. 7, 1983, 2nd period vs. Winnipeg. Jets goaltender was Brian Hayward), Mark Messier (Jan. 4, 1984, 2nd period vs. Minnesota. North Stars goaltender was Gilles Meloche), Wayne Gretzky (Oct. 26, 1984, 2nd period vs. Los Angeles. Kings goaltender was Darren Eliot), Wayne Gretzky (Oct. 15, 1986, 3rd period vs. Quebec. Nordiques goaltender was Clint Malarchuk), Wayne Gretzky (Feb. 18, 1987, 2nd period vs. Toronto. Leaf goaltender was Allan Bester), Wayne Gretzky (Nov. 14, 1987 3rd period vs. St. Louis. Blues goaltender was Rick Wamsley), Wayne Gretzky (March 4, 1988, 1st period vs. Philadelphia. Flyer goaltender was Mark LaForest), Wayne Gretzky (March 7, 1988, 2nd period vs. Winnipeg. Jets goaltender was Daniel Berthiaume). *(NHL Record)*

Most Assists One Period in a Playoff Game: 3—Wayne Gretzky (Apr. 8 1981, 1st period vs. Montreal. Canadiens goaltender was Richard Sevigny), Wayne Gretzky (Apr. 24 1983, 3rd period vs. Chicago. Blackhawks goaltender was Tony Esposito), Paul Coffey (May 4 1985, 2nd period vs. Chicago. Blackhawks goaltender was Murray Bannerman), Randy Gregg (May 4 1985, 3rd period vs. Chicago. Blackhawk goaltender was Murray Bannerman), Paul Coffey (May 14 1985, 2nd period vs. Chicago. Blackhawks goaltender was Murray Bannerman), Wayne Gretzky (Apr. 9 1987, 1st period vs. Los Angeles. Kings goaltender was Roland Melanson), Wayne Gretzky (Apr. 12 1987, 3rd period vs. Los Angeles. Kings goaltender was Roland Melanson), Glenn Anderson (May 13 1987, 3rd period vs. Detroit. Red Wing goaltender was Greg Stefan), Mark Messier (Apr. 6 1988, 3rd period vs. Winnipeg. Jets goaltender was Daniel Berthiaume), Esa Tikkanen (May 4 1991, 1st period vs. Minnesota. North Star goaltender was Jon Casey). *(Ties NHL Record)*

ASSISTS, INDIVIDUAL—FASTEST

Fastest Two Assists in a Playoff Game: 15 seconds—Paul Coffey (May 25 1985, at 1:10 on a goal by Wayne Gretzky and 1:25 on a goal by Wayne Gretzky of the 1st period vs. Philadelphia. Flyer goaltender was Pelle Lindbergh)).

Fastest Three Assists: 1 minute 48 seconds—Wayne Gretzky (February 15 1980, at 13:14 on a goal by Dave Semenko, 14:04 on a goal by Bobby Schmautz and 15:02 on a goal by Blair MacDonald of the 3rd period vs. Washington. Capital goaltender was Wayne Stephenson).

Fastest Three Assists in a Playoff Game: 7 minutes 24 seconds—Wayne Gretzky (April 25 1985, at 0:54 on a goal by Jari Kurri, at 1:18 on a goal by Jari Kurri, at 8:18 on a goal by Glenn Anderson, of the 2nd period vs. Winnipeg. Jet goaltender was Brian Hayward).

Fastest Four Assists: 4 minutes 38 assists—Wayne Gretzky (March 7 1988, at 9:38 on a goal by Esa Tikkanen, 10:38 on a goal by Craig Simpson, 13:46 on a goal by Mark Messier, 14:16 on a goal by Craig Simpson of the 2nd period vs. Winnipeg. Jets goaltender was Daniel Berthiaume).

Fastest Four Assists in a Playoff Game: 21 minutes 18 seconds—Glenn Anderson (May 13 1987, at 18:23 on a goal by Mark Messier, of the 2nd period, at 4:48 on a goal by Mark Messier, at 19:11 on a goal by Kent Nilsson, and 19:41 on a goal by Kent Nilsson, of the 3rd period vs. Detroit. Red Wings goaltender was Greg Stefan).

Fastest Five Assists: 16 minutes 38 seconds—Wayne Gretzky (February 14 1986, at 17:03 of the 2nd period on a goal by Dave Semenko, 1:16 on a goal by Paul Coffey, 2:32 on a goal by Jari Kurri, 12:59 on a goal by Craig MacTavish, and at 13:41 on a goal by Paul Coffey, of the 3rd period vs. Quebec. Nordiques goaltender was Mario Gosselin).

Fastest Five Assists in a Playoff Game: 51 minutes 15 seconds—Wayne Gretzky (April 9 1987 vs. Los Angeles, The assists came at 6:26 of the first period on a goal by Jari Kurri, at 14:09 of the first period, on a goal by Esa Tikkanen; at 14:05 of the second period, on a goal by Kent Nilsson, at 7:30 of the third period, on a goal by Jari Kurri, and at 17:41 of the third period, on a goal by Jari Kurri. Kings goaltenders were Roland Melanson [2] and Darren Eliot [3]).

ASSISTS, TEAM

Most Assists, One Season: 737—1985-86 (in 80 games, on 426 goals).

Most Assists, One Playoff Year: 159—1983-84 (in 19 games, on 94 goals scored).

Fewest Assists, One Season [48 games]: 232—1994-95 (on 136 goals).

Fewest Assists, One Season [80 games, minimum]: 385—1998-99 (in 82 games, on 230 goals).

POINTS, INDIVIDUAL—CAREER

Most Career Points: 1,669—Wayne Gretzky (1979-80 through 1987-88, 583 goals, 1,086 assists, 2.40 points per game).

Most Career Playoff Points: 252—Wayne Gretzky (1979-80 through 1987-88, 81 goals, 171 assists, 2.10 points per game).

Most Career Points Including Playoffs: 1,921—Wayne Gretzky (1979-80 to 1987-88, 664 goals, 1,257 assists in 696 regular season, 120 playoff games, 2.35 points per game).

Most Career Points by a Defenseman: 669—Paul Coffey (1980-81 to 1986-87, 209 goals, 460 assists, 1.26 points per game).

Most Career Playoff Points by a Defenseman: 103—Paul Coffey (1980-81 to 1986-87, 36 goals, 67 assists, 1.10 points per game).

Most Career Points by a Defenseman Including Playoffs: 772—Paul Coffey (1980-81 to 1986-87, 245 goals, 527 assists in 532 regular season, 94 playoff games, 1.23 points per game).

Most Career Points by a Goaltender: 36—Grant Fuhr (1981-82 to 1990-91, 36 assists, .085 points per game).

Most Career Points by a Goaltender in the Playoffs: 11—Grant Fuhr (1981-82 to 1990-91, 11 assists, .099 points per game).

Most Career Points by a Goaltender Including Playoffs: 47—Grant Fuhr (1981-82 to 1990-91, 36 regular season, 11 playoff, .088 points per game).

POINTS, INDIVIDUAL—SEASON

Most Points, Single Season: 215—Wayne Gretzky (52 goals, 163 assists, 2.69 points per game 1985-86 season). *(NHL Record)*

Most Points One Playoff Year: 47—Wayne Gretzky (17 goals, 30 assists, 2.61 points per game, 1984-85 season). *(NHL Record)*

Most Points Including Playoffs, Single Season: 255-Wayne Gretzky (208 regular season points, 47 playoff points, 90 goals, 165 assists, 2.60 points per game 1984-85 season). *(NHL Record)*

Most Points by a Defenseman, Single Season: 138—Paul Coffey (48 goals, 90 assists, 1.75 points per game, 1985-86 season).

Most Points by a Defenseman One Playoff Year: 37—Paul Coffey (12 goals, 25 assists, 2.06 points per game, 1984-85 season). *(NHL Record)*

Most Points by a Defenseman Including Playoffs, Single Season: 158—Paul Coffey (121 regular season points, 37 playoff points, 49 goals, 109 assists, 1.61 points per game, 1984-85 season). *(NHL Record)*

Most Points by a Rookie, Single Season: 75—Jari Kurri (32 goals, 43 assists in 75 games, 1.00 points per game 1980-81 season).

Most Points by a Rookie, One Playoff Year: 12—Glenn Anderson (5 goals, 7 assists, 1.33 points per game, 1980-81 season), Jari Kurri (5 goals, 7 assists, 1.33 points per game, 1980-81 season).

Most Points by a Goaltender, Single Season: 14—Grant Fuhr (14 assists in 1983-84 season).

Most Points One Playoff Series: 18—Wayne Gretzky (4 goals, 14 assists, 3.00 points per game in 6 games vs. Chicago in 1984-85 Conference Final).

First Oiler to Score 50 Points in a Season: Wayne Gretzky—December 26, 1979 vs. Colorado Rockies in Edmonton (Gretzky scored at 13:37 of the 1st period against goaltender Hardy Astrom. Brett Callighen and Blair MacDonald received assists. Gretzky had recorded 18 goals and 32 assists and played in 32 games).

First Oiler to Score 100 Points in a Season: Wayne Gretzky—February 24, 1980 vs. Boston Bruins in Edmonton (Gretzky received the only assist on a goal by Brett Callighen at 5:43 of the 2nd period against goaltender Gilles Gilbert. Gretzky had recorded 35 goals and 65 assists and played in 61 games).

POINTS, INDIVIDUAL—GAME

Most Points in One Game: 8—Wayne Gretzky (3 goals, 5 assists, Nov. 19 1983 vs. New Jersey. Devils goaltenders were Ron Low [5] and Glenn Resch [3]), Wayne Gretzky (4 goals, 4 assists, Jan. 4 1984 vs. Minnesota. North Stars goaltenders were Don Beaupre [4] and Gilles Meloche [4]), Paul Coffey (2 goals, 6 assists March 14 1986 vs. Detroit. Red Wings goaltenders were Greg Stefan and Ed Mio).

Most Points One Playoff Game: 7—Wayne Gretzky (4 goals, 3 assists, Apr. 17 1983 vs. Calgary. Flames goaltender was Don Edwards), Wayne Gretzky (3 goals, 4 assists, Apr. 25 1985 vs. Winnipeg. Jets goaltenders were Brian Hayward [5] and Marc Behrend [2]), Wayne Gretzky (1 goal, 6 assists, Apr. 9 1987 vs. Los Angeles. Kings goaltenders were Roland Melanson [3] and Darren Eliot [4]). *(NHL Record)*

Most Points by a Defenseman, One Game: 8—Paul Coffey (2 goals, 6 assists, March 14 1986 vs. Detroit. Wings goaltenders were Greg Stefan and Ed Mio). *(Ties NHL Record)*

Most Points in the Playoffs by a Defenseman, One Game: 6—Paul Coffey (1 goal, 5 assists, May 14 1985 vs. Chicago. Blackhawks goaltender was Murray Bannerman) *(NHL Record)*

Most Points One Home Game: 8—Wayne Gretzky (3 goals, 5 assists, Nov. 19 1983 vs . New Jersey. Devils goaltenders were Ron

Low [5] and Glenn Resch [3]), Wayne Gretzky (4 goals, 4 assists, Jan. 4 1984 vs. Minnesota. North Stars goaltenders were Don Beaupre [4] and Gilles Meloche [4]), Paul Coffey (2 goals, 6 assists, March 14 1986 vs. Detroit. Wings goaltenders were Greg Stefan and Ed Mio)

Most Points One Road Game: 7—Wayne Gretzky (4 goals, 3 assists, Nov. 6 1983 vs. Winnipeg. Jets goaltender was Doug Soetaert)

Most Points One Home Game Playoffs: 7—Wayne Gretzky (1 goal, 6 assists, Apr. 9 1987 vs. Los Angeles. Kings goaltenders were Roland Melanson [3] and Darren Eliot [4]).

Most Points One Road Game in the Playoffs: 7—Wayne Gretzky (4 goals, 3 assists, Apr. 17 1983 vs. Calgary. Flames goaltender was Don Edwards) Wayne Gretzky (3 goals, 4 assists, Apr. 25 1985 vs. Winnipeg. Jets goaltenders were Brian Hayward [5] and Marc Behrend [2]) *(NHL Record)*

POINTS, INDIVIDUAL—PERIOD

Most Points One Period: 5—Jari Kurri (2 goals, 3 assists, 2nd period, October 26, 1984 vs. Los Angeles. Kings goaltender was Darren Eliot).

Most Points One Period in a Playoff Game: 4—Wayne Gretzky (1 goal, 3 assists, 3rd period, Apr. 12, 1987 vs. Los Angeles. Kings goaltender was Roland Melanson), Glenn Anderson (3 goals, 1 assist, 3rd period, Apr. 6 1988 vs. Winnipeg, Jets goaltender was Daniel Berhiaume). *(Ties NHL Record)*

SCORING POINTS, TEAM

Most Scoring Points, One Season: 1,182—1983-84 (446 goals, 736 assists, 14.8 points per game). *(NHL Record)*

Fewest Scoring Points, One Season [48 games]: 368—1994-95 (136 goals, 232 assists, 7.7 points per game)

Fewest Scoring Points, One Season [minimum 80 games]: 615—1998-99 (230 goals, 385 assists, 7.5 points per game).

Most Scoring Points, One Game: 36—December 11, 1985 (12 goals, 24 assists in a 12-9 win vs. Chicago. Blackhawks goaltenders were Murray Bannerman and Bob Sauve).

Most Scoring Points Allowed, One Game: 31—February 12, 1984 (Hartford scored 11 goals and 20 assists in 11-0 win. Oilers goaltenders were Grant Fuhr and Andy Moog).

Most Scoring Points, One Game (Both Teams): 62—December 11, 1985 (Oilers 12 goals, 24 assists, Chicago 9 goals, 17 assists. Blackhawk goaltenders were Murray Bannerman [30] and Bob Sauve [6], Oiler goaltenders were Grant Fuhr [11] and Andy Moog [15].). *(NHL Record)*

Most Scoring Points, One Playoff Game: 33—April 9, 1987 (13 goals, 20 assists in a 13-3 win vs. Los Angeles. Kings goaltenders were Roland Melanson and Darren Eliot).

Most Scoring Points Allowed, One Playoff Game: 25—April 7, 1982 (Los Angeles scored 10 goals and 15 assists in 10-8 win. Oilers goaltender was Grant Fuhr).

Most Scoring Points, One Playoff Game (Both Teams): 46—April 7, 1982 (Los Angeles had 10 goals, 15 assists, Edmonton had 8 goals, 13 assists. Oilers goaltender was Grant Fuhr, Kings goaltender was Mario Lessard).

Most Scoring Points, One Period: 18—October 18, 1983 (3rd period, Oilers scored 7 goals, 11 assists vs. Vancouver. Canucks goaltender was Richard Brodeur), February 19, 1985 (2nd period, Oilers scored 7 goals and 11 assists vs. Toronto. Maple Leaf goaltenders were Ken Wregget and Tim Bernhardt), December 11, 1985 (2nd period Oilers scored 6 goals and 12 assists vs. Chicago. Blackhawk goaltenders were Murray Bannerman and Bob Sauve).

Most Scoring Points Allowed, One Period: 19—January 17, 1980 (2nd period vs. Boston. Bruins scored 7 goals and 12 assists in a 7-1 win. Oiler goaltender was Jim Corsi).

Most Scoring Points Allowed in One Period, Playoffs: 14—April 10, 1982 (3rd period vs. Los Angeles. the Kings had 5 goals and 9 assists in a 6-5 win. Oiler goaltender was Grant Fuhr), April 28, 1984 (2nd period vs. Minnesota. The North Stars had 5 goals, 9 assists in an 8-5 loss. Oiler goaltender was Andy Moog), May 12, 1985 (1st period vs. Chicago. The Blackhawks had 5 goals, 9 assists in an 8-6 win. Oiler goaltender was Grant Fuhr).

PENALTY MINUTES, INDIVIDUAL—CAREER

Most Career Penalty Minutes: 1,747—Kelly Buchberger (1987-88 to 1998-99 in 795 games. 2.20 minutes per game).

Most Career Penalty Minutes in the Playoffs: 314—Glenn Anderson (1980-81 to 1990-91, in 164 games. 1.91 minutes per game).

Most Career Penalty Minutes Including Playoffs: 1,863—Kelly Buchberger (1,747 regular season, 116 playoff in 873 games. 2.13 minutes per game).

Most Career Penalty Minutes by a Defenseman: 1,236—Kevin Lowe (1979-80 to 1997-98 in 1,037 games. 1.19 minutes per game).

Most Career Penalty Minutes by a Defenseman in the Playoffs: 216—Steve Smith (1984-85 to 1990-91 in 87 games. 2.48 minutes per game).

Most Career Penalty Minutes by a Defenseman Including Playoffs: 1,392—Kevin Lowe (1,236 in regular season, 156 in the playoffs in 1,209 games. 1.15 minutes per game).

Most Career Penalty Minutes by a Goaltender: 54—Grant Fuhr (in 423 games, .128 minutes per game).

Most Career Penalty Minutes by a Goaltender in the Playoffs: 14—Grant Fuhr (in 111 games, .126 minutes per game).

Most Career Penalty Minutes by a Goaltender Including the Playoffs: 68—Grant Fuhr (in 534 games, .127 minutes per game).

PENALTY MINUTES, INDIVIDUAL—SEASON

Most Penalty Minutes by a Defenseman, Single Season: 286—Steve Smith (1987-88 in 79 games, 3.62 minutes per game).

Most Penalty Minutes by a Defenseman One Playoff Year: 64—Don Jackson (1984-85 in 9 games, 7.11 minutes per game).

Most Penalty Minutes by a Defenseman One Year Including Playoffs: 341—Steve Smith (286 regular season, 55 playoffs in 98 games, 1987-88. 3.48 minutes per game).

Most Penalty Minutes by a Forward, Single Season: 281—Kevin McClelland (1987-88 in 74 games, 3.80 minutes per game).

Most Penalty Minutes by a Forward One Playoff Year: 75—Kevin McClelland (1984-85 in 18 games, 4.17 minutes per game).

Most Penalty Minutes by a Forward One Year Including Playoffs: 349—Kevin McClelland (281 regular season, 68 playoffs, 93 games in 1987-88. 3.75 minutes per game).

Most Penalty Minutes by a Goaltender, Single Season: 18—Bill Ranford (1989-90 in 56 games, .321 minutes per game).

Most Penalty Minutes by a Goaltender One Playoff Year: 6—Grant Fuhr (1987-88 in 19 games, .316 minutes per game).

Most Penalty Minutes by a Goaltender One Year Including Playoffs: 22—Grant Fuhr (16 regular season, 6 playoff in 94 games, 1987-88. .234 minutes per game), Bill Ranford (18 regular season, 4 playoff in 78 games, 1989-90. .282 minutes per game).

Most Penalty Minutes by a Rookie, Single Season: 234—Kelly Buchberger (1988-89 in 66 games, .355 minutes per game).

First Minor Penalty on the Road: October 10, 1979 vs. Chicago (Wayne Gretzky, 2 minute minor for slashing, at 5:19 of the 1st period).

First Minor Penalty by Opposition in an Oiler Road Game: October 10, 1979 in Chicago (Terry Ruskowski, at 3:05 of 1st period).

First Major Penalty on the Road: October 10, 1979 in Chicago (Lee Fogolin, a misconduct and Kevin Lowe a fighting major at 17:48 of the 3rd period).

First Major Penalty by the Opposition in an Oiler Road Game: October 10, 1979 in Chicago (Grant Mulvey, fighting major at 17:48 of the 3rd period).

First Minor Penalty at Home: October 13, 1979 vs. Detroit (Dave Hunter, 2 minute minor for hooking at 18:30 of the 1st period).

First Minor Penalty by Opposition in an Oiler Home Game: October 13, 1979 vs. Detroit (Jean Hamel, a two minute minor for hooking at 4:02 of the 1st period).

First Major Penalty at Home: October 13, 1979 vs. Detroit (Brett Callighen, a fighting major at 19:37 of the 2nd period).

First Major Penalty by the Opposition in an Oiler Home Game: October 13, 1979 vs. Detroit (Mike Foligno, a fighting major at 19:37 of the 1st period).

Most Penalty Minutes One Playoff Year: 75—Kevin McClelland (1984-85 in 18 games, 4.17 minutes per game).

First Minor Penalty in the Playoffs on the Road: April 8, 1980 in Philadelphia (Stan Weir, 2 minute minor for hooking at 16:18 of the 1st period).

First Minor Penalty by Opposition in the Playoffs in an Oiler Road Game: April 8, 1980 in Philadelphia (Al Hill, 2 minute minor for fighting at 5:37 of the 1st period).

First Major Penalty in the Playoffs in an Oiler Road Game: April 9, 1980 in Philadelphia (Pat Price, a fighting major at 13:01 of the 3rd period).

First Major Penalty by Opposition in the Playoffs in an Oiler Road Game: April 9, 1980 in Philadelphia (Paul Holmgren, a fighting major at 13:01 of the 3rd period).

First Minor Penalty in the Playoffs at Home: April 11, 1980 vs. Philadelphia (Lee Fogolin, 2 minute minor for crosschecking at 16:42 of the 1st period).

First Minor Penalty by Opposition in the Playoffs in an Oiler Home Game: April 11, 1980 vs. Philadelphia (Behn Wilson, 2 minute minor for hooking at 4:27 of the 1st period).

First Major Penalty in the Playoffs at Home: April 11, 1980 vs. Philadelphia (Dave Hunter a fighting major, Dave Lumley a slashing minor and a fighting major at 17:43 of the 2nd period).

First Major Penalty by Opposition in the Playoffs in an Oiler Home Game: April 11, 1980 (Mike Busniuk a fighting major, and Jim Watson a fighting major at 17:43 of the 2nd period).

PENALTY MINUTES, INDIVIDUAL—GAME

Most Penalty Minutes One Game: 42—Dave Semenko (March 13 1982 vs. Vancouver, and included 1 minor, 2 majors, 2 ten minute misconducts, 1 match penalty).

Most Penalty Minutes One Playoff Game: 30—Dave Semenko (April 17 1983, vs. Calgary, and included 1 major, 1 ten minute misconduct, 1 game misconduct, 1 match penalty).

PENALTY MINUTES, INDIVIDUAL—PERIOD

Most Penalty Minutes One Period: 41—Lee Fogolin (March 28, 1981, 3rd period vs. Detroit, and included 3 minors, 1 major, 1 ten minute misconduct, 1 game misconduct, 1 gross misconduct).

Most Penalty Minutes One Period in a Playoff Game: 30—Dave Semenko (April 17 1983, 1st period vs. Calgary, and included 1 major, 1 ten minute misconduct, 1 game misconduct, 1 match penalty).

PENALTY MINUTES, TEAM

Most Penalty Minutes, One Season: 2,173—1987-88 (in 80 games, 27.2 minutes per game).

Most Penalty Minutes, One Playoff Year: 627—1987-88 (in 18 games, 34.8 minutes per game).

Most Penalty Minutes Including Playoffs, One Season: 2,800—1987-88 (2173 regular season, 627 playoff, 28.6 minutes per game).

Most Penalty Minutes, One Playoff Series: 262—1985-86 Division final vs. Calgary (included 66 minors, 10 majors, 6 misconducts and 2 game misconducts. 37.4 minutes per game).

Most Penalty Minutes, One Playoff Series (Both Teams): 465—1985-86 Division final vs. Calgary (Oilers received 262 penalty minutes, Calgary received 203 penalty minutes. 66.4 minutes per game).

Most Penalty Minutes, One Game: 199—February 28, 1990 vs. Los Angeles (included 27 minors, 7 majors, 6 misconducts, 4 games misconducts and 1 match penalty. The Kings scored one powerplay goal).

Most Penalty Minutes, One Game (Both Teams): 356—February 28, 1990 vs. Los Angeles (Kings received 26 minors, 9 majors, 3 misconducts and 3 game misconducts. Oilers received 27 minors, 7 majors, 6 misconducts, 4 games misconducts and 1 match penalty. Each team scored 1 powerplay goal).

Most Penalty Minutes, One Playoff Game: 111—April 10, 1982 vs. Los Angeles (Oilers received 18 minors, 3 majors, and 6 10-minute misconducts. Oilers allowed 2 powerplay goals).

Most Penalty Minutes, One Playoff Game (Both Teams): 227—April 10, 1982 vs. Los Angeles (Los Angeles received 18 minors, 2 majors, 6 10-minute misconducts and 1 game misconduct. Oilers received 18 minors, 3 majors, and 6 10-minute misconducts. Oilers scored 1 powerplay goal, the Kings 2).

Most Penalty Minutes, One Period: 123—February 28, 1990 (3rd period vs. Los Angeles. Oilers received 9 minors, 3 majors, 5 misconducts and 4 game misconducts. The Kings did not score a powerplay goal).

Most Penalty Minutes in One Period, (Both Teams): 233—January 19, 1980 (2nd period vs. Pittsburgh. Penguins received 9 minors, 7 majors, and 7 game misconducts. Oilers received 5 minors, 8 majors, and 6 game misconducts).

Most Penalty Minutes in One Period, Playoff Game: 82—April 24, 1986 (3rd period vs. Calgary. Oilers received 6 minors, 4 majors, 4 misconducts, and 1 game misconduct. The Flames did not score a powerplay goal).

Most Penalty Minutes in One Period, Playoff Game (Both Teams): 161—April 10, 1982 (3rd period vs. Los Angeles. Kings received 5 minors, 2 majors, 6 10-minute misconducts and 1 game misconduct. Oilers received 3 minors, 3 majors, and 5 10-minute misconducts).

Most Penalty Minutes by Opposition, One Playoff Series: 213—1987-88 Division semi-final vs. Winnipeg (Jets received 64 minors, 5 majors, and 6 10-minute misconducts. The Oilers scored 9 powerplay goals on 37 opportunities).

Most Penalty Minutes by Opposition, One Game: 157—February 28, 1990 vs. Los Angeles (Kings received 26 minors, 9 majors, 3 misconducts, and 3 games misconducts. The Oilers scored 1 powerplay goal).

Most Penalty Minutes by Opposition, One Playoff Game: 116—April 10, 1982 vs. Los Angeles (Los Angeles received 18 minors, 2 majors, and 6 10-minute misconducts and 1 game misconduct. The Oilers scored 1 powerplay goal).

Most Penalty Minutes by Opposition, One Period: 123—January 19, 1980 (2nd period vs. Pittsburgh. Penguins received 9 minors, 7 majors, and 7 game misconducts).

Most Penalty Minutes by the Opposition in One Period, Playoff Game: 90—April 10, 1982 (3rd period vs. Los Angeles. Kings received 5 minors, 2 majors, 6 10-minute misconducts, and 1 game misconduct).

Fewest Penalty Minutes, One Season [48 games]: 1,183—1994-95 (24.6 minutes per game)

Fewest Penalty Minutes, One Season [80 games minimum]: 1,373—1998-99 (16.7 minutes per game).

PENALTIES, INDIVIDUAL—ONE GAME

Most Penalties One Game: 7—Lee Fogolin (March 22 1981 vs. Detroit, and included 3 minors, 1 major, 1 ten minute misconduct, 1 game misconduct, 1 gross misconduct, for 41 minutes).

Most Penalties One Playoff Game: 7—Lee Fogolin (April 18 1983 vs. Calgary, and included 4 minors, 2 majors, and 1 game misconduct, for 28 minutes).

PENALTIES, INDIVIDUAL—ONE PERIOD

Most Penalties One Period: 7—Lee Fogolin (March 22 1981, 3rd period vs. Detroit, and included 3 minors, 1 major, 1 ten minute misconduct, 1 game misconduct, 1 gross misconduct for 41 minutes), Dave Semenko (November 15 1984, 3rd period vs. Calgary, and included 3 minors, 2 majors, 1 match penalty and 1 game misconduct, for 36 minutes).

Most Penalties One Period in a Playoff Game: 4—Dave Semenko (April 17 1983, 1st period vs. Calgary and included 1 major, 1 match penalty, 1 ten minute misconduct, and 1 game misconduct for 35 minutes), Lee Fogolin (April 18, 1983, 1st period vs. Calgary and included 3 minors and 1 major for 20 minutes).

PENALTIES, TEAM

Most Penalties, One Playoff Series: 84—1985-86 Division finals vs. Calgary (Oilers received 66 minors, 10 majors, 6-10 minute misconducts, and 2 game misconducts in 7 games for 262 minutes. Flames won series 4-3).

Most Penalties in One Playoff Series (Both Teams): 155—1985-86 Division finals vs. Calgary (Oilers received 66 minors, 10 majors, 6-10 minute misconducts, and 2 game misconducts for 262 minutes. Calgary received 59 minors, 7 majors, 4 10-minute misconducts and 1 game misconduct for 203 minutes. Flames won series 4-3).

Most Penalties, One Game: 44—February 28, 1990 vs. Los Angeles (Oilers received 26 minors, 7 majors, 6 misconducts, 4 game misconducts, 1 match penalty for 197 minutes). *(NHL Record)*

Most Penalties in One Game (Both Teams): 85—February 28, 1990 vs. Los Angeles (Oilers received 26 minors, 7 majors, 6 misconducts, 4 game misconducts, 1 match penalty for 197 minutes. Kings received 26 minors, 9 majors, 3 misconducts, and 3 game misconducts for 157 minutes). *(NHL Record)*

Most Penalties, One Playoff Game: 29—April 24, 1986 vs. Calgary (Oilers received 20 minors, 4 majors, 4 misconducts and 1 game misconduct for 110 minutes).

Most Penalties, One Playoff Game (Both Teams): 54—April 10, 1982 vs. Los Angeles (The Kings received 18 minors, 2 majors, 6-10 minute misconducts and 1 game misconduct for 116 minutes. The Oilers received 17 minors, 3 majors, and 7 10-minute misconducts for 119 minutes).

Most Penalties, One Period: 21—February 28, 1990 (3rd period vs. Los Angeles. Oilers received 9 minors, 3 majors, 5 misconducts, 4 games misconducts for 123 minutes and lost the game 4-2).

Most Penalties in One Period (Both Teams): 42—January 19, 1980 (2nd period vs. Pittsburgh. Penguins received 9 minors, 7 majors, and 7 game misconducts for 123 minutes. Oilers received 5 minors, 8 majors and 6 game misconducts for 110 minutes. Edmonton won the game 5-2).

Most Penalties in One Period, Playoff Game: 15—April 24, 1986 (3rd period vs. Calgary. Oilers received 6 minors, 4 majors, 4 misconducts, 1 game misconduct for 82 minutes. Oilers won 7-4).

Most Penalties in One Period in a Playoff Game (Both Teams):28—April 20, 1992 (3rd period vs. Los Angeles. The Kings received 9 minors, 1 major and 4 misconducts for 63 minutes. Oilers received 9 minors, 1 major, and 4 misconducts for 63 minutes).

Most Penalties Against, One Playoff Series: 75—1987-88 Division semi-final vs. Winnipeg (Jets received 64 minors, 5 majors, and 6-10 minute misconducts for 213 minutes, in 5 games).

Most Penalties Against, One Game: 41—February 28, 1990 vs. Los Angeles (Kings received 26 minors, 9 majors, 3 misconducts, and 3 game misconducts for 157 minutes).

Most Penalties Against, One Playoff Game: 27—April 10, 1982 vs. Los Angeles (Kings received 18 minors, 2 majors, 6 misconducts and 1 game misconduct for 116 minutes).

Most Penalties Against, One Period: 23—January 19, 1980 (2nd period vs. Pittsburgh. Penguins received 9 minors, 7 majors, and 7 games misconducts for 123 minutes and lost the game 5-2).

Most Penalties Against in One Period, Playoff Game: 14—April 10, 1982 (3rd period vs. Los Angeles. The Kings received 5 minors, 2 majors, 6 misconducts, and 1 game misconduct for 90 minutes. Los Angeles won 6-5), April 20, 1992 (3rd period vs. Los Angeles. The Kings received 9 minors, 1 major and 4 10-minute misconducts for 63 minutes. Los Angeles won 8-5).

MINUTES PLAYED BY A GOALTENDER

Most Minutes Played in Career: 25,004—Bill Ranford (in 449 games).

Most Minutes Played in the Playoffs, Career: 6,528—Grant Fuhr (in 111 games).

Most Career Minutes Played Including Playoffs: 30,436—Grant Fuhr (23,908 regular season and 6,528 in playoffs in 534 games).

Most Minutes Played, Single Season: 4,364—Tommy Salo (2000-01 in 73 games).

Most Minutes Played in Playoffs, Single Season: 1,401—Bill Ranford (1989-90 in 22 games).

Most Minutes Played Including Playoffs, Single Season: 5,440—Grant Fuhr (4,304 regular season, 1,136 in playoffs, in 94 games, 1987-88 season).

Most Minutes Played One Game: 117:34—Tommy Salo (April 27 1999 vs. Dallas, Joe Nieuwendyk of the Stars scored at 57:34 of overtime. Dallas won 3-2).

WINS, GOALTENDER

Most Regular Season Wins, Career: 226—Grant Fuhr (in 423 games, .534 winning percentage).

Most Career Wins in the Playoffs: 74—Grant Fuhr (in 111 games, .667 winning percentage).

Most Wins Including Playoffs, Career: 300—Grant Fuhr (226 regular season, 74 in playoffs, .562 winning percentage).

Most Wins, Single Season: 40—Grant Fuhr (1987-88 for a .533 winning percentage).

Most Wins, One Playoff Year: 16—Grant Fuhr (1987-88, for a .842 winning percentage), Bill Ranford (1989-90, for a .727 winning percentage). *(Ties NHL Record)*

Most Wins Including Playoffs, Single Season: 56—Grant Fuhr (1987-88, 40 regular season, 16 playoff, .596 winning percentage).

LOSSES, GOALTENDER

Most Losses, Career: 192—Bill Ranford (in 449 games).

Most Losses Career, Playoffs: 32—Grant Fuhr (in 111 games).

Most Losses Including Playoffs, Career: 208—Bill Ranford (192 regular season, 16 playoff in 490 games).

Most Losses, Single Season: 38—Bill Ranford (1992-93 in 67 games).

Most Losses One Playoff Year: 8—Bill Ranford (1991-92 in 16 games).

Most Losses Including Playoffs, Single Season: 38—Bill Ranford (all losses in regular season, 1992-93 in 67 games).

TIES, GOALTENDER

Most Ties, Single Season: 14—Grant Fuhr (1981-82 in 48 games).

Most Ties, Career: 57—Bill Ranford (in 449 games).

SHUTOUTS, GOALTENDER

Most Shutouts in a Career: 14—Curtis Joseph (1995-96 to 1997-98 in 177 games).
Most Career Playoff Shutouts: 5-Curtis Joseph (1995-96 to 1997-98 in 24 games).
Most Career Shutouts Including Playoffs: 19—Curtis Joseph (14 regular season, 5 playoff in 201 games).
Most Shutouts in One Season: 8—Curtis Joseph (1997-98 in 71 games), Tommy Salo (2000-2001 in 73 games).
First Shutout at Home: December 9, 1979 vs. Hartford (Eddie Mio made 30 saves. Oilers won 3-0).
First Time Being Shutout at Home: March 12, 1981 vs. N.Y. Islanders (Billy Smith made 36 saves. Islanders won 5- 0).
First Time Being Shutout on the Road: November 17, 1979 in Hartford (Al Smith made 23 saves. Whalers won 4-0).
First Shutout on the Road: January 8, 1985 in Quebec (Grant Fuhr and Andy Moog made 28 saves. Oilers won 4-0).
Most Shutouts in One Playoff Year: 3—Curtis Joseph (1997-98 in 12 games).
First Time Being Shutout in the Playoffs on the Road: The Oilers have never been shutout in a road playoff game.
First Shutout in the Playoffs on the Road: May 10, 1984 in Long Island (Grant Fuhr made 34 saves vs. the Islanders. Oilers won 1-0).
First Time Being Shutout in the Playoffs at Home: May 10, 1983 vs. N.Y. Islanders (Billy Smith made 35 saves. Islanders won 2-0).
First Shutout in the Playoffs at Home: April 8, 1989 vs. Los Angeles (Grant Fuhr made 26 saves. Oilers won 4-0).

GOALS AGAINST AVERAGE, GOALTENDER

Highest Average, Career [minimum 2,400 minutes]: 4.03—Ron Low (1979-80 to 1982-83 in 67 games).
Highest Average in Playoffs, Career [minimum 240 minutes]: 3.13—Andy Moog (1980-81 to 1986-87 in 37 games).
Lowest Average Career [minimum 2,400 minutes]: 2.39—Tommy Salo (1998-99 to 2000-2001 in 156 games).
Lowest Average in Playoffs, Career [minimum 240 minutes]: 2.33—Tommy Salo (in 15 games).
Highest Average, Single Season [minimum 1,200 minutes]: 4.43—Ron Low (1980-81 in 24 games).
Highest Average in Playoffs, Single Season [minimum 120 minutes]: 5.05—Grant Fuhr (1981-82 in 5 games).
Lowest Average, Single Season [minimum 1,200 minutes]: 2.35—Tommy Salo (1999-2000 in 70 games).
Lowest Average in Playoffs, Single Season [minimum 120 minutes]: 2.12—Curtis Joseph (1997-98 in 12 games).

GOALS AGAINST, GOALTENDER

Most Goals Against, Career: 1,470—Grant Fuhr (in 423 games, 3.69 goals against per game).
Most Career Goals Against, Playoffs: 330—Grant Fuhr (in 111 games, 3.03 goals against per game).
Most Goals Against Including Playoffs, Career: 1,800—Grant Fuhr (1,470 regular season, 330 playoffs, 3.55 goals against per game).
Most Goals Against, Single Season: 246—Grant Fuhr (1987-88 in 75 games, 3.43 goals against per game).
First Goal Against on the Road—October 10, 1979 in Chicago (John Marks scored at 1:26 of the 1st period. Oiler goaltender was Dave Dryden).
First Goal Against at Home—October 13, 1979 vs. Detroit (Dan Labraaten scored at 14:16 of the 2nd period. Oiler goaltender was Ed Mio).
Most Goals Against Including Playoffs, Single Season: 301—Grant Fuhr (246 regular season, 55 playoffs, 1987-88, 3.32 goals against per game).
First Goal Against in a Playoff Road Game—April 8, 1980 in Philadelphia (Paul Holmgren scored at 00:56 of the 1st period. Oiler goaltender was Ron Low).
First Goal Against in a Playoff Home Game—April 11, 1980 vs. Philadelphia (Behn Wilson scored at 4:24 of the 2nd period. Oiler goaltender was Ron Low).

GOALS AGAINST, TEAM

Most Goals Against, One Season: 337—1980-81 (in 84 games, 4.01 goals against per game).
Most Goals Against, One Playoff Year: 60—1989-90 (in 22 games, 2.73 goals against per game), 1990-91 (in 18 games, 3.33 goals against per game).
Most Goals Against, Three Game Playoff Series: 12—1979-80 (in Preliminary series vs. Philadelphia, 4.00 goals against per game).
Most Goals Against, Four Game Playoff Series: 21—1991-92 (in Conference final series vs. Chicago, 5.25 goals against per game).
Most Goals Against, Five Game Playoff Series: 27—1981-82 (in Division semi-final series vs. Los Angeles, 5.40 goals against per game).
Most Goals Against, Six Game Playoff Series: 29—1980-81 (in Quarterfinal series vs. N.Y. Islanders, 4.83 goals against per game).
Most Goals Against, Seven Game Playoff Series: 27—1983-84 (in Division final series vs. Calgary, 3.86 goals against per game).
Most Goals Against, One Game: 11—February 12, 1984 (11-0 loss vs. Hartford, Oilers goaltenders were Grant Fuhr and Andy Moog), January 8, 1986 (11-9 loss vs. Toronto. Oiler goaltenders were Grant Fuhr and Andy Moog).
First Powerplay Goal Against on the Road—October 10, 1979 in Chicago (John Marks at 1:26 of the 1st period, on Oiler goaltender Dave Dryden).
First Powerplay Goal Against at Home—October 14, 1979 vs. Vancouver (Lars Lindgren at 3:17 of the 3rd period on Oilers' goaltender Dave Dryden).
First Shorthanded Goal Against on the Road—November 7, 1979 in Boston (Wayne Cashman at 16:24 of the 3rd period on Oilers' goaltender Ed Mio).
First Shorthanded Goal Against at Home—February 8, 1980 vs. Atlanta (Bob MacMillan at 14:37 of the 3rd period on Oilers' goaltender Dave Dryden).
First Game Winning Goal Against in a Road Game—October 10, 1979 in Chicago (John Marks scored at 18:59 of the 1st period vs. Oiler goaltender was Dave Dryden).
First Game Winning Goal Against at Home—October 28, 1979 vs. Washington (Tom Rowe scored at 13:31 of the 3rd period. Oiler goaltender was Ed Mio).
Most Goals Against, One Playoff Game: 10—April 7, 1982 (10-8 loss vs. Los Angeles. Oiler goaltender was Grant Fuhr).
First Powerplay Goal Against in the Playoffs on the Road—April 9, 1980 in Philadelphia (Bobby Clarke at 4:08 of the 2nd period, on Oilers goaltender Ron Low).
First Powerplay Goal Against in the Playoff at Home—April 19, 1981 vs. N.Y. Islanders (Mike Bossy scored at 12:30 of the 2nd period on Oilers' goaltender Andy Moog).
First Shorthanded Goal Against in the Playoffs on the Road—April 16, 1981 in Long Island (Denis Potvin at 10:50 of the 3rd period on Oilers' goaltender Gary Edwards).
First Shorthanded Goal Against in the Playoffs at Home—April 14, 1983 vs. Calgary (Paul Reinhart at 13:01 of the 3rd period on Oiler goaltender Andy Moog).
First Game Winning Goal Against in a Playoff Road Game—April 8, 1980 in Philadelphia (Bobby Clarke scored at 8:06 of the 1st period. Oiler goaltender was Ron Low).
First Game Winning Goal Against in a Playoff Home Game—April 11, 1980 vs. Philadelphia (Ken Linseman scored at 3:56 of the 2nd period. Oiler goaltender was Ron Low).

First Overtime Goal Against in a Playoff Game—April 8, 1980 in Philadelphia (Bobby Clarke scored at 8:06 of overtime vs. Oiler goaltender Ron Low).

First Overtime Goal Against in the Regular Season—December 8, 1984 in Vancouver (Peter McNab scored at 1:24 of overtime on Oiler goaltender Grant Fuhr).

Most Goals Against, One Period: 7—January 17, 1980 (2nd period vs. Boston, Oiler goaltender was Jim Corsi).

Most Goals Against in One Period, Playoff Game: 5—April 7, 1982 (2nd period vs. Los Angeles, Oiler goaltender was Grant Fuhr), April 10, 1982 (3rd period vs. Los Angeles, Oilers goaltender was Grant Fuhr), April 28, 1984 (2nd period vs. Minnesota, Oiler goaltender was Andy Moog), May 12, 1985 (1st period vs. Chicago, Oilers goaltender was Grant Fuhr).

Most Consecutive Goals Against, One Game: 11—February 12, 1984 (11-0 loss vs. Hartford. Oilers goaltenders were Grant Fuhr and Andy Moog).

Most Consecutive Goals Against, One Playoff Game: 6—April 10, 1982 (6-5 loss vs. Los Angeles. Oiler goaltender was Grant Fuhr), May 16, 1992 (8-2 loss vs. Chicago. Oiler goaltender was Bill Ranford).

First Two Goal Game Against on the Road—October 10, 1979 in Chicago (John Marks on Oiler goaltender Dave Dryden).

First Two Goal Game Against at Home—October 13, 1979 vs. Detroit (Mike Foligno on Oiler goaltender Ed Mio).

First Three Goal Game Against on the Road—March 4, 1980 in Long Island (Mike Bossy against Oilers' goaltenders Ed Mio and Jim Corsi).

First Three Goal Game Against at Home—February 8, 1981 vs. Calgary (Ken Houston against Oilers goaltenders Ed Mio and Gary Edwards).

First Two Goal Game Against in the Playoffs on the Road—April 16, 1981 vs. NY Islanders (Clark Gillies on Oiler goaltender Andy Moog).

First Two Goal Game Against in the Playoffs at Home—April 7, 1982 vs. Los Angeles (Marcel Dionne on Oiler goaltender Andy Moog).

First Three Goal Game Against in the Playoffs on the Road—April 17, 1981 in Long Island (Denis Potvin on Oiler goaltender Grant Fuhr).

First Three Goal Game Against in the Playoffs at Home—April 14, 1983 vs. Calgary (Paul Reinhart on Oiler goaltender Andy Moog).

Fewest Goals Against, One Season (48 games): 183—(1994-95, 3.81 goals against per game)

Fewest Goals Against, One Season (minimum 80 games): 211—(1999-00, 2.57 goals against per game)

Fewest Goals Against, Three Game Playoff Series: 5—1985-86 (in Preliminary series vs. Vancouver, 1.67 goals against)

Fewest Goals Against, Four Game Playoff Series: 9—1986-87 (in Division final series vs. Winnipeg, 2.25 goals against per game).

Fewest Goals Against, Five Game Playoff Series: 8—1989-90 (in Cup final series vs. Boston, 1.60 goals against per game).

Fewest Goals Against, Six Game Playoff Series: 15—1991-92 (in Division final series vs. Vancouver, 2.50 goals against per game).

Fewest Goals Against, Seven Game Playoff Series: 16—1997-98 (in Conference quarter final series vs. Colorado, 2.29 goals against per game).

FASTEST GOALS AGAINST, TEAM

Fastest Five Goals Against, One Game: 7 minutes: 49 seconds—October 24, 1979 (1st period vs. N.Y. Rangers. Ron Greschner scored at 3:41, Walt Tkaczuk scored at 4:31, Don Murdoch scored at 5:18, Ulf Nilsson scored at 11:13, and Ron Duguay scored at 11:30. Oiler goaltenders were Ed Mio and Dave Dryden).

Fastest Five Goals Against, One Playoff Game: 8 minutes: 27 seconds—April 28, 1984 (2nd period vs. Minnesota. Brad Maxwell scored at 4:09, Mark Napier scored at 8:48, Mark Napier scored at 10:22, Neal Broten scored at 12:04, and Neal Broten scored at 12:36. Oiler goaltender was Andy Moog).

Fastest Four Goals Against, One Game: 3 minutes: 19 seconds—January 25, 1990 (2nd period vs. Los Angeles. John Tonelli scored at 00:32, Barry Beck at 3:06, Dave Taylor at 3:21 and Tony Granato at 3:51. Oiler goaltender was Bill Ranford).

Fastest Four Goals Against, One Playoff Game: 3 minutes: 48 seconds—April 28, 1984 (2nd period vs. Minnesota. Mark Napier scored at 8:48, and 10:22, Neal Broten at 12:04, and at 12:36. Oiler goaltender was Andy Moog).

Fastest Three Goals Against, One Game: 38 seconds—January 26, 1982 (3rd period vs. St. Louis. Joe Mullen scored at 00:44, Perry Turnbull at 1:09, and Mike Crombeen at 1:22. Oiler goaltender was Ron Low).

Fastest Three Goals Against, One Playoff Game: 1 minute: 26 seconds—May 16, 1992 (2nd period vs. Chicago. Mike Peluso scored at 2:51, Jeremy Roenick at 3:20 and Steve Smith at 4:17. Oiler goaltender was Bill Ranford).

Fastest Two Goals Against, One Game: 4 seconds—December 15, 1995 (2nd period vs. Winnipeg. Deron Quint scored at 7:51 and at 7:55. Oiler goaltenders were Bill Ranford and Joaquin Gage). *(Ties NHL Record)*

Fastest Two Goals Against in One Playoff Game: 11 seconds—April 22, 1990 (1st period vs. Los Angeles. Larry Robinson scored at 19:20 and Todd Elik scored at 19:31. Oiler goaltender was Bill Ranford).

Fastest Three Goals Against From the Start of a Game: 3 minutes: 9 seconds—December 2, 1987 (Brent Ashton scored at 00:47, Gerard Gallant at 1:02 and Shawn Burr at 3:09 vs. Detroit. Oiler goaltender was Grant Fuhr).

Fastest Three Goals Against From the Start of a Playoff Game: 12 minutes: 4 seconds—April 10, 1990 (Mark Kumpel scored at 4:55, Pat Elynuik at 11:42 and Doug Evans at 12:04 vs. Winnipeg. Oiler goaltender was Bill Ranford).

Fastest Three Goals Against From the Start of a Period: 1 minute: 22 seconds—January 26, 1982 (3rd period vs. St. Louis. Joe Mullen scored at 00:44, Perry Turnbull at 1:09 and Mike Crombeen at 1:22. Oiler goaltender was Ron Low).

Fastest Three Goals Against From the Start of a Period in a Playoff Game: 4 minutes, 30 seconds—April 16, 1981 (2nd period vs. N.Y. Islanders. John Tonelli scored at 2:46, Hector Marini at 3:33 and Denis Potvin at 4:30. Oiler goaltender was Andy Moog).

Fastest Two Goals Against From the Start of a Game: 41 seconds—December 5, 1984 (John Tonelli scored at 00:25 and again at 00:41 vs. Islanders. Oiler goaltender was Grant Fuhr).

Fastest Two Goals Against From the Start of a Playoff Game: 2 minutes: 54 seconds—April 24, 1998 vs. Colorado. (Valeri Kamensky scored at 1:22, and Peter Forsberg at 2:54. Edmonton goaltender was Curtis Joseph).

Fastest Two Goals Against From the Start of a Period: 41 seconds—December 5, 1984 (John Tonelli scored at 00:25 and again at 00:41. Oiler goaltender was Grant Fuhr).

Fastest Two Goals Against From the Start of a Period in a Playoff Game: 35 seconds—May 19, 1984 (3rd period vs. Islanders. Pat Lafontaine scored at 00:13 and again at 00:35. Oilers goaltender was Andy Moog.)

SHOTS ON GOAL, INDIVIDUAL

Most Shots on Goal, Single Season: 369—Wayne Gretzky (24.9 % shooting percentage, 1981-82 in 80 games).

Fewest Shots on Goal, Single Season (minimum 80 games): 61—Luke Richardson (1995-96 in 82 games)

Most Shots on Goal per Game, Single Season (40 games minimum); 4.61—Wayme Gretzky (1981-82 in 80 games).

Fewest Shots on Goal per Game, Single Season (40 games minimum): 0.34—Curt Brackenbury (1980-81 in 58 games)

SHOTS ON GOAL, TEAM

Most Shots on Goal, One Season: 2,689—1981-82 (in 80 games, 33.6 shots per game).

Most Shots On Goal, One Playoff Year: 717—1983-84 (in 19 games, 37.7 shots per game).

Most Shots on Goal, One Game: 55—March 21, 1986 (5-4 win vs. Minnesota. North Star goaltender was Don Beaupre).

Most Shots on Goal, One Game (Both Teams): 100—December 11, 1982 (5-4 loss vs. Minnesota. Minnesota had 52 shots, Oilers had 48 shots. North Star goaltender was Don Beaupre, Oiler goaltender was Grant Fuhr).

Most Shots on Goal, One Playoff Game: 54—April 4, 1984 (5-4 win vs. Winnipeg. Jets goaltenders were Doug Soetaert and Mike Veisor).

Most Shots On Goal, One Playoff Game (Both Teams): 97—April 13, 1984 (6-5 loss vs. Calgary. Flames had 50 shots, the Oilers had 47 shots. Flames goaltender was Don Edwards, Oiler goaltender was Grant Fuhr).

Most Shots On Goal, One Period: 24—March 21, 1986 (2nd period vs. Minnesota. North Star goaltender was Don Beaupre).

Most Shots on Goal, One Period (Both Teams): 38—December 16, 1981 (1st period vs. Colorado Rockies. Oilers had 20 shots, the Rockies 18 shots. Rockies goaltender was Glenn Resch, Oiler goaltender was Ron Low).

Most Shots on Goal in One Period, Playoff Game: 22—April 16, 2000 (1st period vs. Dallas. Stars goaltender was Ed Belfour).

Most Shots on Goal in One Period, Playoff Game (Both Teams): 35—April 4, 1984 (1st period vs. Winnipeg. Oilers had 19 shots, Winnipeg had 16 shots. Jets goaltenders were Doug Soetaert and Mike Veisor, Oiler goaltender was Grant Fuhr).

Fewest Shots on Goal, One Season [48 games]: 1,427—1994-95 (29.7 shots per game).

Fewest Shots On Goal, One Season [80 games minimum]: 2,207—1990-91 (in 80 games, 27.6 shots per game).

Fewest Shots on Goal, One Game: 11—October 19, 1989 (3-0 loss vs. Boston. Bruin goaltender was Andy Moog), November 5, 1999 (2-1 loss vs. St. Louis. Blues goaltender was Jamie McLellan).

Fewest Shots on Goal, One Game (Both Teams): 32—October 19, 1989 (3-0 loss vs. Boston. The Bruins had 21 shots, Oilers had 11 shots. Bruin goaltender was Andy Moog, Oiler goaltender was Bill Ranford).

Fewest Shots on Goal, One Playoff Game: 13—April 21, 1999 (2-1 loss vs. Dallas. Stars goaltender was Ed Belfour).

Fewest Shots On Goal, One Playoff Game (Both Teams): 36—May 18, 1988 (2-1 win vs. Boston. Oilers had 22 shots, the Bruins had 14 shots. Oiler goaltender was Grant Fuhr, Bruin goaltender was Andy Moog), May 9, 1998 (2-0 win vs. Dallas. Oilers had 21 shots, Dallas had 15 shots. Oiler goaltender was Curtis Joseph, Stars goaltender was Ed Belfour).

Fewest Shots On Goal, One Period: 0—February 20, 1991 (2nd period vs. Minnesota. North Star goaltender was Jon Casey).

Fewest Shots on Goal, One Period (Both Teams): 5—January 12, 1999 (2nd period vs. Dallas. The Stars had 3 shots, the Oilers 2 shots. Oiler goaltender was Bob Essensa, Stars goaltender was Ed Belfour).

Fewest Shots on Goal in One Period, Playoff Game: 1—April 22, 1990 (1st period vs. Los Angeles. Kings goaltender was Ron Scott), May 4, 1992 (1st period vs. Vancouver. Canucks goaltender was Kirk McLean.).

Fewest Shots on Goal in One Period, Playoff Game (Both Teams): 8—April 23, 1988 (3rd period vs. Calgary. Oilers had 4 shots, Calgary had 4 shots. Oiler goaltender was Grant Fuhr, Flames goaltender was Mike Vernon).

Most Shots on Goal Allowed, One Game: 59—March 17, 1993 vs. New York Rangers (Oiler goaltender was Bill Ranford).

Most Shots on Goal Allowed, One Playoff Game: 56—April 27, 1999 vs. Dallas (Oiler goaltender was Tommy Salo).

Most Shots On Goal Allowed, One Period: 29—November 7, 1979 (2nd period vs. Detroit. Oiler goaltender was Ed Mio).

Most Shots on Goal Allowed in One Period, Playoff Game: 20—May 8, 1992 (1st period vs. Vancouver. Oiler goaltender was Bill Ranford).

Fewest Shots on Goal Allowed, One Game: 14—March 7, 1987 (5-3 win vs. Montreal, Oiler goaltender was Andy Moog), February 2, 1992 (8-2 win vs. Quebec, Oiler goaltender was Norm Foster), February 28, 1993 (4-1 win vs. San Jose, Oiler goaltender was Bill Ranford).

Fewest Shots on Goal Allowed, One Playoff Game: 12—May 20, 1988 (4-2 win vs. Boston, Oiler goaltender was Grant Fuhr).

Fewest Shots On Goal Allowed, One Period: 1—March 13, 1983 (1st period vs. Buffalo. Oiler goaltender was Andy Moog), April 2, 1987 (1st period vs. Calgary. Oiler goaltender was Grant Fuhr), October 4, 1996 (1st period vs. Buffalo. Oiler goaltender was Curtis Joseph), November 7, 1999 (3rd period vs. Anaheim. Oiler goaltender was Bill Ranford)

Fewest Shots on Goal Allowed in One Period, Playoff Game: 0—May 9, 1998 (1st period vs. Dallas. Oilers goaltender was Curtis Joseph).

SHOOTING PERCENTAGE

Highest Career Shooting Percentage (over 100 shots): 25.3%—Craig Simpson (185 goals on 730 shots)

Highest Shooting Percentage, Single Season (over 10 goals): 36.4%—Craig Simpson (43 goals on 118 shots, 1987-88 season)

COACHING RECORDS

Most Seasons Coached: 11—Glen Sather (1979-1988, 1993).

Most Games Coached, Regular Season: 842—Glen Sather (1979-1988, 1993).

Most Games Coached, Playoffs: 127—Glen Sather (1979-1988, 1993).

Most Games Coached, Regular Season and Playoffs: 969—Glen Sather (1979-1988, 1993).

Fewest Games Coached: 18—Bryan Watson (1980-81, 4 wins, 9 losses, 5 ties).

Most Wins, Regular Season: 464—Glen Sather (1979-1988, 1993).

Most Wins, Playoffs: 88—Glen Sather (1979-1988, 1993).

Most Wins, Regular Season and Playoffs: 552—Glen Sather (1979-1988, 1993).

Most Losses, Regular Season: 268—Glen Sather (1979-1988, 1993).

Most Losses, Playoffs: 38—Glen Sather (1979-1988, 1993).

Most Losses, Regular Season and Playoffs: 306—Glen Sather (1979-1988, 1993).

Most Ties, Regular Season: 110—Glen Sather (1979-1988, 1993).

Most Ties, Playoffs: 1—Glen Sather (1979-1988, 1993).

Most Ties, Regular Season and Playoffs: 111—Glen Sather (1979-1988, 1993).

Longest Winning Streak, Regular Season: 9 games—Craig MacTavish (February 20, 2001 through March 13, 2001)

Longest Winning Streak, One Playoff Year: 9 games—Glen Sather (April 10, 1985 through May 7, 1985).

Longest Losing Streak: 11 games—Ted Green (October 16, 1993 through November 7, 1993).

Longest Undefeated Streak: 15 games—Glen Sather (12 wins, 3 ties, October 11 1984 through November 9, 1984).

Longest Winless Streak: 14 games—Ted Green (13 losses, 1 tie, October 11, 1993 through November 7, 1993).

STREAKS, INDIVIDUAL

Longest Consecutive Games Streak: 518—Craig MacTavish (October 12, 1986 through January 2, 1993. The streak came to an end January 3rd when he was out of the lineup with a lower back strain).

Longest Consecutive Games Streak Including Playoffs: 621—Craig MacTavish (521 regular season, 103 playoff, October 12, 1986 through January 2, 1993. The streak came to an end January 3rd when he was out of the lineup with a lower back strain).

Longest Consecutive Goal Scoring Streak: 12 games—Dave Lumley (November 21 1981 through December 16 1981, 15 goals scored during the streak. The streak was stopped by goaltender Pat Riggin of the Calgary Flames).

Longest Consecutive Goal Scoring Streak, One Playoff Year: 6 games—Esa Tikkanen (April 10 1990 through April 20 1990, 7 goals during the streak. Tikkanen's streak was stopped by Kings goaltenders Ron Scott and Mario Gosselin).

Longest Consecutive Playoff Goal Scoring Streak: 6 games—Esa Tikkanen (April 10 1990 through April 20 1990, 7 goals during the streak. The streak was stopped by King's goaltenders Ron Scott and Mario Gosselin).

Longest Consecutive Assist Scoring Streak: 17 games—Wayne Gretzky (November 26 1983 to January 4 1984, 38 assists during streak. The streak was stopped by Greg Millen of the Hartford Whalers), Paul Coffey (November 27 1985 to January 2 1986, 27 assists during streak. The streak was stopped by Mike Liut of the Hartford Whalers). *(NHL Record)*

Longest Consecutive Assist Scoring Streak, One Playoff Year: 9 games—Glenn Anderson (April 20 1985 through May 16 1985, 13 assists during streak. The streak was stopped by Pelle Lindbergh of the Philadelphia Flyers).

Longest Consecutive Playoff Assist Scoring Streak: 9 games—Glenn Anderson (April 20 1985 through May 16 1985, 13 assists during streak. The streak was stopped by Pelle Lindbergh of the Philadelphia Flyers).

Longest Consecutive Point Scoring Streak: 51 games—Wayne Gretzky (October 5 1983 to January 27 1984, 153 points during streak and included 61 goals and 92 assists. The streak was stopped by Markus Mattsson of the Los Angeles Kings). *(NHL Record)*

Longest Consecutive Point Scoring Streak from the Start of a Season: 51 games—Wayne Gretzky (October 5 1983 through January 27 1984, 153 points, 61 goals, 92 assists during streak. The streak was stopped by Markus Mattsson of the Los Angeles Kings). *(NHL Record)*

Longest Consecutive Point Scoring Streak Including Playoffs: 54 games—Wayne Gretzky (May 12 1983 through January 27 1984. Gretzky scored points in the last three Oiler playoff games against the Islanders in the 1982-83 final series and the first 51 games of the 1983-84 season. The streak included 61 goals and 96 assists and 157 points. The streak was stopped by Markus Mattsson of the Los Angeles Kings). *(NHL Record)*

Longest Consecutive Point Scoring Streak, One Playoff Year: 17 games—Wayne Gretzky (April 9 1988 through May 26 1988, 41 points and included 12 goals and 29 assists. Gretzky recorded points in every game in the 1988 playoffs except the first two).

Longest Consecutive Playoff Point Scoring Streak: 18 games—Wayne Gretzky (April 11 1980 through April 9 1983, 42 points and included 17 goals and 25 assists. The streak was stopped by Flames' goaltender Rejean Lemelin).

Longest Undefeated Streak by a Goaltender: 23 games—Grant Fuhr (October 21 1981 through January 13 1982, 15 wins and 8 ties, 76 goals against. The streak was stopped January 16th by the Toronto Maple Leafs).

Longest Undefeated Streak by a Goaltender in His First NHL Season: 23 games—Grant Fuhr (October 21 1981 through January 13 1982, 15 wins and 8 ties, 76 goals against. The streak was stopped January 16th by the Toronto Maple Leafs). *(NHL Record)*

Longest Shutout Sequence by a Goaltender: 192 minutes: 53 seconds—Tommy Salo from March 2 through March 11, 2001. (Minnesota scored at 10:02 of the 2nd period on March 2, 2001. Salo then recorded consecutive shutouts, March 7 and 9 before finally allowing Carolina to score at 2:55 of the third period March 11).

Longest Playoff Shutout Sequence: 166 minutes, 54 seconds—Curtis Joseph (Joseph allowed a goal by Colorado at the 16:20 mark of the first period on April 30 1998, then shutout the Avalanche May 2 1998 and May 4 1998 before allowing a goal at 3:14 of the first period against Dallas May 7 1998).

STREAKS, TEAM

Longest Winning Streak: 9 games—February 20, 2001 through March 13, 2001 (February 20 Oilers 5 L.A. 0, February 24 Oilers 3 Calgary 1, February 25 Oilers 3 Dallas 2, February 28 Oilers 5 St. Louis 3, March 2 Oilers 3 Minnesota 1, March 7 Oilers 4 Toronto 0, March 9 Oilers 4 Buffalo 0, March 11 Oilers 3 Carolina 2, March 13 Oilers 5 Tampa Bay 4)

Longest Winning Streak, One Playoff Year: 9 games—April 10, 1985 through May 7, 1985 (6 at home, 3 on the road).

Longest Home Winning Streak: 8 games—January 19, 1985 through February 22, 1985 (46 goals for, 27 goals against), February 24, 1986 through April 2, 1986 (47 goals for, 22 goals against).

Longest Home Winning Streak, One Playoff Year: 11—April 6, 1988 through May 26, 1988. (55 goals for, 28 goals against).

Longest Road Winning Streak: 8 games—December 9, 1986 through January 17, 1987 (45 goals for, 20 goals against).

Longest Road Winning Streak, One Playoff Year: 6 games—April 11, 1987 through May 11, 1987 (26 goals for, 15 goals against)

Longest Undefeated Streak: 15 games—12 wins, 3 ties (October 11 1984 through November 9, 1984, 81 goals for, 38 goals against)

Longest Home Undefeated Streak: 14 games—11 wins, 3 ties (November 15, 1989 through January 6, 1990. 55 goals for, 33 goals against).

Longest Road Undefeated Streak: 9 games—6 wins, 3 ties (January 17, 1982 through March 2, 1982, 41 goals for, 25 goals against), 7 wins, 2 ties (December 23, 1982 through January 18, 1983, 62 goals for, 29 goals against).

Longest Undefeated Streak From Start of Season: 15 games—12 wins, 3 ties (October 11 1984 through November 9, 1984, 81 goals for 38 goals against) *(NHL Record)*

Longest Losing Streak: 11 games—October 16, 1993 through November 7, 1993 (34 goals for, 61 goals against).

Longest Home Losing Streak: 9 games—October 16, 1993 through November 24, 1993 (21 goals for, 37 goals against).

Longest Road Losing Streak: 9 games—November 25, 1980 through December 30, 1980. (28 goals for, 47 goals against).

Longest Winless Streak: 14 games—October 11, 1993 through November 7, 1993 (13 losses, 1 tie, 34 GF, 61 GA).

Longest Home Winless Streak: 9 games—October 16, 1993 through November 24, 1993 (9 losses, 0 ties, 21 GF, 37 GA).

Longest Road Winless Record: 9 games—November 25, 1980 through December 30, 1980 (9 losses, 0 ties, 28 goals for, 47 goals against), December 12, 1992 through January 23, 1993 (8 losses, 1 tie, 18 goals for, 38 goals against), January 11, 1994 through February 19, 1994 (7 losses, 2 ties, 21 goals for, 34 goals against).

Longest Consecutive Games Streak Without Being Shutout: 229 games—March 15, 1981 to February 11, 1984 (1,218 goals scored during the streak).

Longest Consecutive Games Streak Without Being Shutout Including Playoffs: 198 games—March 15, 1981 through May 3, 1983 (972 goals scored during the streak)

Longest Stretch Without Scoring a Goal: 156 minutes, 31 seconds—

October 25, 1990 (goal scored at 37:35, team was shutout against Washington October 28, 1990, and also was shutout against Winnipeg in overtime October 31, 1990 before scoring a goal against New Jersey, November 3, 1990 at 13:43).

Longest Consecutive Streak Playing a Game in Overtime, Regular Season: 4 games—January 18, 1994 (4-3 loss at Ottawa), January 19, 1994 (1-1 tie at Buffalo), January 24, 1994 (5-4 loss vs. Vancouver in a neutral site game), January 26, 1994 (3-3 tie at home vs. New Jersey).

Longest Consecutive Streak Playing a Game in Overtime, Playoffs: 5 games—April 14, 1991 (2-1 loss at home vs. Calgary), April 16, 1991 (5-4 win at Calgary), April 18, 1991 (4-3 loss at Los Angeles), April 20, 1991 (4-3 win at Los Angeles), April 22, 1991 (4-3- win at home vs. Los Angeles).

TEAM WINS

Most Wins, One Season: 57—1983-84 (in 80 games).

Most Wins, One Playoff Year: 16—1986-87 (in 21 games), 1987-1988 (in 19 games), 1989-90 (in 22 games) *(Ties NHL Record).*

Most Wins Including Playoffs, One Season: 72—1983-84 (57 regular season, 15 playoffs in 99 games).

Most Home Wins, One Season: 32—1985-86 (in 40 games).

Most Road Wins, One Season: 26—1983-84 (in 40 games).

Fewest Wins, One Season [48 games]: 17—1994-95.

Fewest Wins, One Season [minimum 80 games]: 26—1992-93 (in 84 games).

Fewest Wins, One Playoff Year: 0—1979-80 (in 3 games vs. Philadelphia).

Fewest Home Wins, One Season [48 games]: 11—1994-95 (in 24 games).

Fewest Home Wins, One Season [minimum 80 game schedule]: 15—1995-96 (in 41 games).

Fewest Road Wins, One Season [48 games]: 8—1994-95 (in 24 games).

Fewest Road Wins, One Season [minimum 80 game schedule]: 10—1992-93 (in 42 games).

Most Overtime Wins, One Season: 5—1985-86 (of 14 games), 1986-87 (of 14 games), 1989-90 (of 19 games), 1992-93 (of 17 games).

Most Playoff Overtime Wins, One Year: 4—1990-91

Fewest Overtime Wins, One Season (since 1983-84): 0—1984-85 (in 11 games), 1991-92 (in 12 games).

TEAM WINNING PERCENTAGE

Highest Winning Percentage, One Season: .744—1983-84 (57 wins, 18 losses, 5 ties in 80 games), 1985-86 (56 wins, 17 losses, 7 ties in 80 games).

Highest Home Winning Percentage, One Season: .825—1981-82 (31 wins, 5 losses, 4 ties in 40 games), 1983-84 (31 wins, 5 losses, 4 ties in 40 games), 1985-86 (32 wins, 6 losses, 2 ties in 40 games).

Highest Road Winning Percentage, One Season: .663—1983-84 (26 wins, 13 losses, 1 tie in 40 games), 1985-86 (24 wins, 11 losses, 5 ties in 40 games).

Lowest Winning Percentage, One Season: .357—1992-93 (26 wins, 50 losses, 8 ties in 84 games).

Lowest Home Winning Percentage, One Season: .427—1995-96 (15 wins, 21 losses, 5 ties in 41 games)

Lowest Road Winning Percentage, One Season: .274—1992-93 (10 wins, 29 losses, 3 ties in 42 games).

TEAM LOSSES

Most Losses, One Season: 50—1992-93 (in 84 games).

Most Losses, One Playoff Year: 7—1996-97 and 1997-98 (in 12 games).

Most Losses Including Playoffs, One Season: 50—1992-93 (in 84 games).

Most Home Losses, One Season: 22—1993-94 (in 42 games).

Most Road Losses, One Season: 29—1992-93 (in 42 games).

Fewest Losses, One Season: 17—1981-82 (in 80 games), 1985-86 (in 80 games).

Fewest Home Losses, One Season: 5—1981-82 (in 40 games), 1983-84 (in 40 games).

Fewest Road Losses, One Season: 11—1985-86 (in 40 games).

Most Overtime Losses, One Season: 8—1999-2000 in (28 games).

Fewest Overtime Losses, One Season (since 1983-84): 0—1983-84 (in 9 games).

Most Overtime Losses, One Playoff Year: 2—1979-80, 1983-84, 1990-91.

TEAM TIES

Most Ties, One Season: 16—1980-81 (in 80 games), 1999-2000 (in 82 games)

Most Home Ties, One Season: 10—1980-81 (in 40 games).

Most Road Ties, One Season: 11—1981-82 (in 40 games), 1993-94 (in 42 games).

Fewest Ties, One Season [48 games]: 4—1994-95

Fewest Ties, One Season [minimum 80 games]: 5—1983-84 (in 80 games).

Fewest Home Ties, One Season [48 games]: 1—1994-95 (in 24 games)

Fewest Home Ties, One Season [minimum 80 games]: 2—1985-86 (40 games).

Fewest Road Ties, One Season: 1—1983-84 (in 40 games), 1986-87 (in 40 games).

Most Overtime Ties, One Season: 16—1999-2000 (in 28 games).

POINTS, TEAM

Most Points, One Season: 119—1983-84 (57 wins, 18 losses, 5 ties, .744 winning percentage), 1985-86 (56 wins, 17 losses, 7 ties, .744 winning percentage).

Most Home Points, One Season: 66—1981-82 (31 wins, 5 losses, 4 ties, .825 winning percentage), 1983-84 (31 wins, 5 losses, 4 ties, .825 winning percentage), 1985-86 (32 wins, 6 losses, 2 ties, .825 winning percentage).

Most Road Points, One Season: 53—1983-84 (26 wins, 13 losses, 1 tie, .663 winning percentage), 1985-86 (24 wins, 11 losses, 5 ties, .663 winning percentage).

Fewest Points, One Season [48 game season]: 38—1994-95 (17 wins, 27 losses 4 ties, .396 winning percentage).

Fewest Points, One Season [80 games minimum]: 60—1992-93 (26 wins, 50 losses, 8 ties, .357 winning percentage).

Fewest Home Points, One Season [48 games]: 23—1994-95 (11 wins, 12 losses, 1 tie, .479 winning percentage).

Fewest Home Points, One Season [80 games minimum]: 35—1995-96 (15 wins, 21 losses, 5 ties, .427 winning percentage).

Fewest Road Points, One Season [48 games]: 15—1994-95 (6 wins, 15 losses, 3 ties, .313 winning percentage).

Fewest Road Points, One Season [minimum 80 games]: 26—1979-80 (11 wins, 25 losses, 4 ties, .325 winning percentage).

First Games vs. Opposition

At SkyReach Center	***Road***	***Venue***
Nov. 21, 1993 Oilers 2 Anaheim 4	Oct. 13, 1993 Oilers3 Anaheim 4	The Arrowhead Pond
Dec. 12, 1979 Oilers 5 Atlanta Flames 5	Oct. 26, 1979 Oilers 3 Atlanta Flames 7	The Omni
Feb. 25, 2000 Oilers 5 Atlanta Thrashers 4	Mar. 13, 2000 Oilers 3 Atlanta Thrashers 0	Phillips Arena
Nov. 4, 1979 Oilers 1 Boston 2	Nov. 8, 1979 Oilers 2 Boston 4	Boston Garden
	Feb. 27, 1996 Oilers 4 Boston 3 (OT)	Fleet Center
Jan. 13, 1980 Oilers 6 Buffalo 5	Nov. 18, 1979 Oilers 7 Buffalo 9	Memorial Auditorium
	Jan. 24, 1997 Oilers 3 Buffalo 1	Marine Midland Arena
Oct. 22, 1980 Oilers 5 Calgary 3	Dec. 30, 1980 Oilers 3 Calgary 5	Calgary Corral
	Oct. 15, 1983 Oilers 4 Calgary 3	Saddledome
Nov. 12, 1997 Oilers 4 Carolina 6	Mar. 15, 1998 Oilers 1 Carolina 4	Greensboro Coliseum.
	Mar. 15, 2000 Oilers 2 Carolina 2 (OT)	Raleigh E. S. Complex
Nov. 28, 1979 Oilers 4 Chicago 2	Oct. 10, 1979 Oilers 2 Chicago 4	Chicago Stadium
	Jan. 25, 1995 Oilers 1 Chicago 5	United Center
Nov. 20, 1995 Oilers 3 Avalanche 3 (OT)	Dec. 7, 1995 Oilers 5 Avalanche 3	McNichols Arena
	Jan. 3, 2000 Oilers 2 Avalanche 2 (OT)	Pepsi Center
Dec. 26, 1979 Oilers 4 Rockies 3	Dec. 21, 1979 Oilers 4 Rockies 5	McNichols Arena
Jan. 7, 2001 Oilers 4 Blue Jackets 2	Nov. 5, 2000 Oilers 4 Blue Jackets 2	Nationwide Arena
Nov. 29, 1993 Oilers 5 Dallas 6 (OT)	Dec. 5, 1993 Oilers 3 Dallas 4	Reunion Arena
Oct. 13, 1979 Oilers 3 Detroit 3	Nov. 7, 1979 Oilers 3 Detroit 5	Joe Louis Arena
Mar. 9, 1994 Oilers 3 Florida 5	Mar. 18, 1994 Oilers 4 Florida 4 (OT)	Miami Arena
	Dec. 19, 1998 Oilers 1 Florida 3	National Car Rental Arena
Dec. 9, 1979 Oilers 3 Hartford 0	Nov. 17, 1979 Oilers 0 Hartford 4	Hartford Civic Center
Jan. 5, 1980 Oilers 3 Los Angeles 3	Dec. 22, 1979 Oilers 3 Los Angeles 9	Fabulous Forum
	Nov. 9, 1999 Oilers 1 Los Angeles 1 (OT)	Staples Center
Oct. 21, 1979 Oilers 5 North Stars 5	Dec. 5, 1979 Oilers 1 North Stars 6	Met Center
Nov. 3, 2000 Oilers 3 Wild 0	Oct. 15, 2000 Oilers 5 Wild 3	Xcel Energy Center
Dec. 14, 1979 Oilers 5 Montreal 3	Jan. 7, 1980 Oilers 3 Montreal 4	Montreal Forum
	Mar. 23, 1996 Oilers 6 Montreal 5	Molson Center
Nov. 4, 1998 Oilers 3 Nashville 2	Dec. 8, 1999 Oilers 3 Nashville 3 (OT)	Nashville Arena
Dec. 17, 1982 Oilers 10 New Jersey 4	Nov. 11, 1982 Oilers 5 New Jersey 1	Meadowlands Arena
Nov. 2, 1979 Oilers 7 Islanders 5	Oct. 23, 1979 Oilers 3 Islanders 3	Nassau County Coliseum
Jan. 11, 1980 Oilers 2 Rangers 6	Oct. 24, 1979 Oilers 2 Rangers 10	Madison Square Garden
Nov. 3, 1992 Oilers 5 Ottawa 2	Feb. 3, 1993 Oilers 2 Ottawa 3	Ottawa Civic Center
	Mar. 24, 1996 Oilers 3 Ottawa 2	Corel Center
Nov. 24, 1979 Oilers 2 Philadelphia 2	Nov. 15, 1979 Oilers 3 Philadelphia 5	The Spectrum
	Mar. 13, 1997 Oilers 4 Philadelphia 5	First Union Center
Oct. 30, 1996 Oilers 4 Phoenix 1	Oct. 14, 1996 Oilers 6 Phoenix 3	America West Arena
Jan. 23, 1980 Oilers 4 Pittsburgh 3	Jan. 19, 1980 Oilers 5 Pittsburgh 2	Pittsburgh Civic Center
Oct. 19, 1979 Oilers 6 Quebec 3	Jan. 9, 1980 Oilers 2 Quebec 3	Le Colisee
Nov. 29, 1991 Oilers 4 San Jose 4 (OT)	Nov. 8, 1991 Oilers 2 San Jose 6	Cow Palace
	Oct. 26, 1993 Oilers 1 San Jose 3	San Jose Arena
Feb. 6, 1980 Oilers 3 St. Louis 6	Oct. 30, 1979 Oilers 1 St. Louis 2	St. Louis Arena
	Feb. 20, 1995 Oilers 0 St. Louis 4	Kiel Center
Nov. 28, 1992 Oilers 4 Tampa 3 (OT)	Oct. 20, 1992 Oilers 1 Tampa 6	Expo Hall
	Mar. 16, 1994 Oilers 4 Tampa 4 (OT)	Thunderdome
	Dec. 12, 1996 Oilers 2 Tampa 2 (OT)	The Ice Palace
Nov. 11, 1979 Oilers 3 Toronto 6	Nov. 21, 1979 Oilers 4 Toronto 4	Maple Leaf Gardens
	Nov. 27, 1999 Oilers 2 Toronto 5	Air Canada Center
Oct. 14, 1979 Oilers 4 Vancouver 4	Dec. 28 1979 Oilers 5 Vancouver 3	Pacific Coliseum
	Nov. 1, 1995 Oilers 3 Vamcouver 3 (OT)	G.M. Place

At SkyReach Center	*Road*	*Venue*
Oct. 28, 1979 Washington 6 Edmonton 4	Nov. 13, 1979 Oilers 5 Washington 3	Cap Center
	Nov. 8, 1997 Oilers 1 Washinton 2	MCI Center
Dec. 16, 1979 Oilers 3 Winnipeg 4	Dec. 7, 1979 Oilers 3 Winnipeg 8	Winnipeg Arena

Oilers Monthly Record

Month	*Home*	*GF–GA*	*Road*	*GF–GA*	*Overall*	*GF–GA*
October 1979	1–1–3	22–21	0–4–1	11–26	1–5–4	33–47
October 1980	1–3–2	21–25	1–1–1	9–9	2–4–3	30–34
October 1981	5–1–0	41–21	4–3–0	30–29	9–4–0	71–50
October 1982	3–3–1	30–28	1–3–2	29–37	4–6–3	59–65
October 1983	4–0–1	27–16	5–2–0	35–36	9–2–1	62–52
October 1984	6–0–1	45–14	2–0–1	16–11	8–0–2	61–25
October 1985	6–0–0	31–18	2–1–0	17–18	8–1–0	48–36
October 1986	6–0–0	33–13	2–4–0	24–26	8–4–0	57–39
October 1987	3–2–0	24–19	3–3–0	25–22	6–5–0	49–41
October 1988	4–2–1	29–28	1–2–1	14–19	5–4–2	43–47
October 1989	1–3–1	16–18	3–2–2	30–25	4–5–3	46–43
October 1990	2–4–1	17–15	0–3–1	12–17	2–7–2	29–32
October 1991	2–1–2	17–15	3–5–0	24–33	5–6–2	41–48
October 1992	2–3–1	19–22	1–5–0	14–32	3–8–1	33–54
October 1993	2–5–0	19–23	0–5–1	13–25	2–10–1	32–48
October 1994	0–0–0	0–0	0–0–0	0–0	0–0–0	0–0
October 1995	3–1–1	17–14	1–4–0	8–26	4–5–1	25–40
October 1996	4–2–0	18–13	3–3–0	23–22	7–5–0	41–35
October 1997	3–4–1	17–28	2–2–0	9–10	5–6–1	26–38
October 1998	2–2–0	15–8	3–2–0	18–14	5–4–0	33–22
October 1999	3–1–2	15–12	1–4–0	13–16	4–5–2	28–28
October 2000	4–2–2	22–18	2–4–0	16–21	6–6–2	38–39
November 1979	3–2–1	22–20	1–5–1	24–34	4–7–2	46–54
November 1980	2–2–2	30–24	2–6–0	25–38	4–8–2	55–62
November 1981	5–1–0	45–21	3–1–3	43–22	8–2–3	88–43
November 1982	2–1–2	25–18	5–2–1	40–30	7–3–3	65–48
November 1983	5–0–1	48–19	5–2–1	47–34	10–2–2	95–53
November 1984	4–1–0	27–17	6–2–1	38–29	10–3–1	65–46
November 1985	4–1–1	46–15	4–2–2	22–32	8–3–3	68–47
November 1986	4–2–1	29–27	2–4–0	25–29	6–6–1	54–56
November 1987	5–1–0	31–15	3–2–2	33–30	8–3–2	64–45
November 1988	4–1–0	26–12	6–3–1	46–39	10–4–1	72–51
November 1989	4–1–2	26–20	4–4–0	34–35	8–5–2	60–65
November 1990	3–2–0	15–14	2–5–0	23–25	5–7–0	38–39
November 1991	2–2–1	16–16	1–5–1	19–28	3–7–2	35–44
November 1992	3–2–1	20–23	2–2–2	18–25	5–4–3	38–48
November 1993	1–5–0	17–24	1–4–2	20–28	2–9–2	37–52
November 1994	0–0–0	0–0	0–0–0	0–0	0–0–0	0–0
November 1995	1–3–2	16–20	2–4–2	21–26	3–7–4	37–46
November 1996	2–3–1	18–25	4–4–0	33–22	6–7–1	51–47
November 1997	1–2–2	15–14	2–5–3	23–30	3–7–5	38–44
November 1998	3–3–0	17–19	4–2–1	18–14	7–5–1	35–33
November 1999	1–2–2	11–12	1–4–2	18–23	2–6–4	29–35
November 2000	5–1–1	19–10	3–4–0	22–24	8–5–1	41–34
December 1979	3–3–1	25–23	1–4–0	16–31	4–7–1	41–54
December 1980	2–3–1	18–21	0–6–0	18–31	2–9–1	36–52
December 1981	6–1–0	48–28	2–2–3	32–31	8–3–3	80–59
December 1982	6–2–0	48–30	2–1–2	25–18	8–3–2	73–48
December 1983	5–1–1	36–21	4–2–0	33–25	9–3–1	69–46

Month	*Home*	*GF–GA*	*Road*	*GF–GA*	*Overall*	*GF–GA*
December 1984	5–1–0	40–17	2–2–1	20–29	7–4–1	60–46
December 1985	6–2–1	53–36	4–1–0	29–28	10–3–1	82–64
December 1986	5–1–1	37–21	5–1–0	27–18	10–2–1	64–39
December 1987	7–1–1	45–21	2–3–0	22–25	9–4–1	67–46
December 1988	3–4–0	35–30	2–2–1	23–18	5–6–1	58–48
December 1989	8–0–1	37–18	1–2–1	15–12	9–2–2	52–30
December 1990	7–1–0	30–22	4–2–0	28–24	11–3–0	58–46
December 1991	5–3–0	33–28	2–2–2	28–29	7–5–2	61–57
December 1992	3–3–1	23–28	2–6–0	16–26	5–9–1	39–54
December 1993	6–1–0	34–15	1–4–2	16–28	7–5–2	50–43
December 1994	0–0–0	0–0	0–0–0	0–0	0–0–0	0–0
December 1995	3–4–1	22–36	3–4–0	22–33	6–8–1	44–69
December 1996	3–4–1	26–28	1–3–2	14–14	4–7–3	40–42
December 1997	1–3–1	6–11	2–4–2	22–26	3–7–3	28–37
December 1998	2–4–0	15–21	1–4–2	13–18	3–8–2	28–39
December 1999	4–0–2	21–11	2–6–1	17–30	6–6–3	38–41
December 2000	3–1–1	15–11	1–5–2	18–26	4–6–3	33–37
January 1980	3–2–2	29–28	3–4–1	30–26	6–6–3	59–54
January 1981	6–1–1	48–26	2–3–1	22–30	8–4–2	70–56
January 1982	6–0–1	41–24	2–3–3	27–40	8–3–4	68–64
January 1983	5–2–1	45–33	5–1–1	47–26	10–3–2	92–59
January 1984	4–1–1	36–28	6–1–0	39–26	10–2–1	75–54
January 1985	6–1–1	41–32	5–1–1	32–18	11–2–2	73–50
January 1986	5–2–0	37–30	5–2–1	40–34	10–4–1	77–64
January 1987	5–1–1	31–21	5–1–1	38–22	10–2–2	69–43
January 1988	4–1–1	26–17	2–4–3	28–29	6–5–4	54–46
January 1989	2–3–1	20–19	3–5–1	32–38	5–8–2	52–57
January 1990	3–3–1	31–28	2–2–2	23–23	5–5–3	54–51
January 1991	3–2–0	19–15	4–3–1	30–29	7–5–1	49–44
January 1992	2–4–0	22–18	3–4–1	29–37	5–8–1	51–55
January 1993	4–2–2	19–18	1–4–1	17–29	5–6–3	36–47
January 1994	1–3–2	22–24	1–4–1	17–22	2–7–3	39–46
January 1995	1–1–0	4–5	1–3–0	11–18	2–4–0	15–23
January 1996	3–5–0	18–28	2–1–0	11–7	5–6–0	29–35
January 1997	5–1–0	15–7	3–2–1	17–20	8–3–1	32–27
January 1998	4–3–1	25–22	3–2–0	17–11	7–5–1	42–33
January 1999	2–2–2	16–14	2–1–2	18–12	4–3–4	34–26
January 2000	2–3–3	25–17	3–2–1	21–17	5–5–4	46–34
January 2001	4–2–2	20–17	3–4–0	15–25	7–6–2	35–42
February 1980	3–4–1	36–30	2–3–1	16–20	5–7–2	52–50
February 1981	4–3–1	39–31	1–4–1	18–24	5–7–2	57–55
February 1982	5–1–1	47–24	4–0–0	11–8	9–1–1	58–32
February 1983	4–1–1	32–21	2–3–0	21–23	6–4–1	53–44
February 1984	6–1–0	45–25	3–5–0	30–35	9–6–0	75–70
February 1985	3–1–1	21–14	4–3–0	39–35	7–4–1	60–49
February 1986	4–1–0	32–20	3–2–1	27–22	7–3–1	59–42
February 1987	2–1–1	21–12	2–5–0	22–32	4–6–1	43–44
February 1988	3–2–1	32–28	3–2–0	23–22	6–4–1	55–50
February 1989	5–3–0	34–32	2–2–0	11–12	7–5–0	45–44
February 1990	3–2–0	25–19	2–4–2	24–35	5–6–2	49–54
February 1991	3–2–1	26–24	2–6–0	21–31	5–8–1	47–55
February 1992	7–1–0	36–18	2–2–0	18–20	9–3–0	54–38
February 1993	2–2–0	12–5	3–5–0	28–37	5–7–0	40–42
February 1994	4–4–1	32–36	0–3–1	8–14	4–7–2	40–50
February 1995	4–2–1	20–19	1–4–1	13–22	5–6–2	33–41
February 1996	3–3–0	21–18	1–4–1	15–26	4–7–1	46–44
February 1997	4–2–0	23–17	0–4–2	12–25	4–6–2	35–42
February 1998	3–2–0	10–10	0–2–0	6–9	3–4–0	16–19
February 1999	2–4–2	19–19	2–4–0	15–17	4–8–2	34–36
February 2000	4–1–0	21–13	4–2–2	21–19	8–3–2	42–32
February 2001	4–2–0	23–16	2–2–1	14–12	6–4–1	37–28
March 1980	3–2–0	24–20	4–4–0	39–41	7–6–0	63–61
March 1981	1–1–2	14–18	5–2–3	47–40	6–3–5	61–58
March 1982	3–1–2	24–19	2–3–2	26–27	5–4–4	50–46

Month	*Home*	*GF–GA*	*Road*	*GF–GA*	*Overall*	*GF–GA*
March 1983	4–0–0	22–13	7–2–0	50–33	11–2–0	72–46
March 1984	7–2–0	49–26	3–1–0	21–13	10–3–0	70–39
March 1985	2–2–3	30–31	3–4–0	36–36	5–6–3	66–67
March 1986	6–0–0	36–16	5–2–1	42–27	11–2–1	78–43
March 1987	7–1–0	44–27	4–3–0	30–29	11–4–0	74–56
March 1988	5–1–0	29–19	3–3–2	35–34	8–4–2	64–53
March 1989	3–3–1	28–29	3–3–1	25–26	6–6–2	53–55
March 1990	4–2–1	30–27	2–3–1	20–21	6–5–2	50–48
March 1991	4–4–1	27–29	3–3–1	24–27	7–7–2	51–56
March 1992	3–1–2	19–16	3–3–1	26–29	6–4–3	45–45
March 1993	2–6–0	28–38	1–4–0	11–24	3–10–0	39–62
March 1994	2–3–0	18–19	3–2–2	26–25	5–5–2	44–44
March 1995	4–4–0	29–33	1–3–1	14–17	5–7–1	43–50
March 1996	2–3–1	20–20	5–3–0	33–29	7–6–1	53–49
March 1997	2–3–0	13–14	4–4–0	25–22	6–7–0	38–36
March 1998	4–2–0	14–9	4–4–0	22–22	8–6–0	36–31
March 1999	3–3–1	18–21	2–4–1	23–28	5–7–2	41–49
March 2000	2–5–0	14–18	2–2–1	12–10	4–7–1	26–28
March 2001	4–2–0	22–14	4–2–1	29–20	8–4–1	51–34
April 1980	1–0–1	7–3	0–1–0	0–5	1–1–1	7–8
April 1981	1–0–1	11–6	1–0–0	7–2	2–0–1	18–8
April 1982	1–0–0	2–1	0–0–0	0–0	1–0–0	2–1
April 1983	1–0–1	10–5	0–0–0	0–0	1–0–1	10–5
April 1984	0–0–0	0–0	0–0–0	0–0	0–0–0	0–0
April 1985	0–1–1	10–11	1–0–0	6–4	1–1–1	16–15
April 1986	1–0–0	8–4	0–1–1	6–11	2–1–0	14–15
April 1987	0–0–1	4–4	1–0–0	7–3	1–0–1	11–7
April 1988	1–0–1	10–7	0–0–0	0–0	1–0–1	10–7
April 1989	0–0–0	0–0	0–1–0	2–4	0–1–0	2–4
April 1990	0–0–0	0–0	1–0–0	4–2	1–0–0	4–2
April 1991	0–0–0	0–0	0–0–0	0–0	0–0–0	0–0
April 1992	1–1–0	8–10	0–0–0	0–0	1–1–0	8–10
April 1993	0–3–0	11–17	0–3–0	6–13	0–6–0	17–30
April 1994	1–1–0	5–6	2–1–2	14–16	3–2–2	19–22
April 1995	2–4–0	11–21	3–4–1	26–37	5–8–1	37–58
April 1996	0–2–0	4–7	1–3–0	12–14	1–5–0	16–21
April 1997	1–1–2	11–13	0–1–0	4–5	1–2–2	15–18
April 1998	4–0–0	16–9	2–2–0	13–12	6–2–0	29–21
April 1999	3–1–0	13–10	2–1–1	12–11	5–2–1	25–21
April 2000	1–2–0	6–7	2–0–0	11–7	3–2–0	17–14
April 2001	0–0–1	2–2	1–1–1	10–10	1–1–2	12–12
May 1995	0–1–0	5–6	0–1–0	3–5	0–2–0	8–11

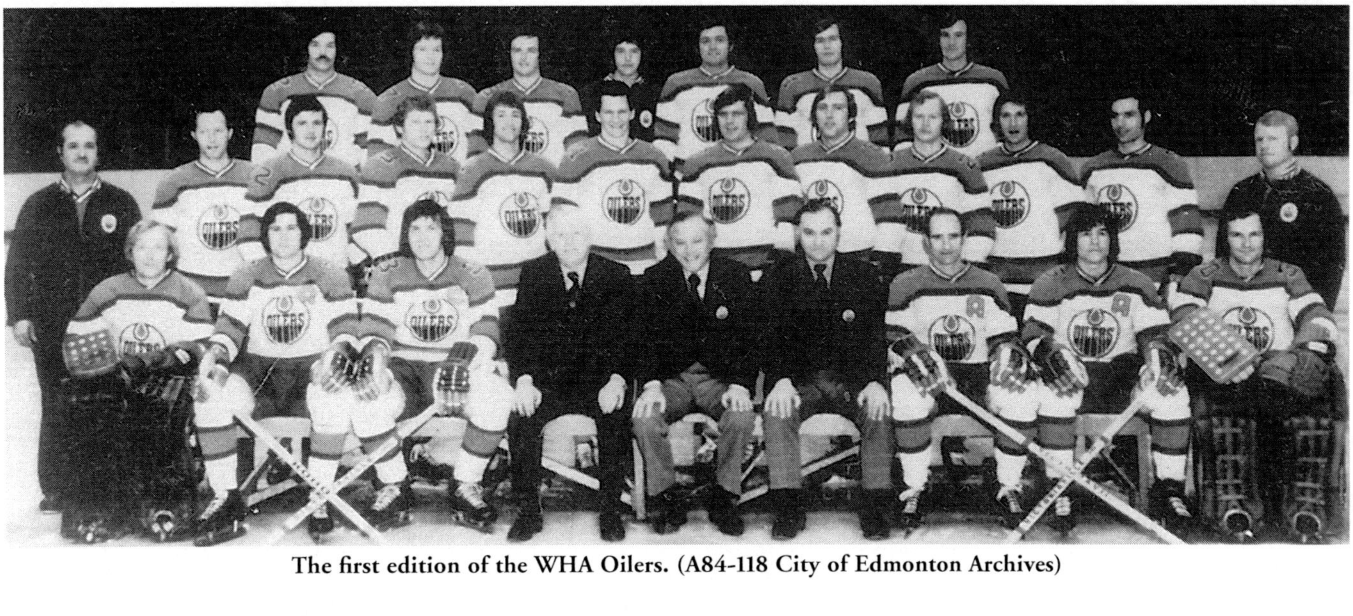

The first edition of the WHA Oilers. (A84-118 City of Edmonton Archives)

The WHA

1972-73

—Edmonton was officially awarded a World Hockey Association franchise on July 12, 1972.
—the team was known in their first year as the Alberta Oilers.
—the franchise awarded to Bill Hunter, majority owner of the Western Canada Hockey League's Edmonton Oil Kings.
—the franchise was then transferred to Edmonton World Hockey Enterprises Ltd. which also took over control of the Oil Kings.
—Chairman of the Board was prominent Edmonton surgeon Charles Allard.
—President was Zane Feldman, Vice-Chairman of Allarco Developments the company run by Dr. Allard.
—Named as Vice-President was E.E. Fitzgibbons, Vice-President and G.M. of Canadian Cablesystems Ltd.
—other board members were W.Z. Estey, Gordon Arnell, and Raymond Barth.
—Bill Hunter remained as Vice-President and G.M. and was in charge of all hockey operations.
—Ray Kinasewich was named as the team's first head coach.
—the team's first office was located on the main floor of the MacDonald Hotel.
—team colors were Royal Blue and Orange.
—the Oilers played in the WHA's first game on October 11, 1972 against the Ottawa Nationals in the Ottawa Civic Center. Ron Anderson of the Oilers scored not only the first goal for the team but the first goal in the league. The Oilers won the game 7-4. The team played their first home game October 17, defeating the Winnipeg Jets 3-2.
—Al Hamilton was named as first Captain, and Doug Barrie was Alternate.
—The Oilers finished their first season with a 38-37-3 record, tied for fourth place in the Western Division.. The team scored 269 goals and allowed 256. They finished last in the league in power play efficiency scoring on only 48 of 284 opportunities for a 16.9% rating. They finished third from the bottom in penalty killing with a 77.7% rating.
—the team was led in scoring by Bonnyville, Alberta born Jim Harrison. The veteran of three NHL seasons, finished the season with 39 goals, 47 assists and 86 points. Harrison was signed to a multi-year contract for a reported $75,000 a season. The previous year he had earned $20,000 playing for the NHL Maple Leafs.
—Although finishing with an identical regular season record as the Minnesota Fighting Saints and despite having a better goals for and goals against record the team was forced to play a tie breaker game to decide a final playoff spot. Minnesota won the game 4-2.
—the Oilers played their first season in the 5,200 Edmonton Gardens.Total attendance was 149,280.
—first season lineup and sweater numbers: **10**-Ron Anderson 73-14-15-29-43, **19**-Ken Baird 75-14-15-29-112, **5**-Doug Barrie 54-9-22-31-111, **22**-Jim Benzelock (traded to the Chicago Cougars for Bernie Blanchette) 26-1-1-2-10, Bernie Blanchette (obtained in a trade with the Chicago Cougars for Jim Benzelock) 23-5-4-9-2, **14**-Brian Carlin 65-12-22-34-6, **20**-Steve Carlyle 67-7-10-17-35, **2**-Roger Cote 61-3-5-8-46, **6**-Bob Falkenberg 76-6-23-29-44, **21**-John Fisher 40-0-5-5-0, **8**-Val Fonteyne 77-7-32-39-2, **3**-Al Hamilton 78-11-50-61-124, **27**-Derek Harker 1-0-0-0-0, **7**-Jim Harrison 66-39-47-86-93, **12**-Bill Hicke 73-14-24-38-20, **16**-Ed Joyal 71-22-16-38-16, **15**-Dennis Kassian 50-6-7-13-14, **18**-Bob McAneeley 51-5-7-12-24, **17**-Rusty Patenaude 77-29-27-56-59, **9**-Ross Perkins 71-21-37-58-19, **4**-Bob Wall 78-16-29-45-20, **11**-Ron Walters 78-28-26-54-37, **1**-Ken Brown (Goal) 20-10-8-0-3.66, **30**-Jack Norris (Goal) 64-28-29-3-3.06.

1973-74

—Brian Shaw took over the coaching reins for the 1973-74 season. Bill Hunter remained as G.M.
—Edmonton finished the season a 38-37-3 record. This was identical to their 1972-73 record but this year it allowed them to finish in third place in the Western Division. The Oilers scored 268 goals and allowed 269.
—the leading scorer was Ron Climie who had 38 goals and 36 assists for 74 points. Last year's leading scorer Jim Harrison scored 24 goals and contributed 45 assists in only 46 games.
—Al Hamilton was named to the WHA's 2nd All-Star Team on defense.
—the Oilers played the Minnesota Fighting Saints in the playoffs losing a best of seven series 4 games to 1. The team lost 2-1, 8-5 and 6-2 in their first three playoff games all played at home, before defeating the Saints 2-1 in Minnesota and then losing their final game 5-4 on the road.
—attendance for the season was 172,737 in the 5,200 seat Edmonton Gardens.
—this season's line-up and sweater numbers: Ron Anderson 19-5-2-7-6, **19**-Ken Baird 68-17-19-36-115, **5**-Doug Barrie 69-4-27-31-214, Brian Carlin 5-1-0-1-0, **20**-Steve Carlyle 50-2-13-15-18, **11**-Ron Climie 76-38-36-74-22, Hal Colborne 2-0-0-0-0, **2**-Roger Cote 59-0-3-3-34, Gary Cunningham 2-0-0-0-0, **6**-Bob Falkenberg 78-3-14-17-32, **21**-Bob Fitchner 31-1-2-3-21, **8**-Val Fonteyne 72-9-13-22-2, **10**-Tom Gilmore 71-17-18-35-191, **3**-Al Hamilton 77-14-45-59-104, **7**-Jim Harrison 46-24-45-69-99, **16**-Eddie Joyal 45-8-10-18-2, Len Lunde 71-26-22-48-8, **18**-Bob McAneeley 52-12-11-23-49, **22**-Jim "Mountain" McCrimmon 75-2-3-5-106, **14**-Blair MacDonald 78-21-24-45-24, **12**-Brian McKenzie 78-18-20-38-66, **17**-Rusty Patenaude 71-20-23-43-55, **9**-Ross Perkins 78-16-40-56-43, Jim Schraefel 34-1-1-2-0, Bobby Sheehan (traded to the Oilers for future considerations) 10-1-3-4-6, **4**-Bob Wall 74-6-31-37-46, Wayne Zuk (traded to Los Angeles for Ian Wilkie) 2-0-0-0-0, Gary Doyle (Goal) 1-1-0-0-4.00, **30**-Jack Norris (Goal) 53-23-24-1-3.21, Ian Wilkie [(Goal)-traded to the Oilers for Wayne Zuk] 5-3-1-0-2.11, **1**-Chris Worthy (Goal) 29-11-12-1-3.80

1974-75

—Brian Shaw began the season as coach and guided the team to a 30-26-3 record, before G.M. Bill Hunter took over behind the bench. The team posted a 6-12-1 record with Hunter as coach.
—the team finished the season with a 36-38-4 record, which, although only 3 points less than they had ended up with in each of the previous 2 seasons, was only good enough for 5th and last spot in the league's tough Canadian Division.
—the team scored 279 goals, while allowing an equal amount.
—Doug Barrie took over as Captain when Al Hamilton was injured. Barry Long and Bruce MacGregor were named as Alternate Captains.
—Rookie Mike Rogers led the team in scoring with 35 goals and 48 assists in 78 games and was named as the league's Most Gentlemanly Player, although losing out to future superstar Anders Hedberg in Rookie of the Year balloting. Hedberg scored 53 goals and added 47 assists in only 65 games
—Barry Long was named to the WHA's 2nd All-Star team on defense.
—the Oilers signed 45 year old goaltender Jacques Plante to a contract. After having sat out the previous season to try his hand at coaching, Plante played in 31 games; winning 15, losing 14 and tying 1, posting a 3.32 average.
—attendance for the 1974-75 season was 428,880 in the new 16,000 seat coliseum. The new venue also played host to the league's annual All-Star Game on January 21, 1975 when the Western Division defeated the Eastern Division 6-4.
—this season's line-up and sweater numbers: **19**-Ken Baird 77-20-28-58-151, **5**-Doug Barrie 78-12-33-45-122, Ron Buchanan (obtained from Cleveland by the Oilers for Jim Harrison and subsequently traded by the Oilers to Indianapolis for Murray Kennett), 22-6-9-15-4 **20**-Steve Carlyle 73-4-25-29-46, **11**-Ron Climie (traded to New England for Tim Sheehy) 49-15-7-42-15, **10**-Tom Gilmore 74-12-19-31-84, **3**-Al Hamilton 25-1-13-14-42, **8**-Don Herriman 33-1-2-3-21, **16**-Eddie Joyal 78-22-25-47-2, **15**-Murray Kennett (traded to the Oilers by Cleveland for Ron Buchanan) 50-4-14-18-17, Doug Kerslake 10-4-0-4-10, **21**-Bill Laing 43-2-4-6-32, **2**-Barry Long 78-20-40-60-116, **12**-Bruce MacGregor 72-24-28-52-10, **22**-Jim "Mountain" McCrimmon 34-1-5-6-50, **14**-Blair MacDonald 72-22-24-46-14, **4**-Ray McKay 69-8-20-28-47, **11**-Bill Morris 36-4-8-12-6, **17**-Rusty Patenaude 56-20-16-36-38, **9**-Ross Perkins 76-7-16-23-33, **18**-Mike Rogers 78-35-48-83-2, **7**-Bobby Sheehan 77-19-39-58-8, **15**-Tim Sheehy (traded to the Oilers from New England for Ron Climie) 29-8-20-28-4, **27**-Ken Brown (Goal), 32-11-11-0-3.48, **1**-Jacques Plante (Goal) 31-15-14-1-3.32, **30**-Chris Worthy (Goal) 29-11-13-3-3.58

1975-76

—The coaching duties were assumed this year by collegiate coaching legend Clare Drake, formerly of the University of Alberta. Drake, whose U. of A. Golden Bears had won the C.I.A.U. championship in 1975, was replaced in mid season by General Manager Bill Hunter. The team posted a 18-28-2 record with Drake behind the bench and only a 9-21-3 record with Hunter as coach.
—the Oilers scored 268 goals while allowing a whopping 345. This was exceeded only by the inept defense of the Toronto Toros who allowed 398 goals.
—41 year old Norm Ullman led the team in scoring with 31 goals and 56 assists in 77 games.
—the Oilers special teams finished in the bottom half of the league with an 18.1% power play while their penalty killers could only manage to kill off 78.8% of their penalties.
—the Oilers met the Winnipeg Jets in the postseason playoffs. Edmonton lost all four games to the Jets, 7-3 and 5-4 in Winnipeg and 3-2 and 7-2 in Edmonton. The second game in Winnipeg went into overtime with the Jets scoring at the 54 second mark of the first overtime period.
—attendance in 1975-76 was 317,234, capacity of the Coliseum this year was 15,273.
—Nelson Skalbania and Peter Pocklington became involved in the ownership group along with Charles Allard and Zane Feldman. Pocklington and Skalbania assumed full ownership at the end of the season.
—this season's lineup and sweater numbers: **19**-Ken Baird 48-13-24-37-87, **5**-Doug Barrie 79-4-21-25-81, **8**-Wayne Carleton (traded to the Oilers with Paul Hurley for Mike Rogers by the New England Whalers) 26-5-16-21-6, **20**-Jack Carlson (obtained from Minnesota) 10-1-1-2-31, **20**-Steve Carlyle 28-0-11-11-10, Bill Evo (traded to Cleveland)-8-0-4-4-0, **3**-Al Hamilton 54-2-32-34-78, **6**-Paul Hurley (traded to the Oilers with Wayne Carleton for Mike Rogers by New England) 26-1-4-5-14, **16**-Eddie Joyal 45-5-4-9-6, **6**-Murray Kennett 28-3-4-7-14, **14**-Doug Kerslake 13-1-1-2-4, Kerry Ketter 48-1-9-10-20, Skip Krake 41-8-8-16-55, **21**-Bill Laing 54-8-12-20-67, **2**-Barry Long 78-10-32-42-66, **14**-Blair MacDonald 25-7-5-12-8 **12**-Bruce MacGregor 63-13-10-23-13, **18**-Bob McAneeley 71-12-16-28-60, **23**-Ted McAneeley 79-2-17-19-71, **22** Peter Morris 75-7-13-20-34, 7-Rick Morris (traded from Ottawa) 33-11-15-26-52 , **26**-Wayne Muloin 10-1-1-2-0, **17**-Rusty Patenaude 77-42-30-72-88, **10**-John Rogers 44-9-8-17-34, **18**-Mike Rogers (traded to New England for Wayne Carleton and Paul Hurley) 44-12-15-27-10, **25**-Bob Russell 58-13-18-31-19, **15**-Tim Sheehy 81-34-31-65-17, **24**-Dan Spring 75-12-11-23-8, **9**-Norm Ullman 77-31-56-87-12, **28**-Dave Dryden (Goal) 62-22-34-5-3.95, Frank Turnbull (Goal) 3-0-1-0-5.09, **30**-Chris Worthy (Goal) 24-5-14-0-4.68

1976-77

—after Skalbania and Pocklington took control of the team, Assistant G.M. Gord Robson moved up to become Executive Vice President and Mitch Klimove remained as President.
—March 2, 1977, Peter Pocklington took control of the team from Skalbania.
—Bep Guidolin began the season as both coach and General Manager. After a 25-36-2 record Guidolin was replaced as coach by Glen Sather but still retained the post of G.M. In Sather's first year as coach the team won 9, lost 7 and tied 2.
—the team scored 243 goals and allowed 304 and finished in fourth place in the Western Division.
—the power play team operated at 20.7% and the penalty killers finished third in the league operating at a 79.1% rate.
—Bryan Campbell and Bill Flett led the team in scoring. Flett socred 34 goals and added 20 helpers in 48 games after coming over from the NHL's Atlanta Flames, while Campbell scored 12 times and added 42 assists in 66 games.
—the Oilers met the Houston Aeros in the first round of the playoffs. Houston won the first two games at home by scores of 4-3 and 6-2. The first game was decided after 13 minutes and 11 seconds of overtime. The next two games were played at home and the Oilers won the first 7-2 but lost the second one 4-1. The Aeros then wrapped up the series by winning the fifth game 4-3 at home.
—attendance this year was 343,868 with capacity being about 15,000.
—this season's lineup and sweater numbers: Mike Antonovich (traded from Minnesota) 7-1-1-2-0, Danny Arndt (traded from New England) 1-0-0-0-0, **19**-Ken Baird (traded to Calgary) 2-1-2-3-0, **5**-Doug Barrie 70-8-19-27-27, **27**-Frank "Seldom" Beaton 68-4-9-13-274, **2**-Gregg Boddy (traded to the Oilers from San Diego for Larry Hornung) 64-2-19-21-60, **8**-Ron Busniuk (traded to the Oilers from New England) 29-2-2-4-83, Bill Butters 7-0-2-2-17, **18**-Brett Callighen (traded from New England) 29-9-16-

25-48, **21**-Bryan Campbell (traded from Indianapolis to the Oilers for Gene Peacosh) 66-12-42-54-18, **12**-Wayne Connelly (traded to the Oilers from Calgary) 38-13-15-28-18, **19**-Bill Flett 48-34-20-54-20, Joe Fortunato 1-0-0-0-0, **3**-Al Hamilton 81-8-37-45-60, **4**-Larry Hornung (traded to San Diego for Gregg Boddy) 21-2-1-3-0, **10**-Gavin Kirk (traded from Birmingham Bulls to the Oilers for Tim Sheehy) 52-8-28-36-16, **20**-Pete Laframboise 17-0-5-5-12, **26**-Dave Langevin 77-7-16-23-94, **2**-Barry Long (traded to Winnipeg) 2-0-1-1-2, **11**-Barry Merrell 10-1-3-4-0, **22**-Peter Morris 3-0-0-0-0, **7**-Rick Morris 79-18-17-35-76, **8**-Bob Nevin 13-3-2-5-0, **17**-Rusty Patenaude 73-25-16-41-57, **24**-Glenn Patrick 23-0-4-4-62, **23**-Dennis Patterson 23-0-2-2-2, **21**-Gene Peacosh (traded to Indianapolis for Bryan Campbell) 11-5-4-9-14, Bill Prentice 3-0-0-0-2, **20**-Randy Rota 40-9-6-15-8, **25**-Bob Russell 57-7-6-13-41, **15**-Claude St. Sauveur (traded to the Oilers by Calgary) 15-5-7-12-2, **14**-Glen "Slats" Sather 81-19-34-53-77, **10**-Ted Scharf 5-0-2-2-14, **15**-Tim Sheehy (traded to Birmingham for Gavin Kirk) 28-15-8-23-4, **16**-Tom Simpson (traded from Birmingham with Gavin Kirk for Tim Sheehy) 15-3-2-5-16, **16**-Paul Stewart 2-0-0-0-2, **9**-Norm Ullman 67-16-27-43-28, **6**-Barry Wilkins 51-4-24-2-75, **12**-Warren "Butch" Williams 29-3-10-13-16, **1**-Ken Broderick (Goal) 40-18-18-1-3.49, **28**-Dave Dryden (Goal) 24-10-13-0-3.26, **30**-Louis Levasseur [(Goal) traded from Minnesota to the Oilers] 21-6-12-3-4.35

1977-78

—Glen Sather took over full time duties as Coach and Director of Hockey Operations. Brian Conacher was named as the team's General Manager.
—the team finished the season with a 38-39-3 record, scoring 309 goals and allowing 307. The Oilers finished in 5th place in the league's single division.
—the season's leading scorer was Ron Chipperfield who scored 33 goals and added 52 assists in 80 games.
—goaltender Don "Smokey" MacLeod assisted on 8 goals in the 33 games in which he played.
—Al Hamilton was named to the league's first All-Star team.
—the Oilers met the New England Whalers in the first round of the playoffs, losing the first two games in Hartford by scores of 6-4 and 4-1. The series then moved to Edmonton for the next two games. The Oilers won the first game, shutting out the Whalers by a 2-0 score. The Whalers more than avenged that shutout by trouncing the Oilers by a 9-1 score. The Whalers then ended the series at home defeating Edmonton 4-1.
—attendance this year was 429,343 with building capacity at 15,273.
—this season's lineup and sweater numbers: Chris Ahrens 4-0-0-0-15, **8**-Ron Busniuk 59-2-18-20-157, **18**-Brett Callighen 80-20-30-50-112, **21**-Bryan "Soupy" Campbell 73-7-13-20-12, 7-Ron Chipperfield 80-33-52-86-48, Jim Cross 2-0-0-0-0, Butch Deadmarsh (traded to Cincinnati for Del Hall and Dennis Sobchuk) 20-1-3-4-32, **5**-Ab Demarco 47-6-8-14-20, Bob Falkenberg 2-0-0-0, **9**-Norm Ferguson 71-26-21-47-2, **19**-Bill "Cowboy" Flett 74-41-28-69-34, **16**-Pierre Guite (traded from Quebec with Don MacLeod for Rick Morris, Ken Broderick and Dave Inkpen) 60-12-21-33-71, **15**-Del Hall (traded from Cincinnati with Dennis Sobchuk for Butch Deadmarsh) 1-0-0-0-0, **3**-Al Hamilton 59-11-43-54-46, **24**-Jerry Holland 14-1-4-5-4, Dave Inkpen (traded to Quebec with Rick Morris and Ken Broderick for Pierre Guite and Don MacLeod) 19-0-1-1-16, **22**-Pierre Jarry 18-4-10-14-4, **26**-Dave Langevin 62-6-22-28-90, Owen Lloyd 3-0-1-1-4, **14**-Blair MacDonald 80-34-34-68-11, **17**-Gary MacGregor 37-11-2-13-29, **17**-Ray McKay 14-1-4-5-4, Dale McMullen 1-0-0-0, **4**-Joe Micheletti 56-14-34-48-56, Warren Miller (traded to Quebec with Rick Morris and Ken Broderick for Pierre Guite and Don MacLeod) 18-2-4-6-18, Rick Morris (traded to Quebec for Warren Miller and Ken Broderick for Pierre Guite and Don MacLeod) 5-1-1-2-7, Gerry Pinder 5-0-1-1-4, **15**-Kevin Primeau 7-0-1-1-2, **20**-Randy Rota 53-8-22-30-12, **2**-Cal Sandbeck 11-1-2-3-39, **27**-Dave "Sammy" Semenko 65-6-6-12-140, **6**-Paul Shmyr 80-9-40-49-100, **10**-Dennis Sobchuk (traded from Cincinnati with Del Hall for Butch Deadmarsh) 13-6-3-9-4, Craig Topolnisky 10-0-2-2-4, **23**-Jim Troy 47-2-0-2-124, **11**-Juha Widing 71-18-24-42-8, **12**-Mike Zuke 71-23-34-57-47, **1**-Ken Broderick [(Goal) traded to Quebec with Rick Morris and Warren Miller for Pierre Guite and Don MacLeod] 9-2-5-0-5.07, **28**-Dave Dryden (Goal) 48-21-23-2-3.49, **1**-Don MacLeod [(Goal) traded from Quebec with Pierre Guite for Rick Morris and Ken Broderick and Dave Inkpen] 33-15-9-1-3.55, Frank Turnbull (Goal) 1-0-1-0-6.00

1978-79

—Glen Sather remained behind the bench as coach and Vice President of Hockey Operations but Larry Gordon took over the G.M. position, replacing Brian Conacher.
—the team finished in first place in the league for the first time in their history, winning 48 games losing 30 and tying two. They also led the league in goals for and goals against, scoring 340 and allowing 266.
—Rookie Wayne Gretzky led the team in scoring with 43 goals and 61 assists in 72 games with the Oilers and won the Rookie of the Year Award. Dave Dryden led the league in goals against average, with an average of 2.89 in 63 games and capped off a spectacular season by winning the league's best goaltender award and the M.V.P. award.
—Dryden was named to the league's first All-Star team in goal. Three Oiler players were named to the second All-Star team: Dave Langevin on defense, Wayne Gretzky at center and Blair MacDonald at right wing.
—a three game All-Star break was scheduled for the Coliseum in January 1979. The WHA All-Stars met a Soviet team and defeated them in all three games.
—after leading the league in points in the regular season the team was expected to win their first WHA championship. They struggled however in the first round of the playoffs against the New England Whalers but eventually defeated them 4 games to 3 in a seven game series. In the first two games at Edmonton the Oilers won 6-2 and 9-5. The series then moved back to Springfield where the Oilers lost to the Whalers 4-1 and 5-1. The Oilers then won 5-2 at home and lost 8-4 back in Springfield. The teams then met in game 7 at Edmonton, with the Oilers emerging victorious by a score of 6-3.
—The Oilers then met Winnipeg in the championship series losing to the Jets 4 games to 2. After losing to the Jets at home by scores of 3-1 and 3-2 the series moved to Winnipeg. The Oilers won the first road game by an 8-3 margin but lost the second game 3-2. The Oilers got right back into the series in the next game at home, trouncing the Jets by a 10-2 score. Edmonton then lost the final game of the series in Winnipeg when the Jets defeated the Oilers 7-3.
—Dave Semenko scored the very last goal in the WHA, at 19:48 of the third period in game 6 of the Winnipeg series.
—attendance for the season was 461,347 with Coliseum capacity at 15,273.
—this season's lineup and sweater numbers: **5**-Claire Alexander 54-8-23-31-16, **17**-Ace Bailey 38-5-4-9-22, **11**-Doug Berry 29-6-3-9-4, **18**-Brett Callighen 71-31-39-70-79, **23**-Steve Carlson 73-18-22-40-50, 7-Ron Chipperfield 55-32-37-69-47, **24**-Peter Driscoll (obtained from Indianapolis with Wayne Gretzky and Ed Mio for cash and future considerations) 69-17-23-40-115, **19**-Bill Flett 73-28-36-64-14, **8**-Wes George (obtained from Indianapolis) 3-0-0-0-11, **9**-Bill Goldsworthy 17-4-2-6-14, **99**-Wayne Gret-

SkyReach Center (the circular building in the background). (EA117-145 City of Edmonton Archives)

zky (obtained from Indianapolis with Peter Driscoll and Ed Mio for cash and future considerations) 72-43-61-104-19, **16**-Pierre Guite 12-1-1-2-8, **3**-Al Hamilton 80-6-38-44-38, **20**-John Hughes 41-2-15-17-82, **12**-Dave Hunter 72-7-25-32-134, **26**-Dave Langevin 77-6-21-27-76, **14**-Blair MacDonald 80-34-37-71-44, **25**-Jim Mayer 2-0-0-0-0, **4**-Joe Micheletti 72-14-33-47-85, **15**-Jim Neilson 35-0-5-5-18, **2**-Cal Sandbeck 6-0-0-0-2, **27**-Dave Semenko 77-10-14-24-158, **6**-Paul Shmyr 80-8-39-47-119, **8**-Risto Siltanen 20-3-4-7-4, **10**-Dennis Sobchuk 74-26-37-63-31, **8**-Rudy Tajcnar 2-0-0-0-0, **21**-Stan Weir 68-31-30-61-20, **28**-Dave Dryden (Goal) 63-41-17-2-2.89, **35**-Hannu Kampurri (Goal) 2-0-1-0-6.67, **31**-Ed Mio [(Goal) obtained from Indianapolis with Wayne Gretzky and Peter Driscoll for cash and future considerations) 22-7-10-0-3.99, **30**-Ed Walsh (Goal) 3-0-2-0-3.75

Skyreach Centre

First opened in 1974, the $15 million coliseum has been home to the Oilers since their third WHA season.

Edmonton's Coliseum was built in what had been, just after the turn of the century, the residential area of Eastwood. The site was adjacent to the grounds of the Edmonton Exhibition Association, which had occupied the site since early in the century, and who would for the first few years operate the facility.

The building originally seated 15,326 fans, but was capable of being expanded to around 17,000. The five level complex would be able to house a 21 story building beneath the ceiling. Some of the original features included high density lighting to accommodate television coverage of events, air conditioning, escalators and elevators to provide access to all three public levels, and a gondola near roof top to accommodate media coverage. There was originally a 200 seat restaurant, cocktail lounges, dressing rooms and a press area.

The first game was a sell out and the team sold out a further five games in the first season in the new building. Attendance the first season would range anywhere from the 15,326 fans attending the first game to the 6,565 attending a January 10, 1975 game against Indianapolis. In 1979-80 the average ticket price was around $10. This was the highest average price in the league.

Capacity would be increased to 15,423 when the team joined the NHL and regularly increased to 17,503 by 1994.

In 1994 the Coliseum underwent a massive $14 million renovation. The new features included a brand new eight sided three story high scoreboard, the addition of new skyboxes, seats and washrooms. With the addition of the skyboxes, seating capacity would now be 17,099.

The summer long project was supervised by architect Bob Walker, and would take the work crews 20 hours a day, 7 days a week to complete. Even at this pace the project might not have been ready for the opening of the 1994-95 season, if not for the player lockout which moved the opening date for hockey to January 20, 1995.

On September 23, 1998 the Coliseum was renamed the Skyreach Centre. Skyreach Equipment Ltd., a business which specializes in aerial work platforms, is based in nearby St. Albert. Skyreach president Barry Weaver is a member of the Edmonton Investors Group.

	Regular Season Attendance						*Playoff Attendance*				
Year	***Cap.***	***G***	***SO***	***Possible***	***Att.***	***%***	***Cap.***	***G***	***Possible***	***Att.***	***%***
2000-01	17100	41	14	701100	640085	91.3	17100	3	51300	51300	100.0
1999-00	17100	41	19	701100	647935	92.4	17100	2	34200	34200	100.0
1998-99	17100	41	19	701100	666641	95.1	17100	2	34200	34200	100.0
1997-98	17099	41	22	701059	666033	95.0	17099	5	85495	85495	100.0
1996-97	17099	41	12	701059	657786	93.8	17099	5	85495	85495	100.0
1995-96	17103	41	7	701223	505734	72.1	The Oilers did not reach the playoffs.				
1994-95	16441	24	0	394584	314972	79.8	The Oilers did not reach the playoffs.				
1993-94	17503	41	3	717623	552581	77.0	The Oilers did not reach the playoffs.				
1992-93	17503	41	6	717623	606677	84.5	The Oilers did not reach the playoffs.				
1991-92	17503	40	7	700120	647170	92.4	17503	8	140024	133513	95.4
1990-91	17503	40	15	700120	673749	96.2	17503	9	157527	156845	99.6
1989-90	17503	40	15	700120	680333	97.2	17503	11	192533	190360	98.9
1988-89	17503	40	13	700120	673800	96.2	17503	3	52509	52357	99.7
1987-88	17502	40	18	700080	678290	96.9	17502	11	192522	190535	99.0
1986-87	17498	40	25	699920	691919	98.9	17502	12	210024	206846	98.5
1985-86	17498	40	40	699920	692771	99.0	17498	6	104988	104393	99.4
1984-85	17498	40	40	699920	699920	100.0	17498	10	174980	172015	98.3
1983-84	17498	40	40	699920	699920	100.0	17498	11	192478	192069	99.8
1982-83	17490	40	40	699600	699920	100.0	17498	9	157482	157482	100.0
1981-82	17490	40	40	699600	696600	100.0	17490	3	52470	52470	100.0
1980-81	17291	40	40	691640	697427	100.8	17490	4	69960	69960	100.0
1979-80	15423	40	40	616920	616717	100.0	15423	1	15423	15423	100.0

The Front Office

Owners-Edmonton Investors Group (1998-
Owner/Governor-Peter Pocklington (1979-1998)
Governor-Jim Hole (1998-2000); Cal Nichols (2000-present)
Alternate Governor-Larry Gordon (1979); Glen Sather (1980-2000); Kevin Lowe (2000-present); Gordon Buchanan (2000-present)
President-Glen Sather (1980-2000); Pat LaForge (2000-present)
Assistant to the President-Ted Green (1994-96)
General Counsel-Lynn Patrick (1979-1981); Gary Frohlich (1981-1992); Bob Kinasewich (1982-84); Bob Lloyd (1985-1992); Lorne Ruzicka (1993-95)
Executive Vice-President-Larry Gordon (1979); Bruce MacGregor (1990-2000)
Assistant to the Vice-Presidents-Bryan Watson (1979)
General Manager-Larry Gordon (1979); Glen Sather (1980-2000); Kevin Lowe (2000-
Assistant General Manager-Bruce MacGregor (1980-2000); Scott Howson (2000-
Vice-President of Hockey Operations-Glen Sather (1979); Doug Risebrough (1997-1999)
Coach-Glen Sather (1979-1988, 1994); Bryan Watson (1980); John Muckler (1989-1990); Ted Green (1991-1993); George Burnett (1994); Ron Low (1995-1999); Kevin Lowe (1999-2000); Craig MacTavish (2000-
Associate/Assistant/Co Coach-Bryan Watson (1980); Billy Harris (1981); Ted Green (1981-84, 86-90, 97-2000); John Muckler (1982-1988); Bob McCammon (1985, 1995-1998); Ron Low (1989-1994); Kevin Primeau (1991-96); Kevin Lowe (1998-99); Craig MacTavish (1999-2000); Charlie Huddy (2000-present); Billy Moores (2000-present)
Goaltender Coach-Pete Peeters (1997-98, 2000-01)
Administrative Assistant Hockey Operations-Kevin Prendergast (1990-94)
Director of Hockey Administration-Steve Pellegrini (1995-1998)
Co-ordinator of Development-Curt Brackenbury (1994-95)
Director of Player Personnel-Bruce MacGregor (1979); Barry Fraser (1982-94)
Director of Player Personnel/Hockey Operations-Kevin Prendergast (1995-
Director of Player Development-Bob McCammon (1986)
Scouting Staff-Barry Fraser (Chief Scout) (1979-2000); Len Lunde (European) (1979-80); Jim Neilson (Western) (1979); Lorne Davis (1980-; Vic Hadfield (1981); Ace Bailey (1981-1993); Bob Freeman (1981-95); Ed Chadwick (1982-; Matti Vaisanen (1985-90); Bucky Kane (1985); Albert Reeves (1986-87, 1989-95); Jan Slepicka (1991-1993); Harry Howell (1991-; Brad Smith (1991-1994); Bob McCammon (1994); Brad MacGregor (1995-96); Pete Mahovlich (1995-96); Chris McCarthy (1995-; Kent Nilsson (1995-; Michael Georges (1996); Brad Davis (1997-; Gilles Leger (1997-; Dave Semenko (1997-; Tom Thompson (1997-1999); Bob Mancini (2000-present); Gord Pell (2000-present); Stuart MacGregor (2000-present)

MEDICAL/TRAINING

Athletic Trainer/Therapist-Peter Millar (1979-1988); Ken Lowe (1989-
Trainer-John Blackwell (1979); Kelly Pruden (1980-81); Barrie Stafford (1982-95)
Assistant Trainer-Lyle Kulchisky (1981-95)
Equipment Manager-Barrie Stafford (1996-
Assistant Equipment Manager-Lyle Kulchisky (1996-
Massage Therapist-Juergen Merz (1987); Stewart Poirier (1989-93, 1997-; Roland Kelly (1995-96)
Team Medical Chief of Staff-Dr. Gordon Cameron (1989-92); Dr. David C. Reid (1993-
Team Physician-Dr. Gordon Cameron (1979-1988); Dr. Don Groot (1989-; Dr. Boris Boyko (1993-; Dr. Steven Aung (1993)
Team Acupuncturist-Dr. Steven Aung (1994-
Physical Therapy Consultant-Dr. Dave Magee (1989-
Team Orthopedic Surgeon-Dr. David C. Reid (1991-
Team Dentist-Dr. Brian Nord (1979-1983, 1988-; Dr. W.M. Taskey (1984-1987); Dr. A.H. Sneazwell (1988-
Fitness Consultant-Dr. Art Quinney (1982-; Daryl Duke (1996-
Dressing Room Attendant-Joey Moss

PUBLIC RELATIONS

Public Relations Manager-Bryn Griffiths (1997-
Director of Public Relations-John Short (1979); Bill Tuele (1980-96)
Vice President, Public Relations-Bill Tuele (1997-
Public Relations Assistant-Dan Taylor (1996)
Public Relations Service Representative-Ryan Gillis (1996)
Public Relations Secretary-Debbie VanOs (1988); Fiona Liew (1989-96)
Community Relations & Communications Co-ordinator-Fiona Liew (1997-

BUSINESS

Executive V.P. Business Operations-Doug Piper (1996-2000)
Manager, Corporate Sponsorship-Brad MacGregor (1996-
Manager, Corporate Sponsorship-Greg McDannold (1996-
Vice President, Sponsorships, Sales and Service-Allan Watt (1997-
Vice President Corporate Communications-Trish Kerr (1997-1999)

SPECIAL MENTION

Radio Voice of the Oilers-Rod Phillips
Anthem Singer-Paul Lorieau

Edmonton Oilers Fast Facts

The WHA Oilers staged the largest of the early player raids on the rival NHL. Edmonton signed defenseman Al Hamilton from the Buffalo Sabres, Ed Joyal from Philadelphia, Brian Carlin and Doug Barrie from Los Angeles, and Bob Wall from Detroit. Edmonton would also sign minor league players Ross Perkins and Roger Cote to contracts. The signing of these players was announced June 6, 1972, and they were the first players signed to contracts by the Oilers.

Unheralded Don Ashby registered 6 points in the March 29, 1980, game against Toronto. Playing on a line with Wayne Gretzky and Blair MacDonald, Ashby scored 3 goals and added 3 assists against Mike Palmateer in the Toronto net. Gretzky also scored 6 points, while MacDonald added four. Gretzky assisted on all three of Ashby's goals, added an assist on MacDonald's goal and also added two goals of his own. Ashby scored 19 points while playing in only 18 games in the 1979-80 season. He would be killed in a car accident, May 30, 1981 near Summerland, British Columbia, just two miles from his home of Kamloops.

The Edmonton Oilers had their own version of a two sport athlete. Jim Corsi, who had a graduate degree in engineering, played 26 games in goal for the Oilers during the 1979-80 season. Several years earlier Corsi had played seven games for the Montreal team of the North American Soccer League as a midfielder and scored one goal for the Olympiques. Corsi also played three years for the Canadian Olympic soccer team and joined the team on a European tour one year. During the 1980-81 season Corsi appeared with the Italian National Team, playing seven games with the team which won the "B" pool of the World Championships.

Dave Semenko, not noted as an offensive player, scored seven of his nineteen points in the 1980-81 season in a span of three games. "Sammy" scored one goal against Billy Smith and the Islanders in a 5–5 tie on October 18. The following night against the Rangers, Semenko scored a hattrick and added one assist against Wayne Thomas in the Rangers' net. The Oilers won 4–2. On October 22, Semenko scored twice more against Daniel Bouchard in the Calgary net and Edmonton won the game 5–3. Wayne Gretzky assisted on all of Semenko's goals and scored the goal on which Semenko assisted. Semenko, who scored only 11 goals all year, scored six of them in this three game stretch.

Rod Phillips has broadcast almost every Oiler hockey game since the 1973-74 season, when the team was still a member of the World Hockey Association. From 1974 until 1992, Phillips broadcast the games on 1260 CFRN radio. For the next three years the broadcast rights were held by 790 CFCW and since the 1995-96 season Phillips has broadcast the games for 630 CHED radio. Though working with a variety of analysts over the years, Phillips himself has missed hardly any games. Prior to the November 25, 1997, game against Chicago, Rod was presented with a silver hockey stick by the Oiler organization to commemorate 25 years of broadcasting the games. He is one of seven individuals to receive such an honor from the team. Wayne Gretzky, Mark Messier, Jari Kurri, Glenn Anderson, Bruce MacGregor and equipment manager Barrie Stafford each received a silver stick from the Oilers to commemorate milestones. Phillips was so overcome by the presentation that he was unable to broadcast the first period of the game against the Blackhawks. Bryan Hall had broadcast the team games for the 1972-73 season, their first in the World Hockey Association, for CJCA radio.

The Oilers uniform had remained substantially the same from when the team first joined the WHA in 1972. The first road uniforms were basically orange with a blue stripe across the shoulders down to an area midway between the shoulder and elbow and running horizontally across the front of the jersey and bordered by a thin white stripe. There was also a blue stripe at the elbows which was bordered by a thin white stripe. The home uniform was white with orange on the shoulders and was bordered by blue. The logo was the familiar white with blue writing and an orange oil drop. As time passed the patches at the shoulders and across the front shrank to cover only the shoulders, and the base color for the road uniform was changed to blue from orange. By the 1978-79 season the logo on the home uniform was orange with "Oilers" written in blue, and the oil drop was white. By the next season when the team joined the National Hockey League the uniform had taken on the look which longtime fans have become familiar with. At the start of the 1996-97 season the team changed its road jersey's colors to a base of Midnight Blue, trimmed with metallic copper, red and white. The home uniform had a base color of white, trimmed with Midnight Blue, white and red. The uniform now also sported a small logo on each shoulder, which showed a stylized representation of an oil worker. In June 2001 it was announced that the team would sport a third uniform, designed by team investor and world famous comic book illustrator Todd McFarlane.

Edmonton native Garry Unger, who played 88 games with the Oilers over a span of three seasons, was at one time the NHL's iron man. Unger appeared in 914 consecutive regular season games from February 24, 1968, until December 21, 1979.

Although he had hurt his shoulder in a game against Winnipeg on December 9, 1979, Unger remained in the Atlanta Flames lineup and was dressed for the Flames when they met St. Louis in the December 22nd game. It was reported that Flames coach Al MacNeil had to physically restrain Unger from going on the ice against his former team. MacNeil was concerned that Unger's preoccupation with the streak had become detrimental to his game. Unger appeared in an additional 35 consecutive playoff games.

Unger's consecutive games streak was subsequently surpassed by Doug Jarvis in the 1986-87 season, Jarvis would play in 964 consecutive regular season games.

Of the Oilers' 22 season opening games, Edmonton has won 11, lost 8 and tied 3. Of the Oilers' 22 home opening games, Edmonton have won 11, lost 7 and tied 4. The Oilers have met Detroit most often in home opening games, playing the Red Wings five times. Edmonton has won one, lost three and tied one, against the Wings in home opening games. At the other end of the schedule, the Oilers have met Calgary 11 times in the last or second last game of the season since 1981. The Oilers have won three, lost five and tied three. Edmonton has also met the Winnipeg Jets eight times in the last or second to last game of a season. The Oilers have won five and lost three of these games

A former member of the Edmonton Oilers who played with the team in the World Hockey Association still participates in over 60 National Hockey League games a year.

Paul Stewart, a rugged 6'1", 205 lb. winger from Boston, Massachusetts, began his major league career with the Oilers, playing two games with the team in 1976-77. The following season while playing for the Cincinnati Stingers, he finished fifth in the league with 241 penalty minutes although he played in only forty games. Eighty-six games and 362 penalty minutes later he ended his playing career. On March 27, 1987, Stewart returned to the league and this former WHA badman began his career as an NHL referee. Since that day he has refereed over 700 games in the National Hockey League.

Stewart's grandfather Bill was also a referee and officiated in the longest NHL game ever played, March 24-25, 1936, in which Detroit defeated the Montreal Maroons 1–0 after 116 minutes, 30 seconds of overtime.

The Oilers nickname was chosen by team owner Charles Allard and General Manager Bill Hunter and was announced June 8, 1972. The name was chosen because of Edmonton's large petrochemical industry. The team was originally to be called the Edmonton Oil Kings, the same name as the local junior team. When Calgary decided not to ice a WHA team in the 1972-73 season, Hunter decided on a name with a more province-wide image.

The Molson Cup is awarded to the player who accumulates the most points in the three star voting at the end of each season in each of the six Canadian NHL cities. The Oilers' Molson Cup winners are as follows: 1979-80 Wayne Gretzky 135 voting points (runner-up Blair MacDonald 70); 1980-81 Wayne Gretzky 145 (Glenn Anderson 75); 1981-82 Wayne Gretzky 175 (Grant Fuhr 70); 1982-83 Wayne Gretzky 210 (Glenn Anderson 80); 1983-84 Wayne Gretzky 155 (Mark Messier 95); 1984-85 Wayne Gretzky 175 (Paul Coffey 85), 1985-86 Wayne Gretzky 200 (Paul Coffey 90); 1986-87 Wayne Gretzky; 1987-88 Wayne Gretzky 135 (Mark Messier 115); 1988-89 Grant Fuhr 105 (Jari Kurri 100); 1989-90 Mark Messier; 1990-91 Bill Ranford (Petr Klima); 1991-92 Joe Murphy; 1992-93 Bill Ranford (Kelly Buchberger, Shayne Corson); 1993-94 Bill Ranford (Jason Arnott, Doug Weight); 1994-95 Bill Ranford (Shayne Corson, Todd Marchant); 1995-96 Doug Weight (Curtis Joseph, Jason Arnott); 1996-97 Curtis Joseph 155 (Ryan Smyth 90); 1997-98 Curtis Joseph 130 (Dean McAmmond 50), 1998-99 Bill Guerin, 1999-2000 Tommy Salo 95 (Ryan Smyth 75), 2000-2001 Tommy Salo 110 (Doug Weight 100).

From 1979-80 to 2000-01 the Oilers have played in 215 pre-season games. Of these 215 games, the team has won 107, lost 82 and tied 26 for a .558 winning percentage.

The Oilers' first Stanley Cup victory celebration took place on May 22, 1984. An estimated 100,000 fans attended the parade and rally in downtown Edmonton. Not only did these events attract huge crowds but downtown Edmonton was pandemonium immediately following the victory over the Islanders. The resulting chaos in the city's downtown area resulted in several arrests.

The fervor and excitement waned in subsequent Stanley Cup winning years. The 1985 rally and parade attracted 25,000 people. The 1987 rally attracted only a measly 5,000 fans. The 1988 rally drew a crowd of 30,000 people, while the 1990 rally attracted 18,000 people. All of the rallies were held at Commonwealth Stadium.

Due to an injury to Grant Fuhr, Mike Zanier was the backup goaltender to Andy Moog in the Oilers' first ever Stanley Cup winning game, May 19, 1984.

Zanier had been living in his home-town of Trail, British Columbia, collecting Unemployment Insurance and playing senior hockey with the legendary Trail Smoke Eaters when he decided to contact all 21 of the NHL's teams, asking for a tryout. Only Edmonton offered him an invitation. He would end up playing only three games with the Oilers, winning one, losing one and tying one.

In 1961 the Trail Smoke Eaters became the last Canadian team to win the world championship until an NHL stocked team won it in 1994.

The Oilers sold out their first 217 straight games at the Coliseum. This included 200 regular season and 17 playoff games. The first time the team played before less than a full house was the April 4, 1984, playoff game against Winnipeg. Attendance then was 17,197.

Country performer Larry Gatlin, who sang the American national anthem prior to the 1985 Oilers' Stanley Cup–winning game, had his own small claim to fame in the world of athletics.

While playing football as a member of the Houston Cougars of the NCAA's Southwest Conference in 1968 Gatlin caught one touchdown pass for the Cougars against the Tulsa Golden Hurricane. While this was not remarkable in itself it did help Houston just squeak by the Hurricane by a score of 100–6. The Cougars set a modern major college record for points scored and points in a half, with 76. The touchdown was not quite the turning point in the game as it made the score 93 to 6. This was Gatlin's only collegiate touchdown.

Houston, which had scored 77 points the previous week, set an NCAA record of 177 points scored in two consecutive games.

Following the Oilers' Stanley Cup victory in 1985, the National Hockey League introduced a piece of legislation (Rule 27D) which at the time was known as the "Oiler Rule." This would, for the most part, eliminate the coincidental four on four manpower situations which the high powered Oilers had become so adept at taking advantage of. With players such as Anderson, Coffey, Gretzky, Kurri and Messier in the lineup, the Oilers would score on almost as many four on four situations as they would on the powerplay.

This was reminiscent of the "Montreal" rule which the league passed in the late 1950s. Before the rule change a player would have to sit out his entire minor penalty whether the attacking team scored or not. The Canadiens of the late 1950s with stars such as Richard, Beliveau, Moore, Geoffrion and Harvey were so dominant on the powerplay that they sometimes scored two or three goals with the man advantage.

Voting for the 1985 piece of legislation was 17–3, with one abstention, in favor of the new rule. Curiously, the New Jersey Devils were one of the three teams not in favor of the new rule. The Devils were one of the major proponents of the "trap" system which had become prevalent in the 1990s and made the game so frustrating to watch.

The Oilers set a league record for the most penalties in a single game by one team which also featured the most penalties in a single game by both teams. In the contest of February 28, 1990, at the Los Angeles Forum the Oilers received 44 penalties (197 minutes) while

Los Angeles received 41 penalties (157 minutes). The penalties were as follows:

1st period: Messier Edmonton (fighting) 1:35, Muni Edmonton (fighting) 1:35, McSorley Los Angeles (fighting) 1:35, Taylor Los Angeles (fighting) 1:35, Krushelnyski Los Angeles (elbowing) 2:35, Murphy Edmonton (roughing and slashing) 5:45, Prajsler Los Angeles (roughing) 5:45, Brown Edmonton (roughing) 8:19, Allison Los Angeles (roughing) 8:19, McSorley Los Angeles (roughing) 8:19, Anderson Edmonton (roughing) 8:43,Watters Los Angeles (roughing) 8:43, Tikkanen Edmonton (hooking) 9:40, Beukeboom Edmonton (hooking) 11:15, Lowe Edmonton (high sticking) 13:18, Steve Smith Edmonton (cross checking) 13:45, Beukeboom Edmonton (high sticking) 16:19, Allison Los Angeles (high sticking) 16:19, Halkidis Los Angeles (holding) 17:19, Benning Los Angeles (cross checking) 19:15.

2nd period: Messier Edmonton (elbowing) 0:41, Tonelli Los Angeles (hooking) 2:07, MacTavish Edmonton (unsportsmanlike conduct) 2:53, Halkidis Los Angeles (unsportsmanlike conduct) 2:53, Granato Los Angeles (holding) 2:53, Prajsler Los Angeles (holding) 10:17, MacTavish Edmonton (holding) 12:56, Prajsler Los Angeles (holding) 13:24, Kurri Edmonton (roughing) 15:43, Allison Los Angeles (roughing) 15:43, Watters Los Angeles (roughing) 15:43, Messier Edmonton (double minor for roughing) 15:43, Brown Edmonton (fighting) 16:05, Halkidis Los Angeles (fighting) 16:05, Anderson Edmonton (match penalty for deliberate attempt to injure) 16:38, Buchberger Edmonton (roughing) 16:38, Lamb Edmonton (roughing) 16:38, Duchesne Los Angeles (roughing) 16:38, Granato Los Angeles (roughing) 16:38, Sandstrom Los Angeles (roughing) 16:38, Steve Smith Edmonton (holding, fighting, 10 minute misconduct) 16:38, Benning Los Angeles (fighting) 16:38.

3rd period: Messier Edmonton (high sticking) 5:11, Beukeboom Edmonton (roughing, fighting, game misconduct) 8:33, Brown Edmonton (roughing, 10 minute misconduct) 8:33, Buchberger Edmonton (roughing, 10 minute misconduct) 8:33, Allison Los Angeles (fighting, 10 minute misconduct) 8:33, Granato Los Angeles (roughing and tripping) 8:33, Watters Los Angeles (roughing) 8:33, Muni Edmonton (roughing) 13:54, Benning Los Angeles (slashing) 13:54, Kudelski Los Angeles (roughing) 14:52, Lamb Edmonton (fighting) 16:26, Elik Los Angeles (fighting) 16:26, Benning Los Angeles (cross checking major, game misconduct) 16:40, Lowe Edmonton (roughing, 10 minute misconduct) 19:34, Halkidis Los Angeles (roughing, 10 minute misconduct) 19:34, Kudelski Los Angeles (roughing, 10 minute misconduct) 19:34, Ranford Edmonton (leaving crease, game misconduct) 19:34, Simpson Edmonton (roughing, 10 minute misconduct, game misconduct) 19:34, Steve Smith Edmonton (fighting, game misconduct) 19:34, McSorley Los Angeles (double fighting major, double game misconduct) 19:34, Scott Los Angeles (leaving crease) 19:34.

The Kings scored 1 goal on 11 powerplay opportunities, while the Oilers were 1 for 10.

In 1985, Mark Napier switched from sweater number 18 to number 65, because he had been named as honorary chairman of the '65 Roses Club. The '65 Roses Club assisted people who were afflicted with cystic fibrosis. Petr Klima chose sweater number 85 because that was the year in which he defected from Czechoslovakia. Wayne Gretzky chose sweater number 99 because as a youngster he had worn sweater number 9 but when he went to the training camp of the Sault Ste. Marie Greyhounds, sweater 9 was taken by Brian Gualazzi so it was suggested that Gretzky wear number 99 instead. For much the same reason Garry Unger wore sweater number 77 when he joined the Oilers. Unger had worn jersey number 7 with St. Louis for nine seasons but Paul Coffey was wearing number 7 when Unger joined the team so Unger had to make do with two sevens. Dave Hunter wore sweater number 27 when he rejoined the Oilers in January of 1988 because the number 12 jersey which he wore for nine seasons was now being worn by Jimmy Carson. Tough guy Georges Laraque wore sweater 27 in honor of former Oiler enforcer Dave Semenko.

The Oilers played a total of 11 exhibition games against NHL opposition while the team was a member of the World Hockey Association. The dates and scores are as follows:

October 6, 1974—Vancouver Canucks 4 Oilers 3; September 26, 1976—Pittsburgh Penguins 3 Oilers 1; September 28, 1976—Pittsburgh Penguins 7 Oilers 3; September 29, 1976—St. Louis Blues 5 Oilers 4; October 3, 1977-Oilers 3 St. Louis Blues 2; October 8, 1977—Oilers 5 Detroit Red Wings 4; October 9, 1977—Cleveland Barons 4 Oilers 2; October 3, 1978—Oilers 4 Minnesota North Stars 2; October 4, 1978—Oilers 5 Vancouver Canucks 3; October 7, 1978—Minnesota North Stars 9 Oilers 3; October 8, 1978—Oilers 6 Colorado Rockies 4.

The Oilers' first appearance on Hockey Night in Canada, a Saturday night institution in Canada, was on October 13, 1979. Play by play was by Jim Robson, while Gerry Pinder added the color commentary. Seven additional games were scheduled to be broadcast on Hockey Night in Canada in the 1979-80 season.

The team's games were also broadcast on a regional basis by CITV for the first 13 seasons, but in 1992-93 CFRN television acquired the broadcast rights and telecast the games for the next five years before the A Channel took over broadcasting the games in 1997-98.

Although Wayne Gretzky holds nearly every conceivable Oilers franchise offensive record he does not hold the record for most points in one game. That mark belongs instead to Jim Harrison.

On January 30, 1973, while the team was still a member of the World Hockey Association, Harrison scored ten points against the hapless New York netminding duo of Gary Kurt and Ian Wilkie. Harrison tallied one goal and one assist in the first period, one goal and two assists in the second period and one goal and four assists in the third period.

The Oilers registered 52 shots on goal, 23 of them in the third period, and defeated the Raiders by a score of 11–3. The game was played in Edmonton before a sparse crowd of 2,846.

Harrison jumped from 22nd place in scoring to 12th due to this offensive outburst.

Oilers superstar Wayne Gretzky had a reputation for not being effective on his breakaway opportunities. While records don't exist to either confirm or deny this, Gretzky did score 51 unassisted goals. Thirty-eight of these goals were scored at even strength, three on the power play, and perhaps most indicative of his prowess on the breakaway, he also scored ten unassisted goals while his team was shorthanded. Many times shorthanded goals are scored when the puck is stolen in the defending team's zone and a player from the shorthanded team races in alone on the goaltender. Gretzky has also scored on two of his five penalty shots.

Not only were the Los Angeles Kings the Oilers' opponent when the team blew its big lead in the infamous game in the Stanley Cup playoffs on April 10, 1982, but the Kings were also the opposing team when the Oilers overcame one of the biggest deficits in team history. In the 1982 game the Oilers were ahead of the Kings by a score of five to zero after two periods. Edmonton was showing the Kings little respect but Los Angeles refused to lie down and die, scoring five unanswered goals in the third period to tie the score at five, before Daryl Evans scored at 2:35 of overtime to win the game for Los Angeles. This game featured over 220 minutes in penalties including 12 misconducts (one to Jari Kurri) and one game misconduct.

In the remarkably similar January 21, 1985, game in Northland's Coliseum Los Angeles had just scored at the 17:21 mark of the second period to put the Kings ahead by a score of six to one. The Oilers then scored two goals in the last minutes of the period to close the score to 6–3. Edmonton then caught fire in the third period, scoring five goals to win the game eight to seven. The biggest difference in the two games aside from the outcome was that the Oilers' victory was in a rather meaningless game in January, while the Kings' victory took place in April in a game which probably turned the tide of the series.

Although the name Wayne Gretzky has become synonymous with the sweater number 99, the "Great One" was not the only nor even the first player to wear that number. As far back as the 1934-35 season the Montreal Canadiens had three players wear the number. Joe Lamb, Leo Bourgault and Desmond Roche all wore the 99 on their jersey at some point during that season. Wilf Paiement of the Toronto Maple Leafs also wore sweater number 99 when he joined the Leafs in the 1979-80 season. The number 99 was retired by the Oilers and the entire league following Gretzky's retirement at the end of the 1998-99 season.

The Oilers' 1st draft pick in the 1987 entry draft, Peter Soberlak, had a narrow brush with death just a few months before being drafted. Soberlak was a member of the 1986-87 Swift Current Broncos team that was involved in a tragic highway accident five kilometers from Swift Current in which four players were killed. In the December 30, 1986, accident the Broncos' team bus flipped over on the icy highway, throwing longtime friends Scott Kruger and Trent Kresse out of the bus to their deaths. S. Scott Mantyka and Brent Ruff were trapped in the bus and died there. Ruff was a native of Warburg, Alberta, and the brother of NHL veteran Lindy Ruff.

All four of the players who died were seated at the back of the bus, while Soberlak was seated just in front of them and was not seriously hurt.

The Oilers have played 73 afternoon games. They have a dismal record in these games. They have won 26, lost 41 and tied 6 for a .397 average. Following is a list of the Oilers' afternoon games (shown is the season, the score and the opposition, Oilers score is listed first). 1980 2–2 Winnipeg, 3–6 Toronto; 1981 5–2 Pittsburgh, 4–2 Detroit, 5–3 Philadelphia, 3–6 Boston, 4–6 St. Louis; 1983 2–3 Vancouver; 1984 3–2 Winnipeg, 2–9 Washington, 1–4 Boston, 0–11 Hartford; 1985 7–3 Chicago; 1986 7–3 Los Angeles; 1987 2–5 Winnipeg; 1988 0–2 Washington, 4–3 Winnipeg; 1989 2–4 New Jersey, 3–3 Winnipeg, 2–5 Boston, 2–4 Calgary; 1990 1–5 Philadelphia, 2–3 Winnipeg, 5–4 Washington, 4–2 Winnipeg; 1991 4–5 Vancouver, 5–4 New Jersey, 3–2 Winnipeg,; 1992 7–0 Vancouver, 8–2 Quebec, 6–4 San Jose, 2–7 Vancouver, 5–8 Philadelphia, 4–2 Winnipeg, 4–3 Boston, 2–6 Washington; 1993 2–3 Quebec, 4–5 Chicago, 5–7 Winnipeg, 2–3 Winnipeg, 5–4 Buffalo, 3–7 Hartford; 1994 4–4 San Jose, 5–2 Winnipeg, 3–6 Anaheim, 1–4 Vancouver, 1–5 Boston, 3–4 Pittsburgh, 5–3 Los Angeles, 1–6 Los Angeles, 1996 1–4 Chicago, 0–2 Islanders, 3–4 St. Louis, 1997 2–4 Chicago, 3–6 Florida, 3–1 Washington, 1–6 Dallas, 4–2 Hartford, 1–4 Anaheim, 1998 0–3 Vancouver, 2–3 Los Angeles, 4–5 Colorado, 1999 3–3 Philadelphia, 4–6 St. Louis, 1–3 Nashville, 5–2 San Jose, 2000 3–1 New Jersey, 2–2 Buffalo, 3–4 Nashville 2001 Minnesota 5–3, Carolina 3–2, Chicago 3–3, Dallas 4–3

Despite the presence of probably over a half dozen future Hall of Fame players on their roster Al Hamilton and Wayne Gretzky are the only two members of the Oilers to have their jersey numbers retired by the team. Hamilton wore the number 3 in the Oilers' first game in the World Hockey Association, and wore it throughout his entire career in Edmonton. Hamilton spent seven seasons with the WHA Oilers and also played on the team in their first NHL, season after which he retired. Following his retirement at the conclusion of the 1998-99 season Wayne Gretzky's number 99 sweater was retired by the league and by the Oilers at the beginning of the 1999-2000 season. Jari Kurri's number 17 was retired at the beginning of the 2002 season.

The Wichita Wind of the Central Hockey League, one of the Oilers' farm teams in 1980-81, was so decimated by injuries and call-ups in one game that they had to take some unusual steps in order to fill out their roster. In a December 27, 1980, game against the Dallas Black Hawks in Wichita, the Wind had to dress goalie Pete LoPresti as a forward, public relations man Mike Milo as the backup goaltender and coach Ace Bailey as a defenseman. Bailey, a former winger, had been retired from the playing ranks for over a year. The Wind were so short of players because the Oilers, their parent team, had been hard hit by injuries themselves and had called up a number of players from Wichita to fill out their own roster. Wichita lost the game 6–3.

The Edmonton Oilers have played six games against international opponents since 1979 when the team joined the NHL. The dates and results of these games are shown below; all games were played at Northland's Coliseum.

January 4, 1980, Moscow Dynamo 4 Edmonton 1; December 28, 1982, Soviet All-Stars 3 Edmonton 4; December 27, 1985, Soviet Red Army 6 Edmonton 3; December 28, 1988, Dynamo Riga 1 Edmonton 2; December 6, 1989, Khimik Voskresensk 2 Edmonton 6; January 6, 1991, Soviet Red Army 2 Edmonton 4.

The Oilers also played ten games against international clubs while the team was a member of the World Hockey Association. The dates and results of these games are shown below; all games were played at Northland's Coliseum.

December 13, 1976, Czechoslovakia 4 Edmonton 6; January 5, 1977, Soviet Nationals 3 Edmonton 2; December 14, 1977, Czechoslovakia All-Stars 1 Edmonton 6; December 21, 1977, Soviet All-Stars 2 Edmonton 5; January 4, 1978, Soviet Nationals 7 Edmonton 2; December 15, 1978, Soviet All-Stars 3 Edmonton 5; December 16, 1978, Vikingarna (Sweden's B Team) 2 Edmonton 11; December 29, 1978, Moscow Dynamo 4 at Edmonton 1; December 30, 1978, Czechoslovakia All-Stars 1 Edmonton 5; March 20, 1979, Finland "Sisu Team" 4 Edmonton 8.

The Moncton Alpines of the American Hockey League were the Oilers' primary farm team for the three years from 1981-82 to 1983-84.

The Wichita Wind had been Edmonton's farm team for their first two seasons in the National Hockey League but the Oilers decided to switch their affiliation to the Nova Scotia–based team. Moosehead Breweries offered the Oilers a large sum of money for the sponsorship rights to the new farm team and thus gained the rights to name them.

The Alpines were not named after any mountain chain in Nova Scotia but after a brand of beer made by Moosehead.

David Shaw was traded to the Oilers from the Rangers on November 12, 1991 and played in his first Oiler game the following night. On November 13 against Pittsburgh, Shaw became the first player to score a goal, an assist, and receive a penalty in his first Oiler game.

On October 6, 1992, Brent Gilchrist matched this feat in a game against the Vancouver Canucks in the team's first game of the 1992-93 season.

The Oilers have had working agreements with nine different teams who were to fulfill the role of farm teams. In chronological order they were the Houston Apollos (1979-80, CHL), Wichita Wind (1979-80 to 1981-82, CHL), Milwaukee Admirals (1980-81 to 1983-84, IHL), Moncton Alpines (1981-82 to 1983-84, AHL), Nova Scotia Oilers (1984-85 to 1987-88, AHL), Cape Breton Oilers (1988-89 to 1995-96, AHL), Fort Wayne Komets (1988-89, IHL), Phoenix Roadrunners (1989-90, IHL), Hamilton Bulldogs (1996-97 to present, AHL).

The Oilers have scored ten or more goals in a game 27 times since joining the NHL In order they are: Nov. 26, 1980—10–3 over Chicago, Feb. 6, 1981—10–4 over Winnipeg, Oct. 31, 1981—11–4 over Quebec, Nov. 25, 1981—11–4 over Los Angeles, Nov. 29, 1981—10–2 over Winnipeg, Dec. 27, 1981—10–3 over Los Angeles, Mar. 17, 1982—10–2 over Winnipeg, Dec. 17, 1982—10–4 over New Jersey, Jan. 12, 1983—10–4 over Chicago, Jan. 15, 1983—10–4 over Minnesota, Feb. 19, 1983—10–7 over Pittsburgh, Apr. 17, 1983—10–2 over Calgary*, Oct. 18, 1983—10–7 over Vancouver, Nov. 2, 1983—11–3 over Washington, Nov. 19, 1983—13–4 over New Jersey, Jan. 4, 1984—12–8 over Minnesota, Feb. 3, 1984—10–5 over Calgary, Mar. 11, 1984—12–2 over Vancouver, May 4, 1985—11–2 over Chicago, May 14, 1985—10–5 over Chicago*, Nov. 8, 1985—13–0 over Vancouver, Dec. 11, 1985—12–9 over Chicago, Mar. 14, 1986—12–3 over Detroit, Apr. 9, 1987—13–3 over Los Angeles, Dec. 6, 1987—10–4 over Minnesota, Dec. 4, 1988—10–6 over the Rangers, and Nov. 26, 1996—10–1 over Calgary. They have outscored the opposition 291-107 in these 27 games.

Edmonton has only been involved in six games in which they have allowed ten or more goals. In order they are: Oct. 24, 1979—10–2 to the Rangers, Mar. 4, 1980—10–4 to Calgary, Feb. 8 1981—10–4 to Calgary, Apr. 7, 1982—10–8 to Los Angeles*, Feb. 12, 1984—11–0 to Hartford, Jan. 8, 1986—11–9 to Toronto.

*Indicates playoff game

The Oilers were not the first Edmonton based team to compete for the Stanley Cup. On December 28, 1909, the Edmonton Thistles as the Western champions traveled east to meet the Montreal Wanderers in a two game total goal series for the Cup. Despite the fact that every member of the team except for one was a "ringer" the Thistles lost to Montreal 7–3 in the opening game. Two days later the Thistles managed to defeat Montreal 7–6 but lost the series 13 goals to 10. Both games were played in Montreal. The Edmonton team played its home games during the regular season at the Thistle Rink.

Craig MacTavish holds the record for most consecutive games played with the Oilers. MacTavish played in 518 straight games for the team from October 12, 1986, until January 2, 1993. "Mac T" also played in all 121 playoff games in which the team was involved during this period. MacTavish was the last ever NHL player to play without a helmet.

Vincent Damphousse, who led the team in scoring in the 1991-92 season with 89 points, is the only player in National Hockey League history to lead three different teams in scoring in three consecutive years. Damphousse, who was the Leafs' 1st choice overall in the 1986 draft, led Toronto in scoring in the 1990-91 season with 26 goals and 47 assists in 79 games. Damphousse was then involved in the blockbuster trade to Edmonton in which the Leafs picked up veterans Glenn Anderson and Grant Fuhr. Damphousse led the Oilers in scoring with 38 goals and 51 assists in 80 games. In August of 1992 the Oilers traded Damphousse to the Montreal Canadiens for Shayne Corson and Brent Gilchrist. Damphousse then led the Canadiens in scoring with 39 goals and 58 assists in 84 games.

Goaltender and future Oiler coach Ron Low almost singlehandedly took the Oilers into the playoffs in their first season. With the team sporting a 20–37–12 record in the first 69 games, the Oilers traded popular center and captain Ron Chipperfield to Quebec for the veteran goaltender. Backstopped by Low, the Oilers won eight, lost two and tied one of their final 11 games. Low allowed 37 goals and posted a 3.37 average. Before the arrival of Low the team had a goals against average of 4.14.

The Oilers' 1988 Stanley Cup–winning team was the youngest NHL team to win the trophy since the league was formed in 1917. The average age of the Oilers roster during the regular season was 24.22 years, although the average age for the team which played in the Cup final was 25.8 years. By contrast the 1966-67 Toronto Maple Leafs, the last team to win the Stanley Cup prior to expansion, averaged 31.74 years of age. The Leafs gained notoriety as being the oldest team to win the Stanley Cup. Since 1967 only one team has come close to this record. The 1998-99 Stanley Cup winning Dallas Stars had an average age of 30.8 years.

Mark Messier, who starred for 12 seasons as an Oiler, was the last former player from the World Hockey Association to play in the NHL. In the 1978-79 season Messier appeared in five games for the Indianapolis Racers and 47 for the Cincinnati Stingers after the Racers folded. "The Moose" scored one goal and added ten assists for the Stingers during this his first pro season.

When the WHA was absorbed into the NHL Messier became eligible for the amateur draft and was taken in the second round of the draft by the Oilers. Messier would go on to a stellar career, playing over twenty seasons with three different teams.

Former Oiler superstar Wayne Gretzky was the second last survivor from the WHA, calling quits to his career following the 1998-99 season.

Oiler defenseman Frantisek (Frank) Musil did not get permission from the Czechoslovakian Ice Hockey Federation to play in North America so he defected. Ever since Minnesota had drafted Musil 38th overall in 1983, North Stars General Manager Lou Nanne had been attempting to get him out of the communist country. In July of 1986, while vacationing in Yugoslavia, Musil met with Nanne and Edmonton based player agent Rich Winter. Leaving his girlfriend behind, Musil and the other two men spent two days driving around Yugoslavia, before acquiring a temporary U.S. work visa. By that afternoon he was in London and by midnight had landed at the airport in Bloomington, Minnesota.

Musil was not the only player ever to suit up with the Oilers from behind the Iron Curtain: Edmonton forward Petr Klima also illegally left Czechoslovakia. The Oilers' Jaroslav Pouzar was one of only around a half dozen Czech players given permission by the Czechoslovakian authorities to play in North America.

The Oilers and Chicago tied the record for most goals scored in a game with 21. On December 11, 1985, at Chicago Stadium the Oilers defeated the Black Hawks 12–9. This tied the previous record set on January 10, 1920, when the Montreal Canadiens defeated the Toronto St. Patricks 14–7. The scoring summary of the Edmonton game is as follows:

1st period: **1**-Edmonton: Anderson (Gretzky, Gregg) 1:35, **2**-Edmonton:Lumley (Carroll, Lowe) 3:19, **3**-Edmonton: Semenko (MacTavish, Napier) 4:58, **4**-Edmonton: McSorley (Gretzky, Jackson) 13:24.

2nd period: **5**-Edmonton: Anderson (Jackson, Gretzky) 1:20, **6**-Edmonton: McClelland (McSorley, Summanen) 3:08,**7**-Chicago: Savard (Larmer, Secord) 5:38 (PP), **8**-Edmonton: Fogolin (McClelland, Summanen) 6:11, **9**-Chicago: Fraser (Troy Murray, Doug Wilson) 6:38, **10**-Chicago: Watson (Yaremchuk, Dupont) 7:11, **11**-Chicago: Troy Murray (Behn Wilson, Brown) 9:36 (PP), **12**-Chicago: O'Callahan (Dupont, Troy Murray) 11:36, **13**-Edmonton: Kurri (Gretzky, Anderson) 14:52, **14**-Chicago: Brown (Olcyzk)

16:07, **15**-Edmonton: McSorley (Fogolin, McClelland) 18:58, **16**-Edmonton: Anderson (Gretzky, Coffey) 19:50.

3rd period: **17**-Chicago: Troy Murray (Olczyk, Brown) 13:22 (PP), **18**-Edmonton: Kurri (Gretzky, Anderson) 15:34, **19**-Chicago: Yaremchuk (Gardner, Behn Wilson) 17:59, **20**-Edmonton: Kurri (Gretzky, Anderson) 19:24, **21**-Chicago: Yaremchuk (Lysiak, Gardner) 19:37

The Oilers had 44 shots on goal and Chicago had 46. The goaltenders for Chicago were Murray Bannerman (who allowed ten goals) and Bob Sauve (who allowed two). The goaltenders for the Oilers were Andy Moog (who allowed five goals) and Grant Fuhr (who allowed four).

The Oilers were also involved in the next two highest scoring games in league history. They defeated Minnesota 12–8 January 4, 1984, and lost to the Toronto Maple Leafs 11–9, January 8, 1986.

After playing parts of six season with the San Jose Sharks Ray Whitney was signed as a free agent by Edmonton, October 1, 1997. He played nine games for the Oilers in the 1997-98 season, scoring one goal and adding three assists before being picked up on waivers by the Florida Panthers. Whitney would score 32 goals and add 29 assists in 68 games for the Panthers in the 1997-98 season. The Fort Saskatchewan native had been the Oilers' stick boy during some of their Stanley Cup–winning seasons.

Ryan Smyth was the stick boy for Team Canada during the squad's training camp in Banff prior to the 1984 Canada Cup series.

Wayne Gretzky registered multiple points in 473 of the 696 regular season games in which he played. "The Great One" had 172 two point games, 142 three point games, 80 four point games, 57 five point games, 14 six point games, 6 seven point games, and 2 eight point games. This accounts for 1,517 of his 1,669 points. Gretzky played in only 152 games in which he scored a single point. He appeared in only 71 games in which he did not register a point. Gretzky had four consecutive five-point games (for 20 points) from February 17, 1982, to February 24, 1982. In comparison, in that same season Garry Unger played 46 games and had 20 points, Stan Weir had 13 points in 51 games, Charlie Huddy had 15 points in 41 games and Tom Roulston had 14 points in 35 games.

In his playoff career Gretzky had 31 single point games, 36 two point games, 18 three point games, 11 four point games, 6 five point games, and 3 seven point games. There were only 15 playoff games in which Gretzky played and did not register a point.

Oiler forward Mike Grier is the son of Bobby Grier, the director of player personnel for the New England Patriots of the National Football League. Ray Whitney is the son of Oilers practice goaltender and Edmonton policeman Floyd Whitney. Matti Hagman was the brother-in-law of former Edmonton Driller soccer star Kai Haaskivi. Chad Kilger is the son of former NHL referee Bob Kilger. Alex Selivanov is the son-in-law of Hall of Famer Phil Esposito and played in Tampa Bay while Esposito was general manager. Frank Musil is the brother-in-law of fellow NHLer Bobby Holik. Mike Comrie is the brother of Paul Comrie.

Chris Ferraro is the twin brother of Boston Bruins center Peter Ferraro. Both brothers have had almost identical careers. Beginning in 1990 they have each played in Dubuque, Waterloo, University of Maine, U.S. National Team, Atlanta and Binghampton before getting a chance to play on the Rangers in 1995-96. Both brothers were drafted by the Rangers in 1992: Peter in the first round, Chris in the fourth.

Tony Hrkac had his number 21 jersey retired by the University of North Dakota where he played for two years with the Fighting Sioux. In 1987 Hrkac scored 125 points in 48 games for North Dakota while leading them to the NCAA Division 1 championship. Hrkac won the Hobey Baker Award as the top collegiate player in the U.S. His team was sometimes called the "Hrkac Circus," and the arena at the University of North Dakota, officially known as the Winter Sports Center, was sometimes referred to as "The House That Herk Built."

Former Oiler defenseman Colin Campbell was named as senior vice president and director of hockey operations for the National Hockey League, on July 20, 1998. Campbell played 72 games while recording 13 points playing on the Oilers' blue-line during the 1979-80 season. He also led the team in penalty minutes during the first season.

The Oilers Investors Group, which purchased the team in 1997, numbers 37 persons. These include Dave Addie, Nal Allen, Jacob Ambrosius, Manuel Balsa, Ted Barrett, Ed Bean, Gordon Buchanan, Paul Burke, Bill Butler, Dick Colf, Mike Dalton, Ernie Elko, Gary Gregg, Don Hamilton, Ron Hodgson, Jim Hole, Linda Hughes, Gerald Knoll, Walter Kuchar, Larry Makelki, Tom Mayson, Tim Melton, Art Mikalcheon, Cal Nichols, Al Owen, Dick Paine, Marcel and Roger Roberge, Harold Roozen, Bruce Saville, Simon Sochatsky, Rusty Stalwick, Barry and Keith Weaver, Jim Woods, and Jim Zanello. There is also one anonymous investor.

While Todd McFarlane was not one of the original 37 investors when the team was purchased from Peter Pocklington in 1997 he does now own part of the team.

Calgary born McFarlane had hopes of a baseball career, but it was cut short due to an injury. McFarlane then turned to art and in 1984 began work for Marvel Comics. He also worked for a time at DC Comics before forming his own company "Image Comics" in 1992. It was there that he created "Spawn."

"Spawn" has since gone on to become the top selling comic book in the world. From that idea has sprung an award winning television show, a movie, toys, videos and C.D.'s.

Former Oiler defenseman Marty McSorley had a bit part in the 1997 Touchstone Pictures release *ConAir*. McSorley played one of the co-pilots of the aircraft which was hijacked by the very criminals it is transporting. McSorley, who is called "Mac" in the movie, had two lines of dialogue. The two lines are "I've got a fire," and "She's reporting it in the rear cabin." McSorley, who was billed as Martin McSorley in the credits, is shot and killed early in the film. The other stars of the film were Nicolas Cage, John Cusack, and John Malkovich.

Wayne Gretzky also had a walk-on part in an American soap opera and appeared in an episode of the Canadian sitcom *Snow Job*. Former Oiler Adam Graves, while a member of the New York Rangers, had a bit part in an episode of the Michael J. Fox sitcom *Spin City*. Graves played himself.

Of the Oilers' 33 goaltenders, four of them have been of African-Canadian heritage. Spruce Grove, Alberta, born Grant Fuhr starred for the team for ten seasons and was a major part in all five Stanley Cup–winning seasons. Eldon "Pokey" Reddick of Halifax, Nova Scotia, played 14 games for the club and backed up Bill Ranford for much of the 1989-90 season. Ottawa born Fred Brathwaite also found himself in the backup role to Ranford for the 1993-94 and 1994-95 seasons. Joaquin Gage of Vancouver, British Columbia, played a total of 18 games over two seasons for the Oilers. These four players represent 80% of the entire population of black goaltenders in the league. Only Kevin Weekes, who played with Florida in 1997-98, has never played on the Oilers.

In September, 1986 the Oilers signed Dartmouth, Nova Scotia, born Darren Beals to a free agent contract. Beals, also of African-Canadian heritage, never appeared in a league game.

On January 1, 2001, in a game against St. Louis, Joaquin Gage replaced Tommy Salo in the Edmonton goal. Gage appeared in the final period and let in two goals in a 5–2 Oiler loss. Gage joined forwards Anson Carter, Mike Grier, Georges Laraque, and defenseman Sean Brown in the Oiler lineup. In the same game the Blues dressed Toronto born forward Jamal Mayers. While the NHL does not keep such records it is no doubt the only time that six black players have appeared in one game and certainly the only time in NHL history that one team has dressed five black players in a game.

In the 1987-88 season Jimmy Carson scored 55 goals as a member of the Los Angeles Kings. At 19 years, 8 months and 5 days, Carson was the second youngest player in NHL history to score 50 goals. Wayne Gretzky, at 19 years, 2 months and 7 days, is the only player younger than Carson to score 50 goals in a season. On August 8, 1988, Carson and Gretzky were the two main players in the huge trade which saw Gretzky leave Edmonton and Carson come to Edmonton.

During the same season which saw Carson score 55 goals, Craig Simpson became the first NHL player to score 50 or more goals in one season while playing for two different teams. Simpson scored 13 goals in 21 games for Pittsburgh before being traded to the Oilers for Paul Coffey. Simpson then scored 43 goals in 59 games with Edmonton, finishing the season with 56 goals. There have only been 80 players in NHL history to score 50 or more goals in one season.

On March 17th, 2001 the Oilers met the New Jersey Devils in an important late season game. This was the first time in 21 seasons and only the eighth time in league history that two teams with at least nine game unbeaten streaks had played against each other.

The Oilers were fresh off of a ten game undefeated streak which saw them win a franchise record nine consecutive victories. The Devils had also set their own franchise mark by winning nine consecutive games. In an exciting contest the Devils defeated the Oilers 6–5 in overtime.

Curiously the Oilers' undefeated streak both began and ended with identical overtime scores. On February 17, the Vancouver Canucks defeated the Oilers 6–5 after 58 seconds of overtime and it was exactly one month later that the Oilers lost to the Devils by the same score.

In a game against San Jose on December 29 2000, Doug Weight received 39 minutes in penalties in the first period. Weight had been hit in the knee by the Shark's Bryan Marchment and took exception to the act. Weight lightly slashed Marchment on the arms and then punched him. The Oilers captain was assessed a two minute minor, a two minute instigator penalty, a five minute major for fighting, a double misconduct and a game misconduct (for slamming his stick on the glass). Referee Paul Devorski neglected to penalize Marchment at all. This meant that the Oilers were shorthanded for nine consecutive minutes. Luckily San Jose had one minute remaining in a penalty which they had been assessed prior to the incident and were also handed a minor near the end of Weight's penalty. San Jose did not score on the power play, while the Oilers managed to register one shorthanded goal.

Poul Popiel, who played only ten games for the Oilers in the 1979-80 season, held the World Hockey Association record for most games played with one team. Popiel played 468 of the scheduled 474 regular season games that the Houston Aeros played from 1972 to 1978, when the team folded. Popiel also played in all 71 of the team's playoff games.

Selected Bibliography

Books

Alberta on Ice: Gary W. Zeman, 1985, Westweb Press, Edmonton, Alberta.

Big Bucks & Blue Pucks: Murray Greig, 1997, Macmillan Canada, Toronto, Ontario.

Champions: The Making of the Edmonton Oilers: Kevin Lowe with Stan and Shirley Fischler, 1988, Prentice Hall, Englewood Cliffs, New Jersey.

Complete Historical and Statistical Reference to the World Hockey Association, Scott Adam Surgent, 1995, Xaler Press, Temple Arizona.

Edmonton: A History: J.G. MacGregor, 1975, Hurtig Publishers, Edmonton, Alberta.

Edmonton Oilers Media Guides: Published annually by the Edmonton Oilers.

The Game of Our Lives: Peter Gzowski, 1981, McClelland and Stewart Limited, Toronto, Ontario.

The Great Gretzky: Terry Jones, 1980, General Paperbacks, Don Mills, Ontario.

Gretzky: From the Back Yard Rink to the Stanley Cup: Walter Gretzky and Jim Taylor, 1984, McClelland and Stewart Limited, Toronto, Ontario.

Hockey Encyclopedia: The Complete Encyclopedia of Ice Hockey: Stan Fischler and Shirley Walton Fischler, 1983, Macmillan Publishing Company, New York, New York.

International Ice Hockey Guide: Tom Ratschunas, Editor, 1980, 1981, 1982, Donald R. Wall, Publisher, Helsinki, Finland.

National Hockey League Official Guide and Record Book: Published annually by the NHL Communications Department and the member clubs of the NHL.

Professional Sports Statistics: A North American Team-By-Team, and Major Non Team Events, Year-By-Year Reference, 1876 through 1996: K. Michael Gaschnitz, 1997, McFarland Publishing, Jefferson, North Carolina.

Total Hockey: Second Edition, Edited by Dan Diamond, 2000, Total Sports Inc. New York, New York.

Periodicals

Edmonton Journal
Edmonton Sun
Hockey Digest
The Hockey News

Online Sources

www/nhl.com
www/Edmonton oilers.com
www/hockey db.com

Index